T0393019

# THE ROUTLEDGE COMPANION
# TO BUSINESS JOURNALISM

*The Routledge Companion to Business Journalism* provides a complete and critical survey of the field of business and economic journalism.

Beginning by exploring crucial questions of the moment, the volume goes on to address topics such as the history of the field; differentiation among business journalism outlets; issues and forces that shape news coverage; globalism; personal finance issues; and professional concerns for practicing business journalists. Critical perspectives are introduced, including gender and diversity matters on the business news desk and in business news coverage; the quality of coverage, and its ideological impact and framework; the effect of the internet on coverage; differences in approaches around the world; ethical issues; and education among journalists. Contributions are drawn from around the world and include work by leading names in the industry, as well as accomplished and rising-star academics.

This book is an essential companion to advanced scholars and researchers of business and financial journalism as well as those with overlapping interests in communications, economics, and sociology.

**Joseph Weber** is the Jerry and Karla Huse Professor Emeritus at the University of Nebraska-Lincoln, USA. He spent 22 years reporting and writing for BusinessWeek, serving in various bureaus and leaving as the Chief of Correspondents.

**Richard S. Dunham** is co-director of the Global Business Journalism program at Tsinghua University in Beijing, China. He is a past president of the National Press Club and the National Press Club Journalism Institute.

# THE ROUTLEDGE COMPANION TO BUSINESS JOURNALISM

*Edited by*
*Joseph Weber and Richard S. Dunham*

Routledge
Taylor & Francis Group

LONDON AND NEW YORK

Designed cover image: Igor Kutyaev/iStock/Getty Images Plus Via Getty Images

First published 2024
by Routledge
4 Park Square, Milton Park, Abingdon, Oxon OX14 4RN

and by Routledge
605 Third Avenue, New York, NY 10158

*Routledge is an imprint of the Taylor & Francis Group, an informa business*

*British Library Cataloguing-in-Publication Data*
A catalogue record for this book is available from the British Library

ISBN: 9781032288864 (hbk)
ISBN: 9781032288833 (pbk)
ISBN: 9781003298977 (ebk)

DOI: 10.4324/9781003298977

Typeset in Galliard
by codeMantra

# CONTENTS

Contents

Contents

Contents

# CONTRIBUTORS

## Editors

**Richard S. Dunham** is the co-director of the Global Business Journalism program at Tsinghua University in Beijing and a visiting professor in the Tsinghua School of Journalism and Communication. He is the author of the textbook "Multimedia Reporting" (Springer, 2020), and the co-editor of Springer's Tsinghua Global Business Journalism book series. A veteran Washington journalist, he was the president of the National Press Club, Washington bureau chief of the Houston Chronicle, White House reporter for BusinessWeek magazine and a Washington correspondent for the Dallas Times Herald. He has trained professional journalists, journalism students and journalism educators in countries, including the United States, China, Finland, the Netherlands, Lebanon and the Philippines. He contributed to six books, including "The Founding City" (Chilton Books, 1976) and "The Almanac of the Unelected" (Bernan Press, 2006). He wrote a new foreword to the 60th anniversary edition of his grandfather Barrows Dunham's classic philosophy book, "Man Against Myth" (2007, National Book Trust of India). A native of Philadelphia, Dunham holds BA and MA degrees in history from the University of Pennsylvania.

**Joseph Weber** is the Jerry and Karla Huse Professor Emeritus at the College of Journalism and Mass Communications at the University of Nebraska-Lincoln. He also taught at Tsinghua University in Beijing and the Shanghai University of Finance and Economics. Before moving into academia in 2009, he worked for 22 years at BusinessWeek, retiring as the Chief of Correspondents and Chicago Bureau Chief after running the magazine's bureaus in Toronto and Philadelphia and working in its Dallas bureau. Earlier, he worked at the Rocky Mountain News in Denver, Dun's Business Month in New York City and at The Home News in New Brunswick, NJ. His work has been published by The Washington Post, the Miami Herald, the National Journal and the Columbia Journalism Review, among other outlets, and in academic journals, including *Human Rights Quarterly*. He is the author of "Rhymes with Fighter: Clayton Yeutter, American Statesman" (University of Nebraska Press 2021), "Divided Loyalties: Young Somali Americans and the Lure of Extremism" (Michigan State University Press 2020) and "Transcendental Meditation in America: How a New Age

Movement Remade a Small Town in Iowa" (University of Iowa Press 2014). He authors a regular commentary on Substack at https://josephweber.substack.com/. Weber earned his bachelor's degree in English at Rutgers College and master's at the Columbia University Graduate School of Journalism.

## Contributors

**Theodora Dame Adjin-Tettey** is a senior lecturer at the Department of Media, Language and Communication, Durban University of Technology, and a research associate at the School of Journalism and Media Studies, Rhodes University, South Africa, and a lecturer at the Department of Communication Studies, University of Ghana. Some of the recent research projects she has been part of the state of the Ghanaian media report, the sustainable journalism in sub-Saharan Africa study and policy brief, the South African country report on government communications during the pandemic, the Konrad-Adenauer-Stiftung (KAS) Foundation-funded study on global strategies to save journalism and the Open Society Foundation's commissioned report on news consumption habits among non-elite audiences in the global south.

**Ángel Arrese** is a full professor of journalism at the School of Communication (University of Navarra, Spain). His main research interests include journalism and society, and economic and financial news. He is the author of "La identidad de The Economist" [The Economist's identity] (1994), "Prensa Económica" [Economic and Financial Press] (2002), and "¿Interesa la economía? Economía, medios y ciudadanía" [Is Economics interesting? The Economy, media and citizens] (2011). He has published on these topics in journals such as *Journalism, Journalism Studies, Journalism Practice, Media History, Discourse & Society, Language & Communication, and Communication and Society*, among others.

**Ashia Aubrey** is a communications strategist and writer with experience in the public and private sectors. She previously worked as a television news reporter, anchor, and multimedia journalist at stations in Nebraska, Virginia, and Washington, DC. Aubrey is passionate about storytelling, and her work has gained the attention of news outlets, including the Huffington Post and local news stations worldwide. She has coordinated and managed communication strategies for an $8.9 million federal grant and led efforts in internal and external communications, branding, and social media. She earned her master's degree in integrated media communications at the University of Nebraska-Lincoln.

**Jake Batsell** is the William J. O'Neil Chair in Business Journalism and an associate professor at Southern Methodist University, USA. He is the author of "Engaged Journalism: Connecting with Digitally Empowered News Audiences" (2015) and has written extensively about nonprofit news startups and the business of digital news in publications ranging from peer-reviewed academic journals to industry periodicals. He previously worked as a reporter for newspapers, including The Dallas Morning News and The Seattle Times.

**Mark A. Bernhardt** is a professor in the history department at Jackson State University. He received his PhD in history from the University of California, Riverside. His research examines how media engage in public discourse about imperialism and its legacy in the transnational North American West, the U.S. involvement in wars, social and cultural issues surrounding crime, representations of workers in labor strikes, and intersectionality through representations of marginalized peoples.

**Kelli S. Boling** is an assistant professor at the University of Nebraska-Lincoln. As a cultural studies scholar, she focuses on the lived reality of media audiences (specifically women, women of color, or victims of domestic violence), how those women are depicted, and how they interpret and make meaning from the media they consume. Her research has been published in *Mass Communication & Society*, *Feminist Media Studies*, *Journalism Studies*, and *Journalism History*. Her research on women in podcast audiences has also been cited by traditional media outlets such as TIME magazine and The Washington Post.

**Alexandra Bregman** is a freelance writer based in New York, NY. She is the author of "The Bouvier Affair: A True Story" (2019) about the $1 billion dollar commission fees procured from a Russian oligarch by a Swiss art advisor, subsequently featured in the art documentary "The Lost Leonardo" (2021). Her research continues to explore the intersection of art and business, and its impact on culture, money, and power worldwide. She has published extensively in art trade and mainstream publications and has lectured at Yale (where she is a Global Justice Fellow), Columbia Journalism School (where she was a teaching associate from 2019 to 2021), Quinnipiac University, and New York University.

**James Breiner** is a bilingual consultant (English-Spanish) on digital journalism and newsroom leadership with three decades of experience on the editorial and business sides of newspapers (www.jamesbreiner.com). His specialty is entrepreneurial journalism, or new financial models for digital media. He has trained journalists in many countries, including Mexico, Spain, China, England, Poland, and Belarus. He has been a consultant for NewsU of the Poynter Institute, the Fundación Nuevo Periodismo Iberoamericano (Garcia Marquez Foundation), International Center for Journalists, American City Business Journals, and Crain Communications.

**Colin H. Campbell**, PhD, is a Washington, DC,-metro area communications professional, academician, journalist, and a 2023-2024 Frederick Douglass Institute teaching fellow at Shippensburg University. As an award-winning scholar, he examines media political economy at the intersection of journalism, technology, and the Black American experience. He is an advocate for ethical A.I. and media accountability. He has published material grounded in his degree concatenate with communications, culture, and media studies. His background as a TV correspondent, presenter, and radio anchor has taken him around the country. He has also worked for several international media outlets during his on-the-ground coverage of four presidencies. He created the Pan-African Report, a growing online digital news network that highlights the African diaspora and its connections to U.S. polisocioeconomic culture.

**Claudia E. Cruz**, MA and JD, is a business reporter and expert in Latino-centric journalism. She shares a National Murrow Award for bilingual pandemic coverage in a small market (2021) and a Silver Telly for a video about the Mexican director of animation for "God of War," PlayStation's award-winning game (2019). At the University of Nevada, Reno's Reynolds School of Journalism, she's the current managing editor of Noticiero Móvil and the director of the internship program. Her most recent published chapter is "Race, Colorism and Policing in Latinx Communities: Getting the Real Story" in *Reporting on Latino/a/x Communities: A Guide for Journalists* (Routledge 2022).

**Ron Culp** is a veteran corporate and agency leader who began his career as a newspaper reporter. He now consults with C-suite executives and is Professional in Residence in DePaul University's graduate Public Relations and Advertising program. He is a founding board member and former chairman of the Plank Center for Leadership in Public Relations and a current board member of the Museum of Public Relations. A recipient of PRSA's Gold Anvil Award for lifetime achievement and the Hall of Fame and Distinguished Service Awards from the Arthur W. Page Society, Culp and DePaul colleague Matt Ragas are co-authors of three books focused on improving the business acumen of strategic communicators.

**David R. Davies** is a professor of journalism in the School of Media and Communication at the University of Southern Mississippi. Before joining Southern Miss, he worked for ten years as a reporter in Arkansas, most recently the Arkansas Gazette. He is a graduate of the Kiplinger Program in Public Affairs Reporting at Ohio State University, where he earned a master's degree in journalism. He also holds a master's degree in American history from The University of Southern Mississippi and a PhD in mass communication specializing in media history from the University of Alabama. His research specialties are the press and the Civil Rights Movement and trends in American newspapers since World War II. He has written two books, "The Press & Race: Mississippi Journalists Confront the Movement" (2001) and "The Postwar Decline of American Newspapers," 1945–1965 (2006).

**Alan Deutschman** is a professor of journalism and Reynolds Chair of Business Journalism at the Reynolds School of Journalism, University of Nevada, Reno. Formerly the Silicon Valley correspondent for Fortune magazine, he is the author of four books, including "The Second Coming of Steve Jobs" (2000).

**Richard S. Dunham** is the co-director of the Global Business Journalism program at Tsinghua University in Beijing and a visiting professor in the Tsinghua School of Journalism and Communication. He is the author of the textbook, "Multimedia Reporting" (Springer, 2020), and the co-editor of Springer's Tsinghua Global Business Journalism book series. A veteran Washington journalist, he was the president of the National Press Club, Washington bureau chief of the Houston Chronicle, White House reporter for BusinessWeek magazine and a Washington correspondent for the Dallas Times Herald. He has trained professional journalists, journalism students and journalism educators in countries, including the United States, China, Finland, the Netherlands, Lebanon and the Philippines. In addition to writing "Multimedia Reporting," he has contributed to six books, including "The Founding City" (Chilton Books, 1976) and "The Almanac of the Unelected" (Bernan Press, 2006). He wrote a new foreword to the 60th anniversary edition of his grandfather Barrows Dunham's classic philosophy book, "Man Against Myth" (2007, National Book Trust of India). A native of Philadelphia, Dunham holds BA and MA degrees in history from the University of Pennsylvania.

**Shant Fabricatorian** has research interests that align at the nexus of communication, sociology and political economy, with a particular emphasis on the media's responses to the economic crises of the 1970s. He holds a master's degree in communications from Columbia University, a master's degree in journalism from the University of Technology Sydney and a bachelor's degree in economic and social sciences from the University of Sydney. He has worked as a journalist, editor and educator in Australia and overseas.

**Ivor Gaber** is a professor of political journalism at the University of Sussex. He has published widely on various aspects of political communication and the UK's news media. He also holds honorary chairs at the universities of London and Canberra. His latest book (with James Curran and Julian Petley) is "Culture Wars: the Media and the British Left" (second edition). His previous journalistic career included senior editorial positions at BBC TV and Radio, Independent Television News and Channel Four News. In 1989, his independent TV production company played a key role in the launch, and first year, of the then Murdoch-owned Sky News in 1989. He currently represents the UK at UNESCO's Communication Sector.

**Kristin Gilger** is the Reynolds Professor in Business Journalism at the Walter Cronkite School of Journalism and Mass Communication at Arizona State University, where she has served as an associate dean and interim dean. She joined ASU in 2002 after a 20-year career in newspapers. She was the deputy managing editor for news at The Arizona Republic in Phoenix, suburban editor at the Times-Picayune newspaper in New Orleans and managing editor of the Statesman-Journal newspaper in Salem, Oregon. She is the co-author of "There's No Crying in Newsrooms: What Women Have Learned About What it Takes to Lead," published by Rowman & Littlefield.

**Paul Glader** is a senior editor at CNN Business, overseeing companies coverage. Before that, he was a professor of journalism and program chair at The King's College NYC for a decade and directed the business reporting program for the Dow Jones News Fund at NYU for several years. Glader was the Laventhol / Newsday Visiting Professor at the Columbia University Graduate School of Journalism in the Spring of 2018, serving as lead professor for the capstone M.A. Seminar in Business. He spent 10 years as a staff writer at The Wall Street Journal, covering beats including technology, health & science, travel, metals & mining and finance. He has written for publications including The Washington Post, The Associated Press, Der Spiegel, Forbes.com and Bloomberg BusinessWeek. Glader received a master's from Columbia University as a Knight-Bagehot Fellow at the graduate schools of business and journalism. He completed his EMBA and served as a media scholar at The Berlin School of Creative Leadership at Steinbeis University in Germany. He lived in Germany from 2011-2013, as a Robert Bosch Foundation Fellow and as a European Journalism Fellow at Freie Universität in Berlin.

**Alexandre Gonçalves** is an assistant professor of journalism at the University of Illinois at Urbana-Champaign. He is interested in the use of computational methods to understand media ecosystems. He has a PhD in Communication from Columbia University and a master's in Comparative Media Studies from MIT. Before graduate school, he worked as a science reporter for mainstream publications in Brazil.

**Desiree J. Hanford** is a professor of journalism and director of academic integrity and appeals at the Medill School of Journalism, Media, Integrated Marketing Communications at Northwestern University. She serves as the faculty adviser for Medill's Accelerated Master's Program (Summer 2022-present), chairs the journalism curriculum committee (Fall 2021-present) and has been an instructor for Medill's Cherubs Program. She teaches undergraduate and graduate courses that include news reporting and business and economics reporting. Hanford is the president for the Society for Advancing Business Editing and

Writing (April 2023-April 2024). She was a contributing editor to the business-to-business Building Operating Management/FacilitiesNet for more than a decade. She also worked as an equities reporter for Dow Jones & Co. for more than ten years and worked for other news organizations and magazines.

**Sophie Knowles** is an associate professor of journalism at Middlesex University. She has written widely on the media's role in the global financial crisis. She co-edited "The Media and Austerity: Comparative Perspectives" (Routledge 2018), and "Media and Inequality" (Routledge 2022). Her book, "The Mediation of Financial Crises: Watchdogs, Lapdogs or Canaries in the Coal Mine," was published in 2020.

**Stephen Kurczy** is a visiting assistant professor at Providence College, where he teaches journalism. He has also taught courses on media law, ethics, and writing at Seton Hall University and The King's College. An award-winning reporter, over nearly two decades, he has written and edited for regional, national, and international publications, including the Cambodia Daily, Christian Science Monitor, and New York Times. A past Knight-Bagehot Fellow in Business and Economics Journalism at Columbia University, where he earned his MS in Journalism, he is also the author of "The Quiet Zone: Unraveling the Mystery of a Town Suspended in Silence" (Dey Street Books 2021).

**Alyson Martin** is a founder and editor of Cannabis Wire, a reader-supported, newsletter-driven news organization that covers policy, regulation, and research focused on the global cannabis industry. Cannabis Wire was launched with grant funding, including a Magic Grant from the David and Helen Gurley Brown Institute for Media Innovation (a collaboration between Columbia University and Stanford University), and a grant from New York City's Office of Media and Entertainment. Martin also co-authored the book "A New Leaf: The End of Cannabis Prohibition" (The New Press). Martin teaches journalism courses at the Columbia University Graduate School of Journalism and runs the Columbia News Service.

**Jill Martin** is an assistant professor of practice at the University of Nebraska-Lincoln College of Journalism and Mass Communications. She teaches reporting and editing. She is the director of the Nebraska News Service and the co-director of the college's Experience Lab. Prior to accepting the position at CoJMC, Martin served as the managing editor of four weekly publications in Southeast Nebraska, including the Seward County Independent, Milford Times, Friend Sentinel and Wilber Republican. Martin holds a bachelor's degree in communication studies and a master's degree in professional journalism from UNL. She has nearly two decades of experience in newspapers, radio and television news, including positions at KLKN-TV in Lincoln and KNOP-TV and KELN/KOOQ in North Platte. She has received numerous awards in the Nebraska Press Association's annual newspaper competition. She is a member of the Nebraska Press Women, the Society of Professional Journalists, Investigative Reporters & Editors, and the Association for Education in Journalism and Mass Communication.

**Joe Mathewson** is a professor at the Medill School of Journalism, Media, Integrated Marketing Communications at Northwestern University, Chicago and Evanston, Illinois. He was a reporter for The Wall Street Journal in New York, Washington and Chicago, covering various industries, the stock market, Congress, and the Supreme Court. He graduated from the University of Chicago Law School and practiced law in Chicago, where he also worked in financial services. He is the author of "Ethical Journalism: Adopting the Ethics of Care" (2021), "A Quick Guide to Writing Business Stories" (2016), "Law and Ethics for Today's Journalist: A Concise Guide" (2013), and "The Supreme Court and the Press: The Indispensable Conflict" (2011). He has taught business reporting and writing to MSJ students for more than 20 years.

**Henrik Müller** is the chair of economic policy journalism at the Institute of Journalism and Mass Media at TU Dortmund University, Germany, where he directs bachelor and master programs at the intersection of economics and journalism studies. He studied economics at the University of Kiel, holds a doctoral degree in economics from the University of the Armed Forces Hamburg, and graduated from German School of Journalism in Munich. Prior to joining the faculty in Dortmund, he worked as a business journalist for two decades, his last position being the deputy editor-in-chief at manager magazin, a monthly. Müller is the author of numerous books on economic policy and is a weekly columnist for Der Spiegel, the German news magazine. In 2023, his book, "Challenging Economic Journalism – Covering Business and Politics in an Age of Uncertainty," was published by Palgrave Macmillan.

**Matthew W. Ragas** (PhD, University of Florida) is a professor of public relations in the College of Communication at DePaul University in Chicago. He was the founding director of the master's in professional communication program. He researches, teaches, and consults on subjects within the fields of corporate communication and strategic communication, including developing business literacy for communicators. With colleague Ron Culp, he has co-authored or co-edited "Business Acumen for Strategic Communicators" (2021), "Mastering Business for Strategic Communicators" (2018), and "Business Essentials for Strategic Communicators" (2014).

**Kaci Richter** is an assistant professor of practice and communication design coordinator at the College of Journalism and Mass Communications. She teaches audio production, podcasting and communication design courses. She worked in commercial radio as on-air talent at KIBZ-FM, KSLI-FM and KLMY-FM in Lincoln, Nebraska. She held various positions off the air, including promotions director and web director at both KSLI-FM and KLMY-FM. Richter began her teaching career at Iowa Western Community College where she served as the Media Studies Program Chair and faculty from 2008 until 2019. She has a bachelor's degree in journalism, a graduate certificate in public relations and social media and a master's degree in professional journalism from the University of Nebraska-Lincoln. She also holds a master's degree in management and leadership from Doane University and is pursuing a PhD in public administration from the University of Nebraska at Omaha. Richter is a published audiobook narrator, producer, podcast host and free-lance audio editor.

**Ceci Rodgers** is a professor of journalism in the Medill School of Journalism, Media, Integrated Marketing Communications at Northwestern University. A former broadcast and print business journalist, her academic appointments include being the Director of Global Journalism Learning at Medill. She is Northwestern's Faculty Senate Past President, after serving as President and President-Elect. Her teaching focuses on business and economics reporting, basic writing and reporting and multimedia reporting. Her work appeared on

CNN, CNNfn, CNBC, NBC, Reuters Insider, the syndicated show BusinessWeek Weekend and the PBSshow CEO Exchange.

**José Luis Rojas Torrijos** is an associate professor of journalism at the University of Seville, Spain. He also participates in the MA programs in journalism and sports communication at Pompeu Fabra University, the European University in Madrid, San Antonio Catholic University in Murcia, Pontifician University in Salamanca and Marca-CEU University. He holds a PhD in Journalism (2010) and a BA in Information Sciences (1994) from the University of Seville. His research focuses on sports journalism, quality journalism, media innovation and digital storytelling.

**Chris Roush** is the former dean of the School of Communications at Quinnipiac University. He spent 17 years at the University of North Carolina at Chapel Hill, where he started its business journalism program. He is the author or coauthor of ten books, including the textbook "Show Me the Money: Writing Business and Economics Stories for Mass Communication" and "The Future of Business Journalism: Why it Matters for Wall Street and Main Street." He has won awards for business journalism teaching and has taught business journalism on five continents.

**Steve Schifferes** is the former Marjorie Deane Professor of Financial Journalism and founder of the MA in Financial Journalism at City University of London, where he is currently an honorary research fellow at City's Political Economy Research Centre. He is also a visiting professor of journalism at Middlesex University. He is the co-editor of three books: "The Media and Financial Crises" (2014), "The Media and Austerity" (2018) and "The Media and Inequality" (2023), all published by Routledge, and the author of the chapter on financial journalism in the "Edinburgh History of the British and Irish Press in the Twentieth Century" (2020). He has written and lectured widely on financial journalism and financial crises across the world. He was a Knight-Bagehot Fellow in Economic Journalism at the Columbia University Graduate School of Journalism and a BBC Fellow at the Reuters Institute for the Study of Journalism at Oxford University. Before his academic career, he covered business and economics for BBC News for two decades, leading the BBC's online coverage of the global financial crisis.

**Anya Schiffrin** is the director of the technology and media specialization at Columbia University's School of International and Public Affairs and a senior lecturer who teaches on global media, innovation and human rights. She writes on topics related to journalism sustainability, impact and online disinformation. Her most recent book is the edited collection "Media Capture: How Money, Digital Platforms and Governments Control the News" (Columbia University Press 2021). She holds a PhD from the University of Navarra.

**Ibrahim Seaga Shaw** is the Chairman and Information Commissioner of the Right to Access Information Commission in Sierra Leone and Chair, Graduate Programme, Faculty of Communications, Media, and Information Studies, Fourah Bay College, University of Sierra Leone. He was a Senior Lecturer in Media and Politics at Northumbria University, U.K., and served as the Secretary General of the International Peace Research Association (IPRA) between 2012 and 2016. He is the author of five books, including "Business Journalism: A Critical Political Economy Approach," (2016), published by Routledge, and "Human Rights Journalism"

(2012), published by Palgrave, and over 40 academic articles and book chapters. He holds a PhD from the Sorbonne. He is also a journalist and publisher/CEO of the Expo Media Group that publishes Expo Magazine (monthly) and the Expo Times newspaper in Sierra Leone.

**Melony Shemberger** is a professor of journalism and mass communication at Murray State University in Murray, Kentucky. She researches and writes about journalism history and the scholarship of teaching and learning. Before entering academia, Shemberger had successful, award-winning careers as an education and business journalist and later in university public relations. Shemberger has a bachelor's degree, with a double major in mass communication, and history and government, Western Kentucky University; a master's in mass communication, Murray State; a master's in management, Austin Peay State University; a master's in instructional systems design, University of Kentucky; and a doctorate in administration and supervision, with a concentration in higher education, Tennessee State University.

**Sara Silver** holds the Alan Abelson Endowed Chair of Business Journalism at Quinnipiac University, where she teaches students to follow the international money trail and established a training partnership with The Wall Street Journal. As an adjunct at Columbia Journalism School, she trains master's students and international journalists to uncover the rich trove of news in financial statements. While at the WSJ, she covered the implosion of telecom equipment giants under pressure from Chinese competition. She began reporting for The Associated Press in Mexico, where she later wrote an award-winning series for the Financial Times that kept a would-be Evita from channeling charity to her campaign to succeed her husband as the president. Silver earned an MBA and an MS in Journalism at Columbia, both thanks to the Knight-Bagehot Fellowship.

**Dean Starkman** is an investigative journalist, media analyst, author, and teacher who focuses on finance, media and the intersection between the two. As a newspaper reporter, he helped lead the *Providence Journal* to the 1994 Pulitzer Prize for Investigations, and covered white-collar crime, corporate governance and general business news for The Wall Street Journal and other major American newspapers; as a magazine writer, he wrote about the financial crisis, business media, and economic inequality for *The New Republic, The Nation, Mother Jones* and other publications. As a media critic, he ran the Columbia Journalism Review's business section, "The Audit," a daily critique of the U.S. business press. He wrote "The Watchdog that Didn't Bark: the Financial Crisis and the Disappearance of Investigative Journalism" (Columbia University Press 2014). He has taught media courses for Central European University's Department of Public Policy. He is currently a senior editor at the Washington-based International Consortium of Investigative Journalists, responsible for overseeing longform investigative stories; prize-winning projects include "Paradise Papers" (2017), "The Implant Files" (2018), The China Cables" (2019), "Luanda Leaks" (2020), "The FinCEN Files" (2020), "The Pandora Papers" (2021), "The Uber Files" (2022), and "The Ericsson List" (2022).

**Nadine Strauß**, PhD, is an assistant professor of strategic communication and media management (tenure track) at the Department of Communication and Media Research at the University of Zurich. From 2019 until 2021, she completed a Marie Sklodowska-Curie Fellowship at the Smith School of Enterprise and the Environment at the University of Oxford, where she studied the role of the news media for sustainable finance. Her research has been published in various peer-reviewed journals, such as Journalism, Digital Journalism, Climatic Change, and Communication Research.

**Alecia Swasy** is a professor and the Donald W. Reynolds Chair in Business Journalism at Washington and Lee University in Lexington, Virginia. She worked as a reporter and editor at the Wall Street Journal and the St. Petersburg Times prior to earning her PhD at the University of Missouri. She is the author of "A Wall Street Guidebook for Journalism and Strategic Communication" (2020), "How Journalists Use Twitter: The Changing Landscape of U.S Newsrooms" (2016), "Changing Focus: Kodak and the Battle to Save a Great American Company" (1996) and "Soap Opera: The Inside Story of Procter & Gamble" (1993).

**Jeffrey Timmermans** holds the Donald W. Reynolds Chair in Business Journalism at Arizona State University's Walter Cronkite School of Journalism and Mass Communication and is the director of the Reynolds Center for Business Journalism. He worked for more than a decade as a reporter and editor at The Wall Street Journal and Dow Jones Newswires. He joined the Cronkite School in 2021 from The University of Hong Kong, where he served as an associate professor and director of the undergraduate journalism program. He has a BA from Colgate University, an MS from Columbia University's Graduate School of Journalism and a PhD from The University of Hong Kong.

**Hai L. Tran** is an associate professor of journalism at DePaul University in Chicago. His research and teaching link theory to practice in journalism, including data-driven reporting, multimedia storytelling, agenda setting and methodology. Tran's scholarship is informed by several years of experience working across platforms in the newsroom. He has published journalism research in top-tier journals such as *Journalism & Mass Communication Quarterly*, *Media Psychology*, *Journalism Studies*, and *Journalism: Theory, Practice and Criticism*, among many others.

**Dan Trigoboff** is on the faculty at St. Augustine's University and has served on the faculties at Elon University and Methodist University, all in North Carolina. He also taught at North Carolina State University, where he earned his PhD. A lawyer and journalist, he covered legal issues for The Los Angeles Daily Journal, American Lawyer Media, and Legal Times, and covered media as a senior editor at Broadcasting & Cable magazine. He began his career at the Taunton Daily Gazette (Massachusetts). His work appears in "Society, Ethics, and the Law: A Reader" (2020), and "Guns 360: Differing Perspectives and Common-Sense Approaches to Firearms in America" (2022).

**Alfonso Vara-Miguel,** PhD, is an associate professor of economics, media management and business journalism at the School of Communication at the University of Navarra, Spain. His main research interests are media management, journalism, and economic and financial news. He has published several papers about these issues in Journalism Practice, Discourse and Society, and Communication and Society, among others. He is the author of "Economía básica para Comunicadores" (2009) and (with Ángel Arrese) "Fundamentos de Periodismo Económico" (2011). Since 1998, he has headed the Seminar of Financial and Business Journalism, a training program for undergraduate students at the university's School of Communication.

**Rob Wells** is an associate professor and PhD Program Director at the University of Maryland's Philip Merrill College of Journalism. His research focuses on business journalism, particularly the trade press. He teaches data journalism, investigative journalism and graduate journalism courses. He is the author of "The Enforcers: How Little-Known Trade Reporters Exposed the Keating Five and Advanced Business Journalism" (University of Illinois Press 2019) and "The Insider: How the Kiplinger Newsletter Bridged Washington and Wall Street" (University of Massachusetts Press 2022). Wells was a reporter and editor for several news outlets, such as The Associated Press, Bloomberg News, and Dow Jones Newswires/ The Wall Street Journal.

# INTRODUCTION

*Joseph Weber*

As we move through the third decade of the 21st century, business and economic journalism endures as a vibrant area of news coverage around the world. Its history is fascinating, dating back to the very earliest publications, as this volume makes clear. And its status today remains rich and varied, even as practitioners contend with the financial and technological challenges (and opportunities) facing all media.

In this book, distinguished journalists and journalism academics explore the field in its wondrous variety. Readers will find information about and analysis of this fascinating corner of the news business from several continents and many countries. The tapestry that emerges in these pages stretches from Asia and Africa to Europe and the Americas, all locales where commerce makes for compelling coverage.

As they range from discussions of the globally important Panama and Pandora papers to the growth of entrepreneurial journalism in the Spanish-speaking world and the challenges facing the field in places such as Ghana, Sierra Leone, and China (as well as across the Western world), the contributors provide unique perspectives drawn from their immersions in those areas. Still others here share their knowledge and reporting about issues such as the rise of women and minorities in the field and the hurdles they've overcome or still face, the difficulties in covering economics in times of great ferment, and the roles public relations specialists play in the reporting of business matters.

Business and economic journalism, of course, touches on all aspects of life and culture. So, along the way, our contributors explore politics, the impact of such individuals as Rupert Murdoch, the role of labor, and the rich history of this field. Some discuss the effects various technologies have had on business reporting, ranging from the influence of television to the growth of the internet and emerging fields such as podcasting. Others paint portraits of the rise and fall of once-powerful media outlets, explore the growth and importance of trade journalism and the coverage of art and sports, and examine the transitions that business journalists make into areas such as public relations or academia.

This effort, nearly three years in the making, involved 44 major contributors and several others who aided them and the editors. Their expertise in the field – whether as current or former practitioners or as academics who study the area – allowed them to provide

DOI: 10.4324/9781003298977-1

exceptional depth in each chapter. Their expertise is as varied as business and economic journalism itself.

While we, as editors, have sought to retain the varied voices of each contributor, in the hope that their varying approaches will reflect their cultures and norms, we also sought some consistency. Thus, the text here adheres to the latest Associated Press style with just a few departures. Bowing to the needs of an academic volume, however, the notes and references adhere to Harvard style.

Our hope is that readers find this volume to be an engaging snapshot of the field at this most important and tumultuous point in its development, as well as a rich accounting of where it has been and where it is heading. It has been a delight and an education to work with the talented folks whose insights have shaped this volume. Enjoy it.

# PART I

# Hot Topics

# 1

# PANDORA PAPERS

## An Insider's View of Cross-Border Collaboration

*Dean Starkman*

### Introduction

Everybody loves cross-border journalism – these days.

At this point, it has arrived. It's an accepted journalism practice. One could even call it a thing.

Many people are saying so.[1]

Who, after all, can be against collaborating? Collaborating to amplify societal impact? Data? Sharing data? Using bespoke, high-end, ultra-secure technology to share the data to collaborate to amplify societal impact? At this point, only oligarchs,[2] arms traffickers,[3] a string of former Honduran presidents,[4] the former Czech prime minister,[5] the Ecuadorian president,[6] Apple,[7] Nike,[8] the offshore services industry,[9] certain global law[10] and accounting firms,[11] the former Icelandic prime minister,[12] Vladimir Putin's judo partners and other flunkies,[13] HSBC, Deutsche Bank, JPMorgan Chase and major global banks,[14] the defunct Estonian branch of a Danish bank[15] and maybe a few others.

Other than that, it's pretty popular. And there are many good reasons for that, which we'll get to.

This paper offers a practitioner's perspective on cross-border journalism collaboration, focusing on the Pandora Papers, the 2021 blockbuster probe of the offshore financial system organized by the International Consortium of Investigative Journalists, the Washington-based news organization where I work as a senior editor.

The Pandora Papers project offers a good opportunity to pause and reflect on the practice of cross-border journalism. By any fair measure – and I realize I have a dog in this fight – it made for a highwater mark for the practice.

The documents were the focus of the largest journalism collaboration in history[16] – and I can testify that publishing a project based on them certainly felt like it.

In terms of raw size, the Pandora Papers leak, at 2.94 terabytes, was bigger than both Panama Papers (2.6 terabytes) and Paradise Papers (1.4 terabytes). If you go by the number of files, the Paradise Papers had more – 13.4 million files, compared to Pandora's 11.9 million.[17]

DOI: 10.4324/9781003298977-3

Unlike the Panama Papers, which came from a single offshore service provider – Mossack Fonseca (now defunct) – the Pandora Papers came from 14 providers based in tax havens around the world from the Seychelles to Cyprus to, well, Panama again.

ICIJ shared the files with 150 media partners, including The Washington Post, the BBC, The Guardian, Radio France, Oštro Croatia, the Indian Express, Zimbabwe's The Standard, Morocco's Le Desk and Ecuador's Diario El Universo. The investigation spanned two years and came to include more than 600 journalists in 117 countries and territories.[18]

I pause to let the "600 journalists" on a single project figure sink in.

## An Insider's View

Here, I offer views on what it's like to work inside one of these projects; the impact it had on the world, from where I sat; and an assessment of where cross-border journalism stands today. It has evolved from admirable idea to core business journalism practice vital to the public interest. Oh, and we need to figure out how to make it sustainable.

Chuck Lewis, a renowned investigative reporter, founded ICIJ and is a historian of the cross-border journalism movement. He traces the practice to at least the founding of the Associated Press in 1846, when four New York newspapers pooled resources to better cover the Mexican-American War. But in a sense, he is being modest, and he quite rightly moves quickly to his own role in founding the Center for Public Integrity in 1989, a non-profit newsroom designed to carve out a space for journalism in the public interest amid the publicly traded, commercially motivated media monoliths of the day. Almost as an outgrowth of its non-profit model, it pioneered the then-radical idea that news organizations might cooperate, when in 1994, it collected some 2,000 pages of paper Indian campaign contribution records, manually typed into a single database, and shared them with a consortium it organized of legacy Indiana news organizations. The project, "Statehouse Sellout: How Special interests Have Hijacked the Legislature," was a hit. A model was born.[19]

Lewis went on to found ICIJ in 1997 to expand the cooperative idea across borders, an idea ahead of its time. Housed in the basement offices at the Center for Public Integrity with just three full-time staffers, ICIJ had produced worthy investigations into tobacco smuggling and the U.S. AIDS policy abroad, among other things.[20]

It's important to pause to remember that ICIJ was born into a different media world than exists today – one of robustly profitable (albeit, yes, flawed) commercial news organizations supporting giant newsrooms. Local markets supported local newspapers, some of them excellent, some of them less so.[21] ICIJ then could be seen as a noble experiment that would supplement the output of the mainstream.

The organization's modern incarnation began just as the old world was cratering, with the arrival in 2008 of accomplished Argentine journalist Marina Walker Guevara and again in 2011, when Gerard Ryle, the investigation editor for the Sydney Morning Herald, arrived as the director of ICIJ. At the time, he was already in possession of a hard drive of containing 2.5 million documents from two offshore financial service providers.[22]

Two years later, an ICIJ-led global collaboration of journalists from nearly 40 news organizations and 46 countries used the hard drive's leaked records to produce an investigation formally called Secrecy for Sale but known internally as Offshore Leaks.[23] The probe was a journalistic landmark, and the leak – as leaks tend to do – generated others, documents from other offshore service providers, banks, law firms and other sources. This remarkable string of gets provided the basis for a string of offshore blockbusters, including Luxembourg

Leaks, based on nearly 28,000 pages of confidential tax rulings granted by the government of Luxembourg to some of the world's largest corporations[24]; SwissLeaks, featuring records from the Swiss branch of one of the world's biggest banks, HSBC[25]; and the Bahama Leaks, in 2016, based on internal documents from the island nation's corporate registry.[26]

The Panama Papers,[27] also published in 2016, have been much remarked-upon and right-fully so. Featuring a massive leak from the now-defunct Panamanian law firm Mossack Fon-seca, they included financial and attorney-client information on more than 214,000 offshore entities, and were anonymously leaked by a confidential source to reporters Bastian Ober-mayer and Frederik Obermaier at the German newspaper Süddeutsche Zeitung, an ICIJ partner. The stories are still powerfully relevant today.[28]

My career in investigative and financial journalism began as a local reporter in Anniston, Alabama, with an investigation into health, safety and labor law violations at a steel plant in nearby Georgia. In the mid-1980s and early 1990s, I worked as an investigative reporter and later investigative chief at The Providence Journal, in Rhode Island, then beset by the twin plagues of public corruption and organized crime. I became fascinated by money – its motivational power, by the mechanics of corruption and its corrosive effects on public trust and democracy itself.[29] Later, as a staff writer at The Wall Street Journal, I reported on white-collar crime, securities law, corporate governance, and later heavy industries and the com-mercial real estate business (where I crossed paths in the early 2000s with Donald J. Trump, then considered a second-tier New York developer). Later, I became a critic of the business press, and while an editor at the Columbia Journalism Review, wrote a book on financial journalism's tragic and glaring failures in the lead-up to the financial crisis.[30]

And while at CJR, I became an admirer of ICIJ and began noting the potential of cross-border collaborations.[31]

So, it felt slightly karmic when, in 2017, ICIJ asked me for editing help for the final stages of the Paradise Papers,[32] based principally on the leak of documents from a high-end offshore provider, the Bermuda-based Appleby law firm. That project was followed by others: Mau-ritius Leaks, an exposé of the tax haven's role in diverting tax revenue away from its African neighbors,[33] Luanda Leaks, on the insider dealings of Africa's richest woman and daughter of Angola's president,[34] the Implant Files, exposing the dangerously underregulated medi-cal devices industry,[35] China Cables, based on leaked Chinese government documents on mass incarceration in Xinjiang,[36] and FinCEN Files, a project with BuzzFeed News on major banks' role in money-laundering.[37] My job as a senior editor consists of working with ICIJ editors and writers to shape the overall project and with the writers to shape the copy of ICIJ's longform investigations.

By the time the Implant Files were published in the fall of 2018, a mere two years after the Panama Papers, cross border had crossed a threshold to the point that CJR's Jon Allsop could write.

When ICIJ published the Panama Papers in 2016, its collaborative model seemed like a bold departure from the old logic of fierce competition. Two years later, pooling resources across organizations no longer feels so novel. News organizations the world over are strug-gling financially; many have folded; those that survive often have such slender resources that ambitious investigative work is beyond their means. In the Trump era, meanwhile, some outlets, especially in the U.S., have started to see each other less as rivals and more as allies in the face of vicious rhetoric attacking the media as a whole. ICIJ's success with the Panama Papers – not to mention its Pulitzer Prize for the work – no doubt fueled this trend, too.[38]

By then I, too, had become acclimated to the routines of cross-border work – mostly working in isolation with copy, or one-on-one with reporters, punctuated by a series of secure video conference calls throughout the week with fellow ICIJ staffers, and, less frequently, with reporters and editors from partner organizations in various time zones.

Work on the Pandora Papers began in early 2021 the usual way: an excited Signal call from Ryle announcing a new leak, except this one was going to be bigger and more explosive than anything that had come before. ICIJ's data team, led by Emilia-Diaz Struck in Washington, had been sifting through what we would later call an "offshore data tsunami": the 11.9 million-plus records were largely unstructured. More than half the files (6.4 million) were text documents, including more than 4 million PDFs, some of which ran to more than 10,000 pages. The documents included passports, bank statements, tax declarations, company incorporation records, real estate contracts and due diligence questionnaires. There were also more than 4.1 million images and emails in the leak. Spreadsheets made up 4 percent of the documents, or more than 467,000. The records also included slide shows and audio and video files.[39]

ICIJ published a methodology of the data work on Pandora[40] but suffice it to say that roughly half of ICIJ's staff on a project are data experts who do the work of stripping out text from PDFs, emails and other documents, weeding out duplicates, formatting them, making make them searchable and – critically – verifying the accuracy of every number in the story, such as, for instance, the number of Russian oligarchs found in the data (46).[41]

Even less visible in the final published project – but no less indispensable – is the work of ICIJ's discrete (and discreet) technology group, which develops the bespoke technology platforms that provide the foundation for both searching data and communicating findings efficiently and securely. Led by Pierre Romera in the Paris office, the group built Datashare, a software that allows reporters to index, search, star, tag, filter and analyze data whatever the format (text, spreadsheets, pdf, slides, emails, etc.). Datashare automatically highlights and extracts the names of people, locations and organizations in documents, as well as email addresses.

Above all, Datashare is secure and can be used locally on personal computers to minimize the risk of interception. Primarily designed for investigative journalists, it can be used by anyone who needs to analyze and explore a set of documents. It's also open-source and free.[42]

The technology group also developed the I-Hub,[43] the social media platform that allows previously vetted partners to share findings securely and, as we learned with the Pandora Papers, can accommodate hundreds of reporters at the same time, all talking at once.

The ICIJ collaborative model is based on previously established relationships with mostly legacy news organizations – e.g., Le Monde, the BBC – and individual professional practitioners. The success and security of the enterprises rise and fall on these trust relationships. I have described ICIJ's model as a form of "professional peer production."[44] In my view, the concept represents an advance from both the old model of an individual news organization acting on its own and the utopian idea once popular in some quarters of crowd-sourced news and investigations.[45]

The rules for partners are simple, but adherence is critical. Once a publication date is established, no one jumps the deadline. And once allowed into the data, partners are expected to share what they find. That's basically it.

Pandora, code named Aladdin, had to overcome a serious handicap: because of COVID, we never met in person. Typically, partners and ICIJ assemble somewhere – Washington for "Implant Files," Paris for "Luanda Leaks," for instance – to hash over initial impressions of the data, draw up potential storylines, vote on a publication date and, importantly, socialize over meals, coffees and drinks to establish or cement relationships.

Instead, we launched with a massive call on a secure communications platform with dozens of partners staring out from small boxes on a screen. Since COVID, the world has become accustomed to living our entire work lives online, for better and for worse. In the cross-border business, remote work is built into the model. It was remote before COVID. It will be remote afterward. I'm unable to add any original insights to the subject of remote work here, except to say in-person newsrooms at least allowed the possibility for humanizing chance encounters that might help resolve lingering tensions. In a remote newsroom, there are no chance encounters or non-transactional conversations. Every communication is deliberate, even calls to "catch up."

But I don't want to idealize newsrooms of the past. There were plenty of tensions there, too, and plenty of ways to avoid people you didn't get along with. The main disadvantages to remote work for me are virtual meetings. The format lends itself more to presentations than conversations or proper give-and-take. Actual feedback and critique are best left to private calls on Signal. Beyond that, and despite everything, my experience in a news organization of moderate size, remote work basically works.

And so it did with Pandora. I work from home in Budapest or at an office provided by the Democracy Institute at the Central European University, with which I am affiliated. From my perch, I worked with ICIJ staffers to shape many of the stories we publish. Our editorial process, which has been refined since I arrived, generally involves reporters digging into data, performing Datashare searches for weeks or even months to find story ideas. While this may sound like a series of glorified Boolean searches, don't kid yourself. It is frustrating – and because it is frustrating – exhausting work. I spent days in the Aladdin data and came up with precisely nothing. It is highly specialized work and the ICIJ bylines you read result from the fact that the authors were able to find the stories in the first place. It took senior reporter Scilla Alecci with help from Pavla Halcova of ICIJ's Czech partner investigace.cz to discover that the then-sitting rightwing prime minister of the Czech Republic, Andrej Babis, had secretly bought a French chateau via complex transactions involving an anonymous shell company registered in Monaco.[46] And ICIJ's Will Fitzgibbon found that while foreign aid was pouring into Jordan, King Abdullah II was secretly buying $100 million in luxury properties in the U.S. and elsewhere. His Swiss and Caribbean wealth advisors referred to his majesty as "you know who."[47]

I've spoken to ICIJ reporters informally about how they do it, and, invariably, and modestly, they chalk it up to instinct, hard work and patience. A fuller accounting of their data searching techniques awaits further study.

My view of the project from Budapest was limited. The nature of remote cross-border work requires each practitioner to work in personal isolation that is mitigated by virtual contacts on a variety of platforms – Rocket Chat groups, WhatsApp and/or Signal groups and direct messages, I-Hub posts and direct messages, emails, sometimes encrypted using the Mailvelope application. I attended weekly internal "Aladdin" calls run by ICIJ's unflappable managing editor, Fergus Shiel, who also serves as the hub for the entire project, managing relationships with partners and mediating any disputes that arise both within ICIJ and among partners.

The project formally launched in April 2021 with a virtual general meeting of partners that already numbered several dozen and began to mushroom from there. Smaller group calls were periodically organized for Eastern Europe, Western Europe, Latin America, Central

Asia, Africa, each group managed by an ICIJ regional coordinator. Newly arriving partners went through Datashare training offered by Jelena Cosic, ICIJ's Belgrade-based training manager who also coordinates Eastern European partners.

Soon, the I-Hub began to fill with more posts, news, tips and excited chatter as stories began to emerge.

Latin America proved a particularly rich vein. Among the 14 offshore service providers whose data was leaked was the prestigious Panama law firm, Alemán, Cordero, Galindo & Lee, which, ICIJ's data team discovered, had set up offshore companies for 160 politicians – nearly half of the 300 or so political figures whose names appear in the leaked records. And of the 35 current and former heads of states who appear in the records, 14 were from Latin America.[48]

Leads popped up around the world. Family members of Sri Lankan President Gotabaya Rajapaksa's family had used shell companies to buy luxury property and artwork.[49] The family of Kenya's reformist president Uhuru Kenyatta secretly had owned a network of offshore companies for decades.[50]

America's largest law firm, Baker McKenzie, turned out to have been a go-to firm for Kremlin-linked companies seeking to evade U.S. sanctions.[51]

And we found, a leading center for offshore finance turns out to be Sioux Falls, South Dakota.[52]

Maybe the richest trove turned out to be the offshore service providers that cater particularly to Russians, including the Cyprus law firm Demetrios A. Demetriades and Seychelles-based Alpha Consulting Limited.[53]

Putin's propaganda chief, Konstantin Ernst, owned a secret stake in a massive, state-funded privatization deal. Herman Gref – the chief executive of Sberbank, Russia's biggest bank – used an offshore operative in Singapore in 2015 to restructure a $75 million family trust tied to a tangle of offshore companies.

And so on, and so forth.

The I-Hub became inundated with posts from all over the world. Newcomers, and even old timers, couldn't be blamed for feeling overwhelmed by the sheer volume of data, and as much as ICIJ struggled to make the information flow coherent, reading the I-Hub could itself become an overwhelming experience. The Russia section alone contained 128 original posts. A single post about a single figure, Putin's alleged mistress, Svetlana Krivonogikh, a former cleaning woman found to have ties to a luxury Monaco apartment,[54] generated 735 posts and comments.

ICIJ meanwhile prepared a staggering budget of more than a dozen longform investigations, each numbering more than 4,000 words, each with countless sensitive facts about dozens of powerful and often litigious subjects.

I worked with reporters on copy, spending sometimes hours at time on a Signal call working with a reporter someplace far away on a document on a secure Google Drive server. The most extreme example of remote working collaboration came on a story that would reveal the offshore holdings of members of the Pakistani military and ministers in the government of erstwhile reformer Imran Khan.[55] Over the course of at least six days, I sat down at 8 a.m. Budapest time for a line-by-line edit of the 4,000-plus word copy with the authors, Margo Gibbs, working on London time, Malia Politzer, working in Spain, and a co-editor, Mia Zuckerlandel, working from 11 p.m. often until 3 a.m. from her base in California. Such is the new normal in the world of cross-border collaboration.

Tension within the project spiked in August when the Russian government declared ICIJ's local partner, Important Stories (known as IStories), along with the independent broadcaster Dozhd, as "foreign agents," an ominous step that came just five months after Russian police had raided iStories' offices and the homes of some of its staff members.[56] IStories is now based outside Russia.[57]

The project built to a crescendo with the beginning of "comment period," the massive, coordinated global effort to contact every subject in every story to provide an opportunity to respond to the findings. The unfolding of the comment period, which began several weeks before publication, began the most intense period of the project, in which reporters both finished and fact-checked their stories while incorporating the responses, or as often happens, grappling with legal threats from high-powered law firms around the world.

So, what in the end was the point of all this work, all this confrontation, all this stress? During media appearances on behalf of ICIJ, or just at a dinner party, someone invariably asks: Why do we bother anyway when nothing ever changes?

Doesn't it?

A week after Pandora Papers was published, a bloc of Czech opposition parties stunned Babis and his party in the national elections, pushing the rightwing government aside and allowing a new coalition to form a government. One media poll suggested that 8 percent of his party's supporters switched their votes as a result of Pandora Papers disclosures.[58]

The project sparked a protest wave throughout Latin America. Honduran voters in the country's presidential election rejected Nasry Asfura, the once-favored ruling party candidate exposed as secretly invested in Panamanian companies[59]; Chilean lawmakers moved to impeach President Sebastián Piñera in response to revelations about his children's offshore dealings[60]; Ecuador's President Guillermo Lasso survived his own impeachment, an effort directly sparked by the probe.[61]

Pandora Papers revelations, on top of a decade of work on Russian oligarchs, became instantly relevant after Russia invaded Ukraine in February 2022. The U.S. and other Western governments began levying sanctions against those named in the Pandora Papers and other ICIJ projects. Among them: the banker Gref, the cellist Sergey Roldugin exposed in the Panama Papers as likely Putin front man,[62] and, significantly from my point of view, the propagandist Ernst,[63] who had largely managed to evade international scrutiny until our exposé.

In February 2022, the U.K. government announced a new economic crime bill that would establish a new registry forcing foreign owners of U.K. property to reveal and verify their identities or face harsh penalties, including prison.[64] Meanwhile, citing ICIJ's FinCEN Files, a government agency published a white paper outlining a long-overdue overhaul of Companies House, the government registry and notorious safe-haven for anonymous shell companies.[65]

In the U.S., the House of Representatives passed the so-called ENABLERS Act that for the first time required trust companies, lawyers, art dealers and other professionals to investigate clients and report suspicious activity to the Treasury Department. The measure was introduced days after the Pandora Papers' publication and was inspired by it, according to the bill's authors.[66]

The list goes on.

Listen, no one is arguing that ICIJ – or all of cross-border journalism put together – is more than just another set of voices in the broader fight for democracy and rule of law in an increasingly authoritarian world. And while the roll call of reform law and other project impact is a point of pride and fair game in the endless fundraising struggle, it's important to keep some perspective. The reforms cited here remain incremental and incomplete. The U.K. registry law is "full of loopholes," some critics say.[67] The ENABLERS Act as of this writing remains stuck in the Senate and faces stiff opposition from the American Bar Association[68] and other powerful interests.[69]

But journalism can be a long game.

In January 2021, Congress passed The Corporate Transparency Act, requiring companies registered in the U.S. to report their true owners to the Treasury Department.[70] The law effectively ended the anonymous shell company business in the U.S. and further discredited the practice in general. And in October 2021, 136 countries of the Organization of Economic Cooperation and Development signed an agreement to tax multinationals at a minimum rate of 15 percent in a bid to clamp down on profit shifting and aggressive tax avoidance.[71]

Both measures are flawed. Both are also landmarks. Both, in my view, are inconceivable without cross-border exposés hammering offshore finance over a decade.

From a journalism perspective, the Pandora Papers stretched the limits of the possible when it comes to cross-border journalistic collaboration and raises the question of how big is too big? In my view, a lot depends on the point person for a project – whoever has overall coordinating responsibility within the organization that is managing all the partners.

The subject calls for further academic research, and I'd suggest that future researchers start with Shiel, my boss, who coordinated for Pandora. By way of preview, I excerpt his response to a recent email exchange with me on the topic:

> Time, technology and complexity are the great limitations to every international investigation. Together with editorial resources, source protection and team safety, they largely dictate the scope and duration of the work. To succeed, you need clear divisions of responsibilities; regular operational meetings; a production schedule; constant technical support: and an immutable bedrock of trust.[72]

The year 2021 also marked a coming out of sorts for collaborative journalism in general. Where the ICIJ model was once a journalism novelty, it has now proliferated in the form of organizations dedicated to the practice, such as European Investigative Collaborations,[73] as well as ad-hoc cooperative efforts. The Facebook Papers,[74] the Pegasus Project[75] and Suisse Secrets,[76] all ad-hoc collaborations, appeared in the months before and after the Pandora Papers. The Facebook Papers, exposing the platform's cynical anger-driven business model, and the Pegasus Project, showing the misuse of NSO Group spyware on journalists, human rights defenders, academics and others, were bona fide blockbusters.

The cross-border field is becoming populated, even crowded. The public is now routinely exposed to projects with alliterative titles, all touting big numbers, the size of the leak, the number of partners and so on.[77] This proliferation is a good thing. ICIJ can take some credit, if I may say so.

But as much as a sign of strength, this proliferation, to Allsop's point above, can also be seen as a response to journalism's financial weakness[78] and its marginalization in minds of huge swaths of the population.[79] That makes the sustainability of cross-border even more of a public interest imperative.

The proliferation also raises questions about where the practice goes from here, whether ad-hoc collaborations have advantages over ICIJ's fixed-hub-and-spoke model, and, if so, how dispersed the model should become. I'm an interested party, but I'd say that there's a good argument for a professional organization with long experience in handling leaks securely, building collaborative platforms, cleaning data and managing projects of vast size and scope. In other words, I'm thinking if ICIJ didn't exist it would probably have to be invented. I realize, as the Wall Street expression goes, I'm talking my book, but there you are.

## Conclusion

The Pandora Papers should be seen as the most recent, and maybe strongest evidence so far, that cross-border journalism has evolved from a status as a useful supplement to professional journalism – a feel-good enterprise that everyone can applaud – into a core competence and indispensable tool for journalism in general and for business journalism in particular. The financial industry and the economy globalized long ago. So, too, did large-scale public corruption, along with the industry that launders the proceeds using anonymous shell companies registered in secrecy jurisdictions. These shell companies then open bank accounts[80] in corrupt regional banks that then – for some reason – are still allowed to shuffle the money through giant global banks in Lower Manhattan with accounts at the Federal Reserve Bank of New York. That's all pretty global.

Business journalism is only now catching up, and it is in large part, thanks to cross-border journalism. Its impact on public debate has only grown and is now manifest. In short, cross-border journalism is no longer nice to have. It is required in the public interest.

Finally, a cautionary note: it's important to remember what cross-border journalism is and isn't. It is a valuable journalism tool. It's not a business model. ICIJ, for instance, relies solely on donor funding,[81] and for the time being its financial success is only very indirectly tied to its journalistic success.

And that makes its future uncertain.

## Notes

1 See, for example: Sambrook, R. (2018) *Global Teamwork: The Rise of Collaboration in Investigative Journalism*, The Reuters Institute for the Study of Journalism ISBN: 978-1-907384-35-6 Available at: https://reutersinstitute.politics.ox.ac.uk/sites/default/files/2018-03/sambrook_e-ISBN_1802.pdf; Heft, A. and Baack, S. (2021) "Cross-Bordering Journalism: How Intermediaries of Change Drive the Adoption of New Practices," *Journalism*, Vol. 23 (11), 1–19. https://doi.org/10.1177/1464884921999540; Hume, E. and Abbott, S. (2017) "The Future of Investigative Journalism: Global, Networked and Collaborative," Center for Media Data and Society, March. Available at: https://cmds.ceu.edu/sites/cmcs.ceu.hu/files/attachment/article/1129/humeinvestigativejournalismsurvey_0.pdf;

Lück, J. and Schultz, T. (2019) "Investigative Data Journalism in a Globalized World," *Journalism Research*, Vol. 2 (2), 93–114. ISSN 2569-152X; cross-border now has at least one funding institution devoted to the practice, e.g., The IJ4EU fund, which supports cross-border investigations of public interest in Europe; see https://www.investigativejournalismforeu.net/; Columbia University Graduate School of Journalism offers post-graduate fellow known as, "The Cross-Borders Data Project': see Investigations.https://journalism.columbia.edu/cross-borders-data, among other examples.

2 Sallah, M. and Kozyreva, T. (2020) "With Deutsche Bank's Help, an Oligarch's Buying Spree Trails Ruin Across the US Heartland," *International Consortium of Investigative Journalists (ICIJ)*, September 22. Available at: https://www.icij.org/investigations/fincen-files/with-deutsche-banks-help-an-oligarchs-buying-spree-trails-ruin-across-the-us-heartland/

3 Michaels, M. and Hudson M. W. (2021), "Pandora Papers Reveal Emirati Royal Families' Role in Secret Money Flows," *ICIJ*, November 16. Available at: https://www.icij.org/investigations/pandora-papers/pandora-papers-reveal-emirati-royal-families-role-in-secret-money-flows/

4  Medina, B. Escudero, J. and Díaz-Struck, E. (2021) "When Latin America's Elite Wanted to Hide Their Wealth, they Turned to this Panama Firm," *ICIJ*, October 3. Available at: https://www.icij.org/investigations/pandora-papers/alcogal-panama-latin-america-politicians/

5  No author (2021), "Pandora Papers: The Power Players)," *ICIJ*, October 3. Available at: https://www.icij.org/investigations/pandora-papers/power-players/

6  Ibid.

7  Bowers, S. (2017) "Leaked Documents Expose Secret Tale of Apple's Offshore Island Hop," *ICIJ*, November 6, 2017. Available at: https://www.icij.org/investigations/paradise-papers/apples-secret-offshore-island-hop-revealed-by-paradise-papers-leak-icij/

8  Bowers (2017) "How Nike Stays One Step Ahead of the Regulators," *ICIJ*, November 6, 2017. Available at: https://www.icij.org/investigations/paradise-papers/swoosh-owner-nike-stays-ahead-of-.the-regulator-icij/

9  No author (2021), "Pandora Papers: The Secrecy Brokers," *ICIJ*, October 3, 2021. Available at: https://www.icij.org/investigations/pandora-papers/secrecy-brokers/

10  Ibid.

11  Hallman, B. et al. (2020), "Western Advisers Helped an Autocrat's Daughter Amass and Shield a Fortune," *ICIJ*, January 19. Available at: https://www.icij.org/investigations/luanda-leaks/western-advisers-helped-an-autocrats-daughter-amass-and-shield-a-fortune/

12  No author (2016): "Official: Iceland PM Resigns Amid 'Panama Papers' Fallout," *CBSNews* (online), April 5. Available at: https://www.cbsnews.com/news/iceland-prime-minister-sigmundur-david-gunnlaugsson-resigns-panama-papers/

13  Gibbs, M., Kranhold, K. and Cosic, J. (2021) "Putin Image-Maker's Role in Billion-Dollar Cinema Deal Hidden Offshore," *ICIJ*, October 3, 2021. Available at: https://www.icij.org/investigations/pandora-papers/vladimir-putin-konstantin-ernst-russia-tv-offshore/; Bernstein, J. et al. (2021), "All Putin's Men: Secret Records Reveal Money Network Tied to Russian Leader," *ICIJ*, April 3, 2016. Available at: https://www.icij.org/investigations/panama-papers/20160403-putin-russia-offshore-network/

14  ICIJ (2020), "Global Banks Defy U.S. Crackdowns by Serving Oligarchs, Criminals and Terrorists"; "Global Banks Defy U.S. Crackdowns by Serving Oligarchs, Criminals and Terrorists," September 20, 2020. Available at: https://www.icij.org/investigations/fincen-files/global-banks-defy-u-s-crackdowns-by-serving-oligarchs-criminals-and-terrorists/

15  Bowers, S., Kehoe, K. and Roonemaa, H., "Inside Scandal-Rocked Danske Estonia and the Shell-Company 'Factories' That Served It," *ICIJ*, September 21, 2020. Available at: https://www.icij.org/investigations/fincen-files/inside-scandal-rocked-danske-estonia-and-the-shell-company-factories-that-served-it/

16  Starkman, D., et al. (2021), "Frequently Asked Questions About the Pandora Papers and ICIJ," *ICIJ*, October 19. Available at: https://www.icij.org/investigations/pandora-papers/frequently-asked-questions-about-the-pandora-papers-and-icij/

17  Ibid.

18  Ibid.

19  Lewis, C. (2018) "Tear Down These Walls: Innovations in Collaborative Accountability Research and Reporting," in Sambrook, Investigative Reporting Workshop, https://archive.investigativereportingworkshop.org/2018/01/26/the-power-of-reporters-working-together/

20  Sadek, N. (2022) "The Inside Story of How the Offshore Leaks Database Became a Go-to Resource on Offshore Finance," *ICIJ*, May 3, 2022. Available at: https://www.icij.org/investigations/pandora-papers/the-inside-story-of-how-the-offshore-leaks-database-became-a-go-to-resource-on-offshore-finance/

21  For a fuller discussion of journalism's transformation, see Starkman (2014), *The Watchdog That Didn't Bark*, Columbia University Press, New York, Chapter 10, "Digitism, Corporatism, and the Future of Journalism: As the Hamster Wheel Turns."

22  Sadek.

23  The "Secrecy for Sale" project is available at: https://www.icij.org/investigations/offshore/secret-files-expose-offshores-global-impact/

24  The "Luxembourg Leaks" project is available at: https://www.icij.org/investigations/luxembourg-leaks/

25 The "Swiss Leaks" project is available at: https://www.icij.org/investigations/swiss-leaks/about-project-swiss-leaks/

26 The Bahamas Leaks project is available at: https://www.icij.org/investigations/offshore/former-eu-official-among-politicians-named-new-leak-offshore-files-bahamas/

27 The Panama Papers project is available at https://www.icij.org/investigations/panama-papers/

28 See Bernstein et al., which exposed a clandestine network operated by Putin associates, including the unlikely figure of cellist and Putin childhood friend, Sergey Roldugin, that shuffled at least $2 billion through banks and offshore companies.

29 The author notes that the governor of the day, Edward D. DiPrete, later imprisoned on corruption charges stemming from the author's reporting, chose to retain as his principal political advisor none other than the young Paul Manafort, then in a consulting firm with Roger Stone, now both key figures in the U.S. ongoing crisis of democracy.

30 Starkman (2014).

31 Starkman (2013) "Investigative Collaboration, Cross-Border Edition," *CJR* (online), April 8. Available at: ttps://archives.cjr.org/the_audit/investigative_collaboration_cr.php?page=all: "A Good Sign That Your Investigation Has Hit the Mark Is When Law Enforcement Agencies Start Demanding to See Your Data."

32 The Paradise Papers project is available here:https://www.icij.org/investigations/pandora-papers/the-inside-story-of-how-the-offshore-leaks-database-became-a-go-to-resource-on-offshore-finance/

33 The "Mauritius Leaks" project is available at https://www.icij.org/investigations/mauritius-leaks/.

34 The "Luanda Leaks" project is available at https://www.icij.org/investigations/luanda-leaks/

35 The "Implant Files" project is available here: https://www.icij.org/investigations/implant-files/

36 The "China Cables" project is available here: https://www.icij.org/investigations/china-cables/

37 The "FinCEN Files" project is available here: https://www.icij.org/investigations/fincen-files/

38 Allsop, J. (2018) "Under the skin of ICIJ's Implant Files," *Columbia Journalism Review*, November 26. Available at: https://www.cjr.org/special_report/behind_the_scenes_icij_implant_files.php

39 Diaz-Struck et al. (2021) "Pandora Papers: An Offshore Data Tsunami," *ICIJ*, October 3. Available at: https://www.icij.org/investigations/pandora-papers/about-pandora-papers-leak-dataset/

40 Ibid.

41 Shiel, F. (2021) "About the Pandora Papers," *ICIJ*, October 3. Available at https://www.icij.org/investigations/pandora-papers/about-pandora-papers-investigation/

42 Ledésert, S. (2019) "What Is Datashare," *ICIJ*, November 4. Available at https://www.icij.org/inside-icij/2019/11/what-is-datashare-frequently-asked-questions-about-our-document-analysis-software/

43 Boland-Rudder, H. and Cabra, M. (2014) "ICIJ to Build Global I-Hub, a New Secure Collaboration Tool," *ICIJ*, July 17. Available at https://www.icij.org/inside-icij/2014/07/icij-build-global-i-hub-new-secure-collaboration-tool/

44 Starkman. (2017) "#ParadisePapers and the Rise of Professional Peer Production," *Center for Media, Data and Society*, November 8, 2017. Available at: https://medium.com/center-for-media-data-and-society/paradisepapers-and-the-rise-of-professional-peer-production-fc56a5ca9a87

45 For a discussion on hopes for socially produced news, see Starkman (2011) "Confidence Game: The Limited Vision of the News Gurus," *CJR*, November/December, an examination of the work of academics Jeff Jarvis, Clay Shirky and Jay Rosen, Where I Address This Debate. Available at https://archives.cjr.org/essay/confidence_game.php

46 Alecci, S. (2021). "Czech Prime Minister Secretly Bought Lavish French Riviera Estate Using Offshore Companies," *ICIJ*, October 3. Available at: https://www.icij.org/investigations/pandora-papers/czech-prime-minister-andrej-babis-french-property/

47 Fitzgibbon, W. (2021) "While Foreign Aid Poured in, Jordan's King Abdullah Funnelled $100m Through Secret Companies to Buy Luxury Homes," *ICIJ*, October 3. Available at https://www.icij.org/investigations/pandora-papers/jordan-king-abdullah-luxury-property/

48 Medina, B. (2021) "Chilean Legislators Impeach President after Pandora Papers Revelations." *ICIJ*, November 9. Available at: https://www.icij.org/investigations/pandora-papers/chilean-legislators-impeach-president-after-pandora-papers-revelations/

49 Hudson and Fitzgibbon (2021) "Pandora Papers Caps off 2021 with Consequences Felt Around the Globe," December 21. Available at: https://www.icij.org/investigations/pandora-papers/pandora-papers-caps-off-2021-with-consequences-felt-around-the-globe/; and Alecci (2021)

"Clamor for Crackdown on Hidden Wealth Jolts Sri Lanka Elite Following Pandora Papers Revelations," *ICIJ*, November 1. Available at https://www.icij.org/investigations/pandora-papers/clamor-for-crackdown-on-hidden-wealth-jolts-sri-lanka-elite-following-pandora-papers-revelations/

50 Olewe, D. and Adamou, L. (2021) "Pandora Papers: Uhuru Kenyatta family's Secret Assets Exposed by Leak," *British Broadcasting Service* (online), October 4. Available at: https://www.bbc.com/news/world-africa-58775944

51 Freedberg, S. (2022) "Baker McKenzie, a Go-to Firm for Kremlin-Linked Companies, Now Says it's Leaving Russia," *ICIJ*, March 15. Available at: https://www.icij.org/investigations/pandora-papers/baker-mckenzie-a-go-to-firm-for-kremlin-linked-companies-now-says-its-leaving-russia/

52 Fitzgibbon, Cenziper, D. and Salwan, G. (2021) "Suspect Foreign Money Flows into Booming American Tax Havens on Promise of Eternal Secrecy, *ICIJ*, October 3. Available at: https://www.icij.org/investigations/pandora-papers/us-trusts-offshore-south-dakota-tax-havens/

53 Woodman. (2022) "How a Network of Enablers Have Helped Russia's Oligarchs Hide Their Wealth Abroad," *ICIJ*, March 22. Available at: https://www.icij.org/investigations/russia-archive/how-a-network-of-enablers-have-helped-russias-oligarchs-hide-their-wealth-abroad/

54 Sonne, P. and Miller, G. (2021) "Secret Money, Swanky Real Estate and a Monte Carlo Mystery," *The Washington Post* (online), October 4. Available at: https://www.washingtonpost.com/world/interactive/2021/putin-monaco-luxury-apartment/?itid=lk_inline_manual_13

55 Gibbs and Politzer (2021) "Prime Minister Imran Khan Promised 'New Pakistan' But Members of his Inner Circle Secretly Moved Millions Offshore," *ICIJ*, October 3. Available at: https://www.icij.org/investigations/pandora-papers/pakistan-imran-khan-prime-minister-allies-offshore/

56 Shiel and Cosci (2021) "Russia brands IStories a 'Foreign Agent' in Independent Media Crackdown," *ICIJ*, August 20. Available at: https://www.icij.org/inside-icij/2021/08/russia-brands-istories-a-foreign-agent-in-independent-media-crackdown/

57 *Organized Crime and Corruption Reporting Project* (2022), "Reporting from Exile: A Webinar with Russian Journalist Roman Anin," *OCCRP*, July 19. Available at: https://www.occrp.org/en/announcements/16481-reporting-from-exile-a-webinar-with-russian-journalist-roman-anin

58 See Hudson and Fitzgibbon (2021)

59 Ibid.

60 Medina (2021) "Chilean President Avoids Removal after Senate Impeachment Vote Sparked by Pandora Papers," *ICIJ*, November 16. Available at: https://www.icij.org/investigations/pandora-papers/chilean-president-avoids-removal-after-senate-impeachment-vote-sparked-by-pandora-papers/

61 Medina (2021) "Ecuador President Survives Removal Effort by National Assembly Following Pandora Papers Revelations," *ICIJ*, December 8. Available at:https://www.icij.org/investigations/pandora-papers/ecuador-president-survives-removal-effort-by-national-assembly-following-pandora-papers-revelations/

62 Bernstein et al.

63 Cosic, J. (2022) "Canada Sanctions 10 Putin Allies, Including Russia's Leading TV Propagandists," *ICIJ*, March 8. Available at https://www.icij.org/investigations/russia-archive/canada-sanctions-10-putin-allies-including-russias-leading-tv-propagandists/

64 *Gov.UK* (2022) "Government Takes Landmark Steps to Further Clamp Down on Dirty Money," Gov.Uk, February 22. Available at: https://www.gov.uk/government/news/government-takes-landmark-steps-to-further-clamp-down-on-dirty-money

65 Kehoe (2022) "UK Moves to Clamp Down on Dirty Russian Money," *ICIJ*, March 4. Available at:https://www.icij.org/investigations/fincen-files/uk-moves-to-clamp-down-on-dirty-russian-money/

66 Toosi, N. (2021) "Lawmakers, Inspired by 'Pandora Papers,' to Push New Anti-Corruption Bill," *Politico*, October 5. Available at: https://www.politico.com/news/2021/10/05/pandora-papers-anti-corruption-bill-515177

67 *The Guardian* (2022) "Register of Offshore Owners of UK Properties Full of Loopholes, Say Experts," *The Guardian*, March 22. Available at: https://www.theguardian.com/money/2022/mar/01/register-of-offshore-owners-of-uk-properties-full-of-loopholes-say-experts

68 *American Bar Association* (2022), "House Passes Sweeping Defense Authorization Bill Imposting Bank Secrecy Act Regulations on Lawyers," July 28. Available at: https://www.americanbar.org/advocacy/governmental_legislative_work/publications/washingtonletter/july-22-wl/enablers-0722wl/

69 "H.R. 5525: ENABLERS Act" (2021), U.S. Congressional Legislation. Govtrack.us (online). Available at: https://www.govtrack.us/congress/bills/117/hr5525

70 Mustafa, A. (2020) "Advocates Celebrate Major US Anti-Money Laundering Victory," *ICIJ*, December 11. Available at: https://www.icij.org/investigations/paradise-papers/advocates-celebrate-major-us-anti-money-laundering-victory/
71 Boland-Rudder and Fitzgibbon. (2021) "136 Countries Agree to Global Minimum Tax for Corporations in 'Historic' OECD Deal," *ICIJ*, October 8. Available at: https://www.icij.org/investigations/paradise-papers/136-countries-agree-to-global-minimum-tax-for-corporations-in-historic-oecd-deal/
72 Shiel, F. (2022) ICIJ managing editor, email to the author, August 4–5.
73 See https://eic.network/
74 For an example of the ad-hoc consortium's output, see Wired Staff (2021) "Inside the Facebook Papers," *Wired* (online), October 25. Available at: (2021https://www.wired.com/story/facebook-papers-internal-documents/
75 *Forbidden Stories* (2021) "About The Pegasus Project," *Forbidden Stories* (online), July 18. Available at: https://forbiddenstories.org/case/the-pegasus-project/.
76 For an example of the project's output, see *The Guardian* (2022), "Suisse Secrets." Available at: https://www.theguardian.com/news/series/suisse-secrets
77 Examples: "Through our partner, German newspaper *Süddeutsche Zeitung*, OCCRP obtained leaked records on more than 18,000 Credit Suisse accounts, the largest leak ever from a major Swiss bank." See https://www.occrp.org/en/suisse-secrets/; and: "An unprecedented leak of more than 50,000 phone numbers selected for surveillance by the customers of the Israeli company NSO Group shows how this technology has been systematically abused for years. The Forbidden Stories consortium and Amnesty International had access to records of phone numbers selected by NSO clients in more than 50 countries since 2016." See https://forbiddenstories.org/about-the-pegasus-project/
78 For a full discussion, see Starkman and Chittum, R. (2021), "The Hamster Wheel, Triumphant," in Schiffrin, A. *Media Capture How Money, Digital Platforms, and Governments Control the News*, Columbia University Press, pages 232–258; and Grieco, E. (2020) "10 Charts About America's Newsrooms," *Pew Research Center*, April 20. Available at: https://www.pewresearch.org/fact-tank/2020/04/28/10-charts-about-americas-newsrooms/
79 For a history of rightwing efforts to discredit the press, see Brock, David (2004) *The Republican Noise Machine: Right-Wing Media and How It Corrupts Democracy*, Crown Publishers, New York.
80 For what it's worth, the author finds it hard to believe that major U.S. banks are still permitted to make dollar transactions between foreign bank accounts owned by anonymous shell companies.
81 For a discussion of philanthropy and journalism, see Benson, R. (2017). "Can foundations Solve the Journalism Crisis?" *Journalism*, Vol. 19 (8), https://doi.org/10.1177/1464884917724612.

## Further Reading

Hamilton, J. (2016). *Democracy's Detectives: The Economics of Investigative Journalism*, Cambridge, MA, Harvard University Press. Groundbreaking study of investigative journalism's positive externalities.
Sambrook, R. (2018) *Global Teamwork: The Rise of Collaboration in Investigative Journalism*, The Reuters Institute for the Study of Journalism ISBN: 978-1-907384-35-6. A multi-faceted exploration of cross-border journalism.
Schiffrin, A. (2021) *Media Capture: How Money, Digital Platforms, and Governments Control the News*, New York, Columbia University Press. A valuable overview of media problems and possible solutions.
Starkman, D. (2014). *The Watchdog that Didn't Bark: The Financial Crisis and the Disappearance of Investigative Journalism*, New York, Columbia University Press. Places business journalism history within a framework that juxtaposes two competing fields: access vs. accountability journalism.

## References

Alecci, S. (2021a). *ICIJ*. Available at: https://www.icij.org/investigations/pandora-papers/clamor-for-crackdown-on-hidden-wealth-jolts-sri-lanka-elite-following-pandora-papers-revelations/
Alecci. (2021b). *ICIJ*. Available at: https://www.icij.org/investigations/pandora-papers/czech-prime-minister-andrej-babis-french-property/

Allsop, J. (2018). *Columbia Journalism Review*. Available at: https://www.cjr.org/special_report/behind_the_scenes_icij_implant_files.php

Benson, R. (2017). *Journalism*. Available at: https://doi.org/10.1177/1464884917724612

Bernstein, J. et al. (2016). *ICIJ*. Available at: https://www.icij.org/investigations/panama-papers/20160403-putin-russia-offshore-network/

Boland-Rudder and Cabra, M. (2014). *ICIJ*. Available at: https://www.icij.org/inside-icij/2014/07/icij-build-global-i-hub-new-secure-collaboration-tool/

Boland-Rudder, H. and Fitzgibbon, W. (2021). *ICIJ*. Available at: https://www.icij.org/investigations/paradise-papers/136-countries-agree-to-global-minimum-tax-for-corporations-in-historic-oecd-deal/

Bowers, S. (2017a). *ICIJ*. Available at: https://www.icij.org/investigations/paradise-papers/apples-secret-offshore-island-hop-revealed-by-paradise-papers-leak-icij/

Bowers. (2017b). *ICIJ*. Available at: https://www.icij.org/investigations/paradise-papers/swoosh-owner-nike-stays-ahead-of-the-regulator-icij/

Bowers, Kehoe K. and Roonemaa, H. (2020). *International Consortium of Investigative Journalists (ICIJ)*. Available at: https://www.icij.org/investigations/fincen-files/inside-scandal-rocked-danske-estonia-and-the-shell-company-factories-that-serve

Brock, D. (2004). New York, Crown Publishers.

*CBS News*. (2016). Available at: https://www.cbsnews.com/news/iceland-prime-minister-sigmundur-david-gunnlaugsson-resigns-panama-papers/

Cosic, J. (2022). *ICIJ*. Available at: https://www.icij.org/investigations/russia-archive/canada-sanctions-10-putin-allies-including-russias-leading-tv-propagandists/

Diaz-Struck, E. et al. (2021). *ICIJ*. Available at: https://www.icij.org/investigations/pandora-papers/about-pandora-papers-leak-dataset/

Fitzgibbon. (2021). *ICIJ*. Available at: https://www.icij.org/investigations/pandora-papers/jordan-king-abdullah-luxury-property/

Fitzgibbon, W. and Cenziper, D. (2021). *ICIJ*. Available at: https://www.icij.org/investigations/pandora-papers/the-cowboy-cocktail-how-wyoming-became-one-of-the-worlds-top-tax-havens/

Fitzgibbon, Cenziper and Salwan, G. (2021). *ICIJ*. Available at: https://www.icij.org/investigations/pandora-papers/us-trusts-offshore-south-dakota-tax-havens/

Freedberg, S. (2022) *ICIJ*. Available at: https://www.icij.org/investigations/pandora-papers/baker-mckenzie-a-go-to-firm-for-kremlin-linked-companies-now-says-its-leaving-russia/

Gibbs, M., Kranhold, K. and Cosic, J. (2021). *ICIJ*. Available at: https://www.icij.org/investigations/pandora-papers/vladimir-putin-konstantin-ernst-russia-tv-offshore/

Gibbs and Politzer, M. (2021). *ICIJ*. Available at: https://www.icij.org/investigations/pandora-papers/pakistan-imran-khan-prime-minister-allies-offshore/

*Govtrack.us* (2022). Available at: https://www.govtrack.us/congress/bills/117/hr5525

Grieco, E. (2020) Pew Research Center. Available at: https://www.pewresearch.org/fact-tank/2020/04/28/10-charts-about-americas-newsrooms/

Hallman, B. et al. (2020). *ICIJ*. Available at: https://www.icij.org/investigations/luanda-leaks/western-advisers-helped-an-autocrats-daughter-amass-and-shield-a-fortune/

Heft, A. and Baack, S. (2021). *Journalism*, 23(11), 1–19. https://doi.org/10.1177/1464884921999540

Hudson, M. and Fitzgibbon. (2021). *ICIJ*. Available at: https://www.icij.org/investigations/pandora-papers/pandora-papers-caps-off-2021-with-consequences-felt-around-the-globe/

Hume, E. and Abbott, S. (2017). "The Future of Investigative Journalism: Global, Networked and Collaborative," Center for Media Data and Society, March. Available at: https://cmds.ceu.edu/sites/cmcs.ceu.hu/files/attachment/article/1129/humeinvestigativejournalismsurvey_0.pdf

*ICIJ*. (2013). "Secrecy for Sale." Available at: https://www.icij.org/investigations/offshore/secret-files-expose-offshores-global-impact/

ICIJ (2014). Available at: https://www.icij.org/investigations/luxembourg-leaks/

*ICIJ*. (2015). "Swiss Leaks." Available at: https://www.icij.org/investigations/swiss-leaks/

*ICIJ*. (2016a). "Bahamas Leaks." Available at: https://www.icij.org/investigations/offshore/former-eu-official-among-politicians-named-new-leak-offshore-files-bahama

*ICIJ*. (2016b). "Panama Papers." Available at: https://www.icij.org/investigations/panama-papers/

*ICIJ*. (2017) "Paradise Papers." Available at:

*ICIJ.* (2020). Available at: https://www.icij.org/investigations/fincen-files/global-banks-defy-u-s-crackdowns-by-serving-oligarchs-criminals-and-terrorists/

*ICIJ.* (2021a). Available at: https://www.icij.org/investigations/pandora-papers/secrecy-brokers/

*ICIJ.* (2021b). Available at: https://www.icij.org/investigations/pandora-papers/power-players/

Kehoe. (2022). *ICIJ.* Available at: https://www.icij.org/investigations/fincen-files/uk-moves-to-clamp-down-on-dirty-russian-money/

Ledésert, S. (2019). *ICIJ.* Available at: https://www.icij.org/inside-icij/2019/11/what-is-datashare-frequently-asked-questions-about-our-document-analysis-software/

Lück, J. and Schultz, T. (2019). Investigative Data Journalism in a Globalized World, *Journalism Research*, 2(2), pp. 93–114. ISSN 2569-152X

Medina. (2021a). *ICIJ.* Available at: https://www.icij.org/investigations/pandora-papers/chilean-president-avoids-removal-after-senate-impeachment-vote-sparked-by-pandora-papers/

Medina. (2021b). *ICIJ.* Available at: https://www.icij.org/investigations/pandora-papers/ecuador-president-survives-removal-effort-by-national-assembly-following-pandora-papers-revelations/

Medina. (2021c). *ICIJ.* Available at: https://www.icij.org/investigations/pandora-papers/chilean-legislators-impeach-president-after-pandora-papers-revelations/

Medina, B., Escudero, J. and Díaz-Struck, E. (2021). *ICIJ.* Available at: https://www.icij.org/investigations/pandora-papers/alcogal-panama-latin-america-politicians/

Mustafa, A. (2020). *ICIJ.* Available at: https://www.icij.org/investigations/paradise-papers/advocates-celebrate-major-us-anti-money-laundering-victory/

Olewe, D. and Adamou, L. (2021), *British Broadcasting Service Online.* Available at: https://www.bbc.com/news/world-africa-58775944

*Organized Crime and Corruption Reporting Project.* (2022). OCCRP.org. Available at: https://www.occrp.org/en/announcements/16481-reporting-from-exile-a-webinar-with-russian-journalist-roman-anin papers/

Sadek, N. (2022). *ICIJ.* Available at: https://www.icij.org/investigations/pandora-papers/the-inside-story-of-how-the-offshore-leaks-database-became-a-go-to-resource-on-offshore-finance/

Sallah, M. and Kozyreva, T. (2020). *ICIJ.* Available at: https://www.icij.org/investigations/fincen-files/with-deutsche-banks-help-an-oligarchs-buying-spree-trails-ruin-across-the-us-heartland/

Sambrook, R. (2018). *The Reuters Institute for the Study of Journalism.* Available at:

Shiel, F. (2021). *ICIJ.* Available at: https://www.icij.org/investigations/pandora-papers/about-pandora-papers-investigation

Shiel (2022) email to the author.

Sonne, P. and Miller, G. (2021). *The Washington Post.* Available at: https://www.washingtonpost.com/world/interactive/2021/putin-monaco-luxury-apartment/?itid=lk_inline_manual_13

Starkman. (2011). *CJR*, November/December. Available at: https://archives.cjr.org/essay/confidence_game.php

Starkman. (2013). *CJR.* Available at: ttps://archives.cjr.org/the_audit/investigative_collaboration_cr.php?page=all: "

Starkman. (2014). *The Watchdog That Didn't Bark: The Financial Crisis and the Disappearance of Investigative Journalism*, New York, Columbia University Press.

Starkman. (2017). *Center for Media, Data and Society.* Available at: https://medium.com/center-for-media-data-and-society/paradisepapers-and-the-rise-of-professional-peer-production-fc56a5ca9a87

Starkman et al. (2021). *ICIJ.* Available at: https://www.icij.org/investigations/pandora-papers/frequently-asked-questions-about-the-pandora-papers-and-icij/

Starkman and Chittum, R. in Schiffrin, A. (ed) (2021). *Media Capture How Money, Digital Platforms, and Governments Control the News*, New York, Columbia University Press, pages 232–258.

*The Guardian.* (2022). Available at: https://www.theguardian.com/money/2022/mar/01/register-of-offshore-owners-of-uk-properties-full-of-loopholes-say-experts

Toosi, N. (2021). *Politico.* Available at: https://www.politico.com/news/2021/10/05/pandora-papers-anti-corruption-bill-515177

Wired Staff. (2021). *Wired.* Available at: https://www.wired.com/story/facebook-papers-internal-documents/

Woodman. (2022). *ICIJ.* Available at: https://www.icij.org/investigations/russia-archive/how-a-network-of-enablers-have-helped-russias-oligarchs-hide-their-wealth-abroad/

# 2
# SHINING A LIGHT ON TAX AVOIDANCE

How the Panama Papers Created Salience
in a World Crowded with Good Causes

*Alexandre Gonçalves, Anya Schiffrin and Shant Fabricatorian*

## Introduction

The Panama Papers, published in 2016, brought the problem of tax avoidance to front pages around the world. A massive leak of documents laid bare the role of lawyers who helped the rich and powerful keep their money in offshore accounts and the International Consortium of Investigative Journalists (ICIJ) showed the costs to society of this tax avoidance. By publishing a series of articles, and following up with other leaks, including Lux Leaks in 2014, Swiss Leaks in 2015 and the Pandora Papers in 2021, the ICIJ helped set the agenda and bring the problem of tax avoidance to the attention of the public. Other journalists have also written extensively on such avoidance, including the 2022 series Suisse Secrets published by the Organized Crime and Corruption Reporting Project.

The reporting by journalists complemented efforts by social justice advocates and campaigns by international non-governmental organizations (INGOs) that had been trying for more than a decade to bring about policy changes. Making this arcane financial topic salient to mass audiences can be difficult, and both journalists and non-governmental organizations (NGOs) have used a range of techniques in order to pique the interest of the public and generate outrage (Keck & Sikkink 1998; Hendrix & Wong 2014). However, the reporting by dozens of outlets belonging to the ICIJ, and their massive release of news on the same day across the globe, captured the world's attention in a way that NGO campaigns did not. A number of studies show the effectiveness of the ICIJ reporting in raising awareness and bringing about political change (Pitt & Green-Barber 2017; Graves & Shabbir 2019; Lublinski 2020).

The ICIJ's reporting has been extensively studied and a number of scholars have highlighted the impact of the papers (Graves & Shabbir 2019). Scholars have looked at the policy changes that resulted (Pitt & Green-Barber 2017; Konieczna & Graves 2020). They have also studied the effects on the journalism profession, including the role of data journalism (Bradshaw 2021), ethics and norms (Cortés and Luengo 2021) and the role of advocacy journalism (Stonbely 2022). In her work on "Global Muckraking," Schiffrin highlighted the long-standing relationship between journalists and NGOs and, using a number of historical examples, argued that journalistic reporting is more likely to bring about change when there

DOI: 10.4324/9781003298977-4

are already INGOs working on solving a social problem, entities that are accountable, and regulators that are able to change government policies (Schiffrin 2014; Stapenhurst 2000). For this reason, it is essential to look at journalism investigations in relation to other efforts already underway (Konieczna & Graves 2020).

Despite the fact an increasing number of journalists identify as advocacy reporters (Powers 2018), there are, of course, differences between journalists and advocates as well as similarities. What the ICIJ shares with the INGOs involved in campaigns against tax avoidance is the desire to catalyze change so that tax avoidance is lessened.[1] By articulating new information, journalists not only raise awareness, but can help change norms and inspire policy makers and regulators who can address the problem. Accordingly, this research employs the definition of media impact laid down by Protess et al. Protess and his colleagues argued that impact unfolds in three phases: personal, deliberative (for example, Congressional hearings) and substantive, such as policy changes or new laws (Protess 1991). Raising awareness and generating public outrage can help bring about change in all three phases that Protess and colleagues described.

We agree with the INGO argument that large-scale tax avoidance and evasion are unfair, deprive governments of revenue needed to fund social services, and undermine voter faith in the legitimacy of the tax system as well as in government. Because we believe that large-scale, long-term tax avoidance presents a threat to democracy, we are particularly interested in understanding the effect of ICIJ's reporting and how it captured public attention. We build on the argument by Barabas and Jerrit (2009) that media coverage does lead to changes in the level of knowledge among the American public. As well as reviewing literature describing how journalists and INGOs attract attention for their campaigns, one of the authors (Gonçalves) studied the response on social media to the ICIJ reporting on tax avoidance as well as the INGO campaigns in order to evaluate their relative importance, frames commonly used, shifts in sentiment and most prominent actors. We found the ICIJ reporting resulted in substantial and sustained media coverage of tax avoidance that endured over time.

## Background on Tax Avoidance

Addressing tax avoidance is a task that has historically relied heavily on reputational shaming, and as such, depends on widespread knowledge of wrongdoing. Although not illegal, certain types of tax avoidance have become tied in public perception to illegal tax evasion (McBarnet 1992) – due in part to what might be termed its "professionalization" by teams of accountants and lawyers working for multinational corporations (MNCs) and high-net-worth individuals.

Of course, efforts to minimize tax burdens are not new, but the problem has been quantified and discussed more in the past decade. In some cases, it is because local regulations encouraged the development of offshore banking, such as in the well-known cases of Switzerland and Panama (Zucman 2015). In other instances, local regulations or loopholes encouraged a race to the bottom by different states, areas or regions. For example, different U.S. states changed their regulations in order to become tax havens. South Dakota began in the 1980s, while Delaware began more than 100 years ago (Roe 2003; Dyreng, Lindsey & Thornock 2013; ICIJ 2021; Salmon 2021).

Despite public anger, and attempts by some regulators to reduce tax avoidance, the internationalization and deregulation of the financial sector in recent decades, as well as the dramatic gains in prosperity of the globe's wealthiest individuals, have provided tax-dodging efforts with new impetus. Globally, revenues lost from tax avoidance are estimated to total some $427 billion annually, and between $21 trillion and $31 trillion in financial assets are sitting offshore in tax havens, according to the Tax Justice Network (Tax Justice Network 2022). According to one estimate, the United States loses $200 billion a year from tax avoidance, and Britain's Labour Party has said the U.K. was deprived of some £13 billion in revenue over five years from 2010 to 2015 (Buchan 2017; Turner 2018). At the same time, there is evidence to suggest that such tax dodging is highly unpopular among the public.

A 2014 study by ActionAid indicated that some 85 percent of British adults considered tax avoidance by large corporations to be morally wrong, even if it was technically legal (ActionAid 2014), and in 2016, the Financial Times reported a shift in business attitudes, noting that only one in five big businesses thought that tax avoidance was acceptable (Houlder 2016). The majority of Americans say that they are bothered a lot by the feeling that some corporations and wealthy people don't pay their fair share in taxes (59 percent each), according to a Pew Research Center survey (Dunn & Green 2021).

The race to the bottom has raised public ire as the discrepancies between different countries' tax policies have become clear. The European Commission has attempted to crack down after reporting in 2013 revealed that Irish law permitted Apple to attribute over $100 billion in profit to its subsidiaries in Ireland in order to avoid paying taxes in the United States. In 2017, Apple was ordered to pay back $15 billion in taxes by the European Commission, while Ireland was accused of depriving other EU members of tax revenue by allowing Apple to attribute nearly all profits generated in the EU to Ireland. Apple later moved two of its three Irish subsidiaries to Jersey, another popular European tax haven (Farrell & McDonald 2016; Drucker & Bowers 2017).

## Exposing Tax Avoidance

Over the past decade, the major voices challenging this trend of large-scale corporate tax avoidance in the global sphere have come from NGOs such as the Geneva-based Tax Justice Network, ActionAid, Christian Aid, Oxfam, and the Independent Commission for the Reform of International Corporate Taxation (ICRICT), along with important reporting by the ICIJ, which published several lengthy series on tax avoidance and the Organized Crime and Corruption Reporting Project. Their reports and series of articles laid bare the extent to which loopholes such as offshore accounts, subsidiary shell companies and declarations of profits in tax havens are widely employed.

## The Role of Transparency

Disclosure and transparency are central to the core beliefs of the journalism community as well as the INGOs that campaign against tax avoidance (Christensen & Murphy 2004; Craft & Heim 2008). Allison Christians, in a discussion of "taxpayer morality," argues that, while an imperfect mechanism, transparency is "the best hope for achieving justice across a wide variety of governance-related failures of which unjust taxation is a prominent example" (Christians 2014). She contends that transparency forms "the central core of all contemporary treatments of the problem of governance, and there is no reason why it should not also define the contours of thinking about what behaviors should be acceptable when it comes to taxation" (Christians 2014). The paradox, however, is that more disclosure can lead to information overload in a world crowded with good causes (Thrall et al. 2014). Thus, journalists and campaigners try to find ways to make the problem meaningful and attract the sustained attention of the public as well as government officials and regulators.

## How to Garner Attention in a World Crowded with Causes – Showing Why It Matters

In the well-known framework outlined by Keck and Sikkink (1998), international advocacy networks use symbolic politics, information politics and leverage politics in order to bring about change. They find potent symbols, provide information to their audiences and push governments to sign international agreements and treaties, and then hold them to these agreements. Part of how such organizations attract attention in a world crowded with good causes is by creating "salience" (Hendrix & Wong 2014; Thrall et al. 2014). In other words, NGOs and journalists need to find ways to make the subject of tax avoidance seem like a problem that affects everyone, and that society needs to fix (O'Sullivan 2017; Quantrill 2017; Siu 2017; Powers 2018).

## Creating Salience

In his study of the political salience of the Tax Justice Network, Dallyn (2017) contends that, notwithstanding the increased prominence of tax avoidance in media coverage in recent years, existing accounting analyses have done "little to explain how some accounting issues acquire political attention and media coverage." He emphasizes the important role of news-papers in translating a complex, often-arcane area into one that has general public resonance. This has also been supported through members of TJN contributing stories to journalistic outlets to help increase exposure (see also Shaxson 2011) and advising politicians about in-ternational policy proposals.

Political salience is used by Dallyn to understand how the practice of corporate tax avoid-ance "emerged as a high profile political issue" (2017). It draws on previous work by Wong (2012) with regard to how and why some accounting issues generate more substantive atten-tion than others; he considers political salience "a concept that operates across different dimen-sions, so as a heuristic it is best assessed through a compound of indicators" (Dallyn 2017).

## Tactics of INGOs – Showing the "Human Cost"

Both INGOs and journalists use a number of tactics to create salience, some of which over-lap. Organizations like the ICIJ and Oxfam, as well as INGOs that focus on public services such as education and health, have tried to frame tax avoidance as a fairness question that has costs for society. Both tax avoidance campaigners and journalists have sought to show how much revenue is being lost through tax avoidance and what else could be done with that lost revenue. By showing the "human face" of tax avoidance, INGOs and journalists hope to show the salience of what may seem, on initial acquaintance, obscure financial jargon (ActionAid, author interview).

Journalists and INGOs show the human costs of tax avoidance in order to make their reporting more salient to broader audiences. For example, The New York Times published a story looking at what the U.S. government could fund if the top 1 percent of the wealthy in the United States paid more taxes. According to the article, the lost revenue would be more than enough to provide free undergraduate college for all, free universal pre-kindergarten, fix all of the U.S. highways, or contribute to health care (Cohen 2015). Other groups like Oxfam, the National Education Association (NEA), ActionAid and Britain's Christian Aid have also quantified the economic effects of tax avoidance, with the NEA noting that of the $222.7 billion lost to the federal government through tax avoidance schemes, $9.8 billion would have gone to public schools and colleges, funding academic support for low-income and disabled students, financial aid, pre-kindergarten programs and jobs in education (National Education Association 2011).

In their reporting, the ICIJ sought to stress the human cost. The Panama Papers stories included a video showing that clinics in Uganda were short of medicines because of tax avoidance.

> We as journalists at ICIJ were very aware that a project like Panama Papers would have limited impact if we didn't try to explain how the offshore world can touch everyday lives. We hope we achieved that, at least to some extent.
>
> *(Schiffrin interview 2018)*

Another tactic related to both information and symbolic politics (Keck & Sikkink 1998) and the notion of the "human cost" is the tendency by journalists and NGOs to "name and shame" particular companies and individuals. A report by ActionAid (Hearson & Brooks 2010) named the multinational brewing company SABMiller and shamed them for paying less taxes than the people that sell their beer. Reporters interviewed a Ghanaian beer stall owner named Marta Luttgrodt who was shocked at the discovery, as it became clear that the international tax system was an enabler of injustice.

## Using High-Profile Spokespeople

In keeping with sociologist Clifford Bob's findings about the importance of INGOs using high-profile spokespeople to gain attention, the key groups campaigning against tax avoidance have recruited high-profile individuals such as Colombian economist and former trade minister José Antonio Ocampo, Member of the European Parliament Eva Joly, and Nobel laureate Joseph E. Stiglitz to write reports and issue statements on the subject of tax avoidance (Bob 2009; ICRICT 2022).

According to Toby Quantrill, then the global economic justice lead at Christian Aid, INGOs have adopted a conscious effort to try to more effectively communicate with the public about the need for reform and enforcement. "We knew that a bunch of NGOs and radicals shouting about 'new paradigms' is relatively easy to dismiss in public debate," he said.

> [T]he theory was that by using a group of highly credible and global voices arguing for the depth of change required, then we could begin to shift public assumptions about what can be done. This needs us to be successful in reaching public ears, and policy makers in as many countries as possible, something we are still working out how to do.
>
> *(Schiffrin interview 2017)*

## Timing the Release of News, Finding and Creating News Hooks

In addition, NGOs seek public attention by timing their news releases in the hope they will have more impact, and ensure they relate the "scandal of the moment" to tax avoidance

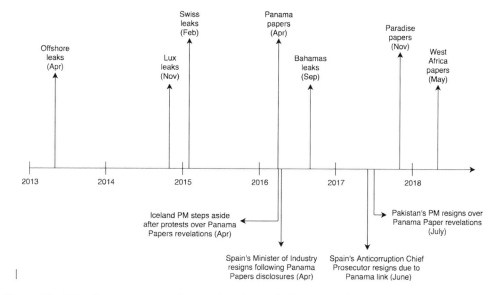

*Figure 2.1*   Major leaks in the past six years (see Appendix for more information).

(Powers 2018). News hooks such as the financial crisis of 2007–2008, Brexit (June 2016) and even natural weather occurrences such as Hurricane Irma, which affected the British Virgin Islands during August and September 2017, can help to conjure the requisite salience that can then be wedded to driving attention toward the need for international tax reform. INGO communications staffers look for any opportunity to tie their case to current events. "[I]n the wake of the international financial crisis and austerity policies, the method was to show that the people were being punished, but MNCs [Multinational Corporations] continued to be able to take advantage of generous tax cuts," said Erika Siu, formerly of the ICRICT (author interview).

The ICIJ made the release of the news, news itself. All the outlets that worked on the Panama Papers stories were told they had to hold the news and publish on the same day. The ICIJ hoped that by having dozens of outlets publish on the same day, the news of the tax avoidance would receive more attention. They succeeded and then at conferences and in trade publications and interviews for years after, the editors talked about the success of their tactic and hailed the rise of a new form of cross-border collaboration (Garside 2016; Umansky 2016). Figure 2.1 presents a timeline for the major tax scandals of the past six years.

## Media vs. Social Media

As part of our ongoing interest in how organizations garner public attention about the problem of tax avoidance, one of our authors (Gonçalves) compared the media and social media attention that resulted from the ICIJ's Panama Papers leak in 2016 and the NGO campaigns dating from 2010 to 2018.

Part of the research tried to gauge whether any of the reporting or campaigning, using the tactics described above, affected the amount and tenor of the press coverage or conversation on social media over time.

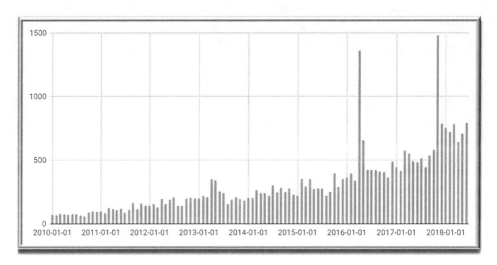

*Figure 2.2* Number of online articles per month for generic search terms and hashtags.

*Table 2.1* Twitter hashtags and Google search terms

| Type | Twitter Hashtag | Google search terms | Start | End |
|---|---|---|---|---|
| generic | #taxavoidance | "tax avoidance" | 2010–01–01 | 2018–07–31 |
| | #taxevasion | "tax evasion" | 2010–01–01 | 2018–07–31 |
| | #taxhaven | "tax haven" | 2010–01–01 | 2018–07-31 |
| | #taxshelter | "tax shelter" | 2010–01–01 | 2018–07–31 |
| specific | #luxleaks | "lux leaks" | 2014–11–01 | 2018–07–31 |
| | #swissleaks | "swiss leaks" | 2015–02–01 | 2018–07–31 |
| | #panamapapers | "panama papers" | 2016–04–01 | 2018–07–31 |
| | #paradisepapers | "paradise papers" | 2017–11–01 | 2018–07–31 |

We collected 762,412 tweets and 652,577 Google search results based on the keywords and hashtags listed in Figure 2.2. The data spanned from January 1, 2010 to July 31, 2018. We extracted all the URLs mentioned in the tweets and Google search results. After excluding duplicate URLs, we removed spurious results with the help of Watson, IBM's AI cloud solution. The resulting data set constituted the corpus of 38,112 online articles that supported our analysis. Finally, we collected the Facebook engagement data for each one of those URLs. We used it as a proxy for article reach and influence (Table 2.1).

## Results and Discussion

In general terms, the observed results were coherent and in line with the authors' initial expectations. At a macro level, Figure 2.2 shows a clear, relatively steady increase in the level of online articles related to tax avoidance/evasion/reform over the assessed period, with two big spikes. Apart from the publication of the Panama Papers and Paradise Papers which were associated with expected spikes, there was no evidence of a singular turning point or "moment" at which overall interest took off and settled at a consistently higher level.

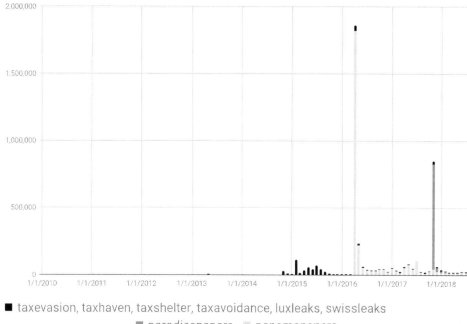

*Figure 2.3*  Number of tweets per month for all hashtags (data from Crimson Hexagon).

Rather, the rise appears to be relatively constant, suggesting that interest is being sustained over time and that the ongoing publishing of articles is itself generating further attention in the topic. This "organic" growth suggests greater resilience for the staying power over the medium-term because it signals rising interest in the subject overall – a desire for information, which is addressed by an accompanying increased level of news production and commentary.

Figure 2.3 shows how news coverage of the major tax scandals was enormously successful in grabbing media attention. In fact, the campaigns organized by INGOs (that usually resorted to the generic hashtags #taxavoidance, #taxevasion, #taxshelter and #taxhaven) pale in comparison to the media storm in the aftermath of the Paradise Papers and, especially, the Panama Papers. In fact, Figure 2.3 reveals that, in the following months, there continued to be a sizable amount of attention dedicated to the Panama Papers revelations.

The generic hashtags (#taxavoidance, #taxevasion, #taxshelter and #taxhaven), despite their poor performance vis-à-vis the Panama and Paradise Papers' hashtags, can shed some light on the strategy of INGOs. Those hashtags surged shortly after Swiss Leaks broke in February of 2015. Notably, the majority of these tweets emanated from domains located in the EU.

According to Will Fitzgibbon, senior reporter at the ICIJ, there is "no doubt" that reporting, along with the disclosure of names, led to reforms and resignations, including that of Iceland's Prime Minister Sigmundur Gunnlaugsson, as well as Michael Grahammer, CEO of Austrian bank Hypo Vorarlberg. "Especially in Europe, there were resignations not because they admitted wrongdoing, but because the 'look and feel' of being associated with [the] Panama Papers was so off," Fitzgibbon said in an email interview.

> There is little doubt in many people's minds that the decision of the Government of Panama to sign up to more international tax information exchange agreements was also related to the Panama Papers. The German parliament also passed the so-called 'Panama Law,' which I think speaks for itself, at least in terms of branding and governments wishing to be seen to respond.
>
> *(Schiffrin interview 2018)*

Our analysis of the top-ranked domains for tax articles, by overall number and Facebook engagement, shows heavy prominence for reporting by The Guardian, which gave the issue a high degree of billing, and could be considered the lead English-language narrative driver on this topic. Along with the BBC, the paper was a leading English-language partner in the Panama/Paradise Papers project, along with Süddeutsche Zeitung, Le Monde, SonntagsZeitung, Falter, La Nación, German broadcasters NDR and WDR, and Austrian broadcaster ORF. The paper also has a strong online presence and no paywall which helped its stories generate high levels of interest both in and of themselves, and through social media shares.

Notable, however, is the prominent number of shares of The Indian Express – a national daily Indian paper that took a leading role in promulgating details of the Panama and Paradise leaks and published numerous articles based on them (258 based on the Panama Papers, 72 from the Paradise Papers), as well as undertaking collaborative work on Swiss Leaks. To some extent, its high ranking may be a function of the simple volume of traffic – India's large population means that a major international story, with multiple local angles, will likely result in a high level of traffic. Nonetheless, they suggest ongoing interest in this story among Indian readers, as does the paper's dedication to publishing such a large number of stories on the subject – perhaps also influenced by the significant number of prominent Indian public figures named in the Papers.

The precise role of international NGOs in driving the narrative is somewhat obscured. It is to be expected that mainstream media publications would outrank articles published by INGOs. The INGOs were involved in exposing tax avoidance years before the Panama Papers were published but they did not spend a lot of time on social media (author interviews). This is reflected in the corpus as the news reporting seemed to generate more interest online than did the earlier INGO campaigns. Much of the INGO effort was behind the scenes and involved negotiation with government officials. It may be that the INGOs paved the way by raising awareness but the reinforcement from the media reporting had more immediate results of forcing government officials to resign and call for parliamentary hearings.

The political campaign of Bernie Sanders in 2016 gave visibility to the problem of tax avoidance, evidenced by Sanders' site being the eighth highest-ranked website as shared on social media, while the refusal of President Trump to release his tax returns allowed the media a news hook to keep returning to the issue. Tax avoidance/evasion articles went viral on Facebook during the 2016 presidential election and in the first year of Trump's presidency. Topics covered included Trump's tax reforms, his refusal to release his returns, and the alleged links of his businesses and aides to tax scandals. To some extent, Trump and his aides brought the topic of tax avoidance and evasion onto the national agenda. Interestingly, those proved the articles with the highest level of Facebook engagement in our corpus.

We also performed topic analysis and keyword extraction in our corpus with the help of IBM Watson. There was a clear evolution in the topics discussed in the six-month periods preceding and immediately following the Panama Papers leak. While many of the key concepts remained constant, there was a noticeable increase in the prominence of negatively-charged concepts, including "crime" (in conjunction with "jury"), "prison" and "Al Capone." Other concepts that included negative charges included mentions of FC Barcelona and La Liga (referencing footballer Lionel Messi's name appearing in the Papers), and Indian Prime Minister Narendra Modi, who saw people close to him implicated in the leaks and was also the leader of a country which saw a relatively large number of high-profile individuals exposed by the leaks.

While raising awareness and generating outrage are not enough on their own to bring about policy change, they can certainly lay the groundwork for such policy change to happen. This has been the argument advanced by INGO campaigners. In his seminal cost-benefit analysis of investigative journalism, James T. Hamilton notes that the stage two deliberative impact outlined by Protess et al. can lead to stage three, which is substantive change. Given that tax avoidance has existed for decades, it certainly appears that the increased attention in the media and the naming-and-shaming process catalyzed the government responses that appeared shortly after.

However, while journalists were pleased with the degree of attention attained, activists were disappointed by some of the regulatory changes, such as the OECD response on BEPS, which fell short of what the INGOs had sought.

## Conclusion

According to the ICIJ, as a consequence of the Panama Papers, 150 inquiries, audits or investigations were announced in 82 countries by police, customs, financial crime and mafia prosecutors, judges and courts, tax authorities, parliaments and corporate reviews. These resulted in the removal of senior politicians in Spain, Iceland, Mongolia, Côte d'Ivoire and Pakistan, and new laws being passed worldwide. For example, in the U.K., it became a criminal offense for lawyers not to report clients' tax evasion, while in the United States, the Corporate Transparency Act was passed, and in Indonesia, the government decreed that all companies must declare their true owners (ICIJ 2019). Beyond that, countries recouped more than $1.36 billion in unpaid taxes, fines and penalties, and $184 million in new money (Fitzgibbon & Hudson 2021).

Measuring the impact of media reporting is extremely difficult, in part because of attribution difficulties and the complexity of establishing causation (Napoli 2014; Lublinski 2015; Schiffrin & Zuckerman 2015). In the case of the campaigns and reporting on tax avoidance, it is relatively easy to see whether discussion on social media increased and more newspaper articles appeared. Our data show there is more coverage of tax avoidance now than before the Panama Papers and the other series of articles were published. It may well be that the reporting helped contribute to the 2021 decision by OECD countries to agree to a global minimum corporate tax in an effort to end the race to the bottom, with countries such as Ireland having become havens for corporate tax avoidance.

The U.S. Congress approved a modified form of the global 15 percent tax on corporations that was agreed to in principle by 131 countries in October 2021. This was a major victory after years of negotiations, although many advocates believe that 15 percent is too low because a global agreement would stop companies from moving their headquarters to countries with low taxes (Rappeport & Alderman 2021). The agreement would also tax companies where they sell goods and services, rather than where their headquarters are located (Rappeport & Alderman 2021). Russia's invasion of Ukraine in February 2022 diverted attention from this critical reform and raised new tensions within the EU. While the global agreement would not address individual tax avoidance, campaigners at ICRICT used the invasion of Ukraine as a way of calling attention to tax avoidance by using the crackdown on Russian oligarchs as a news peg and releasing a letter signed by well-known economists calling for a global registry of assets (ICRICT 2022).

In the case of tax avoidance, INGOs and journalists have made a sustained effort over many years to research the problem and present the facts to the public as well as to government and regulators. The INGOs have also produced policy proposals and assisted governments hoping to address the problem. These efforts have run up against the hard political realities of the polarized world we live in, as well as the wealth and power of major corporations and the authoritarian populists at the head of several of the world's major economies.

The questions raised by the paradox of greater campaigning and more information proving relatively ineffective in producing political change provide fodder for researchers. Both the INGO campaigning on tax avoidance and reporting such as the Panama Papers rely on "naming and shaming" as a mechanism to encourage behavior change and changes in policy. But will these tactics still work in the future? Does the polity become inured to such allegations if they are heard repeatedly, in the same way that compassion fatigue sets in (Moeller 1999; Hafner-Burton 2008; Schiffrin 2014)? Given that much of the reporting has been cross-border in nature and undertaken in multiple languages, further research will need to focus on different regions and languages in order to understand the full magnitude of the campaigns and media coverage.

Even more worrying is the backfire effect. At what point does reporting on corruption not only lead to public fatigue, but also a widespread mistrust of government, leading to the election of demagogues such as Donald Trump and Jairo Bolsonaro who play on fears that the "system is rigged"? Future researchers may want to study the role that perceptions of corruption have on elections and how INGO campaigns and media reporting can lead to solutions for the problem of tax avoidance rather than greater distrust in the political system.

## Acknowledgments

Research assistance: George Grun, Anamaria Lopez and Chloe Oldham, Jenik Radon. Thanks to Lucas Narotzky for his timeline of major events in the INGO campaigns against tax avoidance and Margaret Ng for helping with data collection. We are grateful to Fran Edgerton for her work on the final drafts of this chapter and to Will Fitzgibbon and Toby Quantrill for their time. Sam Dallyn's work inspired us and we are grateful for his comments on an earlier draft of this chapter.

## Note

1 Tax avoidance is generally considered more ethically ambiguous than tax evasion. While the latter is in almost every context a crime, with the negative ethical connotations that generally accompany it, many forms of tax avoidance, or minimization, are entirely legitimate and appropriate forms of recompense – for example, a salaried office worker claiming back travel expenses incurred for work. Such typical examples of legitimate tax minimization fall outside the scope of the reporting by the ICIJ. Rather, their focus, and that of the public, has been on activities which see money stashed in secret offshore accounts located in low-tax jurisdictions.

# Bibliography

Abbott, K., & Snidal, D. (2009). "The governance triangle: Regulatory standards institutions and the shadow of the state," in *The Politics of Global Regulation* (pp. 44–88). Princeton, NJ: Princeton University Press.

ActionAid. (2014). "85% of Brits say company tax avoidance is morally wrong," Accessed October 20, 2018.

Alm *et al.* (1993). "Fiscal exchange, collective decision institutions, and tax compliance," *Journal of Economic Behavior & Organization*, 22, pp. 285–303.

Alm *et al.* (2009). "Getting the word out: Enforcement information dissemination and compliance behavior," *Journal of Public Economics*, 93(3–4), pp. 392–402.

Barabas, J., & Jennifer, J. (2009). "Estimating the causal effects of media coverage on policy-specific knowledge," *American Journal of Political Science*, 53(1), pp. 73–89.

Bedolla, L. G. (2018). "Do voter perceptions of corruption affect voting patterns?" Preliminary paper, shared with authors.

Bob, C. (2009). "Merchants Of morality," *Foreign Policy*, 129, p. 36.

Bradshaw, P. (2021). "Data Journalism with Impact," in *The Data Journalism Handbook: Towards a Critical Data Practice*, Amsterdam: Amsterdam University Press, pp. 388–396.

Buchan, L. (2017). "Tax avoidance cost UK economy £13bn in five years, say labour," *The Independent*.

Campbell, A. F. (2016). "The cost of corporate tax avoidance," *The Atlantic*.

Casal, S. *et al.* (2016). "Tax compliance depends on voice of taxpayers," *Journal of Economic Psychology*, 56, pp. 141–150.

Christensen, J., & Murphy, R. (2004). "The social irresponsibility of corporate tax avoidance: Taking CSR to the bottom line," *Development*, 47(3), pp. 37–44.

Christians, A. (2014). "Avoidance, evasion, and taxpayer morality," *Washington University Journal of Law & Policy*, 44(1), pp. 39–59.

Cobham, A. (2017). *Tax Avoidance and Evasion — The Scale of the Problem*. London: Tax Justice Network.

Cohen, P. (2015). "What could raising taxes on the 1% do? Surprising amounts," *The New York Times*.

Cortés, H. and Luengo, M. (2021). "Data Journalism, Massive Leaks, and Investigation: What the Panama Papers Have Taught Us About Ethics." In M. Luengo (Ed.), *News Media Innovation Reconsidered: Ethics and Values in a Creative Reconstruction of Journalism*, Hoboken, NJ: John Wiley & Sons, pp. 124–137.

Craft, S., & Heim, K. (2008). "Transparency in journalism: Meanings, merits, and risks," in L. Wilkins and C. G. Christians (Eds.), *The Handbook of Mass Media Ethics*. pp. 217–228. New York: Routledge.

Dallyn, S. (2017). "An examination of the political salience of corporate tax avoidance: A case study of the tax justice network," *Accounting Forum*, 41(4), pp. 336–352.

DellaVigna, S., & Gentzkow, M. (2010). "Persuasion: Empirical evidence," *Annual Review of Economics*, 2 (1), pp. 643–669.

Drucker, J., & Bowers, S. (2017). "After a tax crackdown, Apple found a new shelter for its profits," *The New York Times*.

Dunn, A., & Van Green, T. (2021, April 16). "Top tax frustrations for Americans: the feeling that some corporations, wealthy people do not pay fair share." *Pew Research Center*.

Dyreng, S., Lindsey, B., & Thornock J. (2013). "Exploring the Role Delaware Plays as a Domestic Tax Haven," *Journal of Financial Economics*, 108 (3), pp. 751–772.

Farrell, S., & McDonald, H. (2016). "Apple ordered to pay up to €13bn after EU rules Ireland broke state aid laws," *The Guardian*.

Fellner *et al.* (2013). "Testing enforcement strategies in the field: Threat, moral appeal and social information," *Journal of the European Economic Association*, 11 (3), pp. 634–660.

Fitzgibbon, W. (2018, October 22). Email interview with Anya Schiffrin.

Fitzgibbon, W., & Díaz-Struck, E. (2016). "The Panama Papers have had historic global effects — and the impacts keep coming," *International Consortium of Investigative Journalists*. https://www.icij.org/investigations/panama-papers/20161201-global-impact/

Fitzgibbon, W., & Hudson, M. (April 3, 2021). Five years later, Panama Papers still having a big impact. *International Consortium of Investigative Journalists*. https://www.icij.org/investigations/panama-papers/five-years-later-panama-papers-still-having-a-big-impact/

Garside, J. (2016). "Panama Papers: Inside The Guardian's investigation into offshore secrets," *The Guardian*.

Gentzkow, M. (2006). "Television and voter turnout," *The Quarterly Journal of Economics*, 121(3), pp. 931–972.

Gentzkow, M., & Shapiro, J. (2010). "What drives media slant? Evidence from U.S. daily newspapers," *Econometrica*, 78, pp. 35–71.

Gerber *et al.* (2009). "Does the media matter? A field experiment measuring the effect of newspapers on voting behavior and political opinions," *American Economic Journal: Applied Economics*, 1 (2), pp. 35–52.

Graves, L., & Shabbir, N. (2019). "Gauging the global impacts of the panama papers three years later," *Reuters Institute Digital News Report*.

Hafner-Burton, E. M. (2008). "Sticks and stones: Naming and shaming the human rights enforcement problem," *International Organization*, 62(04), p. 689.

Hamilton, J. T. (2016). *Democracy's Detectives: The Economics of Investigative Journalism*, Boston, MA: Harvard University Press.

Hearson, M., & Brooks, R. (2010). *Calling time: Why SABMiller should stop dodging taxes in Africa*, UK: *ActionAid*.

Hendrix, C., & Wong, W. (2014). "Knowing your audience: How the structure of international relations and organizational choices affect amnesty international's advocacy," *Review of International Organizations*, 9(1), pp. 29–58.

Henriksen, L., & Seabrooke, L. (2015). "Transnational organizing: Issue professionals in environmental sustainability networks," *Organization*, 23(5) pp. 722–741.

Henry, J. (2012). *The Price of Offshore, Revisited*. London: Tax Justice Network.

Houlder, V. (2016, August 29). "Public opinion brings shift in business attitudes to tax planning," *The Financial Times*.

Independent Commission for the Reform of International Corporate Taxation (ICRICT). (2015). "Need to go beyond BEPS."

Independent Commission for the Reform of International Corporate Taxation (ICRICT). (2018). Executive summary of the report. "A roadmap to improve rules for taxing multinationals."

Independent Commission for the Reform of International Corporate Taxation (ICRICT). (2022). "Open letter to G20 leaders: It's time for a global asset register to target hidden wealth."

International Consortium of Investigative Journalists. (n.d.). "Victims of offshore: A video introduction to the Panama Papers," *International Consortium of Investigative Journalists*.

International Consortium of Investigative Journalists. (2019). What Happened After the Panama Papers.

Kasper, M. *et al.* (2015). "Tax policy and the news: An empirical analysis of taxpayers' perceptions of tax-related media coverage and its impact on tax compliance," *Journal of Behavioral and Experimental Economics*, 54, pp. 58–63.

Konieczna, M., & Graves, L. (2020). "Everything just went apeshit": Revisiting the "mobilization model" of Journalistic impact," *Journalism Studies*, 21(16), pp. 2343–2359.

Lublinski, J. *et al.* (2015). "Triggering change," *Journalism*, 17(8), pp. 1074–1094.

Lublinski, J. (December 15, 2020). Tracking Success. *DW*.

Napoli, P. (2014). "Measuring media impact: An overview of the field," *Media Impact Project*.

Keck, M. E., & Sikkink, K. (1998). *Activists Beyond Borders*. Ithaca, NY.: Cornell University Press, pp. 1–16.

McBarnet, D. (1992). "Legitimate rackets: Tax evasion, tax avoidance, and the boundaries of legality" *The Journal of Human Justice*, 3, 3 (2), p. 56–74.

Moeller, S. D. (1999). *Compassion Fatigue: How the Media Sell Disease, Famine, War and Death*. New York: Routledge.

National Education Association. (2011). *The Costs of Corporate Tax Avoidance*. Washington, DC: National Education Association.

New South Wales Hansard (Australia). (1986). "Legislative assembly," Friday, November 21.

OECD. (2018). *OECD/G20 BEPS Project*. Paris: OECD Publishing.

O'Sullivan, D. (2017, September 18). Email interview with Anya Schiffrin.

Pitt, F., & Green-Barber, L. (2017). "*The case for media impact: A case study of ICIJ's radical collaboration strategy*," *Tow Center for Digital Journalism*. https://doi.org/10.7916/D85Q532V

Powers, M. (2018). *NGOs as Newsmakers: The Changing Landscape of International News*. New York: Columbia University Press.

Protess, D. *et al.* (1991). *The Journalism of Outrage: Investigative Reporting and Agenda Building in America*. New York: Guilford Press.

Quantrill, T. (2017, September 16). Email interview with Anya Schiffrin.

Rappeport, A., & Alderman, L. (October 2016). "Global deal to end tax havens moves ahead as nations back 15% rate," *The New York Times*. https://www.nytimes.com/2021/10/08/business/oecd-global-minimum-tax.html

Rappeport, A., & Alderman, L. (May 2022). "Yellen Looks to get global tax deal back on track during Europe trip," *The New York Times*. https://www.nytimes.com/2022/05/16/us/politics/treasury-yellen-europe-global-tax.html

Roe, Mark J. (2003). "Delaware's Competition." *Harvard Law Review* 117(2), pp. 588–646.

Salmon, F. (October, 6, 2021). Axios. https://www.axios.com/2021/10/06/south-dakota-global-tax-haven

Schiffrin, A. (Ed.) (2014). *Global Muckraking: 100 Years of Investigative Journalism from Around the World*. New York: The New Press.

Schiffrin, A., & Zuckerman, E. (2015). "Can we measure media impact? Surveying the field," *Stanford Social Innovation Review*, 13 (4), pp. 48–51.

Shaxson, N. (2011). *Treasure Islands: Uncovering the Damage of Offshore Banking and Tax Havens*. New York: St. Martin's Griffin.

Siu, E. (2017, September 17). Email interview with Anya Schiffrin.

Slemrod *et al.* (2001). "Taxpayer response to an increased probability of audit: Evidence from a controlled experiment in Minnesota," *Journal of Public Economics*, 79, pp. 455–483.

Stapenhurst, R., (2000). "'The media's role in curbing corruption," WBI Working Papers, World Bank Institute, Washington, DC.

Stonbely, S. (2022). "*Cross-field collaboration: How and why journalists and civil society organizations around the world are working together*," Center for Cooperative Media School of Communication And Media Montclair State University.

Tax Justice Network. (November 14, 2020). "Tax avoidance and tax evasion," Accessed April 18, 2022.

Thrall, T. *et al.* (2014). "May we have your attention please? Human-rights NGOs and the problem of global communication," *The International Journal of Press/Politics*, 19(2), pp. 135–159.

Turner, G. (2017). "New estimates reveal the extent of tax avoidance by multinationals," *Tax Justice Network*, Accessed October 20, 2018.

Umansky, E. (2016). "Meet the Panama Papers editor who handled 376 reporters in 80 countries," *ProPublica*.

Wong, W. (2012). *Internal Affairs: How the Structure of NGOs Transforms Human Rights*. Ithaca, NY: Cornell University Press.

Zucman, G. (2016). "A Century of Offshore Finance," in *The Hidden Wealth of Nations: The Scourge of Tax Havens*, University of Chicago Press, pp. 8–33.

# 3

# NO LONGER A BOY'S CLUB

*Kristin Gilger and Sophie Knowles*

## Women in Business News: A Value Proposition

As a young business reporter for The Wall Street Journal, Amanda Bennett got a coveted assignment covering the auto industry in Detroit. When she started breaking big stories, some of her male colleagues came up with the only explanation that made sense to them: they assumed she must be sleeping with her sources (Bennett 2022).

The executive director of the Economic Club of New York once told Carol Loomis, who went on to a legendary career at Fortune magazine, that she wasn't welcome at a club dinner because women weren't allowed. He said that the club wanted to stay clear of "any frivolous little Smith girls who are looking for a free dinner and the chance to spend an evening with 1,200 men in black tie." Loomis ended up covering the dinner anyway, but she later sued the club – a suit she lost when the judge ruled that private clubs had a right to set their own rules (Loomis 2022).

Elvina Nawaguna, who has worked for Insider, CQ Roll Call, Market News International and Reuters, was well into her career before she felt comfortable displaying pictures of her children on her desk. She waited for as long as she could before telling anyone that she was getting married, and later, that she was pregnant. She didn't want them to assume that her personal life would interfere with her job (Nawaguna 2022).

Women in the United States who have made their careers in business and financial journalism tell dozens of stories like these. They put up with assumptions that they couldn't hold their own with CEOs or do basic math. They weathered endless mansplaining, warded off sexual advances from sources and colleagues, and tried their best to prove that their value lay beyond checking a box on a diversity plan.

Female business journalists in the United Kingdom paint a somewhat different picture. They say their biggest challenge has been the long hours, coupled with childcare responsibilities. Some feel that they have had to work harder than their male counterparts to achieve success. A prominent U.K. business editor said she feels that she would have done better, and progressed quicker, if she were a man.

The gender dimensions of the business journalism profession are largely unknown. Business journalism as a whole is under-researched (Knowles 2020a), and research on gender in

DOI: 10.4324/9781003298977-5

business journalism is almost untouched (Knowles 2020b). Examining the topic through the lens of women who have practiced business journalism in the United States and the United Kingdom, both of which have well-developed business and financial centers, offers a rich history and lessons from which to draw.

Moreover, both countries score high on the Gender Empowerment Measure scale (the GEM factor), which accounts for the number of women in positions of financial and economic power and parity of wages and income, and low (a positive thing) on the UN Gender Inequality Index, which measures women's empowerment and participation in the labor market. So, in theory, there are similar opportunities in the two countries for women to progress in their careers.

## What the Data Tell Us about Women in Business Journalism

One of the first women, if not the first, to serve in the top role at a U.S. business publication was Arlene Hershman, who in 1984 was named the editor of Dun's Business Month. In 2007, Ellen Pollock was appointed the first female editor-in-chief at Bloomberg Businessweek and has the same distinction now as the business editor of The New York Times. In 2015, Zanny Bedoes became the first female editor-in-chief at the preeminent global magazine The Economist.

From Zany Bedoes' appointment until now, women have continued to step into the top editor posts at the world's most well-known business and financial titles. In 2018, Stephanie Mehta became the first female CEO and first female editor-in-chief at Fast Company, a print and online media company that focuses on technology, business and design. In 2019, Roula Khalaf became the first woman editor at the Financial Times. In 2021, both Fortune and Reuters appointed their first female editors-in-chief: Alyson Shontell at Fortune and Alessandra Galloni at Reuters. Then in 2022, The Wall Street Journal appointed Emma Tucker as the editor. She was previously editor of the U.K. title the Sunday Times. Among the major news providers in the United Kingdom – Daily Mail, Times, Sun, Telegraph, Daily Mirror, Independent, Guardian, BBC, ITV and Sky – three women currently serve in business or financial editor roles.

These appointments have been a huge boon for women. In most cases, these media outlets have a global audience, and they have existed for well over a century. But despite the success stories, it's clear that women have not yet achieved full equity in business journalism. Women are still underrepresented in both editing and reporting ranks.

For instance, a 2021 report by the Women's Media Center based on an analysis of more than 80,000 pieces of content in the U.S. media showed that women had 44 percent of the bylines for business and economic stories, compared to 55 percent for men, with 1 percent unclear (see also Davis 1982; Greenwald 1990). In the United Kingdom, British journalist Grant Feller (2018) found that over the course of one week, women garnered only 2 percent of bylines in the business sections of nine national newspapers.

The data, however, tell only part of the story. In-depth interviews with 20 women in the United States and the United Kingdom – some of them early pioneers and others still in the midst of their careers – reveal a more nuanced picture. These interviews are some of the first with women in business journalism to foreground the issue of gender. Their experiences flesh out a picture of the forces that have propelled women into business journalism, the experiences that have shaped their careers and the challenges that remain for women entering a field that has traditionally been the stronghold of men.

## From the Wild, Wild West to a Brave New World?

Overall, the women interviewed were largely positive about their experiences in business journalism, despite some shocking stories of misogyny described by women in the United States. Women who entered newsrooms in the 1970s and 1980s, in particular, remember them as being macho, rambunctious places with few limits on what people said or did.

"I was definitely treated differently than the guys," Pollock said. "I knew what they were thinking: 'Who is this girl?' It took a long time before some people trusted and accepted me – way longer than it should have. It was a fight for credibility" (Pollock 2023).

"Nobody pulled any punches," said Bennett, who also came up at The Wall Street Journal. A supervisor once introduced her to the newsroom by saying, "'Hey, guys, meet our new bimbo.' There wasn't any sense that it was wrong," she said. "They were just talking to me in the same language they talked to their colleagues."

Another time, Bennett was assigned to fill in for a male reporter whose desk was covered with pictures of naked women. And she will never forget the male source who pushed her against a wall and groped her one night after dinner (Bennett 2022).

Sources were a particular problem, Pollock said. She remembers dodging kisses and avoiding lunges from some of the men she interviewed. "It was bad, and it was ugly, and there wasn't anybody out there to protect us," she said. "It wasn't like you could go to HR" (Pollock 2023).

Susan Lisovicz, former anchor and reporter for CNN and a CNBC correspondent, remembers seeing a message pop up on her computer screen in the newsroom one day in the 1980s. It came from a colleague whose desk was just a few feet from hers. "He was asking me for a very specific sexual act," she said. "I looked up, and I looked at him, and he was laughing. … I don't think that would happen in this day and age, but (things like that) happened a lot" (Lisovicz 2022).

Diana Henriques, who went on to become a senior financial writer for The New York Times, remembers having things explained to her – things she fully understood. "There was just this assumption that I wouldn't know anything when, in fact, I often knew a great deal more than the people sitting across the table," she said (Henriques 2022).

Alice Hancock, an EU correspondent for the Financial Times, said, "In one interview for a job, there were two men interviewing me and one of them said, 'You're a very quiet person, Alice, do you think you have the ability to take on tough male CEOs?'"

But for the most part, women interviewed in the United Kingdom said that they have not encountered the problems described by their American counterparts. "Journalism has always been open; by their nature, journalists are quite open. The men I've interviewed have always been respectful and interested, and I've never had any prejudice," said Maggie Pagano, the executive editor at Reaction and columnist at the Daily Mail. She has has been a business journalist for 40 years at numerous titles, including The Guardian and The Times (Pagano 2022).

To some degree, these results confirm research that indicates women do not always wish to be defined by their experience of gender (Elmore 2007; Knowles 2020; Liao and Lee 2014). Acceptance also may be a byproduct of the resilience that women have built over the years and evidence that women have had to put in more work to succeed when compared to men (Lumsden 1995; Volz and Lee 2013). Finally, there may be cultural differences in the way these issues are discussed that warrant further research (Hanitzsch et al. 2011).

A number of the women in both countries thought that they benefited from efforts to diversify newsrooms. In this sense, their gender may have helped them succeed. "When I started out, there were one or two very well-known female business journalists. It was a male arena," said Merryn Somerset Webb, editor-in-chief of the U.K. personal finance magazine MoneyWeek. "People were looking for women to write things" (Webb 2022).

Kathryn Christensen, who worked for news outlets such as The Wall Street Journal and ABC News for three decades before turning to college teaching, described the environment for women as good when she entered journalism in the 1970s. Companies had "an appetite" for hiring more women, she said, "so if you worked hard and seemed to pay attention, there were some opportunities that weren't there five years earlier and might not have been there 10 years hence" (Christensen 2022).

More recently, newsrooms have evolved into more welcoming places for women as the result of the #MeToo movement, which has served to discourage the kind of language and behavior once common in newsrooms, and has spurred a new generation of young people entering the profession who are demanding change.

Mehta, editor-in-chief at Fast Company, said that she sees a growing appetite for female leadership:

> My sense is that employees want more authenticity from their leaders. They want some-body who is more approachable. They want somebody whose office door is literally or figuratively open all the time. … I don't want to be an imperious leader, and I don't want to come across as somebody who should be feared, who cannot be collaborated with. So, if that is a female style of leadership, I think it will work to my advantage and other female leaders' advantages.
>
> *(Mehta 2022)*

Cesca Antonelli, who was named the editor-in-chief of Bloomberg BNA in 2018 and over-sees more than 200 journalists, agreed:

> Young people today are very interested in career growth, and they want to be coached. …They don't want just an editor who comes in and rewrites copy from top to bottom and then hits the publish button. They want to have a say in what the news-room is going to look like [and] weigh in on policies. They like a lot of training, and they want to grow in their careers.

Women leaders, she said, are often best prepared to meet such demands (Antonelli 2022).

Sometimes, change has come from the top. At the Financial Times, the appointment of Roula Khalaf as an editor led to a proactive diversification of the newsroom, said Alice Hancock, who works there as an EU correspondent. Khalaf "started a huge push for more women and more inclusion of different communities," Hancock said. "You have to be repre-sentative of the people you are going to write about" (Hancock 2022).

## The Problem of Pay

While women are no longer a rarity among business writers or editors and the overt sexism some faced in newsrooms seems to have waned, they still face one persistent problem – that of equal pay.

A 2022 survey conducted by the Donald W. Reynolds National Center for Business Journalism at Arizona State University concluded that the median annual salary for female business reporters and correspondents in the United States lagged behind that of males by $9,167, with women earning $62,498 compared to men's $71,665, a difference of about 13 percent (Donald W. Reynolds Center 2022). The wage gap was bigger in higher-level editing and managerial positions, with female editors or managers reporting earning a median of $79,996 compared to men's $101,997, a gap of about 21 percent.

Some companies have been called out for their wage discrepancies. In 2019, unionized staffers at Bloomberg Industry Group, a largely DC-based segment of the financial news company, conducted a pay survey of non-management employees. It showed that women made up nearly 53 percent of the workforce, but their pay trailed that of their male counterparts by 7 percent (Tani 2020).

The Independent Association of Publishers' Employees (IAPE) scrutinized wages at Dow Jones, publisher of The Wall Street Journal, Barron's and MarketWatch, among others, and also found a gender wage gap. Its review of salary data from 2000 through 2016 showed that women made 86.8 percent of what their male colleagues earned. Dow Jones management disputed the findings, saying that employee pay did not vary because of gender or ethnicity (Davidow 2017).

Company officials at Insider, formerly Business Insider, a financial news website, didn't wait for an outside group to call them to task. They released wage information to their staff in 2020 that showed white female employees earning 88.2 percent and women of color earning 82.4 percent of what male employees earned. The company said that part of the problem could be traced to more diversity in junior positions than in senior positions, where salaries are higher (Lebowitz 2022).

In the United Kingdom, where media companies are now legally obliged to release wage information annually, results are similar. In 2018, the latest year for which information is available, 91 percent of men working in media were paid more than women. Additionally, global financial publications and wire services had some of the widest pay disparities between genders. The gender pay gap at The Economist was 32.5 percent, followed by Dow Jones/Wall Street Journal at 31 percent and the Financial Times at 24.4 percent (Tobitt 2018).

Pay inequity persists in top-level jobs in the United Kingdom as well. A 2020 survey of financial and business newsrooms (Knowles 2020b) showed that 30 percent of women, compared to 4 percent of men, were paid under £30,000.

Women interviewees said that there were times when they suspected they were being paid less than their male predecessors or colleagues, but they often had a hard time confirming that because salaries are shrouded in so much secrecy (Anonymous 2022).

Henriques said that she learned she was earning substantially less than a man who held the identical job before her only after she left the company and the man told her what he was making (Henriques 2022).

Marty Steffens, who had a 30-year career in newsrooms before accepting a chair in business journalism at the University of Missouri, said that she once discovered she was earning less than a male reporter only because she was his boss and had access to that information. When she joined the business desk of the Los Angeles Times as an editor, she said she had a pretty good sense of how fair her pay was because her husband worked at the paper, too. "And I knew what he made" (Steffens 2022).

Mary Kuntz, whose career has included stops at Forbes, New York Newsday, Business-Week and McKinsey & Company, said that she often wondered whether she was getting paid the same as her male colleagues. Her best defense, she said, was to tell her supervisor:

> I want you to promise that I will make at least as much as the lowest-paid man in this job. I'm not sure I always did, but that was my starting point. It's not setting the bar very high, but ... I had too many other things to think about.
>
> *(Kuntz 2022)*

Others, such as Spriha Srivastava (the U.K. Bureau Chief for Insider) and Natasha Turner, editor of ESG Clarity, said that they have had no concerns about pay. Natasha Turner is only six years into her career, but she has written for Citywire, Money Marketing, the New States-man and CityMetric. She said she became a business journalist in part because it paid better than other reporting jobs (Turner 2022).

## Future Challenges

What's still holding women back from full parity in business journalism?

Interviewees cited a range of issues that included lingering pay inequities, insufficient support for working mothers, too few women in leadership roles and newsrooms that lack diversity more generally. They also noted that there are fewer job opportunities as news organizations continue to shrink and that, outside of newsrooms, the business and financial sectors they cover must also recognize the need to pursue equal rights for men and women.

The 24/7 news cycle is hard on both men and women, interviewees pointed out, but it's particularly hard on women who still bear most of the responsibility for raising children and running households. "That's a huge, huge issue," Kuntz said, because it occurs at such a critical point in women's careers, just as they are starting to gain traction in their jobs. Without flexible work schedules, part-time options or decent time-off benefits, women either find themselves dropping out or falling behind (Kuntz 2022).

Diversity is another big concern. Much more needs to be done to encourage people of color and those from underrepresented communities to enter business journalism, multiple interviewees said. Nawaguna put it this way:

> When you think about most of the big economic decisions, the decisions that compa-nies make, who gets affected the most? There's a hierarchy of who gets impacted the most and right at the bottom are people of color, and that perspective almost always gets left out of our reporting.
>
> *(Nawaguna 2022)*

The challenge, Antonelli said, is not to just recruit people of color to the business but to retain them. "We hire people and then we don't hear them," she said:

> We need to be working together to better support women of color in business journal-ism, to understand that their struggles are similar but not identical, and to elevate all the voices. There's still a lot of work to do there.
>
> *(Antonelli 2022)*

Kathleen Graham believes strongly that women, especially women of color, need more support. As an executive director of the Society for Advancing Business Editing and Writing (SABEW), the largest membership organization serving business journalists in the United States, she prioritized programs that help women develop their business journalism skills, navigate newsroom culture and develop as leaders. "It's about positioning women for leadership and highlighting them and their skills," she said. "How do you create a culture that sets women up for success and supports them on the leadership ladder?" (Graham 2022).

Interviewees agreed that culture change, both within and outside newsrooms, may be the biggest challenge of all. "It takes a long time to throw off cultural expectations," said the University of Missouri's Steffens:

> And I think that echoes particularly in business journalism, where you walk onto the floor of the New York Stock Exchange and it's still all male traders, where at the highest levels of [business news], it's still mostly men. … It takes more than one generation.
> *(Steffens 2022)*

Henriques concurred. Wall Street, she said,

> Has always been hostile to women, with this incredible glass ceiling and incredible hostile working environment that would just curl your hair. So, women trying to cover that are subject to the same gender bias that operates in that world.

Another "black hole," she said, is Silicon Valley:

> There are almost no women there, and these are a bunch of tech bros that don't play well with women. There's a lack of women in the ranks of all of the big tech companies, a paucity of women in leadership roles. If you're a business journalist covering technology and you're a woman, you're facing a double bogey. You're facing whatever remains of the gender bias in your own business and the gender bias you're going to meet everywhere you go on the tech beat.
> *(Henriques 2022)*

Henriques' concern about a lack of representation for women in business is very real. A recent analysis of 10,493 companies by Deloitte, an international professional services network, indicates that women occupy just 20 percent of seats on corporate boards globally; at this pace, parity will not be reached until 2045 (Konigsburg and Thorne 2022).

## Business Journalism as a Career Choice

Women in the United States and the United Kingdom agreed that business and financial journalism is a good career for women and that coverage benefits when more women are involved. Women, they said, bring different perspectives and news judgment to the work, producing coverage that is more reflective of audiences.

"I'm interested in how companies run, and in their finances, but I'm also interested in the people and their stories," Pollock said. When a Times' editor told her that he had run into a former business reporter who commented, "You can tell by the coverage that the business section is now run by a woman," she was thrilled, even though she's pretty sure the comment wasn't meant as a compliment. "I really want our stories to be accessible to everyone, and I think that's hard in business journalism. (You're) walking that fine line between sophistication and accessibility. It's tough" (Pollock 2023).

Some research supports the notion that women's news judgment differs in some respects from that of men. A 2020 survey of U.K. business journalists, for example, showed that women turned to different sources in their reporting, relying most on investment institute professionals, followed by company executives. Men used financial analysts most frequently, with a 29 percent difference between the genders. In addition, 20 percent more men than women saw themselves as watchdogs, while 10 percent more women than men saw journalism as a "public forum" that motivates ordinary people to get involved in public debates (Knowles 2020).

But interviewees also noted that business journalism still is not a natural draw for most women. In fact, many said that business journalism was not a career they themselves intentionally chose. It was more likely to be a lucky accident.

Bennett said that she was basically tricked into the profession. She had applied for a scholarship from Dow Jones and, shortly after learning she had won, she got a call from The Wall Street Journal offering her a summer job. She had no interest in covering business, but it was a lot more money than anyone else was offering, and it didn't take her long to fall in love with the job. "I found that the Journal's approach to business was so engaging and so cool," she said (Bennett 2022).

Maggie Pagano said that she was taking her college finals when she learned of an opening in the business section of The Times. She wanted to become a foreign correspondent and write about politics, but when the job offer came through, "I couldn't turn it down," she said. "But I realized from day one it covers everything – politics, economics, social and cultural things. I found it wasn't dry... it's all about the personalities and the characters of the business world" (Pagano 2022).

Similarly, Nawaguna said that she never considered business journalism as a career until she attended an orientation for her master's program at Arizona State University and found herself sitting next to a faculty member who talked her into taking his business journalism course. "Before that, there were two pages I never opened in newspapers – the business pages and the sports pages," Nawaguna said,

> But I went to his class and realized that the reason I was afraid of business journalism before was that I thought it was all numbers. And I realized you can tell complicated economic stories through the voices of people, through the experiences of people. I like writing about people, and I figured I could do both.
>
> *(Nawaguna 2022)*

The reluctance of women to enter business journalism could be related to low financial literacy among young women – a trend found in most countries (Nicolini, Cude, and Chatterjee 2013). Also, new research shows that women are less engaged with financial news than men and that media use has a significant relationship with trust and understanding about financial institutions (Strauß, Knowles and Cinceoglu 2023; Knowles and Schifferes 2020).

Change, if it comes, may depend on college journalism programs. Steffens said many more women are showing up to her business journalism classes at the University of Missouri these days, which is not surprising given that most journalism programs are predominantly female. But she still sees women shying away from business reporting because they fear they don't understand it, or they think they "suck at math." She points out that there are jobs in business journalism and the pay is better. She tells them that if she could do it, they can, too (Steffens 2022).

Christensen used to tell her students something similar before retiring from the University of Nebraska-Lincoln a few years ago. "You know there's a mystique about business journalism that it's terribly hard," she said. "But if you do your homework, which means a lot of studying, especially for somebody like me who didn't have any business training, you can do it." She also tells them that business journalism offers "so much ground to plow. It's not like politics, which is very much a 'he-said, she-said' endeavor. ... If you're going to go into journalism, business journalism is probably the thing to choose" (Christensen 2022).

When Henriques talks to students, she asks them, "How many of you are planning to cover business?" Hardly any hands go up. She tells them:

I've got news for you. Every one of you is going to cover business because business will be part of every single beat you take on. ... Maybe you say, 'I want to cover sports,' to which I would say, 'Sports is a business.' Or 'I want to cover the arts.' Oh, well, that's business.

Henriques offered another compelling reason for young women to consider the profession: Documents, she said, don't care if you're male or female. She said she learned the following as a young reporter:

I can't sit in the hot tub with the county sheriff, but I can read the documents that show that he's been buying land next to a new highway exit that nobody knows is going to be built yet. So, documents are a leveling tool. Business coverage is document-driven in a way that other areas aren't ... I didn't waste time schmoozing. I went directly to the documents.

*(Henriques 2022)*

Ultimately, until young women become convinced that business journalism is a viable career for them, news coverage won't fully reflect the interests or needs of audiences. Women "are the ones who make sure to write about why women aren't getting the same level of investment from investors," Mehta said. They're the ones "who make sure that women's stories are getting told" (Mehta 2022).

## References

Davis, J. 1982. Sexist bias in eight newspapers. *Journalism Quarterly* 59, 456–460.
Davidow, S. 2017. Guild to WSJ: Yes, there is a wage gap. *The News Guild*, July 12. Accessed August 1, 2022. https://newsguild.org/guild-to-wsj-yes-there-is-a-wage-gap/
Elmore, Cindy. 2007. Recollections in hindsight from women who left: The gendered newsroom culture. *Women and Language* 30(2), 18.
Feller, G. 2018. It's none of your business, women. *The British Journalism Review* 29(3), 25–30.
Greenwald, M. S. 1990. Gender representation in newspaper business sections. *Newspaper Research Journal*, 11, 68–73.

Hanitzsch, T., Hanusch, F., Mellado, C., Anikina, M., Berganza, R., Cangoz, I., Coman, M., Hamada, B., Elena Hernández, M., Karadjov, C. D. and Virginia Moreira, S. 2011. Mapping journalism cultures across nations: A comparative study of 18 countries. *Journalism Studies* 12(3), 273–293.

Knowles, S. 2020a. *The mediation of financial crises: watchdogs, lapdogs or canaries in the coal mine?* (Vol. 25). Peter Lang.

Knowles, S., 2020b. Women, the economy and the news: Undeserved and underrepresented? *Journalism Studies* 21(11), 1479–1495.

Knowles, S. and Schifferes, S. 2020. Financial capability, the financial crisis and trust in news media. *Journal of Applied Journalism & Media Studies* 9(1), 61–83.

Konigsburg, D. and Thorne, S. 2022. Women in the boardroom. *Deloitte Insights*, February 2. Accessed July 20, 2022. Women in the boardroom | Deloitte Insights

Lebowitz, Shana. 2022. My company just released employee-pay data, and the salary gap between men and women shows we have a lot of work ahead of us. *Business Insider*, July 22. Accessed July 25, 2022. Gender at Work: How to Reach Pay Equity for Women and People of Color (businessinsider.com).

Liao, Sara X. T. and Lee, Francis L. F. 2014. Do journalists believe in gender specificities of news topics? The impact of professionalism and family status. *Asian Journal of Communication* 24(5), 456–473. Doi:10.1080/01292986.2014.908934.

Lumsden, Linda. 1995. You're a tough guy, mary-and a first-rate newspaperman: Gender and women journalists in the 1920S and 1930s. *Journalism & Mass Communication Quarterly* 72(4), 913–921.

Nicolini, G., Cude, B. J. and Chatterjee, S. 2013. Financial literacy: A comparative study across four countries. *International Journal of Consumer Studies* 37(6), 689–705.

Strauß, N., Knowles, S. and Cinceoglu, V. 2023. Understanding Financial Institutions: The Role of Reading Economic News in Germany and the UK. In Financial Literacy in Today's Global Market. IntechOpen. Available at: http://dx.doi.org/10.5772/intechopen.1002495.

Tani, M. 2020. Bloomberg staffers dispute That he pays women equally. *The Daily Beast*, February 20, 2022. Accessed August 2, 2022. Bloomberg Staffers Dispute That He Pays Women Equally (thedailybeast.com)

Tobitt, Charlotte. 2018. Gender pay gap figures in full. *Press Gazette*, April 5. Accessed August 1, 2022. http://www.pressgazette.co.uk/gender-pay-gap-figures-in-full-conde-nast-telegraph-and-economist-groups among-worst-offenders-for-pay-disparity-in-uk-media/.

United Nations (UN). 2022. Human development reports. Accessed August 1, 2022. Gender Inequality Index | Human Development Reports (undp.org)

Volz, Yong Z. and Lee, Francis. 2013. What does it take for women journalists to gain professional recognition? Gender disparities among pulitzer prize winners, 1917–2010. *Journalism & Mass Communication Quarterly* 90(2), 248–266.

Women's Media Centre. (WMC). 2021. https://womensmediacenter.com/reports/wmc-divided-2021-the-media-gender-gap.

## Interviews

Alice Hancock (2022). Interviewed by Sophie Knowles (Zoom), August 08.
Amanda Bennett (2022). Interviewed by Kristin Gilger (Zoom), April 28.
Anonymous (2022). Interviewed by Sophie Knowles (Zoom), May 20.
Carol Loomis (2022). Interviewed by Kristin Gilger (Zoom), February 16.
Cesca Antonelli (2022). Interviewed by Kristin Gilger (Zoom), April 26.
Diana Henriques (2022). Interviewed by Kristin Gilger (Zoom), March 11.
Ellen Pollock (2023). Interviewed by Kristin Gilger (Zoom), June 7.
Elvina Nawaguna (2022). Interviewed by Kristin Gilger (Zoom), June 2.
Kathryn Christensen (2022). Interviewed by Kristin Gilger (Zoom), May 5.
Kathleen Graham (2022). Interviewed by Kristin Gilger (Zoom), March 10.
Maggie Pagano (2022). Interviewed by Sophie Knowles (Zoom), August 04.
Marty Steffens (2022). Interviewed by Kristin Gilger (Zoom), May 24.
Mary Kuntz (2022). Interviewed by Kristin Gilger (Zoom), Feb. 17

Merryn Somerset Webb (2022). Interviewed by Sophie Knowles (Zoom), August 4.
Natasha Turner (2022). Interviewed by Sophie Knowles (Zoom), June 25.
Susan Lisovicz (2022). Interviewed by Kristin Gilger (Zoom), May 16.
Stephanie Mehta (2022). Interviewed by Kristin Gilger (Zoom), April 25.
Spriha Srivastava (2022). Interviewed by Sophie Knowles (Zoom), August 31.

# 4

# A UNICORN IGNORED

## The Case for Business News Coverage of the U.S. Latino Market

*Claudia E. Cruz*

### Introduction

Business reporters, particularly those who cover the technology industry, have come to be familiar with the term "unicorn." It's commonly used to describe a new company, usually a startup, with a value of more than $1 billion. These companies often sell products or services that have high costs and at least initially, generate limited revenue, so the need for venture investment is critical to their survival.

If it were a company, the Latino community would be a sleeping unicorn. With 62.1 million people in the United States and more than $2 trillion of disposable income (Obolenskaya 2021), Latinos can potentially inject that amount of money into the economy through the consumption of goods and services, and financially boost the nation's gross domestic product (GDP).

But the value of the Latino population in the United States goes far beyond its purchasing power. Consulting firm McKinsey & Company stated that Latino businesses could potentially generate an additional $2.3 trillion in total revenue each year (Pérez 2021, p. vi). Also, if Latinos created 735,000 new businesses, they would support 6.6 million new jobs (p. 3). The report added that if the wage gap between Latino and non-Hispanic white workers closed, 1.1 million Latinos would move into the middle class (p. 11). Higher incomes for Latinos mean the ability to invest in stocks and bonds, retirement accounts and homes, and other income-building mechanisms that would reduce the $380 billion annual wealth gap between Latinos and non-Hispanic whites (p. 8).

Prioritizing Latinos in business strategies is a "win-win," according to McKinsey (Pérez, p. 53). Still, the report contained lots of "buts," "yets" and "howevers" because this community hasn't been a genuinely, prioritized target of the financial sector – and it argues that they should be.

"Addressing the barriers preventing Latinos from fully participating not only is morally right – and in keeping with the essence of the American dream – but presents an opportunity to make the economy more robust for everyone," Lucy Pérez, McKinsey's principal report researcher, said in the executive summary (p. 9).

DOI: 10.4324/9781003298977-6

One such barrier stems from the lack of representation of Latinos in the media where only 4 percent are executives, 7 percent are middle management and 8 percent are broadcasters, writers, reporters and editors (GAO 2022). According to the Government Accountability Office, "relatively few financial resources are dedicated to producing content for Hispanics, which may limit opportunities available to Hispanic workers" in broadcast (Ibid.). A 2022 Pew Research Center survey found that only 7 percent of all economy and business journalists are Hispanic (Tomasik and Gottfried 2023).

This chapter explores, through interviews with Latino business leaders and journalists, the scarce ecosystem of business news publications and media outlets that have targeted Latinos in the United States. The goal is to understand what has worked, what hasn't, why and what can be done next to try and satisfy the growing demand from Latinos to learn about investing in themselves, their companies, and in the prosperity of the country, or as McKinsey states: the American dream.

## Historical Perspectives: Latinos and Business News in the United States

The American Latino population is heterogeneous. It hails – in varying degrees – from the dizzying mix of Spanish colonizers, Indigenous peoples, African slaves and migrant labor from Asia and the Middle East that came together in Latin America post-1492. Latinos have been present in the United States since before the annexation of México in 1848 and the Puerto Rican territory in 1898, the majority of the migration from the Caribbean, Central and South America to the United States took place in the 20th century (Puente et al. 2022).

In their first report to comprehensively focus on this community, McKinsey & Company posits that Latinos have not been allowed to completely participate in driving the U.S. economy forward. The study acknowledges that to "fully harness the economic power and global competitiveness of the nation, we must remove the barriers that prevent Latinos in the United States from reaching their full potential" (Pérez, p. ii).

Whether Latinos arrived in the United States two hundred years ago or two days ago, just like any other group, they need goods, services, plus reliable and effective information to prosper in this society. With more exposure to business news, Latinos – the fastest-growing population in the nation – may be able to achieve similar wealth outcomes as the non-Hispanic white population and, in turn, propel our economy, the biggest in the world, higher.

This doesn't mean that Latinos don't currently consume business news. Some do, but their sources of information don't always stem from the well-funded mainstream U.S. news outlets with access to the analysts, power-players and decision-makers that can affect how and where Latinos invest their money. Instead, Latinos have been hurt by predatory scams in part because they do not have strong financial knowledge or footing in this country (Chávez 2022; Rodriguez 2012).

Latinos with access to the Internet and cable, and who speak Spanish can access global economic news directly from the business sections of many Latin American newspapers and magazines, including copy from The Wall Street Journal Americas and CNN en Español Dinero services. However, if they want more localized economic and financial information that they can leverage to improve their business and personal situations in the United States, they would have a harder time locating these news sources – regardless of language.

A quick search for business news media outlets that aim to inform Latinos, whether in Spanish or in English, leaves one yearning for more options.

The Center for Hispanic Marketing at Florida State University lists several titles, some of which no longer publish, such as Hispanic Market Weekly (HMW), and others that provide demographic information for advertisers to target this market. This includes Hispanic PR Newswire, the first service of its type – it launched in 2000 – to distribute press releases about Latino businesses and industry moves by prominent Latino executives. In fact, for nearly a decade, HMW – created by the now deceased and legendary journalist and publisher Arturo Villar – provided the best business news for and about the Latinx media industry (Baer 2021). "There was very little coverage of our industry at the time and HMW was an essential read for all of us," according to Amazon Prime exec Larissa Acosta (Portada-online 2021).

Digital outlets such as HispanicAd.com, Hispanic Executive, Latin Biz Today and Negocios Now currently publish news, features and profiles about and for Latinos and have tried to fill in the gaps that the mainstream business outlets overlook.

The one major business news program for Latinos is CNN en Español's Dinero, which inherited the former prime time slot of the network's Economía y Finanzas show (Del Valle 2011). However, this broadcast service with on-air talent Xavier Serbiá – a former Menudo boyband-member whose TV personality is Jim Cramer-esque – had been difficult to access without a subscription to a cable service. Serbiá, unfortunately, was laid off in December 2022 as part of the network's restructuring (Villafañe 2023). At the time of publication, CNN en Español Dinero online business news content does not explicitly target the U.S. Latino market, though Serbiá's old videos still exist, including his last: tips for starting 2023 with good financial resolutions (Serbiá 2022).

The other major Spanish-language news networks, Telemundo and Univision (Adams 2021), sprinkle economic news into their evening news programs and those segments are published on their websites, but neither has a single standalone in-depth daily or weekly financial news show.

These Hispanic publishers, broadcasters and – primarily Latino – advertisers have continued the trend of "self-presentation," i.e., the process by which a community portrays itself to others to make a desired impression. Historically, U.S. Latinos have supplemented the coverage from the mainstream media outlets (Dávila 2012), and this is particularly clear when it entails economic and financial information to this population (Ellingrud and Sichel 2022).

Another attempt to inform Latinos about business, and the growing and important technology sector, was CNET en Español, launched by the CBS Interactive division of the major network in 2013. The digital technology news and product review site covered hardware and software trends, published explainers on autonomous vehicles, the chip sector, artificial intelligence, cryptocurrency and smart homes, among other topics, and interviewed Latinos in the science, technology, engineering and mathematics fields (gabosama 2022). It folded in 2020 after the merger of CBS and Viacom and the sale of the CNET brand to Red Ventures.

"I read it as a recognition that there was enough traffic going to CNET en Español that they wanted to redirect to their main website because they wanted those numbers. So good for them," remarked a former Wall Street Journal reporter and CNET en Español's former managing editor, Gabriel Sama, in an interview. "But it's kind of tragic that those seven years of Spanish language tech coverage vanished from the web" (Sama 2022).

Several attempts were made to get a comment from officials at Red Ventures about why they closed this edition and why the content was not archived, but no comment was received prior to publication of this chapter. (Full disclosure: I am a former staff writer for CNET en Español.)

## The Consequences of Keeping Latinos in a Business News Desert

Business journalists track, analyze and interpret commercial, economic and financial data and activities in a society, but not every sector of the United States receives the same level of coverage in print, television, radio or even digitally. Latinos are one such "invisible" community. The omission of the Hispanic community from media sources "creates a void in the narrative, a black hole where stereotypes and bigotry can fester" (Castro 2022).

At the World Economic Forum in January 2020, the president and CEO of the Hispanic Association on Corporate Responsibility (HACR), Cid Wilson, addressed the lack of knowledge and understanding the global community has about Latinos. He tasked the attendees to guess which country had a GDP of $2.8 trillion (Latino Donor Collaborative 2022), no currency risk, a strong financial structure – so that you don't have the regulatory risks; with a relatively low interest rate environment; whose average age is about 28 and the mode age is 11, and that's growing faster than every G-20 country in the world (Wilson 2022).

"Would you invest in a country like that?" Wilson asked the roomful of business leaders in Davos, Switzerland. "Everyone was like 'Yeah! This is a dream economy.' I just described to you the U.S. Latino economy" (Wilson 2022).

Wilson commended CNBC, The Wall Street Journal, Forbes, Fortune, Yahoo Finance and others for recognizing the need, especially since 2020, to give the Latino economy more coverage. But he still critiqued the scarce attention Latinos received generally from the business media community.

"When you see the media covering economies that actually are smaller than our Latino economy and you see the level of attention that those smaller economies get," Wilson said, "you can see the immediate gap in the lack of coverage of the Latino economy" (Wilson 2022).

He noted that a business news media mindful of the power of the Latino economy would almost naturally supplement the educational efforts of organizations such as HACR, the U.S. Hispanic Chamber of Commerce, and those for independent Hispanic legal, healthcare and real estate professionals.

Wilson correlated the sparse representation of Latinos in business coverage with the absenteeism of Latinos on corporate boards and executive positions. He did laud the appointment of Cesar Conde as the chairman, NBCUniversal News Group, the first Latino to ever lead a major English-language television news organization. The immediate impact? Conde launched an initiative to increase the share of women and people of color in newsrooms – including CNBC – to 50 percent of the total employee count (Chang 2020). One recent success story: Carla Vernón was appointed the CEO of The Honesty Company in January 2023. According to her company biography, she's the "first Afro-Latina" of a publicly traded company (The Honest Company 2023).

The McKinsey report supports this assertion. Improving the underrepresentation of Latinos within academia, management, professional careers such as law and medicine, and within STEM fields would close the $288 billion annual income gap between Latinos and non-Hispanics (Pérez, p. 1). This loss of economic opportunity creates barriers to Latino entrepreneurship, wealth attainment and their full participation as consumers (Ibid.). However, frequent news segments that highlight issues such as real estate, labor or insurance with members of these associations as the sources telling their stories would acknowledge Latinos and be more inclusive of the U.S. society, as a whole (Garza 2022).

"The overall coverage is significantly lacking and when there is media, it's often stereo-typical, which perpetuates some of the ultra-right-wing propaganda," Wilson said highlight-ing how Fox News promotes the tropes that Latinos are all "undocumented," "we are not American" and "we do not belong here" (Chávez 2022; Tameez 2022). Comments on Twitter about a recent article in The Economist titled "Why are Latin American workers so strikingly unproductive" include that it evokes dog-whistles about Latinos as "lazy," which the McKinsey report contradicts (The Economist 2023).

U.S. Representative Joaquin Castro, who has taken on the task at the federal level to shed light on the underrepresentation of Latinos in the media, agrees that these harmful depic-tions perpetuate stereotypes that unfairly take away attention from the contributions of this community to society.

> For decades the American media industry has been running an extended commercial about Latinos that focuses on the most harmful stereotypes of who we are. On screen and on the front pages of major newspapers, Latinos are portrayed as gang bangers, as drug dealers and as 'illegals.' These depictions obscure the positive real-life roles of Latinos as essential workers who got us through the early days of the pandemic, im-migrant entrepreneurs giving new life to cities in the Midwest and trailblazers across almost every American industry.
>
> *(Castro 2022)*

With the current movement to incorporate more inclusive content in media, there is an im-petus for business news editors to ensure that their reporters, sources and stories have more Latinos to balance out the original target audience sought by their ads – and promoted by their business model (Rosas-Salas 2019; Tameez 2022). If not, as will be shown later in this chapter, this community will find a way to do so. Historically, it has been Latinos themselves who will fill in the gaps where the major news publications have failed, according to former president of the Society of Professional Journalists Rebecca Aguilar (Castañeda 2022).

### Business Journalism Should Explore Opportunities to Inform the Latino "Unicorn"

Most, if not all, executives and business journalists respect the economic and financial guid-ance of McKinsey analysts and researchers. Therefore, a fair conclusion can be made that their report might behoove more consideration of Latinos in business news because one sentiment continuously jumped out: the tacit exclusion of Latinos from the U.S. economy could hurt the country's financial growth, and this should be urgently addressed.

To help Latinos achieve the American dream, some of McKinsey's suggestions include increasing the pay and benefits afforded to Latinos, improving the quality of their jobs and creating pathways to higher wage-earning opportunities through recruitment, retention and promotion (Pérez, p. 27). A recommendation for the banking sector is to give Latinos more access to capital, support their entrepreneurial spirit with development and guidance, and help them increase their online presence in order to drive business and income back into their communities (p. 39).

For example, Latinos have the "highest entrepreneurship rate of any race," yet despite having similar credit scores to non-Hispanic white merchants, banks lend them less capital to start their businesses (Pérez, pp. 33, 36). One glaring example of the disparity and critique of how capital is invested is the $420 million secured in 2022 by Adam Neuman, the embattled former CEO of WeWork, for his new startups (Sundar and Joyner 2022).

WeWork imploded in 2019 after "investors raised concerns about its financial strength, debt and corporate governance practices" (Miranda 2019). Still, despite Neuman's failures and in contrast to his recent bounty, 90 other startups from Black and Latino founders collectively raised only $225 million, which highlighted the "ongoing disparity in investments flowing towards companies with founders who are women or from underrepresented communities" (Sundar and Joyner 2022).

Further, in 2021, only 1 percent of "all venture capital funding" – and even less in 2022 – went to Black and Latina women because this group is traditionally ignored (Ortakales Dawkins 2023). Still, out of 750 women surveyed, nine have at one point or another raised more than $1 billion dollars, including the Latina actress and entrepreneur Jessica Alba, founder of The Honest Company (Ibid.).

Insofar as the Latino consumer is concerned, McKinsey finds that Latinos would pay for more and better goods and services, especially those that help them build wealth, improve their health and house-purchasing prospects (pp. 50, 53). Lastly, to help Latinos close the wealth gap, the business community can offer retirement and other financial benefits in a worker's compensation packet. Their employers, or other businesses, can also share more estate planning, financial literacy, credit assistance and overall financial information with this community.

## Inclusive Business News Is Good for All Consumers and Investors

Should business newsrooms also integrate these suggestions? Can there be more stories that help Latinos become better consumers of financial products?

To be sure, business news can appear "agnostic" in its delivery despite the lack of socioeconomic diversity of economists (Ryssdal and Hollenhorst 2022). Daily stock market, commodities, currency, labor and consumer price index stories speak to an arguably general public.

While a "brick wall" exists between the newsroom and a media outlets' sales team, implicitly the ads sold and displayed most often reflect the target audience for that publication or broadcaster – a primarily non-Hispanic white and affluent one (Dávila 2012). The market is created, it's a social construction and it can be invented to reach different consumers, just the same way it was developed to exclude racialized communities (Rosas-Salas 2018).

Intentional in-depth journalism from the business news community about the systemic barriers to receiving capital, why Latinos don't get promoted to executive ranks within companies and why better financial products aren't advertised to them, could help dispel the myths and stigmas held by banks, venture firms or government agencies that Latinos are not trustworthy investments or strong business partners (Guynn and Fraser 2022; O'Brien 2018). If 800,000 more Latinos opened up businesses, it would spur 7 million more jobs and contribute nearly $2.3 trillion dollars in revenue to the United States (Ellingrud and Sichel 2022). That's a boom for everyone, not just Latinos.

> The biggest finding that we found is that Latino economic mobility is no longer a Latino issue, it's an American one. If we really want, as a country, to achieve our goals in the decades to come, we need to improve in a significant way the Latino participation in our economy,

said Bernardo Sichel, a partner at McKinsey (Ellingrud and Sichel 2022).

Business news reporters can also investigate why Latinos participate and invest less in long-term financial products – such as IRAs, mutual funds and college education funds. Latinos are also more likely to be unbanked (FDIC 2021, Fields, 2022). The McKinsey report alludes to this disparity: "Latinos are, on average, more dissatisfied with goods and services on offer than non-Latino white people. That's especially true in categories they struggle to access such as banking and financial services, food, housing and healthcare" (Pérez, p. 50).

An example of how a Latina reporter could help reach the community of unbanked using her own personal experience to quell their fears is Nely Galan's episode for her Money Maker podcast on the fall of First Republic Bank (Galan 2023). In this segment, she shares her family's traumatic experience when banks collapsed in Cuba. Despite her past, Galan explains how the Federal Deposit Insurance Corporation does protect client funds and why Latinos should trust the U.S. banking system.

Media scholar Chris Chávez has noticed this imbalance and pointed to the Los Angeles Times, his hometown newspaper, as an example of a regional paper that now reflects its Latino community better and does "probably the best job I've seen."

Since the population of Latinos in L.A. County is 49.1 percent, Chávez believes that the Times' mainstream audience, "is the Latino audience. You just can't ignore it," the professor of advertising and director of the Center for Latina/o and Latin American Studies at the University of Oregon, said in an interview.

> There's more news about Latinos in business, more of the readers are going to be Latinos, and most of the writers are Latinos. It's just so much more of a sophisticated environment because the conditions allow for that. … I think it's a function of just being in L.A. and here you are going to live and die by Latino readers.
>
> *(Chávez 2022)*

More inclusive business news could also help reduce the amount of scams that Latinos fall victim to, especially when it involves predatory lending and the steering of this community to low-end financial purchases versus the high-end investment products that they may want and qualify for (Chávez 2022; Rodriguez 2012). The financial footing of the Latinos in the United States took a big hit during the 2008 housing crisis where the wealth of Hispanic households fell by 66 percent and one-in-four Latinos lost their home to foreclosure compared to 12 percent of non-Hispanic whites (Rodriguez 2012). The lack of targeted and accurate news to Hispanics makes them more susceptible, especially those who struggle with English, to misinformation (Chen 2022; Lehrer and Mochkofsky 2022; Panditharatne 2022).

Latinos in the United States so want to be included in the prosperity they see the white population achieve that some invest in speculative investments. Business journalists from Bloomberg, including crypto managing editor stacy-marie ishmael, noted that

> A lot of those people came from households that had relatively low incomes and almost no access to traditional forms of wealth. So you do have this kind of disproportionate wealth effect of the people who are venture capitalists or who bought Bitcoin when it was like $12, who are totally fine because Bitcoin is still $17,000 and venture capitalists make expensive bets for a living,

ishmael said in the video during the panel.

> The people who bought, you know, some fraction of bitcoin either because a celebrity in a Super Bowl told them to and who are now looking at what was effectively their life savings either dwindling to zero or being caught up in a bankruptcy process.
>
> *(Bloomberg 2023)*

Dozens of Latino crypto investors in Houston, Texas, e.g., have sought the assistance of the U.S. Securities and Exchange Commission to reclaim up to tens of thousands of dollars for the fraudulent practices of a local company called CryptoFX, LLC. One of the alleged victims told ABC 13, "I invested all of my life savings, and my mom did, and now I have to figure out how to pay for things that I wasn't expecting" (Ehling 2022).

Latinos, and the society at large, would benefit from an increase in proper and accurate information that can help in the wealth attainment of this vulnerable population.

> The key message of the [McKinsey] study - and I think it's a critical one - is that while there's evidence that Latinos are pursuing and achieving the American dream in terms of upward mobility, greater education, and middle-class stability, the economic parity of Latinos remains elusive for this group,

said Sichel.

> ... There is still a huge gap to fill, especially compared with whites - and one that needs to be filled quickly if not only this group but also the US economy is going to achieve its goals in the decades to come.
>
> *(Ellingrud and Sichel 2022)*

## Recommendations for Newsroom Practice

- *Make Coverage of Latinos Intentional, not Accidental*

To generate more economic and financial news for the Latino population – which is expected to account for more than 30 percent of workers and be 76 percent U.S.-born by 2060 (Pérez, p. 13) – business publications should encourage their leaders to hire more reporters and editors who have an interest in producing focused coverage about this community. Additionally, they should encourage their reporters to become members of affinity journalism organizations, such as the National Association of Hispanic Journalists (NAHJ).

The Los Angeles Times is one example of a national publication with a diverse reporting team that has successfully told the stories of Latino workers, consumers and entrepreneurs in their region (Chávez 2022). It would make sense that the Times has placed an emphasis in this community as Chicanos and other Hispanics have become the largest ethnic group in California with 15.8 million people of Latino-descent (Krogstad 2022).

Nancy Rivera Brooks, deputy business editor at the Los Angeles Times, explained that compelling business stories about Latinos resonate beyond the Hispanic community and this has incentivized the data-driven company to produce more with journalists who reflect the target audience.

"We have two Latino reporters, and our economy reporter is fluent in Spanish. She does a lot of worker stories and worker stories are a big hit for us. People want to read about work," said Rivera Brooks, adding that aside from entertainment companies such as Netflix, the paper hardly covers earnings reports anymore, in an interview. "We are less company focused, and more people-focused now and worker-focused" (Rivera Brooks 2022).

The Times business section plans to double down on stories for the nearly 4.8 million Latinos in the County of Los Angeles, according to Rivera Brooks. Why? Because it makes business sense.

"We write more about wealth, money, we're trying to build our personal finance arm and there is a wealth of stories about Latinos, that include Latinos, in those stories," she said. "I don't understand why other publications don't hit it as hard as we do because they work" (Rivera Brooks 2022).

Just like Rivera Brooks, newsroom editors can also be more intentional about the stories they assign and how they encourage their reporters to brainstorm ideas and find sources.

They should encourage participation and attendance at Latino industry events and outreach to local Hispanic chambers of commerce to gain access to members and trending data. Also, editors should also establish a frequency for publishing these stories so that they can develop a consistent reader-, viewer- or listenership. Furthermore, editors may want to implement "source maps," where reporters track who they interview. This hopefully will motivate them to diversify their contacts and conduct outreach to Latino analysts, business owners and company executives for quotes. Representation in news stories can help attract and engage a more diverse audience, not to mention, perhaps surprise the general audience with new untold stories and issues (Garza, pp. 146–147; Yost 2022).

"If one network is being very intentional about covering Latino news and others are not, my viewership eyes are going to go to that network," HACR's Wilson said.

> That could attract advertising dollars, especially those that are looking to sell to a very brand loyal community. … Those companies that recognize our growing Latino economic, business and consumer power are going to gravitate toward networks that have a strong following of Latinos.
>
> *(Wilson 2022)*

- ### *English or Spanish, May Not Matter – Just Do it*

Not all Latinos communicate solely in Spanish and not all of them speak only English. Traditionally, newer Latino immigrants to the United States primarily consume news in Spanish, and their children and grandchildren will be either bilingual or prefer English. For example, in 2021, 72 percent of Latinos over the age of five – propelled by the U.S. newborns – spoke English in contrast to 37 percent of Latino immigrants (Krogstad 2022).

To be sure, Spanish-language economic and financial news still has potential and can make business sense if one's target audience is a recent immigrant (Sama 2022). In May 2022, for example, The Weather Channel launched a Spanish-language channel to cover atmospheric sciences and the impact of climate change as it affects this audience around the world. Weather can affect business operations, commodities and infrastructure, both in the short and long term, and information in the Spanish language could permit a small business owner to make wiser decisions based on this coverage, for example.

As has been shown in this chapter, a handful of economic and financial news sources in the United States already exist in Spanish, mostly because immigrants from Latin America first established the current business news publications to service their communities. However, this just means that English-dominant newsrooms have even more opportunities to produce business content for the ever-growing native-born Latinos, especially with Spanish-speakers or Latinos on staff in the newsroom.

"Every time [the mainstream media tries] to tackle ethnic minorities, they tackle it from the perspective of curiosity – 'Look at how different they are from us!' The goal is not to write about Latinos, but for Latinos," the journalist and editor Same said.

> Most editors in mainstream media understand what those stories are for the larger group of society in the U.S., so it's kind of ironic that they have a hard time seeing it from a different perspective and it's why it's important to have a diverse newsroom.
>
> *(Sama 2022)*

- *Do it because it makes business sense – and it's morally right*

The McKinsey report brought to the forefront the urgent need for the U.S. business industry to engage with Latinos. It reminded us that while Latinos have worked hard to improve their status in the United States, it's the "policies and practices" of "America's contribution to that dream [that] is uneven" (Pérez, p. 1).

Some of those policies and practices have caused Latinos to be consistently paid less, offered lower-wage work, face greater challenges to secure loans and start a business, and receive less mentoring and support (pp. 27, 39, 53, 63). The report explicitly states that not addressing these barriers is "morally" wrong (p. 9).

By 2060, the United States will become minority white (44.3 percent), while the Hispanic population would have ballooned to 27.5 percent (Frey 2018). This growth will primarily be driven from the increased birth rate of the native-born Latino population (Funk and Lopez 2022). But the business news media should not wait another 40 years to target this audience because these changes can be witnessed in communities all over the country, not just the major cities and usual spots.

Small town United States is a lot more diverse than it used to be. Since 2010, Latinos have grown the fastest in population in North Dakota – a 155 percent increase – and an impressive 87 percent in South Dakota (Krogstad 2022). In Idaho, between 2007 and 2012, the amount of Hispanic-owned businesses increased by 62 percent (Taros 2020). In Missouri, the Latino population grew 42.6 percent in the decade prior to 2020 (U.S. Census Bureau 2021) and by 2050, almost one in four people in Nebraska will be Hispanic, a treble increase from 2010 (Cusido 2017).

The business news community in the United States could spend more resources covering this community, which not only benefits Latino pocketbooks and wealth planning, but the larger investor community.

Steps are being taken, however. For example, the Society for Advancing Business Editing and Writing (SABEW) has a diversity committee dedicated to expanding the coverage in newsrooms and the diversity of its journalists. Newsrooms such as TechCrunch and Yahoo Finance have partnered with organizations such as NAHJ to recruit for Latino journalists.

### The Future Direction of Business News for the Latino Market

Since mainstream business news coverage in the United States has not traditionally focused on the Latino population, it has been Latinos themselves who have filled this need – then and now.

Some of the most informative business news currently online now is produced by Lyanne Alfaro, founder of Moneda Moves ("moneda" means currency in Spanish), who has a newsletter and podcast, and runs a blog of the same name on Substack. At nearly 160 issues, she covers everything from the blockchain, to NFTs, to personal finance, brand strategy, reducing debt, to entrepreneurship and investing in the stock market. She began to write business news about Latinos because of the underrepresentation of their impact, particularly engineers, in business media.

"I thought that those intersections were always very interesting because when you looked at the popular magazines at the time, especially in the early 2010s, there wasn't much diversity," said the former supervising producer and social content director at Nasdaq, and writer for Business Insider and CNBC. "I don't think I was fully able to pull out those threads and see them as salient until I went full-time into the industry [at the national scale] in New York" (Alfaro 2022).

The Chicago native wanted to explore this lack of representation in the national media where the news cycle repeatedly included the same characters: Bill Gates, Warren Buffett, Elon Musk and Jeff Bezos. According to McKinsey, "less than 5 percent of Fortune 500 board and C-Suite seats are occupied by Latinos" and "as a result, Latinos consumers are often overlooked by companies that do not recognize them as a priority demographic" (Pérez 2022, p. 7).

"While I know these are the biggest titans in terms of the wealth accumulation, I also hear that Latinos have big consumer power and I see a lot of Latino entrepreneurs," Alfaro said. She's been more successful with editors when she pitched stories about people with generational wealth, mainly non-Hispanic whites. "I decided to start Moneda Moves as a way to share stories that weren't being written about Latinos in business" (Alfaro 2022).

Alfaro's Moneda Moves was selected to participate in the 2022 cohort of Google's Podcast Creators Program as one of only seven podcasters chosen to learn new skills and funding strategies from PRX professionals. In fall 2022, she also participated and wrote about L'ATTITUDE, a business convention focused on connecting like-minded Latinos from various sectors, owned by the Hispanic venture capital fund, LAT VC (Alfaro 2022).

Other young Latinas have jumped on popular apps, including Instagram and TikTok, to share financial literacy (SayHolaWealthPodcast 2022), particularly because "many are not taught financial skills" and because they can empathize with the cultural nuances that prevent some Latinos from speaking openly about money issues (Arena 2022; Hiplatina 2022). Latinas have also been critical at supporting one another with access to venture capital (Murillo 2022).

If mainstream U.S. business news editors don't pay attention, they may miss what's already happening with Latinos and the next generation of technologies on the Internet, web 3.0 or web3 (Business Wire 2022). There is a robust and collaborative community of Latino programmers, techies and entrepreneurs doing the work to educate themselves on the blockchain, cryptocurrencies and non-fungible tokens. They take advantage of platforms such as Twitter Spaces to gather and learn about web3 (Holametaverso 2022). There, they host conversations around intellectual property, government regulations and taxation – not just with Latinos in the United States, but with Latin Americans around the world too.

According to McKinsey, the "right combination of structural and immediate interventions can accelerate Latino economic advancement and prosperity" (Pérez 2022, p. 10), so not all is lost for mainstream business news, especially if it has the right leadership.

One particular moment that stands out to HACR's Wilson as a positive inflection point for the mainstream media was the appointment of Cuban American César Conde, as the chairperson of the NBCUniversal News Group, including CNBC, MSNBC, NBC News and all other local affiliate channels.

"There is no question, no doubt that there is a correlation with the diversity-focused coverage on CNBC with the arrival of César Conde," Wilson said.

## Conclusion

As has been explored in this chapter, mainstream U.S. business journalists, editors and publishers can benefit their investing audience through more education about the untapped potential of the Latino consumer, worker, entrepreneur and investor. More information about this potential can be found in many useful sources, as noted here.

## Further Reading

Auger-Domínguez, Daisy. (2022). *Inclusion Revolution: The Essential Guide to Dismantling Racial Inequity in the Workplace*. Seal Press.

Burgos, David and Mobolade, Ola. (2011). *Marketing to the New Majority: Strategies for a Diverse World*. St. Martin's Press.

Carbajal, Frank and Morey, José. (2021). *Latinx Business Success: How Latinx Ingenuity, Innovation, and Tenacity are Driving Some of the World's Biggest Companies*. Wiley.

Childers, N. (2020). The Moral Argument for Diversity in Newsrooms is also a Business Argument – and You Need Both. *Niemanlab*. Available at https://www.niemanlab.org/2020/11/the-moral-case-for-diversity-in-newsrooms-also-makes-good-business-sense/

Gonzalez, Juan and Torres, Joseph. (2011). *News for All the People: The Epic Story of Race and the American Media*. Verso.

## References

Adams, David C. (2021, December 19). "Las brechas que frenan a los latinos: Más de 1 millón podrían estar dentro de la clase media." *Univision*. Available at: https://www.univision.com/noticias/dinero/la-desigualdad-salarial-sigue-frenando-a-los-latinos-segun-un-estudio-de-mckinsey

Alfaro, Lyanne. (2022, April 5). Interviewed by Claudia Cruz [via Zoom].

Alfaro, Lyanne. (2022, October 4). "An inside look at L'ATTITUDE 2022." *Hispanic Executive*. Available at https://hispanicexecutive.com/an-inside-look-at-lattitude-2022/

Arena, Victoria. (2022, March 11). "6 Latina financial experts you should be following on social media." *Latinas in Business*. Available at https://latinasinbusiness.us/2022/03/11/6-latina-financial-experts-you-should-be-following-on-social-media/

Baer, Marcos. (2021, August 30). "Celebrating Arturo Villar's Life." *Portada*. Available at https://www.portada-online.com/feature/arturo-villar-celebrating-his-life-as-a-unique-publisher/

Bloomberg. (2023, February 13). "Why financial news needs more black and brown journalists." Available at https://www.bloomberg.com/news/videos/2023-02-13/why-financial-news-needs-more-black-brown-journalists-video

Business Wire. (2022, February 17). "Encantos and SUMA wealth announce strategic partnership to bring NFTs to the latinx community." Press release available at https://www.businesswire.com/news/

home/20220217005689/en/Encantos-and-SUMA-Wealth-Announce-Strategic-Partnership-to-Bring-NFTs-to-the-Latinx-Community

Castañeda, Laura. (2022). "Reporting on Latinas: 'She' Se Puede!" *Reporting on Latino/a/x Communities: A Guide for Journalists*. Routledge, p. 66.

Castro, Joaquin. (2022, October 5). "NPC newsmaker: Rep. Joaquin castro." *National Press Club Live*. Available at https://youtu.be/2DVNYJ_Yzmg

Chang, Alisa. (2020, July 10). "Nbcuniversal head explains his 50 percent diversity challenge." *NPR*. Available at https://www.npr.org/2020/07/10/889842769/nbcuniversal-head-explains-his-50-diversity-challenge

Chávez, Chris. (2022, June 21). Interview by Claudia Cruz [via Zoom]. *The Center of Hispanic Marketing: Florida State University*. Available at https://hmc.comm.fsu.edu/about-us/external-resources/

Chen, Shawna. (2022, August 30). "Abortion misinformation surges in Latino communities." *Axios*. Available at https://www.axios.com/2022/08/30/latinos-abortion-misinformation-roe-maternal-health

Cusido, Carmen. (2017, April 10). "'A hidden gem': Nebraska Latinos touts its rich history and diversity." *NBC News*. Available at https://www.nbcnews.com/news/latino/hidden-gem-nebraska-latinos-tout-its-rich-history-diversity-n744611

Dávila, Arlene. (2012). *Latinos Inc.: The Marketing and Making of a People*. University of California Press, Berkeley, pp. 56–87.

Del Valle, Elena. (2011, April 4). "CNN en español expanded programming with three new shows." *HispanicMPR.com*. Available at https://hispanicmpr.com/2011/04/04/cnn-en-espanol-expanded-programming-with-three-new-shows/

Ehling, Jeff. (2022, December 14). "'Real consequences happen': Latino families who invested in alleged crypto scheme want justice." *ABC 13 (KTRK)*. Available at https://abc13.com/crytofx-crytocurrency-scheme-ponzi-ftx-investment/12570073/

Ellingrud, Kweilin and Sichel, Bernardo. (2022, September 27). "Empowering economic growth in the Latino community." *McKinsey Podcast*. Available at https://www.mckinsey.com/featured-insights/sustainable-inclusive-growth/future-of-america/empowering-economic-growth-in-the-latino-community

@Eliana_Murillo. (2022, June 23). "Latinas building generational wealth." *Twitter*. Available at https://twitter.com/Eliana_Murillo/status/1540065078812282880

Federal Deposit Insurance Corporation. (2022, November 14). "2021 FDIC national survey of unbanked and underbanked households." Available at https://www.fdic.gov/analysis/household-survey/index.html

Fields, Samantha. (2022, August 22). "Black, Hispanic and poorer families pay the price of being 'unbanked.'" *Marketplace*. Available at https://www.marketplace.org/2022/08/22/black-hispanic-and-poorer-families-pay-the-price-for-being-unbanked/

Frey, William H. (2018, March 14). "The US will become 'minority white' in 2045, census projects." *The Brookings Institute*. Available at https://www.brookings.edu/blog/the-avenue/2018/03/14/the-us-will-become-minority-white-in-2045-census-projects/

Funk, Cary and Lopez, Mark Hugo. (2022, June 14). "A brief statistical portrait of U.S. Hispanics." *Pew Research Center*. Available at https://www.pewresearch.org/science/2022/06/14/a-brief-statistical-portrait-of-u-s-hispanics/

@gabosama. (2022, June 14). "Why we covered latinos in tech." Available at https://twitter.com/gabosama/status/1536758144537268224

Galan, Nely. (2023, June 7). "Inside the traumatic collapse of first republic bank." *Money News Network*. Available at https://moneynewsnetwork.com/podcast/money-maker/inside-the-traumatic-collapse-of-first-republic-bank/

Garza, Melita M. (2022). "Covering Latinos in business and the economy." *Reporting on Latino/a/x Communities: A Guide for Journalists*. Routledge, p. 146.

Government Accountability Office. (2022, September 29). "Workforce diversity: Analysis of federal data shows hispanics are underrepresented in the media industry." Available at https://www.gao.gov/assets/gao-22-104669.pdf

Guynn, Jessica and Fraser, Jayme. (2022, August 2). "Only two Latinas have been CEO of a Fortune 500 company. Why so few Hispanic women make it to the top." *USA Today*. Available at https://news.yahoo.com/only-one-latina-ceo-fortune-090149215.html

@Hiplatina. (2022, August 3). How to save during inflation. Available at https://www.instagram.com/p/Cg0RTElJdZ0/?utm_source=ig_web_copy_link

@holametaverso. (2022, May 15). Weekly Twitter spaces announcement. Available at https://twitter.com/holametaverso/status/1526007902019809280

Krogstad, Jens Manuel, et al. (2022, September 23). "Key facts about the U.S. Latinos for national hispanic heritage month." *Pew Research Center*. Available at https://www.pewresearch.org/fact-tank/2022/09/23/key-facts-about-u-s-latinos-for-national-hispanic-heritage-month/

Latino Donor Collaborative. (2022, September). "LDC U.S. Latino report: Quantifying the new mainstream economy." Available at https://www.latinodonorcollaborative.org/original-research/2022-ldc-u-s-latino-gdp-reportLehrer, Brian and Mochkofsky, Gabriela. (2022, July 20). "Reaching Spanish-language media consumers." *The Brian Lehrer Show, WNYC*. Available at https://www.wnyc.org/story/reaching-spanish-language-media-consumers

Miranda, Leticia, (2019, May 24). "WeWork imploded in 2019. The pandemic brought it back to life." *NBC News*. Available at https://www.nbcnews.com/business/business-news/wework-imploded-2019-pandemic-brought-it-back-life-n1267957

O'Brien, Soledad. (2018, December 16). "Latinos start businesses faster than any other group. So why can't they get capital?" Matter of Fact. *YouTube*. Available at https://www.youtube.com/watch?v=KKMJgORWJUw

Obolenskaya, Christina. (2021, December 21). "Hispanic buying power rising in the U.S., bolstering consumer sectors." *eMarketer*. Available at http://www.emarketer.com/content/hispanic-buying-power-rising-us-bolstering-consumer-sectors

Ortakales Dawkins, Jennifer. (2023, June 4). "Meet the 8 Black and Latina female founders whose startups have topped a $1 billion valuation." *Business Insider*. Available at https://www.businessinsider.com/black-and-latina-female-founders-billion-valuations-vc-capital-2023-3

Panditharatne, Mekela. (2022, August 30). "Latino voters at high risk for misinformation in midterm elections." *Brennan Center for Justice*. Available at https://www.brennancenter.org/our-work/analysis-opinion/latino-voters-high-risk-misinformation-midterm-electionsPérez, Lucy. (2021, December 9). "The economic state of Latinos in America: The American dream deferred." *McKinsey & Company*. Available at https://www.mckinsey.com/featured-insights/sustainable-inclusive-growth/the-economic-state-of-latinos-in-america-the-american-dream-deferred

Perez, Lucy. (2022, November 14). "The economic state of Latinos: Determined to thrive." *McKinsey & Company*. Available at https://www.mckinsey.com/featured-insights/diversity-and-inclusion/the-economic-state-of-latinos-in-the-us-determined-to-thrive

Puente, Teresa, Retis, Jessica et al. (2022). *Reporting on Latino/a/x Communities: A Guide for Journalists*. Routledge, p. 1.

Rivera Brooks, Nancy. (2022, July 20). Interviewed by Claudia Cruz [via Zoom].

Rodriguez, Eric. (2012, March 7). "Assessing the Damage of Predatory Lending by Countrywide: The Fallout for Latino Families." *National Council of La Raza*. Available at https://www.judiciary.senate.gov/imo/media/doc/12-3-7RodriguezTestimony.pdf

Rosas-Salas, Marcela. (2019). "Making the mass white: How racial segregation shaped consumer segmentation." *Race in the Marketplace: Crossing Critical Boundaries*. Palgrave MacMillan, p. 22, 26.

Ryssdal, Kai and Hollenhorst, María. (2022, April 28). "Economics' diversity problem includes socioeconomic diversity." Marketplace. Available at https://www.marketplace.org/2022/04/28/economics-diversity-problem-includes-socioeconomic-diversity/

Sama, Gabriel. (2022, April 11). Interview by Claudia Cruz [via Zoom].

@SayHolaWealthPodcast. (2022, April 15). Available at https://www.instagram.com/sayholawealthpodcast/

Serbiá, Xavier. (2022, December 7). "¿Qué puedo hacer para mejorar mis finanzas en 2023?" *CNN en Español Dinero*. Available at https://cnnespanol.cnn.com/video/resoluciones-financieras-2023-nuevo-ahorro-inversion-dinero-serbia/

Sundar, Sindhu and Joyner, April. (2022, August 23). "How Adam Neumann's $420 million fundraising for his startups this year compares to what Black, Latino and women founders raised." *Business Insider*. Available at https://www.businessinsider.com/how-adam-neumann-funding-compares-black-latino-women-startup-founders-2022-8

Tameez, Hanna. (2022, March 8). "American journalism's 'racial reckoning' still has lots of reckoning to do." *Nieman Journalism Lab*. Available at https://www.niemanlab.org/2022/03/american-journalisms-racial-reckoning-still-has-lots-of-reckoning-to-do/#

Taros, Megan. (2020, May 1). "Latino businesses are the fastest-growing in the U.S., but their voices are seldom heard." *Magic Valley*. Available at https://magicvalley.com/business/latino-businesses-are-the-fastest-growing-in-the-u-s-but-their-voices-are-seldom/article_1e431d9b-2251-5655-942e-32680c22b41c.html

@TheEconomist. (2023, June 9). Available at https://twitter.com/TheEconomist/status/1667203951488532480

The Honest Company. (January 2023). "Bio: Carla Vernón, chief executive officer." Available at https://investors.honest.com/home-leaders/carla-vernon

Tomasik, Emily and Gottfried, Jeffrey. (2023, April 4). "U.S. journalists' beats vary widely by gender and other factors." *Pew Research Center*. Available at https://www.pewresearch.org/short-reads/2023/04/04/us-journalists-beats-vary-widely-by-gender-and-other-factors/

U.S. Census Bureau. (2021, August 25). "Missouri surpassed 6 million population mark last decade." Available at https://www.census.gov/library/stories/state-by-state/missouri-population-change-between-census-decade.html

Villafañe, Veronica. (2023, June 1). "CNN en Español will cut linear programming and jobs, shift production to Mexico City." *Media Moves*. Available at https://www.mediamoves.com/2023/06/cnn-en-espanol-will-cut-linear-programming-and-jobs-shift-production-to-mexico-city.html

Wilson, Cid. (2022, April 4). Interview by Claudia Cruz [via Zoom].

Yost, Billy. (2022, January 24). "Latinos belong in the boardroom." *Hispanic Executive*. Available at https://hispanicexecutive.com/anilu-vazquez-ubarri-tpg-capital/

# 5

# POLITICAL BIAS IN BUSINESS AND GENERAL MEDIA

*Colin H. Campbell*

## Introduction

On January 6, 2021, Capitol Hill was in chaos. During the transfer of power between U.S. President Donald J. Trump and President-elect Joseph R. Biden, Jr., the future of U.S. democracy seemed to be in a tenuous state. Trump had ended his speech at the White House Ellipse as members of ultra-right groups and Make America Great Again (MAGA) loyalists stormed the halls of the U.S. Congress about two miles away. Rioters pushed through fencing and bike racks set up by Capitol Hill Police officers. News media made decisions on whether they were going to cover the events every hour or how the events should be reported on in the days that followed. Coverage varied among various news groups. Media outlets such as Yahoo News, CNN, Breitbart, Business Insider, and many others made decisions on narratives based on their consumer constituencies. Some left-leaning news organizations framed the riots as a mob or siege. Other outlets described the imbroglio as an insurrection or an invasion. Right-leaning news groups downplayed the event altogether or framed it as less deleterious than it realistically was. The coverage was seen around the world and business journalists played a part in that. Business media sought to strike the right tone in their characterization of that moment.

As the nation watched pro-Trump MAGA supporters raucously surge through the Capitol, the news media described the insurrectionists in varying ways that may have been confusing for readers and viewers. However, depending on what news medium a consumer read or watched, one's understanding of the events may have varied. Where some saw chaos, some news sources saw a profit.

"Media bias" is the focused regard engaged by media gatekeepers, such as producers and managers, given to the selection of events and stories that are reported, how they are covered, and many times, framed (Smith & Wakefield 2005). Bias could indicate the entrenched positions within the news organizations. Skewed or biased media suggest a mass media source that may be neglecting other important stories. This lies at the heart of agenda-setting theory, a concept that is fundamental in evaluating media bias (Smith & Wakefield 2005). Media bias has been studied for decades but is getting a new look because of its implications for how our media are informing the public.

DOI: 10.4324/9781003298977-7

   This chapter examines how some business news media, including The Wall Street Journal, Insider, and Forbes, covered the insurrection in Washington, DC, on January 6, 2021. How the media portray such events and the issues they raise may depend on consciously strategic biases. Mainstream mass media sometimes neglect controversial issues, while alternative news outlets may report on them as part of their specialized coverage. Understanding business decisions that media make within their strategies for investigating and sharing information sheds light on what gets covered especially when politics are involved as discussed by Patterson (1997, p. 450). Consequently, we examine mainstream media to discuss the mainstream/alternative spectrum by contextualizing the events of January 6th. Through one perniciously provocative moment in American history, we describe the framing of the insurrection by leading business journalism news outlets that have been initially evaluated for bias. Also, we explore how these business news platforms differ from some general news platforms.

## Historical Perspectives

When media companies consider what to cover, agenda-setting is at the decision-making core. Social scientist Walter Lippmann writes in his book *Public Opinion* (1922) about the fundamentals that lead to agenda-setting theory. Lippmann explains that the news media are gatekeepers who create the visualizations or more descriptively, the "pictures," that provide the concepts that the public uses to create its own opinions about their environment (Shoemaker, Vos, & Reese, 2009). Gatekeepers fill a number of roles, including but not exclusive to, general managers, news directors, executive producers, producers, assignment editors, script editors, and at times, even the reporters themselves, according to Pingree, Quenette et al. (2013, p. 362). Although many attempt to maintain journalistic objectivity, opinions are constantly being formulated by events, issues, and public figures. When media consumers perceive pictures in their minds, they are encouraged to make decisions about what is presented by the media and what they understand to be reality (McCombs & Guo 2014, p. 258). News items are condensed when presented. The truncation of this news can warp the depiction of the action and create a distorted view of events.

   Researcher Maxwell McCombs (2008) remarked on Lippmann's thetical concept that the news media act as a primary link between myriad events occurring at any given time. McCombs posits that "the news media are the primary bridge between the vast array of events in the external world and the truncated views of these events in our minds" (McCombs 2008). Therefore, the collective ethos of the public is responsive to "pictures" introduced by news media, which could differ from reality. Lippmann concludes his initial analysis by calling for an independent, expert organization that would serve policymakers and industry leaders with information they need to make decisions. He suggests that the media were flawed, saying,

> Public opinions must be organized for the press if they are to be sound, not by the press as is the case today. This organization I conceive to be in the first instance the task of a political science that has won its proper place as formulator, in advance of real decision, instead of apologist, critic, or reporter after the decision has been made.
>
> *(Lippmann 1922)*

McCombs' and Donald Shaw's seminal research, later titled "The Agenda-Setting Function of Mass Media," used Lippmann's research as a jumping-off point to define the tenets of agenda-setting theory as it is understood in academia and industry. McCombs and Shaw

FIRST LEVEL AGENDA-SETTING

|  | Media Agenda | Public Agenda |
|---|---|---|
| First Level | Objects ——————> | Objects |
|  | 1. Frequency |  |
|  | 2. Length |  |

*Figure 5.1* An example of first level agenda-setting demonstrating media influence in the public sphere.

cited the work of Kurt Lang and Gladys Engel Lang, whose research found that the "mass media force attention to certain issues. They build up public images of political figures." Lang, Potter et al. (2009) argue that media are constantly presenting objects suggesting what individuals in the mass should think about and have feelings about.

McCombs and Shaw (2008) also connected with the works of Bernard C. Cohen, who contended that the duo offered the most comprehensive explanation of their theorized agenda-setting operations of the mass media (McCombs & Shaw 1972, p. 183) (Figure 5.1). Cohen wrote that members of the mass media "may not be successful much of the time in telling people what to think but are stunningly successful in telling its readers what to think about" (Gormley 1975).

Lang and Lang (1981) heavily influenced McCombs and Shaw's studies when examining agenda-setting function in the 1968 U.S. presidential election. Using the election between Richard M. Nixon and John F. Kennedy as a basis for research, the three social scientists analyzed the correlation of content demonstrated by members of the mass media and the elevation of an issue in the public's minds. They found connections to McCombs' and Shaw's study revealing that "the mass media set the agenda for each political campaign, influencing the salience of attitudes toward the political issues" referenced by McCombs and Shaw (1972, p. 177). McCombs and Shaw were able to find connections between the prominence of a campaign item in the voters' minds as well as the number of mentions that were presented. McCombs and Shaw (1972) posited that, "the political world is reproduced imperfectly by individual news media." McCombs and Shaw state that the evidence in this study that voters tend to share the media's composite definition of what is important strongly suggests an agenda-setting function of the mass media.

## Critical Issues and Topics

Corporate bias theory suggests that news narratives are chosen or written to satisfy the objectives of corporate media owners. Decision-making biases, i.e., the biases that create the motivations, perceptions, or beliefs of the writers, will influence their writing (Broudy & Winter 2016). News agencies and media corporations are run by people with disparate power and influence. Those in control have biases that often influence their news outlets. When those biases are also influenced by neo-liberalism, the results can be an output of skewed journalism reflecting the sociopolitical leanings of its producers, as indicated by Hobbs and Phillips (2009, p. 253).

Were the events of January 6, 2021 the result of an "insurrection" or a "protest?" Georgia Republican Congressman Andrew Clyde said, "there was an undisciplined mob," but argued that "to call it an insurrection in my opinion is a bald-faced lie" (Segers 2021). By contrast, Democratic lawmakers described the events as domestic terrorism. Pam Keith, a former Democratic candidate for Congress, remarked on the disruptions of that day as being one of the worst situations of her life in recent U.S. history. She posted on Twitter: "On 1/6/2021, 9/11/2001 ceased being the worst thing that happened to America in my lifetime" (Keith 2021).

Of course, individuals could characterize the events of that day based on their unique perspectives, but network leaders made choices to characterize or "frame" the events of January 6 in a particular fashion. VisualCapitalist.com (2021) examined the following news services on January 6, 2021, to understand how media described the incident at Capitol Hill: Yahoo! News, CNN, The New York Times, Fox News, The Washington Post, Breitbart, The Epoch Times, BBC, and Business Insider. These artifacts were taken from a sample of more than 180 articles from Alexa's top-ranked news websites in the United States.

Reporters found that The New York Times and The Washington Post used neutral language. These outlets commonly described the event as a "siege" and a "riot," and those who participated in the event as "the mob" and "rioters." In another lexical analysis, The Epoch Times and Breitbart used milder descriptors such as "protesters" and "alleged Trump supporters" when discussing the people and individuals involved that day around the Capitol. The BBC used terms such as "riot" and "stormed," which appeared to be the most common words in the coverage of the melee. These framing considerations were slightly different for business publications that covered the same event.

The Wall Street Journal, owned by Rupert Murdoch's News Corp., is generally considered center or center-right on the media bias scale. AllSides.com describes the U.S.-based Wall Street Journal as a centered news outlet. The same content from the News Corp. publication shifts a little to the right when ranked by Ad Fontes Media.

Insider, formerly known as Business Insider, is an American news website founded in 2007. Despite the recent rebranding, its executives still consider it a multinational financial and business news website consistent with the news/information website's genesis. It operates several international editions, including one in the United Kingdom. Insider, an original publisher and an aggregator, has been nominated for numerous awards. However, it has faced criticism because of its use of clickbait akin to the tradition of yellow journalism where headlines could be misleading.

Forbes magazine is owned by Whale Media Investments and the Forbes family enterprise. Published eight times a year, it focuses on finance, investing, marketing, and industry/trade information. According to AllSides.com, Forbes would be considered as center (Forbes.com 2022). Forbes has a centered media bias rating, meaning that it does not automatically publish news or opinion content taking a partisan side on either side of the political spectrum. When the outlet does tend to report stories, it maintains largely a neutral balance that tends to lean left and right equally at different times.

The publications produce print versions of their products, as well as material on their websites.

## Current Contributions and Research

Communications and business media are flexible fields, which makes them challenging to review within the current literature. Some options need to be evaluated when assessing these areas, including an interrogation of the media progenitor. This section reviews five different studies retrieved from various areas that have suggested how to discuss agenda-setting, best narrative construction approaches, and the need for media literacy even within business journalism outlets.

Cruz and Holman (2022) examine the roles that journalists pursue when shaping public perception of issues through the stages of priming, framing, and ultimately agenda-setting. This study emphasizes the works of foundational theorists. The research suggests that society's professional standards, often supported by business interests and decision-making, manage and control how journalists cover events. At the same time, these accepted professional norms can be influenced by implicit biases and systemic structures that have profound impacts on journalistic practices. However, these results can be provocative when analyzed through the lens of corporate bias. Because of the choices that a journalist or a newsroom makes, the editorial manifestations can further marginalize individuals (Entman & Rojecki 2000, p. 921).

The study then analyzes two structurally different newsrooms that reported on the Black Lives Matter (BLM) movement, combined with the U.S. immigration debate over the Obama-era executive order called the Deferred Action for Childhood Arrivals Act (DACA). Cruz and Holman (2022) use sampled articles and discursive narratives from the Tampa Bay Times, a predominately white newsroom, and the Atlanta Journal-Constitution, a more diverse news organization. The study analyzes articles written the day after Donald Trump was elected president of the United States in 2016 to the period just before Joseph Biden was inaugurated in 2021. The analysis pointed to differences in sourcing, framing, and other societally influential factors in the coverage of DACA and BLM. The study found that the ethnicity of journalists and their culture influences the coverage of Black citizenry and Latino immigrants. The coverage tended to be more sympathetic and the framing more ethical for the BLM stories after the extrajudicial killings of Black and brown people in 2020. The study concluded that specialized reporting would lead to better representation of the issues.

Researcher Steven Jukes (2019) questions whether Anglo-American journalism has exceeded the usual boundary that separates those who "run the business of news" and those who report the news. Jukes posits that the demarcation, often called a "Chinese Wall," is designed to support journalists' professional agency away from neo-liberal commercial interests and the influences of the most senior media gatekeepers. The article concentrates on the usage of Twitter. It analyzes the output of ten political correspondents based in the United Kingdom during the busy party conference season. The study examines how the reporters promoted their own stories on Twitter at the same time as their personal brands. The research observed whether the correspondents stepped over a forbidden line, obfuscating the boundary between news and the business. Paliktzoglou, Oyelere et al. (2021) point out that the research serves as a companion to interviews with political correspondents and an analysis of ethical codes of practice when using social media. To satisfy advertisers, journalists may also be pressed to boost "clicks" by emphasizing sensational news. This could undermine their objectivity and amounts to a new form of yellow journalism (Muller 2016).

Carlson and Lewis (2015) indicate that this examination builds upon a framework of research that inspects news editorial boundaries influenced by business decisions. The findings suggest that the political correspondents are highly individualistic in their Twitter usage. The research also emphasizes that securing a specific news marketing brand in the area of reporting practices has become normalized and validated.

In a third study, Suhonen (2021) posits that the news media industry and its journalistic expression operates more like a business rather than an organic recounting of events and therefore creates a schism between journalistic and managerial styles. The explanation includes the professional boundaries of self-regulation, professional agency, autonomy, public service; managerial responsibility connotes the preference for the business ideal which includes measurable outcomes and systemic efficiency, which is often the objective of business journalism ideals as referenced by Suhonen (2022).

Fredricks and Phillips (2021) contend that media can be heavily influenced by a current governmental situation. "When governments become entangled in the business of licensing and regulating news outlets, news outlets succumb to the pressures of only publishing stories favorable to the current regime" (Fredricks & Phillips 2021). The tendency to publish negative stories could encourage the loss of losing a publishing license. The researchers use Venezuela as an example. Fredricks and Phillips (2021) point out that in the past two decades, the country of Venezuela has misled its people, setting up an environment of "misinformation, confusion, and propaganda."

And lastly, Isom, Boehme et al. (2021) suggest that "media is a primary player in shortening this distance" between extremist views and the understanding of events as they take place. They point to polarization within American society and the embrace of political binarism within media framing decisions. As each new societal division is introduced, there is a new opportunity to connect with a novel and inevitable tangential point of view. The researchers suggest that myriad journalism outlets, including business journalism platforms, are integral in attempting to bridge the divide in people's perceptions and responses to social issues.

The study suggested that it is important for journalists to remain objective, neutral, independent, and able to report without the threat of government censorship, as Wike and Fetterolf (2018) point out. The findings indicate that the media are also under the influence of federal and state governments. A controlling and dominant neo-liberal influence on journalistic expression can cloud editorial neutrality and so allow politicians to bend media to their interests. Instead, the public needs objective news that it can trust for there to be a fully functioning democracy. Without varied voices and the separation of media from business interests, the example of robust debate and diversity declines, as Fredricks and Phillips (2021) contend.

## Main Research Methods

This chapter provides a qualitative content analysis of stories introduced by six news outlets. As outlined in Pallin and Aubel et al. (2021), the codes within the content were measured dichotomously. Wallsten (2007) posits that frames that happen frequently throughout a period of time can have a profound impact on consumers' perceptions and analysis.

The words that the media use are coded by a large number of frames and separate elements. This research restricted the analysis to qualitatively compare the media outlet, timbre, and lexical usage which differed from other news media. Because of news sharing by media outlets and overlap between original and second-hand sourcing, this research eliminated other sources because of lack of accessibility in prominent online formats such as Facebook, YouTube, and others.

Restricted news cycles limit data collection by decreasing news stories online just after the events of January 6, 2021. This research examined the aggregate from prominent news sources and insights that needed continued analysis. This research categorized various media based on their ranking on their popularity and reach within the public. Miscoded sentiments of how just a few words could have influenced the outcomes and revelations of the studied news sources.

This study attempts to provide relevant qualitative context to support the usually quantitative method in which these issues are examined based on the leading news articles pertinent to January 6.

## Descriptions of the January 6 Event From January 7, 2021

*Table 5.1* Descriptors used in printed articles on January 7, 2021, regarding the Capitol Hill insurrection

|  | *WSJ* | *BI* | *Forbes* | *CNN* | *NYT* | *Yahoo!* |
|---|---|---|---|---|---|---|
| Assault |  | 1 |  | 5 | 1 | 5 |
| Attack | 3 | 3 | 4 | 3 | 6 | 3 |
| Breach |  | 1 |  | 4 | 3 | 4 |
| Insurrection | 1 | 6 | 2 | 3 | 1 | 3 |
| Invasion |  | 1 |  |  |  |  |
| Mob | 5 |  | 4 |  |  |  |
| Rampage |  |  | 1 | 1 | 3 | 1 |
| Riot | 8 | 7 | 6 | 9 | 9 | 6 |
| Siege |  | 4 |  | 6 | 7 | 6 |
| Savage |  |  |  |  |  |  |
| Storm | 5 | 8 | 9 | 9 | 6 | 9 |
| Unrest | 1 |  |  |  |  |  |

## Analysis

This analysis sought to understand how news reporting patterns affect the way that business news outlets cover major political issues (Table 5.1). The patterns that emerged for each publication followed previous trends and maintained expected levels of partisanship and news editorial norms. There are variances in how a specific event is framed while also emphasizing its salience and the polarization that derives from different ownership enterprises. In a more fulsome way, this study's analysis regarding specific news coverage contends that there is a general consensus on the realities of what happened on January 6th. While this consensus is not representative of all publications that reported on the events, especially among some of the more fringe publications that were excluded from the article sample, it does demonstrate some observations to note. Media coverage that continues to engage in more partisan discursive expression is a bigger part of the conventional mainstream coverage rather than business media.

Pre-eminent news media influence how our society processes events that dominate the news cycle. To understand better the language used in the coverage surrounding the events of January 6th, this research examined more than 50 printed articles published the following day by the six news outlets named here. In order to measure the descriptions via print media, the articles assessed were published the day after January 6. This time period was chosen so as to include the most salient day of news articles relation to the incident and how the media reacted. The publications were chosen because of their prominence and ratings by various organizations that measure the partisanship of media outlets.

The purposive sampling is important here because it examines the language that the publications used when the events of that day were still fresh. Gatekeepers were deciding and learning how the actions of the antagonistic group would be considered. The content analysis focuses on a number of words and phrasing occurrences within each article as they characterize the events. This method supported a "contextualist approach with a reflexive vision" and followed Culler (1997) via a "close reading" of the news articles that meet certain criteria that Coleman (2020, p. 24) points out. This method of analysis was chosen for this study because of its versatility in identifying specific words within the data, which proves useful in understanding thematic similarities.

The most unanticipated consequence of this analysis was the similarity in which most of the business reporting narratives agreed on the characterizations. The differences between business reporting perspective and more general types of news coverage are not exactly novel, but each publication had its own assessment of how the throngs of Trump supporters and their activities would be described as showing a level of cognitive salience that was not previously realized. The noteworthy observations of a business news outlet maintain Edelman's (1987) assertions that the business norms follow noteworthy and highly suggestive content. News coverage created by The Wall Street Journal is often reported in a fashion that refutes the obvious partisan framing from other rival news outlets such as Forbes.com and Insider.

## Recommendations for Practice

When considering future research, investigators should look at a diverse array of video social media platforms. This chapter touched on the intersection of business practices and editorial media selection based on the agenda-setting nature of gatekeepers to inform the public while simultaneously protecting their interests. As we remember, the primary function of agenda-setting theory reinforces the understanding that an exposure to certain topics leads the audience to consider that the selected topics should be considered as highly important even at the neglect of more pertinent information. However, the subjective nature of story selection is also made with the interests of the business in mind.

The media impact regarding how the public processes events is unequivocal. So paying attention to decisions that corporate media make is vital. The influence of media and public perception is nearly inextricably linked. It is reported that nearly 90 percent of surveyed Americans consider the news an essential tool to stay informed about public affairs. From the January 6th riots to the rhetoric from a former president of the United States, the way that media companies evaluate the U.S. Capitol events leaves an impression on the way consumers process the information and how they think about it. The enormity of an event such as what happened at the capital encourages a high level of saliency (Blake 2021).

Subjectivity makes it difficult to rate neutrality when reporting. Every one of us comes from somewhere, and that somewhere, in part, informs our work. The challenge for journalism and media educators is to balance expectations of objectivity with the realities of doing good journalism. The charge and challenge for journalists and media academicians are to discover balance within expectations of reporting and understanding solid journalism.

Various perspectives can offset the negatives of bias. Instead of ignoring biases as if they do not exist or considering them only as a negative expression of malicious intent, an alternate way to find fairness and objectivity is to permit different voices and ideas to be discovered, shared, and evaluated in a clear and open way. This could make a space for the analysis or the discussion of what creates the bias and what encourages people to make decisions on their own instead of thinking in terms of a singular worldview or support for specific information.

News media should untether as much as possible the corporate interests of what is being covered in deference to how certain events affect individuals. The public should have more interaction with story coverage than just the option to change a channel when certain narratives are not agreeable to the consumer. Similarly, news media can use a process to help understand how warped media depictions of equitable coverage can lead to dubiousness over media convergence. News corporations need to create a complete and more accurate depiction of topical events while providing the most relevant information without the heavy use of filters and corporately influenced censorship.

## Conclusion

Media bias is not always bad when the bias is stated and transparent. Points of view should be as diverse as the society that presents them. The issue, of course, is that obfuscated biases can mislead, manipulate, and divide us. Rather than looking to eradicate widespread news media bias, which would be all but impossible to do, it is better to make it more transparent. Reporters could build a larger audience through increased trust and reflection with more focused reporting from individuals' writing. This scenario would be unlikely as corporations are currently incentivizing outlets to maintain a partisan angle.

Future research should address the effect that corporate sources have on the effect represented in agenda-setting. News items change rapidly in today's media climate. Future research should analyze the implications of how a changing media environment should reflect more of what is interesting to the public rather than what corporate media gatekeepers provide.

## References

AllSides Media Bias Chart. (2022). Don't be fooled by media bias & misinformation. Retrieved through https://www.allsides.com/media-bias/media-bias-chart

Blake, A. (2021). Capitol riot worse for America than 9/11, says failed Florida democratic congressional candidate. *Washington Times*. Retrieved from https://www.washingtontimes.com/news/2021/sep/11/pam-keith-florida-democrat-describes-capitol-riot-/

Broudy, D., & Winter, J. P. (2016). Propaganda in a neoliberal universe: An interview with James winter. *Synaesthasia, SCAC (SYNÆSTHESIA COMMUNICATION ACROSS CULTURES)*, 18–23.

Business Insider. (2022). Retrieved from https://www.businessinsider.com

Carlson, M., & Lewis, S. C. (Eds.) (2015). *Boundaries of journalism: Professionalism, practices and participation*. Routledge.

Coleman, C.-L. (2020). *Environmental clashes on Native American land: Framing environmental and scientific disputes*. Palgrave Pivot.

Culler, J. (1997). *Literary theory: A very short introduction*. Oxford: Oxford University Press

Cruz, C. Y., & Holman, L. (2022). The media and race in the Trump era: An analysis of two racially different newsrooms' coverage of BLM and DACA. *The Howard Journal of Communications, 33*(2), 197–215. https://doi.org/10.1080/10646175.2021.2012853

Edelman, M. (1987). *Constructing the political spectacle*. The University of Chicago Press.

Entman, R. M., & Rojecki, A. (2000). The black image in the white mind: Media and race in America (Book Review). *Journalism and Mass Communication Quarterly, 77*(4), 921.

Forbes.com. (2022). Who we are. Retrieved from https://www.forbes.com/connect/who-we-are/

Fredricks, S. M., & Phillips, J. D. (2021). The media's influence on the government: A case study of Venezuela's media agenda setting with a non-free press and its repercussions. *Journalism and Media, 2*(2), 275. https://doi.org/10.3390/journalmedia2020016

Hobbs, A. P., & Phillips, P. (2009). The hyperreality of a failing corporate media system. *Censored 2010 1*, 251–259.

Isom, D. A., Boehme, H. M., Mikell, T. C., Chicoine, S., & Renner, M. (2021). Status threat, social concerns, and conservative media: A look at white America and the alt-right. *Societies, 11*(3), 72. https://doi.org/10.3390/soc11030072

Jukes, S. (2019). Crossing the line between news and the business of news: Exploring journalists' use of twitter. *Media and Communication, 7*(1), 248–258. https://doi.org/10.17645/mac.v7i1.1772

Keith, P. (2021). Twitter post. Retrieved from https://twitter.com/pamkeithfl/status/1436676637 463097345?lang=en

Lang, G.E., & Lang, K. (1981). Watergate: An exploration of the agenda-building process. In Wilhout, G.C. & de Bock, H. (Eds.), *Mass Communication Review Yearbook* (Vol. 2, pp. 447–468).

Lang, A., Potter, R. F., & Bolls, P. (2009). Where psychophysiology meets the media: Taking the effects out of mass media research. In *Media effects*, 3rd edition (pp. 201–222). Routledge.

Lippmann, W. (1922). News, truth, and a conclusion. In W. Lippmann, *Public Opinion* (pp. 358–365). MacMillan Co. https://doi.org/10.1037/14847-024McCombs, M. (2008). Creating a new news: Opportunities on the internet for broader and deeper journalism. *Brazilian Journalism Research*, *4*(1), 6–17.

McCombs, M. E., & Guo, L. (2014). Agenda-setting influence of the media in the public sphere. *The Handbook of Media and Mass Communication Theory*, *1*, 251–268.

McCombs, M. E., & Shaw, D. L. (1972). The agenda-setting function of mass media. *Public Opinion Quarterly*, *36*(2), 176–187.

Muller, D. (2016). Conflict of interest: Hybrid journalism's central ethical challenge. *Ethical Space*, *13*(2/3), 95–109.

Pallin, R., Aubel, A. J., Knoepke, C. E., Pear, V. A., Wintemute, G. J., & Kravitz-Wirtz, N. (2021). News media coverage of extreme risk protection order policies surrounding the parkland shooting: A mixed-methods analysis. *BMC Public Health, 21*, 1–13. doi: https://doi.org/10.1186/s12889-021-11909-z

Paliktzoglou, V., Oyelere, S. S., Suhonen, J., & Mramba, N. R. (2021) "Social Media: Computing Education Perspectives in Diverse Educational Contexts." *Journal of Information Systems Education*, *32*(3), pp. 160–165.

Patterson, T. E. (1997). The news media: An effective political actor? *Political Communication, 14*(4), 445–455.

Pingree, R. J., Quenette, A. M., Tcherney, J. M., & Dickinson, T. (2013). Effects of media criticism on gatekeeping trust and implications for agenda setting. *Journal of Communication, 63*(2), 351–372.

Segers, Grace. (2021). "Normal tourist visit": Some Republicans downplay January 6 riot amid Democratic objections. *CBS News*. Retrieved from https://www.cbsnews.com/news/capitol-riot-january-6-hearing-lawmakers-clash/

Shoemaker, P. J., Vos, T. P., & Reese, S. D. (2009). Journalists as gatekeepers. In *The Handbook of Journalism Studies* (vol. 73, p. 15).

Smith, K. C., & Wakefield, M. (2005). Textual analysis of tobacco editorials: How are key media gatekeepers framing the issues? *American Journal of Health Promotion, 19*(5), 361–368.

Static Media Bias Chart. (2022). Retrieved through https://adfontesmedia.com/static-mbc/

Statista. (2021). Media use in the U.S. - statistics & facts. Retrieved from https://www.statista.com/topics/1536/media-use/

Suhonen, J. L. (2022). Negotiating journalistic professional ethos in Nordic business journalism. *Media and Communication, 10*, 1.

Wallsten, K. (2007). Agenda setting and the blogosphere: An analysis of the relationship between mainstream media and political blogs. *Review of Policy Research, 24*(6), 567–587.

Wike, Richard, & Janell Fetterolf. 2018. Liberal democracy's crisis of confidence. *Journal of Democracy, 29*, 136–150. [CrossRef]

# 6

# POLITICS AND THE BUSINESS MEDIA

*Paul Glader*

## Introduction

A business story in The New York Times on April 10, 2021, titled "Inside the Fight for the Future of The Wall Street Journal" (Lee 2021), suggested that the nation's largest and most famous business newspaper was too focused on older white men at a time when the United States is growing more racially diverse. The story suggested that the Rupert Murdoch-owned Journal was held back by its conservative editorial page, which champions the motto "free markets, free people" and serves as a daily talking points memo for many in the Republican Party.

> Soon after the killing of George Floyd, staff members created a private Slack channel called 'Newsroomies,' where they discussed how The Journal, in their view, was behind on major stories of the day, including the social justice movement growing in the aftermath of Mr. Floyd's death. Participants also complained that The Journal's digital presence was not robust enough, and that its conservative opinion department had published essays that did not meet standards applied to the reporting staff. The tensions and challenges are similar to what leaders of other news organizations, including The Times, have heard from their staffs,

wrote Edmund Lee, a reporter at The New York Times (Lee 2021).

Lee also reported that an internal strategy team at The Journal suggested "that the paper should try to attract new readers – specifically, women, people of color and younger professionals – by focusing more on topics such as climate change and income inequality." Lee also reported that a few people on the business side and some top editors who had seen the analysis by the strategy team "dismissed it as a 'woke' strategy, given its emphasis on appealing to underrepresented readers, the people said."

The story kicked off a wave of debate among alumni of the WSJ on a private Facebook group, some of whom said that the NYT was projecting its "woke" values on rivals. (As defined by Merriam-Webster, the term "woke" means aware of and actively attentive to important societal facts and issues, especially issues of racial and social justice. To right-wing

DOI: 10.4324/9781003298977-8

critics, it suggests politically liberal in an extreme or unreasonable way.) One former staffer suggested that it's fine for the WSJ opinion pages to remain "anti-woke," while the news pages should remain "not woke." Another former staffer wrote, "The Journal is the last bastion of passion, quality and balance." A former WSJ masthead editor who became the chief executive at Fortune, Alan Murray, wrote to the group, "The Wall Street Journal is the only news outlet that will emerge from this sad period of history with any ability to be trusted by the entire country. Reuters and Pew studies show that." Other former WSJ staffers agreed with the Times report, complaining that the conservative opinion pages at the WSJ were too doctrinaire and arguing that the WSJ news pages should have done more and better investigative work on Donald Trump.

For decades, most business journalism outlets, including The Wall Street Journal, have recognized that they should diversify their staff of reporters and editors – considering race, gender, geography, class and other categories – which helps the outlet to tell diverse stories and to reach broader, diverse audiences. The former effort often helps the latter effort. Yet, a conflict of worldviews and journalistic approaches seems to exist between The New York Times and The Wall Street Journal, as a microcosm of conflict in the news business, on these topics.

This debate relates to business journalism more broadly, which has historically covered markets, economics and all aspects of business. Over time, major titles such as the WSJ, The Economist, Forbes and others developed conservative, classical liberal or libertarian editorial viewpoints. This often has meant championing free trade, wealth creation and big business. It often meant opposing big government, socialism, group think and collectivism. And it often meant that business owners, social conservatives and religious communities often ended up in the same broad political camps. This chapter aims to explore how and why that alignment developed and whether it will remain longer term.

## From the Beginnings of Journalism History

Mitchell Stephens, a journalism professor at New York University, points to business journalism as a beginning of the news business in his book, "A History of News." Humanity emerged from the oral storytelling tradition of Ancient Greeks, tribal societies and European town criers in coffee shops and public houses (taverns). Commerce became an early topic for written news. In the 16th century, Venetian merchants received written reports of the spice trade from India to Portugal. They also learned of movements of the Turkish fleet, which threatened their trade business. Early banking entities from Italy such as the House of Fugger used private written reports and correspondents to provide key information in finance and business as well as movements of the Spanish armada. News sheets emerged in continental Europe (present-day Germany) with Johannes Gutenberg's letter press spawning printed products in religion, commerce and other topics. Early American settlers and colonies relied on written correspondence and, later, on newspapers to transmit prices for crops, livestock and details on ships arriving in port with various goods ranging from ale and cotton to beaver pelts. "In 1815, the banker Nathan Rothschild received advance word on the outcome of the Battle of Waterloo from one of his agents, who had rushed the news across the Channel," Stephens wrote (Stephens 1988). "Rothschild is said to have then used the information to his advantage on the London Stock Exchange." From the beginning, many businesspeople needed and valued quality information to do business. Journalism provided that.

The sociologist Paul Starr at Princeton University notes that newspapers have served as an enormous democratizing and civilizing force in the last 400 years. The printing press and newspapers helped bring communication out of the realm of the wealthy elite and into the hands of a broader public. Starr notes that between 1790 and 1835, the population of the United States grew from 3.9 million people to 15 million people, while the number of newspapers grew 11-fold from 106 to 1,258 during that timeframe, compared to 369 newspapers in the British Isles (Starr 2004). Starr suggests that the development of robust news and information networks in the United States contributed to higher literacy and education rates. He notes that school enrollment rose significantly after the American Revolution to the highest levels in the world at that time. Starr implies that the literacy rates, education rates and newspaper rates played a big role in American progress, innovation and prosperity. "The acute observer will not have missed the fact that in the modern world there are no prosperous and powerful countries with mass illiteracy. The long-term economic payoff of literacy and education is well established," he writes (Starr 2004).

Business journalism has often provided fuel to help grow and develop new technologies and professional practices within broader news journalism that related to progress in business and economics. The telegraph is one example of this phenomenon. In "The Victorian Internet," Tom Standage writes how half of all telegraph messages in the 1850s in London related to the stock exchange. Another third was business related. And telegraph use in America was even more heavily oriented toward investing, business and commercial purposes. Young operators such as Thomas Edison and Andrew Carnegie gained notice for their skill and learned about business and invention from the Telegraph, filing patents, gaining investors and inventing new products. Early news wire services such as The Associated Press and Reuters formed in collaboration with the telegraph. The German-born Paul Julius von Reuter perfected the business of translating stories from various European newspapers and redistributing them. "Businessmen in particular were willing to pay for timely information, so he set up his own operation, using carrier pigeons to supply business information several hours before it could be delivered by mail," Standage writes (Standage 1998).

Meanwhile, the business press developments marched on past the telegraph age as well, with publications forming and printing titles such as "The Journal of Commerce" in 1827. Some 50 years later, The Wall Street Journal began printing but, "some of the most important stories in business journalism during this time ran in mainstream papers," writes Chris Roush in "Show Me The Money" (Roush 2016). Roush explains how early newspapers investigated railroad scandals, fireworks dangers and sour milk. Notable writers of the era such as Upton Sinclair documented unsafe working conditions in the meatpacking industry in his novel, The Jungle. Ida Tarbell wrote muckraking pieces about Standard Oil that led to a breakup of that company by 1911. Roush points to The Boston Post uncovering the financial wrongdoings of Charles Ponzi in 1920, a namesake for the type of fraud practiced by Bernie Madoff and many others.

## Modern Business Reporting and Abundance

Andrew L. Yarrow, a former New York Times reporter, wrote a notable paper in Journalism History in 2006 that explored how economic journalism emerged after the Great Depression and then flourished after World War II, coinciding with a notion of "abundance" in America. "Financial reporting changed from reciting stock quotations, company earnings, and puff

pieces on businessmen and individual companies to broader stories about the national economy and what economic trends meant for average Americans," Yarrow writes.

> The readership of business publications also expanded enormously during the twenty
> years after the war, and economic reporting gained a more prominent place in major
> newspapers and general-interest magazines. What was once intended for a small cogno-
> scenti of businessmen was now geared to the burgeoning postwar middle class.
>
> *(Yarrow 2006)*

As business journalism exploded to wider audiences, its underlying political and economic
philosophies also expanded.

Yarrow notes that financial journalists realized that the big story was America's dramatic
economic growth and mass prosperity that brought changes to American society. And these
forces also ushered in an age of liberty-oriented thinking, debates over small government
versus large government, John Maynard Keynes versus Adam Smith and shareholder capitalism versus stakeholder capitalism.

Yarrow points to Henry Luce's Fortune as an example of postwar optimism with its lavish
prose, photography, tables, charts, diagrams and paintings. Luce brought on star economics
writers such as John Kenneth Galbraith in the 1940s and created a "new capitalism" style
journalism that was "more in tune with the prevailing American Zeitgeist than other publications" such as The Wall Street Journal, BusinessWeek and The New York Times (which was
politically conservative at the time). Over time, The Wall Street Journal and BusinessWeek
magazine joined Fortune in cheerleading economic growth through coverage in the 1950s.

> Capitalism was no longer the exploitive tyranny depicted by Karl Marx, Charles
> Dickens, or Lincoln Steffens but instead it was a new 'people's capitalism' in which
> workers, responsible business people, government, and assorted experts cooperated
> to improve living standards for all, and in which home-owning, stock-owning average
> citizens now owned the means of production,
>
> *(Yarrow 2006)*

Yarrow writes that journalists and popular writers began emphasizing the American "system"
of "free enterprise" and presenting that as counterpoint to the Soviet Union. And business
journalism boomed. After 65 years of limited circulation among elite businessmen, The Wall
Street Journal grew its readership 16-fold from 50,000 in 1945 to 800,000 readers in 1961
under editor Barney Kilgore, who greatly expanded the scope and creativity of reporting in
The Journal. The Journal also became the nation's first truly national paper by opening five
printing plants around the country by 1955, expanding its coverage and reach from Wall
Street to Main Street. The Pulitzer Prize-winning editorial page editor Vermont C. Royster
played a huge role in the Journal championing free-market, Republican-oriented and anti-
Keynesian ideas and policies. "Business, free enterprise, is the economic manifestation of
the free society, the principal reason for America's pre-eminence," Royster wrote according
to Jerry M. Rosenberg's 1982 account "Inside the Wall Street Journal" (Rosenberg 1982).

Yarrow writes that the boom in financial publications caused general interest magazines such
as Life, The Saturday Evening Post and Reader's Digest to publish more business stories to
interest a vast middle-class audience in post-World War II America. Life published articles
with titles such as "The American and His Economy" and "The Good Life." The articles

often featured photos of happy families as consumers, mass production factories and illustrated charts and graphs showing "an upward trajectory of American abundance" (Yarrow 2006).

## The New Deal versus Marketplace of Ideas

Yarrow's history suggests that the business press for most of the 1930s into the 2000s shared the notion that free markets and capitalism were good for national progress, economic growth and individual wealth creation. Economics writers ranging from the post-Keynesian John Kenneth Galbraith at Fortune to the proto-libertarian Henry Hazlitt at Newsweek dueled over the right mix of government involvement versus the small government vision of free-market capitalism.

At the time, some scholars, such as Fred S. Siebert at the University of Illinois Communications Department, observed that press freedom aligned with other tenets of broad liberalism, including economic liberty and free markets. He contributed an essay to a classic journalism textbook, "Four Theories of the Press: The Authoritarian, Libertarian, Social Responsibility, and Soviet Communist Concepts of What the Press Should Be and Do" (Siebert 1956). Siebert called the history of the Anglo-American press freedom a "libertarian theory" and argued that this theory was characterized as the "free marketplace of ideas."

Historian Sam Lebovic writes that "press freedom became a sanctuary for the valorization of laissez-faire economic philosophy at the height of the New Deal order" and the marketplace of ideas concept became "a liberal cause, and a foundational commitment of American political life" championed by conservatives, liberals and centrists alike (Lebovic 2021). Lebovic argues that the Austrian free-market economist Friedrich Hayek made efforts to stretch the arguments for liberty of speech and press to "legitimate a broader vision of economic liberty." Lebovic suggests that the business press inclination toward free-market liberalism and philosophical conservatism was forged by liberalism itself and a complex mixture of news organizations, many of them growing economic entities themselves, defending freedom of the press by championing economic freedoms, progress and growth, all concepts New Deal regulators and liberals found difficult to counter. "Media industries with conservative political philosophies have long dressed up their partisan and economic interests as paladins of civil liberties," Lebovic writes:

> The conservative newspaper industry seeded the long libertarian crusade against New Deal regulation; their successes in presenting a laissez-faire marketplace of ideas as a part of a consistent liberal tradition helped to create dynamics that have defined American political culture into the present.
>
> *(Lebovic 2021)*

Yarrow notes that a small set of voices in publications such as The Atlantic, Saturday Review, The New York Times Magazine saw economics more through a New Deal liberal lens. And left-leaning publications such as Harper's, The New Republic, Commonweal and The Nation offered a more critical take on the juggernaut vision of the rising business press. Particularly, "The Nation, with its tiny liberal readership, was almost alone in taking a more jaundiced view of the idea that a beneficent new capitalism would bring a paradise of ever-rising wealth for all," writes Yarrow (2006, p. 65).

"When the economy collapsed in the Great Depression, that vision and those reform ideas provided the moral energy that propelled FDR's New Deal," writes sociologist Fred

Block from the University of California at Davis in a book review essay in Theory and Society:

> But in the post-World War II decades, marked by an intensification of the Cold War, political liberalism lost its moral and democratic grounding. That is what created the political and intellectual vacuum that was ultimately filled by Milton Friedman, his Mont Pelerin colleagues, and the right-wing think tanks.
>
> *(Block 2013)*

## The Role of Hayek, Friedman and the Austrian and Chicago Schools

Block also reviews a book, "The Great Persuasion: Reinventing Free Markets since the Depression," by the intellectual historian Angus Burgin on the history of the Mont Pelerin Society, a free-market salon and debate society founded by Hayek in 1947. Burgin, aiming to answer the question of how and why the free-market right became so powerful, points to figures such as Walter Lippman and Hayek aiming to identify a "neoliberalism" before and after World War II to challenge the communist and socialism movements on the rise. Hayek wrote his famous treatise, the "Road to Serfdom," in 1944.

Although Hayek considered the German "ordoliberal" approach by his friend Walter Eucken, Hayek ultimately sided with Ludwig von Mises and other libertarians in the Austrian school tradition such as Milton Friedman, a future Nobel Prize-winning economist who taught at the University of Chicago. Block writes that Hayek thought Friedman favored an ordoliberal-style compromise between classical liberalism and the welfare state. "During the course of the 1950s, Friedman moved significantly to the right" and his influence in economics circles grew. Friedman mentored notable economists such as Nobel Prize winners Gary Becker, Robert Lucas Jr. and Robert Fogel and the writer Thomas Sowell, a leading free-market economist and social conservative Black intellectual who influenced many other economists and writers.

One of Friedman's largest intellectual influences on corporate governance came in the form of his theory of "shareholder capitalism," which is sometimes called "the Friedman doctrine." Friedman argued in a New York Times Magazine article in 1970 that executives work for the owners (shareholders or investors) and the only social responsibility a business has is "to use its resources and engage in activities designed to increase its profits so long as it stays within the rules of the game, which is to say, engages in open and free competition without deception or fraud," wrote Friedman (1970, p. 6). In that same essay, Friedman ridiculed businessmen who spoke of the "social responsibilities of business in a free-enterprise system." He wrote that such preaching is "pure and unadulterated socialism," and he called businesspeople who talk this way, "unwitting puppets of the intellectual forces that have been undermining the basis of a free society." Friedman's theory sliced through the confusion of the 1970s and gave clarity to investors, corporate boards and executives about their mission. Hayek won a Nobel Prize in Economics in 1974; Friedman won in 1976. Friedman's theory was so thoroughly welcomed that it would take decades for rival economists, leading business schools and the political and cultural left to form a credible response.

The rise of Anglo-American conservative political figures such as U.K. Prime Minister Margaret Thatcher and U.S. President Ronald Reagan in the 1980s bolstered the Austrian and Chicago School economists such as Hayek and Friedman. The 1980s economic boom suggested a triumph for these economists over their big government Keynesian foes. "Hayek and the Mont Pelerin Society were extraordinarily successful in moving from extreme marginality in the 1940s to global hegemony in the 1970s and 1980s," writes Block (2013, p. 650).

## Ronald Reagan's 1980s

Beyond America's boom into abundance after World War II, the emerging Cold War with the Soviet Union also fueled a right-leaning, pro-capitalism business press from the 1950s into the 1990s. Publications framed economic stories as a contest between two superpowers, a battle between opposite economic and political operating systems in everything from the space race to economic growth to military supremacy. Many saw economic data and American prosperity as the greatest weapon in the Cold War. Many in the business press enjoyed pontificating about the record-breaking progress and unlimited potential of the American economy. As an example, The Wall Street Journal declared in 1954: "Americans are working under better conditions, are making more money, live in better homes, and have a higher living standard generally than their counterparts in any previous period of history" (Yarrow 2006, p. 67). Many in the business press believed that capitalism was the greatest force to eradicate poverty and proponents of this idea used the term "people's capitalism," a phrase The New York Times published 105 times between 1945 and 1965, according to Yarrow (2006, p. 75).

Increasingly, Yarrow notes a subtle shift in language from a producer economy to a consumerist economy in the late 1940s and early 1950s as the business press started to label Americans as "consumers," "homeowners" and "stockowners" rather than "workers" or "citizens" or "people" (Yarrow 2006, p. 69). Yarrow suggests that the heroic story of American progress was a product of traumatic events ranging from World Wars, a Holocaust and atomic bombs that shocked humanity. The big story of growth, progress and abundance in the postwar years of 1950s to 1970s remained in the 1980s as new enemies and forces emerged.

Large, publicly traded companies and executives tended to favor free-market economics and pro-business policies, naturally aligning with the Republican Party. People who became wealthy from starting or leading businesses had a vested interest in their own financial success and in the story of American growth and abundance. Meanwhile, the philosophical and movement conservatism brought by figures such as Barry Goldwater and William F. Buckley Jr. added political force, strategic creativity and a swaggering optimism to the free-market economics influence of Hayek, von Mises and Friedman.

The Democratic Party and political left had difficulty finding traction against the sauntering confidence of the free-market, pro-growth Republicans. Republicans successfully portrayed Democrats as the party of red tape, anti-business and redistributionism of wealth. Republicans derided one-term president Jimmy Carter's for his feeble response to economic malaise in 1979. The Hollywood actor turned California governor, Ronald Reagan, defeated Carter by a landslide a year later.

Once a Democrat, Reagan had been the voice of General Electric Co. advertisements and host of its GE Theater television show from 1954 to 1962. He said the views he encountered at GE from thoughtful Republican executives helped transform him into a free-market conservative who believed in limited government (Glader 2020). While Carter was famously a Baptist Sunday School teacher and many Southern Baptists and other religious groups had voted Democratic for decades, the tables turned as social conservatives and religious voters increasingly flocked to the free-market ideology, anti-socialism and economic optimism of the Republican Party. Leading evangelical figures such as Rev. Jerry Falwell Jr. and Rev. Pat

Robertson brought these religious voters into the Republican camp with TV shows, radio shows and direct mailings. They also influenced the Republican Party to care for moral issues such as abortion (a pro-life/anti-abortion agenda), traditional family values (an anti-LGBTQ agenda) and embracing, or at least accepting, America's Christian heritage (patriarchal structures for some) as tenets within the Republican Party.

Libertarian strains and free-market capitalism continue to populate the thinking of Silicon Valley and big technology companies. One difference, however, is that while Silicon Valley has a free-market, pro-business ethos, fewer tech funders and founders are social conservatives. The birth of the internet and explosion of the internet in the 1990s was seen, once again, as a triumphant moment of American exceptionalism in which free-market ideas, technology and innovations birthed in the developed world offered promise to help and change the developing world.

As technology companies have become arguably the biggest business story in the last five decades, the sector has also changed business journalism itself. As companies such as Facebook, Google and Twitter took over the advertising market, local and metro newspapers lost ad revenue and started closing, consolidating, laying off journalists and reducing business journalism. Meanwhile, many business journalism outlets in large coastal cities have flourished even as local metro newspapers have struggled or collapsed. And new business media outlets – from Bloomberg News, Quartz, Cheddar and Axios to Semafor – are launching, hiring thousands of journalists and serving millions of readers.

## Shareholder Capitalism versus Stakeholder Capitalism

Friedman's ideas of shareholder value became so widespread that The Economist called it "the biggest idea in business" in a 2016 article and said "today's shareholder value rules business." Meanwhile, 50 years after The New York Times published Friedman's famous essay on shareholder capitalism titled "A Friedman Doctrine," it published 22 short responses to that essay by 25 notable people in September of 2020.

Some of the critiques suggested that Friedman's theory was problematic financially, economically, legally, socially or morally. The alternative, some said, is for companies, board and executive to embrace "stakeholder capitalism." Among the respondents, Starbucks founder Howard Schultz writes that

> Starbucks's initiatives included providing part-time baristas with health care and tuition-free college education; volunteering in neighborhoods; talking openly about racism and helping impoverished youth find first jobs. The ethos fueling such efforts – that companies have a responsibility to enhance the societies in which they flourish – was integral to Starbucks's ability to employ great people and attract customers.
>
> *(The New York Times 2020)*

The stakeholder theory, by contrast, is "a view of capitalism that stresses the interconnected relationships between a business and its customers, suppliers, employees, investors, communities and others who have a stake in the organization," according to Stakeholdertheory. org, a site led by several scholars, including R. Edward Freeman, a professor at the Darden School of Business at the University of Virginia who began outlining a stakeholder theory in 1984. This idea has gained traction in recent decades at many top business schools and in the boardrooms, break rooms and Instagram feeds of Fortune 500 companies.

At the same time, the growing willingness for corporate leaders to embrace stakeholder capitalism, to put out statements about racial justice and to speak out about climate change might draw cheers from the left and be seen as silly from the right. And engaging in social justice activism or refusing to engage in such activism brings its own set of perils for corporate leaders and the companies they lead. For example, some employees at the Walt Disney Co. opposed legislation in Florida limiting what can be taught about sex and gender in Florida schools at various grade levels. The LGBTQ community and its allies labeled the legislation the "Don't Say Gay" bill, demanding that Disney condemn the legislation. Disney did so, pledging to fight for a repeal of the bill. In response, Florida's Senate passed legislation to eliminate Disney's ability to govern the 40-square miles of land in Florida where it built its sprawling theme parks, adding back taxes and red tape to the entertainment giant. This incident illustrates some of the pitfalls Friedman outlines in his essay in 1970 that companies and executives face when they stray from their core business and drift into various and sundry "responsibilities" various stakeholders place upon them, which may be detrimental to business and investors.

Defenders of the status quo in business reporting at outlets such as The Wall Street Journal and the Financial Times would suggest that their journalists do cover key issues in society and shifts in corporate behavior with rigor. They say that they are trying to hire competent, diverse staff members and to diversify their coverage within reason. They suggest that their reporting approach is not so much socially conservative so much as an attempt to exercise journalistic standards and ethics by reporting with neutrality on numerous sides of a story or an issue rather than only through a socially progressive lens. Many in the business press, more than in the general press, are just unwilling to be socially liberal or "woke." That may bother some who believe that business should embrace social responsibility and that journalists, including business journalists, should be activists serving progressive left causes.

Some business journalists may be motivated to work for a news organization with a social justice lens on the news. Still, plenty of staff members are content working at publications with a fact-based, economic lens on the world. One former high-level editor at The New York Times told this author The Wall Street Journal may "save journalism" with its traditional separation between news and opinion pages.

As a new outlet, Semafor, launched in October 2022, co-founder Ben Smith, wrote an opening column about The New York Times, his former employer, and its ongoing turmoil driven by battles by activist journalists against traditional journalistic principles, causing some readers to wonder if the progressive left culture of The Times, not the free-market conservative bent of The Journal, poses longer term internal strife.

"Journalists and the company are currently locked in a bitter contract fight, but the convulsions of COVID-19 and the surge of racial justice activism in 2020 left deeper divides," Smith wrote in his inaugural column. "A civil war has slid into a kind of frozen conflict, a distracting identity crisis at the heart of a company."

## References

"Analyse this." *The Economist*, 31 March 2016. Retrieved 15 July 2019.
Block, Fred. 2013. "Review: Think tanks, free market academics, and the triumph of the right." *Theory and Society*, 42 (6): 647–651.
Friedman, Milton. September 13, 1970. "Social responsibility of business to increase its profits." *The New York Times Magazine*. http://websites.umich.edu/~thecore/doc/Friedman.pdf

Glader, Paul. 2020. "Lights out at general electric." *Acton Institute LongForm.* https://acton.org/pub/longform/2020/02/03/lights-out-general-electric

Lebovic, Sam. 2021. "The conservative press and the interwar origins of first amendment lochnerism." *Law and History Review,* 39 (3): 539–567.

Lee, Edmund. 2021. "Inside the fight for the future of the wall street journal." *The New York Times.*

Merriam-Webster Dictionary Online, https://www.merriam-webster.com/dictionary/woke

Rosenberg, Jerry M. 1982. *Inside the Wall Street Journal.* MacMillan, New York.

Roush, Chris. 2016. *Show Me the Money: Writing Business and Economics Stories for Mass Communication.* 3rd Edition, Routledge, New York.

Roush, Chris. February 14, 2011. "The need to be more critical in business journalism." *TalkingBizNews. com.* https://talkingbiznews.com/they-talk-biz-news/the-need-to-be-more-critical-in-business-journalism/

Schultz, Howard. "A free market manifesto that changed the world, reconsidered". *The New York Times,* 11 September 2020. Retrieved 16 September 2020. https://www.nytimes.com/2020/09/11/business/dealbook/milton-friedman-doctrine-social-responsibility-of-business.html

Siebert, Fred S., Peterson, Theodore, and Schramm, Wilbur. 1956. *Four Theories of the Press: The Authoritarian, Libertarian, Social Responsibility, and Soviet Communist concepts of What the Press Should Be and Do.* University of Illinois Press, Urbana.

Standage, Tom. 1998. *The Victorian Internet.* Bloomsbury, New York.

Starr, Paul. 2004. *The Creation of the Media.* Basic Books, Cambridge, MA.

Stephens, Mitchell. 1988. *A History of News.* Viking Penguin, New York.

Yarrow, Andrew L. 2006. "The big postwar story: Abundance and the rise of economic journalism." *Journalism History,* Vo. 32, 2006, Issue 2 58–76.

### Additional Source

Bower, Joseph L., and Paine, Lynn S. (June 2017). "The Error at the Heart of Corporate Leadership." *Harvard Business Review,* 95(3): 50–60. These events illustrate a way of thinking about the governance and management of companies that is now pervasive in the financial community and much of the business world.

# PART II

# From Backwater to Front Page

# 7

# THE HISTORICAL EVOLUTION OF ECONOMIC, BUSINESS, AND FINANCIAL JOURNALISM

*Ángel Arrese*

## Introduction

The economic, business, and financial press has always occupied a marginal place in the history of journalism. Although the price currents and shipping lists of the seventeenth and eighteenth centuries are often cited as the precedents of newspapers (this is the case in virtually all histories of journalism, from the classical (Groth 1928; Weill 1934) to the recent (John and Silberstein-Loeb 2015; Pettegree 2014)), the study of the role of economic journalism and the economic media in different moments of history, or around events of special public relevance, has been very limited. It is only some isolated works, which are nevertheless very valuable, that have tried to explain the importance of economic journalism in the context of economic history and the evolution of economic ideas (McCusker and Gravesteijn 1991; Parsons 1989). Apart from those studies, a few works on the history of the business press have explored the emergence of different types of publications, the prominence of certain journalists, and so on, but always from the point of view of how a field for specialized news was built in different parts of the world (Arrese 2002; Duval 2004; Elfelbein 1969; Forsyth 1964; Henno 1993; Kareithi and Kariithi 2005; Kjær and Slaatta 2007; Quintâo 1987; Roush 2006; Spachmann 2005). More recently, new investigations have been carried out into the role of economic and financial media in times of crisis, when their relevance for the performance of economies is mixed in with their impact in political and social terms (e.g., Arrese 2010; Doyle 2006; Schuster 2006; Tambini 2008). In fact, since the credit crisis of 2008, a growing number of researchers have been working on subjects in this sector of the press, which is nowadays at the center of the process of shaping economic opinion in society (Arlt and Storz 2010; Basu 2018; Basu et al. 2018; Berry 2019; Knowles 2020; Lischka 2016; Mercille 2014; Merrill 2019; Picard 2015; Schifferes and Roberts 2015; Schiffrin 2011; Shaw 2016; Starkman 2014; van Dalen et al. 2019; Vliegenthart et al. 2021).

This neglect of economic journalism in the history of journalism is certainly surprising. Ever since writing helped men and women to manage in society, the recording and transmission of relevant information on events related to his economic and commercial activities have been essential tasks. It is commonplace to go back to the Egyptians, Assyrians, and Babylonians, or even to earlier civilizations, when speaking of the first examples of the dissemination

 DOI: 10.4324/9781003298977-10

of economic information (Forsyth 1964). The list of precedents could continue with the Phoenicians, Carthaginians, Greeks, and Romans, and then to the Middle Ages and the Renaissance, when the occasional publication of handwritten news sheets developed in practically all European countries (Arrese 2002; Blair et al. 2021).

However, it is from the 16th century onward, and especially in the second half of that century, 100 years after Gutenberg developed the use of movable type and during a period of great commercial expansion derived from the discovery and exploitation of the New World, that we can speak of the building of stable and advanced systems for the diffusion of economic information (McCusker and Gravesteijn 1991). At that time, the very possibility of the existence of a newspaper, the most innovative product derived from the printing press, the emergence of commercial capitalism, with the special information needs derived from the mercantile activity of the great merchants, and the appearance, as a consequence, of a certain variety of opinions regarding the economic activity of citizens and countries, were to converge.

Since then, the development of economic journalism has been marked by the intersection of historical events in several interconnected fields: the history of economics and finance, the history of economic thought, and the history of media and journalism.

## Price Currents and Early Economic Controversies in the Press

(From the 1600s to the 1750s)

Between the early 16th and the mid-18th centuries, the spread of economic information underwent its first phase of development. Even before the invention of the printing press, the link between commercial activity and the dissemination of market news was at the origin of the first information networks created by the great bankers and merchants, such as the Függer family in Germany, Simón Ruiz in Spain, and Thomas Gresham in England (Bauer 2011; Elfenbein 1945; Matthews 1959; Müller, 2023; Nieto 1984). All these bankers and merchants organized their own national and international networks of informants, who supplied them regularly and more or less systematically with news on events of interest affecting the markets in which they had or could have commercial and financial interests. In some cases, like that of the Függer newsletters, the news was of a generic nature, about political, social, and economic events; in others, the correspondence was basically composed of commercial dispatches relating to the specific activity of the merchant in question, as in the case of the letters of Simón Ruiz. As for Gresham, he became a true agent of information in London, with the news that he himself gathered and the news of his collaborators in different cities.

With the advent of the printing press, these private information activities became institutionalized around the main markets, such as Amsterdam, with the emergence of various forms of price currents and shipping lists. These early "newspapers" (a paradigmatic example was London's Lloyd's List), which proliferated in Europe and America between the mid-17th and mid-18th centuries and coincided with the development of commercial (merchant) capitalism, constituted the first dominant form of economic news. They were characterized by the regular reproduction, almost without any commentary or interpretation, of tables of data on prices and other variables of commercial and financial interest (McCusker 2005; Neal 1991).

Along with this commercial information, a market for financial news was developed at this time, with the emergence of the modern stock exchanges. With these stock exchanges, in the 17th century, the first financial crises, so important from the point of view of the news business, began to occur in Europe. It was in the 18th century, with the "bubbles" of the South Sea Company in London (1719) and the Mississippi in Paris (1720), that the recurrence of stock market crashes became a constant, and their history began to be definitively associated with the news (Chancellor 1999; Garber 2000). It is significant that, even in such early times, the impact of this type of event on the market for financial news, which grew or retreated around these crises, was already noticeable.

Little by little, even at this time, the incorporation of opinions on and analysis of commercial and financial data represented an important qualitative advance in the development of economic publications. Controversies, such as one that arose in 1713 between the Mercator and the British Merchant over British commercial treaties, were a sign that people and institutions with conflicting commercial interests were becoming aware of the potential of the press to create economic opinion, beyond the dissemination of news about trade and the publication of financial data. Henry Martyn's articles in the British Merchant and Daniel Defoe's in the Mercator were, in a way, precursors of the journalism in defense of free trade and mercantilism that would flourish in Britain and other European countries many years later (Parsons 1989).

## The Emergence of Economic Journals

(From the 1750s to the 1850s)

From the second half of the 18th century, in particular, coinciding with the period of the Enlightenment and the transition from commercial to industrial capitalism (Beaud 2001), the discussion of certain principles of economics jumped into the pages of periodicals generally aimed at the bourgeois class. The polemics between mercantilists and free traders, and the ideas of the physiocrats, the classical economists (Adam Smith, David Ricardo, John Stuart Mill, and so on), and the first socialist thinkers were aired in the press until well into the 19th century.

Between the first publication of the physiocratic Journal oeconomique (1751) and that of The Economist (1843), almost a century passed in which intellectuals of various kinds used the media for their ideological campaigns. Following the spirit of the Enlightenment, publishing ventures were driven by intellectuals and reformists, who defended economic and political changes based on the new ideas of what was soon to be called "political economy." The Cameralists in Germany, the Physiocrats in France, and the first classical economists in England and Scotland used the format of essay magazines (Reviews) to introduce new ideas about economic reforms directly to the public or, better, to the influential elites (Roper 1978). A good example of that phenomenon is the propagandistic activity of the Physiocrats, the first financial journalists in history, according to Schumpeter (1994). Much of the impact on public opinion of physiocratic thinking, in the decades prior to the French Revolution, must be explained by the work of the members of the "School" as magazine publishers or writers (Higgs 2001). In parallel, and also as part of this phenomenon, the precursors of academic publications in economics appeared in various countries toward the end of this period, although even then the difference between one title and another was not great, and it would be necessary to wait until the end of the 19th century for this separation (Augello et al. 1996; Backhaus 2011; Coats and Colander 1989; Cole 1957).

With the emergence of the economic journal, titles such as the French Journal des Economistes (1841), which would become one of the pillars of French economic liberalism, and the Giornali degli economisti (1857) in Italy, played a leading role. In this group of publications,

Britain's The Economist (1843) stands out as one of the first examples of economic journals with a marked journalistic character (Arrese 1995; Dudley-Edwards 1993). The editorial evolution of The Economist, especially under the editorship of Walter Bagehot, is representative of the changes that were taking place in the British journalistic market and in the field of economics as a matter of public and scientific interest. In fact, this model of journal, lying between an academic publication, a doctrinal organ and a journalistic vehicle, would be predominant for much of the 19th and early 20th centuries, and was a reference point for many other journals, from the American Commercial and Financial Chronicle (1865) founded by William Buck Dana, to the Japanese publication Tokyo Keizai Zasshi (The Tokyo Economist) (1879) (Sugiyama 1994), the Swedish Affärsvärlden (Business World) (1901), and the Austrian Der Österreichische Volkswirt (The Austrian Economist) (1908), among many others.

The consolidation of financial information and the debate on political economy as regular and increasingly important parts of the content of the main general newspapers and magazines is a phenomenon that can also be observed between the second half of the 18th century and the first third of the 19th century, from the Times (1785) in London to the New York Journal of Commerce (1827). Parsons (1989), for example, refers to the American case, pointing out the important role played by Hezekiah Niles and his Baltimore Weekly Register in the development of an incipient economic journalism in that country. He also highlights the figures of Gordon Bennett and Henry J. Raymond in their early years as journalists. For his part, Vissink (1985) speaks of a similar situation in the main Dutch newspapers, especially in the Algemeen Handelsblad. The phenomenon was general in many other countries. Schifferes (2020) points out that by the 1820s, most daily London newspapers had a "City page." Spachmann (2005) explains in detail this process in the case of Germany. In Spain, for example, a generalist newspaper such as El Diario de Barcelona had been born in 1792 with the express founding desire to deal extensively with economic and commercial issues; among other things, this was due to the demands of censorship, which prohibited the publication of information on many other topics (Arrese 2002).

## Financial Newspapers and Business Magazines

(From the 1850s to the 1930s)

The development of financial capitalism that characterized the economic imperialism of the most advanced countries during the second half of the 19th century coincided with the progressive professionalization of the activity of economists and journalists. On the one hand, after the marginalist revolution of the 1870s, economics as a science began to create its own bodies for the generation and dissemination of knowledge (academic publications, university studies, etc.), with the result that economists found their own sphere of activity, separate from that of other professionals (Maloney 1985). Something similar, although less clearly, happened with journalists, partly as a consequence of the slow development of the press as an industry, with the creation of mass markets of readers and the configuration of the first modern journalistic companies (Baldasty 1992; Høyer and Lauk 2017; Wiener 1988).

In this context, and in view of the business and financial prominence of big new industries such as railroads, mining, banking, oil, and electricity, the first stable financial newspapers, many of which are still running today, appeared during the last decades of the 19th and the first decades of the 20th century. They had precedents in earlier publications focused on local stock markets (the Parisian Cours de la Bourse et de la Banque – cote Desfossés (1825), or the German Berliner Börsen-zeitung (1855) (Henno 1993; Spachmann 2005)), but the new financial and economic dailies were much more advanced, and the information infrastructure of the markets was more complex. The availability of daily information on the big new industries and companies, centered on data from different stock markets, improved greatly, especially after the provision of financial information by new news agencies. Between 1835 and 1851, for example, the Havas, Wolff, and Reuters agencies were launched (Boyd-Barrett 1980; Palmer 2019; Read 1999).

In this period when economic and financial titles flourished, it is worth noting the births, within a short space of time, of the two most important newspapers in the history of the economic press: The Financial Times (1888) and The Wall Street Journal (1889) (Dealy 1993; Kynaston 1988; Rosenberg 1982; Wendt 1982). The emergence of these financial newspapers in London and New York symbolized the consolidation of financial journalism as a special and peculiar branch of economic journalism that was capable of generating daily publications in practically all markets. It is no coincidence that many of the economic–financial newspapers that have survived to the present day as leading media brands in this field are from this period, between the last third of the 19th century and the first decade of the 20th: The Chugai Bukka Shimpo (1876), precursor of the Nihon Keizai Shimbun (Nikkei); Frankfurter Zeitung und Handelsblatt (1866), predecessor of the Frankfurter Allgemeine Zeitung; Il Sole (1865), one of the two titles that would eventually form Il Sole 24 Ore (Baitari and Carruba 1990); and the current leading economic newspapers in France, Les Échos (1908), Denmark (Børsen 1896), and Finland (Kauppalehti 1898), to give a few examples.

The explosion of financial publications, in an environment in which professionalism in journalism was low, demonstrated that the professed standards of neutrality and objectivity proved hard to maintain, and that acts of bribery, blackmail, puffery, and corruption were the order of the day. In Germany, for example, some publications were owned outright by joint-stock companies, while others relied heavily on advertising from newly incorporated companies; scandals involving financial journalists preoccupied the German public (Radu 2017). In other countries, such as Great Britain and France, multiple scandals plagued financial journalism well into the 20th century (Bignon and Miscio 2010; Jeanneney 1975; Porter 1986, 1998; Taylor 2012, 2013). A century later, and after high-profile cases such as that of Wall Street Journal journalist Robert Foster Winans in the 1980s (Winans 1986), financial and business journalism continues to carry the stigma of conflicts of interest and phenomena such as insider trading and market manipulation. In countries with weaker economic journalism, in particular, ethically reprehensible practices such as "brown envelope" journalism in Africa, the "red envelope" in China, and other forms of "cash for news coverage" or "payment for publicity" in many Eastern European countries, Latin America, and Southeast Asia are still found (Skjerdal 2010).

However, it was not only financial information that had achieved a certain popularity by this time. In fact, a whole sector of technical and professional presses specializing in specific industries had been consolidating since the first decades of the 19th century, meeting the growing demand for news from specialists in each field (Elfenbein 1969; Endres 1994; Forsyth 1964; Greco 1988; Laib 1955). Toward the end of this period, the new role of large corporations in economic life – "the visible hand," in the words of the business historian Alfred Chandler (1977) – justified the emergence of a new type of business publication, represented by titles such as Forbes (1917), The BusinessWeek (1929), and Fortune (1930) (Burlingame 1959; Elson 1968; Pinkerton 2011). Over time, these "Big Three" titles would become the worldwide benchmark and model for the "business magazine" (Arrese 2002). Unlike the technical press, which had a "vertical" view of current affairs by sector or industry, the business magazine sought to offer a "horizontal" information service, with news on subjects of interest to all businesses. Its target audience was the entrepreneur, the businessman, and the manager, all of them protagonists in and recipients of the growing flow of news generated from the world of business and large corporations. At the same time, as a critical response to the power of this corporate "visible hand" and in the same way that the radical and socialist press counterbalanced the influence of liberal publications (Conlin 1974; Hopkin 1978), a critical and combative journalism emerged, whose clearest symbol was the American muckraker who, in a certain way, anticipated modern investigative journalism (Roush 2006; Serrin and Serrin 2002).

## The Consolidation of Economic Journalism

(From the 1930s to the 1980s)

The Great War, the 1929 crisis, and the ensuing international economic depression radically changed the economic landscape. After the failure of the "invisible hand" of the market and the "visible hand" of the large corporations, economic leadership passed into the hands of the state between the 1930s and the 1970s. The state took on the role of the supervision and/or control of national economies, with greater or lesser rigor, depending on the case. Industrial and financial capitalism was replaced by state-led capitalism, in which the search for welfare – through Keynesian policies – and the management of macroeconomic conditions gave a new visibility to the "Economy," with a capital E, as the new protagonist of the news discourse (Emmison 1983, Yarrow 2006).

Macroeconomic, labor, fiscal, monetary, and similar information was mixed with politics in the general media, while the specialized press continued to grow as a sector focused on a specific segment of readers: investors, entrepreneurs, businessmen, and managers. This press, in any case, was also transformed, and the financial newspapers of the 19th century became economic newspapers, with a much broader coverage, while the economic and business magazines began to show their great potential for segmentation by specific audiences and thematic interests. After the 1929 crisis, we can therefore speak of a period of the clear decline of financial news, not only in the Anglo-Saxon sphere but also in other countries (Arrese 2002).

After the bitter interlude of World War II, the 1950s and 1960s were a period of great momentum in the media industry, led by a golden age of advertising. A good example of this situation was seen in the great advance of the economic and business magazine markets. The international expansion of the main Anglo-Saxon titles – The Economist, BusinessWeek, Fortune, and Forbes – was accompanied by the appearance of highly successful titles in most countries: Capital (1962) in Germany, Trend (1969) in Austria, L'Expansion (1967) in France, L'Impresa (1959) in Italy, the Swedish business weekly Veckans Affärer (1965), Exame (1967) in Brazil, and Actualidad Económica in Spain (1958) are examples of important publications that appeared during these years.

Many of the histories of economic journalism in different countries recognize that in the 1950s and 1960s, the structure of a specialized economic, business, and financial sector took shape, with at least one economic–financial daily, some economic magazines, and several business magazines. In fact, in less developed markets, stable financial newspapers were born where they did not exist (for example, Financial Mail (1959) in South Africa, The Seoul

Kyuyjie Shinmun (The Industry and Economic Daily) (1959) in South Korea, and The Financial Express (1961) in India); the number and variety of specialized titles expanded where there were already consolidated brands, especially in Europe and the United States (Arrese 2002; Brand 2010; Kjær and Slaatta 2007; Roush 2006); and new journalistic sub-specializations within the field were boosted, as in the case of personal finance, with paradigmatic publications such as the American Kiplinger Magazine (1947) and Money (1972) (Davidson 2012; Lucht 2013; Wells 2021).

This intense development of the specialized press would not have been so accentuated if economic, business, and financial topics had been equally well established in the general press. But this had not happened. Although it is evident that the coverage of these topics by the main newspapers and magazines improved between the 1930s and the 1960s, this improvement was not comparable to that achieved in other areas (Arrese 2002). At the same time, neither radio nor television, new media that in other journalistic fields produced a major transformation of the printed press (a clear case was sports news), had a significant effect on the specialized press during this period, although they gradually began to devote more time and space to economic issues.

This panorama would begin to change at the beginning of the 1970s, when economics came to the forefront of the news, in both general and specialized media (Arrese 2000). The breakdown of the international economic order established at Bretton Woods, the 1973 oil crisis, and the debate between Keynesians and monetarists, in an environment of the coexistence of high inflation rates, high levels of unemployment, and reduced economic growth, gave a definitive boost to public interest in these issues. In the words of Parsons (1989, p. 7), "a new golden age of economic debate" began, and economic journalism began to cease being the Cinderella of newsrooms (Welles 1973).

Perhaps the spirit of the times was best reflected in the growth of front pages dedicated to economic issues, and in the great reinforcement of the regular economic sections in the large quality newspapers such as The Times, Le Monde, and Frankfurter Allgemeine Zeitung. Particularly symbolic was the creation in 1978 of a third section ("Business Day") in The New York Times (Nelson 1990), although even earlier, in the 1960s, newspapers such as the Los Angeles Times and the Washington Post had "respectable" sections (Quirt 1993). Very important generalist newspapers also appeared in this period, such as La Repubblica (1976) in Italy and El País (1976) in Spain, which made economic news one of their main priorities. Of course, important economic newspapers continued to be founded (such as the Swedish Dagens Industri (1976), the Hong Kong Economic Journal (1973), Cinco Días (1978) in Spain or Ámbito Financiero (1976) in Argentina (Ruiz 2005)). The 1970s were also the years when economic journalism really took off in many African countries (Kareithi and Kariithi 2005).

The efforts made by the press as a whole to report on the economy were gradually joined by those of radio and television. In fact, in almost every news area, the audiovisual media, and especially television, were by now the main source of information for the majority of the population. Economic issues were not exceptional from this point of view. In 1976, a survey conducted in the United States concluded that 83 percent of citizens cited television news as their main source on economics and business issues (Arrese 2002). By then, in addition to taking up more time in radio and television news, economic information had begun to generate a good number of specialized programs in the more advanced markets (for example, the BBC's Money Programme (1965), PBS's Wall Street Week (1970), ARD's Plusminus (1975), and CNN's Moneyline (1980)).

All the advances made during this period in the consolidation of business journalism were key to the professionalization of specialized journalists. Symbolic initiatives of this professionalization, although replicable in other countries, were the creation in the United States in 1964 of the Society of American Business Editors and Writers (SABEW, since renamed Society for Advancing Business Editing and Writing), and the launch of the Knight-Bagehot Fellowship Program in Economics and Business Journalism (Columbia University) in 1975.

## The "Popularization" of Economic, Business, and Financial News

(From the 1980s to the present)

The end of the Keynesian consensus, the new impulse of neoliberal economic thinking (driven by Thatcherism and Reaganomics), and the subsequent fall of the communist economic systems meant the start of a new period in the evolution of the coverage of economic issues in the media. With markets and business as the new paradigms of economic, social, and even political organization (in the face of a certain "end of ideologies"), the last two decades of the 20th century and the beginning of the new century saw a definitive "boom" in economic news – even in countries that had been latecomers to the developments in this field. This boom was mainly in financial and business news, at the expense of a decline in macroeconomic information and, above all, in areas such as labor journalism (Martin 2019; Schifferes 2020). The so-called "popular capitalism" (Saunders and Harris 1994), which led millions of citizens to become investors and entrepreneurs, created an extraordinary broadening in the range of the recipients of economic information. However, undoubtedly the great novelty in the last years of the 20th century was the emergence of the Internet and of the new media, as an essential infrastructure for the dissemination of economic, business, and financial news. In fact, the adaptation of the traditional media to this new electronic environment and to the extraordinary availability of information offered by the network – with an exponential growth of potential issuers of information, journalistic, and otherwise – marked the evolution of the sector (Arrese and Medina 2002).

By the 1990s in many countries, there were two or three economic and financial newspapers, and even a financial weekly, following the model of the veteran Barron's. This expansion of the daily press, although important, was unparalleled in the world of magazines. It can be said that during the 1980s and 1990s, there was a veritable fever of economic and business magazines, in line with the development of increasingly numerous market niches (business in general, entrepreneurship, managers, lifestyle, personal finance, institutional finance, etc.) (Arrese 2002). As in other periods of history with booms around specific industries (the financial bubbles of the 18th century or the railway and mining manias of the 19th), in this period, too, following the technological boom, a whole field of economic journalism emerged around the "new economy" businesses, which in the US market gave rise to successful publications – at least until the dotcom crash – such as Upside (1989), Wired (1992), Red Herring (1993), Fast Company (1995), Business 2.0 (1998), and The Industry Standard (1999). Similarly, globalization and the increasing integration of geographical markets led to the proliferation of new transnational economic publications (e.g., African Business (1982), América Economía (1983), Eurobusiness (1988), and Asia Inc. (1992)), which complemented the role that had been played until then by the main Anglo-Saxon titles (the "dominators," as defined by Roush (2022)). Finally, the change in the economic spirit of the time, symbolized, better than by any other event, by the fall of the Berlin Wall in 1989, meant that the business press also played a special role in the processes of political and economic transition experienced in Russia, China, and other countries with authoritarian regimes (Arrese 2017; Nelson 1999; Shuli 2011).

The renewed prominence of business and finance was reflected in the audiovisual focus of this content. In television, the novelty was the launch of thematic channels, with a strong focus on financial markets. In the United States, Financial News Network (FNN) was launched in 1981, three years after the Dow Jones Index plummeted in 1978; CNBC was established in 1989 in the midst of the dotcom boom but after a sharp drop in stock prices in 1988; and, lastly, Bloomberg Television was established in 1994 after a sharp drop in stock prices in 1991. The phenomenon spread to other latitudes, with the launch of the European Business Channel (1995), the German n-tv (1993), the Italian 24ore-TV (2001), and the Dutch ETV (1998), to give a few examples. Similarly, the idea of a specialized radio station (Bloomberg Radio (1993), BFM Radio (1994) in France, the German FAZ Businessradio (2000), the Dutch Business Nieuws Radio (1998), the Spanish Radio Intereconomía (1994), and the Italian Radio 24 (1999)) became more widespread. The greater popularization of economic information through audiovisual media, even if particularly for specialized audiences, posed an enormous challenge for economic journalism, not only from the point of view of news production and dissemination but also from the perspective of public perception about this journalistic field. The sensationalization and trivialization of audiovisual content – especially around news related to investment decisions – were often the object of harsh criticism (Kurtz 2000).

However, for economic journalism nothing in this period was to be as transcendental as the irruption of the Internet and the development of new communication technologies from the mid-1990s onward. There is perhaps no better symbol of what has happened since then than the birth, development, and extraordinary success of Bloomberg Business News (1991), a brand of global, multimedia, multi-platform business journalism (Bartram 2003; Bloomberg 2019; Machin and Niblock 2010; Palmer 2019; Roush 2022). In one way or another, most established journalistic brands had to adapt to the digital world, develop different content modalities (text, visual, and audio), adapt to different dissemination platforms, and change the way they connected to their audiences, in a context of the overabundance of economic information (with an infinity of new online media, increasingly transparent sources of information (companies, banks, markets, etc.), and search engines and social networks with a central role in the filtering of news) (Arrese and Medina 2002). Unlike other media, the economic media in general defended the role of quality economic journalism by betting on paid, as opposed to free, content, in recognition of the value of that content (Arrese 2016).

In this environment of the expansion and transformation of the sector, and in the wake of the neoliberal wave and the impetus of the new economy, economic journalism had to face the challenges of a period of prosperity marked by crises of various kinds (the long savings and loans crisis in the United States, the collapse of the European exchange rate mechanism in 1992, the Mexican crisis of 1994–1995, the Asian crisis of 1997–1998, the dotcom crash, or the bankruptcy of large corporations such as Enron, Parmalat, and Arthur Andersen at the turn of the century). In all of these crises, economic journalism showed its lights and shadows, but in all cases, its importance for the proper functioning of markets and for a society with a well-informed citizenry became evident (Doyle 2006; Gavin 1998; Kurtz 2000; Madrick 2001; Smith and Emshwiller 2004; Wells 2019). Almost without there being time to react and learn from the mistakes, came the Great Recession of 2007–2008, which put an end to more than three decades of neoliberal consensus and in which economic journalism – perhaps more than at any other time in its history – was a protagonist in the debate on the causes and consequences of the crisis (Davies 2010).

## Conclusion

This is not the place to discuss whether the Great Recession of 2008 was a turning point in the historical evolution of economic journalism. There is no doubt that it was a turning point for professional and academic analysis of its role, its strengths and weaknesses, and its contribution to economic development and the shaping of a better-informed citizenry. As discussed in the introduction to this chapter, and as confirmed by various reviews of the research on the 2008 crisis and the media (Damstra and Vliegenthart 2018; Lee 2014), a growing number of researchers in diverse fields (communication, economics, politics, etc.) have focused on economic journalism and its ability to alert society to possible crises, its role in shaping economic expectations and opinions, and its contribution to the healthy functioning of markets and businesses. The recent COVID-19 pandemic and the war in Ukraine do not augur, at least in the short and medium terms, a hopeful economic future, and this will once again mean that economic journalism must face transcendental challenges.

## References

Augello, M. M., Bianchini, M. and Guidi, M. (eds.) (1996) *Le riviste di economia in Italia (1700–1900). Dai giornali scientifico-letterari ai periodici specialistici.* Milano: Franco Agnelli.

Arrese, Á. (1995) *La identidad de the economist.* Pamplona: Eunsa.

Arrese, Á. (2000) "Economía y medios de comunicación en la década de los setenta," *Comunicación y Sociedad*, 13(2), pp. 9–51.

Arrese, Á. (2002) *Prensa económica, De la lloyd's list al wsj.com.* Pamplona: Eunsa.Arrese, Á. (2016) "From gratis to paywalls. A brief history of a retro-innovation in the press's business," *Journalism Studies*, 17(8), pp. 1051–1067.

Arrese, Á. (2017) "The role of economic journalism in political transitions," *Journalism*, 18(3), pp. 368–383

Arrese, Á. and Medina, M. (2002) "Competition between new and old media in economic and financial news markets," in Picard, R. (ed.) *Media firms: Structures, operations and performance.* New Jersey: Lawrence Erlbaum Associates, pp. 59–75.

Backhaus, J. G. (2011) *The beginnings of scholarly economic journalism. The Austrian economist and the german economist.* Berlin: Springer.

Baitari, P. and Carruba, S. (1990) *La trasparenza difficile. Storia de due giornali economici: "Il Sole' e '24 Ore."* Palermo: Sellerio.

Baldasty, G. J. (1992) *The commercialization of news in the 19th century.* Madison: University of Wisconsin Press.

Basu, L. (2018) *Media amnesia: Rewriting the economic crisis.* London: Pluto Press.

Basu, L., Schifferes, S. and Knowles, S. (2018) *The media and austerity. Comparative perspectives.* London: Routledge.

Bartram, J. (2003) "News agency wars: The battle between reuters and Bloomberg," *Journalism Studies*, 4(3), 387–399.

Bauer, O. (2011) *Zeitungen vor der zeitung. Die fuggerzeitungen (1568–1605) und das frühmoderne nachrichtensystem.* Berlin: Akademie Verlag.

Beaud, M. (2001) *A history of capitalism 1500–2000.* New York: Monthly Review Press.

Berry, M. (2019) *The media, the public and the great financial crisis.* Cham, Switzerland: Palgrave Macmillan.

Bignon, V. and Miscio, A. (2010) "Media bias in financial newspapers: Evidence from early twentieth-century France," *European Review of Economic History*, 14(3), pp. 383–432.

Blair, A., Duguid, P., Goeing, A.-S. and Grafton, A. (eds.) (2021) *Information: A historical companion.* Princeton, NJ: Princeton University Press.

Bloomberg, M. R. (2019) *Bloomberg by Bloomberg.* Revised edition. Hoboken, NJ: Wiley.

Boyd-Barrett, O. (1980) *The international news agencies.* London: Sage.

Brand, R. (2010) "The business of business news: South Africa's financial press and the political process," *Ecquid Novi: African Journalism Studies*, 31(1), pp. 24–41.

Burlingame, R. (1959) *Endless frontiers - The story of McGraw Hill*. New York: McGraw Hill.

Chancellor, E. (1999) *Devil take the hindmost. A history of financial speculation*. New York: Plume.

Chandler, A. D. Jr. (1977) *The visible hand. The managerial revolution in American business*. Cambridge, MA: Harvard University Press.

Coats, A. W. and Colander, D. C. (eds.) (1989) *The spread of economic ideas*. New York: Cambridge University Press.

Cole, A. H. (1957) "Conspectus for a history of economic and business literature," *The Journal of Economic History*, 17(3), pp. 333–388.

Conlin, R. (ed.) (1974) *The American radical press, 1880–1960*, vols. 1 and 2. Westport, Conn: Greenwood Press.

Damstra, A. and Vliegenthart, R. (2018) "(Un)covering the economic crisis?" *Journalism Studies*, 19(7), pp. 983–1003

Davidson, R. (2012) "The emergence of popular personal finance magazines and the risk shift in American society," *Media Culture & Society*, 34(1), pp. 3–20.

Davies, H. (2010) *The financial crisis. Who is to blame?* London: Polity Press.

Dealy, F. X. (1993) *The power and the money: Inside The Wall Street Journal*. Secaucus, NJ: Carol Pub. Group.

Doyle, G. (2006) "Financial news journalism," *Journalism*, 7(4), pp. 433–452.

Dudley-Edwards, R. (1993) *The pursuit of reason. The Economist, 1843–1993*. London: Hamish Hamilton.

Duval, J. (2004) *Critique de la raison journalistique. Les transformations de la presse économique en France*. Paris: Le Seuil.

Elfenbein, J. (1945) *Business journalism: its function and future*. New York: Harper & Brothers.

Elfenbein, J. (1969) *Business journalism*, 2ª Ed. Revised. New York: Greenwood Press.

Elson, R. T. (1968) *Time Inc. The intimate history of a publishing enterprise, 1923–1941*. New York: Atheneum.

Emmison, M. (1983) "The economy: Its emergence in media discourse," in Davis, H. and Walton, P. (eds.) *Language, image and media*. Oxford: Blackwell, pp. 139–155.

Endres, K. (ed.) (1994) *The trade, industrial and professional periodicals of the United States*. Westport, CT: Greenwood Publishing.

Forsyth, D. P. (1964) *The business press in America, 1750–1865*. Philadelphia, PA: Chilton Books.

Garber, P. (2000) *Famous first bubbles: the bundamentals of early manias*. Cambridge: MIT Press.

Gavin, N. T. (ed.) (1998) *The economy, media and public knowledge*. London: Leicester University Press.

Greco, A. N. (1988) *Business journalism: Management notes and cases*. New York: New York University Press.

Groth, O. (1928) *Die zeitung. Ein system der zeitungskunde (Journalistik)*. Mannheim: J. Bensheimer.

Henno, J. (1993) *La presse économique et financière*. Paris: Presses Universitaires de France.

Higgs, H. (2001) *The physiocrats*. Kitchener: Batoche Books.

Hopkin, D. (1978) "The socialist press in Britain," in Boyce, G., Curran, J. and Wingate, P. (eds.) *Newspaper history: From the seventeenth century to the present day*. London: Constable, pp. 294–306.

Høyer, S. and Lauk, E. (2017) "The paradoxes of the journalistic profession," *Nordicom Review*, 24(2), pp. 3–17.

Jeanneney, J.-N. (1975) "Sur la vénalité du journalisme financier entre les deux guerres," *Revue Française de Science Politique*, 25(4), pp. 717–739.

John, R., and Silberstein-Loeb, J. (2015) *Making news. The political economy of journalism in Britain and America from the glorious revolution to the internet*. Oxford: Oxford University Press.

Kareithi, P. M. and Kariithi, N. (2005) *Untold stories: Economics and business journalism in African media*. Johannesburg: Wits University Press.

Kjær, P. and Slaatta, T. (2007) *Mediating business: The expansion of business journalism*. Copenhagen: Copenhagen Business School Press.

Kurtz, H. (2000) *The fortune tellers. Inside the Wall Street's game of money, media and manipulation*. New York: Simon & Schuster.

Kynaston, D. (1988) *The Financial Times. A centenary history*. London: Viking.

Laib, J. (1955) "The trade press," *Public Opinion Quarterly*, 19(1), pp. 31–44.

Lee, M. (2014) "A review of communication scholarship on the financial markets and the financial media," *International Journal of Communication*, 8, pp. 715–736.

Lischka, J. A. (2016) *Economic news, sentiment, and behavior. How economic and business news affects the economy*. Wiesbaden: Springer.

Lucht, T. (2013) *Sylvia Porter: America's original personal finance columnist*. Syracuse, NY: Syracuse University Press.

Machin, D. and Niblock, S. (2010) "The new breed of business journalism for niche global news. The case of bloomberg news," *Journalism Studies*, 11(6), pp. 783–798

Madrick, J. (2001) The business media and the new economy, Research paper D-25, The Joan Shorenstein Center on the Press, Politics and Public Policy, John F. Kennedy School of Government, Harvard University, Boston, MA.

Maloney, J. (1985) *The professionalization of economics*. Cambridge, MA: Cambridge University Press.

Martin, C. R. (2019) *No longer newsworthy. How the mainstream media abandoned the working class*. Ithaca and London: ILR Press.

Matthews, G. T. (ed.) (1959) *News and rumor in renaissance Europe. The Fugger Newsletters*. New York: Capricon Books.

McCusker, J. (2005) "The demise of distance: The business press and the origins of the information revolution in the early modern Atlantic world," *The American Historical Review*, 110(2), pp. 295–321.

McCusker, J. and Gravesteijn, C. (1991) *The beginnings of commercial and financial journalism. The commodity price currents, exchange rate currents, and money currents of early modern Europe*. Amsterdam: Neha.

Mercille, J. (2014) *The political economy and media coverage of the European economic crisis: The case of Ireland*. London: Routledge.

Merrill, G. J. (2019) *The Political content of British economic, business and financial journalism*. London: Palgrave.

Müller, H. (2023) *Challenging economic journalism. Covering business and politics in an age of uncertainty*. Cham: Palgrave Macmillan.

Neal, L. (1991) *The rise of financial capitalism. International capital markets in the age of reason*. Cambridge, MA: Cambridge University Press.

Nelson, D. (1990) "'Business day' & the New York Times: New life for an old priority," *Newspaper Research Journal*, 11(4), pp. 24–30.

Nelson, M. (1999) "Business reporting in Eastern Europe," *Media Business Journal*, Fall, pp. 150–157.

Nieto, A. (1984) *La prensa gratuita*. Pamplona: Eunsa.

Palmer, M. L. (2019) *International news agencies. A history*. Cham, Switzerland: Palgrave Macmillan.

Parsons, W. (1989) *The power of the financial press. Journalism and economic opinion in Britain and America*. Aldershot: Edward Elgar.

Pettegree, A (2014) *The invention of news*. New Haven and London: Yale University Press.

Picard, R (ed.) (2015) *The Euro crisis in the media. Journalistic Coverage of economic crisis and European institutions*. London: I.B. Tauris.

Pinkerton, S. (2011) *The fall of the house of Forbes: The inside story of the collapse of a media empire*. New York: St. Martin's Press.

Porter, D. (1986) "'A trusted guide of the investing public': Harry marks and the financial news 1884–1916," *Business History*, 28(1), pp. 1–17.

Porter, D. (1998) "City editors and the modern investing public: Establishing the integrity of the new financial journalism in late nineteenth-century London," *Media History*, 4(1), pp. 49–46.

Quintâo, A.-S. (1987) *O jornalismo económico no Brasil depois de 1964*. Rio de Janeiro: Agir.

Quirt, J. (1993) *The press and the world of money. How the news media cover business and finance, panic and prosperity, and the pursuit of the American dream*. California: Anton/California-Courier.

Radu, R. (2017) *Auguren des geldes. Eine kulturgeschichte des finanzjournalismus in deutschland 1850–1914*. Gottingen: Vandenhoeck & Ruprecht.

Read, D. (1999) *The power of news. The history of Reuters*, 2ª Ed. Oxford: Oxford University Press.

Roper, D. (1978) *Reviewing before the Edinburgh, 1788–1802*. London: Methuen.

Rosenberg, J. M. (1982) *Inside The Wall Street Journal. The history and the power of Dow Jones & company and America's most influential journal*. New York: Macmillan.

Roush, C. (2006) *Profits and losses. Business journalism and its role in society*. Oak Park: Marion Street Press.

Roush, C. (2022) *The future of business journalism*. Washington, DC: Georgetown University Press.

Ruiz, F. (2005) *El señor de los mercados. Ámbito financiero, la City y el poder del periodismo económico*. Buenos Aires: Editorial El Ateneo.

Saunders, P. and Harris, C. (1994) *Privatization and popular capitalism*. London: Open University Press.

Serrin, J. and Serrin, W. (eds.) (2002) *Muckraking! the journalism that changed America*. New York: The New Press.

Schiffrin, A. (ed.) (2011) *Bad news. How America's business press missed the story of the century*. New York: The New Press.

Schifferes, S. (2020) 'The financial press', in Conboy, M. and Bingham, A. (eds.) *The Edinburgh history of the British and Irish press*, Vol. 3. Edinburgh: Edinburgh University Press, pp. 189–210.

Schifferes, S. and Roberts, R. (eds.) (2015) *The media and financial crisis*. London: Routledge.

Schumpeter, J. A. (1994) *History of economic analysis*. Oxford: Oxford University Press.

Shaw, I. S. (2016) *Business journalism. A critical political economy approach*. London: Routledge.

Shuli, H. (2011) "The rise of business media in China," in Shirk, S. (ed.) *Changing media, chaging China*. Oxford: Oxford University Press, pp. 77–90.

Skjerdal, T. S. (2010) "Research on brown envelope journalism in the African media," *African Communication Research*, 3(3), pp. 367–406.

Smith, R. and Emshwiller, J. R. (2004) *24 days: How two wall street journal reporters uncovered the lies that destroyed faith in corporate America*. New York: Harper Collins.

Spachmann, K. (2005) *Wirtschaftsjournalismus in der presse. Theorie und empirie*. Konstanz: UVK Verlagsgesellscht mbH.

Starkman, D. (2014) *The watchdog that didn't bark: The financial crisis and the disappearance of investigative journalism*. New York: Columbia University Press.

Sugiyama, C. (1994) *Origins of economic thought in modern Japan*. London: Routledge.

Tambini, D. (2008) *What is financial journalism for? Ethics and responsibility in a time of crisis and change*. London: Polis-London School of Economics.

Taylor, J. (2012) "Watchdogs or apologists? Financial journalism and company fraud in early Victorian Britain," *Historical Research*, 85(230), pp. 632–650.

Taylor, J. (2013) "Privacy, publicity, and reputation: How the Press regulated the market in nineteenth-century England," *Business History Review*, 87, pp. 679–701.

Timmermans, J. (2020) "Financial Journalism," in Örnebring, H. (ed.), *The Oxford encyclopedia of journalism studies*. New York : Oxford University Press. Online editon in https://www.oxfordreference.com

van Dalen, A., Svensson, H., Kalogeropoulos, A., Albæk, E. and de Vreese, C. H. (2019) *Economic news. Informing the inattentive audience*. New York: Routledge.

Vissink, H. G. A. (1985) *Economic and financial reporting in England and the Netherlands: A comparative study over the period 1850 to 1914*. Assen/Maastricht, Netherlands: Van Gorcum.

Vliegenthart, R., Damstra, A., Boukes, M. and Jonkman, J. (2021) *Economic news: Antecedents and effects*. Cambridge, MA: Cambridge University Press.

Weill, G. (1934) *Le journal: Origines, evolution et role de la presse periodique*. Paris: La Renaissance du Livre.

Wells, R. (2019) *The enforcers*. Urbana: University of Illinois Press.

Wells, R. (2021) "'Serve it up hot and brief': The journalistic innovations and influence of Willard M. Kiplinger," *American Journalism*, 38(2), pp. 177–201.Welles, C. (1973) "The bleak wasteland of financial journalism," *Columbia Journalism Review*, July/August, pp. 40–44.

Wendt, L. (1982) *The Wall Street Journal: The story of Dow Jones & The nation's business newspaper*. Chicago, IL: Rand McNally & Co.

Winans, R. F. (1986) *Trading secrets. An insider's account of the scandal at the wall street journal*. New York: St. Martin's Press.

Wiener, J. H. (ed.) (1988) *Papers for the millions. The new journalism in Britain, 1850s to 1914*. Connecticut: Greenwood Press, Westport.

Yarrow, A. L. (2006) "The big postwar story," *Journalism History*, 32(2), pp. 58–76.

# 8

# RAKING IT IN

## How the Muckrakers Spurred on Business Journalism

### Chris Roush

### Introduction

The importance of the muckrakers – a group of journalists in the late 19th and early 20th centuries who exposed wrongdoing in society – has been well chronicled since they first began reporting and writing. The muckrakers garnered widespread attention – and scorn from those who they exposed. President Theodore Roosevelt gave them their name in 1906 after being upset with how Cosmopolitan magazine detailed unethical practices by various U.S. senators (Neuzil 1996).

But their role in the development of business journalism in the United States has been all but ignored even though much of their work focused on businesses and economic inequities. Their reporting and writing tactics help set the tone and standard for future coverage of major corporations and economic inequities. Streitmatter (2019, pp. 88–89) noted their "seminal impact" in saving "democracy from the clutches of the robber barons." Filler (1968, p. 30) writes that the main accomplishment of the muckrakers was "the rescue of the individual and the curbing of the corporations."

Some of the most well-known muckraking included Upton Sinclair's (1906) exposure of the meatpacking industry led to government reforms. Ida Tarbell's (1904) use of documents such as lawsuits and corporate records helped bring about the Supreme Court-ordered breakup of the Standard Oil Co. Lincoln Steffens (1903) brought to light the unethical financial dealings between company bigwigs and city government officials. Others exposed issues with child labor and unsafe living conditions, as well as products such as milk. Consumers were aghast to read in Collier's magazine that they were taking medicines that included alcohol, cocaine and morphine.

Their work led to major reforms in industries and individual companies. Serrin and Serrin (2002, p. xx) wrote that "working-class families in the early 1900s would probably have paid much more a year for their kerosene if journalism had not exposed the railroad rebate system." Aramao (2000, pp. 36–37) noted that by 1912, there had been nearly 2,000 articles that could be classified as muckraking, and they included "wrongdoing by insurance companies, poor conditions in tenements, job-related accidents, bank fraud, abuses in the meat-packing industry, mistreatment of minorities and other topics."

DOI: 10.4324/9781003298977-11

Businesses and industries were well aware of the coverage, and in some cases promoted the journalism. The American Medical Association reprinted the work of Samuel Hopkins Adams on patent medicines and distributed 500,000 copies (Cassedy 1964, p. 86). The New York Stock Exchange and Chicago Board of Trade helped other muckrakers expose "bucket shops" and other unsavory Wall Street practices (Cowing 1965, pp. 29–30).

These journalists brought new reporting and writing tactics to how corporate America was covered and set standards for years to come, bringing to light for the first time how big business affected large swaths of society and should be examined. Robert Hunter (1904, p. 184), writing about the railroad industry and its disregard for employees, noted, "The railroads consider the Block System of signals and automatic couplers unwarranted luxuries because profits are more valued than the lives of workmen." They also forced governments to examine new regulations of businesses. Stein (1990, p. 405) noted how early muckrakers "detailed how inadequate or non-existent was state, local and federal government overseeing of technologies that harmed workers or permitted making of bad products."

This chapter examines the importance of the muckrakers from a business journalism perspective, detailing how, for the first time in many cases, they covered topics related to industry and the economy, and how the journalism strategies used by the muckrakers set the tone for future coverage and reporting styles still being practiced today. It explores five key themes in muckraking coverage that, in the 21st century, are considered basic tenets of business journalism.

## *Company and Industry Coverage*

The industrial revolution in the United States in the 19th century dramatically changed society as millions left farms and moved to cities seeking work in factories or plants. Electricity, assembly lines and advanced machinery allowed many companies to produce goods and services at faster rates. As they grew, they expanded their operations to a point where they became the focus of journalists at magazines and newspapers. Much of that coverage was not positive and detailed vast wealth as well as unsavory business practices.

Charles Edward Russell, probably the most productive muckraker, wrote about the beef industry in Everybody's magazine in 1905 and then the tobacco industry two years later in the same magazine, later turning his reporting into books. In "Lawless Wealth" (1908, pp. 278–279), he wrote, "We have given our praise to the money-getters. Then shall we profess astonishment that men do extreme things to get money – now that we are all discovering what that means to the rest of us?" Another Thomas Lawson (1906) took on Amalgamated Copper Company in Everybody's, turning his writing into a book called "Frenzied Finance." What made Lawson's writing so interesting was that he had been a partner in the company's creation and was exposing his business partners.

In the New York World, reporters David Ferguson and Louis Seibold disclosed how Equitable Life Assurance Society executives were taking funds paid by policyholders and making personal investments (Emery and Emery 1984, p. 214). McClure's writer Barton J. Hendrick also documented problems with life insurance companies, and journalist Alfred Henry Lewis wrote about the International Harvester Company in Cosmopolitan and then later wrote a series of articles about how many of the country's millionaires had obtained their wealth.

Companies that concocted medicines and remedies drew special attention from the muckrakers. In a series of articles in Collier's called "The Great American Fraud," Samuel Hopkins Adams (1905) exposed how many of these medicines did not produce the results that their creators claimed, and that many of them included poisonous ingredients. His articles, like many works from the muckrakers, led to government regulations and caused many publications to stop accepting advertising for these products.

One of the most famous pieces of muckraking around a company was one that was suppressed. In October 1906, Cosmopolitan pulled an article by David Graham Phillips about Prudential Life Insurance Company that disclosed that it had helped finance another company – Public Service Corporation – that was owned by its president. The article was pulled after Prudential purchased $5,000 worth of advertising in the magazine. In its place was an article titled "An Aid to Modern Business" that referred to the Prudential president in glowing terms. The switch was later revealed in the New York Call (Reynolds 1979, p. 515).

Prudential tried similar tactics with other publications and was successful except for Collier's, which in December 1906 and January 1907 disclosed how the insurance company had benefitted from special interest laws by New Jersey lawmakers (Sullivan 1906, pp. 16–17, and Editorial 1907a, p. 7).

Before the muckrakers, individual companies were rarely covered in the media. The muckrakers showed the importance of documenting their negatives and positives. Collier's, in another editorial, noted that Prudential was as good as any other company selling insurance (Editorial 1907b, p. 10).

Soon after the muckraking stopped, a series of business magazines launched that made company and industry coverage a mainstay of their content. Forbes started in 1917, and the first issue included an explanation of an interview with John D. Rockefeller with a teaser on the cover, "How Forbes gets big men to talk" (Quirt 1993, p. 86). McGraw-Hill launched The Business Week in September 1929. A section titled "Corporation" that included stories about companies and their strategies was the mainstay of the publication for decades. And Henry Luce launched Fortune in 1930, with its first issue containing stories on the meat-packing and glass industries, as well as one on the Biltmore Hotel and another on entertainment giant RCA.

In today's business journalism, corporate and industry coverage is how many news organizations define beats for reporters. Many business journalists today cover a single company, such as Microsoft Corporation or Apple Incorporated. Others are assigned beats such as social media companies or big banks on Wall Street. The coverage that the muckrakers started is now considered normal.

### Use of Public Documents and Interviews

Sinclair's "The Jungle" is one of the most important pieces to be published during the muckraking period, but it was not what would be considered journalism in the 21st century. In the book, Sinclair wrote about an immigrant working in Packingtown, the area in Chicago where the meat plants were located. One of the biggest criticisms of his work is that it's fiction, a style that Sinclair felt would have a bigger impact on readers, although Sinclair spent months following workers around the plants and observing the conditions. What is often ignored is that Sinclair used extensive documentation to back up his assertions about the unsafe meat. In a March 1906 letter to Roosevelt, Sinclair detailed letters, affidavits and other documents he relied upon in writing "The Jungle." One of the most important documents was a statement from the chair of bacteriology at Illinois State University who oversaw Chicago meat inspections in 1902 and 1903. Another was an affidavit from a former Armour & Co. employee detailing the company's use of "condemned meat."

Sinclair also documented his interviews. In his autobiography, he noted that he talked to workers, lawyers, doctors, dentists, nurses, policemen, politicians and real estate agents for "The Jungle." He used a simple practice to find workers in the meatpacking plants. He wrote:

> I was not much better dressed than the workers, and found that by the simple device of carrying a dinner pail I could go anywhere. So long as I kept moving, no one would heed me. When I wanted to make careful observations, I would pass again and again through the same room.
>
> *(Sinclair 1962, p. 109)*

By the time Sinclair published, another muckraker, Tarbell, had already shown how documents and interviews could be used to expose the business practices of a large organization – in this case, the Standard Oil Company, which once controlled 85 percent of oil refining in the United States. In the preface to her book, Tarbell wrote that she decided to write about the oil giant because it was one of the few businesses whose history could be traced using trustworthy documentation. Weinberg (2008, p. xiv) writes that Tarbell used "hundreds of thousands of pages scattered throughout the nation" and then complemented that reporting by interviewing corporate executives and competitors, as well as government regulators. Those documents included Congressional investigations and state legislature committees in New York and Ohio, as well as lawsuits and correspondence of officers in the Petroleum Producers' Union. She also reviewed 19 volumes of reports from the Interstate Commerce Commission about Standard (Tarbell 1904, pp. xxiv–xxv).

Although Standard Oil founder John D. Rockefeller never spoke to Tarbell, the journalist interviewed many of its executives for her expose. She wrote that there was no part of Standard Oil's history "which I have not discussed more of less fully with officers of the company." Added Kochersberger (1994, p. xii), "She wrote with passion and conviction, always supporting her statements with painstaking research and powerful evidence."

In writing about the major beef companies, Charles Edward Russell also relied in many sources within the industry (Miraldi 2003, p. 115). And after his first article appeared and the companies ordered his sources to stop talking, others came forward. One disclosed to him that a man was carrying messages among the heads of the four major beef companies, confirming their collusion. Another was a source who lived in Packingtown and provided valuable information (Miraldi 2003, p. 115).

While most business journalists today use public documents such as Securities and Exchange Commission filings and make it a practice to interview the executives of companies they write about, the practice was new in the early 20th century. Schudson and Tifft (2005, p. 24) note that interviewing by journalists was a phenomenon of the late 19th century as the field "began to involve more than stenography or observations and sketches." As a result, Weinberg said Tarbell "invented a new form of journalism."

Business journalism in the 21st century relies heavily on the use of public documents, particularly as corporate executives have become more hesitant to grant interviews to reporters (Pearlstein 2018). Internal company documents and communications are often leaked to reporters in addition to the use of court documents, regulatory filings and other public records. The trend away from executive interviews actually is hurting the reputation of their companies as the "media are seen as being analyzers of good management and strategy" (Roush 2022, p. 68). Yet, business journalists do request and hold interviews with executives as part of their work every day.

## *Impact on Consumers and Society*

The launch of a new product such as an iPhone often receives major coverage by business news organizations in the 21st century. So do product recalls, either by a company or ordered by the Consumer Product Safety Commission.

This genre of business news has its origins in the muckraking of the early 20th century, when journalists started examining products being sold to consumers that were harmful or unregulated by the government. Sinclair's writing about the meatpacking industry, for example, paved the way for the creation of the Food and Drug Administration. In 1908, John Spargo published "The Common Sense of the Milk Question," which argued for more sanitary milk.

The coverage of medicine companies and their elixirs is perhaps the best example of this type of coverage. The industry had become a $59 million revenue business by 1905 (Denham 2020, p. 103), and these pills, compounds and liquids had become popular because doctors lacked cures for common diseases such as cholera, smallpox and tuberculosis. They were also less expensive than a visit to the doctor, and usually changed the mental or physical state of those who consumed them, leading consumers to believe that they were having an effect. But they made businessmen rich. As Denham (2020, p. 143) writes, "Muckrakers exposed fake testimonials and described mansions occupied by the owners of patent-medicine companies."

As far back as 1890, the Ladies' Home Journal had warned its readers about the dangers of "patent medicines" – called that because the names had simply been registered with the U.S. Patent and Trademark Office – with columnist Elizabeth Robinson Scovil (1890, p. 11) noting that they "may arrest the development of the child and ruin its health, if not endanger its life." The publication continued warning consumers about the dangers of such medicines throughout the muckraking period (Denham 2020, pp. 118–119).

Collier's took a leading role in warning consumers about these products. Its June 3, 1905, cover of a skull, titled "Death's Laboratory," included a passage that began, "Patent medicines are poisoning people throughout America to-day." Within a year, the Pure Food and Drug Act of 1906 had passed, and the U.S. Postal Service has begun issuing fraud orders against individuals and companies who shipped the products through the mail (Denham 2020, p. 125). Collier's main writer, Samuel Hopkins Adams, continued his reporting by exposing others who claimed to solve blindness and drinking, among other issues, and in 1912, he wrote a four-part series about the continued problems in the patent medicine industry. He continued his work for The New York Tribune in 1915, writing about dishonest advertising that included patent medicines.

Such coverage has since become a mainstay of magazines and other publications. Consumer Reports launched in 1936 has spent decades analyzing products purchased by consumers. Its first issue included an article that criticized Alka-Seltzer, which it considered harmful to consumers. By 1952, it published its first table on the frequency of repairs needed for automobile brands. In 1977, Forbes exposed the Shaklee Corporation, whose salesmen sold hundreds of millions of dollars in food supplements such as protein shakes (Panacea 1977, pp. 83–90).

Business journalists in the 21st century regularly write about the dangers of products. In just one week in July 2022, the media wrote about problems with a skateboarding helmet that did not protect against head injuries, a brand of ice cream that caused a listeria outbreak and dog treats with salmonella contamination, as well product recalls for cheese and a pizza.

## 4. Interaction between Business and Government

The business journalism world of the 21st century includes multiple news organizations that specialize in covering how business and government interact with each other. For example, Bloomberg Government launched in 2011 has hundreds of editorial staffers. Politico, which was founded in 2007, started a new subscription offering called AgencyIQ that focused on the regulation of the pharmaceutical, biotechnology and medical device industries. Its Politico Pro covers other government-related business stories. CQ Roll Call covers congressional legislation, which often focuses on how the government is regulating business.

Journalism about how the business world and the political world operate isn't new. One of the biggest stories of the 1870s was the Credit Mobilier scandal in which members of the U.S. Congress profited from investing in a sham construction company. And its evolution as a mainstream topic for business journalists can be traced back to one of the famous muckrakers, Lincoln Steffens (1904), whose work in McClure's magazine starting in October 1902 was the first to document the often unethical and illegal relationships between business owners and politicians across the country. Those articles were later published in a popular book called "The Shame of the Cities."

The first article focused on St. Louis. Steffens (1902) wrote:

> Business men were not mere merchants and the politicians were not mere grafters. The two kinds of citizens got together and wielded the power of banks, railroads, factories, the prestige of the city, and the spirit of its citizens to gain business and population.

He reported that city leaders loaned money and placed the interest in their private bank accounts, and that public supplies of goods were used by private businesses. Steffens also disclosed that company executives who refused to pay blackmail to city officials left St. Louis.

Steffens then went to other cities – Minneapolis, Chicago, Philadelphia and Pittsburgh were some of them – and wrote about the relationships between government officials and businessmen. In Pittsburgh, the railroads that provided service to the steel mills purchased their rail lines with bribes (Steffens 1903).

Steffens wasn't alone. In March 1906, Cosmopolitan began publishing a series of articles by David Graham Phillips called "The Treason of the Senate" that detailed business relationships and bribes between U.S. senators and business owners. In one example, he wrote how a New York senator had joined the board of directors of seventy companies, receiving more than $50,000. William Randolph Hearst, who owned the magazine, ordered its editors to allow any publication to reprint parts of the articles (Neuzil 1996, p. 34). These articles are what caused President Roosevelt to issue his speech in which he called reporters "muckrakers" for digging up "muck" instead of other news. The magazine responded with a statement that rather than it exposes the politicians through its muckraking, the president "had better use a steam dredge" to dig up the "slime and ooze at Washington" (Cosmopolitan 1906).

Such coverage is now commonplace in the 21st century by business news organizations. In 2021 and 2022, the website Business Insider wrote a series of articles about stock ownership by members of Congress, disclosing what stocks they owned, which politicians were in violation of laws requiring disclosure of stock purchases, and which politicians had decided not to own stocks. (See Levinthal (2022) as an example.) These stories owe a direct lineage to what the muckrakers were reporting on. As Cohen (2004, p. 10) noted, "Steffens would not be surprised by the extent of the alliance between business and government today. But he would be disheartened if the American people did not start to follow his simple electoral prescription."

### *Labor and the Worker*

Coverage in publications of labor and worker issues has been around since the early 19th century when Journeyman Mechanic's Advocate began publishing in Philadelphia. It was soon followed by the Mechanic's Free Press newspaper and others (Emery and Emery 1984, p. 131). But, among mainstream publications in the century, only the New York Evening Post covered labor issues regularly for their readers.

That changed with the muckrakers, who introduced issues about working and living conditions that the masses had never learned about. John Swinton (1894), managing editor of the New York Sun, can be credited with making labor coverage a major news topic when he left the paper in 1883 to start his own newspaper that advocated for the rights of workers. Shortly thereafter, Jacob Riis (1890) published "How the Other Half Lives," which exposed the living conditions of blue-collar workers in New York. Riis argued that forcing construction companies to improve the quality of the housing would help those who lived there. The tenements "throw off a scum of forty thousand human wrecks to the island asylums and workhouses year by year," he wrote (Riis 1963, p. 3).

Other muckrakers focused on child labor. Edward Markham, the author of "Children in Bondage," pointed out that 50,000 children worked in textile mills across the South. They worked 12-hour days covered in lint dust. John Spargo, who published "The Bitter Cry of Children" in 1906, wrote about young boys working in coal mines. He wrote:

Accidents to the hands, such as cut, broken, or crushed fingers, are common among the boys. Sometimes there is a worse accident: a terrified shriek is heard, and a boy is mangled and torn in the machinery, or disappears in the chute to be picked out later smothered and dead (Spargo 1968, p. 175).

Ray Stannard Baker, writing in McClure's magazine, took on the issue of child labor as well, and then wrote about the working conditions of Blacks, a topic that few journalists in the early 20th century covered. John Fitch, writing in American magazine in 1911, criticized the 12-hour workday in the steel industry when other industries were using ten hours as the standard. He focused on U.S. Steel Corp., which was censured by Congress after Fitch's article appeared (Serrin and Serrin 2002, p. 29).

Coverage of worker issues waned in the latter part of the 20th century but has recently seen a resurgence. Coverage of working conditions in Amazon.com Inc. warehouses has been a regular topic for publications such as The New York Times and Bloomberg News. Union movements at companies such as Starbucks, Kellogg and John Deere are drawing widespread coverage, and union drives are even occurring within media companies such as Fortune magazine. Publications such as The Markup and The Financial Times have added labor reporters in recent years. Stories about the minimum wage and threatened, and actual strikes, are now top stories. And as Scheiber (2018) pointed out, labor news coverage is now focusing more on how technology is impacting work.

Their stories, and their beats, draw directly from the work of the muckrakers.

### Conclusion: The Constant Struggle between Business and the Media

Companies large and small often want to be covered by the news media, and research has shown that even negative coverage in the press is beneficial to business. Stories about companies and industries are also important to investors, who seek reliable information when deciding when to buy and sell stock.

The job of a business journalist is to provide that information, even when companies do not want the coverage because they fear a negative reaction by their workers, their customers, or their investors. And executives, and their public relations staff, often try to influence how they are covered in the news media. This struggle between the two sides – business journalism and corporate America – began in earnest with the muckraking of the early 20th century. While the muckrakers were not considered business journalists, they did lay "the groundwork for aggressive business coverage for years to come" (Roush 2006, p. 50).

It continues today, as the lessons, practices and tactics of the muckrakers are used every day by the business journalists of the 21st century.

## Further Reading

"Profits and Losses: Business Journalism and its Role in Society" (Portland: Marion Street Press, 2006) has a chapter about the muckrakers and their role in business news coverage. "Muckraking: Past, Present, and Future" (University Park: Pennsylvania State University Press, 1973) resulted from a conference held in 1970 and provides a reflection of muckraking at that time. Two excellent anthologies of muckraking are "Global Muckraking: 100 Years of Investigative Journalism from Around the World" (New York: The New Press, 2014) and "Exposes and Excess: Muckraking in America, 1900–2000" (Philadelphia: University of Pennsylvania Press, 2004).

## References

Adams, S. H. (1905) "The Great American Fraud," *Collier's*, October 7, 1905.

Arameo, R. (2000) "The History of Investigative Reporting," in M. Greenwald and J. Bernt (eds.) *The Big Chill: Investigative Reporting in the Current Media Environment*, Ames: Iowa State University Press, pp. 37–38.

Cassedy, J. H. (1964) "Muckraking and Medicine: Samuel Hopkins Adams," *American Quarterly*, 16, pp. 85–99.

Cohen, A. (2004) "'The Shame' that Lincoln Steffens Found Has not Left our Country," *The New York Times*, April 11, 2004. https://www.nytimes.com/2004/04/11/opinion/editorial-observer-shame-that-lincoln-steffens-found-has-not-left-our-country.html.

Cosmopolitan. (1906) "An Open Letter to President Roosevelt," July 1906.

Cowing, C. (1965) *Populists, Plungers and Progressives: A Social History of Stock and Commodity Speculation, 1868–1932*, Princeton, NJ: Princeton University Press.

Denham, B. (2020) "Magazine Journalism in the Golden Age of Muckraking: Patent-Medicine Exposures Before and After the Pure Food and Drug Act of 1906," *Journalism & Communication Monographs*, 22(2), pp. 100–159.

Editorial. (1907a) *Collier's*, January 5, 1907, p. 7.

Editorial. (1907b) *Colliers*, January 26, 1907, p. 10.

Emery, E., and Emery, M. (1984) *The Press and America: An Interpretive History of the Mass Media*, Englewood Cliffs, NJ: Prentice-Hall Inc.

Filler, L. (1968). *The Muckrakers: Crusaders for American Liberalism*, Chicago, IL: Henry Regnery Co.

Hunter, R. (1904) *Poverty*, New York: Macmillan Co.

Kochersberger, R. (1994) *More than a Muckraker: Ida Tarbell's Lifetime in Journalism*, Knoxville: University of Tennessee Press.

Lawson, T. (1906) *Frenzied Finance: The Crime of Amalgamated*, New York: Ridgeway-Thayer Co.

Levinthal, D. (2022) "65 Members of Congress Have Violated a Law Designed to Prevent Insider Trading and Stop Conflicts-of-Interest," *Business Insider*, June 29, 2022. https://www.businessinsider.com/congress-stock-act-violations-senate-house-trading-2021-9.

Miraldi, R. (2003) *The Pen Is Mightier: The Muckraking Life of Charles Edward Russell*, New York: Palgrave McMillan.

Neuzil, M. (1996) "Hearst, Roosevelt, and the Muckrake Speech of 1906: A New Perspective," *Journalism and Mass Communications Quarterly*, 73(1), pp. 29–39.

"Panacea, placebo, & nostrum, amen" (1977). *Forbes*, October 15, 1977, pp. 83–90.

Pearlstein, S. (2018) "No Comment: The Death of Business Reporting," *Washington Post*, July 26, 2018. https://www.washingtonpost.com/business/no-comment-the-death-of-business-reporting/2018/07/06/4fbca852-7e31-11e8-bb6b-c1cb691f1402_story.html.

Quirt, J. (1993) *The Press and the World of Money: How the News Media cover Business and Finance, Panic and Prosperity, and the Pursuit of the American Dream*, Byron, CA: Anton/California-Courier.

Reynolds, R. D. (1979) "The 1906 Campaign to Sway Muckraking Periodicals," *Journalism Quarterly*, 56(3), pp. 513–520, 589.

Riis J. (1963) *How the Other Half Lives: Studies Among the Tenements of New York*, third edition, New York: Hill and Wang.

Roush, C. (2006) *Profits and Losses: Business Journalism and its Role in Society*, Portland, OR: Marion Street Press.

Roush, C. (2022) *The Future of Business Journalism: Why it's Important to Wall Street and Main Street*, Washington, DC: Georgetown University Press.

Russell, C. E. (1908) *Lawless Wealth: The Origins of Some Great American Fortunes*, New York: BW Dodge & Co.

Scheiber, N. (2018) "Labor and Technology Reporting: Two Concentric Circles," *The New York Times*, July 11, 2018. https://www.nytimes.com/2018/07/11/insider/workplace-technology-hype-reporting.html.

Schudson, M., and Tifft, S. (2005) "American Journalism in Historical Perspective," in G. Overholser and K. Hall Jamieson (eds.), *The Press*, New York: Oxford University Press, 17–47.

Scovil, E.R. (1890) "Notes for Young Mothers," *Ladies' Home Journal*, June 1890, p. 11.

Serrin, W., and Serrin, J. (2002) *Muckraking! The Journalism that Changed America*, New York: The New Press.

Sinclair, U. (1906a) Letter to President T. Roosevelt. March 10, 1906, National Archives, Records of the Office of the Secretary of Agriculture. https://www.archives.gov/files/historical-docs/doc-content/images/upton-sinclair-letter-t-roosevelt.pdf?_ga=2.214771348.2046502926.1657900981-368662958.1657900981

Sinclair, U. (1906b) *The Jungle*, New York: Doubleday & Co.

Sinclair, U. (1962) *The Autobiography of Upton Sinclair*, New York: Harcourt Brace and World.

Spargo, J. (1968) *The Bitter Cry of Children*, New York: Times Books.

Steffens, L. (1902) "Tweed Days in St. Louis," *McClure's*, October 1902, pp. 577–588.

Steffens, L. (1903) "Pittsburg: A City Ashamed," *McClure's*, May 1903, pp. 24–39.

Steffens, L. (1904) *The Shame of the Cities*, New York: McClure, Phillips & Co.

Stein, H. (1990) "American Muckraking of Technology Since 1990," *Journalism Quarterly*, 67(2), pp. 401–409.

Streitmatter, R. (2019) *Mightier than the Sword: How the News Media have Shaped American History*, New York: Routledge.

Sullivan, M. (1906) "Dryden and the Prudential," *Collier's*, December 29, 1906, pp. 16–17, 26.

Swinton, J. (1894) *Striking for Life: Labor's Side of the Labor Question: The Right of the Workingman to a Fair Living*, New York: American Manufacturing and Publishing Co.

Tarbell, I. (1904) *The History of the Standard Oil Company*, New York: McClure, Phillips and Co.

Weinberg, S. (2008) *Taking on the Trust: The Epic Battle of Ida Tarbell and John D. Rockefeller*, New York: W.W. Norton & Co.

# 9

# "PRAY FOR THE DEAD, AND FIGHT LIKE HELL FOR THE LIVING"

*Alecia Swasy*

## Introduction

Advocacy newspapers that supported organized labor helped American unions grow from the mid-1800s until the 1970s.

Coverage of striking workers at Pittsburgh steel mills and Kentucky coal mines showed the dangerous workplaces where men, women and children toiled for low wages and little time off. These dispatches from the front lines ultimately helped union leaders win strikes, change labor laws and enforce safety standards.

The publications also helped unify an extremely splintered set of labor movements across the United States. National labor unions such as the AFL-CIO grew out of smaller, regional groups, giving the working class more power from Congress to Wall Street.

## Exposing Evils with the Help of Children

In July 1903, labor activist Mary "Mother" Jones gathered 400 men, women and children striking at textile mills in Philadelphia's Kensington neighborhood for a three-week trip by foot and wagons to New York City. Traveling behind fife and drum players, Jones led the group to show "the sharks of Wall Street," as she called them, the evils of child labor. The goal was to march to President Theodore Roosevelt's Sagamore Hill summer home on Long Island to demand a 55-hour workweek and a ban on nighttime work by women and children.

"I am going to show President Roosevelt the poor little things on which the boasted commercial greatness of our country is built," Jones said (The Labor World 1903).

Jones' march was chronicled on page one of The Labor World, a labor advocacy newspaper published in Duluth, Minnesota. Editors spared no opinions and drama in the retelling of Jones' "crusade of children." The marchers, logging 12 miles a day, were on strike in protest of long workdays and abuse of children in the mills, "living examples of a child slavery system which seems so firmly fixed on the little ones of Pennsylvania," the story said.

DOI: 10.4324/9781003298977-12

"The sight of little children at work in mills when they ought to be at school or at play, arouses me," the paper quoted Jones as saying:

> I found the conditions in Philadelphia deplorable and I resolved to do what I could to shorten the hours or tell of the striking textile workers so as to gain more liberty for the children and the women. An earlier parade through the city-the cradle of liberty-but the citizens were not moved to pity by the object lesson.
>
> The curse of greed so pressed on their hearts that they could not pause to express their pity for future men and women who are being stunted mentally, morally and physically so that they cannot possibly become good citizens. I cannot believe that the public conscience is so callous that it will not respond. ... I am going to show Wall Street the flesh and blood from which it squeezes its wealth:
>
> *(The Labor World 1903)*

At Sagamore Hill, Jones and a delegation of five strikers were turned away by the president's secretary, but scholars credit the labor organizer with advancing the anti-child labor movement. In 1905, Pennsylvania toughened its child labor laws. Jones became a legend for her decades of work to win workers' rights, with many adopting her cry: "Pray for the dead, and fight like hell for the living" (Gorn 2001).

Mother Jones became a staple of advocacy newspapers, such as The Labor World (and, decades later, in 1976, had her name adopted as the title of a crusading magazine that still publishes). Coverage of such labor leaders and issues helped the advocacy press grow, as waves of immigrants came to the United States from mid- to late 19th century to work in mines, steel mills and railroads. The publications played an important role in capturing the stories of key players like Jones, advocating for labor rights against the stronghold of industry titans who curried favor with the mainstream media.

Karla Kelling Sclater, a scholar of labor history, estimates that thousands of labor and radical publications circulated between 1880 and 1940. "Early labor papers commanded political and social recognition, calling for reduced working hours, public education, and the abolishment of debtors' prisons," Sclater wrote in "The Labor and Radical Press: 1820-present." Circulation of labor periodicals reached about 15 million in the late 1940s. Demand for correspondents was high. Indeed, young women who attended the Hudson Shore Labor School in New York City could take classes on how to gather and publish labor news for unions.

Scholars who've studied the advocacy press critique the publications' journalistic quality as uneven, at best. This is not surprising, given the unstable funding stemming from unions getting buffeted by economic downturns, internal fighting, world wars and political shifts. The "Immigrant Labor Press in North America, 1840s–1970s," a three-volume set, lists hundreds of advocacy newspapers published by immigrants. One such publication was Alarm, which was published monthly by the Scandinavian Propaganda League for just three years. It started in 1915 in Seattle, then moved to Minneapolis because of "insufficient financial support" and a greater concentration of Scandinavian workers and organizations in the Midwest city (Hoerder 1987).

While most advocacy newspapers survived a few years, the longevity award surely goes to the ones that changed focus over the years. One of the longest-running publications that started as an advocacy media outlet is The Economist, which started as a pro-working class pamphlet before morphing into a business and politics magazine still in worldwide circulation.

The Economist pamphlets circulated in London by the Anti-Corn Law League in the 1840s. The founder was James Wilson, a hat maker from Hawick, Scotland, who advocated for "free trade, internationalism and minimum interference by government, especially in the affairs of the market" (The Economist 2021).

Specifically, Wilson founded the publication in 1843 to defeat laws that taxed grain imports, making bread expensive and exacerbating food shortages in Britain. At the time, Brits spent about half of their wages on food, prompting the era to be dubbed "the Hungry Forties." Wilson believed Adam Smith's "invisible hand" in the market benefitted "profit-seeking individuals and society alike," according to the prospectus for The Economist.

The Corn Laws were ditched by the House of Commons in 1846, but Wilson and his succeeding editors broadened The Economist's mission as a publication to influence "men of business." His son-in-law, Walter Bagehot, the editor from 1861 to 1877, was a banker who favored political writing, especially about the British constitution. He's also credited with expanding the coverage and interest in the United States.

## An Awakened Working Class

The dissident press has deep roots in the United States. Many believe its birth coincided with Andrew Jackson's election to the White House in 1828, reflecting "an awakened working class during a time of social, economic and political turbulence," wrote Rodger Streitmatter in "Voices of Revolution: The Dissident Press in America" (Streitmatter 2001).

"The common purpose of the publications was to ensure that American workers did not become an industrial underclass merely adding to the power and abundance of their overlords, the merchant capitalists," Streitmatter wrote.

One such newspaper was Mechanics' Free Press, which was published in Philadelphia from 1828 to 1831, reaching a circulation of about 2,000. The Press grew out of the Mechanics' Union of Trade Associations, a group of 15 different tradesmen. The Press was one of the first labor union newspapers and increased laborers' political force, according to Streitmatter.

William Heighton, a shoemaker, was the founder and editor, hoping to "raise the productive classes to that condition of true independence and equality." Heighton started small with an April 1827 pamphlet published under the pseudonym "A Fellow Labourer."

He deemed working people the "blood, bone, sinew of the nation." Like Mother Jones, Heighton quoted Bible verses to condemn industrialists, likening them to money changers who should be driven away from the "temple of freedom."

Some of its causes were shorter workdays – ten hours a day – and less child labor in factories. Heighton had been a child laborer and believed the "sun to sun" workday prevented time for study or enjoyment of the outdoors. To support his cause, Heighton in 1830 published a study linking child labor with illiteracy. The study reported that five of six factory workers couldn't read or write their own names.

He considered education for all children to be the "first and most important" mission of the newspaper. Indeed, the Philadelphia union encouraged all to deepen their education, maintaining a library with "reading and debate rooms" (Arky 1952).

Such dissident papers attracted a following, as educated workers read the news columns to illiterate workers gathered on street corners, or inside churches and town halls. Increasingly disenfranchised workers had a "sense of fraternity" from the gatherings, Streitmatter wrote.

Historians such as Arky considered Heighton's work critical to the early days of the U.S. labor movement, noting that previous attempts by trade societies had few results. He believed education of "producers or working people" who understand the economic order so they could gain greater benefits from their work. Heighton was quite critical, including a broad spectrum of professions in his classification of "non-producers." That group included theologians, jurists, the military, manufacturers, commercial people, the gentry and legislators. Arky characterized Heighton's view of legislators as most guilty of subjugating producers because "they were the most influential and intelligent." And they were "usually lawyers, a class of notorious nonproducers."

Unlike most advocacy newspapers, the Mechanic's Free Press went to the extreme of telling workers to establish their own political party so they could get their own representatives in seats of power. Heighton wanted a workingmen's press and library in every U.S. city. The political group disbanded in 1832, a year after the Free Press stopped publishing. But historians such as Streitmatter note that the paper achieved some of its goals, such as a ten-hour workday established in Philadelphia in 1831.

## Untold Stories from Mines and Mills

The advocacy newspapers were often the only place to get the unions' side of the story, as titans such as John D. Rockefeller, who built Standard Oil, hired public relations firms to spread misinformation that helped them quash union organizers and break strikes. The robber baron financed one of the earliest corporate PR campaigns following investigative reporter Ida Tarbell's exposé on Rockefeller's monopolistic business practices. Tarbell's reporting for McClure's magazine prompted the U.S. Department of Justice to file a lawsuit against Standard Oil. The U.S. Supreme Court ruled that Standard Oil violated anti-trust laws and forced the company to split into 34 separate companies (Swasy 2020).

Rockefeller hired publicist Ivy Lee, a former business reporter, who is credited with creating corporate press releases during the titan's battle with the United Mine Workers organizing 11,000 miners at Colorado Fuel & Iron Co. Rockefeller persuaded Colorado's governor to dispatch the National Guard to handle the striking miners. Devastating fires broke out at miners' camps, leaving 66 people dead. Lee issued press releases blaming miners for the violence and a fake report blaming a faulty stove for the mine campfires.

Likewise, accounts of the historic and bloody Homestead, Pennsylvania, steel strike in 1892 favored the company, Carnegie Steel, the world's largest manufacturing company in the late 1800s. The Amalgamated Association of Iron and Steel Workers had more than 20,000 members, but it had previously lost a major strike to Carnegie across the Monongahela River in Braddock, Pennsylvania, in 1889.

The union and company were at odds over wages, which were pegged to the sales price of steel. The company wanted to reduce the wage scale and wouldn't budge. In late June 1892, workers were locked out and the mill was protected by a tall fence, nicknamed "Fort Frick" after Carnegie CEO Henry Clay Frick (Trump 2017).

In early July, a barge carrying 300 Pinkerton detectives arrived to fight with striking workers. The workers defeated the Pinkertons that first day, causing them to retreat. Official reports said half of the Pinkertons were injured, but none died. But some of the strikers were killed, prompting ministers to condemn Carnegie's hired guns as "a blot on civilization." The battle eventually attracted mainstream media, which labor histories described as reporting "sympathetic to the strikers."

The workers were dealt a serious blow when Pennsylvania's governor dispatched the National Guard to Homestead. The troops patrolled as Carnegie hired scores of non-union workers to replace the strikers. By October, many of the skilled workers went back to the mill. Unskilled workers had already crossed picket lines because they faced starvation. In November, the remaining strikers voted to end the dispute and returned to work.

The victory by Carnegie Steel was cited as a reason for the continued exploitation of workers, and their continued strikes.

Laborers had good reason to be unhappy with working conditions and pay. "Steelworkers in America: The Non-Union Era" by David Brody reported that workers at blast furnaces in 1882 averaged 77 hours per week. By 1910, they were working about 84 hours a week. The demand for industrial materials to fuel World War I meant factories and mills were humming seven days a week. But even after the war ended, 12-hour workdays were common in steel mills. The steel industry had 76 strikes just in 1919 (Brody 1960).

Mother Jones continued to make headlines in advocacy press for her visits to striking workers in and around Pittsburgh, the heart of the modern steel industry. Jones, who lost her four children and husband to a yellow fever epidemic, worked as a dressmaker until her small shop was destroyed in the Chicago fires of 1871. By the early 1900s, Jones had devoted her days to nurturing and organizing laborers to fight for their rights. Dressed in antique black dresses, she was known as Mother instead of her first name of Mary. She earned a stipend from the United Mine Workers Union and traveled the country from mine to mills. "My address is like my shoes," she told a congressional committee. "It travels with me wherever I go" (Gorn 2001).

Jones went to Homestead, once again home to labor unrest, in late August 1919. She called Homestead a "tyrannical borough along the Monongahela river" and "at the head of the list as the most despotic principality of them all." Not surprising, Homestead was quite dependent on steel companies, even for services such as street repairs and snow removal (Labor World 1919).

The Labor Day edition of the Labor World newspaper featured a page-one story of 89-year-old Jones' visit with workers. The story said labor organizers had applied for the required meeting permit but were told by municipal officials they couldn't meet because Slavic interpreters were used at a previous gathering. Officials cited a "no foreign languages spoken" rule for the decision to ban the meeting. And owners of the hall were notified they, too, risked jail time if they rented space without written permission of "the burgess," a British term for magistrate.

Undaunted, Jones spoke to workers gathered in the street, who were "simply electrified" by the elderly woman. "Even the police were awestruck for a moment," the reporter said. But the police obviously didn't remain in awe; they arrested Jones and took her to a "filthy jail cell," according to the news report.

## Labor Coverage in the Mainstream Media

Pittsburgh had seven daily newspapers at the time of the steel strike. One analysis of the papers showed coverage favored U.S. Steel by relying heavily on company press releases, while little ink was given to workers' grievances. Indeed, scholars who have studied labor coverage in the mainstream, metropolitan and national newspapers often concluded that publishers such as William Randolph Hearst and Frank Gannett, owners of multiple city papers, were firmly opposed to unions. But the rise of unions' influence on politics and the economy meant that they couldn't be ignored, especially during peak union membership of the 1930s–1950s when membership grew to one-third of the nonagricultural workforce.

Some editors and publishers proved sympathetic to unions. In 1940, a high-ranking editor at the Scripps-Howard newspaper group issued a memo that said stories "should be undertaken with a sympathetic attitude toward unionism."

Beyond sympathy, coverage of union issues helped sell newspapers, especially in cities like Philadelphia or Akron, Ohio. These union hubs were home to newspapers owned by legendary newspaperman John S. Knight, who saw the business potential of appealing to a larger audience, including blue-collar workers who were often union members (Glende 2020). Knight built a company with just one newspaper, The Akron Beacon Journal, into the Knight Ridder chain, with papers in Miami, Charlotte, Detroit and San Jose.

Meanwhile, journalism was undergoing changes as reporters were encouraged to add background information and explanation to give greater context to daily events. Another factor that shaped public opinion of unions was the growth of public relations campaigns by Lee and other hired press agents, who helped Carnegie and other industrial titans spin their side of labor disputes.

Union papers occasionally got help from former professional reporters such as Gordon Cole, who worked at daily newspapers, including The Wall Street Journal for 15 years. Cole, who was past president of the Washington Newspaper Guild, became the editor of The Machinist, the weekly publication of the International Association of Machinists. While he encouraged union members to press for favorable coverage in mainstream papers, he was a realist about the influence of money. "As long as newspapers are supported by the advertising of business corporations," they are "always going to favor the employer in any showdown," Cole said (Glende 2020).

One New York City paper, Commercial Advertiser, called advocacy press editors "poor and deluded" men who were "the slime of this community." Editors at the Mechanic's Free Press countered that general-circulation papers spoke only for the "aristocracy and wealth" neglecting poor people (Streitmatter 2001).

Even the best, national newspapers missed some key labor stories. For instance, the mainstream media took decades to acknowledge some of the bloodiest confrontations, including the Battle of Blair Mountain, part of a series of coal mine wars in West Virginia's hollows.

The New York Times revisited West Virginia in 2021 to retell the story unknown to most. Coal was mined by men paid only with company scrip, spendable only at the company store and on company housing and medical care. Miners went on strike, but few knew about it even though it was "the largest insurrection since the Civil War," according to the Times' account (Robertson 2021).

"It is one of the most amazing confrontations between workers and bosses ever in this country and no one knows about it," said Cecil Roberts, the president of the United Mine Workers of America and a descendant of those who fought the company in 1921. Indeed, state officials scrubbed West Virginia's official history with a 1931 law that governed "the study of social problems" and the Mine Wars was left out of school history textbooks. It took until 2018 to get the Blair Mountain battleground site placed on the National Register of Historic Places.

Labor news came to newspapers' front doors once their own workers joined unions. In some cases, those employees unionized and founded their own competing newspapers. The Workingman's Advocate was first published in 1864 by the Chicago Typographical Union, which was on strike against the Chicago Times. The strikers believed that the Times wasn't giving their cause enough coverage.

The Advocate promoted itself as "devoted exclusively to the interests of the producing classes." But historians note that the paper also had a lot of articles not relevant to labor or strikes. Some mused that it was "possibly a sign that the editors, although experts on the printing side of newspaper publishing, struggled with news-gathering" and filled space with poetry, fiction and essays (https://www.library.illinois.edu/illinoisnewspaperproject/workingmans-advocate/).

The strike against the Times ended just eight months after it started, but the Advocate continued to publish, thanks to Andrew Cameron, a member of the Typographical Union, who broadened his activism to a national stage with the National Labor Union (NLU). Cameron used the Advocate to publicize the NLU and issues such as an eight-hour workday. The Advocate joined with the Industrial Congress but stopped publication in 1879. Historians consider the Advocate one of the most successful advocacy publications because of its broader influence on the overall labor movement of the era. Besides, it published for 15 years, far longer than most of the other advocacy papers.

## Farmers Unite in Midwest, but Divisions Remained

Some advocacy newspapers grew out of anger far from the industrial hubs. Monopolistic transportation practices angered midwestern farmers, causing them to unite as the "Grangers" after the Civil War. The Grangers attracted farmers who were tired of high rates set by granaries, which were owned by the railroads. In 1871, Illinois farmers succeeded in getting the state legislature to enact anti-price fixing laws, setting a maximum price that grain operators could charge to handle farmers' crops. Other states soon followed with similar laws.

This led to the formation of farmers' political parties in various states. Ignatius Donnelly, one of the organizers, was a Philadelphia attorney who moved to Minnesota and edited the Emigrant Aid Journal in both English and German to attract settlers to the state. A Republican, Donnelly, eventually dropped that party affiliation in favor of smaller independent parties such as the Grangers. In 1874, he founded the Anti-Monopolist newspaper, using it to routinely attack bankers, who he labeled as public enemies.

The Litchfield News reviewed the Anti-Monopolist "as unlike other journals as Donnelly is unlike other men." The mixed review deemed it "as dangerous a plaything as a porcupine. It is always erudite, humorous, sarcastic and generally logical" (Minnesota Historical Society).

Donnelly also fought for independent causes as a politician, seeking office 17 times and winning nine of them, including his bid for U.S. Congress and Minnesota's lieutenant governor.

Financial problems forced the paper to fold in 1878. And the Granger movement membership dwindled to around 100,000, although the National Grange remains as a fraternal organization for farmers. By 1970, nine states had Granges representing 800,000 farmers (Britannica 2020).

One issue that vexed small, advocacy newspapers was the lack of unity and communication among the various tradesmen, their unions, Grangers and Socialists. One publisher, John Swinton, saw this problem and began a new publication called John Swinton's Paper in New York in late 1883. His goal was to bring organization to labor protests, reform efforts to pass legislation and overall organizing of labor, according to Frank Reuter, a former instructor of history at West Virginia University (Reuter 1960).

Swinton wrote that America belonged to workers, not the "coming billionaires." Swinton became acquainted with Karl Marx, author of "The Communist Manifesto." And he was friends with Samuel Gompers, and first and longest-serving president of the American Federation of Labor (AFL), which grew to 50,000 members in 1886 (AFL-CIO, undated).

## Post-World War II Growth of Unions

The return of soldiers from World War II fueled boom times for America's labor unions. That growth was chronicled by the AFL-CIO News, which started as a weekly paper in December 1955 after the merger of AFL and CIO unions.

George Meany had been unanimously elected the president of the merged union at its first convention at an armory on Park Avenue and 34th Street. The AFL-CIO was a formidable group with 15 million members from 135 different unions.

At the meeting, Meany urged repeal of "right to work" laws in 18 states and heard addresses by Eleanor Roosevelt, U.S. Labor Secretary James P. Mitchell, New York Gov. W. Averell Harriman and presidential hopeful Adlai Stevenson. President Dwight D. Eisenhower addressed the group via telephone from his Gettysburg farm (AFL-CIO News 1955).

The AFL-CIO News ceased publication in 1996 with the final issue highlighting the same topics that continue to vex working Americans – a working wage and health benefits. AFL-CIO President John J. Sweeney spoke to journalists at the National Press Club in Washington about the need for a "new social compact between business and labor" that can grow the U.S. economy and "bridge the growing gap between the great majority of Americans who are working longer and harder for less and fortunate few who are prospering as never before" (Byrne 1996).

Sweeney reflected on the post-World War II era when "we prospered together" to create the largest middle class and "the most successful society this world has ever known." Back then, government leaders understood "a rising tide lifts all boats," he said, quoting President John F. Kennedy.

In the 1990s, however, corporate America "too often squeezed the last possible ounce of productivity out of American workers, and then threw them on the scrap heap of unemployment or old age, with reduced pensions and health coverage."

He quoted headlines of banks' mergers that resulted in 12,000 people losing their jobs and the combined company's stock rising. "Does a rising tide now sink all ships – except for the luxury yachts?"

The paper's coverage of Sweeney's address seemed to be a plea for mainstream journalists to fill the void created by the lack of advocacy press, which had withered along with U.S. union membership.

"For American workers and their families, these are snapshots from hell," Sweeney said. "They paint an ugly portrait of an economy that has lost respect for workers and the jobs they do."

## Conclusion

Most of the advocacy publications folded as the U.S. labor movement was stymied by Reagan-era policies that gave employers in the 1980s more power to fire striking workers. But the spirit of those early organizers lives on in magazines such as Mother Jones, named in honor of the firebrand woman who wore out her shoes marching from one cause to another to improve the plight of workers.

In addition, larger news organizations, such as The New York Times and The Washington Post, assign reporters to cover the occasional strike and the overall plight of low-paid workers, such as Dollar General or Walmart employees. And they've provided in-depth coverage of how tougher economic times of 2022 have rekindled union organizing.

Indeed, workers at a Staten Island, N.Y. Amazon warehouse voted in July 2022 to form a union. Labor activists hope the victory will increase organizing elsewhere inside the giant online retailer and other companies.

Harvard labor economist Lawrence Katz talked with the Harvard Gazette about the significance of union victory at Amazon. "Does this lead to a broader movement of independent unions or increased success for existing unions in organizing at Amazon and other major employers, or is it an outlier?" Katz said in the story. "That's an open question."

## Further Reading

Colin, J. R. *The American Radical Press, 1880–1960.* London: Greenwood Press, 1974. (Overview of early advocacy newspapers.)

Gorn, Elliott J. *Mother Jones: The Most Dangerous Woman in America.* New York: Hill and Wang, 2001. (Biography of labor organizer and activist Mother Jones.)

## References

Adamczyk, J. "Homestead Strike," *Encyclopedia Britannica,* 4 March, 2020. https://www.britannica.com/event/Homestead-Strike

AFL-CIO. Samuel Gompers biography, undated, https://aflcio.org/about/history/labor-history-people/samuel-gompers

Arky, L. H. (1952) "The Mechanics' Union of Trade Associations and the Formation of the Philadelphia Workingmen's Movement," *The Pennsylvania Magazine of History and Biography,* 76(2), pp. 142–176.

Brody, D. (1960) *Steelworkers in America: The Non-Union Era,* Cambridge: Harvard University Press.

"For Social Justice, Economic Reform and Political Progress," *The Labor World,* 30 August, 1919.

Glende, P. (2020) "Labor Reporting and Its Critics in the CIO Years," *Journalism & Communication Monographs,* 22(1), pp. 4–75.

Granger movement, *Encyclopedia Britannica,* 20 July, 1998. https://www.britannica.com/event/Granger-movement

Hoerder, D. (1987) *The Immigrant Labor Press in North America, 1840s-1970s, Vol. 1.,* New York: Greenwood Press.

"Little Babes In A Crusade-Mother Jones is To Storm Wall Street," *The Labor World,* 18 July, 1903.

"Mother Jones Arrested By Homestead Police While Speaking to Steel Men," *The Labor World,* 28 August, 1919.

Pazzanese, C. "Will the Message Sent by Amazon Workers Turn Into a Movement?" *The Harvard Gazette,* 7 April, 2022.

Reuter, F. T. (1960) "John Swinton's Paper," *Labor History,* 1(3), pp. 298–307.

Robertson, C. (2021) "A Century Ago, Miners Fought in a Bloody Uprising. Few Know About it Today," *The New York Times*, 5 September, 2021. https://www.nytimes.com/2021/09/06/us/coal-miners-blair-mountain.html

Sclater, K. K. *The Labor and Radical Press: 1820-Present*. Labor Press Project, University of Washington. https://depts.washington.edu/labhist/laborpress/Kelling.htm

Streitmatter, R. (2001) *Voices of Revolution: The Dissident Press in America*, New York: Columbia University Press.

Swasy, A. (2020) *A Wall Street Guidebook for Journalism and Strategic Communication*, Alecia New York: Routledge.

Sweeney, J. "Sweeney Urges U.S. Return to Social Compact," *AFL-CIO News*, 8 January, 1996. https://archive.org/stream/mdu-labor-040713/labor-040713_djvu.txt

The Anti-Monopolist, Minnesota Historical Society, https://www.mnhs.org/newspapers/hub/anti-monopolist

"The Corn Laws at 175: An Anniversary for Free Traders," *The Economist*, 26 June, 2021. https://www.economist.com/finance-and-economics/2021/06/24/an-anniversary-for-free-traders

Trump, R. The Battle of Homestead, The Battle of Homestead Foundation, 25 January, 2017. https://battleofhomestead.org/the-battle-narrative-in-pdf/

Working Man's Advocate, University of Illinois Digital Newspaper Collection.

## *Other Sources*

Boudreaux, D. and Irwin, D. "Corn Laws Repeal at 175," *The Economist*, 25 June, 2021.

Feuer, L. S. and McLellan, D. T. Karl Marx, *Encyclopedia Britannica*, https://www.britannica.com/biography/Karl-Marx.

Friedman, G. (2014) "March of the Mill Children," *The Encyclopedia of Greater Philadelphia*. https://philadelphiaencyclopedia.org/archive/march-of-the-mill-children/

Mansfield, J. (2011) *Worktime in the United States Steel Industry, 1870–1939*. https://dsc.duq.edu/etd/871

Rose, J. D. (2001) *Duquesne and the Rise of Steel Unionism*, Chicago: University of Illinois Press.

# 10

# SIDING AGAINST LABOR IN THE LAST GREAT AMERICAN UNION TOWN

## Coverage of the 1984 Casino Workers Strike by the Las Vegas Review-Journal and Las Vegas Sun

*Mark A. Bernhardt*

### Introduction

With the early 19th-century emergence of the business model by which newspapers generate revenue from setting advertising rates based on circulation, covering labor unrest became a balancing act for newspapers seeking to make inroads with the working class to bolster circulation. Publishers of what is known as the Penny Press, because the papers sold for a penny on the street to reach a mass audience across class lines through affordability (Huntziker 1999; Mindich 1998; Stevens 1991; Tucher 1994), faced the challenge that their readers and advertisers may have different perspectives on strikes based on their own financial stakes in the matter. Consequently, they had to navigate the competing interests of the business community and working-class readers in the way they presented strikes (Huntziker 1999; Mindich 1998; Stevens 1991; Tucher 1994), with individual publishers establishing standards for how and when they would support a specific side (Bernhardt 2016). As the 19th century progressed, the Penny Press gave way to other journalistic forms, such as New Journalism and Yellow Journalism, that practiced similar methods for strike reporting.

Placing such newspapers within the context of national trends, overall, the press sometimes proved more favorable to business and other times more favorable to labor in covering strikes, with national events, political moods, new business practices, and new publishers guiding the trajectory. This vacillation continued until the late 1960s, at which point, media studies scholar Christopher Martin argues, a transition took place within the industry. Newspaper companies sought to increase advertising revenue by changing the target audience from one that had a place for the working class to one that was exclusively middle and upper-middle class, aligning themselves more closely with business interests and altering narratives about the working class in the U.S. journalism in the process (Martin 2019).

Using the New York Penny Press as a frame of reference for how the media attempt to balance business and labor interests began and Martin's conclusions about how it ended, this study analyzes what the local coverage of the 1984 Las Vegas casino workers strikes reveals about the newspapers' views on organized labor. Las Vegas offers an insightful case

 DOI: 10.4324/9781003298977-13

study for exploring labor-press relations in the post-industrial, neo-liberal-era United States, given the city's unique position as a large urban center dominated by a single heavily unionized industry and because Las Vegas casino workers were part of the middle class that Martin says the press coveted. While referred to as the last great American union town (Davis 2002), union power and middle-class status did not translate into press support, with the Las Vegas press' position on labor fitting the national norm Martin describes. Both the Las Vegas Review-Journal, then owned by Arkansas Democrat Witt Stephens and his Republican brother Jackson, and the Las Vegas Sun, owned by Republican Hank Greenspun, backed the corporate-owned casinos that provided a large source of advertising revenue for area media outlets. Over the course of the strike, the tone of most of the articles they published was hostile toward the unions. As such, the presentation of the strikes was geared toward readers whose economic interests were different than those of the casino workers. Both papers emphasized that the unions hurt the local economy, engaged in violence, and were out of touch with public opinion. In this way, they made clear that the casino resort ownership groups had Las Vegas's best interests in mind, not the casino workers' unions.

## Historical Perspectives

In 1840, workers building New York City's Croton Aqueduct went on strike. Initially, the New York Herald and New York Sun, published by James Gordon Bennett and Moses Yale Beach, respectively, supported the strikers' push for higher wages and freedom from having to use the company store. However, the two publishers eventually shifted to supporting the contractors and grew increasingly critical of the strikers. Both papers printed the contractors' statement about the issues involved and cast the strikers as violently obstructing others from working (Bernhardt 2016). This strike coverage reveals that the Penny Press and organized labor had an unsteady relationship "in a particularly insightful way because of the strike's complexity, not just pitting employees against employers, but also dividing unskilled workers from skilled, strikebreakers from strikers, and Irish immigrants from the general population" (Bernhardt 2016, p. 9).

The Penny Press' emergence in the 1830s with papers for the masses had important ramifications for the working class. An economic depression crippled the labor press after 1837 and the Penny Press became the primary newspapers supporting labor (Buchholz and Thompson 2008; Schiller 1981). However, the Penny Press wavered on supporting labor activism (Bernhardt 2016). Because they did not receive financial support from political parties or generate revenue from upper-class subscribers (Huntziker 1999; Stevens 1991), the papers could take any side they wanted on a given issue. However, in taking one side, they potentially alienated those who supported the other (Bernhardt 2016). Because they were dependent on sales and advertising, the Penny Press had to find a way to serve "heterogeneous audiences without alienating any significant segment of audience" (Schiller 1981, p. 3) as well as consider the interests of advertisers (Buchholz and Thompson 2008; Maras 2013; Mindich 1998; Schiller 1981;). Complicating this, the Penny Press' targeted working-class and middle-class audiences were not unified. Within the working class, skilled and unskilled workers, as well as the native-born and immigrants, all recognized their exploitation by employers; however, they also had volatile relationships with each other. Likewise, within the middle class, merchants, manufacturers, and artisans had interests that did not always align (Bernhardt 2016, Schiller 1981). Thus, for Penny Press papers like the Herald and Sun to succeed financially by expanding circulation, they had to find ways to navigate the diverse views of their readers in covering labor issues. Bennett and Beach specifically did this by supporting the right to organize and strike (but strike only as a last resort), supporting the right to work, and opposing the destruction of private property (Bernhardt 2016).

With time, some mass-audience papers did provide more support for the working class, with publishers actively advocating to improve living standards and working conditions. Following the Civil War, the national press paid more attention to labor issues and many publishers supported workers in labor struggles (Martin 2019). However, labor reporting and advocacy began to decline in the early 20th century (Martin 2019). It increased again during the New Deal and remained strong into the 1960s. Finally, through the 1970s and 1980s, it all but disappeared, with only a few newspapers keeping reporters specifically assigned to cover labor news on staff (Martin 2019) and support for strikes became rare. Not coincidentally, labor reporting declined at the same time the corporatization of newspaper ownership expanded. Newspapers themselves had an interest in resisting their own workers' demands and keeping labor costs low (Martin 2019), and this carried over into how they generally portrayed organized labor.

With corporatization, newspapers in sizeable metro centers emphasized a consumer orientation rather than a citizen orientation in the 1970s with their focus on profits (Martin 2019). In the late 1970s, these newspapers shifted to tailoring the news for the upscale audiences that advertisers coveted, promoting themselves as reaching the "right type" of people – those with more disposable income than typical television watchers (Martin 2019). Connecting this transition to the political and economic trends of the time, Martin states, "The rise of individualistic consumerism as a news frame in the 1970s fit nicely with the aims of the larger project of political conservatism in the late 1970s and 1980s. They successfully used 'consumer interest' as the selling point for deregulation of transport and other industries, corporate tax cuts, and attacks on labor unions" (Martin 2019, p. 119).

This resulted in a change in how newspapers presented labor issues and strikes to readers. Most often, papers described how strikes inconvenienced the public, which cast organized labor as a menace (Martin 2019). While Martin's study specifically focuses on transit strikes, his assessment is relevant to strikes generally regarding public perception due to press coverage. "The consumer-oriented frame communicated a new sense of privilege for the transit passengers, giving them the implicit permission to express their irritation, annoyance, anger, and disgust at a labor dispute," writes Martin. "Consequently, this consumer-oriented perspective served management's interest more than labor's because what the consumer wants is for workers to stop complaining and end the strike immediately, no matter the damage to their bargaining position" (Martin 2019, p. 119). The Las Vegas Review-Journal and Las Vegas Sun used such methods in presenting the 1984 strike, supporting the corporate resorts and depicting the unions as harming the city.

## Main Research Methods

To analyze the press coverage of the strike, this study includes every issue of the Las Vegas Review-Journal and the Las Vegas Sun from April 1 to June 8, starting just before and ending just after the period of the main strike (conducted by the Culinary Union), which lasted from April 2 to June 7. In all, 119 articles about the strike appeared in the Review-Journal and 191 articles in the Sun. Based on an assessment of the language used to discuss the strike and the themes addressed in each article, the study counts the percentage of articles that were positive, neutral, and negative in their presentation. Articles were deemed positive when they focused on union successes, portrayed resort owners as unwilling to compromise, and portrayed the unions as engaging in peaceful striking. Articles were deemed negative when they focused on violence committed by strikers, police arrests, the strike as hurting the economy, and portrayed union leaders as unwilling to compromise. Neutral articles presented no information that could be deemed positive or negative or presented information that was both positive and negative. The charts below show the percentage of positive, neutral, and negative articles for each paper (Figures 10.1 and 10.2).

Overall, the press coverage was more negative. The Las Vegas papers disregarded that the city had a heavily unionized population, presenting the strike in a way that supported the resorts and blamed striking workers for damage to the local economy. With the casino resorts

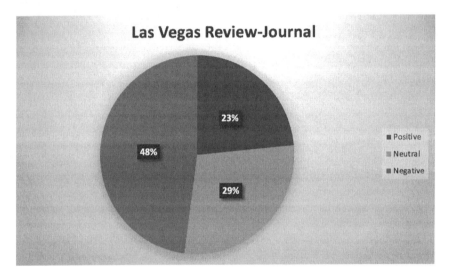

*Figure 10.1*   Presentation of Union Activity in Las Vegas Review-Journal.

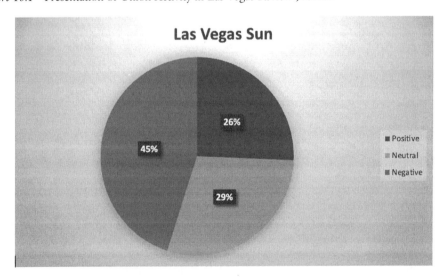

*Figure 10.2*   Presentation of Union Activity in Las Vegas Sun.

among the two newspapers' largest advertisers (Kraft 2010), the papers had a financial interest to support owners against workers. They also fit the trend Martin identifies regarding the abandonment of organized labor but complicate it in that many Las Vegas casino workers had incomes that placed them within the target class audience newspapers coveted.

Finally, it is possible that the owners' political views played a role as well, particularly for the Sun, which was owned by Republican businessman Greenspun. President Ronald Reagan's firing the nation's striking air traffic controllers in 1981 highlighted Republican hostility to unions in the era. For the Review-Journal, how the owners' political views may have influenced the strike coverage is ambiguous. Arkansas Democrat Witt Stephens and his Republican brother Jackson owned the paper as part of the media arm of their business empire, and both expressed pro-business views. While that position might have influenced the papers' stance on the strike, given that they were not from Nevada, the question of how much they cared about the happenings in Las Vegas to take a hands-on role in the coverage of events complicates discerning to what extent the Review-Journal's reporting reflected their personal views. It is worth noting, though, that the Review-Journal published a slightly higher percentage of negative articles than the Sun.

### The 1984 Casino Workers' Strike

Nevada's tourism industry had a complex relationship with unions, which set the stage for the 1984 strike and its presentation in the Review-Journal and Sun. The Nevada legislature passed a right-to-work law in 1952. Support for the law stemmed from a 1949 Reno strike (Kraft 2010). Las Vegas resorts though had a better relationship with unions. In 1956, the owners formed the Nevada Industrial Council (NIC) to serve as a negotiating entity in bargaining with unions (Kraft 2010), specifically the Culinary Union Local 226 (Alexander 2002). Because the mob, which had significant investments in Las Vegas resorts, desired labor peace, the resorts and their unions maintained good relations (Davis 2002). The unions provided casino workers with a middle-class lifestyle, with work in the Las Vegas resort industry paying much more than anywhere else in the country (Rothman 1998). Hattie Canty, a maid who started working in the 1970s and went on to become a union labor organizer in the1980s and president of the Culinary local in the 1990s, remarked:

> In this town I am living proof that a maid can own a home, she can buy her cars, she can pay taxes on that home, she can send her kids to college. These jobs represented stability to me and every other maid out there in this town.
>
> *(Goodwin 2014, p. 133)*

Starting in the late 1960s, union relations with the casino resorts changed. The Nevada legislature amended the state's gaming code to allow corporate resort ownership (Kraft 2010). Howard Hughes pioneered the way, purchasing the Desert Inn in 1967 (Schwartz 2003). Employer-employee relations began to deteriorate as more resorts became corporate-owned (Davis 2002; Kraft 2010). The breakdown of familial treatment made employment in the industry less desirable, despite the high pay (Rothman 1998). These corporate-owned resorts established the Nevada Resort Association (NRA) in 1968 as the entity for dealing with the unions, and the NRA took a harder stand against unions compared to the NIC (Kraft 2010). This led to a series of labor conflicts that the unions tended to win, as was the case with a one-day general strike in 1969, a three-day strike in 1970, and a nine-day strike in 1973 (Kraft

Mark A. Bernhardt

2010). Casino workers remained heavily unionized through the 1970s, with two-thirds of resort workers having union membership (Kraft 2010).

However, as the 1970s progressed, Las Vegas's tourism industry faced new challenges, which put pressure on the unions. A spike in oil prices and an economic recession crimped tourism and the legalization of gambling in Atlantic City created competition (Moehring 2014). With tensions getting worse, a 16-day strike in 1976 had major ramifications for the local economy, but ultimately both sides made concessions to end the strike (Kraft 2010).

In the wake of the economic recession in the early 1980s, combined with a pair of major hotel fires and lackluster new casino resorts opening that led to a drop in tourism (Rothman 1998), during contract renewal negotiations in 1983, the NRA insisted on the need to freeze wages for two years and reduce benefits (Kraft 2010). The NRA also wanted to strengthen sympathy strike restrictions, increase the time before sympathy strikes could occur from the 1976 agreement of ten days to six months (Kraft 2010), acquire more control of the union health insurance fund, eliminate the 40-hour work week, and reduce tip guarantees (Alexander 2002). Some independent owners agreed to new contracts that averted strikes at their resorts (Evensen 1984, "Pact inked"), but they were contingent on the final agreement reached between the NRA and the casino workers unions (Kraft 2010).

On April 2, 1984, 20,000 members of several unions went on strike at the hotels that refused to settle for a new contract (Kraft 2010). The Culinary Union was by far the largest, with 26,000 total members. Other unions involved included the 800-member Bartenders Local 165, 1,500-member Musicians Local 369, and 900-member Stagehands Local 720 (Cling 1984, "Vegas poised"; Peters 1984, "Midnight sit-down"). Other unions backed the strike, with the AFL-CIO calling for a boycott of Las Vegas and honoring picket lines (Cling 1984, "AFL-CIO"; Peters 1984, "Food, garbage"), and labor leader Cesar Chavez visited and gave his support (Evensen, J.D.1984, "Cesar Chavez"; Riley, O'Driscoll, and Levin 1984), bringing more national attention to the conflict. Resorts managed to replace a significant number of strikers and threatened permanent replacement with nonunion workers (Kraft 2010; Glisch and Evensen 1984, "Strikers receive"; Cling 1984, "Strike drags on"), signs the strike would not end quickly. One new employee said, "If they don't want their jobs, I'll be happy to take it for them" (Cornett and Harrison 1984, "Resort leaders," p. 1A). Some union members also chose to cross the picket lines and stay on the job because they were unwilling to make the financial sacrifice, such as waitress Erika Hayes, who was profiled by the Sun (O'Driscoll 1984, "Waitress fights").

In their earliest articles, the papers established different tones for the three sides involved in the strike – unions, owners, and local government. The unions are presented as hostile, with representatives quoted making militant statements, threatening to shut down the resort industry to get what they want. Stagehands president Dennis Kist stated: "There's no point in hitting selectively. If we're going to shut the town down, shut it down" (Cling 1984, "Vegas poised," p. 4). Regarding replacement workers, Culinary Union president Joe Hays vowed that they would "have to fight their way into the hotels and we'll make them fight their way out" (Cling 1984, "Vegas poised," p. 4). Jeff McColl of the Culinary Union went so far as to tell "scabs" to steal from the hotels (Glisch and Evensen 1984, "Culinary leader"). Although the Sun noted McColl's willingness to negotiate anytime the NRA was willing, the paper highlighted his vow for a long and bitter strike (Peterson 1984, "Midnight sit-down"). Emphasizing union militancy, the Review-Journal published an article about the violence committed during the 1976 strike and detailing that the police did not have the resources to handle a long strike that could cost the department $100,000 per day (Evensen 1984, "Police stand").

Comparatively, the resort owners and the Las Vegas Convention and Visitors Authority (LVCVA) are presented as looking out for the interests of the local economy. Owners asserted that their proposal was needed to streamline operations so that Las Vegas would remain competitive with Atlantic City and other tourist destinations (Cling 1984, "Vegas poised"). Exemplifying the view of local government, Herbert Lehrter, the LVCVA advertising director, said that a strike would drop casino revenue and affect gaming and room taxes. Furthermore, he asserted that visitor volume had been increasing and a strike could reverse that, noting that some businesses and individuals had already canceled their convention and visitation plans just due to the threat of a strike (Cling 1984, "Vegas poised," p. 4). The Sun reported that the LVCVA had launched a media blitz to try to assure tourists that Las Vegas was still a good place to visit (Levin 1984, "LVCVA begins"). The papers also pointed out that state representatives defended the resorts' position. When Rep. William Clay (D-Mo.) blamed the casinos for prolonging the strike, then-Rep. Harry Reid (D-Nev.) said that he disagreed and that this was not the time to assign blame (Diaz 1984).

The main way in which the papers attacked the unions was by drawing attention to union efforts to hurt resort business. Sun editorialist Brian Greenspun blasted the unions for hurting business just as Las Vegas was recovering from the early 1980s recession (Greenspun 1984). Hilton Hotels Corporation executive vice president Henri Lewin said that "the bottom line is total disaster," further saying that neither management nor labor could win (Zamont 1984, "Gambling tourists"). The Review-Journal published an article by a New York travel agent blasting the unions for writing agents to tell them not to book at hotels under strike (Cornett 1984, "N.Y. travel"), and the casinos sued the unions for such actions (Borders 1984). Travel agents around the country reported significant drops in customers looking to book trips to Las Vegas as the strike dragged on (Cling 1984, "LV hotel"). Along with tourism, the strike hurt convention business ("Walkout forces"1984). A representative of the National Association of Broadcasters said that the organization, which brought 33,000 convention goers to Las Vegas, would look for a new site after completing their contracted obligation for 1985. Specifically, they wanted a location with fewer labor problems (Werner and Cling 1984). Although some independent hotel owners signed contracts with the unions to avoid their workers walking out, the papers stated that the strike was hurting those hotels just as much as those under strike because the strike was scaring off tourists and conventions (Zamong 1984, "Gambling tourists"; "The damages" 1984), with the independents blaming the corporate-owned hotels for destroying the Las Vegas economy (Cornett 1984, "Hotel exec."; Zambost 1984, "NRA proposals"). Las Vegas Councilman Paul Christensen asserted that the strike was undermining Las Vegas' efforts to improve its image with the traveling public since the MGM fire that killed 85, making the money spent on national advertising a waste (Glisch and Cling 1984). Additionally, both the Review-Journal and Sun reported the strike hurt other local businesses. While restaurants and low-end retail stores saw sales increase, most businesses saw decreases in revenue as families curtailed spending and fewer tourists came to shop. For example, car sales fell 30 percent (Morrison and Cling 1984). Likewise, the hotels spent less, and this trickled down to businesses that supplied them with every type of product (Hurley 1984).

The strike did have the potential to devastate the local economy. Tourism had been vital to Las Vegas' development as a city. Hoover Dam and the relegalization of gambling and drinking in the 1930s began the process (Moehring 2014). In the 1950s, the hotel/casino resorts appeared on The Strip, and hotel construction boomed through the 1950s and 1960s to keep up with tourist demand (Moehring 2014). By the 1970s, hotels and casinos employed one-third of the Las Vegas workforce and other tourist-related businesses employed another one-third (Kraft 2010). In the early 1980s, the resort industry employed 70,000 people (Kraft 2010). The papers noted how much strikes hurt tourism in the lead up to the 1984 strike. The Review-Journal and Sun reminded readers that the 1976 strike led to a drop of 310,000 visitors. The tourism industry lost $23 million and the local economy as a whole lost $131 million (Peters 1984, Negotiators try). The LVCVA estimated that the planned 1984 strike could cost the economy $3.2 million per day (Cling 1984, "Vegas poised"; Glisch 1984 "LV culinary"). Throughout the 1984 strike, the papers gave regular reports on how much tourism was down compared to the same time the previous year (Glisch, Cling, Harrison 1984; Peters 1984, "Strike news").

Building on the way in which the strike hurt the city's economy, another means by which the papers attacked the unions was by drawing attention to the violence that broke out periodically. The press specifically used confrontations between police and picketers to focus on union violence. In all, the police arrested nearly 1,000 picketers (Alexander 2002). In doing so, the Review-Journal and Sun portrayed the unions as hurting the city's reputation and scaring off tourists. Tourists reported harassment by picketers who they said banged on cars, spit at guests, and hurled profanities (Cornett, Russell, and Pattee 1984).

While the Review-Journal described the first day as peaceful (Glisch 1984, "LV culinary"), only noting that strikers prevented workers from entering hotels, the Sun claimed that violence began immediately (Hyman 1984, "Flashes"), citing acts of vandalism. Incidents the second day resulted in arrests. When picketers tried to enter the Las Vegas Hilton, security guards and the Las Vegas Police stopped them, with both sides using force. Police arrested 19 strikers and charged several union leaders with inciting a riot. They arrested another seven strikers in a separate incident for swinging clubs at passing cars (Glisch and Harrison 1984, "Union leaders"; Levin, Peters, and Hyman 1984). After a while, the papers noted that the strikers became less confrontational toward resort employees, guests, and taxi drivers (Pattee 1984, "Teamsters support"). The peace only lasted for a week though, with the violent confrontations picking up again (Evensen 1984, "Cops haul").

The papers also highlighted more serious threats. One striker was arrested outside the Showboat Hotel with lightbulbs filled with flammable liquid (Gisch and Harrison 1984, "Picket line"; Peter 1984, "Metro"). Both reported that bomb threats became a tactic some strikers used to shut down hotels temporarily (Glisch and Evensen 1984, "Strikers receive"; Hyman 1984, "Pickets thin"). Even more so than confrontations with police, these types of reports had the potential to turn public opinion against the strikers due to the fear that there could be a loss of life.

Some articles did offer the unions sympathy by focusing on statements by strikers accusing the police of brutality and provoking violence in confrontations with strikers (Gisch and Harrison 1984, "Picket line"; Levin, Peters, and Hyman, "Restraints"). According to union officials, the police worked in collaboration with the resort owners to prevent picketers from exercising their right to strike. They claimed that the police arrested picketers without cause and strip-searched female strikers (Glisch 1984, "Culinary, NRA"). However, the Review-Journal also published an editorial accusing the unions of staging such violent confrontations with police for publicity ("The damages" 1984).

A final way in which the papers attacked the unions was by drawing attention to both opposition and indifference to the strike. By 1980, Las Vegas was attracting middle- and upper-middle-class professionals and retirees who were not connected directly to the tourism industry (Moehring 2014). The Review-Journal published a University of Nevada, Las Vegas poll showing that residents largely opposed the strike (Standerfer 1984, "Las Vegas"). Additionally, the paper noted that national media attention had waned since the first few days of the strike. Only CNN continued to report on it regularly (Harrison 1984). In these ways, the papers asserted that the unions were failing in the court of public opinion and largely were not even being heard outside of Las Vegas.

A specific issue that turned public opinion against the unions was that the police department exhausted its overtime pay fund and threatened that it would need to make cutbacks in other areas if the strike continued (Pattee 1984, "Police overtime"; Levin 1984, "9 arrested"). The risk that the strike would prove detrimental to public safety was a strong anti-union angle for the press. It made it seem as though the unions were recklessly selfish. Ultimately, the police sought state funding to make up for the extra expenditures ("Police seeking" 1984; O'Driscoll 1984, "Metro").

Another issue that the Review-Journal used to try to turn public opinion against the strikers was the depletion of foodbank resources. The paper described how foodbanks had run out of food and money attempting to feed the additional families in need due to the strike (Standerfer 1984, "Strike strains"). The tone of the article implied that union selfishness had brought the foodbanks to this point and that union members were taking resources from families who had real financial need, not self-induced problems. Relatedly, the Sun emphasized that the hotels were giving jobs to people in need, thus performing a public service, noting that some hired to replace striking workers had been suffering from long-term unemployment (O'Driscoll and Riley 1984, "Unions question").

Emphasizing the social toll of the strike further, the Sun ran an article on the impact the strike had on union families (Coleman 1984). It noted that the financial strain families faced led some to lose custody of their children. This happened for several reasons. In some cases, stress led to child abuse. In other cases, the inability to afford basic necessities resulted in removal of children for neglect. Additionally, when families ended up homeless because they could not pay mortgages or rent, the children were removed from the situation. Though this article could be read as an indictment of corporate greed leading to family breakups, it could just as easily be interpreted as an indictment of striking workers refusing to give up on the union cause and finding a way to support their families.

Further suggesting that the unions failed to win supporters, many hotel guests were indifferent to the strike (Kraft 2010). Cecil Campell of Lansing, Michigan, stated, "I haven't been outside yet. The strike doesn't bother me" (Zamost 1984, "Gambling tourists"). The Sun noted that convention organizers also felt indifferent to the strike and claimed that they experienced no issues holding their conventions in Las Vegas ("Photo marketing" 1984). The Review-Journal pointed out that some guests did express disappointment that their vacations would not be all that they had hoped for, especially regarding show cancelations (Cornett, Russell, and Pattee 1984, "Resorts struggling"). Some tourists said that they had no intention of coming back after their bad experiences, connecting this issue with that of unions causing economic damage.

## Conclusion

The first break in the strike came when Baron Hilton backed out of the NRA agreement and negotiated a contract with the unions (Kraft 2010). A few other resorts followed suit (Cling,

Pattee, and Evensen 1984, "Hilton strikers" and "Caesars, Gaughan"; Peters 1984, "Strike may"), with 6,000 employees returning to work in early May (Kraft 2010). In June, the main strike finally ended. The unions and remaining resorts agreed on a five-year contract with a one-year wage freeze and a 26 percent increase over the remaining four years. Employers could ask certain employees to perform other job duties outside of their job description for three hours per day. Sympathy strikes could only take place after 90 days (Kraft 2010). The Musicians and Stagehands union lost out, however, with resorts gaining the right to use recorded music in specific situations and use traveling groups. This eliminated a sizable number of jobs (Kraft 2010). Overall, although the resort corporations attempted to destroy the Culinary Union in the 1984 strike, they failed, and the union came back stronger in the years following (Alexander 2002). In 1987, under new leadership, the Culinary Union began restrengthening (Alexander 2002).

Giving support to the casino resorts, the Las Vegas Review-Journal and Las Vegas Sun primarily covered the strike in ways that cast the unions in a bad light. While the various casino workers unions provided a middle-class lifestyle for tens of thousands of employees, union members and nonmembers alike, as well as their families, the two main papers in the city presented them as a threat to the city's economic well-being. As Martin points out, this was the direction the press had gone since the late 1960s as the post-industrial, neo-liberal economy solidified itself in the United States. If the press in any city might have gone in another direction though, it was Las Vegas. No other city was so dominated by a single industry that was so heavily unionized. Given the political views of the Sun's owner, expecting support in that venue may have been too much for unions to hope for. Yet, they did not receive favorable coverage from the Review-Journal either. Both papers chose to solidly back the resorts that provided advertising revenue, not even feigning neutrality for the sake of potentially avoiding alienating readers who were union members. A century-and-a-half before, covering labor unrest was an economic challenge for publishers balancing the interests of readers with advertisers. The 1984 Las Vegas casino workers strike suggests that challenge has faded into history.

## References

Alexander, C. 2002, "Rise to Power: The Recent History of the Culinary Union in Las Vegas," in *The Grit Beneath the Glitter: Tales from the Real Las Vegas*, Rothman, H.K. and Davis, M. (eds.), Berkeley: University of California Press.

Bernhardt, M. 2016, "Taking Sides in the 'Bloodless Croton War'": The Coverage of the Croton Aqueduct Strike and Labor's Relationship with the Penny Press," *New York History* 97: 1, pp. 9–33.

Borders, M. 1984, "LV Resorts Sue Over Boycott Letters," *Las Vegas Sun* 34: 326 (May 19), p. 1B.

Buchholz, M. and Thompson, S. 2008, "The Penny Press, 1833–1861," in *The Media in America*, Sloan, W.D. (ed.), Northport, AL: Vision Press.

Cling, C. 1984a, "AFL-CIO Vows Boycott of LV," *Las Vegas Review-Journal* 80: 8 (April 9), p. 1A and 4A.

Cling, C. 1984b, "LV Hotel Strike Puts Tourism on the Skids," *Las Vegas Review-Journal* 80: 14 (April 15), p.1B and 4B.

Cling, C. 1984c, "Strike Drags On: Hotels Eyeing Permanent Replacements," *Las Vegas Review-Journal* 80: 42 (May 14), p. 1A and 4A.

Cling, C. 1984d, "Vegas Poised for Hotel Strike," *Las Vegas Review-Journal* 79: 366 (April1), p. 1A and 4A.

Cling, C., Pattee, P. and Evensen, J. 1984a, "Caesars, Gaughan Accept Union Pact," *Las Vegas Review-Journal* 80: 33 (May5), p. 1A and 4A.

Cling, C., Pattee, P. and Evensen, J. 1984b, "Hilton Strikers Return to Work," *Las Vegas Review-Journal* 80: 32 (May4), p. 1A and 4A.

Coleman, J. 1984, "Strike Stress Overcrowds Child Haven," *Las Vegas Sun* 34: 340 (May 31), p. 1B.

Cornett, R. 1984a, "Hotel Exec: Corporations Strangling LV Economy," *Las Vegas Review-Journal* 80: 9 (April 10), p. 1B.

Cornett, R. 1984b, "N.Y. travel Agent Blasts Union Letter," *Las Vegas Review-Journal* 80: 4 (April 5), p. 1B.

Cornett, R. 1984c, "Resort Leaders Accept Union Challenge," *Las Vegas Review-Journal* 80: 9 (April 10), p. 1A.

Cornett, R., Russell, D. and Pattee, P. 1984, "Resorts Struggling Through Strike," *Las Vegas Review-Journal* 80: 3 (April 4), p. 1B.

Davis, M. 2002, "Class Struggle in Oz," in *The Grit Beneath the Glitter: Tales from the Real Las Vegas*, Rothman, H.K. and Davis, M. (eds.), Berkeley: University of California Press.

Diaz, J. 1984, "Casinos Blamed for Prolonging Strike," *Las Vegas Review-Journal* 80: 26 (April 27), p. 4A.

Evansen, J.D. 1984a, "Cesar Chavez Gives Boost to Strikers," *Las Vegas Review-Journal* 80: 13 (April 14), p.1B.

Evansen, J.D. 1984b, "Cops Haul in Strip Protestors," *Las Vegas Review-Journal* 80: 14 (April 15), p. 1A and 3A.

Evansen, J.D. 1984c, "Pacts Inked with Independent Hotels," *Las Vegas Review-Journal* 79: 366 (April 1), p. 1A.

Evansen, J.D. 1984d, "Police Stand Ready to Prevent Strike Mayhem," *Las Vegas Review-Journal* 79: 366 (April 1), p. 1B.

Glisch, J.J. 1984a, "Culinary, NRA Talk Unfruitful," *Las Vegas Review-Journal* 80: 13 (April 14), p. 2A.

Glisch, J.J. 1984b, "LV Culinary Workers Strike," *Las Vegas Review-Journal* 80: 1 (April 2), p. 1A and 4A.

Glisch, J.J. and Cling, C. 1984, "Resorts, Unions Set New Talks," *Las Vegas Review-Journal* 80: 18 (April 19), p. 1A and 4A.

Glisch, J.J, Cling C. and Harrison, C. 1984, "Culinary Workers Approve Contract," *Las Vegas Review-Journal* 80: 46 (May 18), p. 1A and 4A.

Glisch, J.J. and Evensen, J.D. 1984a, "Culinary Leader Urges 'Scabs' to Steal," *Las Vegas Review-Journal* 80: 53 (May 25), p. 1A and 4A.

Glisch, J.J. and Evensen, J.D. 1984b, "Strikers Receive Termination Notices," *Las Vegas Review-Journal* 80: 5 (April 6), p. 1A and 4A.

Glisch, J.J. and Harrison, C. 1984a, "Union Leaders Seek Probe of Confrontation," *Las Vegas Review-Journal* 80: 3 (April 4), p. 1A and 4A.

Glisch, J.J. and Harrison, C. 1984b, "Picket Line Battle Shifts to the Court," *Las Vegas Review-Journal* 80: 4 (April 5), p. 1A and 4A.

Goodwin, J.L. 2014, *Changing the Game: Women at Work in Las Vegas,1940–1990*, Reno: University of Nevada Press.

Greenspun, B. 1984, "Where I Stand: Las Vegas Is On Roll," *Las Vegas Sun* 34: 271 (April1), p. 1A and 2A.

Harrison, C. 1984, "National Media Coverage Wanes As Strike Wears On," *Las Vegas Review-Journal* 80: 15 (April 16), p. 1B.

Huntziker, W.E. 1999, *The Popular Press,1833–1865*, Westport, CN: Greenwood Press.

Hurley, J. 1984, "Hotel Suppliers See Fewer Orders," *Las Vegas Sun* 34: 276 (April 5), p. 2C.

Hyman, H. 1984a, "Flashes of Violence Mark First Day of Picketing," *Las Vegas Sun* 34: 273 (April 3), p. 1A and 4A.

Hyman, H. 1984b, "Pickets Thin Out After Restraining Order Issued," *Las Vegas Sun* 34: 278 (April 7), p. 1A and 2A.

Kraft, J.P. 2010, *Vegas at Odds: Labor Conflict in a Leisure Economy, 1960–1985*, Baltimore: Johns Hopkins University Press.

Levin, P. 1984a, "9 Arrested in Strike-Related Altercations," *Las Vegas Sun* 34: 283 (April 11), p. 1A and 4A.

Levin, P. 1984b, "LVCVA Begins Media Blitz as Teamsters Sign," *Las Vegas Sun* 34: 273 (April 3), p. 1A and 5A.

Levin, P., Peters, P. and Hyman, H. 1984, "Restraints on Pickets Denied," *Las Vegas Sun* 34: 275 (April 4), p.1B and 2B.

Maras, S. 2013, *Objectivity in Journalism*, Malden, MA: Polity Press.

Martin, C.R. 2019, *No Longer Newsworthy: How the Mainstream Media Abandoned the Working Class*, Ithaca: IRL Press.

Mindich, D.T.Z. 1998, *Just the Facts: How "Objectivity" Came to Define American Journalism*, New York: New York University Press.

Moehring, E.P. 2014, *Reno, Las Vegas, and the Strip: A Tale of Three Cities*, Reno: University of Nevada Press.

Morrison, J.A. and Cling, C. 1984, "Month-Long Strike Affects Business – for Better or Worse," *Las Vegas Review-Journal* 80: 34 (May 6), p. 1B and 2B.

O'Driscoll, M. 1984a, "Metro Will Ask State for Funds to Defray Strike Expenses," *Las Vegas Sun* 34: 293 (April 20), p. 1B.

O'Driscoll, M. 1984b, "Waitress Fights Against Pickets, Continues on Job," *Las Vegas Sun* 34: 300 (April 26), p. 1A.

O'Driscoll, M. and Riley, L. 1984, "Unions Question Resorts' 'Rosy' Outlook," *Las Vegas Sun* 34: 284 (April 12), p. 1A and 6A.

Pattee, P. 1984a, "Police Overtime Pay Running Low," *Las Vegas Review-Journal* 80: 17 (April 18), p. 4A.

Pattee, P. 1984b, "Teamsters Support Praised by Strikers," *Las Vegas Review-Journal* 80: 9 (April 10), p. 4A.

Peters, P. 1984a, "Food, Garbage Drivers Honor Picket Lines," *Las Vegas Sun* 34: 281 (April 10), p. 1B.

Peters, P. 1984b, "Metro Can Handle Pickets," *Las Vegas Sun* 34: 276 (April 5), p. 1A and 5A.

Peters, P. 1984c, "Midnight Sit-Down Stalls Strike," *Las Vegas Sun* 34: 272 (April 2), p. 1A and 4A.

Peters, P. 1984d, "Negotiators Try to Avert Strike Tonight," *Las Vegas Sun* 34: 271 (April1), p. 1A and 5A.

Peters, P. 1984e, "Strike may last through middle of May," *Las Vegas Sun* 34: 294 (April21), p.1A and 2A.

Peters, P. 1984f, "Strike News Hurting LV Economy," *Las Vegas Sun* 34: 273 (April 3), p. 1A and 4A.

"Photo Marketing Convention Begins," *Las Vegas Sun* 34: 276 (April 5), p. 2C.

"Police Seeking Reserve Funds for Strike Duties," *Las Vegas Review-Journal* 80: 52 (May 24), p. 8B.

Riley, L., O'Driscoll, M. and Levin, P. 1984, "Union Leaders Reject Latest Proposal," *Las Vegas Sun* 34: 286 (April 14), p. 1A and 2A.

Rothman, H.K. 1998, *Devil's Bargains: Tourism in the Twentieth-Century American West*, Laurence: University Press of Kansas.

Schiller, D. 1981, *Objectivity and the News: The Public and the Rise of Commercial Journalism*, Philadelphia: University of Pennsylvania Press.

Schwartz, D.G. 2003, *Suburban Xanadu: The Casino Resort on the Las Vegas Strip and Beyond*, New York: Routledge.

Standerfer, S. 1984a, "Las Vegas Residents Give Views on State of the City," *Las Vegas Review-Journal* 80: 14 (April 15), p. 1B and 3B.

Standerfer, S. 1984b, "Strike Strains Services," *Las Vegas Review-Journal* 80: 49 (May 21), p. 1B.

Stevens, J.D. 1991, *Sensationalism and the New York Press*, New York: Columbia University Press.

"The Damages Done Across the Country," *Las Vegas Review-Journal* 80: 4 (April 5), p. 4B.

Tucher, A. 1994, *Froth and Scum: Truth, Beauty, Goodness, and the Ax Murder in America's First Mass Medium*, Chapel Hill: University of North Carolina Press.

"Walkout Forces Demos to Move"1984, *Las Vegas Sun* 34: 273 (April 3), p. 2B.

Werner, L. and Cling, C. 1984, "Strike Negotiations Moving Slowly," *Las Vegas Review-Journal* 80: 29 (May 1), p. 1A and 4A.

Zamost, S. 1984a, "Gambling Tourists Not Bothered by LV Strike," *Las Vegas Sun* 34: 273 (April 3), p. 1B and 2B.

Zamost, S. 1984b, "NRA Proposals 'Unreasonable' – Circus Exec," *Las Vegas Sun* 34: 281 (April 10), p. 1A and 4A.

# 11
# THE COVER CURSE

*Sara Silver*

### Introduction and Definitions

Business journalists have a tough job. While money is sexy, numbers aren't. Novice reporters – many of whom never sought to cover business and shrink from math – are taught to tell human stories to draw in readers. Business magazines by the 1980s regularly humanized their offerings – and boosted online sales – by featuring a dynamic CEO on the cover. Celebrity CEOs, including Elon Musk of Tesla, SpaceX and Twitter, and Facebook and Meta founder Mark Zuckerberg, are clickbait for online media. As with all media, that portrayal often means taking a world of gray and rendering it dramatically in black and white.

"You needed to have a human in the story that you could either glorify or vilify on the basis of their performance," John A. Byrne, who wrote 58 cover stories for BusinessWeek magazine, said in an interview with this author (Byrne 2022). "By the time a business journalist recognizes that a CEO is successful, they are at the top of their careers. So for many … they're on their way down."

CEOs who flame out after being vaunted are deemed victims of "The Cover Curse." There is nothing supernatural about this. Indeed, academic research shows that The Cover Curse is real and is rooted in more than the misjudgments of individual journalists. Behavioral finance gives many reasons why celebrating CEOs – on covers, through awards, or online in echo chambers – dents their performance. This happens within months of being heralded in the press (Wade 2006).

This chapter examines The Cover Curse as it relates to CEOs celebrated in business media, whether on the cover, or through publications' awards such as Entrepreneur of the Year or Best Manager. Although the concept started with print magazines, the "Curse" has intensified in cable business news, online outlets and social media.

The Curse can work frighteningly quickly. Theranos founder Elizabeth Holmes appeared in her signature black turtleneck on the June 2014 cover of Fortune (Parloff) – followed by Forbes, Inc., and, with windswept hair, on The New York Times Style Magazine T. By October 2015, The Wall Street Journal revealed that her incredible claims to run dozens of medical tests on a few drops of blood were, in fact, not to be believed (Carreyrou).

DOI: 10.4324/9781003298977-14

Fortune magazine featured Enron founder and CEO Kenneth Lay on its January 10, 2001, cover as his company topped the list of the "100 best companies to work for." His successor Jeffrey Skilling was on the February 12, 2001, cover of BusinessWeek as "The Power Broker." By the end of that year, Enron was bankrupt.

"Whom the gods would destroy, they first put on the cover of BusinessWeek," wrote Nobel economist Paul Krugman that year (2001).

As this chapter shows, fundamental changes in media have intensified the pressure on journalists to make big calls and have made The Curse harder to avoid. Through the 1980s and 1990s, more people began to invest their retirement savings through 401(k)s or IRAs, expanding the audience for company news. A slew of TV shows on CNN, CNBC, Bloomberg and Fox Business all competed for scoops, while the internet allowed in new entrants Yahoo! Finance, TheStreet.com and Business Insider. Then social media spread the cult of the CEO, and the attendant Curse, to new, unmediated platforms, including Twitter and Substack.

All want to mirror the mood – what readers believe in that moment – and use a well-known individual to explain a complicated situation. "Journalism's goal is to be powerful and compelling, both as narrative and as truth-telling," Nicholas Lemann, former dean of Columbia Journalism School, said in an interview (Lemann 2022). When these goals conflict, "too often the narrative goal wins."

At worst, business media and CEOs engage in mutual endorsement in which certain outlets can celebrate their own prestige and access to interview celebrity executives, while gutted newsrooms struggle to critique the prevailing wisdom.

Is it fair to fault journalists, who have mostly not been trained to understand financials, for missing frauds that auditors and sophisticated investors missed? Probably not, but more journalists need to learn to read the numbers for themselves, and no longer depend on star Wall Street analysts, whose ranks have been gutted on much the same scale as newsrooms.

The book "24 Days: How Two Wall Street Journal Reporters Uncovered the Lies that Destroyed Faith in Corporate America" showed how quickly Enron Corp., whose platform enabled bets on future energy prices under deregulation, collapsed under the scrutiny of journalists who had the skill – and the editorial resources – to read financial statements.

The authors, Rebecca Smith and John R. Emshwiller, noted that hundreds of stories on the Houston-based energy trader had seemed rote "with the same anecdotes repeated over and over and the same quotations appearing from the same executives" (Smith and Emshwiller 2004 p. 34). Reporters had relied on Wall Street analysts, some earning $500,000 or more a year, to sift through the numbers, "yet they apparently weren't reading the financial statements very thoroughly" (p. 34).

"Business reporters bought too much of what CEOs said without verifying it," said Chris Roush, former dean of Quinnipiac University's School of Communications. "And that's because a lot of business journalists are not taught how to read financial statements and know where companies' money is coming from."

Indeed, journalists make little use of the most detailed reports that companies issue each year, the 10-Ks, in which management details their finances and risks.

There were plenty of mistakes, even at BusinessWeek, whose internal mantra was: "No story is ever 100 percent positive or 100 percent negative" (Weber 2022). "Oops!" lamented a BusinessWeek cover on November 5, 1984, that chronicled the failures of companies profiled in the book, "The Search for Excellence."

Often, business publications have gotten it right, as they did when focusing on executives who shaped our world, such as Jeff Bezos, Warren Buffett, Bill Gates or Steve Jobs.

During the dot-com boom, reporters gushed over companies worth billions on paper that had yet to make a single sale. The subsequent jailing of top executives from such darlings as Enron, WorldCom Inc. and Tyco International Ltd. soured many on the celebratory cover.

Since then, editors have worked even harder to ensure that positive features are balanced. "I felt editors always wanted to know: 'What's the weakness?'" said Terri Thompson, long-time director of the Knight-Bagehot Fellowship at Columbia Journalism School and a former BusinessWeek writer. "If I couldn't find one, they wouldn't print the story."

Even as business magazines pulled back from heralding, broadcast, online and especially social media still lionized companies and their CEOs. Fearful, perhaps, of courting The Curse, some CEOs have declined to appear on likely laudatory covers. The ill fate of some who appeared on the cover of The Globe and Mail's "Report on Business" magazine led others by the early 2000s to decline politely, in true Canadian spirit. One worried that "hogging the spotlight" might jeopardize a deal in the works; another felt he was too new in the job "to be seen to be grandstanding," and the CEO of a large retailer said he didn't want to invoke "the curse of the Report on Business cover" (Salewicz 2009).

Former Fortune Staff Writer Cora Daniels recalls the reluctance of candidates for "The 50 Most Powerful Black Executives in America" to be interviewed and photographed as they didn't want to be known as "black executives." When the story was published in 2002, Dick Parsons was the CEO of AOL Time Warner, Ken Chennault was the CEO and Chairman at Amex, and Stan O'Neal was the COO of Merrill Lynch, in line for the top job.

"It was part of why the article needed to be written," Daniels said in a 2023 interview. "It was the racism that permeated every single pore." You had folks who were CEOs asking, "Who else are you going to talk to?"

Beyond balance, journalists need to understand their potential as kingmakers, the consequences of cheerleading and the risks of hype. More need to learn to analyze financial disclosures, to keep companies honest, to offer readers a more complex view of successful companies, and to avoid playing into a self-reinforcing loop.

This chapter reviews the many explanations that have been offered for the persistence of The Curse.

## Historical Perspectives

Magazines long used senior business figures to attract the attention of readers on the newsstand. Alfred P. Sloan, the legendary CEO of General Motors, became the first chief executive to appear on Time Magazine's cover on December 27, 1926.

Still, most business magazines used actual art – abstracts, landscapes, high-design – as cover art through the 1950s. CEOs began to appear on covers in the 1960s.

As businesses took a more prominent role in society, CEOs grew into celebrities. For many, the first was Lee Iacocca, famed for turning around Chrysler in the late 1970s. New stars followed: "Neutron Jack" Welch of General Electric Co., Robert Goizueta of The Coca-Cola Co., Bill Gates of Microsoft Corp., John Chambers of Cisco Systems Inc., Steve Jobs of Apple Inc., Meg Whitman of eBay Inc., Jeff Bezos of Amazon.com Inc., Mark Zuckerberg, founder of Facebook, and Elon Musk of Tesla Inc., Twitter/X and SpaceX (Space Exploration Technologies Corp.).

The urge to read about CEOs combined an interest in celebrities with a need to understand the factors that shape our society and our lives (Lovelace 2018).

Like sports and gaming, journalism uses narratives "to get content sutured to the human consciousness," Columbia's Lemann said. But "to get the public that wants to be informed, you have to traffic in these heroes and villains and that pushes you away from understanding what's going on in the world."

CEOs seemed more exciting as they grew more powerful in the 1970s. Back in 1961, CEOs were paid 21 times as much their average employee (Mishel and Kandra 2021). That multiple had risen to 61 by 1989, and by 2020 it reached 351. From 1978 to 2020, CEO pay grew by 1,322 percent. This outstripped growth in the economy or the S&P 500, which grew 817 percent, according to realized compensation data from Bloomberg.

A broader shift in capitalism brought waves of layoffs due to foreign competition, automation and cost-cutting, which took hold in earnest under President Ronald Reagan. This generated keen interest in global business and how it affected one's pocketbook.

CEO retirement benefits ballooned, often at the cost of worker pensions (Schultz 2011). Companies stopped offering defined-benefit pensions, which guaranteed a certain payout to retirees, and moved to defined-contribution savings plans in which the employee assumed all the risk. This meant anyone with a 401(k) or an Individual Retirement Account suddenly needed investment skills.

As outlets aimed to satisfy this demand, they found readers now wanted an opinion, or a clear take on which stocks they should invest in. Journalists generally lacked the qualifications needed to examine company accounts and were always at risk of being manipulated by Wall Street analysts, but they still tried to satisfy the demand for clear investment takes.

Beyond magazines and The Wall Street Journal, the rise of new media intensified the focus on personalities. "Wall $treet Week," with Louis Rukeyser on PBS, created the genre of TV business shows in 1970, to be followed by dozens of news broadcasts devoted to money and investment. Television needs pictures, and is often based around interviews, so the emphasis on personalities intensified. With the sound turned down, some business shows could be confused with pre-game sports analysis, in which gesticulating men in suits in parse team strategy to pick winners and losers.

In 1989, the trends merged as "Neutron" Jack Welch of GE, the brightest star CEO of his era, bought a news start-up and dedicated it to covering the stock market. It became the CNBC cable network. In the late 1990s, the internet brought social media, initially in the form of Yahoo! chat rooms, and a proliferation of new providers who could handle business developments far faster. Costs of entry dropped; even a humble blogger could become an influential pundit.

Newspapers in the 1990s more than doubled the space dedicated to business news, from 7 percent to 15 percent (Simons 1999). Much of it was devoted to lists of the largest companies and richest investors, including telecom and tech evangelists heralding a new age. And they could all now write about the new heroes, 20-something dot-com multimillionaires, and students, retirees and truck drivers using new technology to make fortunes day trading.

A 20-year study of coverage through 2002 deemed 26 percent of BusinessWeek's cover stories "negative," more critical than those of Forbes (14 percent) or Fortune (8 percent). Fortune was the sunniest, with 77 percent of the covers deemed "positive," more than the 69 percent at Forbes and the 59 percent at BusinessWeek (Arnold 2007).

Whatever the take, most of those CEOs were white men. Black reporters at Fortune struggled to get representation on the covers.

It took a lot of persuasion for the Black list to make the cover, even though Fortune had showcased an annual Women's List since 1998. "The mold for business journalism at that time was 'The Great White Hope,' saving companies, turning them around," Daniels said. Stories that didn't fit the mold required demonstrating to editors that they would interest the magazine's audience.

Stan O'Neal appeared on Fortune's July 22, 2002 cover, months before he was promoted to CEO and oversaw the foray into subprime mortgage debt and other multibillion-dollar errors that led to the firm's demise and eventual sale to Bank of America.

Business journalists themselves became celebrities, such as CNBC's Maria Bartiromo, known as the Money Honey. Dave Kansas, recruited from The Wall Street Journal by the CNBC personality Jim Cramer to edit TheStreet.com, became a multimillionaire on paper from chronicling tech multimillionaires. Much of this wealth evaporated with the dot-com crash of 2000.

The collapse of the dot-com bubble made the cover jinx apparent. Sometimes, a business model stopped working; sometimes, the CEOs were revealed as frauds. Their success stories really had been too good to be true. "Top executives and shrewd investors are good bets to emerge as media heroes, unless or until they appear headed for prison," wrote Norman Solomon (2002).

A notorious example was Bernard Ebbers, a high school basketball coach who built a Mississippi reseller of phone calls into the second-largest U.S. long-distance company. The company, WorldCom, completed dozens of acquisitions, including the $37 billion purchase of MCI in 1997. Ebbers was hailed as the "Telecom Cowboy" on the cover of BusinessWeek before a whistleblower revealed accounting tricks that had inflated profits by $11 billion.

In the wake of these disasters, financial coverage grew more skeptical, a process that accelerated with the Global Financial Crisis of 2008. Business magazines edged away from laudatory covers, in favor of warnings and criticism.

Media had another problem. They grew more skeptical of business after 2008, but also found a collapse in advertising. Newspapers, among the main sources of news gathering, saw their revenue drop from $60 billion in 2006 to less than $20 billion in 2020, and shed 60 percent of their employees, with employment dropping from 74,000 in 2006 to 31,000 in 2020, according to the Pew Research Center (2021).

This critically hampered publications' ability to fund deep reporting and financial analysis to counteract companies' PR machines. "Hollowing out newsrooms gave us the ability to create science fiction in the corporate space," said Peter Atwater (Atwater 2022), whose 2012 book "Moods and Markets" explores confidence-based decision-making.

Journalists still need a good story. A group of scholars led by Jeffrey B. Lovelace at the University of Virginia found that the press had moved from celebrating successful CEOs to those that embody dramatic archetypes: creators of innovations, transformers who steer their firms from problems, rebels who veer from established norms and saviors who rescue failing companies (2018).

"Unicorns," start-ups worth $1 billion or more before going public, made myth-making easier. They present compelling stories without public disclosures to check the facts.

Witness Sam Bankman-Fried, who made the cover of the 2021 Forbes 400 a year before his crypto exchange FTX, filed for bankruptcy. Fortune's cover featured his black ringlets and youthful cheeks over the question: "The Next Warren Buffett?" just months before his co-founders said Bankman-Fried had been channeling customers' money to a sister trading firm, prompting many to ask if he was actually the next Bernie Madoff. The writer of the Fortune cover later said he wished he'd "pushed harder for the documents. I asked but didn't insist on them" (Klein 2022).

To be sure, the crypto whiz became a media darling who fooled plenty of sophisticated investors who poured $2 billion into FTX, which had pitched a take-it-or-leave-it opportunity. During a video call with Sequoia Partners, one partner effused in the chat: "I LOVE THIS FOUNDER" (Griffith and Yaffee-Bellany 2022).

Or take Theranos' Elizabeth Holmes – who appeared on the covers of Forbes, Fortune, Inc. Bloomberg Businessweek and even Glamour and was subject of a New Yorker profile – before her blood-testing company imploded. The Fortune profile cover story, "This CEO's out for blood," repeated Holmes' claims about the accuracy and cost of the tests as a fact, without the journalistic conventions of inserting "said" or "claimed." In 2022, she was convicted on four charges of fraud.

WeWork's Adam Neumann became the Emperor with No Clothes when he tried to take his company public, only to reveal billions in losses previously hidden.

All three built their companies away from the scrutiny of public markets and sold compelling stories – the son of Stanford law professors whose crypto-wealth would fund "effective altruism," the Stanford drop-out whose great idea came from a fear of needles and the sight of blood, and the kibbutznik who revolutionized the world of office space.

Atwater compares celebrity CEOs to circus barkers trying to sustain a crowd. Another example is Elon Musk, who through his Tweets and his melodramatic purchase of Twitter makes the celebrity surreal. "At some point, the two-headed lady has 13 heads and the obscenity is glaringly obvious," he said. "The danger is that in order to sustain the crowd, the act has to get more and more ridiculous."

## Critical Issues

Journalists face practical obstacles to treating CEOs with the skepticism they deserve. Beyond the lag between spotting a story and bringing it to fruition, it's a lot easier to write a positive piece about a celebrity CEO than a negative one. Editors challenge negative stories more and send them to be vetted by lawyers, making the bar harder to clear.

"It requires proof and courage, and it goes through a series of hurdles, editors and lawyers, that make a journalist less productive," said Byrne, who went on to edit Fast Company (2022). "When you're looking for positive pieces, you're shooting fish in a barrel. It's a challenge to find, in the sea of journalism, the negative pieces that broke ground."

While challenging, Byrne counts important negative stories among his BusinessWeek covers. He took on "Chainsaw Al" Dunlap, the notorious asset-stripper whose mass layoffs boosted profits at Scott Paper and Sunbeam, until massive fraud was discovered (Byrne 1998) and criticized how John Chambers of Cisco Systems Inc. accounted for acquisitions (Byrne and Elgin 2002).

Forbes Magazine, where he also worked, took pride in finding companies on the way down, by vetting reported revenues and earnings for signs of financial manipulation, or spotting companies whose debt had juiced returns in the short-term, but risked a later fall. Forbes promoted the idea "that it's of no value to recognize a successful company at its high. You need it when it's poised to break through," Byrne said.

This is undeniably true – but few business reporters are trained to do this. There are now many fewer business reporters than public relations staffers, and they are often paid less (Roush 2022). CEOs are increasingly belligerent toward the press, often bypassing it (Roush, pp. 64–65) to get their message out.

The dynamic is akin to the internet's impact on the music industry, where the ability to upload their own work enabled more musicians to find an audience without the intermediary of a record label. But it limited labels' budgets, leading them to focus their recording and marketing dollars on sure bets. Top 40 radio stations now concentrate on a narrower range of stars and sound more like the Top 25.

Another factor channeling attention is search engine optimization (SEO). As print publications aimed to increase their online audience, reporters learned that including certain keywords would drive traffic to their stories. As a reporter covering the cellphone maker Motorola Inc. for The Wall Street Journal in the late 2000s, this writer learned that including the word "iPhone" in any story would multiply the number of readers. Names such as Musk and Jamie Dimon, longtime CEO of J.P. Morgan, have a similar effect, so journalists have an incentive to write more about them.

Among Byrne's best-known BusinessWeek covers is "Jack," on Jack Welch, whom Fortune magazine would name "Manager of the Century." He turned GE into the world's most valuable corporation through ruthless layoffs, outsourcing, offshoring, acquisitions and a shift from manufacturing to finance. Dozens of Welch's trainees took his aggressive management style to corporations they led.

That focus on market returns may have made sense for an audience of investors. But even some of them are now re-evaluating Welch's legacy, saying that his success at GE became a model for an unsustainable economy and polarized politics. "Wages stagnated and jobs moved overseas. CEO pay went stratospheric and buybacks and dividends boomed. Factories closed and companies found ways to pay fewer taxes" (Gelles 2022). After he retired, Welch became an internet "troll" and GE later settled with the Securities Exchange Commission on charges of longstanding accounting fraud. Welch died on March 1, 2020.

The critical question becomes whether the creation of CEO cover stars does damage. We know it is correlated with subsequent poor performance; does it cause this to happen?

## Current Contributions and Research

Much of the academic research about the decline in performance of celebrated CEOs has focused on their companies' stock after they appeared on covers, won awards or garnered praise in print. This section reviews the literature and the role of the press in "kingmaking."

A 2007 study found that troubled companies had hit bottom – and that outperformers had reached their peak – by the time their strength or weakness became the subject of cover features (Albert, Earl and North 2007). The University of Richmond, Virginia, academics found that companies' appearance on the covers of BusinessWeek, Fortune and Forbes for the 20 years ending in 2002 signaled the end of their exceptional performance, whether good or bad. The signal, however, was weaker for negative cover stories, and not strong enough to support a contrarian investment strategy.

Stephen L. Baker, a BusinessWeek writer for 23 years, noted how long it takes to put together a solid story.

> But by the time we've marshalled our evidence and put together our product, the actors in the drama – from investors to competitors (inside the company and out), are

already responding to the conditions we've been busy documenting. Their responses bring the period of "extreme" behavior to an end.

*(2007)*

Other studies suggest that it is the limelight itself, rather than a lag in identifying and reporting trends, that depresses performance.

A 2006 paper, "The Burden of Celebrity: The Impact of CEO Certification Contests on CEO Pay and Performance," found that chief executives' performance dropped within months of being named CEO of the Year. Firms with medal-winning CEOs had lower market returns than firms with non-medal winners at the helm (Wade et al. 2006).

The dot-com boom created new competition for top CEOs and, in the process, superstars who command a greater share of attention and income, according to Ulrike Malmendier of University of California Berkeley and Geoffrey A. Tate of the University of Maryland. Their paper "Superstar CEOs" studies the intersection of fame and marketing: "CEOs have become the faces of their corporations, starring in ad campaigns, courting regular media coverage, and making cameo appearances on prime-time television shows," such as Bill Gates in "Frasier" and Lee Iacocca in "Miami Vice" (2009, p. 1593).

The experts in behavioral finance examined 250 CEOs who had won awards between 1975 and 2002 such as Best Entrepreneur or CEO of the Year from 10 publications and organizations. They then matched each winner to a similar but uncelebrated peer, in effect creating a control group with another 250 CEOs. They found that fame proved a crucial distraction, lowering superstars' performance by 15 percent to 26 percent and denting the returns of shareholders in the three years after their award. The non-winners' performance declined much less, showing winners' drop was not a mere reversion to the mean.

They found award winners spent more time writing books and memoirs. Andrew Grove of Intel – featured on the covers of BusinessWeek, Forbes and Fortune and Time magazine's Man of the Year for 1997 – wrote three books during the time studied. Star CEOs were also more likely to sit on five or more other corporate boards, a level of outside commitment that irks governance experts. They also engaged in more earnings management to boost near-term results, especially in firms with weak corporate governance. And they had a lower golf handicap, implying more time on the fairway than their uncelebrated peers.

Media awards created a "tournament," enabling star CEOs to demand greater compensation – an average of $7.8 million more in stock options than their matched peers, and a boost not shared by other executives at the same firm.

The authors say that the media "play a causal role in fostering a celebrity culture" (p. 1597) among CEOs who then revel in their role as TV pundits and their jet-set lifestyle: "By increasing CEO status, the media enable CEOs to take actions that destroy value" (p. 1598).

Management experts have documented this process. "The truth is, people do get distracted. You can almost see them start to grow weary of the business and thrilled with the adulation," said Jeffrey Sonnenfeld, who founded the Yale School of Management's Chief Executive Leadership Institute, in an interview with Forbes (Linden 2005).

Miller and Xu (2016) compared CEOs featured as successes on the covers of prominent business magazines and found that, overall, they failed to sustain performance. "Readers would be wise to remember that journalists tend to capture subjects when they do something exceptional, a pursuit that is difficult to sustain" (p. 295). That exceptional achievement often comes from higher risk.

Mergers and acquisitions gain attention for CEOs, and overconfident CEOs tend to overpay for assets. Celebrity feeds hubris and leads CEOs into mergers that destroy value because they overestimate the cost savings the combinations can achieve. In a 2008 study, behavioral finance experts Malmendier and Tate compare the CEOs portrayed in the press as "confident" or "optimistic" to those characterized as "frugal," "prudent" or "conservative" and find that the press overinflates egos.

BusinessWeek itself tackled the issue of hubris in an April 1, 1991, cover story called "CEO Disease" that explored how the job goes to one's head.

> Symptoms are all too familiar: The boss doesn't seem to understand the business anymore. Decisions come slowly, only to be abruptly changed. He (there are only two women in the BusinessWeek 1,000) feels he can do no wrong and refuses to concede any mistake.
>
> *(Byrne et al, 1991 p. 52)*

A further issue is that once a CEO has been widely lauded for a particular approach, they face pressure to "stay true to type." This hinders their ability to shift gears when needed and dents firm performance (Lovelace 2018).

For example, Ginni Rometty, the first woman to lead International Business Machines Corp., gained persistent praise for wringing profit from a shrinking IBM. She appeared on the covers of Bloomberg Businessweek (the successor to BusinessWeek), Fortune ("Can IBM ever be cool?" Cover of 50 Most Powerful Women) and with Jamie Dimon and Alex Gorsky (Change the World Issue: "Profits and Purpose: Can Big Business have it all?") and Barron's ("IBM's Vision. Naysayers are ganging up on Ginni Rometty. They are right that it's not easy for a 103-year-old company to remain nimble. But we think her plan will work. Here's why.").

Rometty's compensation grew to $33 million per year, as IBM repeatedly laid off, outsourced and invested in acquisitions rather than research. Revenues fell in every quarter of her tenure. She lapped the track in a 2023 memoir "Good Power: Leading Positive Change in Our Lives, Work, and World."

A recent area of research covers CEOs' efforts to attain celebrity by making themselves available to reporters. (Bankman-Fried of FTX was still answering reporters' inquiries even after his arrest.)

Lovelace et al. (2022) examine a swath of media – including newspaper, online, and social media – and find that CEOs "push" themselves into the limelight, with little regard to their actual performance, and that journalists "pull" into view the stories of atypical CEOs who embody dramatic archetypes – the creator or innovator, the rebel, the transformer and the savior. Under-resourced journalists are more likely to focus on CEOs who are already famous than those whose rising fortunes might help readers invest their retirement funds better. Since journalists get story ideas from colleagues and competitors at other outlets, this increases the echo chamber of celebrity.

## Recommendations for Practice

Business journalists need to know how to analyze financial disclosures to hold power to account. It's the basis for our skepticism and the first line of defense against the PR machinery lionizing corporate clients. It also makes it easier to stop glorifying CEOs just because someone else has. Reporters should seek safety in the corporate numbers, not in the numbers of other journalists providing cover. The press also often keeps its focus on certain executives far too long. Celebrity fund manager Cathie Wood, whose Arkk investment fund gained some 380 percent in less than a year after the COVID shutdown of March 2020 still gets huge interest from the press even after Arkk gave up all of those gains.

Numbers can break the "he said, she said" mold. When Elon Musk offered to buy Twitter in April 2022, for example, the media rushed to speculate about how he would change Twitter, rather than questioning whether Musk was serious. At the time, his electric vehicle company Tesla, whose stock he sold to finance the purchase, was worth more than every other automaker combined. Its shares dropped by half by the end of the year, accentuating the impression that the bid had been a ruse to let him sell stock while the price was high.

Obviously, it takes time and space to do this kind of analysis, and reporters have ever more demands as their ranks shrink.

Comedy news opens new space for this kind of reporting, by making it more fun to digest bad news, and by using executives' and politicians' own words caught on tape plus unflattering photos, to undercut the mythology. Examples include John Oliver's takedown of coal magnate Bob Murray and Hasan Minhaj's slashing of Turbotax and its former, CEO Bob Smith, for tricking customers into paying to file taxes that it promises can be done for free.

One other way is to ask if something would be news if it were about a less famous figure. For example, would a story mentioning Jamie Dimon, the famous CEO of JPMorgan, be as newsworthy if the name Robert Corbat, a successful CEO of Citigroup, were substituted? If not, why is it such a great story?

Journalists need to be conscious that they can make people famous. But even if their colleagues have made some CEO famous, that's no reason to treat stories about that CEO on anything other than the merits.

# References

Arnold, T., Earl, J. and North, D. (2007) "Are Cover Stories Effective Contrarian Indicators?" *Financial Analysts Journal*, 63(2), pp. 70–75. https://www.tandfonline.com/doi/abs/10.2469/faj.v63.n2.4520 [Accessed October 10, 2021]

Baker, S. (2007) "The Cover Curse: Explained," *Bloomberg.com*, July 20. https://www.bloomberg.com/news/articles/2005-04-24/businessweek-cover-curse [Accessed: November 20, 2021]

Byrne, J. (1998) "How Al Dunlap Self-Destructed," *BusinessWeek*, July 6, pp. 58–65.

Byrne, J. and Elgin, B. (2002) "Cisco Behind the Hype," *BusinessWeek*, January 21, pp. 54–61.

Byrne, J., Symonds, W. and Siler, H. (1991) "CEO Disease," *BusinessWeek*, April 1, p. 52.

Gelles, D. (2022) "How Jack Welch's Reign at G.E. Gave us Elon Musk's Twitter Feed," *The New York Times*, May 21. https://www.nytimes.com/2022/05/21/business/jack-welch-ge-ceo-behavior.html

Griffith, E. and Yaffee-Bellany, D. (2022) "Investors Who Put $2 Billion into FTX Face Scrutiny, Too," *The New York Times*, November 11. https://www.nytimes.com/2022/11/11/technology/ftx-investors-venture-capital.html

Klein, C. (2022) "A Sam Bankman-Friend Media Reckoning Is Underway," *Vanity Fair*, November 11. https://www.vanityfair.com/news/2022/11/a-sam-bankman-fried-media-reckoning-is-underway [Accessed December 20, 2022]

Krugman, P. (2001). "Reckonings; Enron Goes Overboard," *The New York Times*, August 17. Section A, Page 19. https://www.nytimes.com/2001/08/17/opinion/reckonings-enron-goes-overboard.html

Linden, D.W. (2005) "Cancel That Cover Shoot," *Forbes*, 175(2), p. 60. https://search-ebscohost-com.ezproxy.cul.columbia.edu/login.aspx?direct=true&AuthType=ip&db=bth&AN=15723324&site=bsi-live (Accessed September 3, 2022)

Lovelace, J. *et al.* (2018) "The Shackles of CEO Celebrity: Sociocognitive and Behavioral Role Constraints on 'Star' Leaders," *Academy of Management Review*, 43(3), pp. 419–444. https://doi.org/10.5465/amr

Lovelace, J. *et al.* (2022) "The Push and Pull of Attaining CEO Celebrity: A Media Routines Perspective," *Academy of Management Journal*, 65(4), pp. 1169–1191. doi:.5465/amj.2020.0435.4

Malmendier, U. and Tate, G. (2008) "Who Makes Acquisitions? CEO Overconfidence and the Market's Reaction," *Journal of Financial Economics*, 89(1), July 2008, pp. 20–43. https://www.sciencedirect.com/science/article/abs/pii/S0304405X08000251

Malmendier, U. and Tate, G. (2009) "Superstar CEOs," *The Quarterly Journal of Economics*, 124(4), November 2009, pp. 1593–1638. https://doi.org/10.1162/qjec.2009.124.4.1593

Miller, D., & Xu, X. (2016) "A Fleeting Glory: Self-Serving Behavior Among Celebrated MBA CEOs," *Journal of Management Inquiry*, 25(3), pp. 286–300. https://doi.org/10.1177/1056492615607975

Mishel, L. and Kandra, J (2021). "CEO Pay Has Skyrocketed 1,322% Since 1978," *Economic Policy Institute*, August 10. https://www.epi.org/publication/ceo-pay-in-2020/ [Accessed July 20, 2022]

Parloff, R. (2014) "This CEO's Out for Blood," *Fortune*, June 12. https://fortune.com/2014/06/12/theranos-blood-holmes/ [Accessed December 29, 2022]

Pew Research Center. (2021) "Newspapers Fact Sheet," June 29. https://www.pewresearch.org/journalism/fact-sheet/newspapers/

Roush, C. (2022) *The future of business journalism: Why it matters for Wall Street and main street.* Washington, DC: Georgetown University Press.

Salewicz, G. (2009) "The Curse of the Cover," *The Globe and Mail*, April 24. https://www.proquest.com/docview/194512908?accountid=10226&parentSessionId=yWhgOKOVa07T2XdywkzpPIcW3BPD%2BHLB%2BXr2tKomqa0%3D [Accessed September 1, 2022]

Schultz, E. (2011) *Retirement heist: How companies plunder and profit from the nest eggs of American workers.* New York: Penguin.

Simons, L. (1999) "Follow the Money," *American Journalism Review*, November, p. 56.

Smith, R. and Emshwiller, J. (2004) *24 days: How two Wall Street Journal reporters uncovered the lies that destroyed faith in corporate America.* New York: HarperBusiness.

Solomon, N. (2002) "Money Makes Headlines in Today's News Coverage," *Neiman.org.* https://nieman.harvard.edu/articles/money-makes-headlines-in-todays-news-coverage/ (Accessed June 10, 2022)

Wade, J. et al. (2006) "The Burden of Celebrity: the Impact of CEO Certification Contests on CEO Pay and Performance," *Academy of Management Journal*, 49(4), pp. 643–660. https://doi.org/10.5465/amj.2006.22083021

YouGov poll, taken second quarter of 2022. https://today.yougov.com/topics/economy/explore/public_figure/Elon_Musk

## *Interviews*

Atwater, P. (2022) Interviewed by author on August 29.

Byrne, J. (2022) Interviewed by author on June 30.

Roush, C. (2022) Interviewed by author on September 1.

Thompson, T. (2022) Interviewed by author on September 9.

Lemann, N. (2022) Interviewed by author on September 11.

Weber, J. (2022) Interviewed by author on June 28.

# 12

# THE "BIG THREE" (FORTUNE, FORBES, AND BUSINESSWEEK)

## A Study in Competition

*Alan Deutschman*

## Introduction

For the eight decades from 1930s to the early 2000s, the American market for business magazines was dominated by the "Big Three" of Fortune, Forbes, and BusinessWeek (which was founded as The Business Week and changed its name to Business Week, to Business-Week and ultimately to Bloomberg Businessweek (Coy et al. 2019)). A study of their long and lucrative reign reveals the factors that can sustain oligopolistic competition. Each title differentiated itself through its primary subject matter as well as its dominant editorial voice. Forbes focused on investing, Fortune on corporate management, and BusinessWeek on news. Forbes' voice was frequently acerbic, while Fortune's was literary, even Olympian, and BusinessWeek's was strictly factual rather than flashy. While this differentiation helped segment the market, the editors of the Big Three readily copied whatever innovations proved particularly successful at their rivals, such as when the popularity of the Fortune 500 ranking of America's biggest companies inspired the Forbes 400 listing of the wealthiest American citizens. And so, over time, the three magazines became similar in many important ways even while holding on to key elements that set apart their personalities.

The history of the Big Three is an intriguing case study of the dynamics of competition in the media business, and it shows the outsized influence of a small number of extraordinary individuals who shaped their field through the innovativeness of their thinking, the forcefulness of their personalities, and, in some cases, the longevity of their leadership: B.C. Forbes, Malcolm Forbes, and James Michaels at Forbes; Henry Luce, Ralph Ingersoll, and Archibald MacLeish at Fortune; and Stephen Shepard at BusinessWeek.

## Fortune

Henry Luce was raised in China as the son of Presbyterian missionaries from the northeastern United States. In 1922, at age 23, he co-founded Time, the weekly newsmagazine, together with Britton Hadden, who had been his college classmate and a fellow editor at the Yale Daily News. Time magazine quickly became a commercial success, but sharp tensions developed between the business partners, and by 1928 they communicated mainly through

DOI: 10.4324/9781003298977-15

intermediaries. Haddon ran the editorial side of Time. Luce oversaw the business aspects. Meanwhile Luce nurtured his own ideas for a new magazine about the drama, romance, and grandeur of the business world – a magazine where he could express his own creative vision. Haddon opposed the idea, arguing the Time still needed the full attention of both founders. But in September 1928, he let Luce assign two Time editorial staffers to work full-time developing the idea (Brinkley 2010, p. 148).

The new venture would likely have been blocked by Haddon's disapproval, but Haddon fell seriously ill, probably from a bacterial infection, in December 1928. On February 7, 1929, while Haddon was far too sick to make an assessment, Luce submitted his detailed and exceptionally ambitious vision for Fortune to the company's board of directors, beginning: "1. It will be as beautiful a magazine as exists in the United States. If possible, the undisputed most beautiful. 2. It will be authoritative to the last letter. 3. It will be brilliantly written…" (Elson 1968, pp. 128–130).

Haddon died from sepsis and heart failure on February 27. In May, the board gave Luce the go-ahead to launch Fortune. The immediate response from the publishing industry was eager interest: Luce's staff signed up 30,000 subscribers by November (Brinkley 2010, p. 153) and sold an impressive 763½ pages of advertising before the publication of the magazine's first issue in February 1930. To serve as Fortune's advertising manager, Luce tapped F. Du Sossoit Duke, who had played football for Dartmouth College and the New York Giants. Duke only hired salesmen who were at least six feet tall. Even more remarkably, he offered a money-back guarantee to advertisers if they weren't satisfied after six months. Only two very small advertisers later claimed their refunds (Elson 1968, p. 134).

At its launch, Fortune faced an entrenched competitor: World's Work, which had already been publishing for five decades, was a general-interest business magazine with a circulation of 100,000 and writing that aspired to high quality, even though the attitude toward business was relentlessly boosterish. While Luce was an ardent capitalist, and already a successful businessman himself, he said that Fortune would be "neither puffer or booster" but would "attempt to write critically, appraisingly…with unbridled curiosity." Luce's approach proved fortunate, since World's Work's unwavering optimism would seem badly outdated during the economic crisis of the 1930s, and the magazine stopped publishing in 1932 (Brinkley 2010, pp. 149–153).

Striving to make Fortune "brilliantly written," Luce confronted the challenge of finding poetic writers who could understand a subject matter that had been considered prosaic – and who also had a grasp of numbers. "There are men who can write poetry, and there are men who can read balance sheets," Luce said.

> The men who can read balance sheets cannot write. That, happily with some exceptions, is the general rule. Of necessity, we made the discovery that it is easier to turn poets into business journalists than to turn bookkeepers into writers.
>
> *(Elson 1968, p. 137)*

He meant this literally. For Fortune's writing staff, Luce recruited several distinguished poets, including Archibald MacLeish and Russell Davenport, who had both been writing verse while living in Paris. MacLeish went on to win the Pulitzer Prize for poetry in 1932 for his book-length poem, "Conquistador," which he finished while working full-time at the magazine (Elson 1968, pp. 137–138).

Luce also hired the brilliant Dwight Macdonald, a recent Yale graduate with great literary aspirations. After college, Macdonald had joined the executive training program at Macy's, the big New York retail establishment, with a plan "to make a lot of money rapidly and retire to write literary criticism," he said (Elson 1968, p. 139). He quickly soured on retail and joined the writing staff at Fortune, where Luce was recruiting young alumni of Ivy League colleges even though they lacked experience as professional journalists. Macdonald soon brought along his friend James Agee, an aspiring poet, novelist, and critic who also needed a way to make money.

Luce offered high salaries to writers, an especially strong draw after the 1929 stock market crash and the onset of the Great Depression (Brinkley 2010, p. 153). But Luce's literary men typically harbored left-wing political passions that would ultimately clash with Luce's own center-right Republicanism. When asked why he hired so many "Reds," Luce griped: "God-damn Republicans can't write" (Starkman 2014, p. 71). At that time, the leading newspaper of business, The Wall Street Journal, was hiring "timorous high-school graduates," wrote Dean Starkman in "The Watchdog That Didn't Bark," but "Fortune's staff was a cantankerous group of bohemians and intellectuals, mostly leftists" (Starkman 2014, p. 71).

In his quest to create America's "most beautiful" magazine, Luce commissioned cover art by some of the most celebrated painters of the era, including the Mexican muralist Diego Rivera and the French cubist Fernand Leger. Throughout the inside pages of the magazine, many stories were illustrated by original oil paintings. Luce also recruited the 25-year-old photographer Margaret Bourke-White, who wasn't yet well-known but had already shown an extraordinary talent with her starkly beautiful pictures of American industrial buildings. To showcase the full glory of all this remarkable art and photography, Fortune was printed on expensive paper with oversized dimensions that made it seem more like a coffee-table book than a typical magazine. And to pay for these exceptionally high production values, Fortune sold for one dollar an issue at a time when most magazines cost only a nickel or dime.

Fortune faced a crisis early on when its first managing editor, Parker Lloyd-Smith, killed himself by jumping naked from a hotel room in 1931, a tragedy that was "startling and unexplained," writes Columbia University historian Alan Brinkley. He was succeeded by Ralph Ingersoll, who had worked as a managing editor at the New Yorker magazine. Ingersoll wanted Fortune to be as much of a "writer's magazine" as the New Yorker, and he encouraged his staff to express not only their own literary voices and but also their progressive political outlooks in their stories (Brinkley 2010, pp. 160–161).

Fortune quickly became a commercial and creative success. Fortune "remained true to many of its initial goals," wrote Brinkley, 2010, in "The Publisher: Henry Luce and His American Century." "It was almost certainly…the most beautiful broad-circulation magazine in America." And by the mid-1930s, Brinkley, 2010, wrote, Fortune "was often strikingly iconoclastic in its approach to the capitalist world it had set out at first to celebrate" (Brinkley 2010, pp. 160–161).

One of Fortune's greatest contributions to the history of business journalism was its pioneering and mastery of the "long-form" business story – works of deep reporting presented with uncommon literary skill. From early on, Fortune developed as its signature format "the corporation story" – detailed profiles of individual companies or industries. Several would often appear in a single issue of the magazine. The field reporting for these stories was done by young women, who held the titles of "researcher" at the magazine and traveled around the country to conduct interviews and collect facts and figures. All of the writers and editors back at headquarters in New York were men. With a few notable exceptions, this would remain the case until the magazine's women organized and brought a class-action lawsuit in the 1970s.

The visits by Fortune's female reporters to headquarters presented two considerable challenges to a company's executives: First, they weren't used to divulging corporate financial information and other operating details to journalists. Second, they were unaccustomed to being around women as colleagues – and uncomfortable with being questioned by them. Fortune's "corporation stories," while often generally admiring in tone, could also be highly critical, and they looked not only at a company's financial performance but also at the working conditions of its factories and even the sociology of its workers' towns. Luce said:

> Fortune's crusading point was in effect this: 'God damn you, Mrs. Richbitch, we won't have you chittering archly and snobbishly about Bethlehem Common [stock] unless you damn well have a look at open hearths and slagpiles – yes, and the workers' houses of Bethlehem, Pa.'
>
> *(Brinkley 2010, p. 160)*

Despite being a staunch Republican, Henry Luce was initially enthusiastic about President Franklin Delano Roosevelt, whom he saw as a charismatic leader. Luce and MacLeish visited Roosevelt at the White House in late 1933 and conducted an off-the-record interview. "As we came down the stairs," MacLeish later recalled, "Harry grabbed me by the arm, stopped me, faced me and said, his face young and open as a boy's, 'What a man! What a man!'" (Elson 1968, p. 208).

Through the early 1930s, MacLeish and his fellow leftists turned Fortune into a remarkable document of the social history of the Great Depression. But by 1936, Luce had soured on FDR and the New Deal, which he thought had turned against capitalism. What's more, Fortune's advertisers complained about the magazine's anti-business tone. As the Spanish Civil War incited heated debates among Fortune's staffers, the editors struggled to tone down the writers' political passions. Meanwhile, the researchers, who had to fact-check the stories, were often caught in the crossfire. An anonymous poem, titled "The Fortune Researcher's Dilemma, or How Can A Girl Help Not Going Wrong," was published in Time Inc.'s Newspaper Guild union bulletin, with the lines: "The writers are left and the editors right ... the writers all say/I'm in Morgan's pay/And the editors say I'm in Stalin's" (Elson 1968, p. 319).

As Luce pushed to ensure that Fortune was solidly pro-capitalist, he began losing his star writers. MacLeish had been personally close to Luce, whose intelligence and curiosity he greatly admired, but Macdonald and Agee had remained uneasy about their bargain. In 1936, Macdonald resigned his position at Fortune. That same year, the magazine refused to publish Agee's long, poetic essay about poor white sharecroppers in Alabama. The story later gained literary fame when it was published in book form as "Let Us Now Praise Famous Men" along with its iconic photographs by Walker Evans (who worked as a writer and photographer for Fortune). In 1938, MacLeish left Fortune, too, "unhappy with the direction the magazine was taking and disappointed in Luce," wrote Brinkley. MacLeish became the curator of Harvard's Nieman Fellowships in journalism and then was recruited by FDR to serve as the Librarian of Congress (Brinkley 2010, pp. 163–164).

Despite these high-profile defections, Fortune remained a commercial success, reporting a profit of nearly $500,000 in 1937 (Roush 2006, p. 96). And even without its greatest literary lights, the magazine remained an important innovator and a product of unmatched quality. Starkman wrote that

> Even as it navigated a tamer course, Fortune represented a sharp departure from the business news that had preceded it, if for nothing else than its emphasis on original reporting, factual rigor, extensive use of surveys, close attention to narrative and story-telling, and experimentation with graphics, art, and photography. Just as important, it set a new standard in business reporting for maintaining critical distance and editorial independence from the institutions that it covered and their powerful leaders.
>
> *(Starkman 2014, p. 74)*

Henry Luce revisited his ideas about Fortune in the late 1940s. The magazine had enjoyed strong ad sales during World War II, profiting from America's industrial war machine, but sales fell off sharply when peace resumed. Fortune lost more than $600,000 in 1946 and 1947 combined, then lost $805,000 in 1948 alone. Its staff projected an even larger loss of $984,000 for 1949. So, in 1948, Luce cut the magazine's workforce as a cost-saving measure, often finding jobs elsewhere at Time Inc. for the displaced staffers. The result: Fortune returned to profitability by 1951 (Elson 1973, pp. 197, 262–263).

As part of Luce's rethinking of the magazine, Fortune produced a "Reprospectus" in 1948. While the magazine would remain a monthly with long-form stories and an oversized format to showcase art and photography, its editorial mission would include more coverage of topics such as labor, science, technology, and economics (Pendergast 1986, pp. 178–179).

While Luce continued to talk about Fortune's mission as promoting American capitalism, he was quietly committed to publishing the work of important intellectuals who were often quite critical of the system, such as Daniel Bell and John Kenneth Galbraith. A Fortune staff writer, William H. Whyte, wrote a series of stories that evolved into the influential book "The Organization Man" about the culture of conformity in American business. The result was that Fortune in the post-war era would publish "some of the most challenging and often contrarian views of capitalism to be found in journalism," wrote Alan Brinkley (Brinkley 2010, p. 327).

Fortune's formula worked well into the mid-1960s, but by then it was facing pressure from competition in the Big Three. "Fortune still stood in a class by itself in the depth of its reporting and lavishness of its presentation – an expensive magazine to produce, circulating to a relatively small audience and commanding premium advertising rates," wrote Curtis Pendergast in the third volume of "Time Inc.: The Intimate History of a Publishing Enterprise" (the company's authorized history).

> But it was being pressed hard. Not only was Business Week offering a larger circulation guarantee than Fortune's 330,000, but the fortnightly Forbes was edging up. The newsweeklies, Time included, were beginning to compete with Fortune for business and corporate advertising.
>
> *(Pendergast 1986, p. 177)*

In response, Fortune's editors tried to give closer looks at current news. Benefiting from the prosperity of the 1960s, Fortune's circulation rose to 515,000 in 1969, but BusinessWeek had emerged as a strong competitor for advertising (Pendergast 1986, p. 475).

By the 1970s, Pendergast wrote, "The package that Fortune offered was handsome... it remained a lavish production" with "large pages" and a

Huge editorial 'well' of 40-plus pages uninterrupted by advertising, made for the stunning display of the expansive text pieces and picture spreads in color that distinguished Fortune from its rivals. No other business publication was in a position to deal in panoramic fashion with large subjects...Nor did Fortune's rivals tackle at comparable depth the major questions of public policy or social development that affected American business.

Pendergast added that "Fortune was regarded as editorially authoritative." Nonetheless, Fortune's considerable heft – both physical and intellectual – could make it intimidating to the harried businessperson (Pendergast 1986, p. 475).

In response, Fortune's editors transformed it into a smaller physical package through the decade: In 1972, Fortune reduced the size of its pages to 9 by 11 inches, which made it only a little bigger than its rivals. A few years later, beginning with the issue of January 16, 1978 (actually published in December 1977), Fortune switched from monthly to fortnightly publication to make its articles closer to developments in the news and to give its advertisers more opportunities to reach readers. The move was also motivated by Fortune being eclipsed in circulation by the fortnightly Forbes (Pendergast 1986, p. 484).

In the 1980s and 1990s, "Fortune remained a source of literate storytelling and pungent stories on the business world—if tamer than in the Dwight Macdonald era," wrote Starkman. "The 'corporation story' remained a Fortune strength," he wrote, and "Fortune continued the tradition of stories that probed deeply into mismanagement, screw-ups, and manipulation at corporations" (Starkman 2014, p. 94).

## Forbes

Forbes magazine's founder, Bertie Charles Forbes (known professional as B.C. Forbes), was born in 1880 in a village in Scotland, the sixth of ten children of a tailor and a blacksmith's daughter. In 1903, at age 23, he emigrated to New York City, where he found work as a journalist. He ultimately became the business editor of William Randolph Hearst's newspaper, the New York American, where he specialized in publishing flattering profiles of the wealthy. "Forbes soon made the paper's financial section almost as popular as the sports pages," wrote Stewart Pinkerton in his history, "The Fall of the House of Forbes." B.C. Forbes also profited by writing a syndicated column about business, which he maintained even when he left his position at the Hearst paper to launch his own magazine, Forbes, which debuted in September 1917 (Pinkerton 2011, pp. 58–69).

For the magazine's start-up costs B.C. "hit up for loans many of the prominent men that he'd gotten to know and had written about favorably over the years," wrote Pinkerton (Pinkerton 2011, p. 68). The editorial formula was

Heavy doses of investment advice; stock market data and forecasts; inspirational stories; how to succeed (where others fail); lists of notable executives; finger-waving guidance on how to be more productive in your job; adoring profiles of the most favored; and nasty attacks on people or companies the editor-in-chief felt were unworthy. It was the template that succeeding editors would follow for years.

*(Pinkerton 2011, p. 75)*

From the start, the professional ethics at Forbes magazine were questionable. B.C. Forbes accepted the gift of a top-of-the-line car from the president of Dodge, for example (Starkman 2014, p. 75).

Forbes faced formidable new competition with the debuts of The Business Week in 1929 and Fortune in 1930. Forbes magazine struggled financially during the Great Depression, when B.C. Forbes resorted to giving his employees what was known as the "Scottish vacation" – working for four weeks but getting paid only for three (Pinkerton 2011, p. 47). He relied on the income from his syndicated column to subsidize the magazine (Pinkerton 2011, p. 79). In a 1936 survey by the McCann Erickson ad agency, B.C. Forbes ranked as the second most popular feature writer in New York newspapers, eclipsed only by Damon Runyan (Pinkerton 2011, pp. 74–75).

B.C.'s personal renown helped promote the magazine that bore his name. Still, by the end of the 1930s, the magazine's circulation of 102,000 lagged well behind The Business Week at 192,000 and Fortune at 248,000 (Pinkerton 2011, p. 79). By the 1950s, Forbes "was not much more than a quaint, second-tier stock tip sheet," wrote Pinkerton. "It was type-heavy, gray, and often quite boring to read" (Pinkerton 2011, p. 101).

In the post-World War II era, Forbes magazine would be transformed by two charismatic figures: B.C. Forbes' son Malcolm, who would show a genius for marketing and promotion, and the man that Malcolm picked as the managing editor, James Michaels, a brilliant, feisty journalist who would lead the magazine throughout a long run.

Malcolm's career in journalism began inauspiciously when, as an undergraduate at Princeton University in the late 1930s, he tried out for the campus newspaper, the Daily Princetonian, but wasn't picked for a position there. After college, he fought in World War II and was injured by German machine-gun fire. When his father died in 1954, Malcolm became the editor of Forbes magazine, while his brother Bruce became the publisher (Pinkerton 2011, pp. 83–93).

At the time, the magazine "faced two major perceptual obstacles," wrote Christopher Winans in his biography "Malcolm Forbes: The Man Who Had Everything."

> First, part of B.C.'s legacy was that many business people viewed him as a blackmailer. They believed failure to buy advertising in Forbes could result in punishment by editorial lambasting. Though one would be hard pressed to prove this ever happened, the perception affected Forbes staffers' ability to report.

The second obstacle was a perception that the magazine's reporting was inaccurate and had little impact (Winans 1990, pp. 46–47).

The magazine's editorial content would be transformed by Michaels, who took over as the top editor in 1961. He was born in 1921 in Buffalo, New York, where his father owned the Palace Burlesque Theater. Michaels graduated from Harvard in 1942 and drove an ambulance in Burma during World War II. After the war, he worked as a reporter for the United Press International wire service's bureau in New Delhi. He traveled by horseback to report on the war in Kashmir, and in 1948 he climbed over a stone wall to get inside the cordoned-off telegraph office and become the first foreign journalist to report the news of the assassination of Mahatma Gandhi (Pinkerton 2011, pp. 98–99). Despite these scoops, he failed to land a position at the prestigious Fortune when he returned to the United States. Instead, he joined the underdog Forbes in 1954 (Pinkerton 2011, pp. 103–104). As an editor, Michaels saw himself as a wary watchdog for would-be investors, bringing a new emphasis on investigative reporting into mismanagement and financial corruption at companies. "The more contrarian the story, the better," wrote Pinkerton. "Michaels loved to take down big companies riding high on Wall Street and being gushed over by the competition" (Pinkerton 2011, p. 120).

In 1964, when Bruce Forbes died of bladder cancer at age 47, Malcolm Forbes took control of the business side of Forbes as well as the editorial operations. By 1972, he had increased the magazine's circulation to 625,000, exceeding Fortune's readership by 75,000 (Winans 1990, p. 82).

By the mid-1970s, Winans wrote, Michaels had transformed Forbes into

A magazine that prided itself on its willingness to stick its neck out with strongly worded—and preferably negative—pronouncements about businesses and their managers. It was during this time that Forbes was reaching its peak as an abrasive, tough-minded critic.

One Forbes writer said that, "Anything positive was viewed as puffy, which was the reputation Business Week had" (Winans 1990, p. 103).

For a long time, Malcolm Forbes envied Fortune's success with its "Fortune 500" annual ranking of America's 500 biggest companies, which it began publishing in 1955. The phrase "Fortune 500" had become a commonly recognized term in business parlance, and the annual issue bulged with advertising pages. In 1981, Malcolm Forbes conceived of the "Forbes 400" ranking of the 400 wealthiest Americans. Michaels opposed the idea, predicting (correctly, it would turn out) that the feature would be difficult and costly to produce and that the estimates of individuals' net worths would be unreliable. Nonetheless, Malcolm Forbes went ahead with the idea, and the so-called "Rich List" was an instant hit when it debuted in 1982. Fortune responded by coming out with a ranking of the world's billionaires in 1985 (Pinkerton 2011, pp. 110–116).

Malcolm Forbes also proved shrewd at promoting the magazine through his high-profile lifestyle, positioning himself as an advertisement for the good life afforded to the winners of American capitalism. He entertained guests on an elegant company-owned yacht, The Highlander, and at a French chateau. He flew hot-air balloons, rode motorcycles, and hosted lavish parties with celebrity guest lists. After his divorce, he attracted publicity by hobnobbing with the movie idol Elizabeth Taylor, while the tabloids speculated about their romantic ties. (After Malcolm's death, Winans' biography would claim that Malcolm was a closeted gay man with a long but secret history of sexually harassing his male employees.) (Winans 1990, p. 12).

By the early 1980s, Malcolm Forbes and Jim Michaels had been so successful in their missions that the leaders of both Fortune and BusinessWeek found themselves competing with Forbes for editorial impact as well as advertising sales. Forbes had become an equal player in the Big Three.

Forbes' journalistic ethics were still questioned by many in the profession. Newsweek reported about Forbes magazine: "While small companies (and the government, of course)

continue to be attacked, large firms with large ad budgets tend to get off" (Winans 1990, p. 179). Starkman wrote that Forbes

> Never fully shook its reputation, earned in Bertie's day, for trimming its editorial content for favored advertisers and, later, friends of Malcolm Forbes. The magazine's 'unspoken dialogue' with advertisers – whether ad dollars would buy leniency – would continue on a very subtle level for years.
>
> *(Starkman 2014, p. 88)*

## BusinessWeek

James McGraw and John Hill got their starts separately as publishers of trade newspapers for industries such as the railroads at the end of the 1800s and the beginning of the 1900s. They merged their companies in 1917 to create McGraw-Hill. In 1929, only weeks before the "Black Monday" stock market crash, the company launched The Business Week, inspired partly by the newsmagazine format pioneered a few years earlier by Time. Like Forbes, The Business Week struggled financially in the Great Depression, losing $1.5 million from 1929 to 1935 (Roush 2006, pp. 91–92).

While Forbes focused on investing and Fortune was known for in-depth features on corporations, The Business Week had its own niche in reporting the breaking news about business in a fairly comprehensive way. From the start, The Business Week paid close attention to economics – until 1961, a picture of a thermometer appeared on the cover of every issue of the magazine, measuring the "temperature" of the American economy (Roush 2006, p. 91).

The Business Week was also distinctive in its approach to circulation. In "Profits and Losses: Business Journalism and Its Role in Society," Chris Roush wrote:

> It was not sold on newsstands, but instead the magazine solicited subscriptions from corporate management. When applying for a subscription, the reader had to provide his or her title and employer, information that was used by ad salesmen to show that readers were executives. The subscription strategy changed in the 1970s, when the magazine began soliciting readers outside the business world.
>
> *(Roush 2006, p. 93)*

From the 1940s through the 1970s, BusinessWeek embraced a "bland, meat-and-potatoes style," wrote Starkman. A BusinessWeek editor explained that business magazines should be like bankers: "One of the reasons you trust bankers is because they are sober and boring. If bankers wore Hawaiian shirts and long hair, you wouldn't trust them" (Starkman 2014, p. 89).

The New York native Stephen B. Shepard was a young journalist when he took a job at the magazine in 1966. At that time, the publication was "highly successful," he recalled in his memoir. BusinessWeek ran 5,000–6,000 pages of advertising a year, "vying with the New Yorker for first place among all magazines in the United States." The reporting was "very strong," drawing on a network of bureaus around the world. But "the writing was generally bland, and the overall look paled beside Fortune," he wrote, and "an even bigger shortcoming, I soon realized, was its soft, sometimes puffy coverage of individual corporations. There was little investigative reporting" (Shepard pp. 39–40).

The magazine began a transformation around the time that Shepard – who had left for stints at other publications, including one of the top jobs at Newsweek – returned to BusinessWeek, as it was then known, in 1983. "The magazine, though still deeply reported and solidly profitable, was in dire need of editorial change," he wrote.

> It looked drab, all black and white even as other magazines had embraced four-color photography, illustration, and graphics. The writing, with some notable exceptions, was uninspired. And most dangerous of all, BusinessWeek increasingly stressed nuts-and-bolts stories, all too often abandoning the big-picture approach that had distinguished it.
>
> *(Shepard pp. 91–92)*

While the editor-in-chief Lew Young presided over a redesign that gave the magazine a bolder look, with bold-type headlines and prominent color photography, Shepard pushed for a "newsier, more narrative approach that brought out the drama and personality of business" (Shepard, p. 95).

In 1984, Young retired at age 60 after a 15-year tenure, and Shepard took over as the top editor. His mission was to stop the magazine's decade-long losses of market share to Forbes. Shepard immediately gave BusinessWeek a strong infusion of attitude. The cover of his first issue had the attention-getting headline "OOPS!" for a story about the considerable troubles at many of the supposedly model companies profiled in Tom Peters' bestselling book, "In Search of Excellence."

In addition to giving the magazine a livelier tone, Shepard supported investigative reporting. He also emulated the "list journalism" popularized by Fortune and Forbes: In 1988, reporter John Byrne created an influential ranking of the top business-school MBA programs.

Shepard ran the magazine until 2005. During his 20-year run as its leader, BusinessWeek's circulation peaked at 1.2 million and it earned more than $1 billion in operating profits (Shepard, pp. 99–100). While the rise of the digital media in the 1990s was a foreshadow of the demise of "old media," the decade was nonetheless a booming time for the Big Three magazines, which swelled with advertising pages from Internet technology companies until the "dot-com" stock crash of 2000.

### The Decline of the Big Three

The heyday of the Big Three came to an end in the early 21st century with the shift of media content and advertising from print to digital formats and the swift collapse of the business model for magazines. In 2006, years after the death of Malcolm Forbes (in 1990) and the end of James Michaels' tenure as the top editor (in 1998), the Forbes family sold a 40 percent stake in their media empire to Elevation Partners, a California private equity firm. The price of $250 million implied a total value for the company at $650 million (Pinkerton 2011, p. 213). In retrospect, their timing was excellent, since they sold before the 2008 stock market crash, the Great Recession, the ascendancy of the smart phone, and the newfound dominance of advertising revenues by Google and Facebook. The advent of instant news on the Internet seemed to make the weekly or fortnightly formats of the Big Three all but irrelevant at the same time as the economic downturn challenged them financially.

Under its new co-owner from Silicon Valley, Forbes attempted to leverage its prominent brand name into success in the online realm. Forbes.com relied on short, quickly written posts and click-bait "listicles" by bloggers who were paid per-click rather than investigative stories by well-trained, salaried reporters. It was widely regarded as a journalistic embarrassment as well as a financial disappointment (Pinkerton 2011, pp. 226–227).

BusinessWeek made a strong push into online news, but by 2007, it was in the red for the first time since the Great Depression. It lost $44 million in 2008 and was projected to be on course to lose as much as $60 million in 2009 (Shepard 2013, pp. 182–183). McGraw-Hill's chief executive officer at the time was Harold W. ("Terry") McGraw III, the great-grandson of the co-founder. He sold the magazine to Bloomberg in 2009 for a reported $5 million, a token price. The magazine was renamed Bloomberg Businessweek and became a small part of the global business news service, a journalistic endeavor that had been subsidized by the company's lucrative rentals of computer terminals customized for sophisticated financial traders. By 2016, the magazine, which still relied on print advertising, was losing an estimated $20 million to $30 million a year (Alpert 2016). Its print circulation had declined from nearly 1 million in 2012 to 316,000 at the end of 2021, and its digital subscriptions stood at about 370,000, up about 58 percent from the prior year, according to the Poynter Institute (Edmonds 2022). The Economist, the London-based weekly with a strong American readership, did well in signing up paid digital subscriptions – and, in contrast, remained profitable every year while its American counterparts were losing money (Somaiya 2015).

Fortune's parent, Time Inc. – the legacy of Henry Luce – was bought in 2017 by Meredith Corporation, which sold Fortune the following year for $150 million to Chatchaval Jiaravanon, a Thai billionaire. Fortune's financial worth came largely from staging lucrative conferences for executives, which by 2019 brought in around $40 million annually, more than 40 percent of its total revenues. The brand name had retained a certain prestige, but the magazine itself, while still producing fine journalism, was cut back to publishing only six times a year (Trachtenberg 2019).

## Conclusion: Competitive Dynamics of a Media Oligopoly

Looking at the history of the Big Three, we can see that their competitive dynamic was driven by elements of both imitation and differentiation. Fortune's outsized success with the Fortune 500 created a long-term trend toward "list journalism" with the Forbes 400, the Business-Week business-school ratings, and many other popular annual features. The superior editorial quality of Fortune and BusinessWeek through the early 1960s created pressure on Forbes, which greatly improved its reporting and writing during the Jim Michaels era. In turn, Forbes' enhanced competitiveness pushed Fortune to increase the frequency of its issues in the 1970s, and Michaels' knack for investigative reporting with a cheeky tone helped to inspire the editorial redirection of the Steve Shepard era at BusinessWeek beginning in the early 1980s.

And yet, despite these many imitations of each other's successful innovations, all three magazines maintained the distinctive cores of their identities through the decades: Forbes kept its focus on investing and its willingness to strike an aggressively critical tone; Fortune sustained its excellence in long-form storytelling and its Olympian voice; and BusinessWeek continued its emphasis on comprehensive news reporting and the unmatched reach of its network of bureaus around the world. And all three publications achieved a high level of editorial excellence in the 1980s and 1990s before technological shifts thoroughly undermined the basis of their business models and ended the long heyday of print magazines as a media format.

Today, the former Big Three still receive recognition for the quality of their journalism, often performing well in the annual "Best in Business" awards competition of the Society for Advancing Business Editing and Writing (SABEW). But these publications no longer enjoy the cultural impact of their heyday. Still, today's readers have many excellent options for business news and investing advice, many of which come from digital-native outlets as well as legacy publishers that adapted better to the changing environment, such as The Wall Street Journal, New York Times, and Financial Times. Perhaps the biggest deficit left by the Big Three is in long-form business narrative, a genre that was also greatly diminished by the Wall Street Journal's discontinuation of its famed front-page "leders." Still, even this gap has been filled, at least partly, by the burgeoning field of podcasting as well as by continued vibrancy in business books, which provide daily beat reporters the opportunity to tell their stories with greater depth and storytelling power.

## References and Further Reading

Alpert, L. (2016) "Bloomberg changes businessweek leaders, ends political TV program," *Wall Street Journal* (Online), November 17, 2016.

Brinkley, A. (2010) *The Publisher: Henry Luce and His American Century*, New York: Knopf. (The definitive biography of the publishing mogul, written by a Columbia University historian).

Coy, P., Ellis, J., Dwyer, P. and Joel Weber. (2019) "Businessweek at 90: Covering business through the decades," *Bloomberg Businessweek*, December 20, 2019, accessed at https://www.bloomberg.com/news/features/2019-12-20/businessweek-at-90-covering-business-through-the-decades?leadSource=uverify%20wall

Edmonds, R. (2022) "How bloomberg media beat the pandemic blues with explosive growth," March 9, 2022, accessed at https://www.poynter.org/business-work/2022/bloomberg-media-success-pandemic-explosive-growth/

Elson, R. T. (1968) *Time Inc.: The Intimate History of a Publishing Enterprise 1923–1941, Volume 1*, New York: Atheneum. (While this book and its two sequels are the authorized corporate history, they're highly informative, carefully researched, and often even critical).

Elson, R. T. (1973) *Time Inc.: The Intimate History of a Publishing Enterprise 1941–1960, Volume 2*, New York: Atheneum.

Pendergast, C. with Colvin, G. (1986) *Time Inc.: The Intimate History of a Publishing Enterprise Volume Three 1960–1980*, New York: Atheneum.

Pinkerton, S. (2011) *The Fall of the House of Forbes: The Inside Story of the Collapse of a Media Empire*, New York: St. Martin's Press. (Insightful book by a former editor at Forbes and The Wall Street Journal).

Roush, C. (2006) *Profits and Losses: Business Journalism and Its Role in Society*, Oak Park, Illinois: Marian Street Press. (Includes a historical overview of the three magazines by a well-respected journalism professor).

Shepard, S. B. (2013) *Deadlines and Disruption: My Turbulent Path From Print to Digital*, New York: McGraw-Hill. (Memoir by the influential Business Week editor).

Somaiya, R. (2015) "Up for sale, the economist is unlikely to change its voice," *New York Times*, August 4, 2015.

Starkman, D. (2014) *The Watchdog That Didn't Bark: The Financial Crisis and the Disappearance of Investigative Journalism*, New York: Columbia University Pres. (One of the most important books about business journalism in America—and its ultimate failures).

Trachtenberg, J. A. (2019) "Fortune magazine to add paywall, increase cover price," *Wall Street Journal*, May 30, 2019.

Winans, C. (1990) *Malcolm Forbes: The Man Who Had Everything*, New York: St. Martin's Press. (Revealing biography by an investigative reporter at the Wall Street Journal).

(1980) *Writing For Fortune: Nineteen Authors Remember Life on the Staff of a Remarkable Magazine*, New York: Time Inc.

# 13

# HOW BUSINESS BOOKS BECAME BESTSELLERS

*Alan Deutschman*

## Introduction

Books about business were a backwater in the modern American publishing industry until the early 1980s, when they emerged not only as blockbusters but also, in some cases, as works of considerable literary interest. The Eighties catalyzed the popularity of three categories of business books that have shown enduring appeal over the decades: The business narrative, which gained prominence with Tracy Kidder's "The Soul of a New Machine" in 1981; the Chief Executive Officer (CEO) memoir, which was reinvented by Lee Iacocca and his ghostwriter William Novak with "Iacocca: An Autobiography" in 1983; and the business guru book, a popularization of ideas from business-school professors or MBA-wielding management consultants, which was reimagined by Tom Peters and Robert H. Waterman Jr. with "In Search of Excellence" in 1982. Years later, in 2000, a writer for the New Yorker magazine, Malcolm Gladwell, pioneered a fourth category with "The Tipping Point": Books that popularized research from academic social scientists that could be useful to executives in management or marketing.

## The Business Narrative

The literary potential of the business narrative was demonstrated by the legendary journalist Lillian Ross in "Picture," which first appeared as a series of five articles in the New Yorker in 1952 and was later republished in book form. Ross had initially intended to write a magazine story on the Hollywood director John Huston, who agreed to give her unfettered behind-the-scenes access as he shot a film version of the classic novel "The Red Badge of Courage." Ross' editor, William Shawn, suggested that instead of a personality profile, she should write a narrative about the making of a movie at a big studio (Ross 1998, p. 89). Ross wound up staying in Hollywood for a year and a half to follow the story to its conclusion – partly because she was fleeing the amorous advances of Shawn, an older man who was already married and had three children (Ross 1998, pp. 80–88).

In "Picture," Ross revealed the inner workings of the MGM studio in extraordinary detail, from itemizing the movie's production costs to showing the infighting among rival

DOI: 10.4324/9781003298977-16

executives. Her work read like a compelling realist novel with scene-by-scene construction, extensive dialogue, vivid visual descriptions, and richly drawn portrayals of her real-life characters.

"Picture" became a model for the practitioners of the "New Journalism" of the 1960s and 1970s. Truman Capote credited its approach as an inspiration for his 1965 book "In Cold Blood." But as the 1960s burst into countercultural splendor, the new wave of narrative nonfiction writers didn't look to business as their subject matter: Tom Wolfe wrote about hippies and astronauts, and Ross' friend Norman Mailer followed Capote's lead and wrote about a killer. Gay Talese gained renown writing about celebrities and mobsters, though he did explore the inner workings of a big organization in "The Kingdom and the Power" (1969), his book on The New York Times.

But the real breakthrough for the business narrative was Tracy Kidder's "The Soul of a New Machine" in 1981. Kidder spent 18 months as an observer at Data General Corporation in a suburb of Boston, where he watched Tom West, a manager, lead the design of a new computer code-named Eagle. Kidder brilliantly captured the subculture (then still obscure) of youthful techno-geeks who wore blue jeans to the office and worked day and night under extreme deadline pressure. These "Microkids" often found creative satisfaction in their obsessive work. The New York Times' reviewer, Samuel C. Florman, said that Kidder "has endowed the tale with such pace, texture and poetic implication that he has elevated it to a high level of narrative art" and that the book should be considered "literature" rather than merely "nonfiction."

Kidder's timing was propitious as well. "Soul of a New Machine" was published after a decade of economic malaise. In the 1970s, Americans' morale was hurt by the shock of the OPEC oil embargo, the onset of a mystifying "stagflation" (brutally high inflation and high unemployment at the same time), the dismaying trend of manufacturers closing factories and sending jobs overseas, the spectacle of Japanese carmakers humiliating Detroit's Big Three, and the nation's shift from trade surplus to trade deficit. Ronald Reagan had just begun his first term as the president, and Americans were eager for harbingers of economic hope.

> At a time when American productivity is in decline, when the nation's innovative powers are said to be waning, and nobody seems to be able to motivate himself or anybody else, the experience of the people who created Eagle merits attention,

Florman wrote in the Times review. "Not that life can be lived in a state of perpetual commotion. But in microcosm the Eagle team exhibits the intensity and high spirits that pontifical social commentators keep saying Americans have lost." After some of America's youth had looked to rock music, psychedelic drugs, and sexual liberation for a sense of transcendence in the 1960s and 1970s, Kidder showed those in a new generation who were seeking a new kind of "high" in the creative outlet of work.

As the American economy recovered and then boomed in the 1980s, and many voters embraced President Ronald Reagan's optimistic vision and his pro-business attitude, the market for business books became vibrant. In the narrative category, Kidder's success was followed by "The Partners: Inside America's Most Powerful Law Firms" by James B. Stewart in 1983. Stewart was a Harvard-educated attorney who had quit his position as an associate at one of Wall Street's most prestigious law firms, Cravath, Swaine & Moore, to become a journalist at the American Lawyer, a startup publication founded by Steven Brill. When Stewart's first stories were disappointing, Brill worried that perhaps he had ruined the life of young man with a promising career. But Stewart quickly developed into a masterful reporter and writer, and he benefited from his consummate insider's knowledge of the corporate world.

In "The Partners," Stewart told the tales of eight of the most important legal cases of the 1970s. Like Kidder in "Soul of a New Machine," Stewart's stories captured a sense of drama and excitement about working in the corporate realm. "Mr. Stewart's prime interest is not in the law but in the lawyers," wrote Neal Johnston, The New York Times' reviewer:

> And he is at his best in conveying the exhausting, exhilarating, giddy way they work. (A Cravath associate flying to California was once able to bill IBM for 27 hours in a single day, thanks to well-placed time zones.) Young associates abandon youth in the library. Marriages fail under pressure. Truth and law alike are bent to and perhaps beyond the breaking point.

In the 1980s, CEOs were becoming popular culture heroes – the new "rock stars" – but no CEO was more youthful or exciting than Apple Computer co-founder Steve Jobs. The college dropout had become worth $250 million at age 24 when his company had its initial public offering of stock in 1980. Jobs gave interviews and offered extensive behind-the-scenes access at Apple to Michael Moritz, the San Francisco correspondent for Time magazine. Jobs had thought that Time would name him as its "Man of the Year" for 1982, but Moritz found that Jobs, while brilliant and charismatic, would berate his colleagues and had refused to support his out-of-wedlock daughter. So the magazine picked "The Computer" as its "Machine of the Year" and ran a sidebar article by Moritz about Jobs' dark side. Moritz tapped his reporting about Apple for a masterly book-length narrative, "The Little Kingdom," published in 1984.

As the Eighties progressed, the business press chronicled the machinations of Wall Street's new titans, who were reshaping America's economy through corporate takeovers under the lax regulatory environment of the Reagan era – and, in some cases, engaging in criminal conspiracies. While these stories filled the pages of the Wall Street Journal and the top business magazines, the tales were later told in their fullest with compelling blow-by-blow narrative detail in a series of outstanding business books, including: "Greed and Glory on Wall Street" by Ken Auletta in 1986; "The Predator's Ball" by Connie Bruck in 1988; "Liar's Poker" by Michael Lewis in 1989; "Barbarians at the Gate" by Bryan Burrough and John Heylar in 1989; and "Den of Thieves" by James B. Stewart in 1991. The market for business narratives was so hot that even a historical tome, "The House of Morgan" by Ron Chernow, became a bestseller in 1990.

While the fervent interest in Wall Street's "masters of the universe" subsided by the early 1990s, by that point, many journalists, book publishers, and readers had grasped the potential of the business narrative, which became a category of enduring interest. The format worked especially well when investigative journalists who broke important stories for newspapers or magazines could tell the tales at length between hard covers: In 1999, John Byrne of BusinessWeek published "Chainsaw" about "Chainsaw" Al Dunlap, an executive who was cheered by Wall Street investors for boosting short-term corporate profits through brutal cutbacks and layoffs. Bethany McLean, who sounded an early alarm about Enron in Fortune magazine, told the full story about financial scandals at the energy firm in "The Smartest Guys in the Room" in 2003 (co-authored with Peter Elkind). John Carreyrou, who exposed fraud at the Silicon Valley startup Theranos in The Wall Street Journal, expanded on his narrative in "Bad Blood" in 2018. The book format also was especially well-suited for postmortems of major news events such as the 2008 stock market meltdown, which was chronicled by The New York Times reporter Andrew Ross Sorkin in "Too Big to Fail" in 2009 and by the perennially bestselling Michael Lewis in "The Big Short" in 2010.

## The CEO Memoir

Before the 1980s, the corporate executive hadn't been seen as a glamorous figure in postwar America. He (and back then it was almost always a "he") was the alienated "Man in the Gray Flannel Suit" (the title of a 1955 novel by Sloan Wilson), the conformist "Organization Man" (the title of a 1956 study by Fortune writer William H. Whyte), or the ridiculous bureaucrat of "How to Succeed in Business Without Really Trying" (the satirical 1952 novel by Shepherd Mead that inspired the 1961 Broadway musical). So it was surprising when an executive's memoir appeared on the bestseller lists in 1964: "My Years With General Motors" by Alfred P. Sloan, the former CEO of the giant automaker.

The book was ghostwritten by Fortune writer John MacDonald. GM sued to block publication, and MacDonald countersued. MacDonald also withstood pressure from executives at Fortune's parent company, Time Inc., which feared losing GM's lucrative advertising. MacDonald won the five-year legal battle. When the book was finally published in 1964, its sales benefited greatly from the publicity generated by the controversy. "My Years With General Motors" graced The New York Times bestseller list for six months even though it was a dry book about management methodology that revealed little about Sloan himself as a person.

The real breakthrough for CEO memoirs was "Iacocca: An Autobiography" by Lee Iacocca with William Novak, which was published in September 1984. Iacocca was a familiar name and face in American households from starring in television commercials for Chrysler, where he was the CEO. In retrospect, he seems an unlikely figure to emerge as a business hero: He saved the failing company only by pleading with the federal government to guarantee $1.1 billion in loans. The real savior was Uncle Sam. Nonetheless, Iacocca was an appealing figure on TV, where he came across as a straight talker.

Initially, Iacocca was uninterested when Bantam Books approached him about writing a memoir. Then, Stuart Applebaum, Bantam's vice president for publicity, realized that he and Iacocca had the same barber: Gio Hernandez at the Bergdorf Goodman department store. After Applebaum asked Hernandez to give a nudge to Iacocca, the automobile executive agreed to meet with Bantam's team, and the project was underway.

Bantam editor Nessa Rapoport had grown up in a suburb of Toronto with William Novak, who in 1982 was a struggling writer in Massachusetts. Novak was thinking of taking a job in corporate public relations to help support his family. Instead, he accepted a flat fee of $45,000 for two years of work as Iacocca's ghostwriter. He taped 48 hours of interviews with Iacocca over 20 months. Shaping the storyline, Novak relied on two classic plots: The immigrant family success story (Lee was an Americanization of "Lido," and his parents came from Italy) and the cycle of rise, fall, and resurrection: Iacocca had become the president of Ford Motor Company, then was fired, then reemerged triumphant when he took over and rescued Chrysler.

Rapoport rejected Novak's first draft of the manuscript because it was "too well written" and didn't sound enough like Iacocca talking. "Go back to the transcripts," Rapoport told Novak. "Make it sound more like conversation."

In June 1985, nine months after publication, The Washington Post reported that the book had 1.85 million copies in print and had spent 32 weeks at No. 1 on The New York Times nonfiction bestseller list: "With the exception of the Bible, and perhaps some reference books and cookbooks, 'Iacocca' is the biggest selling nonfiction hardback ever." Like "The Soul of a New Machine," Iacocca's memoir benefited from its portrait of the can-do spirit of an American hero emerging out of the economic dislocation and Japanese challenge of the previous decade.

Publishers strived to emulate the success of "Iacocca." In 1987, Apple's CEO, John Sculley, published "Odyssey: Pepsi to Apple" with BusinessWeek's John A. Byrne as his co-author. Like Novak before him, Byrne shrewdly tapped into two archetypal storylines: On one level, he fashioned Sculley's life into a tale of the Old World falling in love with the New World (which Vladimir Nabokov once described as the theme of his classic novel "Lolita"). In Byrne's version of the story, Sculley left his job as the president of a stuffy old-line East Coast company, PepsiCo, to become the CEO of a dynamic new West Coast upstart, Apple Computer. He was personally recruited by Apple co-founder Steve Jobs, who famously asked him: "Do you want to spend the rest of your life selling sugared water or do you want a chance to change the world?"

Sculley's memoir had a dramatic plot twist: After he and Jobs came together for a while blissfully as partners, they fell out acrimoniously – and Sculley edged aside Jobs and took control of the company himself. It was an intriguing story, and "Odyssey" told it with a depth beyond what had already appeared in the media.

Another aspirant for Iacocca's mantle was a 41-year-old real estate developer, Donald Trump, who published "Trump: The Art of the Deal" in 1987. Trump wasn't well-known yet nationally, but he was a familiar figure in New York City, the epicenter of the book publishing industry. While "Iacocca" was about a businessman saving the beleaguered industrial heartland, "The Art of the Deal" cast Trump as a businessman rescuing the nation's greatest city from the urban decay of the 1970s, when the Big Apple was in a financial crisis. In one scene, Trump showed how he was called on to renovate Wollman Rink, the ice-skating facility in Central Park, which had languished in disrepair while politicians were too incompetent to fix it. Trump solved the problem with a quick phone call to a Canadian hockey team.

Trump's book held the No. 1 spot on The New York Times bestseller list for 13 weeks, sold more than a million copies, and "expanded Trump's renown far beyond New York City, making him an emblem of the successful tycoon," wrote Jane Mayer in the New Yorker. In 2016, after Trump was elected the president, Mayer interviewed Tony Schwartz, the ghostwriter of "Art of the Deal": "I put lipstick on a pig," Schwartz said. "I feel a deep sense of remorse that I contributed to presenting Trump in a way that brought him wide attention and made him more appealing than he is."

The major business magazines – Fortune, Forbes, and BusinessWeek – were a powerful force for turning CEOs into pop-culture heroes and setting them up for bestselling memoirs. Fortune's John Huey wrote an admiring 1991 cover story that helped raise the profile of Walmart's founder Sam Walton, whom he portrayed as a folksy character, a zillionaire who nonetheless drove an old pickup truck and piloted his own small Cessna propeller plane around the American heartland to drop in on stores in remote small towns and hobnob with workers. Huey later co-authored Walton's memoir, "Sam Walton: Made in America," published in 1992.

The CEO memoir craze continued into the Nineties and the 2000s with "Losing My Virginity: The Autobiography" by Virgin CEO Richard Branson in 1998; "Jack: Straight From the Gut" by General Electric CEO Jack Welch with John A. Byrne in 2003; "Delivering Happiness: A Path to Profits, Passion, and Purpose" by Zappos CEO Tony Hsieh in 2010; "Onward" by Starbucks CEO Howard Schultz in 2011; and "Shoe Dog" by Nike CEO Phil Knight in 2016.

Why have CEO memoirs exerted such enduring appeal for book buyers? Sometimes, the person's life is, quite simply, a really good story, especially if it's written skillfully by the journalist who serves as a co-author or ghostwriter. What's more, publishers know that the CEOs have strong name recognition as well as the ability to promote their books through appearances in the national media. Journalists who write unauthorized biographies rarely get to plug their books through live interviews to millions of viewers on television, for example, but CEOs easily command that kind of attention. Another factor: Many book readers want to listen to their hero's distinctive voice on the page, and they believe that the memoir will give them the inside scoop that hasn't appeared yet in the media. The reality, of course, is that memoirs tend toward revisionism, while unauthorized books by investigative reporters are far more likely to show the CEOs' darker sides and what really happened behind-the-scenes, such as The New York Times reporter David Gelle's 2022 revisionist history of Jack Welch, "The Man Who Broke Capitalism," or the 2022 postmortem on the tragic demise of Tony Hsieh, "Happy At Any Cost" by Wall Street Journal reporters Kirsten Grind and Katherine Sayre.

## The Business Guru Book

Before the 1980s, the most popular and influential author of books about how to run the modern corporation was Peter F. Drucker. He was born in 1909 in Vienna to Jewish parents who converted to Christianity and raised him as a Lutheran. The family hosted soirees for artists and thinkers, such as the great economist Joseph Schumpeter. The young Drucker worked as a journalist. With the rise of Nazism, he emigrated to England in 1933 and then to America in 1937. During the 1940s, he spent two years as an observer inside the halls of General Motors, where he was working as a consultant. The experience served as the basis for his 1946 study of GM, "The Concept of the Corporation," which launched him into decades of writing prolifically for a general readership. While he was an astute analyst of business, he was also an old-school European intellectual, and his writing was filled with knowledgeable references to the arts and humanities. His 1954 book, "The Practice of Management," was an enduring classic that influenced generations of corporate executives.

But none of Drucker's books rivaled the phenomenal sales of "In Search of Excellence: Lessons From America's Best-Run Companies," which was published in November 1982. The book was based on a study conducted at the McKinsey & Company consulting firm by Tom Peters and Robert H. Waterman Jr. They wrote about 43 companies with track records of outstanding financial performance over a 20-year period, including IBM, Procter & Gamble, Merck, Delta Airlines, and McDonald's. The authors analyzed eight traits of these "excellent" companies – management practices that they labeled with catchy phrases such as "a bias for action."

Harper & Row ordered a modest but respectable first printing of 15,000 units. The book went on to sell 1.4 million copies in hardcover, the most ever in the publisher's 168-year history. The New York Times reported that it was the biggest-selling hardcover book of the year in the United States in any category in 1983, eclipsing even novels by James Michener, John Le Carré, and Stephen King. Much like "Iacocca" and "The Soul of a New Machine," it offered a sense of reassurance that major American companies could still innovate and compete despite the economy's harrowing decline and the looming threats from the Japanese and other rivals.

Inevitably, the stunning success provoked backlash. In 1984, BusinessWeek magazine ran a cover story with the bold-type headline "Oops!": The article documented how 14 of the 43 companies were no longer performing well financially only two years after the book's publication. The following year, when Tom Peters was interviewed for an article about Peter

Drucker at age 75, Peters confessed that he had reread "The Practice of Management" and found to his own "amazement" that everything he and his co-author Waterman had written had already appeared in "some corner or other" of Drucker's book almost 30 years earlier.

The success of "In Search of Excellence" was duplicated in the following decade by two Stanford University business-school professors, Jim Collins and Jerry I. Porras, in their 1994 book "Built to Last: Successful Habits of Visionary Companies." The new book was almost a remake of "In Search" with the word "visionary" replacing "excellence" as the favored superlative. Instead of selecting the companies based on quantitative measures, Collins and Porras conducted a survey of 1,000 CEOs. Rather than choosing 43 companies, they came up with a more select list of only 18, though a few were carryovers from the McKinsey consultants' book (including IBM, Procter & Gamble, and Merck). While "In Search of Excellence" had eight traits with memorable catch-phrases, "Built to Last" came up with nine, including most famously the BHAG (pronounced BEE-hag) for setting and pursuing "Big Hairy Audacious Goals."

The formula continued to succeed fantastically. Seven years after its initial release, "Built to Last" was still selling 300,000 copies a year, and the publisher only offered it as an expensive hardcover and hadn't yet issued a lower-priced paperback. During its first ten years in print, "Built to Last" sold 3.5 million copies. An article in Fast Company, "Was 'Built to Last' Built to Last?," found that "almost half the companies on the list have slipped dramatically in performance and reputation" (Reingold and Underwood, 2004). Another prominent critic was Daniel Kahneman, a professor of psychology at Princeton University. "Knowing the importance of luck, you should be particularly suspicious when highly inconsistent patterns emerge from the comparison of successful and unsuccessful firms," Kahneman wrote in "Thinking Fast and Slow" in 2011.

Collins followed "Built to Last" with a solo effort in a similar vein, "Good to Great," which analyzed seven characteristics that had enabled 11 companies to improve the performance of their stocks. The book sold more than 4 million copies, and like its predecessors in the genre, it provoked considerable backlash as well. Steven D. Levitt, a professor of economics at the University of Chicago, wrote in 2008 in his "Freakonomics" blog that two of the 11 companies, Fannie Mae and Circuit City, had seen their stock prices fall by 80 percent since the book's publication. Fannie Mae was facing bankruptcy, and Circuit City had been beaten badly by rival Best Buy. Meanwhile, only one of the 11 companies, Nucor, had dramatically outperformed the market.

Assessing both "Good to Great" and "In Search of Excellence," Levitt wrote that

> The implicit message of these business books is that the principles that these companies use not only have made them good in the past, but position them for continued success. To the extent that this doesn't actually turn out to be true, it calls into question the basic premise of these books, doesn't it?

### "The Gladwell Effect"

In 2000, Malcolm Gladwell, a young journalist at The New Yorker magazine, published his debut book, "The Tipping Point," which would start a trend of books that popularized research from academic social scientists and, in the process, often revealed valuable new insights to business executives. To understand the significance of Gladwell's breakthrough, it's useful to go back three years earlier and consider an article by Herbert J. Gans, a sociology professor at Columbia University and the former president of the American Sociological Association.

In 1997, Gans set out to find how "informative" his profession had been to the general public. To take a "first cut" at answering that question, he conducted a study of how many books by sociologists had become best-sellers over the previous 50 years. He defined "sociologists" as authors who held advanced degrees or teaching positions in sociology or in related social science fields, such as anthropology, which employ similar methodologies.

It turned out that in a half-century, only a single book by sociologists had sold more than a million copies, the benchmark for a publishing "blockbuster": "The Lonely Crowd: A Study of the Changing American Character" by David Riesman, Nathan Glazer, and Reuel Denny, which had debuted way back in 1950. The Yale University Press had commissioned a first printing of only 3,000 copies, a more likely expectation for sales of a serious book by social science professors. By the time Herbert Gans conducted his study in 1997, "The Lonely Crowd" had sold an astonishing 1.4 million copies.

How could other academic sociologists replicate that kind of public exposure and influence for their important ideas? Gans had some insight into this matter, especially since he had studied with David Riesman as a young scholar, and since one of Gans' own books had been an unusually big seller: "Urban Villagers," a 1962 study of a working-class Italian-American community in Boston's West End, sold more than 150,000 copies, ranking it in the top 20 books in the 1997 sales study.

What were the keys to reaching large audiences? Gans claimed that it was "fairly obvious" that books by professors would sell better if they were "jargon-free" and "written in a language that at least educated general readers can understand" and "emphasize narrative over abstraction."

But could – or should – brilliant sociology professors try to write those kinds of popularizing books themselves? While Gans found that his profession "still has a long way to go before it makes a significant impression on the general public," he nonetheless maintained that the academic sociologists themselves should not attempt to publish bestsellers. Instead, they should continue to "publish intellectually," and if they can "produce more relevant findings and influential ideas," then they "may even be able to attract popular writers, including sociologists, who can report our work to the general public better than we can." For some reason, this phenomenon had already happened in the natural sciences, Gans observed, which implied that his own branch of academia could surely follow that example.

Very soon, it would, as Gladwell published "The Tipping Point" in 2000 and launched an industry trend of bestselling books that popularized previously obscure academic research from sociology and other social sciences disciplines. While the academic researchers were furthering knowledge, the Gladwellians would bring their new ideas to large audiences – and created a profitable new business segment for the major New York book publishing houses that embraced the trend.

By early 2006, when Rachel Donadio profiled Gladwell for The New York Times article titled "The Gladwell Effect," "The Tipping Point" had sold 1.7 million copies and the author's newer book, "Blink," had already sold 1.3 million after only a year. "Gladwell has become an all-out international phenomenon," Donadio wrote, "and has helped create a highly contagious hybrid genre of nonfiction" with its

Counterintuitive look at pop culture and the mysteries of the everyday....With writerly verve and strong narrative powers, he leavens serious social science research with zany characters and pithy, easily digestible anecdotes. Gladwell selects his anecdotes from a wide range of sources — the military, business, food, music, romance — and diverse locales, a tactic that broadens his books' appeal.

157

Explaining himself to interviewers, Gladwell told London's Guardian newspaper: "I've always been a kind of academic wannabee. I realized I didn't have the temperament to be an academic. But I thought I could at least be a liaison to the rest of the world." And he told an interviewer for Powells.com, the website of the Portland bookstore:

> To say I'm a popularizer of other people's academic ideas is to me the highest praise you can offer. That's exactly what I am, and I'm proud to be it. And by the way, it's not easy. It's actually quite difficult. Not difficult in the same way doing academic research is, but it's a craft. Some of these studies, in their virgin form, are pretty dry. You have to be quite creative to find ways to make them come alive. If that's what my talent is, I'm the happiest man in the world.

Gladwell's success inspired the major New York publishing houses to commission and release a wave of new books that the Times described as being in the "Gladwell vein" and the website The Daily Beast later described more cheekily as "Gladwell clones and wannabees."

By far the most successful of the bunch was "Freakonomics: A Rogue Economist Explains the Hidden Side of Everything," in which the journalist Stephen Dubner, a former New York Times Magazine editor, lent his own considerable writerly verve and narrative powers to popularize the counterintuitive findings of his co-author, Steven Levitt, an economics professor at the University of Chicago. Malcolm Gladwell enthusiastically endorsed the book with a blurb that ran on its cover: "Prepare to by dazzled." When a somewhat confused reader stopped Gladwell at the Toronto airport and asked him to sign a copy of "Freakonomics," Gladwell sent an email to Levitt exulting: "We are totally co-branded!" "Freakonomics" and its follow-up "Super Freakonomics" went on to sell 7 million copies combined by 2014.

The performance of these Gladwellian blockbusters inspired similar approaches not only by accomplished journalists (such as Gladwell's New Yorker colleague James Surowiecki with "The Wisdom of Crowds") but also from distinguished professors who, it turned out, could write compellingly for popular audiences if given the opportunities and the right incentives. While academics had long been motivated by publishing papers in highly specialized journals as a way of pursuing tenure and promotion as well as the approbation of their scholarly peers, now they had the chance to achieve considerable recognition, money, and public influence by popularizing in the Gladwellian vein. The trend attracted the likes of the Swarthmore psychology professor Barry Schwartz with his fascinating 2003 book, "The Paradox of Choice," and even Princeton's Kahneman, a Nobel Prize winner in economics, in "Thinking Fast and Slow."

I must confess that I, too, wrote a book that was rather obviously inspired by the Gladwellian boom. I expanded my 2005 cover story for Fast Company magazine, "Change or Die," into a 2007 book (with the same title) about the psychology of behavioral change and organizational change. It told the stories of characters from a far-flung range of unusual settings – from heart surgery survivors trying to adhere to vegan diets…to formerly heroin-addicted felons learning to live without drugs or violence at a San Francisco halfway house… to the workers and managers learning to get along better at General Motors' most troubled automobile factory. The anecdotes were intended to illuminate counterintuitive ideas from academic research across the fields of psychology, cognitive science, and neuroscience. Almost every major New York publisher bid in an auction for rights to publish the book, which wound up selling more than twice as many copies as any of my four other books.

## Conclusion

While there's hasn't been a business book in recent years to rival the blockbuster sales of "In Search of Excellence," "Iacocca," or "The Tipping Point," the category has endured, and publishers have continued to churn out the titles in impressive numbers. Some of the highest-profile CEOs haven't (yet) written memoirs, including Google's co-founders Sergey Brin and Larry Page, Amazon's Jeff Bezos, Apple's Tim Cook, and Tesla's Elon Musk (who prefers to post prolifically on Twitter). But the subgenre of business narratives has remained vibrant: The New York Times reporters Jodi Kantor and Meghan Twohey told the story of how they exposed a long history of sexual harassment by film mogul Harvey Weinstein in "She Said" (2019), which was the basis for a Hollywood movie in 2022. Their Times colleagues Sheera Frenkel and Cecilia Kang revealed the inner workings of Facebook in "An Ugly Truth" (2021). Bloomberg editor Bad Stone took on Internet mogul Jeff Bezos in "Amazon Unbound" (2021). And Wall Street Journal reporters Eliot Brown and Maureen Ferrell chronicled the fall of WeWork in "The Cult of We" (2021). Looking ahead, it seems likely that beat reporters in top newsrooms will continue to look to books as a way of telling their stories in the fullest depth and with the greatest narrative power – and, in some cases, of attracting interest from producers of podcasts and movies, too.

## References and Further Reading

Adams, Tim, "The Man Who Can't Stop Thinking," *The Guardian*, 15 November 2008. (Insightful interview with Malcolm Gladwell).

Behr, Peter, "New Lessons in Corporate Excellence," *The Washington Post*, 1 November 1984.

Deutschman, Alan. *How Steve Jobs Changed Our World*, New York: St. Martin's Press, 2011.

Donadio, Rachel, "The Gladwell Effect," *The New York Times*, 5 February 2006.

Easterbrook, Gregg, "He Wrote the Book," *The New York Times*, 16 June 2002. (Behind-the-scenes detail about the embattled publishing history of *My Years With General Motors*).

Florman, Samuel C. "The Hardy Boys and the Microkids Make a Computer," *The New York Times*, 23 August 1981.

Gans, Herbert J. "Best-Sellers By Sociologists: An Exploratory Study," *Contemporary Sociology*, Vol. 26, No 2, pp 131–135 (March 1997).

Grobel, Lawrence. *Conversations With Capote*, New York: Dutton, 1985.

Huey, John. "America's Most Successful Merchant," *Fortune*, 23 September 1991.

Johnston, Neal. "Lawyers At Work," *The New York Times*, 6 March 1983.

Kahneman, Daniel. *Thinking Fast and Slow*, New York: Farrar, Straus and Giroux, 2011.

Levitt, Steven D. "From Good to Great...to Below Average," *Freakonomics.com*, 28 July 2008

Mayer, Jane, "Donald Trump's Ghostwriter Tells All," *The New Yorker*, 18 July 2016. (A fascinating inside look at the journalist's troubled collaboration with the businessman).

McDowell, Edwin. "Publishing: 'Search' Heads 1983 Hard-Cover List," *New York Times*, 3 February 1984.Mitchell, Dan. "'Blink' Meets 'Freakonomics,'" *New York Times*, 21 May 2005.

Reingold, Jennifer and Ryan Underwood. "Was 'Built to Last' Built to Last?" *Fast Company*, 1 November 2004.

Romano, Lois. "Bill Novak, Galloping Ghost," *The Washington Post*, 12 June 1985.

Ross, Lillian. *Here But Not Here*, New York: Random House, 1998. (While Ross was criticized for writing revealingly about New Yorker editor William Shawn, who prized his privacy, her memoir provides fascinating insight into how their collaboration helped to change journalism).

Schott, Webster, "How to Succeed in Business By Really Trying," *The Washington Post*, 26 May 1985.

Whitfield, Debra, "Peter Drucker: Guiding Light to Management," *Los Angeles Times*, 14 April 1985.

Wyden, Peter, "The Blockbustering of Lee Iacocca," *The New York Times*, 13 September 1987.

"A Few Thin Slices of Malcolm Gladwell," *Powells.com*, 8 February 2005.

"Jonah Lehrer, David Brooks & More Malcolm Gladwell Wannabees (Photos)," *TheDailyBeast.com*, 1 August 2012.

# 14

# A HISTORY OF ART BUSINESS JOURNALISM

*Alexandra Bregman*

## Introduction

Like many fields (i.e., war, political, or science reporting) art news evolved with the subject itself. Each of these contexts is predicated on analysis with the aim of approval, and in the case of art reporting, ensuring that wealthy and influential art world players acknowledge and approve of the material in some form is essential to survival in an industry-specific field. This does present obstacles: opacity and red tape force the importance of relationships, and in so doing, challenge the veracity of unfettered content.

By 2022, the fine art market had become a $65.1 billion industry[1] and with that came a complicated task for business reporters. After centuries of well-heeled commentary, stripping art to its asset-worthiness may seem crude. Yet, tiers of seasoned and burgeoning industry-focused journalists alike cover the ups and downs of auctions and private sales, of gallery and art fair transactions, and, increasingly, the colorful financial transactions framed by fascinating lives.

The cultural value and collective consciousness of present-day art analysis inevitably colors reporting by myriad sources. Journalists take many forms: lawmakers and archaeologists are almost equally influenced and prone to publishing as traditional beat reporters. Therefore, art business is rarely reported on dispassionately, even in the financial section. Rather, passion has always framed the chronicling of art.

## Origins of the "Cult of Artistic Personality" in Art Criticism

Englishman Jonathan Richardson was the first to be credited as an art "critic."[2] He coined the term "art criticism" in 1719 and attempted to "rank" artworks, prompting other English-speaking writers to veer into art commentary (Close 2021).

A successor, Victorian writer John Ruskin, canonized the art world in his day. Best known for "Modern Painters" (1843–1860), he produced 39 volumes in just nine years, heralding a new era of art critical publishing.

A trend of antagonism against art writers developed. Rather than applaud the specificity of the new field, the idea of a Renaissance scholar well-rounded enough to comment thoughtfully

DOI: 10.4324/9781003298977-17

on art was occasionally regarded with skepticism and disdain. British playwright and screen-writer Tom Stoppard (born 1937) said he doubted if "art needed Ruskin any more than a moving train needs one of its passengers to shove it," defining art critics as, "men who have failed in literature and art" (Diakparomre 2011).

Yet, the sheer volume of work that Ruskin produced acted as a precursor to the current state of art business writing. As printing scaled, the ability to mass produce ideas and critiques matched. Twentieth- and 21st-century art writers were responding to the pace of media, and a cult of personality proliferated among the most profuse, apparently inexhaustible art critics.

## Diaspora and Rupture in the Post-War Art World

Prior to the Nazi takeover, Europe enjoyed a golden age of art analysis. Viennese psychoana-lyst Sigmund Freud was particularly fascinated by old masters and their psychological pro-files, presuming Leonardo da Vinci to be homosexual in the 1916 "Leonardo da Vinci and a Memory of His Childhood" (later confirmed in Walter Isaacson's biography) and analyzing Michelangelo's Moses in 1914 after reading Vasari's "Lives" (Strachey 1957).

In the lead-up to World War II, German and Austrian Jews were celebrated art patrons, often acquiring works by more experimental Abstract Expressionists artists...many of whom were Jewish. Art aside, some of the most brilliant minds of the era – Albert Einstein, Freud, and Karl Marx – were German-speaking Jews. But with art exhibition and criticism, the busi-ness of what was good art became a matter of life and death.

Along with the rise of fascism came the complete takedown of "degenerate" Jewish schol-ars and Abstract Expressionists.[3] This culminated in the Entartete Kunst (Degenerate Art) show near the local zoo in 1937, juxtaposed with "Great German Art," Nazi-approved con-temporary paintings in the style of Northern Renaissance Old Masters.

The showcase received a ton of press, successfully ushering in an era of ethnic cleansing that extended to the art itself. It revealed the danger of art criticism's tendency to define art as "good' and "bad," nefariously coopted by fascism, then commodified into a political agenda and the business of war and extermination.

During the Nazi reign, confiscations of Jewish art collections were prevalent. Before Jewish people were sent to their deaths, Nazi soldiers inventoried and sometimes even dis-played their art, or banished it to secret vaults in Switzerland, salt mines in Germany and Austria, and private collections. Wartime politics necessitated a lack of press around these transactions, and lists of confiscated art works were only first released in 1985. From there, the onus was on surviving descendants to recover their losses (Kulenović 2017).

Retribution news reporting only followed much later, predicated on a legal framework honoring both the intrinsic value of the works and the victims and casualties of Nazi raids. Most famously, Maria Altmann tirelessly advocated for the return of five paintings by Vien-nese painter Gustav Klimt from Vienna's Belvedere castle museum, best known among them Portrait of Adele Bloch Bauer I (Woman in Gold), which featured her aunt. In 2000, with the help of her lawyer Randy Schoenberg (grandson of Austrian composer Arnold Schön-berg), Altmann pursued the matter from Los Angeles, and by 2006, the paintings were awarded to her as their rightful heir. Within the year, Altmann sold the Woman in Gold to Neue Galerie Museum founder Ronald Lauder for $135 million, making it one of the most expensive paintings of all time (Vogel 2006). A feature film, "Gustav Klimt and Adele Bloch-Bauer: The Woman in Gold," later canonized their journey and brought it to the mainstream (Gustav Klimt and Adele Bloch-Bauer 2015).

Confiscated works continue to emerge, such as the 1,500 paintings by Chagall, Picasso, and Matisse found in the collection of Nazi art dealer Hildebrand Gurlitt's descendants in November 2013, estimated to be worth about $1.35 billion according to the Jewish Virtual Library. Freud had fled to London to influence a new generation of English-speaking psychoanalysts and critics, including art writers. Yet, Marxist art history particularly appealed to one such art critic, New York-based Clement Greenberg, and created a new pathway of discourse on what he deemed "the avant-garde" (Greenberg 1961, p. 3).

Greenberg's 1939 essay "Avant-Garde and Kitsch" employed Marxist theory to discuss the commercialization of kitsch, defined as "raw material" used for "vicarious experience and faked sensations." He wrote that kitsch, because it could be turned out mechanically, had "become an integral part of our productive system in a way in which true culture could never be, except accidentally" (Greenberg 1961, pp. 10–11). He eschewed the monetary value of art in favor of "detaching itself from society," as perhaps the first art writer to discuss valuation both critically and financially. Analytical to the point of skeptical, Greenberg nevertheless acknowledged the business of art as much as he sought to remove his thought processes from it. Speaking of kitsch, he wrote:

> While it is essentially its own salesman, a great sales apparatus has nevertheless been created for it, which brings pressure to bear on every member of society.
>
> *(Greenberg 1961, p. 11)*

Greenberg went on to great success as an art critic – credited with analyzing, endorsing, and singlehandedly furthering the career of Jackson Pollock. The impact of Greenberg's words on Pollock's success reveals the challenges of writing about art without business in mind in the 20th century, and the "cult of celebrity" of which Vasari was accused proved ever more prevalent in the modern and contemporary eras.

## The Trade Media Trap

What began as Greenberg's championing of Pollock's artistry quickly became a championing of himself. He wove an incredible tale rife with fanfare, in which he "took one look" at Pollock's painting and realized that he "was the greatest painter this country has produced" (Adams 2009). Greenberg was deemed "the voice of the new American painting" and endures as one of the foremost figures not just in art criticism, but in contemporary art altogether. In 2011, art writer Jonathan Jones wrote of Greenberg, "The late American writer and thinker was no Ruskin, but … Greenberg has achieved immortality of a kind" (Jones 2011).

In a 1981 interview with British art historian T. J. Clark on Modern Art Practices & Debates, an aged and celebrated Greenberg said boldly:

> You don't ask anything of art except that it be good. You don't prescribe; you don't make specific demands – 'art do this; art do that.' When it's good, it's does everything … Only your eye could tell you. Nothing else.
>
> *(Clark 1981)*

The evolution of Greenberg's 1939 musings that threw away the old guard was starting to sound remarkably like it, with "good" and "bad" once again acting as limiting categories. Perhaps this was because Greenberg had become a foremost expert on taste by the 1980s, with cultural and political influence far beyond writing and critiquing for its own sake.

From Marxist and Trotskyist, Greenberg is thought to have eventually participated in the CIA's Center for Cultural Freedom, with his propagation of Pollock intended to act counter a symbol of liberty acting counter to the Russian state. He would convince his friends to buy art, such as former classmate turned Wall Street stockbroker Saul "Puggy" Schwamm[4] who purchased The Blue Unconscious, estimated by neighbor Gwen Davis' eyewitness account to be worth $200 million in 2017. At the height of Pollock's career, Greenberg dated artist Helen Frankenthaler (from 1950 to 1955), then curated a show that included her work in 1964. No one explicitly detracted from his reputation by addressing any perceived conflict of interest in his critique, neither personal nor financial (Kammen 2012).

One could argue that the incestuous nature of Greenberg's business ventures was a by-product of the creation of a new canon of media to rival Ruskin's early literature. Hyde's Weekly Art News was founded in New York just two years after Ruskin's death, in November 1902, and today continues to circulate as ARTnews. Its website boasts a 2022 readership of 180,000 key industry players in 124 countries. In the first issue, a modest but prominent sales column featured purposefully along the front-left page. Although sale language was indeed peppered into the issue, it remained mostly listings, with majority of the text focusing on upcoming exhibitions and lectures. Art in America followed suit in 1913, with much more intellectual and lofty reviews (Hyde's Weekly Art News 1904).

Artforum, founded in 1962 in San Francisco (moving headquarters to New York five years later), was a relative newcomer to the more established publishing scene, which perhaps emboldened them to criticize Greenberg's group exhibition. Editor John Coplans noted that Greenberg's 1964 exhibit, "fail[ed] to make its point," and that "Frankenthaler d[idn't] belong in the show" (Coplans 1964).

Like Greenberg, another art theory export from World War II was grappling with the discord between the cultural and the financial. Hans Neuendorf, born in 1937, was entrepreneurial partly out of necessity, trading farmers for food in the bleak post-war years as a German national. A budding passion for the Modernists married his interests, and he sold his first painting in Hamburg at 18 years old – soon regularly selling at a 50 percent markup to finance his education. Neuendorf then staged the first Pop Art show in Germany with Paris-based gallerist Ileana Sonnabend.

When interviewed by Andrew Goldstein in his 80s, Neuendorf remained conflicted about whether the art or the money was the dominant revolutionizer. But as was the case for Neuendorf himself, the necessity of survival and the complexity of the financial situation infiltrated the cultural shift. He was a personal witness to the evolution of Switzerland as an art capital, cynically [or realistically] drawing attention to its profitability:

> Germans were bringing their black money to Basel to deposit it there, so … it would be a good idea to sell them some art, because art is liquid, and you can ship it. Nobody was paying any attention, because no one thought it was worth anything. So that's how Beyeler's business evolved, with that German black money.… It was more of a cultural event than a monetary event. I actually think that all the money that's coming into the art world now is really distorting the whole thing, to a degree that is already very dangerous.
>
> *(Goldstein 2019, part 2)*

In 1989, Neuendorf founded artnet as an art prices database, intending to both expose opacity in the art market and efficiently shape the new frontier of digital art viewing and buying.

The platform included artnet's magazine, the first-ever online publication catering specifically to art market players.

Forever intertwined with the rapid rise of this digital sphere, Neuendorf acknowledged a concurrent shift in the nature of art business reporting:

> It's popularity that counts now, not quality. When something is popular, it sells, and when it sells, the prices go up. And then the press has a reason to report on it. That's how the art world functions nowadays. That's very different even from how it was when I started artnet. At the time, we were still innocent and idealistic, but this money thing has completely ruined everything.
>
> *(Goldstein 2019, part 2)*

In 1990, the online and print publication The Art Newspaper followed suit, founded by Umberto Allemandi and Anna Somers Cocks in London (in partnership with the 1983 publication Il Giornale dell'Arte). A New York office opened in 1992, then a Russian language issue in Moscow in 2012, a Chinese language issue in Shanghai in 2013, French in Paris in 2018, and Hebrew in 2019. The monthly print edition is over 100 pages, but now the daily online news service, newsletter, and podcast disseminate much more quickly. Pertinent business topics include current events, cultural heritage, news … and of course, watershed sales values.

Certainly, the post-war climate of money as survival and money as futurism did much to stimulate both the art world and its peripheral trade reporting arm. However incestuous, the astronomical sums were changing the face of everything, with culture the least immune.

Money culture in art was as risky as it was stimulating. For people such as Greenberg and Neuendorf, it was nearly impossible to remain objective when art – specific art – was making them richer. Until gradually, then suddenly, the money was so much that it was all anyone talked about.

### The Moneyed Evolution of 21st-Century Art Business Journalism

"In the art world, asking 'What is a museum for?' is like asking, 'What is money for?' at a Wall Street dinner, says philosopher Alain de Botton," quoted by Brian Bethune in a 2015 article for Maclean's (Bethune 2015).

Suddenly, Wall Street had more in common with the 21st-century art market than its museums, and the New York art world ushered in a new induction of art stars with banker buyers behind them.

The record-breaking 1973 Robert and Ethel Scull sale was the first to be reported largely for its astronomical value: $2.2 million overall, sold at Sotheby's auction house. Their wealth had been the subject of prior articles to the extent that a 1970 New York Times article was blatantly titled, "When Ethel Scull Redecorates, It's Art News" (Curtis 1970).

Just as Greenberg had made Pollock in the 1950s, 1980s gallery titans such as Larry Gagosian, David Zwirner, and Mary Boone used their networks and strategies to catapult talent into the multi-million-dollar stratosphere. Among these stars were the writers themselves: press agencies such as Fitz & Co., Nadine Johnson, and Resnicow & Associates planned elaborate VIP dinners and trips where the writers hobnobbed with moneyed collectors.

The process was dazzling, especially when considering that the average salary for an editor at a trade publication such as artnet or ARTNews rarely exceeded $50,000 in the early 2000s, and freelance writers were paid by no more than $1 per word for 600-word pieces (per Glassdoor self-reporting). Essentially, art writers were paid in wine nights and society photography, a glamorous but ultimately problematic catering structure. Because by blinding a struggling writer with events in a world of billionaires, especially one who is not officially permitted to accept gifts or bribes, the moral line thins. How can you remain objective toward a market that financially owns you?

Even if art writers weren't actively working at galleries like those they covered (which was common), they still formed essential relationships. The annual ARTnews Top 200 list was a good example of their necessity, based on survey responses from industry professionals about high-net-worth individuals with whom they do business. By 2018, ARTnews itself was corporatized, changing owners in 2014 for the first time since 1972, then merging offices with Art in America under another buy-out and reducing the print edition to quarterly, and finally moving to Penske Media in 2018.

Outside of the trade journals, the select few who were paid well enough to cover art for mainstays such as The Wall Street Journal (Kelly Crow), the Financial Times (Georgina Adam and Melanie Gerlis), and Bloomberg (Katya Kazakina) stayed in coveted positions for decades. With the early 2000s came slightly shifted demographics, as the caricatured bespectacled academic gave way to female faces, but still the pool was still white and extremely small.

A March 2019 survey conducted by Nieman Reports determined just how small. More than a third of respondents believed Roberta Smith of The New York Times to be the most influential art critic in the United States. At the time of writing in 2022, her career had endured 45 years (Schumacher 2019).

Another art market writing veteran, Georgina Adam, cited statistician and art historian Geraldine Keen Norman. Norman launched the Times-Sotheby Index, which used an averaging technique to speculate auction values since 1950 from 1967 to 1971, as prices were not published after sales.

Adam's 2014 book, "Big Bucks: The Explosion of the Art Market in the 21st Century," referenced James Roundell of Christie's, who recollected the state of anonymity and opacity:

> …It was generally the convention that auctioneers did not disclose, as the sale was going along, whether a lot was unsold. Instead, they would call out a fictious name from a prepared list, for example players for Chelsea football club! If buyers at an auction could not tell what was being sold and what was not, then it made the sale seem to be going better than it in fact was.
>
> *(Adam 2014)*

In a 1971 New York Times article called "In Sotheby-land the graphs go up," Norman was panned by a fellow female journalist for her subsequent book.

"The Index cannot pretend to any precise degree of accuracy," wrote Grace Glueck.

> It measures order of magnitude, rather than small variations … I heartily recommend [the book] to those who collect not art, but money, and can afford to shell out $20 for a book that is really nothing more than a cumbersome advertisement for Sotheby's.
>
> *(Glueck 1971)*

When asked to name four other influential critics, more than half of the mentions went to Smith and just five other writers. A similar poll by Prowly revealed only two of five influencers to be traditional art critics (Patricia Bickers at Art Monthly Magazine and Peter Schjedahl at The New Yorker). The others – Sarah Douglas, Editor-in-Chief at ARTnews, Jonathan Jones, U.K.-based writer at The Guardian, and Jerry Saltz, Senior Art Critic at New York Magazine – all had been enmeshed in the climate of art market commentary (Schumacher 2019).

Saltz (born 1951) proved an instrumental figure at the apex of this art market. Prone to incendiary tweets and Instagram posts, the critic harnessed the power of social media to create a 21st-century cult of personality, belatedly seen as an enfant terrible – at once celebrated and a fire starter among elites.

Saltz and his wife, Roberta Smith, rank among the most influential art critics in the world. Both were nominated for the Pulitzer Prize in 2018 … and Saltz won. Nieman Reports cited an outcry focused on Smith's being the more serious writer, attributing her loss to being a woman.[5]

Keeping up with the newfound speed of art writing proved difficult. Whereas Smith and fellow Times critic Holland Cotter maintained their livelihoods and reputations for many years, not all could do so. Carol Vogel, an art business correspondent at The New York Times from 1983 to 2014, stepped down after allegations she plagiarized from Wikipedia (Genocchio and Jovanovic 2014).

In Vogel's defense, the content churn in art often lends itself to secondary reporting (with appropriate citation). Artnet and Art Observed both reshare and repurpose content from breaking news regularly as a means of circulation. Art blogging and the onset of social media platforms created a frenzy, and the nature of the content adapted to the audiences seeking faster and newer "narrative experiences."

But while money was speaking for itself, art critical writers were moving into post-colonial and gendered contexts. This was a postmortem of the World War II Abstract Expressionist absence of identity, now reexamining the origins and ethics of works to better resonate with changing audiences. From feminist theory to queer theory, challenging the discourse was becoming the discourse itself.

### Vested Financial Interests of Art as an Asset Class

Under a shifting racial lens, it must be said that in the current art world climate, money is colorblind in the most problematic sense of the word.

Hong Kong-based Orientations magazine was founded in 1969[6] as a travel and lifestyle magazine, shifting to arts in 1981, while The Asian Art Newspaper was founded in 1997. They each catered to East and South Asian antiquities collectors. By the late 2000s, an unprecedented Chinese collector boom turned these lesser-known insider publications into powerhouses with much larger readerships, and burgeoning Chinese language publications were invited to New York and London showcases on a grander scale. This dynamic sparked a stronger tie to financial publications, as those looking to cover Asian financial markets had to know what was happening in art.

Somewhat concurrently, Russian investment during the 2008 Great Recession also sparked record-breaking sales numbers at Western auctions. GARAGE Magazine was founded by Dasha Zhukova in 2011, then the wife of Russian oligarch Roman Abramovich, as an offshoot of a museum of the same name. These relationships were instrumental in the market reporting of the late 2000s, even as they have now largely dissolved due to changing financial tides and Russian sanctions amidst the Ukraine War. Today, it is owned by VICE media (Garage 2022).

The Asian market also fell under scrutiny, particularly surrounding the increasing controversy around owning objects from the ancient world. Several inflection points included the Iraq War and perceived negligence around protecting the Baghdad Museum, and the 2006 Pulitzer Prize finalist investigations into the unlawful acquisitions of the Getty Museum by Los Angeles-based Jason Felch and Ralph Frammolino (The Pulitzer Prizes 2006).

These were watershed moments that served to challenge the entire market and radicalized the social consciousness of market reporting.

Arguably, the laser focus on museum practices spurred vigilante justice against the Sackler wings of famous museums when the family was held responsible for the opioid crisis. Protesters stormed the Metropolitan Museum of Art as a way to demand justice in 2018 (Walters 2018). The following year, the Smithsonian Institution "rebranded" the Freer and Sackler galleries in Washington, DC, as the National Museum of Asian Art, although the original names remained legally and in small print (McGlone 2019).

The ripple effect of this market challenge meant that art market writing was slowly moving away from money-only reporting into socially conscious truth-telling. With this shift, art moved out of the trade publications and into the mainstream. The heritage of art propaganda had given away to arts journalism as its very antidote.

Beyond the social mores, the forensic reporting on forgery investigations allowed technical studies to factor into art market reporting. "Technical art history" as a field only really developed around 1997 and is an emerging and controversial area of study for established arts professionals (Cardinali 2017).

Modern institutions such as Deloitte, which has published an annual art finance report since 2014, and UBS' collector forecasting, prevailed as the largest sponsors of financial art market documentation. They funded the reports and the art fairs because they reflected their existing clients and brought in new clients (which was, ultimately, the point). The 2022 Arts Economics report noted that 43 percent of high-net-worth collectors were motivated to sell by "Investment returns," and an additional 19 percent on "financial motivations." That meant that "content motives" at 27 percent were in the extreme minority (McAndrew 2022).

Ultimately, data serves as a truthteller. The increasingly quantified art market has taken many forms, notably the Mei Moses Indices (founded by Michael Moses in 2002, with its roots in the Times-Sotheby Index), the projections and summaries of Art Tactic (by Norwegian-English economist Anders Petterson in 2000), and Irish founder Clare McAndrew of Arts Economics in 2005. Numerous art investment firms, such as Athena Art Finance, Winston Art Group, and more recently, Masterworks, designed to replicate partial-share investment strategies for moderate rather than high-net-worth individuals, served a model previously monopolized by the banks.

Evan Beard, formerly of Deloitte to Bank of America as Head of Art Services, and now at Masterworks, a partial-share investment startup to add art to a portfolio, has been a firsthand witness to the evolution of money in the market. He discusses art valuations with his collector clients, reviewing asset strategies such as taking out collateral on multi-million-dollar paintings to funnel it back into businesses.

In a July 2022 interview, Beard described himself as, a "voice for folks covering this market to try and unpack what's going on here," decoding "financial chicanery" of market manipulation and peering behind the curtain of private sales. He sees the current art historical lineage of coverage as business-based at its core, from Andy Warhol's "business as art" to the sudden recognition of Jean-Michel Basquiat.

Warhol is famously quoted as saying, "Making money is art and working is art and good business is the best art" (Gopnick 2020). He was a good friend of Peter Brant, the paper heir who founded Interview Magazine, and together they discovered and nurtured Jean-Michel Basquiat. As time went by, Brant continued to hold more power in the arts, and the value of his collection began to correspond.

As a member of these elite circles, Beard feels that art market coverage is increasingly reported by those with economics training rather than art historical. "This idea where the market followed the critic, that's been turned on its head, where the market is kinda leading it, and the collector has the real power," Beard told me. "…The financial press has had to play catch-up."

Furthermore, Beard has access to private indexes and documents to receive accurate market information, and he is not impressed with the ability of art journalists to cull information – some poorly trained, others simply unable. "I always laugh when these financial journalists walk around the art fairs and rattle off these numbers of what we sold this for," he told me. "It's almost always wrong, and it's almost always the gallery kind of pumping up their artists or their programs as a way to get more consignments."

Beard believes that art business reporters are "sidetracked" by big headlines, unable to probe deeper and do their own calculations: "Art reporters go with the easy headline when they see something big. They don't really have time to go the next level down."

Through Masterworks, Beard has access to the Mei Moses Indices and collector data, neither of which the average art writer can review – especially when considering who owns what: Moses' database was acquired by Sotheby's in 2016 (Sotheby's 2022).

Petterson now teaches at Sotheby's Institute of Art and McAndrew at Christie's. Can the reporting itself be truly ethical on a loop back to vested interests? Looking at the hard, cold numbers on an arts economics report, did anyone care about anything other than the money anymore? Had art critics become irrelevant? (Christie's Education 2020).

The obsession with billionaire tastes has driven both the market and its subsequent reporting. A culmination of market behavior was in the $450 million sale of Leonardo da Vinci's Salvator Mundi (Savior of the World) at Christie's in 2017 by Russian oligarch Dmitry Rybolovlev. In what became known as "The Bouvier Affair," the story of the astronomical sum had its roots in a commission scandal eventually extensively reported, now taught in law and art courses for those seeking to understand the market.

This realm has gone global. Frieze Art Fair, historically in London and New York, plans to open in Seoul in 2022. Chinese investors were increasingly at the forefront of this new market-motivated universe, and they will be replaced when dealers and media follow the next emerging market.

However, art business journalism responds to this 21st-century changing tide, balance is essential – both in content streams and in ethics. Diversity of thought, artistic consciousness, and financial reporting to probe the incestuous and personality-motivated industry will be essential. If this journalistic sensitivity can be taught, all the better.

## Conclusion: Art Market Writing As a Chosen Career

Today, art journalism is a taught field. Motivated by creativity, an interest in writing, and values of truth-telling and integrity, all can be found as much in the word as the process. Although creativity may be seen at odds with the hard-hitting nature of beat journalism, the process itself is as artistic as creating a painting or sculpture, deducing and adding to finalize a masterpiece. By its disruptive climate, understanding is illuminated.

Yet, the field of art writer education is surprisingly new. Columbia Graduate School of Journalism's Master of Arts program in arts journalism, for instance, was launched in 2005, in association with the National Endowment for the Arts' new Arts Journalism Institute in fall 2004, and The National Arts Journalism Program (founded in 1994). The goal was "to advance the quantity and quality of arts coverage in the press" (Columbia Journalism School 2022).

The Columbia website continues: "During the 'culture wars' years, inadequate news coverage had contributed to apathy about the arts at a time when artists, art institutions, and the idea of government arts funding were coming under attack."

Professors invite specialty experts on subjects such as, "how to decipher arts funding, delineate artistic movements, map essential context" and "how to capture an artist's personality with nuance and verve."

The School of the Art Institute of Chicago (SAIC) also offers a Master of Arts in Arts Journalism program, coming more from the art side than the news side. Similarly, Sotheby's Institute of Art and New York University offer courses in Art Business and Arts Administration, although without a focus on newsworthiness. But in 2021, Amherst College taught "The Art Market," one of the first top-ranked American colleges to do so.

Courses specifically designed around business reporting in the arts may become the norm. It is the inescapable trajectory of centuries of navigating wealth and power in a creative field and being able to report it accurately and truthfully – no matter what comes next.

## Notes

1  $65.1 billion represents aggregate sales of art and antiques by dealers and auction houses by Clare McAndrew's annual report, published by UBS. It is important to note that what was formerly known as Union Bank of Switzerland is a private company, but one of few with the bandwidth to accurately sponsor and quantify the broad arc of the art market. This authorship unto itself signifies the challenges associated with art market reporting for public consumption, and the availability of information outside of the inner collector circle.
2  Not a confirmed relative of Picasso biographer Sir John Patrick Richardson (1924–2019).
3  This piece will not be addressing Soviet or Maoist propaganda posters, but they have ties to Nazi imagery and messaging.
4  A nickname reportedly coined by antisemitic colleagues.
5  Cis-gendered, female-identifying.
6  Original Orientations founder, Indonesian Adrian Zecha, gradually became known as a hotelier. He is now known as the founder of Aman Resorts.

## References

Adam, G. 2014. *Big Bucks: The Explosion of the Art Market in the 21st Century*. Farnham: Lund Humphries, pp. 1–30.

"Art theory, criticism, and historiography." Europe, 1450 to 1789: Encyclopedia of the Early Modern World. Retrieved June 22, 2022 from Encyclopedia.com: https://www.encyclopedia.com/history/encyclopedias-almanacs-transcripts-and-maps/art-theory-criticism-and-historiography

Adams, H., 2009. *Decoding Jackson Pollock*. [online] Arts & Culture. Available at: https://www.smithsonianmag.com/arts-culture/decoding-jackson-pollock-142492290/ [Accessed July 2022].

Bethune, B. 2015. "So, Alain de botton, what is art for?" *MACLEAN'S*. https://www.macleans.ca/culture/arts/so-alain-de-botton-what-is-art-for/ [Accessed July 2022].

Cardinali, M. 2017. "Technical art history and the first conference on the scientific analysis of works of art" (Rome, 1930). *History of Humanities*, 2(1), pp. 221–243.

Christie's Education. 2020. "Dr Clare McAndrew." *Online Courses Team.* https://education.christies.com/online/faculty/clare-mcandrew [Accessed July 2022].

Clark, T.J. 1981. "Clement Greenberg on Pollock with T J Clark, modern art practices & debates, 1981." https://www.youtube.com/watch?v=IYyVo2XPn1Y [Accessed July 2022].

Close, C. 2021. "Artists vs art critics: An age-old combative yet symbiotic relationship." https://www.artandobject.com/articles/artists-vs-art-critics-combative-yet-symbiotic-relationship.

Columbia Journalism School, Arts and Culture. 2022. "Programs of study." *Columbia Journalism School.* https://journalism.columbia.edu/arts-and-culture [Accessed July 2022].

Coplans, J. 1964. "The long-awaited Greenberg exhibition fails to make its point." *The Online Edition of Artforum International Magazine.* https://www.artforum.com/print/196406/the-long-awaited-greenberg-exhibition-fails-to-make-its-point-37824 [Accessed July 2022].

Curtis, C. 1970. "When ethel scull redecorates, it is art news." [online] *New York Times.* Nytimes.com. https://www.nytimes.com/1970/02/27/archives/when-ethel-scull-redecorates-it-is-art-news.html [Accessed July 2022].

Diakparomre, A. M. 2011. "Art criticism and art history: A symbiotic relationship." [online] *SJ Magazine of Contemporary Arts & Culture in East Africa.* https://startjournal.org/2011/02/art-criticism-and-art-history-a-symbiotic-relationship/#_edn3 [Accessed July 2022].

Garage. 2022. https://garage.vice.com/en_us/page/garage-about [Accessed July 2022].

Genocchio, B. and Jovanovic, R. 2014. "Veteran arts writer Carol Vogel resigns from the New York times." *Artnet News.* https://news.artnet.com/art-world/veteran-arts-writer-carol-vogel-resigns-from-the-new-york-times-188263 [Accessed July 2022].

Goldstein, A. 2019a. "The story of artnet: How founder Hans Neuendorf rose from the rubble of World War II Germany to transform the art market." *Artnet News.* https://news.artnet.com/the-big-interview/hans-neuendorf-story-of-artnet-interview-part-1-1664431#:~:text=Founded%20in%201989%20as%20a,gallery%20network%20served%20as%20many [Accessed July 2022].

Goldstein, A. 2019b. "The story of artnet, part 2: How founder Hans Neuendorf helped invent the Art Fair in a more 'innocent' time." *Artnet News.* https://news.artnet.com/the-big-interview/hans-neuendorf-story-of-artnet-interview-part-2-1664434 [Accessed July 2022].

Goldstein, A. 2019c. "The story of artnet, part 4: How hans neuendorf and an unlikely crew created artnet and changed the art market." *Artnet News.* https://news.artnet.com/the-big-interview/hans-neuendorf-story-of-artnet-interview-part-4-1664440 [Accessed July 2022].

Gopnik, B. 2020. "Andy Warhol offered to sign cigarettes, food, even money to make money." *Artnews,* April 21, 2020. https://www.artnews.com/art-news/market/andy-warhol-business-art-blake-gopnik-biography-excerpt-1202684403/

Glueck, G. 1971. "In Sotheby-land the graphs go up." *New York Times.* https://www.nytimes.com/1971/11/07/archives/money-and-art-a-study-based-on-the-timessotheby-index-by-geraldine.html [Accessed July 2022].

Greenberg, C. 1961. *Art and Culture: Critical Essays.* https://cpb-us-.e2.wpmucdn.com/sites.uci.edu/dist/d/1838/files/2015/01/Greenberg-Clement-Avant-Garde-and-Kitsch-copy.pdf

Hyde's Weekly Art News, 1904. pp. 1–26. https://archive.org/details/sim_artnews_november-29-1902-april-30-1904_1-2_1-26/page/n9/mode/2up?view=theater

Institute for Advanced Study. n.d. *Erwin Panofsky: Life, Work, and Legacy.* [online] <https://www.ias.edu/erwin-panofsky-life-work-and-legacy> [Accessed July 2022].

Jewish Virtual Library: A Project of AICE. n.d. *Holocaust Restitution: Recovering Stolen Art.* [online] <https://www.jewishvirtuallibrary.org/recovering-stolen-art-from-the-holocausthttps://www.jewishvirtuallibrary.org/recovering-stolen-art-from-the-holocaust> [Accessed July 2022].

Jones, J. 2011. "Clement Greenberg: The art critic who refuses to flatline." *The Guardian.* https://www.theguardian.com/artanddesign/jonathanjonesblog/2011/mar/11/clement-greenberg-art-critic [Accessed July 2022].

Kammen, M. 2012. "Open marriage chez Clem: A life with Clement Greenberg." *LARB.* https://lareviewofbooks.org/article/open-marriage-chez-clem-a-life-with-clement-greenberg/ [Accessed July 2022].

Kulenović, S. 2017. "Degenerate art - modern artworks dismissed by the Nazi as 'filth'." [online] *Widewalls.* https://www.widewalls.ch/magazine/degenerate-art-nazi-artworks [Accessed July 2022].

McAndrew, C. 2022. *The Art Market 2022,* p. 18. https://www.artbasel.com/about/initiatives/theartmarket2022pdf

McGlone, P. 2019. "Don't call it the freer/sackler. Call it the National Museum of Asian Art." *The Washington Post*, December 4, 2019. https://www.washingtonpost.com/entertainment/museums/dont-call-it-the-freersackler-call-it-the-national-museum-of-asian-art/2019/12/04/ce6bbc78-160c-11ea-9110-3b34ce1d92b1_story.html

National Gallery of Art, nga.gov. 2022. *Patrons and Artists in Late 15th-Century Florence.* [online] https://www.nga.gov/features/slideshows/patrons-and-artists-in-late-15th-century-florence.html [Accessed July 8, 2022].

Ronald S. Lauder Neue Galerie. 2015. "Gustav Klimt and Adele Bloch-Bauer: The woman in gold," 2015. https://www.neuegalerie.org/gustav-klimt-and-adele-bloch-bauer-woman-gold

Schumacher, M. L. 2019. "Visual arts journalism: Newsroom pressure and generational change." *Nieman Reports.* https://niemanreports.org/articles/visual-arts-journalism-newsroom-pressure-and-generational-change/ [Accessed July 2022].

Sotheby's Institute, Our Faculty: Anders Petterson. MA in Art Business - London. https://sothebysinstitute.com/why-sothebys/our-faculty-and-guest-speakers/anders-petterson/ [Accessed July 10, 2022].

Sothebys. 2022. "The Sotheby's Mei Moses Indices." *Sothebys.com.* https://www.sothebys.com/en/the-sothebys-mei-moses-indices [Accessed July 10, 2022].

Spencer Museum of Art, 2012. "Giorgio Vasari & court culture in late renaissance Italy." [online] https://spencerart.ku.edu/exhibitions/vasari/michelangelo [Accessed July 2022].

Strachey, J., ed. 1957. *The Standard Edition of the Complete Psychological Works of Sigmund Freud*, Vol. XI. https://www.sas.upenn.edu/~cavitch/pdf-library/Freud_Leonardo.pdf, pp. 60-137

The Pulitzer Prizes. 2006. https://www.pulitzer.org/finalists/jason-felch-and-ralph-frammolino

The Warburg Institute. n.d. "About us." [online] https://warburg.sas.ac.uk/about-us [Accessed July 2022].

Variety Staff. 2018. "PMC buys ARTnews, art in America." *Variety.* https://variety.com/2018/biz/news/pmc-artnews-art-in-america-1203027153/ [Accessed July 2022].

Vogel, C. 2006. "Lauder pays $135 Million, a record, for a klimt portrait." *New York Times.* https://www.nytimes.com/2006/06/19/arts/design/19klim.html

Walters, J. 2018. "Artist Nan Goldin stages opioids protest in Metropolitan Museum Sackler wing." *The Guardian.* https://www.theguardian.com/us-news/2018/mar/10/opioids-nan-goldin-protest-metropolitan-museum-sackler-wing [Accessed July 2022].

## Other Resources

Benowitz, S. 2021. "History of art basel." *MiamiandBeaches.com.* https://www.miamiandbeaches.com/events/art-basel/history-of-art-basel-miami-beach [Accessed July 2022].

Cascone, S. 2022. "'I see pace taking a lot of really interesting risks': Writer and curator Kimberly Drew on why she's joining the gallery world." *Art Market - Artnet News.* https://news.artnet.com/art-world/kimberly-drew-joins-pace-gallery-2070448 [Accessed July 2022].

Conisbee, P. 2009. *French Paintings of the Fifteenth through the Eighteenth Century*, The Collections of the National Gallery of Art Systematic Catalogue, Washington, DC, p. 246.

Court, A. 1990. "The legend of Jack the Dripper: JACKSON POLLOCK an American Saga, by Steven Naifeh and Gregory White Smith (Clarkson N. Potter: $29.95; 944 pp., illustrated)." [online] *Los Angeles Times.* https://www.latimes.com/archives/la-xpm-1990-02-25-bk-2003-story.html [Accessed July 2022].

Drew, K. 2012. @MuseumMammy. https://twitter.com/museummammy [Accessed July 2022].

Elias, J. and Rizvi, K. 2010. *Key Themes for the Study of Islam.* Oxford: One World, pp. 6–25.

Ferretti, F. 1973. "Scull's U.S. art brings record $2 million." [online] *Nytimes.com.* https://www.nytimes.com/1973/10/19/archives/sculls-us-art-brings-record-2-million.html [Accessed July 2022].

Graddy, K. 2021. "You can now buy a share of a masterpiece. Is it worth it?" *Brandeis NOW.* https://www.brandeis.edu/now/2021/september/art-shares-graddy-conversation.html [Accessed July 2022].

Greenberger, A. 2022. "Pace gallery names Kimberly drew as associate director Amid hiring spree." *ARTnews.com.* https://www.artnews.com/art-news/news/kimberly-drew-pace-gallery-1234618297/ [Accessed July 2022].

Harries, G. and Wahl-Jorgensen, K. 2007. The Culture of Arts Journalists. SAGE Publications, 8(6), pp. 619–639. https://journals.sagepub.com/doi/10.1177/1464884907083115

Hester, R. 2018. *Historical Research: Theory and Methods*. United Kingdom: EDTECH.

Hodne, L. 2020. "Winckelmann's depreciation of colour in light of the querelle du coloris and Recent Critique." *Konsthistorisk Tidskrift/Journal of Art History*, 89(3), 191–210. https://doi.org/10.10 80/00233609.2020.1788636

Jones, C. 2008. *Eyesight Alone*. Chicago, IL: University of Chicago Press.

Kinsella, E. 2020. "Miami's art fairs can account for 50 percent of a gallery's annual sales. Here's how dealers are coping with their cancellation." *Artnet News*. https://news.artnet.com/market/art-basel-miami-cancelled-fallout-1908967 [Accessed July 2022].

Postema, S. and Deuze, M. 2020. "Artistic journalism: Confluence in forms, values and practices." *Journalism Studies*, 21(10), 1305–1322. https://doi.org/10.1080/1461670X.2020.1745666

Lancaster, C. (1952). "Keys to the understanding of Indian and Chinese painting: The "six limbs" of Yaśodhara and the "six principles" of Hsieh Ho." *The Journal of Aesthetics and Art Criticism*, 11(2), 95–104. https://doi.org/10.2307/426036

McGath, C. 2010. "Art journalism in the twenty-first century: Where is it headed? Open enrollment." https://magazine.art21.org/2010/06/23/art-journalism-in-the-twenty-first-century-where-is-it-headed/#.YoZYb5PMJ-U [Accessed July 2022].

Morgan T. and Purje, L. 2017. "An illustrated guide to Linda Nochlin's 'why have there been no great women artists?'" *Hyperallergic*. https://hyperallergic.com/377975/an-illustrated-guide-to-linda-nochlins-why-have-there-been-no-great-women-artists/ [Accessed July 2022].

Schulz, B. 2016. "Forgotten history: Bernhard Schulz on contemporary art museum in Berlin after the war." [online] The Art Newspaper - International art news and events. https://www.theart-newspaper.com/2016/04/23/forgotten-history-bernhard-schulz-on-contemporary-art-museum-in-berlin-after-the-war [Accessed July 2022].

Sofroniou, A. 2016. "Sleeping & dreaming explained by arts and science." *Lulu.com*, p. 140.

Surowiecki. J. 2005. "Cash for Canvas." *The New Yorker*. https://www.newyorker.com/maga-zine/2005/10/17/cash-for-canvas [Accessed July 2022].

van Damme, W. (2000). "African verbal arts and the study of african visual aesthetics." *Research in African Literatures*, 31(4), 8–20. http://www.jstor.org/stable/3821074

# PART III

# Setting Themselves Apart

# 15

# TELEVISION BUSINESS NEWS

## Growth and New Audiences in an Evolving Industry

*Ceci Rodgers*

### Introduction

Just as print business journalism has grown in the past several decades, so has business news on television. From modest beginnings on nightly network news in the 1960s and 1970s, TV business news has exploded to include 24-hour business news channels, syndicated broadcast shows and streaming news and video on laptops and phones, available almost anywhere at any time. The revolution can be traced to the 1970s and 1980s, when the fall of Bretton Woods and the gold standard led to hyperinflation and high interest rates, putting economic matters in the news. The invention of individual retirement accounts heralded the era of "popular capitalism" and the "citizen investor" (Arrese and Medina 2002). At least one journalist dubbed the 1978 law that created the 401(k) retirement savings account the "Financial Journalists' Redeployment Act," (Saporito 1999a) because it meant that consumers would now have to know more about investing. Shows such as Wall Street Week and Nightly Business Report were born in this era and attracted devoted audiences of newly minted investors. The fact that audiences for these offerings were more educated and affluent than a mainstream network news audience was not lost on TV executives (Kurtz 2000, p. 31). Financial News Network, which broadcast seven hours of news during market hours on UHF stations, soon followed, and later, as individual stock ownership soared, CNBC, Bloomberg TV, CNNfn, and Fox Business Network (FBN).

Along with rapid growth, the TV business news industry has grappled with questions about its role and efficacy, questions that deserve careful examination. Are investors helped or hurt by the minute-by-minute coverage of stock price moves on cable channels? Do business TV channels inappropriately cheerlead the stock market? Or do they fulfill their journalistic watchdog role by warning of trouble and holding business to account? Much of the academic research on business news concerns their impact on stock prices. Several studies (Pari 1987; Beltz and Jennings 1997; Ferreira and Smith 2003) found that stocks recommended on certain business shows enjoyed a bump higher in price in the days following the show. The value to investors of star anchors (Jim Cramer, Maria Bartiromo, Lou Dobbs) has been a subject of debate, with some extolling the benefits of drawing individual investors to financial news, and others criticizing the outsized impact of such personalities, some more political than financial. This chapter details the history of business news on television and attempts to answer, and challenge, the criticisms. As Sabine Tan observed in 2011 and which still holds today, business news discourse has been an under-theorized area of academic inquiry:

> In an era in which business and finance news has become increasingly complex and difficult to represent, we know – as yet – very little about the relationship of reporting financial and business data in the medium of print (or the medium of hypertext, for that matter), and financial reporting in the medium of television.
>
> *(p. 170)*

Over time, TV business news has ebbed and flowed with stock prices, but it's always found new audiences and better ways to deliver news to them, proof of its staying power in an evolving industry.

## TV Business News: History and Development

The first regular TV news shows appeared in 1948 with the launch of daily evening newscasts on CBS and NBC. In these early years, there was little direct business coverage other than a reading of the closing price of the Dow Jones Industrial Average, if that (Saporito 1999). A decade later, little had changed, perhaps because top editors and producers had a limited understanding of economics and business stories (Samuelson 2002) and thus thought them too complex for a general TV audience. That attitude often left business reporters struggling to get their stories on the air. Business stories were also famously challenging to visualize, because "what you want to talk about isn't there to see," according to Robert Krulwich, a former CBS Morning News business correspondent (Morgan 1986). Technology was not yet sophisticated enough to allow for eye-catching graphics, and until that changed, it was going to be difficult for economic stories to get traction on TV. Edward R. Murrow has been credited with laying the groundwork for economic and business coverage on broadcast news with his award-winning 1960 documentary on CBS Reports, "Harvest of Shame," about poor working conditions for migrant farm workers (Roush 2006, p. 120). The in-depth investigative report laid the groundwork for later investigative reports and investigations of business abuses on such shows as CBS 60 Minutes and PBS Frontline, and on CNBC.

By the end of the 1960s, the booming U.S. economy was a major national story. In 1968, Louis Rukeyser was named economics editor at ABC News, and two years later, frustrated with the little coverage given business, he launched the weekly syndicated public television show Wall Street Week. Only 15 percent of Americans owned stock in 1970, but that was exponentially more than the 2 percent who had owned shares in 1950 (Samuelson 2002). Rukeyser, who helmed the show for 32 years, made investing and the markets more accessible, starting with his weekly signature pun-filled opening commentary. Wall Street Week effectively debunked the myth that financial news was too complex and dull for viewers.

In 1971, NBC named its first full-time on-air network business correspondent. Irving R. Levine would cover an economy that was in deep turmoil after President Richard Nixon announced the temporary suspension of the U.S. dollar's convertibility to gold. The dollar promptly cratered, and the Bretton Woods system of foreign exchange was effectively dissolved (IMF.org 2022). This was followed by the Organization of Petroleum Exporting Countries' oil embargo in 1973. High inflation, a gasoline shortage, and unemployment hit the average American hard and suddenly the economy was a "priority public interest issue"

(Arrese and Medina 2002). Long lines of cars at gas stations gave television vivid and dramatic pictures to air and suddenly, Levine was appearing frequently on Nightly News. The hardships of the time had made economics a kitchen table issue and Levine proved that TV news could effectively tell those stories to a general viewer (Lissit 1994). Similarly motivated by the urgent economic news of the day, Miami's WPBT launched the daily business news show Nightly Business Report in 1979. It immediately found a receptive audience, as it delivered stock quotes, business news, and analysis a few hours after the market close (O'Bryan 2019). In 1981, Nightly Business Report was nationally syndicated on public TV stations across the country. By the 2000s, the staid show faced fierce competition from cable news business networks and it had trouble getting corporate sponsors (Jensen 2010). The show was sold to CNBC, where it aired from 2013 until its cancellation in 2019. Nightly Business Report was on the air for 40 years – still the longest-running business news show on television.

By the mid-1970s, ABC, NBC, and CBS each had correspondents assigned to a business and the economy beat. A 1981 study (Dominick) showed that over a two-year period, the evening newscasts devoted 9–10 percent of their evening newscasts to business and the economy, which was comparable to the time devoted to other major news categories, such as politics and natural disasters. The Tyndall Report analyzed nightly network newscast data from 2010 to 2019 and found that the economy was the fourth most-prevalent story across the three major networks (2019). The three networks have since increased their coverage of business news, a topic that will be covered later in this chapter. The growth of cable television in the late 1970s paved the way for niche channels. In 1980, CNN launched the first 24-hour news network and along with it, a 30-minute primetime business show. Lou Dobbs anchored Moneyline, while Myron Kandel, managing editor of CNN business news, delivered stock commentary. The show drew a well-heeled audience that attracted advertisers, and while the audience was small, Moneyline soon became CNN's most profitable show (Solomon 2002). All-day market coverage on cable was still several years away, but it had already arrived on KWHY, a UHF station in Los Angeles. The station was the first to carry Quotron's stock ticker scroll with delayed quotes from the three major U.S. stock exchanges (Rich 1966). Individuals didn't have access to stock quotes at that time, so beaming them over TV airwaves was a crucial development. Financial News Network grew out of the early UHF station experiments in 1981. Four years later, FNN moved to cable TV with seven hours of market coverage daily (Barmash 1982). FNN and CNN both saw ratings and revenue soar during the 1987 stock market crash (Moss 1987). CNN was awarded the George Foster Peabody award for its breaking coverage of the crash – a distinction that raised its profile.

In 1989, NBC launched Consumer News and Business Channel, or CNBC, in a joint venture with Cablevision. Two years later, FNN was forced to put itself up for sale after an accounting scandal jeopardized its funding. CNBC stepped in and with the addition of FNN's channel space on 3,500 cable systems, instantly doubled its potential audience (Ponce de Leon 2015, p. 222). Roger Ailes became the president of CNBC in 1993 and focused on making the network's daytime market coverage more exciting to watch for its predominantly male audience. Ailes hired attractive on-air female talent, including Maria Bartiromo, later given the sexist nickname "Money Honey," and he modeled CNBC's programming after ESPN's Sports Center (Kurtz 2000, p. 31). Even the show names suggested a sports theme: Opening Bell, Half-Time Report, Fast Money. The network developed star hosts: David Faber, who broke mergers-and-acquisitions stories; Jim Cramer, the colorful former hedge manager; and Bartiromo, who reported stock scoops live from the floor of the New York

Stock Exchange. The formula worked, and at the end of the decade, Fortune Magazine dubbed CNBC a television phenomenon (Serwer 1999).

Researchers Clark, Thrift, and Tickle (2004) called the growing business news audience a "new constituency" driven by rising financial literacy. By the end of the decade, 60 percent of Americans owned shares of stock, according to Gallup poll data (Saad 2022). At the same time, the Internet was transforming peoples' lives and minting tech millionaires. Arrese and Medina (2002) called the 1990s the decade of the free market and popular capitalism, creating a "new stardom" of economic and financial news on television. In 1994, Michael Bloomberg expanded Bloomberg News into cable television. It was a money-loser, but Bloomberg didn't care. He saw the channel as a "loss leader" for the highly profitable Bloomberg terminal (Kurtz 2000, p. 98). The following year, CNN jumped into the 24-hour business news race. The company's board, which had passed on buying FNN's assets three years prior, approved the launch of the stand-alone business network CNNfn and put Moneyline anchor Lou Dobbs in charge. The network's challenge from the beginning was poor distribution: It started with just 5.5 million homes (Reuters 1995) and by 1999, it could reach only 12 million households to CNBC's 70 million households (Arrese and Medina 2002). CNNfn went after younger viewers and people beyond Wall Street with shows such as Business Unusual (Kurtz 2000, p. 106).

The formula, later called "bland" by Broadcasting & Cable (Higgins 2004), failed to attract viewers. In 1999, the height of the dot-com boom, Dobbs left the network to launch Space.com. Without its star anchor, Moneyline's ratings fell 25 percent as a new co-anchor team competed head-to-head with CNBC's Business Center (Los Angeles Times 2001). When Dobbs returned to the network in 2001, the dot-com bust and resulting stock market swoon had depressed ratings for business shows overall (CNBC's viewership had fallen 15 percent during daytime hours from its 2000 peak). In 2005, CNN pulled the plug on CNNfn, as executives in Atlanta had lost faith in the network (Ponce de Leon 2015, p. 223). Dobbs stayed on, but the show increasingly focused on hardline positions against illegal immigration and fallacious theories about President Barack Obama's birthplace. CNN delivered an ultimatum, according to The New York Times: Either he would have to stop espousing his views on television or leave CNN (Stelter and Carter 2009). CNN, which had once devoted one-quarter of the network's 24-hour schedule to business news, now had virtually none.

The field was down to CNBC and Bloomberg TV, but not for long. Rupert Murdoch had wanted to launch an all-business news channel for years and in 2007, he convinced then-Fox News CEO Roger Ailes to do so. FBN was conceived as a destination for regular Main Street investors – "average folks," Neil Cavuto, the managing editor, later said (Pon 2017). At the outset, the network was more politically neutral than its Fox News sibling (Tani 2017). A few months after the launch, a Columbia Journalism Review piece called some of its fare "just plain dumb," criticizing such offerings as Happy Hour, a daily after-market show broadcast from Waldorf-Astoria's Bull and Bear bar (Featherstone 2008).

The timing of FBN's launch was another problem. Viewership was plummeting at CNBC after the financial crisis (between 2008 and 2013, the network lost half its daytime audience), and though Fox Business had secured distribution on Time Warner Cable, its daytime viewership was less than a quarter of its rival's (Steinberg 2011; Hagey and Launder 2013). Ailes took Bill Shine, who had helped guide Fox News Channel to success, and put him in charge of Fox Business's programming (Ariens 2014). In a blow to rival CNBC, Fox Business snagged Maria Bartiromo and at the beginning of 2014, the network announced a new daytime lineup featuring the "Money Honey." FBN replaced many of its lighter shows with hardcore business and market programming, including Coast to Coast with Stuart Varney at midday and Maria in the Morning (Steinberg 2014). Fox Business started gaining ground and in fall 2016 it began beating CNBC in weekly total viewers. This was despite the network's 2016 sexual harassment scandal that led to the ouster of Roger Ailes and others (Ailes died the following year).

Fox Business scored its first yearly ratings win in 2017, according to Nielsen, averaging 195,000 total viewers during the business day, a gain of nearly 30 percent from 2016, compared with 166,000 total viewers for CNBC. CNBC was still ahead in the key 24- to 54-year-old demographic, however (Malone 2018). FBN owed its ratings supremacy to right-leaning, opinionated content on shows anchored by Varney, Dobbs (who had joined the network in 2011), Bartiromo, and Trish Regan, and its embrace of Donald Trump and his presidency, rather than the network's 2014 pivot to more urgent business and market news (Malone 2018, Tani 2017). While it boosted ratings, the opinionated content became a problem for FBN in 2021. The network and three of its hosts – Lou Dobbs, Maria Bartiromo, and Jeanine Pirro – were named in a $2.7 billion defamation lawsuit filed by the election technology company Smartmatic for repeating false claims that the company's voting machines had enabled fraud in the 2020 election. Fox immediately canceled Dobbs's top-rated show (Grynbaum 2021). Larry Kudlow, Trump's Council of Economic Advisors chair and a former CNBC host, replaced Dobbs. In May 2023, his show, Kudlow, topped the Fox Business ratings with the kind of bombastic rhetoric that Fox viewers had come to expect. However, FBN was no longer the overall ratings leader. CNBC's daytime ratings in the critical 24- to 54-year-old demographic was more than double that of FBN and it held the top spot for average total daytime viewers (138,000 versus 103,000) (2023).

## TV Business News: Critical Issues

A central issue for business news on television is whether the content helps viewers profit from their stock investments. Studies of stocks recommended on popular TV business shows have shown mixed results. Engelberg, Sasseville, and Williams (2012) studied CNBC's Mad Money, hosted by Jim Cramer, whose "raucous" antics attract a loyal fanbase of individual investors (Kadlec 2005). They found that Cramer's stock recommendations between June 2005 and February 2009 had a powerful short-term impact: The prices rose significantly in the after-hours market, often beginning during the show, for an average "excess" return of 2.4 percent. Within 100 days, though, the return fell to less than 1 percent. Using Nielsen Media Research ratings and demographic data, they found that when Mad Money ratings were higher, and when more of the viewers were high earners (over $60,000), the recommended stocks had the biggest positive overnight reactions, sometimes as high as 20 percent. One could conclude that short-term investors, or day-traders, could benefit from Mad Money but that long-term investors should watch the show for its entertainment value.

Earlier studies of the Wall Street Week program, in which guests made positive or negative stock recommendations, showed a similar short-term pattern. Pari (1987, cited in Ferreira and Smith 2003), Beltz and Jennings (1997), and Ferreira and Smith (2003) found a positive "information effect" on the recommended stocks' prices on the first trading day after the show, ranging from 0.6 percent to more than 1 percent. After several days, however, the stock returns were either flat or negative. Beltz and Jennings (1997) made qualitative judgments on the "conviction" of the Wall Street Week guests and found that more emphatic recommendations led to a greater likelihood that stocks retained their short-term gains, with the caveat that those stocks usually had positive momentum going into the show. However, they found that negative recommendations were more accurate in the long run. The prices of the negative stocks failed to move like those of positive stocks though, suggesting that viewers didn't act on the information. Beltz and Jennings concluded that viewers were unable to discern which Wall Street Week recommendations had value. Ferreira and Smith (2003) extended the previous one-year study period to two years, and studied stocks recommended on the show in 1997. The stocks were "meaningfully" higher at the end of the two-year period. Separately, a study of stock price movements following CEO interviews on CNBC showed a similar short-term pattern of stock gains in the three days following the interview, but a cumulative negative return in the ensuing ten trading days (Kim and Meschke 2014). The conclusion from the research-to-date: Stocks that were either recommended on popular shows, or that gain attention through CEO interviews, rose in the days immediately following the attention, but later fell back to their original level or below. Long-term stock price trends were less clear.

Another important issue is whether viewers are harmed by the kind of rapid-fire coverage found on cable business channels. As previously discussed, big personalities have often dictated a business channel's success, as the star anchors drive ratings and profits for their corporate owners. Business channels draw about $1 billion in annual ad revenue, according to Kagan (cited by Snider 2017), often making up for losses in other news divisions. Critics say the cult of personality has led to finance becoming a "media event, with its breathless reporters and star anchorpersons more often approximating Entertainment Tonight" (Clark, Thrift, and Tickell 2004). The stock market had become "a spectator sport" (Barber 2018). Dean Starkman called the trend the "CNBC-ization" of business news and said that it marked a retreat to the early 20th century, when the business press acted as a "servant" to the markets rather than as "watchdog" (2012). Narratives about rising asset prices, when shared on the news, can have a "high-five effect" which is the "vicarious thrill of cheering on a winner" (McGinn 2007, quoted in Shiller 2019, p. 217).

During the dot-com boom, some on Wall Street called CNBC "tout TV" for helping push Internet stocks higher by showcasing analysts who praised Internet stocks publicly while calling them "crap" privately (Brady 2003). Business media, including television, were also blamed for not warning investors that the housing market in 2006 was in a bubble and that the financial system was at risk (Starkman 2012). A 2022 study questioned whether that criticism was valid. Researchers Rios-Rodriguez, Dios-Vicente, and Lopez-Iglesias (2022) found that while journalism can influence the economy in certain ways, for example by reinforcing consumer sentiment, it's the real economy that determines the tone of media coverage, not the other way around (p. 190). They concluded that news outlets could have influenced public policy, assuming the financial crisis was due to regulatory failure, but they couldn't have prevented "the structural dynamics of capitalism that lead to cyclical crises" (p. 195). Roush (2008) studied the work of business journalists written before the financial crisis and concluded that some had sounded the warning, but that the public didn't pay attention.

One conclusion to draw from the research is that cable TV business channels do act as giant megaphones, reflecting investors' euphoria when asset prices are sharply increasing. In this way, an unfortunate feedback loop seems to develop and may be difficult to break (ratings soar during bull markets, generating more revenue and profit for networks). But just as the Federal Reserve must pull the punchbowl away when the party is in full swing, business journalism on cable TV must find a way to better meet its obligation to the viewing public, which it serves, during euphoric bull markets.

Long-form documentary production is one area of business journalism on television that hasn't been explored deeply in this chapter but deserves mention. Frontline and CNBC have produced award-winning documentaries that excel at post-mortem analysis of major business and financial stories, such as Frontline's Inside the Meltdown (2009) and The Madoff Affair (2010), which won the George Foster Peabody Award. CNBC's long-form documentaries, which appear on the network in primetime, include David Faber's Peabody award-winning The Age of Walmart (2005) and an in-depth look at the financial crisis, House of Cards (2009). The deeply reported, unembellished but captivating stories of business and finance have been used extensively in education. Frontline's Inside the Meltdown website includes teaching materials and supplemental stories aimed at improving financial literacy. Business documentary units perform a critical service for business journalism, then, much as business investigative units do on the text side.

## State of the Industry and the Future

In 2021 and 2022, broadcast news networks ABC, NBC, and CBS announced new investments in their streaming services to capture viewers who were increasingly moving online and who fell into a younger demographic sought after by advertisers (Weprin 2022). This created a larger news "hole" for business news, which was major news throughout the pandemic. ABC and NBC staffed separate units to produce business stories for general news audiences for all its platforms (Kaplan 2022). Both boosted their staffs during the 2020 pandemic to cover the economic fallout from COVID (Petski 2020). CBSNews.com launched a streaming version of CBS MoneyWatch in 2009 that offers anchored TV segments that mostly focus on personal finance. The business cable channels CNBC and Bloomberg offered viewers the same live stream that's on cable – with a paid subscription to their websites. Fox Business streamed selected segments from its live cable channel programming. Cheddar News, an online-only streaming business news channel, was conceived for a post-cable and linear-TV world and targeted 20- to 30-year-old viewers with the tagline "The Voice of What's Next" (Pierce 2017). The millennial news network, launched in 2016 by former Buzzfeed president Jon Steinberg, grew quickly on streaming services such as Sling and Apple TV (Schouten 2017). In 2019, cable-operator Altice bought Cheddar for $200 million to expand its streaming platforms.

The following year, Altice cut costs by consolidating Cheddar's two news networks and laying off one-third of its staff (Rodriguez 2020). It was an open question in 2023 whether Altice, hammered by declining cable revenue, would invest in re-growing Cheddar. The demand for business journalists who can explain and simplify the economy and business for a viewing audience seems only to be growing. The evidence for this is the growth of business news of all kinds on television: Kitchen table business coverage on the major broadcast and streaming networks; and hardcore market, economic and financial news on cable news business channels. CNBC, Bloomberg, and Fox Business, however, seem destined to see their fortunes rise and fall with the ups and downs of the stock market, as they have from their inception. The quality remains arguable, at least for programming built around stock recommendations, but the growth of long-form business and economic coverage promises more substance for viewers.

# References

Ariens, C. (2014) 'Roger Ailes Promotes Bill Shine and Brian Jones at Fox Business', 14 August. Available at: https://www.adweek.com/tvnewser/roger-ailes-promotes-bill-shine-and-brian-jones-to-lead-fox-business/236586/ (Accessed: 1 July 2022).

Arrese, A. and Medina, M. (2002) 'Competition Between New and Old Media in Economic and Financial News Markets,' in Picard, R. (ed.) *Media Firms: Structures, Operations, and Performance,* pp. 59–73, Mahwah, NJ: Erlbaum.

Barber, L. (2018) 'Too Big to Fail: FT Editor Lionel Barber on the Future of Financial Journalism', *Financial Times,* 23 November. Available at: https://www.ft.com/content/d2a3e50e-ef07-11e8-89c8-d36339d835c0 (Accessed: 1 July 2022).

Barmash, I. (1982) 'Chairman Steps Down at Financial News Network', *The New York Times,* 13 July. Available at: https://www.nytimes.com/1982/07/13/business/business-people-chairman-steps-down-at-financial-network.html (Accessed: 21 June 2022).

Beltz, J. and Jennings, R. (1997) 'Wall $treet Week with Louis Rukeyser' Recommendations: Trading Activity and Performance', *Review of Financial Economics,* 6(1): 15–27.

Brady, R. (2003) 'Makeover: CNBC Fell From Grace When the Bubble Burst. How Does it Look Now?' *Columbia Journalism Review,* 42(4): 50–51.

*Cheddar News.* (2022) 'Where to Watch'. Available at: https://get.cheddar.com/where-to-watch/ (Accessed: 30 July 2022).

Clark, G., Thrift, N. and Tickel, A (2004) 'Performing Finance: The Industry, the Media and Its Image', *Review of International Political Economy,* 11(2): 289–310. (Accessed 26 July 2022).

*CNBC.* (2022). Available at: https://populartimelines.com/timeline/CNBC (Accessed 14 June 2022).

Dominick, J. (1981) 'Business Coverage in Network Newscasts', *Journalism and Mass Communication Quarterly,* 58(2): 179–191. https://doi.org/10.1177/107769908105800201.

Engelberg, J., Sasseville, C. and Williams, J. (2012) 'Market Madness? The Case of Mad Money', *Management Science,* 58(2): 351–364. http://dx.doi.org/10.1287/mnsc.1100.1290.

Featherstone, L. (2008) 'Happy All the Time: Fox Business Network's Populist Sensibility Is Refreshing, But Nobody's Watching. Here's Why', *Columbia Journalism Review,* 46(6): 31.

Ferreira, E. and Smith, S. (2003) 'Wall $treet Week: Information or Entertainment?', *Financial Analysts Journal,* 59(1): 45–53.

Fox News Media. (2022) *Fox Business Network Overtakes CNBC.* Available at: https://press.foxnews.com/2022/06/fox-business-network-overtakes-cnbc-as-leader-in-business-television-delivering-highest-rated-quarter-since-2020 (Accessed: 1 July 2022).

Grynbaum, M. (2021) 'Lou Dobbs's Show Is Canceled by Fox Business', *The New York Times,* 5 February. Available at: file:///C:/Users/cecir/Zotero/storage/LMZMXBFE/lou-dobbs-fox.html (Accessed: 28 June 2022).

Hagey, K. and Launder, W. (2013) 'Ratings Sag for Cable-TV Business News', *The Wall Street Journal,* 2 December. Available at: https://www.wsj.com/articles/SB10001424052702303332904579224390854395388 (Accessed: 31 July 2022)

Higgins, J. (2004) 'Why CNN Failed', *Broadcasting & Cable,* 1 November, p. 6.

*House of Cards.* (2009) CNBC. Available at: https://www.cnbc.com/id/28984151 (Accessed: 30 July 2022).

*Inside the Meltdown.* (2009) *Frontline.* Available at: https://www.pbs.org/wgbh/pages/frontline/meltdown/ (Accessed: 30 July 2022).

Jensen, E. (2010) 'Nightly Business Report Sold by PBS Station', *The New York Times,* 19 August. Available at: https://www.nytimes.com/2010/08/19/business/media/19pbs.html (Accessed: 23 July 2022).

Kadlec, D. (2005) 'Stock-Raving Mad', *Time,* 8 August. Available at: https://content.time.com/time/subscriber/article/0,33009,1090899,00.html (Accessed: 15 July 2022)

Kaplan, E. (2022) 'Business, Technology and Media Producer', *NBC News,* Interview via LinkedIn, 1 July 2022.

Kim, Y. and Meschke, F. (2014) 'CEO Interviews on CNBC', presented at Fifth Singapore International Conference on Finance. http://dx.doi.org/10.2139/ssrn.1745085

Kurtz, H. (2000) *The Fortune Tellers: Inside Wall Street's Game of Money, Media, and Manipulation*, New York: The Free Press.

Lissit, R. (1994) 'Not Just Another Pretty Face', *American Journalism Review,* July/August 16 (6): 44.

'Lou Dobbs to Host Moneyline Again', (2001) *Los Angeles Times.* Available at: https://www.latimes.com/archives/la-xpm-2001-apr-11-fi-49530-story.html (Accessed: 14 June 2022).

Malone, M. (2018) 'Energized Fox Business Aims High in 2018', *Broadcasting & Cable,* 15 January. Available at: https://www.nexttv.com/news/energized-fox-business-aims-high-2018-171100 (Accessed: 15 July 2022).

Morgan, T. (1986) 'A Decade of Change for Business News on TV', *The New York Times,* 13 April. Available at: https://www.nytimes.com/1986/03/13/arts/a-decade-of-change-for-business-news-on-tv.html (Accessed: 29 June 2022).

Moss, B. (1987) 'Cable's FNN: The little network that could', *New York Daily News,* 26 October, print, p. 72.

*News and Research.* (2022) Bloomberg LP. Available at: https://www.bloomberg.com/company/news-and-research/ (Accessed: 30 June 2022).

O'Bryan, L. (2019) 'Remembering Nightly Business Report, a Business Journalism Pioneer', *Talking Biz News,* 21 November. Available at: https://talkingbiznews.com/business-media-news/remembering-nightly-business-report-a-business-journalism-pioneer/ (Accessed: 1 January 2022).

Pierce, David (2017) 'Inside Cheddar, the Would-Be CNBC of the Internet', *Wired,* 30 March. Available at: https://www.wired.com/2017/03/inside-cheddar-cnbc-internet/ (Accessed: 13 November 2022).

Petski, D. (2020) 'Deirdre Bolton Moving to ABC News From Fox Business Network', *Deadline,* 13 April. Available at: https://deadline.com/2020/04/deirdre-bolton-moving-to-abc-news-from-fox-business-network-1202906908/ (Accessed: 30 June 2022).

Ponce De Leon, C. (2015) *That's the Way It Is: A History of Television News in America*, Chicago: The University of Chicago Press. Chapter 1, 'Beginnings', Available at https://press.uchicago.edu/books/excerpt/2015/De_Leon_Thats_Way_It_Is.html (Accessed: 1 June 2022).

Rich, A. (1966) 'Allen Rich', *Valley Times,* 1 November, p. 24, Available at: https://www.newspapers.com/clip/46585778/allen-rich/ (Accessed: 21 June 2022).

Rios-Rodriguez, R., Dios-Vicente, A. and Lopez-Iglesias, E. (2022) 'Can the Media Prevent Economic Crises by Alerting of their Risk? A Debate on the Limited Effects of the Watchdog', *Communication & Society,* 35(2): 185–200. https://doi.org/10.15581/003.35.2.185-200

Rodriguez, A. (2020) 'Cheddar Insiders Describe Its Growing Pains Since Being Acquired by Altice for $200 Million and the Future of its 'Post-Cable' Network Model,' *Insider,* 16 October. Available at: https://www.businessinsider.com/inside-cheddar-growing-pains-future-of-post-cable-network-model-2020-10 (Accessed: 13 November 2022).

Roush, C. (2006) *Profits and Losses: Business Journalism and Its Role in Society,* Oak Park, IL: Marion Street Press, pp. 119–122.

Roush, C. (2008) 'Unheeded Warnings', *American Journalism Review,* December 2008/January 2009. Available at: https://www.academia.edu/396959/Unheeded_Warnings (Accessed: 18 July 2012).

Saad, L. and Jones, J. (2022) 'What Percentage of Americans Owns Stock?', *Gallup, Inc.,* 5 May. Available at: https://news.gallup.com/poll/266807/percentage-americans-owns-stock.aspx (Accessed: 21 July 2022).

Samuelson, Robert. (2002) 'Moving Toward the Mainstream: Economics and Business Reporting Has Increased in Quantity and Improved in Quality', *Nieman Reports,* 56 (2, Summer 2002): 22–24.

Saporito, B. (1999) 'The Business Century: How the Economy Became Hot News in the Last 100 Years', *Columbia Journalism Review,* 37 (6 March/April 1999): 47–52.

Schouten, C. (2017) 'Behind Cheddar's Wager on the Future of TV News,' *Columbia Journalism Review,* 17 May. Available at: https://www.cjr.org/business_of_news/cheddar-television-business-news.php (Accessed: 13 November 2022).

Serwer, A. (1999) 'I Want My CNBC', *Fortune,* 24 May, 139–141. Available at: https://archive.fortune.com/magazines/fortune/fortune_archive/1999/05/24/260244/index.htm (Accessed: 1 July 2022).

Shiller, R. (2019) *Narrative Economics,* Princeton, NJ: Princeton University Press, p. 217.

Snider, M. (2017) 'Fox Business Network Rides Politics and Punch to Cable Ratings Success', *Dayton Daily News,* 13 October. p. Z5.

Solomon, N. (2002) 'Money Makes Headlines in Today's News Coverage', *Nieman Reports*, (56)2, Summer 2002: 17-19.

Starkman, D. (2012) 'A Narrowed Gaze: How the business press forgot the rest of us', *Columbia Journalism Review*, January/February 2012. Available at: https://archives.cjr.org/cover_story/a_narrowed_gaze.php (Accessed: 11 March 2014).

Steinberg, B. (2011) 'FBN Still Trying to Make a Name for Itself in Cable Market', *Ad Age*, 2 May. Available at: https://adage.com/article/media/fox-business-network-make/227332 (Accessed 28 June 2022).

Steinberg, B. (2014) 'Fox Business to Launch New Daytime Schedule Feb. 24 as Bartiromo Debuts', 5 February. Available at: https://variety.com/2014/tv/news/fox-business-to-launch-new-daytime-schedule-feb-24-as-bartiromo-debuts-1201088208/ (Accessed: 28 June 2022).

Stelter, B. and Carter, B. (2009) 'Lou Dobbs Abruptly Quits CNN', 11 November. Available at: https://www.nytimes.com/2009/11/12/business/media/12dobbs.html (Accessed: 28 June 2022).

Tan, Sabine. (2011) 'Facts, Opinions, and Media Spectacle: Exploring Representations of Business News on the Internet', *Discourse & Communication*. 5(2): 169–194. https://doi.org/10.1177/1750481311399511

Tani, M. (2017) 'How Fox Business Is Beating CNBC by Embracing Politics', *Business Insider*, 17 October. Available at: https://www.businessinsider.com/fox-business-beating-cnbc-embracing-politics-2017-10 (Accessed: 1 July 2022).

Weprin, A. (2022) 'CBS News Overhauls Streaming Service', *The Hollywood Reporter*, 24 January. Available at: https://www.hollywoodreporter.com/tv/tv-news/cbs-news-streaming-service-person-to-person-1235079026/ (Accessed: 3 August 2022)

*The Age of Walmart*. (2005) CNBC. Available at: https://peabodyawards.com/award-profile/the-age-of-wal-mart-inside-americas-most-powerful-company/ (Accessed: 30 July 2022).

*The End of the Bretton Woods System*. (2022) IMF.org. Available at: https://www.imf.org/external/about/histend.htm#:~:text=End%20of%20Bretton%20Woods%20system,-The%20system%20dissolved&text=In%20August%201971%2C%20U.S.%20President,the%20breakdown%20of%20the%20system. (Accessed: 27 June 2022).

*The Madoff Affair*. (2010) *Frontline*. Available at: https://www.pbs.org/wgbh/pages/frontline/madoff/ (Accessed: 30 July 2022).

Tyndall, A. (2019) 'Tyndall Report Decade in Review 2010s'. Available at: http://tyndallreport.com/decadeinreview2010s/ (Accessed: 21 June 2022).

*U.S. Cable TV Network and Program Rankings*. (2023) *National Media Spots Inc*. Available at: https://www.nationalmediaspots.com/media-stats.php (Accessed: 16 June 2023).

# 16

# THE SOUND OF BUSINESS JOURNALISM

## How the Field Thrives on Audio Platforms

*Jill Martin and Kaci Richter*

### Introduction

Audio content has long been a ubiquitous part of the media landscape. From Oersted to Faraday's work in electromagnetic theory, Maxwell to Hertz's work in electromagnetic waves and Marconi's transatlantic signal, audio transmissions have had two centuries of innovation. Since Fessenden's first transmission of voice and music in 1906, audio has been a consistent source of news and entertainment. From traditional radio's pervasiveness to podcasting's niche fandom, audio content still thrives today through local radio broadcasts in rural enclaves to on-demand audio content listened to by millions weekly. Radio news, consistently the most popular radio format for persons 6 and older according to Neilsen data, is particularly important to the public (Tops of 2019: Radio).

Business and economic journalism provide the public with resources once reserved for government officials, the well-connected or the rich – economic news and data. The Carolina Business News Initiative website bizjournalismhistory.org notes newsletters were exchanged between trading families to inform all parties about prices and availability of goods in the 1700s. Port information, pricing of goods and other business information could be found in newspapers across Europe in the 1700s, and The New York Herald dedicated a full page to business, thus the first "business section" in 1835 (History of Business Journalism). Business journalism in the United States dates back at least to the late 1800s with the Kiernan News Agency, which operated from 1869 to 1893. The agency trained reporters Charles Dow, Edward Jones and Charles Bergstresser. The Dow Jones News Service launched in 1882, and later The Wall Street Journal (Wells 2020).

Journalists verify information, report on trends and analyze business and economic information, providing much-needed data for citizens to participate fully in financial systems, plan for their future and understand the more significant economic systems in their world. This understanding includes macroeconomic issues such as economic growth, inflation, government spending and microeconomic issues from company behavior down to "kitchen-table" decisions.

While business and economic news is not new, the availability of business journalism on various media – including print, television, radio, online and new media options such as

 DOI: 10.4324/9781003298977-20

social media content and podcasting – has provided multiple ways for the public to access once gatekept information.

McQuail defines medium as "any vehicle for carrying meaning, with some distinctive characteristics in respect of technology, form, manner of use, means of encoding or social definition" (McQuail 2010). The medium by which information is delivered is inextricably tied to the content provided. Medium drives content in editing, distribution and consumption – all of which depend significantly on whether the content is visual, auditory, photographic, interactive or any combination of media. Reich argues that the distinctiveness of each medium is present in early news production stages (including research and information-gathering) as opposed to media serving as "unique packaging houses of similarly-obtained raw materials" (Reich 2016).

Audio requires different types of planning, research and execution than its print or visual counterparts. But that is not to say all audio-based journalism is a monolith. An hourly news report means constant scanning of the environment and less time to develop stories after journalists have begun to pursue them. The same is true for daily podcast or radio show offerings, which may have only one daily deadline (similar to old-fashioned print) but different in the number of post-production resources once a topic is chosen (Reich 2016). Beyond best practices in audio gathering, storytelling and frequency of production, audio-based products differ in audience and scope. In summary, audio-based journalism encompasses everything from breaking news reports broadcast on local news/talk radio stations to on-demand podcasts boasting hundreds of episodes and millions of listeners worldwide.

American Public Media's "Marketplace" has been a staple of the business journalism sector since its first episode on January 2, 1989. Usher's research at Marketplace reveals extensive energy put into finding topics and assessing relevance. The study details the variety of newsroom pressures experienced at Marketplace, but hardly unique to it. Those pressures include time constraints of the production schedule and final project total run time, audience demands, organizational hierarchy, availability of sources and source bias, and brand uniformity. These pressures, coupled with the audio medium's unique features, mean reporters "employ particular or unique practices to obtain their raw information," according to particularists, those who subscribe to medium-based logic that "print, broadcast, and online news operations have developed different cultures in which they do news" (Usher 2013; Reich 2016). In this view, the process of assessing relevance, news gathering and interviewing, scripting, editing and any production elements cannot be divorced from the medium because the medium is in the DNA of the piece and is as central to the story as the news hook.

Naturally, the importance of medium to the preparation and production of audio content and the popularity of business content has led to some successful examples of business journalism in audio formats. Terrestrial radio has syndicated hits such as Planet Money and Marketplace, which have both spun off into additional traditional radio properties and podcast offerings. Business as a podcast genre is consistently in the top ten most popular categories for listeners (Research 2019).

What makes these business audio offerings different from their print or television counterparts? Factors including the intimacy of the medium, ease of use, convenience and portability all contribute to making business content on audio platforms unique and successful. Audio-based content can take many forms; however, the most prominent are in traditional radio applications – whether commercial or public, and in podcasts, which are still understood as "radio-like" (Berry 2016).

## Historical Perspectives

Audio news is categorized by two delivery modes: terrestrial, or traditional radio programming, and digital formats, including online audio and podcasting. Traditional radio has reached the U.S. populations for decades, and listenership reminds high. "In 2020, 83 percent of Americans ages 12 or older listened to terrestrial radio in a given week" (Pew 2021). Most business content airs on News/Talk radio stations, whose target audience trends older than other radio formats. The MRI Simmons, 2021 fall survey, shows that 81.3 percent of "All News," 83.4 percent of "All Talk," 78.2 percent of "News/Talk" and 67.1 percent of "Public/Non-Commercial" listeners are 45 or older (Radio Advertising Bureau|Why Radio Research, no date). All genres above are slightly different in programming and specific target audience; however, the larger national trend shows news and talk-based content attracts an older audience than its music or sports-based counterparts. For those listeners over 45, radio listening is often habitual. For most of their lives, the radio was on at work, while tidying the house and during the commute. In fact, most terrestrial radio station programming schedules are still built around "drive time." Developments in technology cut into radio's long-enjoyed monopoly on in-car entertainment. Dashboard 8-track, cassette and CD players gave consumers other ways to listen to music, but news and talk programming was still largely accessed through the AM and FM dials. Consumers under 45 have not built those same radio habits. New vehicles are often without a CD player and instead offer systems such as uConnect Sirius or Sync, which use the driver's mobile device for navigation, entertainment, and communication. The habit then is plugging in a phone and circumventing the radio altogether. This shift has been met with traditional radio outlets offering programming in podcast or audio report form on online platforms where younger listeners who may not be habitual terrestrial radio listeners can access them.

Online audio programs and podcasting have evolved over the past 15 years both in the number of offerings and genre. The business podcast genre has continued to grow in popularity. The sector now includes offerings specifically targeting smaller, niche audiences such as millennial women, Black entrepreneurs and budding real estate investors. Apple Podcasts subdivides the business podcast genre into subcategories like careers, entrepreneurship, investing, management, marketing and non-profit, making searching for niche content simple for the listener (Apple Podcast Business Chart 2022).

Audio content is everywhere, but what makes it so popular?

## Sound as a Mode of Delivery

People experience different forms of communication through their senses. "Sound is a mode of communication that slows the interpretation of words and ideas, heightens awareness of an environment and encourages quiet interiority. It punctuates buildings, workplaces, leisure complexes and family life" (Brabazon 2016). The sensory mode of exchanging information through audio creates a unique experience for the human brain and thought process. Brabazon (2016) posits that sound learning is effective but underestimated due to a lack of research on auditory literacy. In her study, Brabazon explores teaching and learning through sonic materials, placing contemporary audio content, specifically podcasting, in line with other sonic materials and auditory cultures. Audio content, consumed through only one sense, can create what Flichy calls a "communication bubble" wherein a listener experiences content in a private sphere within a public space (Flichy 1995). From the introduction of the Sony Walkman in 1979, consumers have been taking audio content with them, engaging with content privately while physically participating in the public world (Menduni 2007).

Podcasting and audio-based content create an intimate connection between the content creator and listener that is challenging to replicate through other platforms. According to Chignell (2009), comfortable space in podcasting fosters a repertoire of radio's performative "para-social interaction" with "the characteristics of intimacy in face-to-face interaction" (sincerity, attentiveness, empathy, caring). Lingren (2016) talks about how "radio's capacity to privilege the unique and emotional qualities of the human voice" has driven the popularity of podcasting and the popularity of narrative storytelling in the medium. Podcasting offers an intimacy to the listener experience. It's a well-constructed bridge to an audience (Soto 2022).

## "Easy" Listening

The simplicity of audio learning, with its lack of visuals, can lead to an undervaluing of the potential of the medium (Brabazon 2016). Shastry and Gillespie attribute the popularity of podcasts to ease of use, stating that "audio has become an easy way to consume information without much effort" (Podcasting for Trainers and Educators n.d.). However, a lack of visual processing required to consume audio content and the simplicity of accessing audio content should not be conflated with it being less intellectually stimulating.

Alina Selyukh, a business correspondent for National Public Radio, says that while business journalism in an audio format can include complex terminology, the key is to break information down into human stories and short, easy-to-understand sentences (Selyukh 2022). This approach gives the listener the feeling of ease while consuming complex stories or ideas. Selukh says audio-based programs, such as Planet Money and its offshoot Planet Money Indicator, approach the audience through human-oriented storytelling and an understanding that the audience is both curious about the world around them but too busy to dig into every detail about a particular story. Maria Altman, editor for Harvest Public Media, says that the key for reporters is to think about which audio will set the scene and put the listener into the room with them.

> Like any writing you want it to be compelling, and you want to put characters (people) at the center because people just connect with other people's stories. That's the critical thing, I think, to getting people to kind of perk up and really listen to a story.
>
> *(Altman 2022)*

Selukh says, "The simplest sort of approach is that there are, maybe, only two to three things that people will take away from your story," which informs the production of audio-based business offerings (Selyukh 2022). Producers write in stories, use simple sentences and focus on two to three takeaways to ensure listener comprehension. Signposting, the practice of using audible transitions to tell the listener that the host is moving from one part of the story to the next, is essential in the audio format because they provide a smooth conversationality and an audible roadmap to the listener (Kern 2012; Joyce 2015). Similarly, using "gold coins" – an interesting detail, memorable sound bite or an otherwise novel moment in scripting or sound – keeps listeners engaged in the audio (Selyukh 2022). The best audio offerings are written and produced with intimacy and audience engagement in mind, which provides a stimulating, non-laborious listening experience.

Similar to print publications, audio content can be intended for a general audience or a more niche group of listeners. Some business journalism in audio formats is specifically targeted to those working in finance, economics and associated fields. For example, Selukh says reporting for Reuters means communicating to an audience that is plugged into financial and economic content and seeks it, rather than being served content via terrestrial radio such as that on National Public Radio. In her reporting on NPR, Selukh says:

> On the radio, more often than not, a person is listening to my story while doing something else. They don't voluntarily solicit this content, and you're assuming that they're just as interested in abortion laws nationwide as they are in extreme flooding in South Korea.
>
> *(Selyukh 2022)*

In this regard, there is a different sort of listener contract between the radio listener and the podcast listener. Radio listeners choose a particular radio station and agree to listen to the content programmed for them. That content is intended for a general audience and is limited in length and depth to accommodate the listening habits of the general audience. Podcast offerings, however, are discovered and sought out by the listener with a built-in commitment to either the show topic or the overall brand. Flichy's "communication bubble" exists for audio content of all kinds, but its meaning is amplified when paired with talk-based content that is not passively consumed from a traditional linear source like a radio station but rather sought out by the listener as in the case of a podcast.

The spectrum of business-related audio offerings ranges from extremely general to hyper-niche. However, no matter the audience size or level of commitment to the topic, audio provides an easy way to access information. Audio content is generally free to access, integrated seamlessly into common devices like smartphones and vehicles and portable in ways visual content is not.

## Building Trust and Intimacy

Audio is a unique medium with a method of delivery that allows it to be taken anywhere the listener goes. Pat Safford, podcast network director of Hurrdat Media, said that radio hosts are taught to talk to just one person instead of the entire audience. In doing so, "It's just you (the host) and that person." Safford said that this approach "creates trust and intimacy," which allows listeners to connect to hosts and their content (Safford 2022b). Audio hosts understand how to harness the intimacy of the medium and foster a connection between the host and the listener (Kern 2012).

Audio media – including traditional radio, audiobooks and podcasts – split listeners' attention. Listeners are often commuting or participating in a second activity while listening to audio content. However, Safford said that "rather than being a weakness of the medium, it is a strength." You can't drive and read a book or watch YouTube, but when you're on a treadmill you can listen to a podcast. "There really aren't any barriers to reaching an audience with podcasting and with audio" (Safford 2022b).

Selukh says producing audio stories also allows the host or reporter to be part of the story, which is typically impermissible in print journalism. Selukh says, "With audio, you're inevitably in the story;" certainly even casual listeners of audio-based journalism have heard hosts and reporters introduced as characters in the narrative. This acknowledgment of the active participation of the reporter is, in itself, an act of storytelling and builds intimacy with the audience (Selyukh 2022). In an audio medium, the audience can develop a better understanding of the natural sound, speech patterns and conversationality between a reporter and an interviewee, a host and guest or host and co-host. This understanding is deeply connected to the way humans communicate through more than words but through sound, mannerisms and vocal patterns (Kern 2012). Altman says, "there's something about hearing the human voice." "You can get a lot of information across not just with your words but with how you say things" (Altman 2022). Hearing the conversation between a journalist and a homeowner who is underwater on their mortgage during a housing crisis or a farmer whose crops were decimated in a natural disaster is powerful and intimate in a way that print or images alone cannot capture.

## The Rise of Podcasting

The advancement of smartphones and audio content has created a whirlwind of possibilities for content producers and listeners. "Podcast journalism uses narrative elements forged around emotions and first-person reporting to build intimate relationships between the journalist and the listener" (Lindgren 2021). It is through those elements that the public has quickly latched onto podcasting as a news and entertainment platform.

What we know as podcasting emerged in the late 1990s and was described by scholars as an extension of radio (Berry 2006; Menduni 2007; Madsen 2009). The name "podcast" is a portmanteau of "iPod" and "broadcast" first used by Ben Hammersley, a columnist for The Guardian, in a 2004 piece titled "Audible revolution" chronicling "a new boom in amateur radio" based on the rise of mp3 players like the iPod, online self-publishing via blogs and widely available audio production software (Hammersley 2004). It was at that time podcasting began "as a self-driven community of web and audio enthusiasts that relied primarily on open-source RSS (or Really Simple Syndication) technologies for distribution" (Wade Morris 2021a). Since the distribution of podcast content was not controlled by a particular company or proprietary technology, aggregator sites would become a valuable tool for listeners to find podcasts and creators to list podcasts for consumption. This history illustrates a difference between the rise of self-driven audio content and self-driven video content, wherein the former, using RSS technology, was "anti-platform," and the latter emerged on the YouTube platform, acting as the central repository for content. As Sullivan notes, "While RSS made it technically possible for users to subscribe via podcatcher software such as iPodder, the process was cumbersome and not well understood outside communities of tech enthusiasts" (Sullivan 2019a).

In 2005, podcasting received a mainstream boost when Apple added a podcast directory to its iTunes 4.9 software (Aufderheide 2020). Apple CEO Steve Jobs called podcasting "TiVO for radio" and the directory allowed users to subscribe to RSS-enabled audio feeds (Sullivan 2019a). Apple Podcasts remains the most popular way to access podcasts, a remnant of its "first to market" position (Sullivan 2019b, "The Complete History of Podcasts" 2020). The nature of the decentralized platforms on which podcasts were hosted meant a lag in monetization compared to their video counterpart (Wade Morris 2021b). However, in recent years, podcasting has grown into an industry of its own, in what Tiziano Bonini calls "The 'Second Age' of Podcasting" (Bonini Baldini 2015). Media companies specializing in podcasts have moved the sector forward in terms of offerings for consumers and monetization for both creators and distributors.

The podcast sector now includes individual creators, podcast-based media companies and traditional broadcasting properties looking to diversify and repurpose materials for new audiences (Aufderheide et al. 2020). Noncommercial radio properties can also take advantage of podcast advertising dollars in a way not permitted over the air.

## Business Journalism: From On-Air to Apps

### *Planet Money*

Planet Money began as an episode of the long-running radio show This American Life. The episode titled "The Giant Pool of Money" aired on May 9, 2008, with a mission to cover the financial crisis. In it, Alex Blumberg and Adam Davidson explore the subprime mortgage crisis. Blumberg and Davidson sought to answer the question, "why are they lending money to people who can't afford to pay it back?" (355: The Giant Pool of Money – This American Life, no date). The episode was so successful and compelling that in 2020 it was deemed "culturally, historically, or aesthetically significant" by the Library of Congress and selected for preservation in the United States National Recording Registry, making it the first podcast to be added (This American Life [@ThisAmerLife] 2021).

Planet Money continues as of this writing on air and online. Over time, the episode's topics have expanded and broadened to a wider range of financial and economic issues. Planet Money was ranked ninth among Edison Research's top 50 most listened-to U.S. podcasts of 2020, indicating a growing need among the public for financial clarity and understanding. NPR brands the show as a clear and easy way for anyone to understand the economy. "The economy explained. Imagine you could call up a friend and say, 'Meet me at the bar and tell me what's going on with the economy.' Now imagine that's actually a fun evening" (NPR 2022). As of 2021, Planet Money "podcasts had nearly 1.4 million listeners" (Sloan.org 2021). NPR's weekly podcast audience in 2021 was 12 million, a substantial increase from 3.5 million in 2016 (readymag.com).

### *Marketplace*

Marketplace began airing in 1989 as a 30-minute program produced by American Public Media. Currently, the seven-and-a-half-minute-long Marketplace Morning Report, hosted by David Brancaccio, airs on many public radio stations during the last segment of the NPR program Morning Edition. Marketplace has produced a number of spin-off programs, including Marketplace Weekend (formerly Marketplace Money and Sound Money). Additionally, the Marketplace team produces a number of podcasts, including Make Me Smart with Kai and Molly, featuring anchor Kai Ryssdal and regular contributor Molly Wood, as well as podcast versions of the radio broadcast and extended podcasts built around regular segments from the radio show, such as Views from the Corner Office.

### *In Pod We Trust*

According to Edison Research, 79 percent of Americans are familiar with the term "podcast." "Podcasting as a term is more familiar than ever, as the word continues to penetrate the consciousness of America" (Research 2022), and 177 million Americans aged 12 and older have sampled a podcast. This shows substantial growth from another Edison study in 2018, wherein 64 percent of Americans aged 12 and older were familiar with the term "podcasting," but only 17 percent (48 million) had recently sampled a podcast (Research 2019). Podcasting as a medium has also diversified its listener base in age, gender, race and ethnicity over time, making room for more diverse content and platforming a generation of diverse creators (Research 2019, 2021, 2022; Tops of 2019: Radio, no date).

Both Edison and Nielsen research tracks demographics related to podcast listening, the popularity of individual podcasts, podcast listening habits (including devices used, time spent listening and location listening) and podcast genres by reach.

Business as a podcast genre is consistently in the top ten genres of audiences 12 and up and 18 and up. Moreover, in Nielsen Podcasting Today 2021, "business" held the number seven spot in persons 18–34, persons 18–49 and persons 25–54. When broken down by gender, "business" as a podcast genre ranks even higher, with men at number four behind comedy, news and sports (Research 2021). Podcasting has "rejuvenated talk programming," according to Brabazon. Indeed, the most popular genres of podcasts are talk-based.

Safford attributes the success of business, economic and financial podcasts to trust, intimacy and convenience. Whether listeners want information on how to invest, what an NFT is, or how to make extra money, he says:

> They don't have time to take a class, they don't have time to sit down and read 15 blogs while they're working, so again it's the ease of access for people wanting to get information and learn new things, and they can do it anytime they want with a podcast.
> *(Safford 2022a)*

Menduni argues that podcasting is more "individualized than radio listening" because hosts "are not seen as institutions but as peers." The ability for listeners to subscribe, skip, listen on demand and discover new podcasts set the user experience apart from traditional linear radio listening (Menduni 2007). Audiences who enjoy podcasting for its on-demand accessibility may use platforms such as Spotify and features like "Daily Mix" to act as an aggregator for mixed content playlists that combine music, news and information elements. Altman says that approach is one way to encourage listening that is not so prescriptive in genre or theme and to give listeners some information quickly if they are not inclined to turn on the radio. However, the downside is that it limits listeners' perspectives to that which they already know. As Altman says, "you don't know what you don't know until you hear it or you read it" (Altman 2022). She continues, "Any service operating from an algorithm is primarily concerned with confirmation and engagement based on previous behavior instead of exposure to new ideas." Berry (2016) states the "combination of active decision-making and highly privatized listening gives reasonable grounds to consider audio podcasting as a highly personal and intimate medium – one which is similar to, but not the same as radio."

## How the Pandemic Influenced Podcast Listening

According to Edison Research's The Infinite Dial, smartphone ownership peaked in 2021 and 2022, with 88 percent of Americans reporting that they owned smartphones. The Infinite Dial is the longest-running survey of digital media consumer behavior in America. Gabriel Soto, director of research at Edison Research, says that the country has seen a boom in podcasting in the last decade, beginning in 2014 with entertainment shows, specifically with male podcasters in their homes. As interest grew, industry leaders, including NPR and The New York Times, began offering podcasts. Soto says the advancement of smartphones also contributed to the industry's growth.

Today, more than 40 percent of people have listened to podcasts in the last month. And in 2021, 33 percent of Americans, 12 and older, reported owning a smart speaker. Soto says research indicates the recent pandemic contributed to the increase in podcast listeners. "Podcast listening occurs most often at home. And that's different to radio" (Soto 2022). Soto says companies such as Netflix saw a spike in the pandemic because people were stuck at home, but people still listen to podcasts in the car, so he doesn't think people will stop listening to podcasts as people return to normalcy after the pandemic.

Soto says there's a sizable group who listens to podcasts in their car, but the group of people listening from their homes is a lot larger. The Spoken Word Audio Report conducted by Edison and NPR measured the shift from time spent listening to music to time spent listening to spoken word audio. The 2020 report resulted in three themes: (1) multitasking: taking care of children, cleaning and cooking; (2) new perspectives and (3) connection: people returning home to listen to topics they felt they couldn't talk to about with friends (LGBTQ, race, politics, intimate topics (Soto 2022)).

Soto says he thinks historians will say the pandemic served as a catalyst for an increase in podcasting. "It was a time when people were trying new things. And podcasting was one of them" (Soto 2022). At the height of the pandemic, people were consuming information about health, social distancing and vaccinations. Another emerging theme during the pandemic was social issues, like diversity, spurred on by George Floyd's death and the public outcry that resulted.

> When we're going to look back and say this pledge was actually true. People are sticking with it. People care about the diversity and podcasting. They care about representation among black podcast listeners. They care about the representation of Latino podcast listeners, LGBTQ and podcasting was already a very inclusive community, very collaborative.
>
> *(Soto 2022)*

The percentage of people who listen to business podcasts in Edison podcast metrics has slightly increased. Twenty percent of the sample said they listened to business podcasts in the third quarter of 2021. That grew to 25 percent in the second quarter of 2022. Soto said about 22 percent of the sample says they listen to business podcasts, and that number has remained relatively flat since 2020 with a slight increase. Soto says that the number may fluctuate given the economy.

What goes up must come down and the podcast industry slowed in 2022 and 2023. In 2020, Spotify boasted 1 million podcasts, ballooning to 4.7 million in September 2022 (Shaw & Carman 2023). This growth was not unique to Spotify and the sector-wide expansion was so explosive that it is reasonable to expect contraction. The low barrier to entry (inexpensive hardware, software and distribution) allowed everyone from individuals to large media companies to try their hand at podcasting, some more successfully than others. When the market became flooded, individuals and companies began to cut the podcasts that were not making the impact and revenue expected and cool expansion plans. Sirius XM, Spotify, Amazon Music have pulled back on budgets and slowed new podcast development and distribution deals with existing properties (Shaw & Carman 2023).

The podcast market has reached a point of maturity that calls for different kinds of innovation and investment, chiefly in monetization strategies. According to Acast, advertising dollars typically go to the top 500 of more than 2 million English-speaking podcasts in the United States. Those programs only account for 12 percent of monthly reach, leaving marketing and advertising professionals to diversify their ad strategy and seek out different podcasts that may provide the same targeted ad experience, albeit to a smaller audience, for a more reasonable price. Additionally, podcast ad loads are lower than those in TV, streaming music and streaming video, increasing share of voice and leading to better return on ad spend. One important innovation has been the shift to dynamically inserted ads rather than "baked in" or testimonial style ads, which went from 48 percent dynamically inserted in 2019 to 84 percent in 2021 (U.S. Podcast Advertising Revenue Study 2021). The same study notes that podcast ads are beginning to "mirror the digital industry standard ad length" of 15–30 seconds, an indicator that the normative understanding of listener tolerance for advertising is not all that different from that in terrestrial radio.

The stagnation, and in some cases downturn in podcasting, has impacted those employed in the sector. "The Media Titans 30 Index, which includes audio companies like Spotify and SiriusXM, is down nearly 40 percent over the past year, shedding more than $300 million in market value" (Shaw & Carman 2023). SiriusXM, Spotify and National Public Radio all cut staff in 2022 and 2023, aligned with other tech companies, including Meta, Google and Amazon who have all cut jobs in the post-COVID era (Lee 2023). Still, podcast listening time continues to rise, as does the U.S. podcast advertising revenue, which passed the $1 billion mark in 2021 and is predicted to surpass $4 billion in 2024, according to the Interactive Advertising Bureau (U.S. Podcast Advertising Revenue Study 2021). YouTube is also entering the space and many companies hope to expand but distributing and marketing popular shows to international audiences (Shaw & Carman 2023).

## Conclusion

While audio listenership remains strong, consumer behaviors are shifting. Edison research notes AM/FM radio listening in the car dropped from 81 percent in 2020 to 73 percent in 2022 while podcast listenership in the car increased from 28 percent to 32 percent in the same time frame (Beniamini 2022). The same study estimates 177 million U.S. podcast listeners 12+ but notes a drop off in monthly listeners from 41 percent in 2021 to 38 percent in 2022 (Beniamini 2022). The number of radios in a household continues to drop; 96 percent of U.S. households have at least one radio in 2008, whereas only 61 percent have at least one radio in 2022. However, that doesn't mean audio listenership is dwindling. Smart speakers continue to grow in usage, up from 7 percent ownership in 2017 to 35 percent ownership in 2022 (Beniamini 2022). Twenty-five percent of the total U.S. population 12+ owns neither, a number that has held steady since 2018. Business podcasts and news podcasts dropped in ad revenue percentage between 2020 and 2021, likely correlated with the increase in revenue in podcasts categorized as arts, society and culture and sports which roared back as COVID restrictions on sports eased in 2021 and 2022 (U.S. Podcast Advertising Revenue Study 2021).

While much research exists on listenership trends and the production of audio content, more information about business and financial journalism trends on audio platforms is needed. The pandemic appears to have created an uptick in podcast listening, and listenership, specifically to business journalism, remains consistent. The popularity of audio content such as Planet Money (NPR) and Marketplace (American Public Media) shows a need among American consumers for financial and business guidance and information. The pandemic appears to have influenced audio content trends, but much research still needs to be conducted to have a concrete understanding of the changes. The rise in podcasting and an increase in listening while multitasking is something experts and researchers are watching closely.

# References

*355: The Giant Pool of Money - This American Life* (no date). Available at: https://www.thisamerican-life.org/355/transcript (Accessed: 7 September 2022).

Altman, M. (2022) 'KCUR-FM'. Zoom Interview by Kaci Richter. August 5, 2022.

*Apple Podcast Business Chart.* (2022). Available at: https://www.apple.com/apple-podcasts/ (Accessed: 17 October 2022).

Aufderheide, P. *et al.* (2020) 'Podcasting as Public Media: The Future of US News, Public Affairs, and Educational Podcasts', *International Journal of Communication*, 14, p. 22.

Beniamini, N. (2022). The Infinite Dial. Available at: http://www.edisonresearch.com/wp-content/uploads/2022/03/Infinite-Dial-2022-Webinar-revised.pdf

Berry, R. (2006) 'Will the iPod Kill the Radio Star? Profiling Podcasting as Radio', *Convergence*, 12(2), pp. 143–162. Available at: https://doi.org/10.1177/1354856506066522.

Berry, R. (2016) 'Part of the Establishment: Reflecting on 10 Years of Podcasting as an Audio Medium', *Convergence*, 22(6), pp. 661–671. Available at: https://doi.org/10.1177/1354856516632105.

Bonini Baldini, T. (2015) 'The "Second Age" of Podcasting: Reframing Podcasting as a New Digital Mass Medium', *Quaderns del CAC*, 17, pp. 21–30.

Brabazon, T. (2016) 'Press Learning: The Potential of Podcasting Through Pause, Record, Play and Stop', *Knowledge Management & E-Learning: An International Journal*, 8(3), pp. 430–443.

Flichy, P. (1995) *Une Histoire de la Communication Moderne*. La Découverte, p. 281. Available at: https://halshs.archives-ouvertes.fr/halshs-00438894 (Accessed: 29 July 2022).

Hammersley, B. (2004) 'Audible Revolution', *The Guardian*, 12 February. Available at: https://www.theguardian.com/media/2004/feb/12/broadcasting.digitalmedia (Accessed: 19 July 2022).

*History of Business Journalism* (no date). Available at: http://bizjournalismhistory.org/ (Accessed: 3 August 2022).

Joyce, C. (2015) *Campfire Tales: The Essentials of Writing for Radio, NPR Training + Diverse Sources Database*. Available at: https://training.npr.org/2015/03/20/campfire-tales-the-essentials-of-writing-for-radio/ (Accessed: 7 September 2022).

Kern, J. (2012) *Sound Reporting: The NPR Guide to Audio Journalism and Production*. University of Chicago Press.

Lee, W. (2023, January 23). 'Spotify Reduces Staff by 6%, Chief Content Officer Dawn Ostroff to leave', *Los Angeles Times*. Available at: https://www.latimes.com/entertainment-arts/business/story/2023-01-23/spotify-layoffs-dawn-ostroff-rogan-markle

Madsen, V. M. (2009) 'Voices-Cast: A Report on the New Audiosphere of Podcasting with Specific Insights for Public Broadcasting'. In *ANZCA09 Conference Proceedings* (pp. 1191–1210).

McQuail, D. (2010) *McQuail's Mass Communication Theory*. SAGE Publications.

Menduni, E. (2007) 'Four Steps in Innovative Radio Broadcasting: From QuickTime to Podcasting', *Radio Journal:International Studies in Broadcast & Audio Media*, 5(1), pp. 9–18. Available at: https://doi.org/10.1386/rajo.5.1.9_1.

*Podcasting for Trainers and Educators* (no date). Available at: https://learning.oreilly.com/library/view/podcasting-for-trainers/0132320401/ (Accessed: 29 July 2022).

*Radio Advertising Bureau | Why Radio Research* (no date). Available at: https://www.rab.com/whyradio/reportresults.cfm (Accessed: 18 October 2022).

Reich, Z. (2016) 'Comparing News Reporting Across Print, Radio, Television and Online', *Journalism Studies*, 17(5), pp. 552–572. Available at: https://doi.org/10.1080/1461670X.2015.1006898.

Research, E. (2019) 'Comedy, News, and Society and Culture Podcasts Most Listened-to Genres in Podcasting', *Edison Research*, 16 December. Available at: https://www.edisonresearch.com/comedy-news-and-society-and-culture-podcasts-most-listened-to-genres-in-podcasting/ (Accessed: 19 July 2022).

Research, E. (2021) 'The Top 50 Most Listened to U.S. Podcasts of 2020', *Edison Research*, 9 February. Available at: https://www.edisonresearch.com/the-top-50-most-listened-to-u-s-podcasts-of-2020/ (Accessed: 7 September 2022).

Research, E. (2022) 'Comedy Is Top Podcast Genre in U.S.', *Edison Research*, 12 May. Available at: https://www.edisonresearch.com/comedy-is-top-podcast-genre-in-u-s/ (Accessed: 4 August 2022).

Safford, P. (2022a) 'Hurrdat Media'. Zoom Interview by Kaci Richter. July 21, 2022.

Safford, P. (2022b) 'Podcasting Intimacy and Trust'. Zoom Interview by Kaci Richter. July 21, 2022.

Selyukh, A. (2022) 'NPR'. Zoom Interview by Kaci Richter. August 10, 2022.

Shaw, L., & Carman, A. (2023, January 4). 'The Great Podcasting Market Correction', *Bloomberg.Com*. https://www.bloomberg.com/news/articles/2023-01-04/the-great-podcasting-market-correction

Sullivan, J. L. (2019a) 'The Platforms of Podcasting: Past and Present', *Social Media+ Society*, 5(4), p. 2056305119880002.

Sullivan, J. L. (2019b) 'The Platforms of Podcasting: Past and Present', *Social Media+ Society*, 5(4), p. 2056305119880002.

'The Complete History of Podcasts' (2020) *Voices*, 21 July. Available at: https://www.voices.com/blog/history-of-podcasts/ (Accessed: 7 September 2022).

This American Life [@ThisAmerLife] (2021) 'We Were Thrilled to Learn that Our Show "The Giant Pool of Money" Will be Among the Audio Recordings Added to @Librarycongress this Year. It's the First Podcast Ever Named to the #NatRecRegistry! https://bit.ly/31huqDO https://t.co/GUMx632E8A', *Twitter*. Available at: https://twitter.com/ThisAmerLife/status/1374694774461054984 (Accessed: 7 September 2022).

*Tops of 2019: Radio* (no date) *Nielsen*. Available at: https://www.nielsen.com/insights/2019/tops-of-2019-radio/ (Accessed: 4 August 2022).

U.S. Podcast Advertising Revenue Study. (2021). Available at: https://www.iab.com/wp-content/uploads/2022/05/IAB-FY-2021-Podcast-Ad-Revenue-and-2022-2024-Growth-Projections_FINAL.pdf

Usher, N. (2013) 'Marketplace Public Radio and News Routines Reconsidered: Between Structures and Agents', *Journalism*, 14(6), pp. 807–822. Available at: https://doi.org/10.1177/1464884912455903.

Wade Morris, J. (2021a) 'Infrastructures of Discovery: Examining Podcast Ratings and Rankings', *Cultural Studies*, 35(4–5), pp. 728–749. Available at: https://doi.org/10.1080/09502386.2021.1895246.

Wade Morris, J. (2021b) 'Infrastructures of Discovery: Examining Podcast Ratings and Rankings', *Cultural Studies*, 35(4–5), pp. 728–749.

# 17

# THE NET BROADENED THE BASE

## How Technology Expanded Audiences for Business News

*Jake Batsell*

### Introduction

During the tumultuous summer of 2020, as the world endured pandemic lockdowns and as protests across America spurred a reckoning for social justice, Katherine Bell seized the moment by urging fellow business journalists to rethink their purpose. Six months into her new post as the editor-in-chief of Quartz, Bell (2020) called for a fundamental reshaping of her field in a column provocatively headlined, "It's time for business journalism to break from its conservative past." Bell, who previously held leadership positions at Barron's magazine and Harvard Business Review, lamented that news organizations have long catered their business and economic reporting to serve disproportionately white audiences and power structures. She did not exempt herself from these transgressions. "We have not only failed to expose the extent of the inequities and injustices in business and the economy," she wrote, "we have reinforced and perpetuated them." She called for a "more progressive" form of business journalism that appeals to more inclusive and diverse audiences, accounts for racial and social inequities, and points to possible solutions.

Quartz, which launched in 2012 as a mobile-first business news site, is among a cohort of digitally native media outlets that propelled new forms of business journalism aimed at audiences beyond C-suite executives, savvy investors and Wall Street money managers. Consider the path of Business Insider, founded in 2007 as Silicon Alley Insider, which evolved from a tech-industry blog into a global media enterprise now simply known as Insider, courting the attention of millennials with a mix of business, lifestyle and general-news coverage. Cheddar News has been live-streaming financial news directly to social media feeds and digital platforms since 2016. And in August 2020, as the coronavirus pandemic inflicted disproportionate economic impacts on women and people of color, nonprofit news startup The 19th debuted with a lead story on its homepage declaring "America's first female recession" (Carrazana 2020).

Twentieth-century legacy media outlets approached business and economic news with the presumption that the average American "owned stocks and shares, played the market, and made private investments in business" (Hayes 2014, p. xviii). The interests of this presumed audience were reflected in the traditional staples of business news coverage – quarterly

DOI: 10.4324/9781003298977-21

earnings stories, daily recaps of stock-market fluctuations, dispatches chronicling the latest mergers and executive shakeups. The Internet and mobile devices equipped the 21st-century investing public with a myriad of faster tools and platforms to monitor market data and corporate news, prompting print and broadcast media to incorporate real-time market data into their websites and apps. But as financial publications and cable networks devised new ways to serve the digital information needs of investors, their target audience remained largely the same: affluent, plugged in and familiar with the rhythms of Wall Street.

Meanwhile, a crop of digital news startups began to push the field of business journalism more fundamentally beyond its traditional roots. At a time when the country was becoming more diverse and inequalities in wealth were widening, innovative editors and media entrepreneurs spotted an opportunity to deliver business news to broader and younger audiences who had a stake in the American economy. These newcomers endured their share of turbulence as they navigated between niche and mainstream coverage, often under ownership structures that were constantly shifting during an era of unrelenting digital disruption. But collectively, their staying power through the early 2020s proved that business news outlets could successfully appeal to broader audiences online. This chapter examines some of the key players in that evolution.

## Moving beyond Friedman's Shareholder Capitalism

In her column challenging business journalists to become more progressive, Bell noted that modern corporate culture is shifting to acknowledge and accept the reality that companies are accountable not just to their owners but to a wide array of stakeholders – employees, customers, suppliers and communities. This mindset rejects the doctrine of "shareholder capitalism" championed 50 years earlier by economist Milton Friedman, who, in his famous New York Times Magazine essay (1970), argued that executives' primary responsibility was simply "to make as much money as possible" for a company's owners and shareholders while conforming to society's basic rules.

Throughout the late 20th century and well into the 21st, media outlets' framing of business news coverage largely aligned with Friedman's doctrine. Business journalists, envisioning their core audience as the investing public, often settled into well-worn routines of chronicling stock prices, dividends, transactions and corporate announcements while seeking insider scoops from executives and publicists. Investigative journalist and author Dean Starkman traces the roots of what he calls "access reporting" as far back as the Industrial Age, when shipping news journals and commercial newspapers "functioned as the circulatory system of the market" and "served as a voice for the rising merchant, commercial, and industrial class" (Starkman 2014, p. 41). The early financial press' cozy relationship with power eventually led to an institutional ethos among business journalists that favored access over accountability: "Access reporting tends to talk to elites; accountability, to dissidents … In business news, access reporting focuses on investor interests; accountability, on the public interest" (p. 10).

This pattern of providing access-driven reporting to an affluent audience distracted business journalists from recognizing the systemic failures that produced the 2007–2009 financial crisis, Starkman argues in his book "The Watchdog That Didn't Bark: The Financial Crisis and the Disappearance of Investigative Reporting." He also blames the click-chasing, ad-centric business model of the early digital news era for prizing quantity over quality and creating a "hamster wheel" with "remorseless productivity demands" that are incompatible with time-intensive accountability journalism (Starkman and Chittum 2021, p. 233). When that nonstop quest for digital ad impressions eventually proved to be fruitless for local newspapers, they recentered their business models around digital subscriptions, targeting an audience that continued to be older, elite and generally white – in other words, according to media scholar Nikki Usher, "those who are both willing and able to pay for news" (2021, p. 51).

Against this challenging backdrop, a number of digitally native outlets elbowed their way into the crowded universe of business and financial news with a journalistic approach that moved beyond "shareholder capitalism." Some began with a niche focus and gradually became more mainstream; others brought an economic lens to broader topics from the outset. None were weighed down by the trappings of traditional legacy media business models. And all sought the attention of an audience that was younger and more diverse than the traditional Wall Street Journal subscriber.

## From Tech Blog to "Monster Digital Enterprise": Business Insider's Evolution

During the summer of 2007, tech-industry analyst Henry Blodget and two colleagues launched Silicon Alley Insider, working out of another startup's elevator loading dock. While the site began with a narrow niche focus, its approach to content was similar to preceding "native digital" sites such as Gawker and Huffington Post, which sought to draw audiences through a mix of aggregation, quick-take commentary, and pieces from outside contributors, in addition to original reporting (Bennett 2016, p. 181). Spared from the weight of analog products to distribute, or entrenched newsroom routines to maintain, Blodget and his co-founders felt empowered to fully embrace the digital realm:

> For us, the web is not a side business — something we're doing because we feel like we have to or because we're worried that our traditional business may die. Unlike print and broadcast companies, we don't have a "core business" cash cow to protect, so we are free to let the capabilities of the medium take our product development wherever we think it should go.
>
> *(Blodget 2011)*

The venture soon added several more financial news verticals and rebranded under the name Business Insider. Four years after launching, Blodget reported that the network of sites was drawing nearly 10 million monthly unique visitors per month. But it also gained a reputation for clickbait tactics, drawing criticism for its reliance on aggregated content and "frequently misleading sensationalism" (Starkman 2014, p. 290).

Undeterred in its approach, Business Insider continued to attract massive audiences and was drawing 76 million unique monthly readers by 2015, when it was acquired by German publishing company Axel Springer (Bomey and Yu 2015). Two years later, it dropped "business" from its corporate name, rebranding as Insider Inc. in a strategic move designed to broaden the company's appeal to millennials through niche coverage of non-business topics. "Our ambitions are way beyond business," Blodget told The Wall Street Journal. "And we feel like our strength is native digital storytelling" (Mullin 2017).

By 2020, Insider Inc. had matured into what Poynter called "a monster digital enterprise" that was among the upper echelon of digital publishers (Edmonds 2020). While Business Insider continued to cover corporate and financial news, the parent company had widened its reach globally to around 375 million monthly uniques, expanding its coverage of lifestyle topics and establishing itself as a serious competitor to general-news contemporaries such as BuzzFeed and Vice. On top of ad revenues, the company's fortunes were bolstered by a growing base of 200,000 paid subscribers as well as more commerce and licensing deals. At a start-of-the-decade meeting, Blodget announced an ambitious goal to eventually double the editorial staff to 1,000 and challenged his employees to propel the company toward a pair of gaudy milestones: a million paid subscribers, and a billion monthly unique visitors (Edmonds 2020). The company also acquired a majority stake in Morning Brew, a growing network of newsletters and podcasts aimed at business-minded millennials (Fischer 2020).

By 2021, Insider Inc. had phased out the "Business Insider" name and logo altogether, cementing the company's 15-year evolution from a pure business site into a broader network of verticals covering topics, including politics, lifestyle and travel (Fischer 2021). Not all topical coverage resonated with readers – in 2023, Insider's Washington, DC, bureau, "all but collapsed" after attempting an aggressive push into political scoops three years earlier (Bolies 2023). And in April 2023, on the same day digital pioneer BuzzFeed shut down its news division, Insider Inc. sent out a company memo announcing that the company was laying off 10 percent of its workforce, citing "economic headwinds" that were bedeviling the digital advertising landscape (Bolies 2023b).

Nevertheless, what began in 2007 as a focused source of tech-industry news had morphed into a digital juggernaut that kept covering business while also broadening its scope to general-interest topics ranging from parenting advice to sports scoops to product reviews. To thrive in the digital age, Business Insider continuously reset its audience ambitions further and further beyond the traditional consumers of financial journalism.

### Cheddar: The "CNBC for Millennials"

While Business Insider's path toward broader coverage was a gradual journey, Cheddar's audience strategy was more expansive from the outset. Cheddar, a live-streaming television network described as "The CNBC for millennials," launched in April 2016 with live dispatches from the New York Stock Exchange. Cheddar intentionally avoided cable as a distribution mechanism, billing itself as a "post-cable network" that would serve cord-cutters by streaming content online via Facebook Live and its own website. "I take the belief that no one coming out of college is going to get a cable box," proclaimed Cheddar's CEO and founder, Jon Steinberg (Shontell 2016).

Initially positioning itself as an alternative to legacy cable channels such as CNBC, Fox Business News and Bloomberg, Cheddar quickly signaled its intentions to move beyond business coverage. Just four months after its initial launch, the company opened a second studio in Manhattan's Flatiron Building to introduce a new series called "Cheddar Life" focusing on health, wellness and fashion in addition to business news (Henry 2016). Steinberg, a former executive at BuzzFeed and The Daily Mail's U.S. operations, explained that the addition of lifestyle content supported his vision to build a streaming network "focused on this intersection of business, tech, media and culture." By the time Cheddar unveiled its second studio in late 2016, the company already had amassed a regular audience of roughly 100,000 daily viewers while establishing video streaming partnerships with Amazon Prime and Vimeo.

In 2017, Cheddar went even more mainstream by introducing Cheddar Local, a service providing business news segments tailored to local TV stations. And in 2018, it launched a second streaming network, Cheddar Big News, available via YouTube TV. In a company news release, Steinberg said devoting a second network to non-business topics, including politics, sports, science, weather and human-interest stories marked Cheddar's arrival as a "full suite news offering."

Barely two years into its existence, Cheddar was "here, there and everywhere," as a Nieman Journalism Lab headline put it (Schmidt 2018). In addition to the second network, the company was producing 20-second video segments for gas-station TV screens, airing interviews from remote studios at WeWork locations around the world, and streaming on platforms ranging from Sling TV to Amazon to Twitch. By early 2019, Cheddar's two networks – renamed as Cheddar Business and Cheddar News – were available to 40 million homes through various streaming services. Cheddar's growing popularity within the coveted 25-to-34 demographic soon enticed cable operator Altice USA to purchase the company for $200 million (Vlessing 2019).

After the acquisition, Cheddar's trajectory would become considerably bumpier. About a month into the coronavirus pandemic in 2020, Altice announced widespread layoffs that included the permanent closure of Cheddar's Los Angeles studio and the consolidation of the two networks (Chan 2020). And in early 2023, an exclusive investigation by Insider, of all outlets, found that a shift in strategy to prioritize social media content led to an "identity crisis" at Cheddar News, prompting many staffers to quit (Alexander and Low 2023). Still, as 2023 came to a close, the onetime "CNBC for millennials" continued to court the attention of its target audience not just with business coverage, but a broad mix of stories spanning topics that included culture, sports, science and politics. As it built and maintained an audience of business-savvy young adults, Cheddar took on many flavors.

## Quartz: From "Obsessions" to Navigating the "Mushy Middle"

In contrast to Business Insider and Cheddar, which combined millennial-friendly business news with heavy helpings of mainstream side dishes, Quartz's quest for broader audiences was anchored by a more cerebral and global philosophy. The Atlantic launched Quartz in 2012 as a mobile-first news site whose coverage was anchored around a series of "obsessions," defined by the founding editor-in-chief Kevin Delaney (2012) as "core topics and knotty questions of seismic importance to business professionals." Instead of assigning reporters to traditional financial beats, Quartz organized its coverage around emerging subjects like climate change and the lingering impacts of the financial crisis, aimed at an audience of sophisticated, upwardly mobile global professionals.

Built around an advertising-driven business model fueled by custom native ad campaigns for high-end clients, including Boeing and Credit Suisse, Quartz billed itself to readers and sponsors as "a free and digital Economist for the budding millennial business elite" (Perlberg 2020). Within a year of launching, Quartz actually had surpassed The Economist in web traffic with more than 2 million pageviews. By 2015, its global expansion had reached as far as India and Africa, and Delaney announced that monthly pageviews had swelled to 22 million with an overall audience of more than 100 million when including platforms such as email, apps and social media.

Quartz also developed a buzzy reputation as an early practitioner of digital news innovations, offering experimental products, including chatbots and a mobile app that sent a daily "Markets Haiku" poem via push notifications after the closing bell. "It doesn't take much/A hint from the UAE/And oil prices soar," read one haiku in early 2016, followed a day later by "Don't care what they say/No good reason stocks went up/But hey, we'll take it."

In 2018, Atlantic Media sold Quartz to Japanese media company Uzabase for a sum ranging between $75 million and $110 million, depending on performance (Mozur 2018). Delaney and founding publisher Jay Lauf stayed on as top managers as Quartz altered its business model to target more paying subscribers, reducing dependence on advertising. However, the next several years would be volatile. Delaney departed the company in late 2019 and Lauf shifted to an advisory role. By mid-2020, the company laid off roughly half of its staff and shut down bureaus around the world as Quartz tallied losses tied to dwindling advertising sales exacerbated by the pandemic. While Quartz had succeeded in appealing to a digital audience that extended far beyond the readership targeted by financial wire services and pricey business publications, its value proposition was faltering. As Digiday's Steven Perlberg (2020) put it:

> As industry layoffs and furloughs continue, Quartz has joined a growing club of publications that seemingly got caught in the mushy middle of 2010s digital media, like Mic and Mashable. Not quite niche enough to be essential to a small group of readers, but not quite big enough to compete at scale. Coronavirus didn't help.

The Uzabase era ended with a management-led buyout in November 2020 when the Japanese company sold Quartz to its CEO, Zach Seward, and Bell, along with the rest of the company's staff. Then, in April 2022, the ownership structure changed yet again, as Quartz executives sold the company to G/O Media – a network of websites, including Deadspin, Gizmodo and Jezebel – for an undisclosed amount (Mullin and Robertson 2022). In reporting the 2022 sale, The New York Times noted that while Quartz had suffered declines in revenue throughout the pandemic and was not expected to break even until 2023, the site's reputation for high-quality business journalism made it an attractive acquisition as digital publishers consolidated to compete with tech titans Google, Meta and Amazon. After a decade of experimentation and vacillating between different business models and owners, Quartz nonetheless matured into an enduring and trusted news source for a diverse, global audience that was drawn to Bell's more inclusive style of business journalism.

Soon after the 2022 sale to G/O Media, Bell stepped down as Quartz's editor-in-chief, later announcing that she would lead a team of journalists to produce content for Goldman Sachs. During her two and a half years at the helm of the Quartz newsroom, her defining editorial philosophy, captured in her 2020 column, called for business journalism to "break from its conservative past" and prove its relevance to more diverse audiences by explaining how systemic factors have created inequities and injustices. "If we want a better, more inclusive economy, we need a new, more demanding form of business and economic journalism," Bell wrote. "... In other words, we need business journalism to be more progressive."

## Digital Pathways to More Diverse Audiences

Bell's column noted that business and financial media outlets are staffed by disproportionately white journalists who report on companies and markets populated by disproportionately white leaders, investors and economists. "Not surprisingly," she wrote, "the readers we reach are also disproportionately white." Bell did not call out any particular publications, but the central themes of her column laid bare industry-wide tensions that would play out over the next year during a high-stakes battle over the future of The Wall Street Journal.

In July 2020, the same month that Bell's column was published, an internal strategy team at the Journal presented a draft report to top editor Matt Murray. The team, tasked with finding ways to gain new digital subscribers, recommended that the Journal should pivot from overserving the needs of heavy readers and instead focus more on broadening its reach, according to The New York Times:

> The report argued that the paper should attract new readers – specifically women, people of color and younger professionals – by focusing more on topics such as climate change and income inequality. Among its suggestions: "We also strongly recommend putting muscle behind efforts to feature more women and people of color in all of our stories."
>
> *(Lee 2021)*

The Journal ultimately adopted only parts of the report, called "The Content Review," which never was shared officially with newsroom staffers. The editor who oversaw the report, Louise Story, left the paper in July 2021. The Times' Edmund Lee (2021) reported that Journal executives remained wary of alienating the newspaper's established subscriber base of business leaders.

Indeed, the Journal is perhaps the most iconic among a quintet of elite-serving media outlets that that author Chris Roush (2022) calls "The Dominators" of modern business news – a group that also includes Bloomberg News, Reuters, the Financial Times and CNBC. Importantly, Roush notes that Bloomberg and Reuters subsidize their journalism operations with revenues from proprietary terminals used by traders and bankers to access real-time financial data (Roush, p. 177).

Meanwhile, digital news startups – unburdened by the legacy of subscriber relationships accumulated over decades and exempt from the esoteric world of real-time terminals – had wider freedom to target more inclusive audiences. The broader audience approaches deployed by Business Insider, Cheddar and Quartz varied in their tactics and delivery, but all ultimately proved attractive to new corporate owners by demonstrating the power of harnessing digital platforms to provide business coverage to younger, more diverse readers. And as the pandemic's sprawling economic consequences continued to unfold, another digitally native venture with an inclusive audience strategy quickly carved out a distinct space within the business news ecosystem.

## The 19th: Chronicling "America's First Female Recession"

On August 2, 2020, after several months of publishing content in The Washington Post during its soft-launch phase, The 19th unveiled its own self-standing website. Named after the 19th Amendment to the U.S. Constitution, which granted women's suffrage and was marking its centennial that month, The 19th entered the media landscape as a nonprofit news organization with a mission to cover the intersection of gender, politics and policy. However, the new venture added an asterisk to its logo to acknowledge the amendment's "unfinished business" of ensuring and protecting the right to vote, especially for women of color. The 19th's founders, Emily Ramshaw and Amanda Zamora, both formerly served as top editors at the nonprofit Texas Tribune.

The lead article marking the debut of The 19th's website signaled how the new outlet would approach economic coverage through a gender-focused lens. The story, headlined

"America's first female recession," documented how the unemployment rate for women had climbed disproportionately during the initial months of the coronavirus pandemic. This disparity was even more pronounced among women of color, who are more likely to work low-income jobs while serving as their family's sole breadwinner. The story also cited a study documenting how working mothers were four to five times more likely than fathers to reduce their hours as a result of child-care demands created by pandemic-related lockdowns. And women, the story noted, continued to earn wages at a fraction of their male counterparts. "When the economy crumbled," the article bluntly declared, "women fell – hard" (Carrazana 2020).

As the pandemic unfolded, The 19th's economy reporter, Chabeli Carrazana, continued to center the experiences of women as they navigated the turbulent financial landscape. Another Carrazana article highlighted a national survey's findings that even as the unemployment rate was leveling out, nearly half of Latinas – double the rate of white women – had wiped out their savings to make ends meet during the first year of the pandemic. Latinas, the article noted, are overrepresented in low-wage fields, where they earn only 55 cents for every dollar earned by white men and accumulate far less institutional wealth. The article humanized the survey's statistics by chronicling the struggles of a housekeeper and airport restaurant server, both of whom had been laid off and saw their savings dwindle as they struggled to obtain unemployment benefits. Paraphrasing a nonprofit executive, Carrazana wrote that Latinas' sobering financial losses during the pandemic "reflect what happens when pressure is put on a system that has always been inequitable, and has always made it more difficult for Latinas to secure the financial stability that families build on from generation to generation" (Carrazana 2021).

Later in 2021, The 19th observed Black Women's Equal Pay Day by publishing an article examining why Black women earn 63 cents for every dollar a white man makes. And as the federal eviction moratorium ended, another story examined the looming economic impacts on LGBTQ+ people, who are more likely to experience housing insecurity. Meanwhile, as they documented economic inequality, reporters at The 19th were encouraged to share their personal backgrounds with readers: Carrazana shared during a question-and-answer column that she immigrated to the United States from Cuba when she was five years old, and LGBTQ+ reporter Kate Sosin wrote a first-person essay that reflected on bringing a transgender perspective to the beat.

It all added up to a growing national reputation for coverage that challenged the formulaic, impersonal, institution-friendly, shareholder-centric norms of traditional economic journalism. Washington Post media columnist Margaret Sullivan observed that "unlike many established news organizations, The 19th encourages its reporters to bring their own experiences to their work and writing, rather than attempt to present themselves as ideological blank slates for the sake of old-style objectivity" (Sullivan 2021).

With story after story spotlighting structural inequities and humanizing the pandemic's unequal financial toll, The 19th had established itself with an editorial approach embodying the "more progressive" style of business journalism that Bell had publicly championed just a month before The 19th officially launched. And the nonprofit's early financial health was comfortably viable: according to audited statements available on its website, The 19th generated $10.9 million in total revenue during 2020 through a combination of philanthropic donations, sponsorships, events and memberships, while yearly expenses amounted to just $3.1 million ("Financial Statements" 2021, p. 6).

## Conclusion

The quartet of digital news startups profiled in this chapter understood from the start that entering the 21st-century media landscape would require more than parroting the typical market recaps, earnings stories and other well-worn staples of business journalism. Business Insider, Cheddar, Quartz and The 19th all bucked the traditional "shareholder capitalism" mindset and routines that long defined mainstream economic news coverage.

Each of these digitally native ventures traveled their own unique path in earning the attention of their audiences. Still, when collectively analyzing how all four of them rose to prominence, some common factors emerge:

- **A clean slate, free of legacy media baggage.** The looming prospect of driving away longtime traditional subscribers continues to haunt efforts to innovate at iconic American business publications. "We can no longer allow the fear of losing current audiences to hold us back from digital success and growth," an internal Wall Street Journal strategy team warned in July 2020, according to a leaked report ("The Content Review" 2020, p. 3). Such hesitation did not apply to these four digital upstarts, who were unencumbered by existing subscriber relationships or fixed print distribution costs, and did not maintain a fleet of proprietary real-time terminals. This allowed them the freedom to experiment with purely digital approaches to reach untapped audiences – an advantage often mentioned by their founders.
- **A willingness to embrace general-interest topics.** Instead of limiting themselves to standard business coverage or expanding to arcane niches, each of the four outlets profiled here added mainstream topics to their repertoire of coverage. They hired reporters to cover nontraditional beats like caregiving and LGBTQ+ issues (The 19th); lifestyle topics like health, wellness and travel (Cheddar, Business Insider); and, in the case of Quartz, "obsessions" like the climate economy and fixing capitalism.
- **A deliberate strategy to reach audiences beyond Wall Street.** As Bell forcefully argued in her 2020 column, the American business press, as an institution, "reinforced and perpetuated" systemic inequities for too long by catering coverage to the interests of disproportionately white readers who already were well-situated within financial power structures. By intentionally targeting millennials, women, and more diverse and global audiences beyond Wall Street's orbit of white older men, these four startups found new ways to make business news relevant to nontraditional audiences.

It may take a while longer for the legacy business press to fully break from its conservative past, if it ever does. Old habits die hard, as "The Content Review" episode in 2020 at The Wall Street Journal plainly showed. But Business Insider, Cheddar, Quartz and The 19th leveraged their advantages as digitally native publications to earn the attention of a broader audience for business news. Collectively, this cohort pushed the field of business journalism along the path to a more inclusive – and, yes, progressive – future. By conceding establishment-driven coverage and instead striving to make economic news more accessible, all proved themselves to be formidable and tenacious challengers to more traditional business news outlets such as the Wall Street Journal, Bloomberg and Reuters.

Within elite circles, there will always be demand for niche, markets-based business journalism. But as traditional audience habits fade away, increasingly diverse populations will seek out more comprehensive economic coverage that resonates with their lives. To stay relevant in our digital age, established business news outlets and newcomers alike will need to continue to broaden their base.

# References

Alexander, R. and Low, E. (2023) 'Inside the turmoil at Cheddar News, where an editorial 'identity crisis' and misfired social-media strategy divided the newsroom and pushed staffers to exit', *Insider*, 9 January. Available at: https://www.businessinsider.com/cheddar-news-kristin-malaspina-employees-quit-altice-social-media-strategy-2023-1 (Accessed: 27 March 2023).

Bell, K. (2020) 'It's time for business journalism to break from its conservative past', *Quartz*, 16 July. Available at: https://qz.com/1878256/what-is-the-purpose-of-business-journalism (Accessed: 8 July 2022).

Bennett, W. L. (2016) *News: The Politics of Illusion*. Chicago, IL: University of Chicago Press.

Blodget, H. (2011) 'Why and how we founded Business Insider', *Business Insider*, 4 May. Available at: https://www.businessinsider.com/founding-of-business-insider-2011-4 (Accessed: 8 July 2022).

Bolies, C. (2023a) 'Inside the collapse of insider's much-hyped D.C. team', *The Daily Beast*, 30 January. Available at: https://www.thedailybeast.com/inside-the-collapse-of-insiders-much-hyped-dc-team (Accessed: 27 March 2023).

Bolies, C. (2023b) 'Insider to lay off 10% of staffers, company says', *The Daily Beast*, 20 April. Available at: https://www.thedailybeast.com/insider-to-lay-off-10-percent-of-staffers-company-says (Accessed: 16 May 2023).

Bomey, N. and Yu, R. (2015) 'German publisher Axel Springer acquires business insider', *USA Today*, 29 September. Available at: https://www.usatoday.com/story/money/2015/09/29/german-publisher-axel-springer-acquires-business-insider/73018290 (Accessed: 8 July 2022).

Carrazana, C. (2020) 'America's first female recession', *The 19th*, 2 August. Available at: https://19thnews.org/2020/08/americas-first-female-recession (Accessed: 8 July 2022).

Carrazana, C. (2021) 'How the pandemic has widened the Latina wealth gap', *The 19th*, 19 April. Available at: https://19thnews.org/2021/04/latinas-wealth-gap-pandemic-unidos-report (Accessed: 8 July 2022).

Chan, J.C. (2020) 'Cheddar permanently shuts down Los Angeles studio amid layoffs', *The Wrap*, 24 April. Available at: https://www.thewrap.com/cheddar-permanently-shuts-down-los-angeles-studio-amid-mass-layoffs (Accessed: 8 July 2022).

Delaney, K. (2012) 'Hello, world. A welcome letter from our editor-in-chief', *Quartz*, 24 September. Available at: https://qz.com/6014/hello-world-a-welcome-letter-from-our-editor-in-chief (Accessed: 8 July 2022).

Edmonds, R. (2020) 'Business Insider grew in 12 years to a monster digital enterprise. Now CEO Henry Blodget has plotted a new wave of expansion', *Poynter*, 15 January. Available at: https://www.poynter.org/business-work/2020/business-insider-grew-in-12-years-to-a-monster-digital-enterprise-now-ceo-henry-blodget-has-plotted-a-new-wave-of-expansion (Accessed: 8 July 2022).

'Financial Statements'. (2021) *The 19th News*, December. Available at: https://19thnews.org/wp-content/uploads/2021/12/2020-audit-report-the-19th-news.pdf (Accessed: 14 July 2022).

Fischer, S. (2020) 'Insider Inc. buys majority stake in Morning Brew in all-cash deal', *Axios*, 29 October. Available at: https://www.axios.com/2020/10/29/insider-inc-buys-majority-stake-morning-brew (Accessed: 12 July 2022).

Fischer, S. (2021) 'Insider Inc. to drop business insider name amid massive global expansion', *Axios*, 2 February. Available at: https://www.axios.com/business-insider-name-logo-change (Accessed: 8 July 2022).

Friedman, M. (1970) 'A Friedman doctrine -- The social responsibility of business is to increase its profits', *The New York Times Magazine*, 13 September. Available at: https://www.nytimes.com/1970/09/13/archives/a-friedman-doctrine-the-social-responsibility-of-business-is-to.html (Accessed: 8 July 2022).

Hayes, K. (2014) *Business Journalism: How to Report on Business and Economics*. New York: Apress Media.

Henry, Z. (2016) 'Why a former BuzzFeed exec launched Cheddar, a news streaming service for millennials', *Inc.*, 5 August. Available at: https://www.inc.com/zoe-henry/why-a-former-buzzfeed-exec-launched-cheddar-news-streaming-service.html (Accessed: 8 July 2022).

Lee, E. (2021) 'Louise Story, a top editor at The Wall Street Journal, is leaving', *The New York Times*, 27 July. Available at: https://www.nytimes.com/2021/07/27/business/media/louise-story-wsj.html (Accessed: 8 July 2022).

Mozur, P. (2018) 'Quartz, Atlantic Media's business news start-up, is sold to Japanese firm', *The New York Times*, 2 July. Available at: https://www.nytimes.com/2018/07/02/business/dealbook/quartz-atlantic-media-uzabase.html (Accessed: 8 July 2022).

Mullin, B. (2017) 'Business Insider Inc. drops 'business' from its name as company broadens coverage, distribution', *The Wall Street Journal*, 14 December. Available at: https://www.wsj.com/articles/business-insider-drops-business-from-its-name-as-company-broadens-coverage-distribution-1513249201 (Accessed: 8 July 2022).

Mullin, B. and Robertson, K. (2022) 'G/O Media, owner of Gizmodo and Deadspin, buys business site Quartz', *The New York Times*, 28 April. Available at: https://www.nytimes.com/2022/04/28/business/media/quartz-sale.html (Accessed: 11 July 2022).

Perlberg, S. (2020) 'Caught in the mushy middle: How Quartz fell to earth', *Digiday*, 15 June. Available at: https://digiday.com/media/caught-in-the-mushy-middle-how-quartz-fell-to-earth (Accessed: 8 July 2022).

Roush, C. (2022) *The Future of Business Journalism: Why It Matters For Wall Street ad Main Street.* Washington, DC: Georgetown University Press.

Schmidt, C. (2018) 'Cheddar is here, there, and everywhere — and now reporting on local NYC news for CUNY TV', *Nieman Journalism Lab*, 18 October. Available at: https://www.niemanlab.org/2018/10/cheddar-is-here-there-and-everywhere-and-now-reporting-on-local-nyc-news-for-cuny-tv (Accessed: 8 July 2022).

Shontell, A. (2016) 'Former BuzzFeed president Jon Steinberg launches Cheddar, a CNBC for millennials, with $3 million in funding', *Business Insider*, 19 February. Available at: https://www.businessinsider.com/jon-steinberg-launches-cheddar-tv-2016-2 (Accessed: 8 July 2022).

Starkman, D. (2014) *The Watchdog That Didn't Bark: The Financial Crisis and the Disappearance of Investigative Reporting.* New York: Columbia University Press.

Starkman, D., and Chittum, R. (2021) 'The hamster wheel, triumphant', in Schiffrin, A. (ed.) *Media Capture: How Money, Digital Platforms, and Governments Control the News.* New York: Columbia University Press, pp. 232–258.

Sullivan, M. (2021) 'It's been one pivot after another for the 19th — the start-up news site about gender and politics', *The Washington Post*, 4 August. Available at: https://www.washingtonpost.com/lifestyle/media/the-19th-website-gender-politics/2021/08/03/d6a061ae-f39c-11eb-9738-8395ec2a44c7_story.html (Accessed: 8 July 2022).

'The Content Review'. (2020) *The Wall Street Journal*, July. Available at: https://int.nyt.com/data/documenttools/the-content-review-introduction-july-2020/481ac63bd24c1905/full.pdf (Accessed: 8 July 2022).

Usher, N. (2021) *News for the Rich, White, and Blue: How Place and Power Distort American Journalism.* New York: Columbia University Press.

Vlessing, E. (2019) 'Altice USA buys digital news service Cheddar for $200M', *The Hollywood Reporter*, 30 April. Available at: https://www.hollywoodreporter.com/tv/tv-news/altice-usa-buys-cheddar-200-million-1205959 (Accessed: 8 July 2022).

# 18

# TRADE JOURNALISM
## Underappreciated and Often Prescient

*Rob Wells*

## Introduction

Trade journals play a foundational role in business journalism and commerce, a role largely overlooked by scholars and underappreciated in the mainstream journalism community. Publications such as Advertising Age, American Banker, Computerworld and Billboard deliver specialized reporting on select industries, profiling leaders, examining new lines of business and government regulations.

In a sense, trade journals are a form of community journalism, and journalists working for them treat a particular industry as the equivalent of a city or a town beat. Since the 1500s, trade publications have supplied the lifeblood of capitalism, the information that allows for price discovery and efficient operation of financial markets. This close connection to industry leads to criticism that trade journalists are captive to the industries they cover and they do not perform the traditional watchdog or surveillance role over powerful interests. New research challenges this critique by illustrating important independent journalism, such as Willard Kiplinger's reporting during the New Deal and the National Thrift News's pioneering reporting during the savings and loan crisis (Wells 2021, 2019). Trade journalism can be a lucrative business, generating $37 billion in revenue in 2021.

May Belle Flynn, in her 1944 New York University doctoral dissertation examining the business press, offered a concise definition of the trade press: "Business papers are periodicals published for the purpose of producing profit by fostering commercial enterprise. Their principal appeal is to purchasing agents who buy for business purposes, rather than for personal consumption" (Flynn 1944, p. 1). Historian Julien Elfenbein (1952) said that interpretation and analysis are prime news needs for trade press readers. General news can't just be repeated; trade press articles must say how an issue affects them and their business. The trade press also serves an oversight function on the companies or industries they are covering. "The modern corporation needs a critical business press," Elfenbein wrote, saying that the business press has a watchdog role comparable to the press' role in politics. "The modern corporation needs the free – that is, free to be critical – press just as much as the government does; it needs it as one of the fundamental checks and balances of a free enterprise economy."

DOI: 10.4324/9781003298977-22

## Size and Scope of the Industry

As a business, the trade press brings in far more money than the newspaper industry and major cable television and network news programs combined. Business-to-business publications brought in an estimated $37 billion in revenue in 2021, of which 84 percent represented print and digital advertising revenue, according to Outsell Inc., a consulting firm (Giusto 2022). By comparison, mainstream cable and network news, plus newspaper advertising, brought in about $28 billion in 2020, according to the Pew Research Center. Major cable and network television reaped $5.6 billion in advertising revenue in 2020, a figure that includes Fox News, CNN and MSNBC, network television morning and evening news brought in $1.3 billion, while the newspaper industry reported $20.7 billion in advertising and circulation revenue in 2020, according to the Pew Center (Barthel and Worden 2021; Walker & Forman-Katz 2021; Worden and Walker 2021).

Even though the trade press revenue overshadows the better known media, the results are depressed due to the COVID-19 pandemic causing cancellation of industry conferences and events, which in recent years was about half of the B2B Media and Business industry revenue, Outsell reported. The entire B2B industry saw a 29 percent decline in revenues in 2020 due to cancellation of industry conferences but was poised to rebound and grow by nearly 9 percent in 2021.

These figures include results from a wide range of business information players such as IDG Inc., publisher of ComputerWorld and Informa Plc, publisher of Lloyd's List and Aviation Week. With complex companies such as Informa, Outsell's estimates, derived from public company filings and estimates of private businesses, focus on print and digital revenue and events but not the results from divisions such as book publishing. The trade press is not immune from the broader media industry challenges, such as a decline in print revenues. While Outsell didn't specify print advertising, the company reported total digital and print advertising fell 5.2 percent in 2018, in line with other industry estimates.[1]

Because of the downturn in advertising, the trade press industry in recent years has expanded significantly into selling data and providing events and conferences. The lines between these activities are blurring. Relx Group Plc, the parent of database giants Lexis-Nexis and Elsevier, also publishes specialized magazines such as Lancet, holds conferences and uses data to provide risk management tools for insurance companies, banks and other corporations. It generated $9.6 billion in revenue in 2020 (RELX PLC 2021). Some 87 percent of its 2020 revenue was from electronic sources, primarily subscriptions, and just 8 percent was from print. In 2000, just 22 percent of revenue was from electronic and 64 percent was from print. Some firms positioned businesses as consultants, offering their news and information for market research, data analytics, management consulting or regulatory and compliance risk management. The overall trend in the B2B Media Industry is a blurring of lines, with news, data, events and consulting type services playing some role in business strategy. As a result, a pure industry publishing figure is difficult to obtain.

## Economic Necessity of Trade Journals

Trade journals play a foundational role in business journalism, commerce, and the evolution of capitalism. Since the 1500s, trade and business publications have provided information that allows for price discovery and efficient operation of financial markets. Perhaps the earliest known business publication involved newsletters produced by Phillip Edward Fugger, a

German financier who wrote about general business and economic matters centered around mid-European trade (Elfenbein 1969, p. 196). Simple "price current" publications, which reported on prices of barrel staves, tanned leather and other commodities, proliferated as commerce evolved. "These price currents have been found in the archives of every important European city," historian John McCusker wrote (McCusker 2005, p. 307). Lloyd's List, launched in 1734 from a London coffeehouse, supplied shipping intelligence and stock quotes to leading businessmen, which allowed them to assess commercial ventures (Wright 1928, p. 73). Lloyd's List developed as the economic Lloyd's of London insurance market grew to become a backbone of global finance. As commerce evolved in Colonial America, price current publications appeared in South Carolina (1774), Philadelphia (1783), then New York (1786) (McCusker 2005, p. 314).

The price current publications generally were tabular lists, devoid of narrative, and were akin to the stock price tables in a modern newspaper. Business journalism evolved as a more narrative form in the 1843 with the launching of The Economist magazine. It became a political and intellectual force under Editor Walter Bagehot, who advocated for open markets and provided analytical reporting that influenced others in the field for years to come ("Our history," no date). In the United States, Henry Varnum Poor took an analytical approach to business journalism as editor of the American Railroad Journal and suggested ways the industry could improve and evolve (Chandler 1981, p. 1). This publication represented a new direction for business journalism in the 19th century, the emergence of specialized publications to serve specific business sectors as the industrial revolution transformed the economy and society. As trade journalist Don Gussow observed, "Historically, the appearance of trade papers has tended to accompany the beginnings of industries" (Gussow 1984, p. 7). These publications assumed an explicit functional mission to help businesses evolve and expand. Consider the title of one of the first railroad newspapers: American Railroad Journal and **Advocate of Internal Improvements** (emphasis added).

The trade press had grown to such a size by 1893 that the American Economist carried an article that sought to distinguish trade press from mainstream media. "The trade journal is useful; the general newspaper is entertaining...The trade journal stimulates investigation and reflection; the general newspaper creates and feeds the appetite for what is superficial and often frivolous" (Mason 1893). The trade publications helped educate market participants by describing new industry innovations in production or management. "Such papers became the 'colleges' and 'trade schools' of the early period," Gussow wrote (Gussow 1984, p. 10). As such, these publications played a leadership role and "have been able to shape the direction of the industries they serve" (Gussow 1984, p. 129).

The American Banker, founded in 1836 under the title Thompson's Bank Note Reporter, provided a valuable service to businesses, banks and merchants: investigating fraudulent and unsafe banks and reporting on legitimate and illicit bank notes and currency (Endres 1994). "All though industrial history, there is a close relationship between basic inventions, the subsequent development of industries founded upon such inventions and finally, the emergence of publications to represent that industry," Flynn observed (Flynn 1944, p. 7). Thus, the early years of trade publications showed how journals prioritized building up the professions and did not self-identify as aggressive watchdogs over the industries they covered. "The trade press is one of the most successful business builders in the country," the Federation of Trade Press Association said in 1907 congressional testimony (Federation of Trade Press Associations 1907, p. 717).

Following the U.S. Civil War, trade journalism began to expand. In the 1870s, some 50 trade newspapers were launched, and by the next decade, some 107 trade newspapers were started, according to Jesse H. Neal, executive secretary of the Association of Business Papers in New York, in a 1922 history that is among the first to survey the field[2] (Neal 1922, p. 1245). Neal had worked at United Publishers Corp., a forerunner of the Chilton Co., a longstanding force in trade journalism. One of the early trade associations for this genre of journalism was the Federation of Trade Press Associations, founded in 1906 by James H. McGraw and John A. Hill of McGraw-Hill publishing fame. Trade papers, the group argued, provided a valuable form of technical education for business people at a time when trade or industrial schools were not common in the early 20th century. The National Conference of Business Paper Editors Inc. was founded in 1919 at future president Herbert Hoover's request. One leading trade press association now is the American Society of Business Publication Editors, or ASBPE, founded in 1964. The group runs an extensive annual awards contest known as the Azbee Awards of Excellence. One of the group's goals is to "develop editorial excellence standards and codes of ethics to help editors better serve their readership and marketplace" (American Society of Business Publication Editors, no date).

## Understanding Trade Journals

In a sense, trade journals are a form of community journalism, and trade journalists treat a particular industry as the equivalent of a city or a town beat. James McGraw, a founder of the iconic McGraw-Hill publishing enterprise, said modern business publications serve several functions, such as collecting and disseminating "the experience of those engaged in a certain industry, profession or trade" and acting "as an interpreter of events and developments" while serving "as a leader of sound thought and policy" (McGraw 1930, p. 299). These business publications, in addition to providing news, offer a source of education and even assistance to businesses seeking to market their products through advertising. The Federation of Trade Press Associations argued that trade journal advertising played a much different role in educating an industry, serving as "a necessary medium of communication between the manufacturer, jobber and retailer" (Report of Postal Commission 1907).

There is limited academic literature on this subject but several sources describe how the trade press can be ahead of its mainstream counterparts. Robert Freedman and Steven Roll provided several contemporary examples about the impact of enterprising trade journalism. Revelations about an influence peddling scandal involving James Watt, a lobbyist and former U.S. Interior Secretary, and the U.S. Department of Housing and Urban Development first arose in 1988 in Multi-Housing News. The Washington Post and other mainstream newspapers picked up this story, and the resulting publicity led to reform legislation (Freedman 2006, p. 16). Stanley Strachan, editor of the National Thrift News, was first to report that five U.S. senators were pressuring banking regulators to ease up on enforcement of financier Charles Keating and his troubled Lincoln Savings and Loan. Newspapers generally ignored the National Thrift News reporting for two years until Lincoln Savings collapsed in 1989, which eventually cost U.S. taxpayers $125 billion to clean up. The National Thrift News won a George Polk Award for its reporting of the savings and loan crisis (Wells 2019).

Ann Hollifield observed the trade press may function as "an insider channel of communication in the early stages of industry-related policy processes" (Hollifield 1997, p. 760). Top industry executives find trade press to be a better source of information than the mainstream press, and the trade media set the news agenda for the mainstream press, she added.

Gussow described several normative features of trade journalists, which included reporting skills typical of mainstream journalists but with specialized knowledge and close and frequent contact with industry they are covering (Gussow 1984). Such specialized skills make trade journalists attractive prospects for top newspapers such as *The New York Times* or *The Wall Street Journal.*

Many trade publications deliberately keep a narrow focus on their particular industry. Historian Janet Laib wrote, "If they dilute the subject matter with political coverage and other supported irrelevancies, they will get a diluted audience, and a diluted audience would weaken their appeal to advertisers who want to reach a specialized market of readers" (Laib 1955).

## Critique

This close connection to industry leads to criticism that trade journalists are captive to the industries they cover and they do not perform the traditional watchdog or surveillance role over powerful interests. A handful of surveys revealed a lack of editorial independence and a willingness to accede to advertiser demands. Robert Hays and Anne Reisner found about two-thirds of some 190 farm journalists surveyed said advertisers have threatened their journals on occasion, and about one-half say that advertising has actually been withdrawn. Some advertisers sought to influence coverage by providing journalists with gifts and free meals. Hays and Reisner found 64 percent of journalists they surveyed agreed with the statement: "Some media seem to bend over backwards to some of the commercial outfits to butter up sponsors, advertisers and the like" (Hays and Reisner 1990, p. 939). Advertisers can exert a disproportionate influence in the trade press, which tends to have a narrow base of potential advertisers. "Our study offers clear evidence that advertiser-related pressure on farm magazine writers is a serious problem, although it is one not always recognized by those more seriously affected" (Hays and Reisner 1990, p. 941).

Timothy Hubbard, in a 1966 survey of business newspaper editors, found they "seem curiously resigned to trimming their editorial sails to the edicts of the ad department" and some 23 percent of business editors said "as a matter of routine they were compelled to puff up or alter and downgrade business stories at the request of the advertisers" (Hubbard 1966, p. 703). C. Ann Hollifield, in her 1997 study of the trade press, found "evidence that the trade media may be reluctant to write about the negative impact that industry-related expansion and development may have on individuals and society" (Hollifield 1997, p. 759).

New research is challenging that narrative, however, with evidence of investigative and accountability reporting in this genre. One prime example is a small mortgage industry newspaper, the National Thrift News, which broke the story of developer Charles Keating and his ring of political corruption during the savings and loan crisis. This newspaper's aggressive reporting contributed to the downfall Keating, chairman of American Continental Corp. and owner of Lincoln Savings and Loan. As a result, the National Thrift News defied a longstanding narrative that trade publications are captive to the industries they cover (Wells 2019). There are numerous examples of trade journalists standing up to the powerful industries. The Timothy White Award, bestowed annually by the Software & Information Industry Association, recognizes trade press editors who display "extraordinary courage, integrity, and passion" (Software & Information Industry Association 2018). The winner in 2011 was a magazine for the swimming pool industry, Aquatics International. Editor Gary Thill directed investigations that uncovered a pattern of sexual abuse by swimming coaches (ibid.).

## Influential Trade Publications

The following vignettes of major trade publishers provide a sense of the range of activities in this genre of journalism:

### Crain Communications Inc.

One of the most important and influential trade publishing companies is Crain Communications Inc., which counts among its titles Ad Age, Automotive News, Modern Healthcare, Pensions & Investments, and the Crain's business publications in Chicago, New York, Cleveland and Detroit. The company, founded by G.D. Crain Jr. in 1916 in Louisville, Ky., published 22 different titles, employed more than 1,000 people and reported total sales of $249 million in 2021 (Mergent Online 2022). As a reporter for the Louisville Herald newspaper, G.D. Crain supplemented his income as a correspondent for two insurance trade publications, National Underwriter and Western Underwriter. The experience opened his eye to the potential for business publishing as a career and also showed how some important innovators in trade journalism, such as Willard Kiplinger, had their roots in mainstream journalism (Goldsborough 1992).

Crain's first publication was Hospital Management magazine in 1916, shortly followed by Class, a magazine aimed at advertising in the trade publication arena. As he gained experience in the advertising industry, Crain launched an ambitious new publication, Advertising Age, in January 1930, just weeks after the spectacular Black Tuesday meltdown in the stock markets. In doing so, he was challenging a venerable title, Printer's Ink, which covered the publishing and advertising industry (Goldsborough 1992, p. 25). Other trade publishers, ranging from Kiplinger of the Kiplinger Washington Letter to Stan Strachan of the National Thrift News, created multiple specialized publications as they gained experience in the market and saw new opportunities in business niches. Crain saw a space for his publication to report on public policy involving the advertising industry. In 1939, he opened a Washington bureau for Advertising Age to cover the emerging regulations of the industry by the Federal Trade Commission and the then-Federal Drug Administration. Crain maintained a high profile in the industry with leadership roles in the National Industrial Advertisers Association and speaking appearances at industry conferences. For example, Crain told the Cleveland Advertising Club in 1942 about ways that advertisers could help support the war effort and prepare the markets for postwar developments (Goldsborough 1992, p. 45).

The Crain publications took leadership roles on controversial issues from time to time. In 1968, in wake of the assassination of U.S. Senator and presidential candidate Robert F. Kennedy, Crain's Advertising Age decided to take a stand. It published a June 10, 1968, editorial, "Guns Must Go," and ran a second anti-gun editorial the following week on the front page. A company history recalled the episode: "And later editorials urged readers to write their congressmen urging the enactment of gun-control legislation" (Goldsborough 1992, p. 45). Advertising Age received criticism from some of its readers but lost little advertising from the incident, the company history said.

### Fairchild Publications

John B. Fairchild was not a typical trade press publisher. In 1960, when he took over Women's Wear Daily from his father, the younger Fairchild proclaimed, "What I want," he said, wildly waving a copy of the latest issue, "is for people to come into their office and pick up the paper and become so furious with what they read they just crumple it up and throw it out the window!" (Sheinman 2015). Fairchild went on to transform a trade publication devoted to the fashion industry into a cultural force, illustrating how a trade editor can provide leadership in an industry. "For more than three decades, from 1960 to 1997, Mr. Fairchild was one of the most powerful, and mercurial, people in the fashion business," according to his obituary in The New York Times (Bernstein 2015). Fairchild's publication brought attention to designers such as Bill Blass, Oscar de la Renta and Yves Saint Laurent, "and whacked down those who did not meet his exacting standards" (Bernstein 2015).

Fairchild's grandfather, E.W. Fairchild, co-founded the company in 1891, and established Women's Wear Daily. Along the way, the company counted publications as diverse as Daily News Record, Home Furnishings Daily, Electronics News, Footwear News and Supermarket News. John Fairchild's insistence on irreverent and aggressive news coverage made Women's Wear Daily a leading force in the field. For example, in July 1966 the White House provided journalists the embargoed details and a sketch of the wedding dress of Luci Baines Johnson, President Lyndon Johnson's daughter, who was to be wed in August. Fairchild refused to attend the briefing since it wanted to bring the news of the dress and designer to its readers well before the end of a lengthy news embargo period. The magazine shortly landed the scoop: "On July 14, it published a front-page sketch with the headline 'Luci's Wedding – First Report.' Not everything in the sketch was accurate, but it was close enough for a furious White House to bar the paper from the wedding" (Sheinman 2015).

> What ensued was a flood of newspaper editorials, columns and cartoons in cities all over the U.S., supporting WWD for refusing to accept embargoed material and for upholding the highest traditions of good journalism by going after the story on its own,

Women's Wear Daily journalist Mort Sheinman wrote in Fairchild's obituary. The Fairchild family sold the company in 1968 to Capital Cities Broadcasting Corp. for a deal then valued at $37.2 million, or about $317 million in 2023 dollars (Sheinman 2015, usinflationcalculator.com). The company then was sold to its current owner, Advance Publications, in 1999 for $650 million, or $1.16 billion in 2023 dollars (ibid.).

## Arizent

Arizent is one of the major publishers of financial journalism, counting the American Banker, The Bond Buyer, Financial Planning, and National Mortgage News under its publishing umbrella. The American Banker, founded in 1836 under the title Thompson's Bank Note Reporter, is one of the oldest trade newspapers in the country (The New York Times 1936). Publisher John Thompson helped influence passage of banking regulations in the 19th century. In 1863, for example, Thompson encouraged then Treasury Secretary Salmon Chase, serving in President Abraham Lincoln's administration, to support the National Banking Act of 1863 ("The American Banker: 150th Anniversary" 1986, p. 14). Such activism is consistent with a normative behavior of the trade press as a servant to business, where journalists often sought to modernize the industries they cover (Wells 2019, p. 33). "Specialized business publications that are engaged in leadership activities have been able to shape the direction of the industries they serve," Gussow observed (Gussow 1984,

p. 129). The newspaper advocated for creation of the American Bankers Association, which occurred in 1875.

The publication evolved with the industry and became a daily newspaper in 1925 with the growth of the markets during that decade. The American Banker regarded itself as a community newspaper and, at times, would seek to understand how the banking business was interacting with the broader society. William Zimmerman, a former American Banker editor, recalled in the 1960s that he was urged to cover the civil rights movement and its implications for the banking industry. "Find the bank leaders who are trying to do something about the problem of minorities ... Get them to talk about how they are tackling the job so that other people in the industry can learn from their experiences," Zimmerman wrote (Zimmerman 1986, p. 12). He recalled interviewing Black and Hispanic activists "who felt locked out of the free enterprise system and complained about not having fair access to the banking system" and then got the view from the bankers themselves. Zimmerman said he hoped his reporting "helped at times bring the two polarized sides together to talk for the first time to each other and learn from each other" (Zimmerman 1986, p. 12).

## The McGraw-Hill Cos.

James McGraw began a storied publishing career when he quit his school teaching job in 1884 to sell advertisements for The American Journal of Railway Appliances and Street Railway Journal. He witnessed how the trade press evolved around its industry. In the mid-1880s, the Street Railway Journal "was devoted to the interests of the horse, its care and its car," he wrote (McGraw 1930, p. 296). McGraw said technology was changing the industry: soon, railcars would be powered by electricity, not horses. He pushed for the next editor to have expertise in electricity. The publication eventually changed its name to the Electric Railway Journal. "Industry is always ready for leadership," McGraw concluded. "The editor's responsibility, in other words, is not merely to reflect current views and opinion, but to provide a vehicle for advancing thought" (McGraw 1930, p. 297).

McGraw entered an alliance with John A. Hill, whose publications specialized in the mechanical and engineering fields. In 1917, the McGraw-Hill Publishing Company Inc. emerged, and would eventually count such titles as the Engineering Record, Power, Coal Age, and, in 1929, The Business Week (as it was first known), in its stable. One study of the McGraw-Hill company described the independent nature of its journalism, citing Engineering News and its 1907 coverage of an industrial disaster, the collapse of the Quebec Bridge, which killed 75 workers. Engineering News conducted an investigation, which included interviews and even performed engineering calculations. The publication discovered design flaws behind the bridge collapse. "The tragedy, the News candidly stated, was an indictment on the entire profession" (Burlingame 1959, p. 335).

The company later would expand into academic publishing, purchasing Macmillan and the education division of Random House, making it among the largest academic publishers in the country (Bhasin 2011). In 1966, McGraw Hill entered the financial data and analytics business with the purchase of Standard and Poor's financial services. In 2013, McGraw Hill sold its education division to Apollo Global Management, LLC, a major private equity firm. Much of the remaining business, known as McGraw-Hill Financial, was renamed in 2016 as S&P Global Inc and it operates primarily as a financial data business ("Who We Are" 2022). In a sense, this is a return to its trade industry roots.

## Conclusion

Trade journalism has faced its economic challenges with the downturn in advertising revenue since 2006. Still, the industry's basic business model of focused coverage and multiple revenue streams from data and conferences has influenced mainstream news media. Look at the explosion of newsletters, for example. The Wall Street Journal, Washington Post, The New York Times, Boston Globe and many other publications have launched specialized digital newsletters in recent years to help attract and retain readers (Schouten 2020). Cory Schouten, now editor-in-chief of Crain's New York Business, said that newsletters allow a publication to "showcase deep subject-matter expertise and unique voices" and allow closer engagement with readers (Schouten 2020). One leading practitioner is Axios, the Arlington, Virginia-based news service that is now expanding its newsletter operation to more than a dozen cities as varied as Atlanta, Philadelphia, and Bentonville, Arkansas. The tightly edited newsletters are optimized for reading on cellphones in a format the company calls "smart brevity." The company offers a mix of free and paid newsletters, with the premium content geared toward business and political leaders in their decision-making process. Axios expects to bring in $100 million in revenue in 2022 (Robertson 2022). The Axios business model and emphasis on analytical reporting borrows a page from one of the most influential business publications in the U.S. history, the Kiplinger Washington Letter. The Kiplinger letter, founded in 1923, developed a quirky writing style he called "sweep line" that enabled busy executives to scan a page quickly and capture the essential points of an article. Like Axios today, Kiplinger saw a market opportunity to serve readers who were overwhelmed with news and information – and this was during President Calvin Coolidge's administration, decades before television news and the internet.

The broader question facing the future of trade journalism involves how this valuable, specialized information can be more widely distributed to better society. The National Thrift News, for example, uncovered a major fraud in the savings and loan industry; had this news reached a broader audience earlier, many innocent consumers could have acted to protect their life savings. Trade journalist John Heltman offered a cautionary note about trends in this genre of journalism: "Ironically, as the trade press has gotten bigger and better resourced, its inclination to do longer, deeper enterprise journalism appears to be declining" (Heltman 2015). This is a challenge the talented trade journalists need to confront as soon as possible.

## Further Reading

Historian John J. McCusker provides a definitive examination of the early origins of the business and trade press in Renaissance-era Europe. His 2005 article in The American Historical Review, "The Demise of Distance: The Business Press and the Origins of the Information Revolution in the Early Modern Atlantic World," is particularly noteworthy (McCusker 2005). Wayne Parsons offered a broader view of the mainstream and specialty business press in his 1990 "The Power of the Financial Press" (Parsons 1990) that is carefully written and offers excellent insight. For a broader historical context about the forces leading to the rise of the business press and the evolution of capitalism, Gerald F. Davis's "Managed by the Markets How Finance Reshaped America" (2009), Angus Burgin's "The Great Persuasion: Reinventing Free Markets since the Great Depression" (2012) and Kim Phillips-Fein's "Invisible Hands: The Businessmen's Crusade Against the New Deal" (2010) are invaluable.

The author has documented the unusual role of investigative journalism in the trade press with "The Enforcers" (Wells 2019). This examination of the trade press and its broader impact on society was expanded with "The Insider: How the Kiplinger Newsletter Bridged Washington and Wall Street" (Wells 2022), which examined Willard Kiplinger's Kiplinger Washington Letter and its impact on the New Deal.

## Notes

1 The Software Industry Information Association reported B2B print advertising fell 2.6 percent to $4.9 billion in 2017. Current SIIA data is not available. Matt Kinsman, "Revenue Up 5.4% for B2B Media & Information Industry in 2017" (*SIIA* August 30, 2018). https://www.siia.net/blog/index/Post/76816/Revenue-Up-5-4-for-B2B-Media-Information-Industry-in-2017.
2 Mott also observed an upswing in business, economic, political and social issues in magazines from 1885 through 1905 (Mott 1957).

## References

American Society of Business Publication Editors. (no date) "American Society of Business Publication Editors Constitution and Bylaws," *American Society of Business Publication Editors.* Available at: https://asbpe.org/american-society-of-business-publication-editors-consitution-and-bylaws/.

Barthel, M. and Worden, K. (2021) "Newspaper Fact Sheet," *Pew Research Center Journalism & Media*, 29 June. Available at: https://www.pewresearch.org/journalism/fact-sheet/newspapers/ (Accessed: 30 May 2022).

Bernstein, J. (2015) "John B. Fairchild, 87, Dies; Edited a Bible of Fashion," *The New York Times*, 25 February, p. D6.

Bhasin, K. (2011) "How McGraw-Hill Went From Publishing Railroad Journals To Downgrading The US Debt," *Insider*, 8 August. Available at: https://www.businessinsider.com/mcgraw-hill-textbooks-standard-poors-2011-8.

Burlingame, R. (1959) *Endless Frontiers - The Story of McGraw Hill.* New York: McGraw Hill.

Chandler, A.D. (1981) *Henry Varnum Poor: Business Editor, Analyst, and Reformer.* New York: Arno Press.

Elfenbein, J. (1952) *Business Paper Publishing Practice.* New York: Harper & Brothers.

Elfenbein, J. (1969) *Business Journalism.* New York: Greenwood Press.

Endres, K. (1994) "Research Review: The Specialized Business Press," *The Electronic Journal of Communication*, 4(2–4). Available at: http://www.cios.org/EJCPUBLIC/004/2/004211.html.

Flynn, M.B. (1944) *The Development of Business Papers in the United States.* Doctoral dissertation. Graduate School Business Administration New York University.

Freedman, R. and Roll, Steven. (2006) *Journalism that Matters: How Business-to-Business Editors Change the Industries They Cover.* Oak Park, IL: Marion Street Press.

Giusto, R. (2022) *Historical B2B Media & Business Information Market.* Burlingame, CA: Outsell Inc.

Goldsborough, R. (1992) *The Crain Adventure.* Lincolnwood, IL: NTC Business Books.

Gussow, D. (1984) *The New Business Journalism: An Insider's Look at the Workings of America's Business Press.* San Diego, CA: Harcourt Brace Jovanovich.

Hays, R.G. and Reisner, A.E. (1990) "Feeling the Heat From Advertisers: Farm Magazine Writers and Ethical Pressures," *Journalism and Mass Communication Quarterly*, 67(4), pp. 936–942.

Heltman, J. (2015) "Confessions of a Paywall Journalist," *Washington Monthly*, December, pp. 15–21.

Hollifield, C.A. (1997) "The Specialized Business Press and Industry-Related Political Communication: A Comparative Study," *Journalism & Mass Communication Quarterly*, 74(4), pp. 757–772.

Hubbard, T.W. (1966) "The Explosive Demand for Business News," *Journalism Quarterly*, 43(Winter), pp. 703–708.

Kinsman, M. (2018) "Revenue Up 5.4% for B2B Media & Information Industry in 2017," *SIIA*, 30 August. Available at: https://web.archive.org/web/20200919134540/https://www.siia.net/blog/index/Post/76816/Revenue-Up-5-4-for-B2B-Media-Information-Industry-in-2017.

Laib, J. (1955). "The Trade Press," *Public Opinion Quarterly*, 19(1), 31–44.

Mason, D. H. (1893, July 7). "The Distinguishing Features of the Trade Journal as Compared with The General Newspaper," *American Economist.*

McCusker, J.J. (2005) "The Demise of Distance: The Business Press and the Origins of the Information Revolution in the Early Modern Atlantic World," *The American Historical Review*, 110(2), pp. 295–321. Doi:10.1086/531316.

McGraw, J. (1930, March). "The Business Paper Grows Up, (ar) Scribner's Magazine March 1930," *Scribner's*, 295–300.

Mergent Online. (2022) *Crain Communications Inc.* Mergent Online. Available at: https://www.mergentonline.com/privatecompanyreports.php?pagetype=p.

Mott, F.L. (1957) *A History of American Magazines, 1885–1905.* Cambridge, MA: Harvard University Press.

n/a (no date) "About Us," *American Society of Business Publication Editors.* Available at: https://asbpe.org/about-us/.

Neal, J.H. (1922) "A Review of Business Paper History," in *N.W. Ayer & Son's American Newspaper Annual & Directory.* Philadelphia, p. 1245. Available at: https://play.google.com/books/reader?id=qadEAQAAMAAJ&printsec=frontcover&output=reader&hl=en&pg=GBS.PP1.

"Our history" (no date) *The Economist Group.* Available at: https://www.economistgroup.com/what_we_do/our_history.html.

Parsons, W. (1990) *The Power of the Financial Press.* New Brunswick, NJ: Rutgers University Press.

Phillips-Fein, K. (2010) *Invisible Hands: The Businessmen's Crusade Against the New Deal.* New York: W.W. Norton.

RELX PLC. (2021) "Form 20-F For the Fiscal Year Ended December 31, 2020." *U.S. Securities and Exchange Commission.* Available at: https://www.sec.gov/Archives/edgar/data/929869/000119312521047466/d848056d20f.htm.

Robertson, K. (2022) "Axios Wants Us to Read Everything in Bullet Points," *The New York Times*, 7 March. Available at: https://www.nytimes.com/2022/03/07/business/media/axios-local.html.

Schouten, C. (2020) "(News) Letter Perfect," *Quill.* Available at: Quillmag.com.

Sheinman, M. (2015) 'John B. Fairchild Dies at 87', *Women's Wear Daily*, 27 February. Available at: https://wwd.com/fashion-news/fashion-features/john-b-fairchild-dies-at-87-8235783/.

Software & Information Industry Association. (2018) *Timothy White Award, Timothy White Award.* Available at: https://www.siia.net/neals/Leadership-Awards/Tim-White-Award.

n/a, "The American Banker: 150th Anniversary" (1986) in *The American Banker: 150th Anniversary.* New York: American Banker Incorporated, p. 192.

*The New York Times.* (1936) "Banking Paper 100 Years Old," 31 March, p. 35.

Walker, M. and Forman-Katz, N. (2021) "Cable News Fact Sheet," *Pew Research Center Journalism & Media*, 30 July. Available at: https://www.journalism.org/fact-sheet/cable-news/ (Accessed: 30 May 2022).

Wells, R. (2019) *The Enforcers: How Little-Known Trade Reporters Exposed the Keating Five and Advanced Business Journalism.* Champaign, IL: University of Illinois Press.

Wells, R. (2021) "'Serve It Up Hot and Brief": The Journalistic Innovations and Influence of Willard M. Kiplinger," *American Journalism*, 38(2), pp. 177–201. https://www.tandfonline.com/eprint/UTIJCBBSBHEN3WG3JPKD/full?target=10.1080/08821127.2021.1912982.

Wells, R. (2022). *The Insider: How the Kiplinger Newsletter Bridged Washington and Wall Street.* University of Massachusetts Press. https://www.umasspress.com/9781625347039/the-insider/

Worden, K. and Walker, M. (2021) "Network News Fact Sheet," *Pew Research Center Journalism & Media*, 13 July. Available at: https://www.pewresearch.org/journalism/fact-sheet/network-news/ (Accessed: 30 May 2022).

Wright, C. (1928) *A History of Lloyd's from the Founding of Lloyd's Coffee House to the Present Day.* London: Published for the corporation of Lloyd's by Macmillan and company limited. Available at: https://archive.org/details/historyoflloydsf0000wrig/page/72/mode/2up.

Zimmerman, W. (1986) 'Editor's Personal View of the American Banker', in *The American Banker: 150th Anniversary.* New York: American Banker Incorporated, p. 12.

# 19

# KIPLINGER'S CHANGING TIMES

## A Case Study in the Evolution of Personal Finance Journalism

*Rob Wells*

### Introduction

Kiplinger's Personal Finance magazine, founded in 1947, was the first magazine focused on personal finance and it helped establish a new genre of business journalism. Along with early pioneers Sylvia Porter, the first personal finance journalist, and the product review and testing service Consumer Reports, the Kiplinger magazine was part of a journalistic movement to inform, protect, and empower consumers in the post-World War II consumer society (Wells 2021). The magazine, the dominant personal finance magazine until the launch of Money in 1972, helped generations understand how to finance a home, save for the children's college tuition, and build a retirement nest egg. It represented an attempt to serve consumers as an independent journalistic enterprise, one that didn't take advertising for its first 33 years and was willing to criticize powerful businesses when necessary. The company used its deep consumer finance expertise to branch out into a variety of distribution channels, including VCR tape programs, radio broadcasts, television content, tax preparation software, and its website, Kiplinger.com. The company even published educational materials for school children. The Kiplinger magazine was widely admired by its peers, including personal finance journalist and best-selling author Jane Bryant Quinn. "I love it," Quinn said in an interview. "What can I say? It's so down to earth. I just think it's a really clear, solid magazine" (Roush & David 2005).

This chapter provides a case study of the Kiplinger magazine, known for four decades as Changing Times, to understand the broader economic and societal forces involved with creation of the personal finance journalism genre.[1] This chapter is based on internal documents, interviews, and unpublished manuscripts held by the Kiplinger family and provides the first published details about the Kiplinger magazine and its origins.

The Kiplinger magazine marked a new direction for a company whose foundational work in the 1920s involved advice and forecasts to help business leaders navigate Washington politics and policies. Launching this new magazine was difficult for the Kiplinger organization as it struggled with editorial direction and lost millions of dollars for the first dozen years. The Kiplinger magazine eventually found its voice and mission in personal finance, and continually innovated by finding new distribution channels as media technology evolved from radio to television, personal computers, and the Internet.

 DOI: 10.4324/9781003298977-23

## Definitions

The genre of personal finance journalism came into focus in the early 20th century with the publication of Stuart Chase and F.J. Schlink's "Your Money's Worth: A Study in the Waste of the Consumer's Dollar" (1927) and the launching of Consumer Reports in 1936 (Cron 1997). Historian Tracy Lucht, in her analysis of journalist Sylvia Porter, defines personal finance journalism as "a form of service journalism, often written as a column, that advises readers on financial matters directly affecting their lives" (Lucht 2007, p. 2). Personal finance articles often address saving, investing, managing debt, paying taxes, buying houses and cars, and any myriad of consumer activities, Lucht wrote. "This type of journalism helps readers decide what to do with their money and warns them what not to do" (Lucht 2007, p. 2).

Lucht provided a typology that focuses on audiences to address the confusion about terminology and definitions in the field of business journalism. According to Lucht's typology, "business journalism" examines "corporate structure, small-business trends, executive performance, marketing, industry, and labor." Then, "financial journalism" would mainly cover "the stock, bond, and commodity markets; its readers are investors." For "economic journalism," this "is more political in focus, explaining the policies of presidential administrations and the Federal Reserve." And then "consumer journalism" would cover "products and business practices of interest to buyers" (Lucht 2007, p. 25). Grant Hannis has a broader definition of consumer journalism as "any text made available to the general public on current issues affecting consumers" (Hannis 2007, p. 13).

Even Lucht's useful definitions tend to blur in practical applications in the newsroom. An article about a tax reduction bill could cut across all four categories of business, financial, economic, and consumer journalism. As described later, the Kiplinger magazine initially had a mix of articles on politics, public policy, social and economic trends, but eventually settled on a personal finance focus with articles on retirement, wealth creation, taxes, and investing along with articles on a family's daily living, such as schools and health.

## Rise of Consumers and a Movement

The emergence of the consumer economy in the 19th century formed the foundation of and created the necessity for personal finance journalism. O'Barr traced marketing of consumer goods through advertising to handbills for the sale of coffee in London in 1657 (O'Barr 2005). Limited advertising appeared in the U.S. colonial newspapers, such as Benjamin Franklin's Philadelphia Gazette, in the early 1700s, but generally lacked illustrations, a description of price or a discussion of brands, which would emerge in the following century. In the U.S., the rise of large urban centers in the U.S. in the 1840s allowed formation of mass circulation newspapers, increasingly financed by advertising over the course of the decade. A consumer class began to arise following the Civil War, and companies began targeting consumers with mass advertising for products, ranging from soap to razors, in the 1880s. Consumers also encountered personal sales pitches from door-to-door salesmen in the mid-1800s, some of whom used wild exaggeration and deception to close a deal (O'Barr 2005). Such abuses led to the emergence of a consumer movement in the early 20th century.

As the national economy transformed, so did consumers' demand for fair treatment and compensation from abuse in the marketplace. Journalists eventually would enter this field to provide articles and information to assist consumers. Grant Hannis argues that British author Daniel Defoe, writing in his Review in the early 18th century, made a "trailblazing contribution to the world of consumer journalism" (Hannis 2007, p. 13). Articles in the Review criticized mercantile prices and monopolies, offered advice on public health, and identified scams (ibid.).

Some journalists focused reporting to serve consumers' desire for fair play in the market. Samuel Hopkins Adams, writing in Collier's magazine, was among those exposing consumer frauds, particularly in the advertising of patent medicines (Kennedy 2000). Journalism exposing phony drug claims and filth in the meatpacking industry contributed to the 1906 passage of the Pure Food and Drug Act, which regulated claims on product labeling (Food and Drug Administration 2019). Progressive-Era journalists such as Ida Tarbell and Lincoln Steffens took a more systemic approach and examined antitrust and issues with competition in the marketplace. Tarbell's iconic reporting on John D. Rockefeller and his monopoly control through Standard Oil was followed by a landmark antitrust lawsuit that led to the breakup of Standard Oil in 1911.

The rise of personal finance journalism tracked the emergence of consumer activism. Robert Mayer described three eras of consumer activism in the U.S., with the first arising due to complaints about fake medicines and spoiled food at the turn of the 20th century. The second era, in the 1920s and 1930s, responded to a need for objective information on products. The third era in the 1960s and 1970s focused on product safety, social impact of advertising, and consumer rights for redress (Mayer 1989, p. 13). As described later in this chapter, Kiplinger's magazine found its voice with articles that provided objective information about savings, investment, taxes as well as occupational advice such as job interviewing strategies or lifestyle issues such as child-rearing, health, and travel.

Besides questionable food, drugs, and products, consumers faced another risky realm in the investment world. The U.S. public participation in the stock and bond markets rose significantly following World War I. The U.S. economy grew a torrid 42 percent from 1918 to 1929,[2] and the number of U.S. shareholders quadrupled to 10 million from 1924 to 1930, many hoping to get rich by investing in common stocks (Davis 2009; Smith and Sylla 1993, p. 28). This growth took place despite the risks of market crashes and bank failures. Major banking and financial panics occurred in 1873, 1884, 1890, 1893, 1901, 1907, and 1929. Until the 1913 creation of the Federal Reserve System, the U.S. lacked a central bank to control and respond to such problems, and there was little critical journalism covering the markets during this era.

A landmark in the emerging consumer movement was the 1927 publication of Chase and Schlink's "Your Money's Worth," which described the modern consumer's dilemma when trying to discern the truth from claims in advertising: "We are all Alices in a Wonderland of conflicting claims, bright promises, fancy packages, soaring words, and almost impenetrable ignorance" (Chase & Schlink 1927, p. 2). Schlink, an engineer working for the National Bureau of Standards, teamed with economist Chase to publish Your Money's Worth, which led to the founding of the Consumers' Research product testing organization in 1929.

Arthur Kallet left Schlink to start Consumers Union and in 1936, he published Consumer Reports, which featured product testing and remains one of the most influential publications of its type (Mayer 1989). The idea of a magazine engaging in product testing predated Consumer Reports, however. Good Housekeeping began testing products in 1909 and provided its iconic seal of approval for goods that met the test in return for a licensing fee (Cron 1997, p. 346; "Definition of Good Housekeeping Seal" 2022). Still, Consumer Reports was innovative with its advocacy for consumers combined with an extensive product testing and research operation. Journalist Ernie Smith described it as "of the most important magazines on the shelves" (Smith 2018). Other newspapers caught on, with many publishing articles "to help consumers cope with adversity, scarcity, poverty and fear" through the Great Depression and World War II, journalist Theodore Cron observed (Cron 1997, p. 347).

This genre of journalism saw increasing demand following the end of World War II as returning service members bought houses in new suburban developments, purchased cars, home appliances, and patronized new shopping malls. As historian Andrew Yarrow observed, "This was a period during which a new 'ideology of abundance' was articulated by the media, political and business leaders, educators, and other opinion-shapers that linked American greatness and 'identity' with quantitatively defined prosperity" (Yarrow 2006, p. 59). From 1947 to 1965, the U.S. per capita income jumped 234 percent, while the economy, as measured by the gross domestic product, grew 212 percent (Geisst 2012). Porter and Kiplinger saw an opportunity for journalists to advise this growing middle class on how to manage money and navigate the markets. "Financial reporting changed from reciting stock quotations, company earnings, and puff pieces on businessmen and individual companies to broader stories about the national economy and what economic trends meant for average Americans" (Yarrow 2006, p. 58).

Cron said that "during this period, consumer journalism and consumer advertising developed a partnership" whereby newspapers and women's and service magazines offered advertisers special pages sections and editions focusing on consumer needs (Cron 1997, p. 348). Some newspapers employed public relations writers who specialized in consumer goods to produce the content. Kiplinger's magazine and Consumer Reports did not engage in these practices as they both published independent journalism, relied on subscription revenue, and didn't accept advertising.[3]

The consumer movement evolved further in the 1960s as the public raised concerns about faculty products and industry's damage to the environment. Ralph Nader's 1965 exposé, "Unsafe at Any Speed," was a best seller that influenced a debate about lack of car safety features, such as seat belts. Rachael Carson's "Silent Spring" (1962) described the environment damage from pesticide use. The growing consumer culture benefitted The Wall Street Journal, which saw its circulation rise from 100,000 in 1947 to 615,000 by 1956. Other more specialized publications such as BusinessWeek, Forbes, and Fortune fed the demand from this expanding managerial class. These were very good economic times for the media industry. By one measure, paid daily newspaper circulation in 1965 was about 60 million, equivalent to 105 percent of households; by 2010, it dropped to 43 million or about 37 percent of households (Communic@ations Management Inc., 2011).[4] By the mid-1960s, some 81 percent of daily newspaper and business editors surveyed said their readership's demand for business news has "increased substantially" since 1960, while one in four (27 percent) of those indicating an increase estimated that the demands of their readership had "more than doubled" (Hubbard 1966, p. 703).

Personal finance journalism gained a further boost in the 1970s with the beginning of financial deregulation and the onset of high inflation which created consumer demand for how to navigate quickly changing markets. Time Inc. launched Money magazine in 1972, which, along with Kiplinger's Changing Times, became a dominant personal finance magazine. The trend accelerated in the 1980s and 1990s, particularly with the emergence of USA Today and its heavy emphasis on personal finance news and information to assist the typical business traveler (Simons 1999). "Our strategy is all about focus – to be first and to write it so ordinary people can understand," USA Today business editor John Hillkirk II said (Simons 1999, p. 59). The 1980s and 1990s saw a burst of new entrants such as

SmartMoney from Dow Jones and Hearst, Bloomberg Personal Finance, Worth from Fidelity Investments, and many others.

## Sylvia Porter

The Kiplingers eventually created the first magazine devoted to personal finance, but journalist Sylvia Porter helped invent the genre of personal finance journalism (Hazard 1978, Chapter 23–1; Lucht 2007). Porter began as a bond market reporter for the New York Post in 1935. Due to gender discrimination in the era, she went by the byline was "S. F. Porter" (Lucht 2007, p. 50). Once on the beat, Porter mastered financial topics and focused her mission on her readers. She wrote for multiple audiences, ranging from bankers to homemakers. She began focusing on personal finance during World War II as she informed readers how to get the most for their money and support the war effort. Lucht described Porter's cultural and journalistic significance: "Here was a woman who did not fit our cultural memory of the fifties. She was rich, she was respected, and she was not a housewife" (Lucht 2007, p. 4). By 1975, Porter's journalism blanketed the county, with her column appearing in 350 newspapers reaching 40 million readers. She wrote best-selling books such as "Sylvia Porter's Money Book," published in 1975, which eventually sold more than 1 million copies (Fowler 1991; Lucht 2007, p. 1).

Porter's intelligence and ambition made her a household name. "Few journalists have done more to put financial news on the map than Sylvia Porter, and none has done more to advance the cause of women in this area of journalism," historian John Quirt observed (Quirt 1993, p. 252). Porter had initial success with launching a magazine, Sylvia Porter's Personal Finance, in 1983. The magazine initially published six times a year, launched with a circulation of 250,000. Austin Kiplinger, in a 1989 letter to Porter, said her magazine "set a good fast pace for the rest of us and that's all to the good" (Kiplinger 1989). It led Changing Times, Forbes, BusinessWeek, and Inc. in newsstand sales, but never reached the 1 million subscribers of Changing Times or the nearly 2 million of Money. Sylvia Porter's magazine, along with other personal finance magazines, suffered a sharp drop in advertising following the Oct. 19, 1987, stock market decline. The publisher, Davis Publications, sought a buyer, and ironically, it was Kiplinger's Changing Times that purchased the Porter magazine list of 400,000 subscribers in 1989 for $2.2 million, which ended publication of Sylvia Porter's Personal Finance magazine (Lucht 2013, p. 156; Secrest 2022). "I'm glad you have taken over the magazine in its terminal stages," Porter wrote to Austin Kiplinger. "I think it was a good magazine. As you know, the stories behind this conclusion go deep and wide. I shall now devote myself to forgetting them" (Porter 1989).

The consumer journalism genre evolved further in the 1980s and 1990s with an expansion of lifestyle coverage that combined personal finance, health, medical, wellness, and physical fitness reporting (Cron 1997, p. 349). Columnist Jane Bryant Quinn, whose carefully researched syndicated columns were published for 27 years nationwide, was a dominant force in personal finance journalism in the 1980s and 1990s. Her "Making the Most of Your Money" (Quinn 1997) was a New York Times bestseller. Quinn was a contributing editor to Newsweek, reported on business issues for "CBS Evening News with Dan Rather," and hosted "Take Charge," a television show on money management produced by KQED in San Francisco (Roush & David 2005). She won many awards, including the Gerald Loeb Lifetime Achievement Award in 1997, one of the top honors in journalism.

## Launching the Magazine

Willard M. "Kip" Kiplinger, a former Associated Press economics reporter in Washington, made his mark in journalism with the creation of The Kiplinger Washington Letter in 1923, an influential newsletter that provided concise analysis and forecasting of Washington events for businesspeople. The newsletter became highly successful during the New Deal and remains profitable today. By the end of World War II, Kiplinger was one of the best-known business journalists in the U.S. Throughout the New Deal, Kiplinger's newsletter told readers how the government was expanding into the daily lives of businesspeople, a theme that was central to his 1942 best-selling book, "Washington is Like That." In addition, he had published The Kiplinger Tax Letter since 1925, which analyzed both business and consumer tax issues.

As World War II ended, Kiplinger began thinking of launching a new publication. "I think he was tremendously impressed with the need for a publication that would talk about the economic impact on individuals and what they could do about it," said Austin Kiplinger, son of Willard Kiplinger (Hazard 1978, Chapter 21–2). Before the war, Austin had been a reporter for the San Francisco Chronicle and wrote for the Ithaca (N.Y.) Journal during college. Austin had recently finished his service in World War II as a Navy torpedo bomber and was weighing his future when his father proposed starting the magazine. At 28 years old, Austin became the first executive editor of the new Kiplinger magazine.

Austin Kiplinger described a mission statement for the publication:

> Give the reader ideas about his business, his home, his community, his children's schools, his county government, his taxes. Everyday economics. Practical economics. Subjects which help him to make some sense out of the problems of making a living. Everything directed straight at the lay reader, not at a specialist. Ideas helpful and provocative.
>
> *(Hazard 1978, p. 24)*

One problem: his father initially didn't exactly share this vision. Willard Kiplinger wanted his magazine to serve the needs of readers but he also described a parallel and sometimes competing mission: "I am going to publish a magazine, a monthly, intended primarily for businessmen, devoted to business and economic matters" (Hazard 1978, Chapter 22–11).

In addition, Willard Kiplinger believed the magazine could cement his personal and journalistic legacy. "The motive behind the magazine is not primarily a money-making motive. Instead, it is essentially journalistic or professional, with a strong element of the personal," Kiplinger told his board of directors in June 1946 (Hazard 1978, Chapter 22–1). At age 55, Kiplinger began thinking about retirement and was looking to move beyond the weekly production of The Kiplinger Washington Letter. "Let me remind you once again I am fed up with the letter job," Kiplinger wrote. "I want to do something else. I want to do the magazine, even if it does mean loss of money" (ibid). Austin Kiplinger believed his father wanted a new outlet to write more expansively than the terse and telegraphic prose of the newsletter. "W.M. Kiplinger was a writer to the core...He was tired of doing the same job week after week and wanted an option to expand a little and do some writing that was not quite as confining," Austin Kiplinger said (Hazard 1978, Chapter 21–1).

The mix of these personal priorities and disagreement over the mission led to a lack of focus. While Willard Kiplinger said he wanted the magazine to be brief and useful to the individual, he then would order a major article about business opportunities under the Marshall Plan to rebuild western Europe following World War II. Willard Kiplinger "had a certain number of conflicting ideas about the magazine," Hazard said (Marshall 1977, p. 13).

"Several managing editors came and went, and each one tried to put out the kind of magazine he had previously edited – not the one that the Kiplingers had in mind," Hazard wrote (Hazard 1978, 21–4). Amid these conflicting visions, Willard Kiplinger became angry at how his son and other senior editors were managing the project. In the fall of 1947, the first year of publication, he wrote a scathing, ten-page single spaced memo to the magazine's top three editors, including Austin, "which was loaded with uncharacteristic bitterness" (Hazard 1978, Chapter 22–10). With such fundamental disagreements, combined with the typical heavy expense for any magazine to build circulation, it's little surprise that the magazine initially was a major money loser. The business model was challenging: no advertising and content produced by full-time staff, not freelance writers. Income from 30,000 subscribers "was far from enough to meet expenses," Hazard wrote (Hazard 1978, Chapter 21–10). "By the fall of 1947, half a million dollars had been lost on the venture and it still far lacked the quality that the owner aspired to," Hazard wrote (ibid). Those losses would equal about $6.5 million in 2022 dollars (usinflationcalculator.com 2022).

The first issue's letter to readers said the magazine "has no advertising, and never will have. We shall work solely for readers" (Kiplinger Magazine 1947). This was a departure from typical practice for magazines then and now. The subscription price was $6 per year, or about $79 in 2022 dollars. By the end of 1947, the magazine had 50,000 subscribers, and three years later, it reported 75,000 (Kiplinger 1987, p. 7). Even as circulation rose, the annual losses continued throughout the 1950s, totaling a cumulative $3.7 million for 1947 through 1960, or about $34 million in 2022 dollars.[5] The magazine's losses were offset by The Kiplinger Washington Letter and related newsletters, and overall the Kiplinger company remained profitable (Kiplinger 2022c).

Kiplinger "kept it going from 1948 to 1960 without actually making money. And, of course, he resisted a lot of pressure in the early years to scrap it," said Hazard, author of an unpublished company history (Marshall 1977, p. 14).[6] Hazard recalled, "there was considerable dissatisfaction amongst the directors. … At one point, Kip was actually thinking of stopping the magazine or turning it into a mimeograph sheet or something like that" (Coit 1977, p. 19).

## Family Split

Throughout 1947 and 1948, Willard Kiplinger and Austin clashed over management and editorial direction of the magazine. In an unpublished interview for a company history, Austin Kiplinger recalled how his father

> had the habit of passing responsibility without authority … I was doing all the firing and the dirty work on the magazine and he was having all the fun… He used to accuse me of disloyalty if I had a different view of something.
>
> *(Austin Kiplinger 1977)*

Austin Kiplinger nominally oversaw administration, circulation, and operations, but was undercut by his father. "I felt it was simply an untenable position for anybody, and particularly for me because he took advantage of our personal relationship to some degree," Austin

Kiplinger said (Austin Kiplinger 1977). The father and son tension was visible to the rest of the staff. "I think Kip used to get after Austin unmercifully," said George Bryant, a senior editor (Bryant 1976).

Compounding this stress was a high-profile editorial blunder by Willard Kiplinger in the 1948 presidential election. Kiplinger forecast Thomas Dewey as the winner over Harry Truman in the presidential election and had ordered up a special November edition of the magazine, with the cover "What Dewey Will Do" as president. Willard Kiplinger ordered the issue mailed to subscribers before election day, a bold and risky step that he thought would show the magazine's foresight and confidence. He did so despite misgivings and skepticism from his staff. Other newspapers also erroneously reported Dewey as the winner, but the price for Kiplinger was steep. Subscriptions to The Kiplinger Washington Letter fell by 23,496, or 13 percent, in the year after the 1948 election, and the magazine also faced cancelled subscriptions (n/a 1977).

Austin Kiplinger said the workplace tension and his friction with Willard Kiplinger's third wife, LaVerne Tucker Kiplinger, prompted him to leave the family business. Austin Kiplinger moved his young family to Chicago, his wife's hometown. "It was a terribly painful decision, I guess about as painful a decision as I ever really made in my life," Austin Kiplinger recalled. "We were deeply attached to each other" (Austin Kiplinger 1977). Bryant recalled how Willard Kiplinger was badly shaken by his son's departure.

> Kip got back over to the office and he couldn't talk. He went in and typed out just a little memo to the staff announcing Austin's decision and that was it. We didn't know what to say or to do.
>
> *(Bryant 1976)*

Austin Kiplinger enjoyed considerable success in Chicago where became a columnist for the Journal of Commerce and later an ABC Radio network national commentator, local television anchor, and network television correspondent for ABC and NBC News. At his father's invitation, Austin Kiplinger returned to the company as vice president in 1956 and became president in 1959, expanding on new editorial and marketing ventures.

## Personal Finance

The Kiplingers came across the personal finance formula through a bit of trial and error. The magazine initially focused on business themes but the July 1948 issue carried an article entitled "What a Young Man Should Do with His Money – If Any." Hazard wrote "it was the first of the 'how to' articles for just people and families that in subsequent years were the magazine's bread and butter and gave it a reputation as the country's leading consumer publication" (Hazard 1978, Chapter 23–1).

Hazard, a former Wall Street Journal reporter, conceived the story idea after a conversation with an investment counselor who said he would only accept clients with at least $100,000 to invest ($1.23 million in 2023 dollars). Hazard found this revelatory. "The ordinary young family simply did not have available the kind of professional investment and financial advice that was available to wealthier people," Hazard recalled. "Perhaps the Kiplinger Magazine could supply it" (Hazard 1978, Chapter 23–2). The July 1948 article drew a favorable response from readers and led to a gradual change in editorial course, with the magazine writing about how to retire, how to buy stocks, and how to buy life insurance.

Other articles in the July 1948 issue address personal finance, such as "New Trends in Paid Vacations" and "How They Measure The Cost of Living." Further, a "Questions & Answers" section that fielded reader questions also focused on personal finance issues, with readers asking about ways to save on the cost of building a home and potential savings from a recent tax bill, a reader-driven section that's a common feature in the genre. By May 1949, the magazine came out with a new name, Changing Times (subtitled The Kiplinger Magazine), and a new format. "The staff was hitting regularly on the practical 'how to' theme which became the editorial center-line," according to a 1963 internal history (The Kiplinger Washington Editors 1963, p. 2). The name change allowed the magazine "develop its own life and character without regard to its older brother, the Kiplinger Letters" (Changing Times May 1949, p. 50). A stronger focus on personal finance is evident, with the December 1949 issue focusing on a hot-button issue: "What Every Woman Should Know About Her Husband's Finances." The cover art pictured a woman's hand in the pocket of a man's slacks. The article contained a check list for a family's financial affairs, where readers could fill in savings account numbers and balances, names of stocks and other assets and debts. An October 1949 cover story also explored gender and finance issues: "Working Women ... Do They Get a Fair Break?" In both articles, Kiplinger was bridging the worlds of personal finance with lifestyle coverage.

The magazine also touched on important societal issues, such as a January 1950 article, "Help Alcoholics – They're Sick" or a February 1948 article about the business potential within minority communities: "14 Million Negro Customers." Other notable changes in the fall 1949: the current business conditions column was pushed to the back of the magazine to make way for more personal finance coverage in front.

After a 13-year struggle, Changing Times began to turn profitable in 1961. "In 1965, for the first time in company history, the operating earnings of the magazine surpassed those of the Kiplinger Letters," wrote Knight Kiplinger, Austin's son who later oversaw the company (Kiplinger 2022c). Annual earnings for Changing Times in 1970 and 1971 exceeded $1 million each year (or $7.9 million in 2023 dollars). Yet, high inflation in the 1970s hurt as it posted operating losses from 1973 through the early 1980s due to rising postage, pager, and editorial expenses (ibid). This forced Kiplinger to end the subscriber-only model after 33 years in March 1980, and Changing Times began accepting advertising to supplement the subscription revenues (Kiplinger 1987, p. 7). The magazine "never really made serious money. It never made nearly as much money as the newsletters, until the 1990s ... the magazine was always a labor of love," Knight Kiplinger said (Kiplinger 2022).

## Innovation and Distribution

The company sought new ways to reach its audience through emerging technologies of the era, interesting marketing, and partnerships. In 1952, Changing Times was the first magazine sold on television, according to Knight Kiplinger, and the first advertiser on NBC's "Today" show (Codel 1952; Kiplinger 1987, p. 7). While the Kiplinger organization had been writing and publishing books since the 1930s, the pace picked up in the 1950s. "Success With Your Money" appeared in 1956, and "Boom and Inflation Ahead" in 1958, published by Simon and Schuster, sections of which were syndicated in 30 major newspapers (The Kiplinger Washington Editors 1963, p. 3). Kiplinger published two more books in 1959, "Kiplinger's Family Buying Guide," as well as "Your Guide to a Higher Income." The expansion efforts paid off as Changing Times reported its subscriber base reached 1 million by 1961 (Knight Kiplinger 1987, p. 3).

In 1969, Kiplinger founded a consumer education project later known as the Changing Times Educational Service, to provide multimedia teaching materials for elementary, junior high, and high school students in partnership with the Council for Family Financial (Kiplinger 2022). These lesson plans offered instruction in math; reading, writing, and financial literacy were an outgrowth of a broader consumer education trend in the country. One lesson kit entitled "The Marketplace" covered smart shopping, and how to avoid fraud, understand warranties, and decipher ads (ibid). "Its purpose was to help young people acquire some of the savvy that our magazine provided for their parents," Austin Kiplinger said (Kiplinger 1996). It was never a highly successful business due to the lengthy process of getting classroom material adopted by state and local education boards. Kiplinger sold the business to EMC Publishing of St. Paul, Minnesota, in the early 1980s (Kiplinger 2022).

Austin's son Knight Kiplinger joined the company as corporate vice president in 1983, marking the third generation of family leadership. He had spent 13 years in newspapers, including Washington bureau chief of the Ottaway Newspapers, the former local newspaper division of Dow Jones & Co. Knight became the president of the parent company a decade later and Austin remained as the chairman until the early 2000s. Knight Kiplinger sought to capitalize on new technology and new distribution channels. He struck a deal with the Associated Press to deliver Changing Times content, "making Changing Times the most broadly syndicated of all personal finance magazines" (Knight Kiplinger 1987, p. 7). The company also had a revenue-sharing content distribution agreement in the early 1990s with The New York Times Syndicate. A two-minute "Changing Times Personal Finance Report" was syndicated to some 200 stations on the Mutual Radio Network beginning in 1985. By the 1980s, Kiplinger created series of VCR tapes and guidebooks, sold primarily to its subscribers, that were published in conjunction with the Arthur Young accounting firm (Kiplinger 2022).

In 1990, Kiplinger began creating content for personal computer users via the electronic bulletin board Prodigy, a paid online subscription service that preceded America Online and, a decade later, the commercial Internet. Kiplinger provided personal finance content and moderated Prodigy's personal finance and investing chat rooms. The business at one point yielded nearly $1 million a year in revenue for Kiplinger's organization (Kiplinger 2022).

In 1991, Changing Times was renamed Kiplinger's Personal Finance Magazine and the company sought to build that brand identity by launching a TV syndication program called "Kiplinger's Personal Finance Report," a series of 90-second personal finance features sold to local television stations. Eventually some 100 stations had signed up including major markets in New Orleans, Cleveland, San Francisco and Phoenix (Kiplinger 2022). The service was discontinued in the early 2000s due to declining broadcast advertising during a recession.

In 1992, Kiplinger expanded into the computer software field partnering with the technology firm MECA to provide tax information and advice to the TaxCut program. The partnership was an extension of Kiplinger's expertise in this field with The Kiplinger Tax Letter. H&R Block, the dominant tax preparation firm, purchased MECA in 1993 and promoted the Deluxe Kiplinger TaxCut program. TaxCut was popular but was second to the market leader TurboTax, published by Intuit. Kiplinger parted ways with H&R Block and in 2006 it formed a new relationship with Intuit to provide content to TurboTax software and to its website. This relationship continued until about 2011 when Intuit decided to write its own tax advice for TurboTax, and Kiplinger ended its involvement with tax preparation software (Kiplinger 2022). Kiplinger had a foray into personal money management software with a program called Kiplinger's CA-Simply Money, designed by Computer Associates, that began in 1993 and ended in the late 1990s.

"We always viewed new-product development as a way to serve our readers with useful content in whatever format they liked best, whether print or electronic. Every brand extension was supposed to pay for itself," Knight Kiplinger said (Kiplinger 2022c). The new ventures could lead to new subscribers to the newsletter or magazine. The commercial Internet launched in the mid-1990s and the company staked its claim by launching Kiplinger.com. The site saw a rise in the profitability in its online advertisements that corresponded with the decline in print advertising in Kiplinger's Personal Finance magazine. The era of family ownership ended in 2019 when the entire Kiplinger company was sold to London-based Dennis Publishing, which, in turn, sold it to Future PLC in London in 2021.

## Conclusion

The Kiplinger magazine was a pathbreaker in the field of personal finance journalism, the dominant publication in the genre from its inception until the launch of Money in 1972. Despite a rocky start and a dozen years of losses, the publication succeeded due to its focus on the individual consumers' needs and the ability of the Kiplinger organization to subsidize the publication due to the profitability of the Kiplinger Washington Letter. The magazine stabilized in the 1960s and expanded into new ventures such as the Changing Times Educational Service, which provided personal finance education curriculum and materials to school districts nationwide. Some of its reporting touched on important societal issues, albeit through a practical lens. A 1963 article, "New Opportunities for Negroes," gained the eye of a local African American magazine, Flare, which reprinted the Kiplinger report in its October 1963 edition. Today, Kiplinger's Personal Finance is focused on delivering detailed and objective reporting on all aspects of an individual's financial life.

Personal finance journalism can provide a vital source of independent information for individuals trying to make consequential decisions in a society steeped in neoliberalism, which values self-regulation and market-based solutions to curtail the excesses of capitalism. Magazines such as Kiplinger's Personal Finance can be a lifeline for an individual who has to puzzle through the proper investment selections for a 401(k) plan but can't afford the price of hiring a financial advisor. Columnist Jane Bryant Quinn, in a 2005 interview with Professor Chris Roush, described the dilemma:

> Today, everyone is responsible for themselves. You've got to make financial choices. If you make bad ones, it's too bad, you should have known better than to buy that mutual fund. This is an era where people absolutely must have knowledge of personal finance and an area where people are still easily mistaken. A lot of money gets lost all the time.
>
> *(Roush and David 2005)*

At a time when the Internet is flooded with sophisticated "sponsored content" from major corporations touting its products, or insidious undisclosed paid product reviews posted on blogs, reputable personal finance publications and Web sites provide a hope that a consumer can have a fighting chance in our complex modern markets.

## Further Reading

One iconic work in the history of personal finance journalism is the 1927 "Your Money's Worth: A Study in the Waste of the Consumer's Dollar" (The Macmillan Company 1927) by Stuart Chase and F.J. Schlink, a work that set the stage for the emerging genre. Tracy Lucht's "Sylvia Porter: America's Original Personal Finance Columnist" (Syracuse University Press 2013) is a highly readable and important scholarly work that documents the evolution of personal finance journalism through one of its great practitioners. Andrew Yarrow provided a solid and readable overview situating the growth of U.S. financial journalism in broad economic changes during the post-World War II era in "The Big Postwar Story" (Journalism History 2006). Theodore Cron documented the major trends in consumer journalism in a chapter in "Encyclopedia of the Consumer Movement" (ABC-CLIO 1997). The author documented the story of Willard Kiplinger in "'Serve It Up Hot and Brief': The Journalistic Innovations and Influence of Willard M. Kiplinger" (American Journalism 2021) and the forthcoming "The Insider: How the Kiplinger Newsletter Bridged Washington and Wall Street" (University of Massachusetts Press 2022). Back issues of Kiplinger's Magazine/Changing Times/Kiplinger's Personal Finance are available through August 2010 via Google Books and make highly enjoyable reading, especially in the early years.

## Notes

1 The magazine has gone through the following name changes: from January 1947 through April 1949, it was Kiplinger Magazine; from May 1949 through June 1991, it was Changing Times. Since July 1991, it has been Kiplinger's Personal Finance.
2 GDP measured in the Geary–Khamis dollar, or international dollar: $593.97 billion in 1918, $843.33 billion in 1929. Maddison, A. (2021). Maddison Database 2010. University of Groningen. https://www.rug.nl/ggdc/historicaldevelopment/maddison/releases/maddison-database-2010
3 The Kiplinger magazine didn't accept advertising for its first 33 years until March 1980.
4 While circulation was high relative to today's levels, the mid-1960s marked the beginning of a decline of newspaper circulation as a percentage of households (Communic@ations Management Inc. 2011).
5 Calculation uses 1960 as a base year.
6 The magazine started publishing on January 1947, not in 1948. Hazard's comments in this section were found in interview transcripts with Kiplinger employees, part of a broader project to write a comprehensive company history in the late 1970s. That manuscript was never published but Knight Kiplinger made the unpublished manuscript and interviews available to the author. In these interviews, Hazard would offer extended comments about his recollections of the magazine or about Willard Kiplinger himself, even though he was supposedly interviewing an employee for the company history.

## References

*Changing Times.* (1949) "Changing Times, The Kiplinger Magazine," May.
*Changing Times.* (1950) "Some Editors Are Hogs," February.
Chase, S. and Schlink, F.J. (1927) *Your Money's Worth: A Study in the Waste of the Consumer's Dollar.* New York: The Macmillan Company. Available at: https://hdl.handle.net/2027/mdp.39015063999240.
Codel, M. (1952, January 19). Television Digest with Electronics Reports. *Television Digest with Electronics Reports.* Kiplinger Personal Papers, Seneca, MD.
Cron, T.O. (1997) "Journalism, Consumer," in Brobeck, S., Mayer, R.N., and Herrmann, R.O. (eds) *Encyclopedia of the Consumer Movement.* Santa Barbara: ABC-CLIO, pp. 342–349.

Davis, G.F. (2009) *Managed by the Markets: How Finance Reshaped America*. New York: Oxford University Press.

"Definition of Good Housekeeping Seal" (2022) *Allbusiness Your Small Business Advantage*. Available at: https://www.allbusiness.com/barrons_dictionary/dictionary-good-housekeeping-seal-4946758-1.html.

Fowler, G. (1991) "Sylvia Porter, Financial Columnist, Is Dead at 77," *The New York Times*, 7 June, p. B6.

Geisst, C.R. (2012) *Wall Street: A History*. Oxford: Oxford University Press.

George Bryant. (1976, October 4). *Company History—George Bryant* [Interview]. Kiplinger Personal Papers, Seneca, MD.

Hannis, G. (2007) "Daniel Defoe's Pioneering Consumer Journalism in the Review," *Journal for Eighteenth-Century Studies*, 30(1), pp. 13–26. https://doi.org/10.1111/j.1754-0208.2007.tb00323.x.

Hazard, J. (1978) *Hazard Draft - KWE History – Unpublished*. Washington, DC.

Hubbard, T. W. (1966). "The Explosive Demand for Business News," *Journalism Quarterly*, 43(Winter), pp. 703–708.

Kennedy, S.V. (2000) "Adams, Samuel Hopkins," *American National Biography* [Preprint], article.1600013. https://doi.org/10.1093/anb/9780198606697.

Kiplinger, A. (1977, April 21). *Company History Interview—Austin Kiplinger* [Interview]. Kiplinger Personal Papers, Seneca, MD.

Kiplinger, A. (1989, May 12). *Letter to Sylvia Porter*. Kiplinger Personal Papers, Seneca, MD.

Kiplinger, A. (1996). *Re. Acquisitions by KWE and some approaches that misfired*. Kiplinger Personal Papers, Seneca, Md.

Kiplinger, K. (1987) "Ahead of the Times: Kiplinger's Changing Times Magazine Celebrates 40 Years of Personal-Finance Journalism," *Ahead of the Times*.

Kiplinger, K. (2022a) "Interview with Knight Kiplinger, June 21, 2022."

Kiplinger, K. (2022b) "Notes for Rob Wells - Kiplinger's/Changing Times' Leadership in Consumer Advice and Personal-Finance Information."

Kiplinger, K. (2022c) "Notes on Kiplinger Magazine History."

*Kiplinger's Magazine* (1947) "From the Editor," January. Available at: https://books.google.com/books?id=nP4DAAAAMBAJ&source=gbs_all_issues_r&cad=1.

*Kiplinger's Magazine / Changing Times / Kiplinger's Personal Finance* (1947) "Browse All Issues," January. Available at: https://books.google.com/books?id=nP4DAAAAMBAJ&source=gbs_all_issues_r&cad=1&atm_aiy=1940#all_issues_anchor.

Lew Garrison Coit. (1977, Circa). *Company History—Lew Garrison Coit* [Interview]. Kiplinger Personal Papers, Seneca, MD.

Lucht, T.L. (2007) *Sylvia Porter: Gender, Ambition, and Personal Finance Journalism, 1935-1975*. Doctoral dissertation. Philip Merrill College of Journalism, University of Maryland, College Park, MD. Available at: http://drum.lib.umd.edu//handle/1903/7617 (Accessed: 27 September 2013).

Lucht, Tracy. (2013) *Sylvia Porter: America's Original Personal Finance Columnist*. Syracuse.

Mayer, R.N. (1989) *The Consumer Movement: Guardians of the Marketplace*. Boston, MA: Twayne Publishers.

n/a (1977) "KWL Circulation 1925-1976," Kiplinger Personal Papers, Seneca, Md.

O'Barr, W.M. (2005). A Brief History of Advertising in America. *Advertising & Society Review*, 6(3), doi:10.1353/asr.2006.0006.

Porter, S. (1989, May 26). *Letter to Austin Kiplinger*. Kiplinger Personal Papers, Seneca, Md.

Quinn J. B. (1997). *Making the Most of Your Money*. New York: Simon & Schuster.

Quirt, J. (1993) *The Press and the World of Money: How the News Media Cover Business and Finance, Panic and Prosperity, and the Pursuit of the American Dream*. Byron, CA: Anton/California-Courier.

Robert Marshall. (1977, July 21). *Company History—Robert Marshall* [Interview]. Kiplinger Personal Papers, Seneca, Md.

Roush, C. and David, E. (2005) "Jane Bryant Quinn Q&A," *Business Journalism History*. Available at: http://www.bizjournalismhistory.org/history_quinn.htm.

Secrest, R. (2022) "Porter, Sylvia," *American Women Writers: A Critical Reference Guide from Colonial Times to the Present*. Cengage. Available at: https://www.encyclopedia.com/arts/news-wires-white-papers-and-books/porter-sylvia-field.

Simons, L.M. (1999) "The State of The American Newspaper Follow the Money," *American Journalism Review*, November.

Smith, E. (2018) 'Consumer Conflict," *Tedium*, 15 February. Available at: https://tedium.co/2018/02/15/consumer-reports-history-origin/.

Smith, G. David. and Sylla, R. Eugene. (1993) *The Transformation of Financial Capitalism: An Essay on the History of American Capital Markets*. Cambridge, MA: Blackwell.

The Kiplinger Washington Editors. (1963) *The 1st 40 Years of The Kiplinger Story, 1923-1963*. Washington, DC: The Kiplinger Washington Editors Inc., p. 4.

U.S. Food & Drug Administration. (2019) "Part I: The 1906 Food and Drugs Act and Its Enforcement," *U.S. Food & Drug Administration*, 29 April. Available at: https://www.fda.gov/about-fda/changes-science-law-and-regulatory-authorities/part-i-1906-food-and-drugs-act-and-its-enforcement.

Wells, R. (2021) "'Serve It Up Hot and Brief": The Journalistic Innovations and Influence of Willard M. Kiplinger," *American Journalism*, 38(2), pp. 177–201. https://www.tandfonline.com/eprint/UTIJCBBSBHEN3WG3JPKD/full?target=10.1080/08821127.2021.1912982.

Yarrow, A.L. (2006) "The Big Postwar Story," *Journalism History*, 32(2), pp. 58–76.

# 20

# STARTING FRESH

## Entrepreneurism and Business Journalism

*Alyson Martin*

### Introduction

Business journalism closer to the form as we know it was catapulted into the modern age when three men founded Dow, Jones & Company. Charles Dow, a journalist at the Kiernan News Agency, Edward Jones, who came from the Providence Star, and Charles Bergstresser, the silent partner who brought the financial backing, founded the organization as a financial news bureau in 1882 (Library of Congress undated, Baker 2014, Conklin 1999). The company, while thriving and diversified today, initially existed to deliver the financial news of the day to the budding business community on Wall Street in New York City. It created The Wall Street Journal, which published its first edition in 1889.

Dow, Jones & Company's reputation was built on a foundation of uncompromising reporting on the most pressing financial interests of the day. In 1884, Charles Dow launched the Dow Jones Transportation Average, which focused overwhelmingly on behemoth railroad companies (Crossen 2007, Dow Jones Transportation Average, undated). Then, in 1896, he launched the Dow Jones Industrial Average, comprising a dozen industrial companies selected to represent various slices of the American economy. It included companies such as the American Tobacco Company and General Electric. Dow, Jones & Company sat at an interesting intersection that was one part news, one part practical information about how stocks were faring.

Back during the time of the founding of Dow, Jones & Company, the country was experiencing great economic change and some degree of turmoil as industrialization took hold in America (Library of Congress, undated). Americans moved to cities, expanding them substantially as they industrialized. Specifically, the iron, steel, and oil industries saw great growth in numbers, and with this, the number of publications that covered them. Trade journals became "very popular" in the 1800s, and this popularity led to yet another rise in the number of these publications in the 1900s. Whatever trades were taking shape at the time, there was almost certainly a publication dedicated to it. Or, as magazine historian Frank Luther Mott noted, aside from "bootblacks, nursemaids, and janitors... practically every department of human endeavor had its periodical organs by 1885" (New York Public Library guide 2022).

 DOI: 10.4324/9781003298977-24

As business journalism grew and evolved, it began to serve a wider range of audiences. Today, there are publications aimed at general audiences, along with those focused on niche interests, say, those aiming in part to help the average American invest for their future. On the other end of the spectrum are trade publications, relevant only to stakeholders in particular industries. The audience type often determines the business model.

This spectrum of business journalism – publications such as The Wall Street Journal serving the broader business community on the one side, and publications dedicated to specific trades on the other – persists today, even as the broader journalism industry has undergone significant change. For most publications, the core business models have remained largely the same: advertising and subscriptions. Organizations such as Bloomberg earn revenue primarily from the investment community, and trade publications, with their particularly defined audiences, have a similarly distinct set of revenue streams – and they sometimes leverage the information they publish in different formats.

For example, a trade publication about the business of construction might publish a piece about the latest advancements in cheaper, more durable hempcrete, a product made from the newly legalized hemp. It might then publish, for an additional cost, a special report on this material and its future use in construction. And the release of this report might be timed with an event, with paid tickets, on the same topic, which some of these companies might sponsor, also at a cost paid to the publication. Additional revenue could come from a classified section that lists jobs in construction, or equipment for sale, or from a calendar of construction-specific meetings and events. All these efforts combined create multiple channels for revenue for this publication.

Trade publications are no small part of the journalism landscape. Even Hearst, best known for its diverse portfolio of ownership of newspapers and local news stations, also counts a large section of trade publications as revenue drivers. Among them: Floor Covering Weekly, Used Car Guides, Homecare Homebase, a hospice care journal, and Electronic Engineers Master Catalog (Hearst undated).

Business journalism has been, and will increasingly be, transformed by the internet, which dramatically increased the speed with which business news could be delivered. The internet made publishing both faster and cheaper, eventually enabling any journalist to turn their expertise into a publication. Gone are the days of waiting with coffee at the front door for a newspaper to be chucked onto the front lawn. Instead, hitting refresh at a computer, or on a phone, or even a watch, could serve up the latest stock numbers.

## Critical Issues and Topics: What the Internet Took

The journalism industry has long been supported by three main sources of revenue: classified, display advertising, and subscriptions. And all three legs of the journalism stool took a beating from the internet – advertising in particular (Tow Center 2017).

Suddenly, companies could advertise across billions of online pages instead of, say, A4 of this broadsheet newspaper or A5 of that one. Not only did publishers have to compete with the entire internet for advertisers, but they could not expect to earn as much from those ads. An online reader's eyeballs were worth less, as publishers traded print dollars for digital dimes, as the saying went.

It took the emergence of just one new website, Craigslist, to meaningfully erode classified ad sales slots, as younger users were much more likely to place an ad on the internet than they were at a newspaper (Jones 2009).

And readers began to wonder why they should pay for a subscription to a newspaper, in print or online, when they could just find similar information for free somewhere else on the web.

How bad was the internet's erosion of revenue for the journalism industry? In 2000, the total print advertising revenue for newspapers came to nearly $49 billion (Federal Communication Commission 2011). A decade later, it dropped by half, to roughly $23 billion, a stunning loss in such a short period of time.

Then came the tech platforms that became household names in the early 2000s, too: Google and Facebook. As these companies came to dominate Americans' time spent on the internet, they slowly gobbled up online advertising dollars, too. Today, Google and Facebook receive more than three-quarters of online advertising dollars.

Still, where there's an advertising opportunity – often – publications will arrive as their vehicle. In this new advertising ecosystem where scale was rewarded, publications like Buzz-Feed and Huffington Post were launched.

This period was also marked by plenty of innovation in response to the new tools and formats provided by the internet. It was around this time that news games, for example, emerged as a compelling way for journalists to experiment with storytelling (Tow Center 2015). These games take many forms, but broadly, they reimagine complex data in a gamified form to help explain complicated policies, like healthcare or budget constraints (Nieman Reports 2016). Of course, while news games enabled audiences to interact and engage with complex issues, like immigration policy and federal budgeting, the innovation that publishers needed was around revenue.

Still, even in this environment, most business publications have a powerful variable that general news outlets don't: a niche audience. Ben Thompson, author of the tech-focused newsletter Stratechery, wrote in January 2019 about the need to narrow focus to survive and thrive. He wrote:

> Success used to come from being broad-based with a geographic monopoly. The content of the vast majority of newspapers was largely duplicative (as the success of the wire services proved). On the Internet, though, success comes from being narrow while reaching the whole world. It is the exact opposite.
>
> *(Fischer 2019)*

Thompson's sentiments were prescient. BuzzFeed bought HuffPost in 2020, and the following year, announced layoffs at HuffPost (Wagner 2021).

Then, in April 2023, BuzzFeed CEO Jonah Peretti announced that BuzzFeed would be shuttering its news division, telling staffers in an email that "the company can no longer continue to fund BuzzFeed News as a standalone organization" (Wile 2023).

Peretti added that he put so many resources to the news division "because I love their work and mission so much." He added: "This made me slow to accept that the big platforms wouldn't provide the distribution or financial support required to support premium, free journalism purpose-built for social media."

## Current Contributions: What the Internet Gave

The internet took a great deal from the journalism industry. But it also gave. And for entrepreneurial journalists, it continues to give. With an internet connection, a business plan, and some kind of expertise, more and more journalists are launching their own startups.

And, those same companies that have taken advertising revenue from publishers, such as Facebook and Google, now enable news entrepreneurs to reach audiences once only accessible to publications that could afford the costs of printing and distribution.

In this ecosystem, plenty of business journalism startups have emerged that are more than weathering the market and broader journalism difficulties. One reason credited for their success is in their specialization.

Tech publication founders were some of the earliest adopters of the startup route. For instance, All Things Digital, which published tech-related news and analysis and opinion, showed the power of intrapreneurship as it grew from within The Wall Street Journal. One of its main revenue streams was the All Things D Conference (later Recode), which brought together the biggest household names in tech for "open conversation." This work was available to readers with a Wall Street Journal subscription, and later, when Recode was acquired by Vox, available for free to Vox readers (Topolsky 2014; Suba 2013).

In recent years, events have become a growing revenue stream for many journalism startups, including business journalism startups. That means that these companies had to weather the Covid-19 pandemic lockdowns that interrupted events and travel for people worldwide (James 2020).

Tech publication The Information builds a case for its reader-supported model through access to "exclusive" events (The Information, Undated). It has a strict paywall that is difficult to circumvent and a subscription fee of $399 a year.

Founder Jessica Lessin has spoken at length about The Information's business model, often offering hope to other founders seeking to strike out on their own, whether through a focus on events, subscriptions, or membership models. Lessin told Harvard University's Nieman Lab:

> There's been a proliferation of outlets and entrepreneurs building new media businesses. I've felt that we're on the cusp of a golden age for journalism and the news business, which has been a little contrary to others' points of view about the space. We've seen a huge uptick in the number of entrepreneurs we're working with. In some cases, it's a little more formal. In other cases, we host publications for Zoom calls. We had one last week on the very sexy topic of funnel optimization.
>
> *(Scire 2021)*

Lessin pointed to "differentiated" journalism as a path to success for founders and emphasizes that even in the area of tech – which is arguably the most saturated – there was room to be different through deep dives.

What counts as a startup business publication today can range from a site covering the business of sports to one covering the business of hip-hop. Sportico, which launched in 2020, covers the business of sports, which includes new sectors at the intersection of sports and finance, such as sports betting (Rodriguez 2020). In its own words, the company will be "championing the innovation and creativity that will change not only the business of sports, but the world" (Sportico undated).

And then there's Trapital, where readers "gain insights from the business of hip-hop." The publication invites readers to "follow hip-hop's growing influence with a brief weekly email memo that cuts through the noise and keeps you informed on the latest news" (Trapital undated). Founder Dan Runcie turned a profit through a mix of advising and consulting as well as sponsorship of a weekly newsletter with 10,000 plus subscribers (Tameez 2021).

"It's easy for the media and others to dismiss [entertainers] as just being famous, and whatever they sold was a benefit of their fame and not necessarily the business insights that came from that," Runcie told Harvard's Nieman Lab.

> When we double down on the fact that these are Black entertainers and all of the challenges there, especially when it comes to rising up, money, economic empowerment, there wasn't as much credit given and therefore, there wasn't as much coverage. There was definitely a big inspirational aspect of wanting to start Trapital as well.

Amid all this change, business journalism continues to evolve to match the business of the day. In the 1800s, it was railroads. In 2022, it was the ill-fated area of cryptocurrency. Soon, publications could be commonplace in the metaverse.

> Several publications set out to cover the business of crypto. CoinDesk specializes in bitcoin and digital currencies and "provides guides to bitcoin for those new to digital currencies" (CoinDesk undated). The news organization has a number of newsletters, including one called "State of Crypto" that notes that readers can expect "probing" at the "intersection of crypto and government." Decrypt is a "guide to Bitcoin, Ethereum & Web 3.0." and offers the latest headlines, like this one in early July: Yes, Hostess Really Made Crypto-Themed Twinkies Called $TWINKcoin. It also offers an easy onramp for people looking to learn more about the blockchain and coins, though, through free online courses that cover bitcoin and ethereum (Hayward 2022).

While niche publications are seldom household names such as the Wall Street Journal or the Financial Times, and they often serve smaller audiences, their deep focus enables a type of reporting for which a more broadly focused business publication might not have the bandwidth. It was in fact CoinDesk that broke one of the biggest business stories of 2022: the collapse of FTX (Allison 2022).

## A Case Study: Cannabis Wire

There exists a well-worn path for business publications: produce journalism about a particular business for an audience that needs to know about that business, often for professional reasons. While the type of business being covered must be taken into consideration in the formation of a newsroom's specific editorial and revenue strategies, two publications covering, say, energy and cannabis, will have more strategic overlap with each other than they would with, say, the Los Angeles Times.

Another example of a publication that emerged in response to the changing business landscape is one that I co-founded in 2014 called Cannabis Wire. I developed an expertise on the topic while reporting on the United States' changing medical and adult use cannabis laws for a book that came out in 2014. Prior to the book's publication, I decided to launch a publication on the topic. Publishing just moved too slowly, and editors at major publications were wary of pitches that delved too deeply into the topic of cannabis.

237

I pitched stories such as: why are veterans, looking for an alternative to opioids, struggling to obtain medical cannabis? That story was tentatively accepted by a national publication, then ultimately rejected because it didn't devote enough space to the potential harms of cannabis for these veterans. It was tough to get deeply reported and analytical pieces about cannabis published during this time. So, I took the leap.

In my mind, there were two opportunities. The first was that I could apply my experience as a local news reporter who knew quite a bit about how laws were made and implemented to the topic of cannabis to fill a gap in the landscape of cannabis coverage. Cannabis was very quickly turning into a policy and business story but was often still treated as a culture story. And the second opportunity was a business one: a new industry was taking root.

There were many considerations as I decided to launch a news organization. Should it be a non-profit, for example? While we didn't form Cannabis Wire as a non-profit, we were able to launch through grant funding, the first of which was a Magic Grant through the Brown Institute, a partnership between Columbia University Graduate School of Journalism and the Stanford School of Engineering. The next was a grant from the Mayor's Office of Media and Entertainment, and another from Civil, a short-lived blockchain journalism project. In all of these cases, to nod to a cliché, we happened to be prepared as we arrived at the right place at the right time.

Even with the grant funding, we also needed to think, hard, about revenue streams. So far, we've been reader-supported. We decided on a reader-supported, newsletter-forward approach because we wanted to have a direct relationship with our readers. It's worked well for us. Our audience is sticky and engaged. And we went with a reader-supported model because cannabis policy is evolving, and so are the advertising rules, which are murky at best. We are diving into the events space, which rebounded considerably after the pandemic.

I also spent a great deal of time ahead of the launch with my co-founder, dry erase marker to whiteboard, laying out scope of editorial coverage. For example, High Times already existed, and the world didn't need another cannabis grow magazine (and I didn't want to run one). After covering the launch of several state's industries, we knew the importance of a focus on policy and regulation. I also appreciated research as one of the fulcrums of the beat, too, because it's also at the heart of so many cannabis business stories.

Today, Cannabis Wire is busy. Our newsroom covers the global cannabis industry, centered in policy, regulation, and research. The majority of Americans live in a state with legal cannabis, either for recreational or for medical use. Some of the biggest businesses in the world – Altria, the maker of Marlboro cigarettes, and Constellation, which owns alcohol brands like Svedka vodka and Corona beer – are now players in the cannabis industry. There is no shortage of stories on the ever-changing cannabis beat, maybe just hours in the day.

Cannabis Wire is evolving with the business of cannabis, too. It's a micro and macro trend: as the landscape of business journalism evolves with business, the approaches of industry-specific publications evolve with the industry.

## Newsletters

Cannabis Wire is in good company when it comes to newsletters, which represent a fascinating merging of new technologies and old habits. In other words, the internet (new) made making money off newsletters (old) easy. Today, newsletters are a promising piece of the journalism landscape.

The Reuters Institute at Oxford notes that there's been a "sharp rise" in newsletter efforts at news organizations. "Email newsletters offer news organisations a chance to maintain a strong direct relationship with readers, a high degree of targeting, better showcasing of existing content and original analysis and commentary," Andrew Jack wrote for the Institute (Jack 2016).

While newsletters have more recently emerged as a tool for mainstream news organizations aiming to build a more direct relationship with readers in an effort to drive subscription revenue amid declining ad revenues, newsletters have been more common in the world of trade publications and business journalism.

Law360, which offers "news and analysis on the business of law and lawyers," grew from a tiny newsletter in 2006 to a LexisNexis acquisition in 2012 (LexisNexis 2012). Law360 offers plenty of legal analysis on policy, deals, and ongoing litigation, as well as lists of top leaders in the legal space – geared toward its audience of practicing lawyers (who doesn't want to know who made the list?).

Morning Brew started in 2015 as an email that the co-founders Alex Lieberman and Austin Rief started sending to their friends while college students at the University of Michigan. Over time, it grew into a suite of newsletters that aims to make "business news better." The business-focused news organization now reports 4 million subscribers to its "main newsletter" (there are many off-shoot newsletters) and also reported more than $50 million in revenue in 2021 (Sherman 2022).

"We want to make business news more enjoyable to read," Morning Brew co-founder Austin Rief told CNBC in an interview. "We view our competition as everybody and nobody. It's an attention economy, so we are competing with everyone. But in terms of direct competitors, we don't have one" (CNBC 2022).

Today, as market forces on journalism are pushing more reporters toward going solo or starting their own newsrooms, the newsletter format has become a lifeline. Substack, a popular home for newsletters, launched in 2017, and it bills itself as a platform that makes "subscription publishing simple." On its homepage, the platform urges writers to "Start your Substack at breakfast; start bringing in revenue by lunchtime" (Substack, Undated). Substack hosts dozens of newsletters on business and tech, many by prominent journalists who bet that their existing audiences at major news outlets would follow them to their inboxes.

Founder Hamish McKenzie made headlines when Substack started to attract major names in journalism. Its roster now includes journalists and writers such as Matt Taibbi, Matt Yglesias, Judd Legum, and Roxane Gay.

"We didn't start Substack because we were looking to build a giant company that could one day go public and make us rich," McKenzie wrote (McKenzie 2022).

> We started Substack because we believed it was important to offer writers and readers a way out of the media systems that were serving them poorly. We wanted to show that there can be something better than the attention economy, the incentives of which were leading to the types of content and behavior that corrode trust and comity; that turn readers into mindless doomscrollers; and that strip writers of their financial dignity.

On Substack, a reader can filter newsletters by topic, such as politics or technology. Among them: business and finance. A reader can stumble upon The Ankler, a publication about the business of Hollywood, in short, whose editor-in-chief Janice Min was formerly the co-president of the Hollywood Reporter-Billboard Entertainment Group, or The Fintech Blueprint, a newsletter that aims to help readers "find and build the next Fintech & DeFi unicorn with unbiased and expert insights on financial innovation."

Newsletters have been a shot in the arm for business journalists and journalism, but the reality is that the "solopreneur" route has risen in tandem with rising instability in the journalism industry. Journalists seeing declines in the legacy media have launched such individual products, with mixed success, as a way to protect themselves at a time of downsizing industry-wide.

## New Research and Technologies

Another change is on the horizon for business journalism: the rise of robots in newsrooms, and artificial intelligence. It's likely that any readers of this book will have read at least one story written by code, maybe even this week. Major news outlets, including the BBC, Reuters, Bloomberg, The Washington Post, and The Associated Press, all use AI to some extent (Blankespoor 2017). Where some news organizations have dipped their toes into the AI waters, the AP has taken a big leap.

The AP was "one of the first news organizations to leverage artificial intelligence and automation to bolster its core news report," and the organization's use of AI has sprawled to now include "machine learning along key points in our value chain, including gathering, producing and distributing the news." One way that the AP uses AI is through the automation of video transcripts, with the goal of allowing their journalists to focus their time and attention on more important reporting. The AP's journalists are also deploying natural-language processing to help analyze social media posts, too.

"The impact of AI is like a third wave, following the introduction of electronic publishing and then the internet," said Jim Kennedy, Senior Vice President of Strategy and Enterprise Development at the AP (Kung 2021). Kennedy helps guide the AP's AI efforts. "In every case, the imperative is to learn fast and harness the power of digital transformation early."

The AP has a number of projects currently underway. One involves image recognition to "improve the keywords on AP photos, including the millions of photos in our archive, and improve our system for finding and recommending images to editors" to "create the first editorially-defined taxonomy for the news industry."

One that has the potential to elicit a mixed response from journalists is use of natural language generation on corporate earnings stories for all publicly traded companies in the United States, "increasing our output by a factor of 10 and increasing the liquidity of the companies we covered," the AP notes (Associated Press, Undated). "We have since applied similar technology to over a dozen sports previews and game recaps globally."

The AP is now offering training courses for journalists and editors in newsrooms that want to learn more about how AI can "supercharge" their newsroom. And plenty of startups have emerged to tackle the challenge, including Cortico, Narrative Science, News Whip, and True Anthem, among others.

Some computational journalists at the helm of AI endeavors at news organizations argue that algorithms will play a big role in the future of journalism, with editors functioning as puppeteers (Cools 2021). Computational journalism uses data and computer science techniques and tools to report, perhaps through information gathering, dissemination of data or information, or distribution.

Over time, computational journalism has allowed journalists to take mind-boggling amounts of data and analyze it in faster and new ways. For example, The Associated Press took its financial news coverage from monitoring 300 companies to more than 4,000 through the use of "smart machines," and saw its errors dwindle, too (Cools 2021).

"Computational journalism is the future of news," computational journalist and researcher Francesco Marconi told News Lab.

This doesn't mean that the future of journalism is about letting the machines run loose. It's the opposite. Computational journalists are still the ones who decide what weights, parameters and transparency principles to apply to their machine learning models. Optimal computational journalistic performance happens somewhere between finding these new data signals and having humans validating and contextualizing them.

## Conclusion

Business journalism has come a long, long way from the days of the reports about shipping arrivals and departures. Today, the innovations have driven the field to a point of contending with, and finding ways to harness, artificial intelligence. While the future remains unclear, as long as money is involved, we can expect still more innovations in business, and in business journalism.

## Further Reading

### *Books*

Diakopoulos, N. (2019), "Automating the News: How Algorithms are Rewriting the Media," Harvard University Press

Marconi, F. (2020) "Artificial Intelligence and the Future of Journalism," Columbia University Press

Nielsen, R.K. and Ganter, S.A. (2022) "The Power of Platforms Shaping Media and Society," Oxford University Press

### *Reports*

Bell, E.J. et al. (2017) "The Platform Press: How Silicon Valley Reengineered Journalism," Tow Center for Digital Journalism

Gottfried, J. et al. (2022) "Journalists Sense Turmoil in Their Industry Amid Continued Passion for Their Work," Pew Research Center

Newman, N. (2021) "Journalism, Media, and Technology Trends and Predictions 2021," Reuters Institute, University of Oxford

## References

Allison, I. (2022) "Divisions in Sam Bankman-Fried's Crypto Empire Blur on His Trading Titan Alameda's Balance Sheet," *CoinDesk*, New York, 2 November 2022. Available at: https://www.coindesk.com/business/2022/11/02/divisions-in-sam-bankman-frieds-crypto-empire-blur-on-his-trading-titan-alamedas-balance-sheet/ (Accessed: 25 July 2023).

Associated Press. (Undated) "Leveraging AI to Advance the Power of Facts," Available at: https://www.ap.org/discover/artificial-intelligence (Accessed: 28 July 2022).

Baker, G. (2014) "WSJ Editor in Chief: A Letter to Readers," *New York, The Wall Street Journal*, 8 July, 2014. Available at: https://www.wsj.com/articles/wsj-editor-in-chief-a-letter-to-readers-1404787773 (Accessed: 1 June 2022).

Blankespoor, E. (2017) "Robo-Journalism and Capital Markets," Stanford Graduate School of Business, Stanford, 10 May 2017. Available at: https://www.gsb.stanford.edu/faculty-research/working-papers/robo-journalism-capital-markets (Accessed 1 May 2022).

CoinDesk. (Undated) Available at: https://www.coindesk.com/ (Accessed: 25 July 2022).

Conkin, M. (1999) "IF IT HAD BEEN THE DOW JONES BERGSTRESSER, WOULD IT HAVE HIT," *The Chicago Tribune*, Chicago, 24 March, 1999. Available at: https://www.chicagotribune.com/news/ct-xpm-1999-03-24-9903240029-story.html (Accessed: 1 June 2022).

Cools, H. (2021) "Computational Journalist Francesco Marconi On How Editorial Algorithms will Transform the News Industry," *Newslab*, New York, 12 May 2021. Available at: https://newlab.com/articles/computational-journalist-francesco-marconi-on-how-editorial-algorithms-will-transform-the-news-industry/ (Accessed: 17 July 2022).

Crossen, C. (2007) "It All Began in the Basement of a Candy Store," *The Wall Street Journal*, New York, 1 August, 2007. Available at: (Accessed: 1 May 2022).

Digital News Report. (2021) Reuters Institute, University of Oxford, Oxford. Available at: https://www.digitalnewsreport.org/ (Accessed: 17 July 2022).

Dow Jones Transportation Average. (Undated) Available at: https://web.archive.org/web/20090414063748/http://www.djaverages.com/?view=transportation&page=overview Web archive (Accessed:1 June 2022).

Eater Wine Club. (Undated) Available at: https://eaterwineclub.com/ (Accessed 20 July 2022)

Economic Liberties. (2021) "The Courage to Learn," Washington, DC. Available at: https://www.economicliberties.us/wp-content/uploads/2021/01/Courage-to-Learn-Final.pdf (Accessed 1 June 2022).

Federal Communications Commission. (2011) *The Media Landscape*, Washington, DC. Available at: https://transition.fcc.gov/osp/inc-report/INoC-1-Newspapers.pdf https://www.fcc.gov/general/information-needs-communities (Accessed: 2 June 2022).

Fischer, S. (2019) "The Future of Media Is Niche, and Beware Raising Too Much from VCs," *Axios*, New York, 29 January 2019. Available at: https://www.axios.com/2019/01/29/the-future-of-media-is-niche-1548772147 (Accessed: 1 June 2022).

Georgia Tech. (2019) Available at: https://www.ic.gatech.edu/news/628399/newly-endowed-chair-underscores-value-computational-journalism (Accessed: 1 March 2022).

Hayward, A. (2022) "Yes, Hostess Really Made Crypto-Themed Twinkies Called \$TWINKcoin," *Decrypt*, New York, 12 July 2022. Available at: https://decrypt.co/104983/yes-hostess-really-made-crypto-themed-twinkies-called-twinkcoin (Accessed: 17 July 2022).

Hearst. (Undated) Available at: https://www.hearst.com/hearst-health (Accessed 1 June 2022).

Jack, A. Reuters Institute. (2016) *Editorial Email Newsletters The Medium Is Not the Only Message*, Oxford: University of Oxford, November 2016. Available at: https://reutersinstitute.politics.ox.ac.uk/our-research/editorial-email-newsletters-medium-not-only-message (Accessed 1 June 2022).

James, S. (2020) "Newspapers Fighting for Survival as COVID-19 Ravages ad Spending," *S&P Global Market Intelligence*, 27 April 2020 Available at: https://www.spglobal.com/marketintelligence/en/news-insights/latest-news-headlines/newspapers-fighting-for-survival-as-covid-19-ravages-ad-spending-58306183 (Accessed: 1 June 2022).

Jones, S. (22 May 2009) *Online Classifieds*, Washington, DC: Pew Research Center. Available at: https://www.pewresearch.org/internet/2009/05/22/online-classifieds/ (Accessed: 1 June 2022).

Kung, E. (2021) "How AI Can Help Overworked Journalists and Deliver Better Journalism," *RTDNA*, Washington, DC, 14 October 2021. Available at: https://www.rtdna.org/article/how_ai_can_help_overworked_journalists_and_deliver_better_journalism (Accessed 15 July 2022).

LexisNexis (2013) 'LexisNexis Acquires Law360," New York, 20 March 2012. Available at: https://www.lexisnexis.com/community/pressroom/b/news/posts/lexisnexis-acquires-law360 (Accessed: 17 July 2022).

Library of Congress. (Undated) *This Month in Business History: Dow Jones Industrial Average First Published*. Washington, DC: Library of Congress. Available from https://guides.loc.gov/this-month-in-business-history/may/djia-first-published#:~:text=In%20the%20years%20since%20the,conditions%20in%20the%20United%20States (Accessed: 1 June 2022).

Library of Congress. (Undated) *America at Work, America at Leisure: Motion Pictures from 1894 to 1915.* Washington, DC: Library of Congress. Available at: https://guides.loc.gov/this-month-in-business-history/may/djia-first-published#:~:text=In%20the%20years%20since%20the,conditions%20in%20the%20United%20States (Accessed: 1 June 2022).

McKenzie, H. (2022) "Escape from Hell World," *Disjointed*, San Francisco, 9 June 2022 Available at: https://hamish.substack.com/p/escape-from-hell-world#:~:text=We%20didn't%20start%20Substack,that%20were%20serving%20them%20poorly.(Accessed: 17 July 2022).

New York Public Library. (Last Updated: 9 February 2022) *How to Research a Family Business: Newspapers and Trade Journals*, New York: New York Public Library. Available at: https://libguides.nypl.org/familybusinessresearch/newspapers (Accessed 1 June, 2022).

Rodriguez, A. (2020) "Inside the Launch of Sportico, Penske Media's New Sports-Business Brand that Fast-Tracked its Debut as Live Sports Shut Down," *Business Insider*, New York, 21 July 2020 Available at: https://www.businessinsider.com/inside-sportico-penske-medias-new-sports-business-media-brand-2020-7 (Accessed: 17 July 2022).

SABEW. (2013) "New Coverage Challenges in Business Journalism," *SABEW*. Available at: https://ahbj.sabew.org/story/04042013-new-coverage-challenges-in-business-journalism/ (Accessed: 1 March 2022).

Scire, S. (2021) "The Information's Jessica Lessin Built a Newsroom She Wanted to Work in — and Coaches Other Journalists-Turned-Founders on Doing the Same," *Nieman Lab, Cambridge.* 4 February 2021. Available at: https://www.niemanlab.org/2021/02/the-informations-jessica-lessin-built-a-newsroom-she-wanted-to-work-in-and-coaches-other-journalists-turned-founders-on-doing-the-same/ (Accessed: 15 April 2022).

Sherman, A. (2022) "Morning Brew Tops 4 Million Newsletter Subscribers as it Looks to Expand With M&A," *CNBC*, New York, 28 March 2022. Available at: https://www.cnbc.com/2022/03/28/morning-brew-tops-4-million-subscribers-as-it-looks-to-expand-with-ma.html (Accessed: 15 July 2022).

Sportico. (Undated) About us. Available at: https://www.sportico.com/about-us/ (Accessed: 17 July 2022).

Suba, R. (2013) "All Things Digital Bids Farewell," *Tech Times*, New York, 28 December 2013. Available at: https://www.techtimes.com/articles/2301/20131228/all-things-digital-bids-farewell.htm (Accessed: 1 June 2022).

Substack. (Undated) Available at: https://substack.com/ (Accessed: 25 July 2022).

Tameez, H. (2021) "With Trapital, Dan Runcie Found a Way to Cover the Business of Hip-Hop and Make it Sustainable," *Nieman Lab*, Cambridge, 26 April 2021. Available at: https://www.niemanlab.org/2021/04/with-trapital-dan-runcie-found-a-way-to-cover-the-business-of-hip-hop-and-make-it-sustainable/ (Accessed: 17 July 2022).

The Information. (Undated) "The Information's WTF Summit: What's Next," *The Information*, San Francisco. Available at: https://www.theinformation.com/events/wtf-2022 (Accessed 15 May 2022)

TheSkimm, About Us. (Undated) Available at: https://www.theskimm.com/general/about-4FfFyf05JeQwdPdhgCkWcr-post (Accessed: 25 July 2022).

Topolsky, J. (2014) "Walt Mossberg and Kara Swisher Launch Re/Code News Site, Code Conference Series," *The Verge*, New York, 2 January, 2014. Available at: https://www.theverge.com/2014/1/2/5264506/walt-mossberg-and-kara-swisher-launch-recode-code-conference (Accessed: 1 June 2022).

Tow Center. (2015) *The Novelty of the Newsgame*, New York: Columbia University. Available at: https://towcenter.gitbooks.io/play-the-news/content/history_and_discourses/the_novelty_of_the.html (Accessed 1 June 2022).

Tow Center. (2017) "The Platform Press: How Silicon Valley Reengineered Journalism," Columbia University, New York, 29 March 2017. Available at: https://www.cjr.org/tow_center_reports/platform-press-how-silicon-valley-reengineering-journalism.php Accessed: 25 July 2022.

Trapital. (Undated) Available at: https://trapital.co/ (Accessed 20 July 2022).

Wagner, L. (2021) "Jonah Peretti Lays Off 47 HuffPost Staffers In Latest "Bloodbath," *Defector*, New York, 9 March, 2021. Available at: https://defector.com/jonah-peretti-lays-off-47-huffpost-staffers-in-latest-bloodbath (Accessed: 25 June 2023).

Wile, R. (2023) "BuzzFeed News Is Shutting Down," *NBC News*, New York, 20 April, 2023. Available at: https://www.nbcnews.com/business/business-news/buzzfeed-news-shutting-down-rcna80656 (Accessed: 25 June 2023).

# PART IV

# The Political Economy of Business Journalism

# 21

# BUT IS IT SUSTAINABLE? EXPLORING JOURNALISTS' COVERAGE OF SUSTAINABLE FINANCE

*Nadine Strauß*

## Introduction

Sustainable finance (SF) has become one of the most trending topics on the financial markets and in the financial news media, respectively, in the past years. Large amounts of investment have been flowing into the so-called ESG (environmental, social, governance) funds world-wide (Kerber & Jessop 2021) and the news media have reacted to this shift by covering the topic more often and by creating specialized news outlets (for example, the Moral Money newsletter by the Financial Times and the online news platform Responsible Investor). Despite the potential of channeling financial capital into sustainable industries and corporations, as highlighted by key political figures at the UN Climate Change Conference (COP26) in Glasgow 2021 (e.g., Marc Carney, former governor of the Bank of England), there has been mounting criticism toward SF regarding the market practices labeled as ESG, the definition of the term (Berg et al. 2020), the trustworthiness (Dupre & Roa 2020), and the impact of such investments on the environment and climate (Schütze & Stede 2021), biodiversity, and society at large.

Considering that several studies in financial and business journalism have criticized journalists for their failure to act as watchdogs before, during, and after the Global Financial Crisis (GFC) 2007–2009 (Knowles et al. 2017; Tambini 2010; Usher 2013), the question arises: How have journalists been covering this new, emerging trend of SF? Do they live up to their watchdog role regarding SF practices on the financial markets? How do they perceive their role in reporting on sustainability and the financial markets? And how do they cover SF with regard to the topics, actors, and sentiment?

The uniqueness of SF in combining an environmental with a financial topic makes the investigation of journalistic practices in covering SF intriguing, as it challenges journalists not only regarding their knowledge, role perceptions, and sources in the financial realm, but also requires them to think about financial topics and their relationships with climate change and the environment.

DOI: 10.4324/9781003298977-26

## Sustainable Finance and the Role of Financial News Reporting

SF can generally be understood as "the process of taking **environmental, social and governance (ESG) considerations** into account when making investment decisions in the financial sector, leading to more long-term investments in sustainable economic activities and projects" (European Commission 2022, highlights in the original). While the term SF has emerged in the past decade, "socially responsible investments" have already been around since the 1970s, followed by the terms "social and ethical investments" in the 1980s, "green investment/finance" in the 1990, and since the 2000s the diversification of the discipline in various fields, such as "impact investment," "micro finance," or "climate finance" (Cunha et al. 2021). With the proliferation of terms related to SF, the financial sector has also increased its product range in the field of sustainable investments, ranging from funds to bonds, certificates, impact investments, or blended finance products. In fact, depending on the definition, ESG-related funds range between $3 trillion and $31 trillion worldwide, and ESG-linked debt issuance more than tripled to $190 billion in 2021, according to the IMF (Gautam et al. 2022).

Not only do the financial news media report about these developments continuously, but they are also co-creating and co-shaping the discourse about SF. The news media in general and journalists in particular play a crucial role in establishing, maintaining, and moderating debates around evolving issues such as SF (cf. Brüggemann 2017). Following Engesser and Brüggemann (2016) and Olausson (2018), I argue that financial journalists take a participating role in the process of anchoring and objectifying the social representations of SF. In other words, they are shaping the understanding and representation of SF by embedding and juxtaposing the new concept vis-à-vis existing knowledge and by making the concept more accessible through the use of concrete examples, actors, and illustrations in their coverage. For example, a recent study that has researched frames about SF between 1998 and 2018 by using a network technique identified five frames: responsible investment, risks and opportunities, climate finance, critical frame, and integrated frame (Dimmelmeier 2021). However, Dimmelmeier (2021) took a broad industry perspective, looking at various sorts of documents (e.g., industry reports, news documents, interviews), but not at the concrete representation of SF in the news media. Thus, the way journalists cover SF and how they perceive their own role in this crucial discourse has not been extensively researched so far.

## Combining Financial News with a Sustainable Angle

In the past, scholars have often pointed out a lack of research on financial journalism (Knowles et al. 2017, Lee 2014). However, a number of empirical studies in journalism research have been published that investigate the content of economic news, even dating back to the 1960s and 1980s (Barkin 1982; Griggs 1963). Other research has studied the quality of financial news reporting in times of crises (Knowles et al. 2017; Tambini 2010), the interrelationship of financial journalists with their sources (Davis 2005; Doyle 2006), their role perceptions (Damstra & De Swert 2020; Knowles 2018; Strauß 2019; Usher 2013), and their relationship vis-à-vis the stock market (Lee 2014; Strauß 2019). Particularly since the Great Financial Crisis, scholars have investigated the ways in which financial and business journalists have or have not lived up to their watchdog role in holding the financial sector to account. By making use of observational studies, interviews and surveys, scholars have concluded that financial journalists failed to enact their watchdog role (Knowles et al. 2017; Manning 2013;

Starkman 2014; Tambini 2010). While some research has found that journalists are eager to ascribe themselves the role of a watchdog, their day-to-day practices and working environment, characterized by limited resources and time, often do not allow them to live up to their ideals (Knowles 2018; Strauß 2019).

However, there is a growing concern about greenwashing practices on the financial markets, implying that financial institutions communicate positively about their environmental performance although the performance of their investments is poor (cf. greenwashing definition: Delmas & Burbano 2011). Greenwashing is often understood as "the activity (for example by corporate lobby groups) of giving a positive image to practices that are environmentally unsound" (Oxford Reference 2022). In the field of SF, many voices have been raised regarding greenwashing activities, such as the lack of transparency of sustainable investments (Schrader 2006), inconsistent definitions (Paetzold et al. 2015), and incoherent measurements and ratings (Berg et al. 2020), as well as the dilution of financial sustainability regulation (e.g., EU Taxonomy: Webb 2021). Thus, given the risk of greenwashing in the financial sector regarding SF and some occasional speculations about a "green bubble" that could burst and risk the stability of the market (Jones 2021; The Economist 2021), studying journalistic practices and role perceptions regarding SF coverage becomes of systemic importance.

More recently, there has been a growing field of journalism in reporting the energy sector, with a particular focus on the impact of and the solutions offered in this sector on the climate crisis, albeit the economic aspects of this discussion have been found to remain neglected (Kim et al. 2014; Mercado-Sáez et al. 2022). Likewise, the field of environmental and climate change journalism has enjoyed growing attention in the past two decades (see for an overview: Schäfer & Painter 2021), probably due to the increased scientific evidence of climate change (e.g., IPCC), public pressure (e.g., Greta Thunberg's Fridays for Future), and more frequent and intense weather events that make global warming a more direct experience for individuals (Vautard et al. 2020). Scholars in the field of environmental journalism have provided compelling evidence how role perceptions have shifted from gatekeepers to curators (Fahy & Nisbet 2011), how skeptics and climate change deniers have fallen silent more recently in the U.K. (Tobitt 2021), and how the communication of climate change advocates has become more professionalized (Williams 2015). Thus, given the increasing relevance of covering financial topics with an environmental angle in face of the climate crisis, the second part of this chapter presents findings from an empirical study that content analyzed the coverage of SF in news in the U.K. The findings are contextualized based on two related publications that are based on 33 interviews with financial and environmental journalists in Europe who covered SF in 2019 and 2020 (Strauß 2021a, 2021b).

## Methodological Approaches and Data

The empirical data reported in this chapter stem from a content analysis of news articles about SF in the U.K. between 2019 until mid-2020 (n = 714 articles). Making use of a pre-defined search string with words related to SF, news articles from mainstream and financial news outlets in the U.K. (the Financial Times, The Guardian, The Times, The Telegraph, The Sunday Times, the Daily Mail) were retrieved from the database Factiva. The articles were coded by three English-speaking coders, using a pre-defined codebook. After two rounds of test coding, the inter-coder reliability scores were acceptable for most of the categories (percentage agreement: 70–100 percent), but below average for more complex codes (e.g., tone, evaluation of politics: approx. 60 percent). Despite the exploratory character of this project, some of the findings therefore need to be considered with caution. Although the definition for SF was kept very broad in this research (green, sustainable, responsible, ethical), the findings in the following only refer to "sustainable" to ease the reading.

## Distribution of News Coverage of Sustainable Finance

The manual content analysis of 714 news articles shows that the news coverage differs substantially in the way SF is reported in the U.K. Spikes in the news coverage can be spotted in January 2020, and after that with consistent spikes every two weeks. This can be explained by the introduction of the Moral Money newsletter by the Financial Times, which was regularly introduced in the beginning of 2020 and had a special report on the World Economic Forum in Davos in January 2020. As expected (see Figure 21.1), the Financial Times reported the most about SF (564 articles), followed by mainstream news outlets such as The Guardian (54 articles), The Times (36 articles), The Telegraph (30 articles), The Sunday Times (15 articles), the Daily Mail (11 articles), and The Independent (4 articles).

The majority across the news outlets were regular news articles (613), followed by commentaries by experts from the industry (62), commentaries by journalists (23), and others (e.g., interviews, news agency article, announcements). In fact, the prominence of the Financial Times and the high quality of its news reporting on topics related to SF have also been mentioned by other financial and environmental journalists interviewed in Europe (Strauß 2021a, 2021b). However, at the same time, it has been criticized that the content in the Financial Times and the Moral Money newsletter is hidden behind a paywall, only addressing an elite audience. In fact, and with regard to the audience of SF news, some journalists spoke of an "elite audience," meaning a group of readers largely limited to political and financial

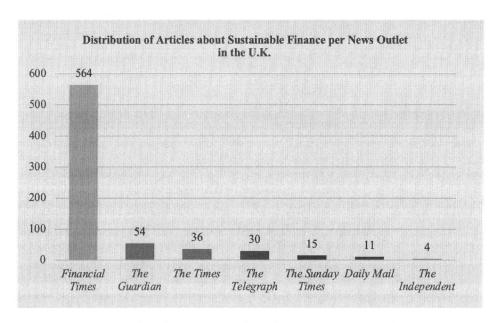

*Figure 21.1* Distribution of articles per news outlet in the U.K. (01/01/2019–30/06/2020).

opinion-leaders such as CEOs or corporate decision-makers, prominent financial market actors (e.g., large asset managers), and influential political figures.

## Financial Instruments and Divestment as Main Topics

Regarding the main topics, the top 12 topics coded for the U.K. news were (see Figure 21.2) sustainable investments (9.5 percent), sustainable bonds (8.4 percent), ESG criteria (6.3 percent), divestment (6.0 percent), environmental actions of companies (5.5 percent), impact investment (4.9 percent), sustainable funds (3.8 percent), legislation (3.4 percent), SF in general (3.1 percent), COVID-19 crisis (3.1 percent), COVID-19 recovery package (3.1 percent), and greenwashing (3.1 percent). More generally, divestments were mentioned in 107 articles, carbon neutrality in 210 articles, the U.N. Sustainable Development Goals in 58 articles, the Paris Agreement in 85 articles, and ESG in 233 articles. The focus on these topics can be supported by the insights from the interview study (Strauß 2021a, 2021b). The journalists indicated here that most of the coverage is driven by external political and financial events, rather than by themselves as journalists (or by their editors). In addition, the journalists in the interviews highlighted that the articles about SF should fit with the overall news cycle, that they should present a fit with the editorial line of the news outlet, and that they should offer a link to recent events or (political) discussions. This becomes prevalent by topics such as the COVID-19 crisis or the discussion about divestments in the U.K. in 2020 by various actors (e.g., pension funds, universities). In fact, much of the inspiration of news articles, according to the interviewees, comes from observing the financial markets or following the political discussions about (potential) new regulations and frameworks.

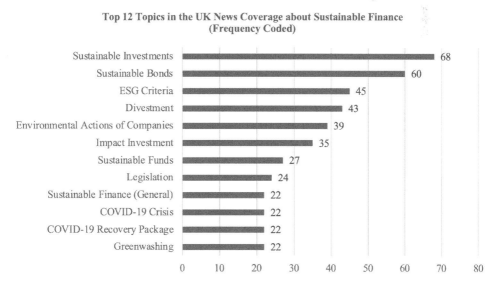

**Top 12 Topics in the UK News Coverage about Sustainable Finance (Frequency Coded)**

*Figure 21.2* Top 12 main topics coded for the U.K. news coverage about sustainable finance (number of times coded as main topic of an article).

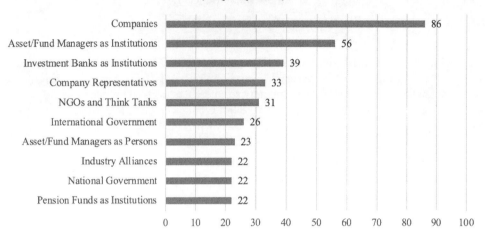

*Figure 21.3* Top ten main actors coded for the U.K. news coverage about sustainable finance (number of times coded as the main actor/initiator of an article).

## Focus on Financial Actors and the Financial Markets

The top ten actors coded in the news coverage about SF in the U.K. were (see Figure 21.3) companies (12.0 percent), asset/fund managers as institutions (7.8 percent), investment banks as institutions (5.5 percent), company representatives (4.6 percent), NGOs and think tanks (4.3 percent), international government (3.6 percent), asset/fund managers as persons (3.2 percent), industry alliances (3.1 percent), national government (3.1 percent), and pension funds as institutions (3.1 percent). The prevalence of companies also becomes apparent, given that a company was mentioned in 455 out of 714 articles. Most of the companies covered in the news stem from the financial industry (291 times), followed by energy (59 times), consumer staples (28 times), information technology (27 times), or consumer discretionary (19 times). In only a few cases, other industrial sectors were mentioned such as consultancy (11 times), materials (eight times), telecommunications (six times), real estate (five times), or industrials (one time) and health care (one time).

The strong focus in the U.K. news on financial actors is also reflected in the responses by journalists in the interview study (Strauß 2021a, 2021b). Here, journalists stated that they mostly rely on financial experts, and sources with whom they have established a year-long, trusted relationship. However, even though the journalists admitted being dependent on the financial sources, most of them also emphasized that they try to present a balanced picture by also giving voice to NGOs and other counter-voices. This is particularly reflected in the prominence of NGOs, think tanks and governmental actors as coded for the U.K. coverage.

## Neutral Sentiment but Limited Criticism

Overall, the articles about SF were mostly presented in a neutral or balanced tone overall (53.1 percent). However, with regard to the way SF was presented in particular, 35.7 percent of the news articles were written in a positive style, whereas only 12.5 percent were explicitly negative. In terms of diversity, striking 90.6 percent of the articles conveyed more than one viewpoint. However, only 37.4 percent of the articles included a call to take action with regard to SF (e.g., need for regulation, measurement, taxonomy), and in only about half of the articles, the coverage referred to a conflict regarding SF (47.2 percent).

The focus on neutral and balanced reporting is also reflected regarding the role perceptions that journalists reported in the interviews (Strauß 2021a, 2021b). The most common role that interviewees ascribed themselves was that of an informant, educator, or chronicler. Overall, most journalists saw it as their main job to describe and reflect market events to their audiences, to provide a complete picture of the subject, and to illustrate the development of the market trend to their readers. At the same time, journalists writing for specialized and financial news outlets indicated that they see their role in contributing to the discussion among decision-makers in the field of SF. By providing the most recent information on SF, and by inquiring and giving voice to industry experts and politicians, these journalists attributed themselves the role of a "facilitator" who provides a platform for the exchanges among these decision-makers, even having an influence on opinion-leaders by raising critical questions.

With regard to the evaluation of the politics of SF in the U.K. news coverage, most articles did not express any assessment (45.8 percent). Yet if present, the U.K. news mainly evaluated politics regarding SF in a neutral or balanced tone (70.0 percent). Interestingly, when the performance of SF investment products was discussed (17.5 percent), 82.4 percent of the articles presented SF as performing better than traditional investments. Similarly, the explorative coding of characteristics being attributed to SF in the news coverage revealed that positive attributes were more prevalent than negative attributes (see Figure 21.4): relevant (236 mentions), forward-looking (213 mentions), impactful (167 mentions), opportunity (166 mentions) vs. complicated (183 mentions), unclear/fuzzy (69 mentions), untrustworthy (66 mentions), and unsuccessful (43 mentions). However, the most prevalent criticism regarding SF in the U.K. news seems to be that it is perceived to be a complicated concept. In fact, many of the journalists in the interview study (Strauß 2021a, 2021b) indicated that the topic is rather perceived as complex, cumbersome, and boring by their audiences. Particularly the positive framing of most of the stories in the field of SF would make it challenging, according to some journalists, to add a twist and to captivate the readership.

This issue regarding the overall positive tone about SF has repeatedly been highlighted by journalists interviewed in Europe (Strauß 2021a, 2021b). When journalists narrated about the process of writing articles about SF and their professional roles, the strong dependence on financial sources and the dilemma between acting as a chronicler and watchdog emerged. As many journalists indicated, public relations material about SF is constantly flooding their email boxes, filled with information promoting the newest ESG fund, climate pledge, or financial sustainability initiative. On the one hand, journalists are challenged in filtering out relevant information from marketing to report adequately and neutrally about the new market trend in their role as chroniclers of SF. On the other hand, journalists indicated that they do not want to provide a free marketing platform for unsubstantiated PR about SF. Accordingly, some journalists identified it as part of their main job to cut through the PR material and distinguish market-relevant information from pure marketing.

However, although the moral standard of not acting as the mouthpiece for the financial markets was strongly pronounced among the journalists in the interviews (Strauß 2021a, 2021b), none of the journalists reported that they had the time and resources to undertake

**Characteristics of Sustainable Finance as Covered in the U.K. News (Frequency Coded)**

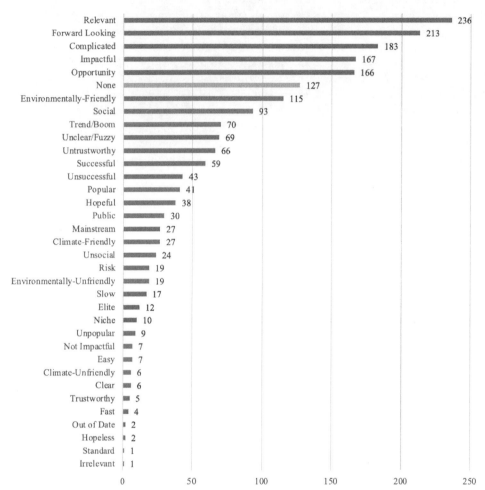

*Figure 21.4*  Explorative coding of characteristics ascribed to SF in the U.K. news coverage (number of times coded in articles; multiple characteristics could be coded per article).

investigative research or reporting. In fact, the role description of being a watchdog was almost absent in the interviews with the journalists, except for one case. Similarly, the content analysis of SF news coverage in the U.K. showed that not only the sentiment of articles about SF was overall rather neutral – if not even pre-dominantly positive regarding the performance of SF – but that also topics such as greenwashing or criticism of SF overall ranked rather low in the reporting. One issue that journalists identified in this regard is that in 2019/2020, the news about SF strongly circulated about the reporting of pledges and promises to act more sustainably or about introducing new products and practices, which are generally more positive news stories. Accordingly, journalists highlighted that enacting the watchdog role would not be possible at that stage and should come at a later point (e.g., in five or ten years) when they are able to investigate and trace back whether the financial sector and its actors have lived up to their promises.

## Conclusion and Future Research

This chapter provides a short overview of the ways in which journalists in Europe (particularly in the U.K.) have reported about SF between 2019 and 2020. The increased relevance of discussing financial and economic topics regarding climate change impacts increasingly requires from financial and business journalists to integrate an environmental perspective in their reporting.

The overview of findings from one empirical study (content analysis of U.K. news articles), coupled from insights from an interview study (Strauß 2021a, 2021b), has shown that the topic has gained growing attention in the past years, and particularly since the beginning of 2020. The content analysis revealed the direct influence of financial and corporate actors and events on the news media reporting about SF in the U.K. Likewise, journalists themselves stated in the interview study (Strauß 2021a, 2021b) that the news agenda is largely driven by industry and political events in the realm of SF. In fact, given the strong role of London as an international financial center, the prevalence of financial and corporate actors in the media discourse about SF is natural.

In addition, the findings indicate that although the reporting is overall rather neutral and balanced, the sentiment regarding the performance of SF is characterized by a positive tone. Moreover, it can be concluded from the interviews with journalists that although SF remains an elite debate in the financial news realm, specialized news outlets have the potential to co-create and co-shape political and financial decision-making by providing a platform for key market voices. However, the absence of an active watchdog role among journalists covering SF and the limited coverage of SF from a more critical perspective (e.g., greenwashing) give reasons for concern. If some of the market warnings about a "green bubble" turn out to be substantiated (Jones 2021; The Economist 2021), (financial) journalists would again have failed to live up to their watchdog role and warn the public of potential fraud, speculation, and instability of the market.

Although this overview has shown some preliminary insights into the coverage of SF in the U.K., the findings of the content analysis only apply to one country and are therefore not generalizable. Future research could expand the geographical focus, given that cultural differences not only exist in news media reporting, but even in the way SF is understood and acted upon (Nadler et al. 2019). What is more, the presented analyses did not take digital news media (e.g., social media, online news) into account. Automated content analyses (e.g., topic, actor, networks) could provide illuminating insights into the interrelationships and dynamics of the SF discourse across countries and platforms. Likewise, a more detailed qualitative analysis of certain issues related to SF (e.g., discourse of greenwashing) could yield a more differentiated account of how such issues are discussed in the mediated public sphere. Furthermore, future research should also focus on the audience perspective and gain a deeper understanding of how news users and private investors perceive, understand, and evaluate SF and how economic news use relates to this respectively. Eventually, following up on the pledges made by journalists to enact their watchdog role in the future, as argued in the interview study (Strauß 2021a, 2021b), research should revisit the reporting and self-reports by journalists at a later stage when the sustainability pledges by the financial and corporate sector have passed their expiry date (e.g., carbon neutrality by 2025).

## Acknowledgments

This work was supported by the European Union's Horizon 2020 research and innovation program under the Marie Skłodowska-Curie grant agreement No 834638. The author also thanks Alex Benham and Marcus Alburez Myers for helping with coding the articles.

## Further Reading

Ferua Rotaru, C. (2019), "Challenges and opportunities for sustainable finance", *The Journal of Contemporary Issues in Business and Government*, 25(1), pp. 1–13, gives a great overview for the field of SF on the potentials and pitfalls. Similarly, Lagoarde-Segot (2019), "Sustainable finance. A critical realist perspective," *Research in International Business and Finance*, 47, 1–9, responds to the epistemological challenges of SF. Boehnert, J. (2016), "The green economy: Reconceptualizing the natural commons as natural capital," *Environmental Communication*, 10(4), pp. 395–417, shows how the "green economy" has already been used in the past to obscure dominant discourse of neoliberalism. My article "Communicating sustainable responsible investments as financial advisors: Engaging private investors with strategic communication," *Sustainability*, 3161, offers a model to communicate SF more effectively.

## References

Barkin, S. M. (1982) "Changes in business sections, 1931–1979," *Journalism Quarterly*, 59(3), pp. 435–439.

Berg, F., Kölbel, J. F. and Rigobon, R. (2020) "Aggregate confusion: The divergence of ESG Ratings," Available SSRN. Forthcoming *Review of Finance*. Available at http://dx.doi.org/10.2139/ssrn.3438533

Brüggemann, M. (2017) "Post-normal journalism: Climate journalism and its changing contribution to an unsustainable debate," in P. Berglez, U. Olausson and M. Ots (eds.), *What Is Sustainable Journalism? Integrating the Environmental, Social, and Economic Challenges of Journalism*, Peter Lang, New York, pp. 57–73.

Cunha, F. A. F. S., Meira, E. and Orsato, R. J. (2021) "Sustainable finance and investment: Review and research agenda," *Business Strategy and the Environment*, 30(8), pp. 3821–3838.

Damstra, A. and De Swert, K. (2020) "The making of economic news: Dutch economic journalists contextualizing their work," *Journalism*, 22(12), pp. 3083–3100.

Davis, A. (2005) "Media effect and the active elite audience: A study of communication in the London stock exchange," *European Journal of Communication*, 20(3), pp. 303–306.

Delmas, M. A. and Burbano, V. C. (2011) "The drivers of greenwashing," *California Management Review*, 54(1), pp. 64–87.

Dimmelmeier, A. (2021) "Sustainable finance as a contested concept: Tracing the evolution of five frames between 1998 and 2018," *Journal of Sustainable Finance & Investment*, 13(4), pp. 1–24.

Doyle, G. (2006) "Financial news journalism: A post-enron analysis of approaches towards economic and financial news production in the U.K," *Journalism*, 7(4), pp. 433–452.

Dupre, S. and Roa, P. F. (2020) "Impact washing gets a free ride. An analysis of the draft EU ecolabel criteria for financial products," *2 Degrees Investing Initiative*. Available at https://2degrees-investing.org/wp-content/uploads/2019/06/2019-Paper-Impact-washing.pdf (accessed 18 May 2022).

Engesser, S. and Brüggemann, M. (2016) "Mapping the minds of the mediators: The cognitive frames of climate journalists from five countries," *Public Understanding of Science*, 25(7), pp. 825–841.

European Commission. (2022) "Overview of sustainable finance," *European Commission*. Available at https://ec.europa.eu/info/business-economy-euro/banking-and-finance/sustainable-finance/overview-sustainable-finance_en#what (accessed 18 May 2022).

Fahy, D. and Nisbet, M. C. (2011) "The science journalist online: Shifting roles and emerging Practices," *Journalism*, 12(7), pp. 778–793.

Gautam, D., Goel, R. and Natalucci, F. (2022) "Sustainable finance in emerging markets is enjoying rapid growth, but may bring risks," *IMFBlog*. Available at https://blogs.imf.org/2022/03/01/sustainable-finance-in-emerging-markets-is-enjoying-rapid-growth-but-may-bring-risks/ (accessed 18 May 2022).

Griggs, H. H. (1963) "Newspaper performance in recession coverage," *Journalism Quarterly*, 40(4), pp. 559–564.

Jones, M. (2021) "Central bank group BIS warns of green asset bubble risk," *Reuters* (online) 20 September 2021. Available at: https://www.reuters.com/business/sustainable-business/global-markets-bis-esg-urgent-2021-09-20/ (accessed 14 May 2022).

Kerber, R. and Jessop, S. (2021) "Analysis: How 2021 became the year of ESG investing," *Reuters* (online), 23 December 2021. Available at: https://www.reuters.com/markets/us/how-2021-became-year-esg-investing-2021-12-23/ (accessed 14 May 2022).

Kim, S. H., Besley, J. Oh, S. H. and Kim, S. Y. (2014) "Talking about bio-fuel in the news: Newspaper framing of ethanol stories in the United States," *Journalism Studies*, 15(2), pp. 218–234.

Knowles, S. (2018) "Financial journalists, the financial crisis and the 'crisis' in journalism," in L. Basu, S. Schifferes and S. Knowles (eds.), *The Media and Austerity*. Routledge, Oxon, pp. 183–195.

Knowles, S., Phillips, G. and Lidberg, J. (2017) "Reporting the global financial crisis: A longitudinal tri-nation study of mainstream financial journalism," *Journalism Studies*, 18(3), pp. 322–340.

Lee, M. (2014) "A review of communication scholarship on the financial markets and the financial media," *International Journal of Communication*, 8, pp. 715–736.

Manning, P. (2013) "Financial journalism, news sources and the banking Crisis," *Journalism*, 14(2), pp. 173–189.

María-Teresa Mercado-Sáez, M.-T., Sebastián Sánchez-Castillo, S. and Pou-Amérigo, M. J. (2022) "Framing energy: A content analysis of Spanish press energy issue coverage from an environmental approach in the context of climate change," *Journalism Studies*, 23(11), pp. 1396–1414.

Nadler, C. and Breuer, W. (2019) "Cultural finance as a research field: An evaluative Survey," *Journal of Business Economics*, 89, pp. 191–220.

Olausson, U. (2018) "'Stop blaming the cows!': How livestock production is legitimized in everyday discourse on Facebook," *Environmental Communication*, 12(1), pp. 28–43.

Oxford Reference. (2022). Greenwash. Retrieved from https://www.oxfordreference.com/view/10.1093/oi/authority.20110803095906807 (accessed 10 August 2022).

Paetzold, F., Busch, T. and Chesney, M. (2015) "More than money: Exploring the role of investment advisors for sustainable investing," *Annals in Social Responsibility*, 1(1), pp. 195–223.

Schäfer, M. and Painter, J. (2021) "Climate journalism in a changing media ecosystem: Assessing the production of climate change-related news around the world," *WIREs Climate Change*, 12(1), e675.

Schrader, U. (2006) "Ignorant advice – customer advisory service for ethical investment funds," *Business Strategy and the Environment*, 15(3), pp. 200–214.

Schütze, F. and Stede, J. (2021) "The EU sustainable finance taxonomy and its contribution to climate neutrality," *Journal of Sustainable Finance & Investment*. https://www.tandfonline.com/action/showCitFormats?doi=10.1080%2F20430795.2021.2006129

Starkman, D. (2014) *The Watchdog That Didn't Bark. The Financial Crisis and the Disappearance of Investigative Journalism*, New York: Columbia University Press.

Strauß, N. (2021a, online first) "Covering sustainable finance: Role perceptions, journalistic practices and moral dilemmas," *Journalism*, 23(6), 1194–1212.

——— (2021b) "Devil's advocate or agenda setter? The Role of journalists covering sustainable finance in Europe," *Journalism Studies*, 22(9), pp. 1200–1218

——— (2019) "Financial journalism in today's high-frequency news and information era", *Journalism*, 20(2), pp. 274–291.

Tambini, D. (2010) "What are financial journalists for?" *Journalism Studies*, 11(2), pp. 158–174.

The Economist. (2021) "A green bubble? We dissect the investment boom," *The Economist* (online), 20 May 2021. Available at https://www.economist.com/finance-and-economics/2021/05/17/green-assets-are-on-a-wild-ride (accessed 14 May 2022).

Tobitt, C. (2021) "How U.K. press moved from denial to acceptance and now action on climate Change," *Press Gazette.* Available at https://www.pressgazette.co.U.K./U.K.-media-climate-change/ (accessed 14 May 2022).

Usher, N. (2013) "Ignored, uninterested, and the blame game: How The New York Times, Marketplace, and TheStreet distanced themselves from preventing the 2007–2009 financial crisis," *Journalism*, 14(2), pp. 190–207.

Vautard, R. et al. (2020) "Human contribution to the record-breaking June and July 2019 heatwaves in Western Europe," *Environmental Research Letters,* 15(9), pp. 1–9.

Webb, D. (2021) "Daily ESG briefing: Investors urge EU not to let gas into taxonomy," *Responsible Investor.* Available at: https://www.responsible-investor.com/articles/daily-esg-briefing-investors-urge-eu-not-to-let-gas-into-taxonomy (accessed 29 March 2020).

Williams, A. (2015) "Environmental news journalism, public relations and news sources," in A. Hansen and R. Cox (eds.), *The Routledge Handbook of Environment and Communication.* Routledge, Oxford, pp. 197–206.

# 22

# THE CAPITAL, QUALITY SIGNALS, AND LEGITIMACY OF AWARDS IN BUSINESS JOURNALISM

*Melony Shemberger*

## Introduction

Journalists in the United States – print, broadcast, and online – vie for more than 200 national, state, and local media contests annually (Volz 2013). Deemed the heart of newsroom culture, journalism awards are "an integral part of American journalism" (Shepard 2000, p. 24). "Every industry values its awards. Awards and recognition are ubiquitous to the human race," said Henry Dubroff (2023), editor and publisher of the Pacific Coast Business Times in Santa Barbara, California, and past president of the Society for Advancing Business Editing and Writing (SABEW). "Within the profession, awards matter." Such awards, staples of the profession since the beginning of the 20th century when the Pulitzer Prizes were launched (Jenkins and Volz 2018), establish credibility for a news organization, as well as for an individual journalist whose expertise may be noticed publicly. Further, journalism awards are signals for quality, increasing the demand for excellence in journalism (Wellbrock and Wolfram 2021).

Business journalism is no different, with its own contests that award monetary prizes or public recognition as a way to reward journalists for their reporting and writing excellence about business, economics, and related fields. Many journalism awards contests are not administered by journalism groups, but are sponsored or designed by businesses, unions and related groups. Interest groups organize news awards as a way they desire to influence "journalism conventions" (Volz 2013, p. 392). Regardless of who sponsors the contests, reporters and editors view these prizes as models of excellence, possibly influencing how topics of economic importance are presented, or even framed, to the public (Welles 1979).

Professional awards are designed to identify and recognize publicly what is regarded as the best practice for the field (Volz 2013). Plus, the awards serve as an agent of legitimation (Tuchman 1978), or a way to make them acceptable measures of success. "I wish the public cared more about the awards," said Dubroff (2023), an expert in local business news operations. "There is a professional development aspect to the awards. When a financial journalist wins a Pulitzer, it's a big deal." Journalism contest prizes also count as quantifiable measures of success by editors, who sometimes craft or support internal newsroom policies that encourage prize-seeking (Coulson 1989). However, the awards present "fundamental value

 DOI: 10.4324/9781003298977-27

problems for juries, for winners, for their peers, and for others concerned with recognition processes" (Heinich 2009, p. 86). Further, news consumers might not be able to identify quality journalism, making decisions based on other factors such as price rather than quality (Wellbrock and Wolfgram 2021). Volz (2013) discussed how some media critics view journalism awards "as the disease of, and not the cure to, perceived journalistic problems" (p. 392). From this perspective, awards and prizes tend to get in the way of, and minimize the purpose of, journalism, becoming a reporter's or a news organization's focus. Journalism awards, however, carry value and should be seen as "a prime site of contention," both ideologically and economically speaking, because reporters and news media are competing for recognition and resources – internally and externally – that could "maximize their social and economic positions" (Volz 2013, p. 391). This is a form of symbolic capital – that is, the awards carry economic, cultural, and social reinforcement that influences the professional significance of journalists (Lanosga 2015).

This chapter begins with an exploration of the different awards contests that business journalists may enter, such as SABEW's Best in Business. Entering this and other prize competitions tends to influence business journalists who strive to aim for better journalism. The kinds of business journalism contests are discussed, providing a historical lens to see how prizes and awards have shaped the journalism culture. This historical foundation sets the stage to examine the judging structure that shapes these contests and the journalism quality that awards could signal. Recommendations for practice and future directions are also offered.

## Specific Business Journalism Contests

Organizations help to define excellent journalism through awards. For business journalism, this is observed through different organizations, all of which play a role in defining excellent business journalism. Over the years, awards contests have been launched, while others have folded. Dubroff (2023), who from 1995 until 1999 was editor of The Denver Business Journal, a weekly newspaper that covers business in Colorado's fast-growing economy, said there is a hierarchy in business awards that many of the large news organizations (e.g., The Wall Street Journal, Reuters, Bloomberg, among others) tend to follow, starting with the well-known Pulitzer Prizes at the top. This section identifies and explains some of the other major business journalism contests that are available for reporters across the nation to enter.

- **Society for Advancing Business Editing and Writing**

Perhaps the most highly regarded business journalism awards come from SABEW, an independent, nonprofit organization that encourages thorough reporting of business and economic news. SABEW honors excellence in business journalism through its annual Best in Business awards competition, recognizing outstanding journalism among professionals and students in the United States. In addition, according to its awards page on its website, SABEW members in Canada are eligible to compete in the Canadian Best in Business Awards after the all-member contest closes in early February (Society for Advancing Business Editing and Writing n.d.). The Best in Business contest features 31 contest categories, including investigative, feature, and data journalism, to name a few. Each category is judged by a panel of business journalists.

- **Barlett & Steele Awards**

SABEW's Best in Business awards program, while established and regarded highly in the field, is not the only contest available to business journalists. Other awards programs exist and have a storied history on how they were formed.

One is the Barlett & Steele Awards, administered since 2007 by the Donald W. Reynolds National Center for Business Journalism, which honor journalists and news organizations for excellence in business reporting in three categories: national and global audiences, regional or locally focused news organizations, and, beginning in 2022, journalists under the age of 30. Gold, silver, and bronze awards are given in each category. The awards are named for the investigative business journalist team of Donald Barlett and James Steele, contributing editors at Vanity Fair, who worked together for more than 40 years, first at The Philadelphia Inquirer (1971–1997), where they won two Pulitzer Prizes and other national journalism awards. During their time together at Time magazine from 1997 to 2006, they earned two National Magazine Awards, becoming the first journalists in history to win both the Pulitzer and its magazine equivalent.

- **Gerald Loeb Awards for Distinguished Business and Financial Journalism**

Another prize opportunity for business journalists is available through the Gerald Loeb Awards for Distinguished Business and Financial Journalism. These awards were established in 1957 by the late Gerald Loeb, a founding partner of E.F. Hutton. Loeb appreciated the significant role that journalists fulfilled in society and created the awards to encourage and support reporting on business and finance that informs and protects both private investors and the public. The Anderson School of Management at the University of California, Los Angeles, administers the awards with the G. and R. Loeb Foundation. Business journalists at print, online and broadcast media outlets may submit entries in 12 competition categories.

- **Jesse H. Neal Awards**

The Jesse H. Neal Awards, established in 1955, recognize and reward editorial excellence in business media. The awards were named after Jesse H. Neal, the first managing director of American Business Media (ABM). The award-winning content reports on major industry issues of the time. Winners of the Neal Awards have exposed corruption and conflicts of interest. Plus, they have drawn attention to major trends, leadership, innovations, and key developments in global businesses.

State press associations also invite their member newspapers to submit entries for their annual awards contests, many of which include categories focusing on excellence in business reporting. In addition, state broadcast associations also organize contests that feature business news categories.

- **New York State Society of CPAs**

Each year, the New York State Society of CPAs (NYSSCPA) administers its Excellence in Financial Journalism awards to recognize the year's most distinguished reporting that contributes to a comprehension of accounting, finance, and business topics.

In place for more than 30 years, the NYSSCPA competition includes 13 awards in ten categories that include enterprise reporting, general reporting, opinion, and public service, among others (New York State Society of CPAs n.d.). Print, broadcast, online, and social platform entries are eligible to be submitted in any category. NYSSCPA members and journalists judge the entries. The winners are honored at a luncheon.

## Critical Issues and Topics

Prizes awarded for excellence in business journalism set the stage for recognition of journalists and organizations that demonstrate superior news reporting. However, the accolades might differ in their functions. This section examines how awards are capital and signals of quality, but the legitimacy of such metrics should be considered as well.

## Awards as Capital

Prizes awarded to journalists each year serve as a way to recognize the work they complete as determined by their peers who serve as judges (Lough 2021). Through this recognition, these awards become a form of capital – or reinforcement or significance – that convey what is regarded as quality that shapes the field of journalism (Jenkins and Volz 2018). This construct of capital includes economic, symbolic, or cultural dimensions. For instance, a journalism award translates to economic capital for reporters and editors when it comes to newsroom employee promotions and hiring and performance evaluations (Coulson 1989; Lough 2021). In addition, journalism awards have social capital, bringing peer recognition (Beam, Dunwoody, and Kosicki 1986; Jenkins and Volz 2018). If the judges are employed as journalists, the awards are regarded as being more legitimate (Jenkins and Volz 2018), building cultural capital.

Journalism awards are important to reporters and news outlets because of the economic, social, and cultural capital that they bring, but they also shape the field of journalism (Beam, Dunwoody, and Kosicki 1986; Lanosga 2015; Willig 2013). Award-winning news stories institutionalize the construct of capital, shaping what it means to practice journalism (Lough 2021) and creating a mutual relationship between awards and journalism (Jenkins and Volz 2018; Lanosga 2015). This relationship is amplified in the news itself, particularly when a news outlet wins an award (Beam, Dunwoody, and Kosicki 1986). While the awards are traction for a prize culture within the journalism field (Shepard 2000), journalists especially are able to define and justify their work through awards contests, possibly helping them to shape their identity in the profession. "Awards can be life changing for careers," Dubroff (2023) said.

## Awards as Quality Signals

Awards are celebrated as signals of recognition and distinction (Gallus and Frey 2017). Characteristics not articulated and deemed hidden, such as dedication and professionalism, become visible to individuals as a result of awards (Frey and Neckermann 2010). However, the public must be able to recognize and process awards as signals in ways that are not complex; otherwise, the signal – the outcome effect of awards – might be limited (Bloom and Reve 1990).

In the digital era, identifying high-quality business journalism is difficult for several reasons. News content is available online, sometimes for free. News outlets once seen as separate entities, such as television and print, have converged in many markets. Competition also is more global (Siapera 2012). These contribute to the challenge of building a quality product in journalism that would become evident to the news consumer (Akerlof 1970; Siapera 2012). Journalists who are nominated for an award and those who win an honor for their work are deemed as having journalistic quality. Their recognition could help offset "quality uncertainty" (Wellbrock and Wolfgram 2021, p. 2532). When news consumers are not able to assess the quality of a news product, quality signals can enhance the product's attributes and assist the consumer to determine whether to buy or use the news product (Kirmani and Rao 2000). Quality signals are actions or items that organizations and individuals use to showcase a product's attributes (Kirmani and Rao 2000).

Wellbrock and Wolfgram (2021) posit that journalism awards are quality signals that can increase consumer demand for quality journalism. Signals can build trust (Schnoor 2000). For awards and certificates to become trustworthy quality signals, they must be seen as independent, reliable and transparent (Cox 1967). Judges for awards contests often are editors and reporters from several diverse news organizations. Judges and other award juries act as expert influencers who increase the effectiveness of awards in terms of signaling quality (Gemser, Leenders, and Wijnberg 2008), likely being more effective in judging news quality more than consumers could do. However, while journalists can hope to earn recognition for their news reports, an award should not be a reason whether a business news story is pursued. "Are we doing a certain business news story for the award or are we doing this to make society more transparent?" asked Dubroff (2023). Consumers also rely heavily on the signal that is most relevant in determining the product quality (Dawar and Parker 1994). Journalism awards tend to be the necessary quality signals, but the signal effect is also dependent on the legitimacy of the award.

## Legitimacy of Awards

The legitimacy of industry-sponsored journalism awards contests should not be questioned unfairly. However, identifying a group's motive might help to pinpoint the degree to which an organization is using an awards contest to enhance its image and reputation. An organization not affiliated with journalism that sponsors a journalism awards contest could use the awards as a public relations tactic – that is, to reward stories favorable to a cause rather than showcase journalistic excellence in a beat or subject such as business journalism.

Industry-sponsored organizations should consider a few factors to enhance and preserve the legitimacy of awards contests that they sponsor or conduct. One is judging structure. Some interest groups that are not in the news business but conduct awards contests might structure the judging by placing their own company personnel on panels or select individuals with little business journalism experience. Another factor is the type of stories that often win. The stories that often are declared winners in industry-sponsored contests are those that offer an analysis of economic trends and noncontroversial business developments. Business misbehaviors or malfeasance sometimes are not regarded as highly among judges. For instance, the Loeb Awards lean toward recognizing entries that advance discussions of public policy to support a position popular with business interests. This does not mean that such news stories should not be published or broadcast, but the question, rather, is whether an award should be given.

The reputation of an awards contest also should be considered when discussing legitimacy. Awards from a contest victory can improve a publication's reputation immediately.

However, not winning awards could damage a news organization's profile (Shepard 2000). Further, awards contests can motivate newspapers to do meaningful projects, encouraging reporters to plan and pursue business news stories that they might not have considered. Some business news projects might be carried out with awards in mind, but winning awards could support a case for additional resources (Shepard 2000).

A final dimension that deserves attention in journalism award culture regarding legitimacy is when the media gives awards as part of a branding strategy to attract advertisers and build audience appeal. These awards include "Best in Community" honors that recognize businesses voted on by readers or viewers. The news organization might publish a special section that contains feature news stories about the winners and allots space for the award recipients to purchase advertising space so that they may place messages of gratitude to those who voted them the best in their respective fields or sectors.

## Recommendations for Practice

Business journalism awards as quality signals are critical to organizations, regardless of their affiliation with journalism. However, organizations that are not affiliated as business news outlets and sponsor awards should be encouraged to re-evaluate how awards are determined and presented. As journalism advances in the open spaces brought on by the digital era, consumers will have more liberty to choose news products that resonate with them, and they could have stronger voices in shaping news content and editorial directions. To respond to this, an idea is to design a judging process similar to what the Pictures of the Year International and the Best of Photojournalism contests practice. Their judging process is open to the public and available online. This gives a rare opportunity for the public to observe the deliberation as judges select the winning entries (Lough 2021).

An organization that participates in journalism awards contests in some way might consider preserving the effects of the award beyond the contest. The awards, already quality signals, can be connected with other quality signals, such as marketing and advertising campaigns, to attract additional news consumers or build a stronger relationship with an existing consumer base.

## Future Directions

Journalism awards possess power that translates to social influence and economic value, but these dimensions can vary in different social contexts (Bourdieu 1983; English 2005). In addition, how business journalism is shaped by the awards culture deserves greater exploration. Therefore, a specific research focus on the impact of business journalism awards on journalists and news organizations is encouraged. Studies could extend the research of these awards by examining the intersection between journalism and the socio-political institutions in which they function (Volz 2013). Interviews with business journalists and judges could be conducted for content analysis, or field research during the judging process could be planned to study the processes of awards contests.

In addition, scholarship could rely on diverse research methods to examine the complete process of business journalism awards. For instance, interviews of award winners could be collected to identify the how the honors enhanced their professional reputation in journalism. Ethnographic studies could focus on how contest rules are established and how judges are selected. A content analysis of winning entries in business could highlight observations in story structure or other journalistic standards. These ideas are among numerous others that could elevate understanding of the relationship that business journalism awards have in relation to the economic forces in a business community and to a journalistic legitimacy that business reporters have with their audience.

Business journalism awards contests should be competitive, and reporters and news outlets deserve to be recognized for the business news they disseminate. However, until the exploration on business journalism awards deepens, news organizations and business reporters should weigh their decision to enter an awards contest according to the capital – economic, symbolic, or cultural – that a business journalism award could bring. In addition, an award's quality signal could position the business reporter or the organization in a positive manner, but the legitimacy of awards contests should also be considered to determine the degree of award quality.

## Further Reading

English, J. (2005) *The Economy of Prestige: Prizes, Awards, and the Circulation of Cultural Values.* Cambridge, MA: Harvard University Press.

## References

Akerlof, G. A. (1970) "The market for 'lemons': Quality uncertainty and the market mechanism." *The Quarterly Journal of Economics* 84(3), pp. 488–500.

Beam, R. A., S. Dunwoody and G. M. Kosicki (1986) "The relationship of prize-winning to prestige and job satisfaction." *Journalism Quarterly* 63(4), pp. 693–699.

Bloom, P. N. and T. Reve (1990) "Transmitting signals to consumers for competitive advantage." *Business Horizons* 33(4), pp. 58–66.

Bourideu, P. (1983) *The Field of Cultural Production.* New York: Columbia University Press.

Coulson, D. C. (1989) "Editors' attitudes and behavior toward journalism awards." *Journalism Quarterly* 66(1), pp. 143–147.

Cox, D. D. (1967) "The sorting rule model of the consumer product evaluation process." In: Cox D. F. (ed.) *Risk Taking and Information Handling in Consumer Behavior.* Boston, MA: Division of Research, Graduate School of Business Administration, Harvard University, pp. 324–369.

Dawar, N. and P. Parker (1994) "Marketing universals: Consumers' use of brand name, physical appearance, and retailer reputation as signals of product quality." *Journal of Marketing* 58(2), pp. 81–95.

Donald W. Reynolds National Center for Business Journalism. (n.d.) *A Stellar Track Record: Barlett & Steele Awards.* Available at https://businessjournalism.org/barlettandsteeleawards.

Dubroff, H. (2023) Interview by Melony Shemberger [telephone], 12 January.

English, J. (2005) *The Economy of Prestige: Prizes, Awards, and the Circulation of Cultural Values.* Cambridge, MA: Harvard University Press.

Frey, B. S. and S. Neckermann (2010) Awards as signals. CESifo Working Paper Series, Working paper No. 3229. Munich: CESifo.

Gallus, J. and B. S. Frey (2017) "Awards as strategic signals." *Journal of Management Inquiry* 26(1), pp. 76–85.

Gemser, G., M. A. A. M. Leenders and N. M. Wijnberg (2008) "Why some awards are more effective signals of quality than others: A study of movie awards." *Journal of Management* 34(1), pp. 25–54.

Heinich, N. (2009) "The sociology of vocational prizes: Recognition as esteem." *Theory, Culture & Society* 26, pp. 86–107.

Jenkins, J. and Y. Volz (2018) "Players and contestation mechanisms in the journalism field: A historical analysis of journalism awards, 1960s to 2000s." *Journalism Studies* 19(7), pp. 921–941.

Kirmani, A. and A. R. Rao (2000) "No pain, no gain: A critical review of the literature on signaling unobservable product quality." *Journal of Marketing* 65(2), pp. 66–79.

Lanosga, G. (2015) "The power of the prize: How an emerging prize culture helped shape journalistic practice and professionalism, 1917–1960." *Journalism* 16(7), pp. 953–967.

Lough, K. (2021) "Judging photojournalism: The metajournalistic discourse of judges at the Best of Photojournalism and Pictures of the Year contests." *Journalism Studies* 22(3), pp. 305–321.

New York State Society of CPAs. (n.d.) *Excellence in Financial Journalism Awards.* Available at https://nysscpa.secure-platform.com/a

Schnoor A. (2000) *Kundenorientiertes Qualitäts-Signaling: Eine Übertragung auf Signaling in Produkt-Vorankündigungen.* Wiesbaden: Deutscher Universitätsverlag.

Shepard, A. C. (2000) "Journalism's prize culture." *American Journalism Review* 22(3), pp. 22–31.

Siapera, E. (2012) *Understanding New Media.* Los Angeles, CA: Sage.

Society for Advancing Business Editing and Writing (n.d.) *Awards.* Available at https://sabew.org/contestsawards/

Tuchman, G. (1978) "Professionalism as an agent of legitimation." *Journal of Communication* 28, pp. 106–113.

Volz, Y. (2013) "Journalism awards as a site of contention in the field of journalism." *Chinese Journal of Communication* 6(4), pp. 391–396. Doi: 10.1080/17544750.2013.854820

Wellbrock, C-W. and M. Wolfgram (2021) "Effects of journalism awards as quality signals on demand." *Journalism* 22(10), pp. 2531–2547.

Welles, C. (1979) "Business journalism's glittering prizes." *Columbia Journalism Review* 17(6), pp. 43–45.

Willig, I. (2013) "Newsroom ethnography in a field perspective." *Journalism: Theory, Practice & Criticism* 14(3), pp. 372–387.

# 23

# BUSINESS JOURNALISM AND PUBLIC RELATIONS

## A Delicate Dance

*Hai L. Tran and Matthew W. Ragas*

### Introduction

Some things rarely change. Journalists mutter that public relations people are "flacks." PR professionals grumble reporters are "hacks." While the relationship between journalism and public relations is strained at times, the reality is that – more often than not – they need each other as part of their respective roles and routines (Supa 2014; Zoch and Molleda 2006). According to survey data, 60 percent of journalists describe their relationship with PR professionals as mutually beneficial and 8 percent go further to call it a partnership (Muck Rack 2022).

In a groundbreaking 1979 study of elite media and news production, Herbert Gans concluded that "the relationship between sources and journalists resembles a dance, for sources seek access to journalists and journalists seek access to sources" (Gans 1979, p. 116). Sometimes, sources lead, and other times journalists lead, but it "takes two to tango." To wit, PR professionals often serve as spokespeople, providing official information to journalists, and gatekeepers, granting access (or not) to senior executives for interviews. In turn, while digital media platforms provide new options for companies to take their messages directly to the public, businesses still seek the visibility and credibility that media coverage provides (Kleinnijenhuis et al. 2015). Consequently, effective media relations remain an essential component in corporate reputations (Kleinnijenhuis 2015).

Each day, a delicate dance takes place between business journalists and their sources, including corporate communication professionals (Kerrigan 2020; Roush 2016, 2022). As such, there is practical and societal value in business journalists and corporate communication professionals understanding the dance moves of each other and developing more mutually beneficial, symbiotic relationships (Callison and Seltzer 2010; Nothhaft et al. 2020; Zoch and Supa 2014).

The authors of this chapter have spent the past decade studying the inner workings of the business news ecosystem, including agenda-building influences and the source-journalist relationship (Ragas and Tran 2015, 2019; Tran and Ragas 2018). Pulling data from a series of national surveys of business journalists conducted over the years, we offer insight into the role of media relations and corporate communication efforts in shaping business news

 DOI: 10.4324/9781003298977-28

coverage. Furthermore, drawing from the opinions of surveyed journalists, we provide specific recommendations on how to improve the quality of media relations in the business beat. With seismic shifts in stakeholder expectations around business and society underway (Business Roundtable 2019; Fink 2022), PR professionals and business journalists would be well served to learn to "dance" better together.

## Literature Review

### *Agenda-Building Theory and Story Idea Generation*

The accumulation of empirical evidence over 50-plus years of agenda-setting research has demonstrated that the patterns of media coverage can influence public opinion (McCombs and Shaw 1972; Perloff 2022). As a corollary, researchers have also analyzed the drivers of the media agenda, including the strategic efforts by public relations and advertising to shape the news. This is called agenda building, which is defined as "the overall process of creating mass media agendas" (Berkowitz and Adams 1990, p. 723).

While agenda-setting and agenda-building theories have their roots in political communication and public affairs (McCombs and Valenzuela 2021), scholars have also documented these processes and effects in the context of corporate communication. An extensive literature review of agenda-setting scholarship within the corporate sphere concludes that media coverage has at least a modest agenda-setting influence on both what the public thinks about and how the public thinks about financial matters. In some cases, findings suggest that the business news agenda may even impact "what the public thinks – and does" (Ragas 2014, p. 274). So far, most agenda-building scholarship has focused on the volume, valence and/ or content of media coverage. Meanwhile, news stories are a tangible output of the news production process, which uses inputs such as source-journalist interactions, journalistic news values, and cross-checking elite media outlets to inform editorial decisions. Story ideas, in particular, do not come out of thin air. Thus, understanding the resources that journalists utilize for story ideas is important. In our view, "the reliance on resources for story ideas, the first step of news production, can be defined as formative agenda building" (Ragas and Tran 2019, p. 4468).

### *Source Influence through Public Relations*

Journalism scholars agree that news content is shaped by a range of resources, sometimes described as a hierarchy of influences (Reese and Shoemaker 2016). Pioneering agenda-setting scholar Max McCombs (1992) has used the metaphor of a multi-layer onion to explain the interconnected forces that help shape news coverage. At the core of the onion is the media agenda. Peeling the layers of the onion reveals the following: (1) the interactions by journalists with external news sources, such as public relations and corporate communication professionals and the information they provide; (2) the interactions and influences of journalists inside and outside the newsroom on each other; and (3) the professional norms and routines taught in journalism school and codified on the beat.

Existing research has demonstrated how pre-packaged public relations materials, known as information subsidies (Gandy 1982), successfully lowered the cost and time of news gathering by journalists (McCombs and Valenzuela 2021). Companies spend millions of dollars each year on corporate communication departments and public relations agencies crafting news releases, briefing documents and other materials. Approximately, from 25 percent to as much as 80 percent of news content is initiated by PR sources, such as corporations and government agencies, and the subsidies they produce (Neill et al. 2018).

The flack-to-hack ratio in recent years would seem to favor even greater corporate influence, as employment data show a rise in the number of PR professionals and a decline in the size of newsroom staffs (Walker 2021). According to the U.S. Census Bureau, there were 6.4 PR people for every journalist in 2018 compared to 1.9× just 20 years ago (Tanzi and Hagan 2019). As summed up by Chris Roush, "the battle between PR and business journalism is being won lately by a rise in public relations staffers, making them more common than the reporters who cover the companies they represent" (Roush 2022, p. 53).

## Source Credibility

Journalists consult a range of information resources for story idea generation (Len-Ríos et al. 2009). The actual resources used at this early stage of reporting may include news trends and subjects highlighted by elite media, tips from the audience, trending topics in social media, PR pitches, or new releases distributed by various entities. Financial news people often rely on numerous sources for news gathering, including other journalists, government and nongovernmental officials, academic experts, and corporate spokespeople, ranging from PR professionals to senior executives (Roush 2016).

Meanwhile, journalistic norms dictate that reporters seek out sources they deem credible (Reese and Shoemaker 2016). Credible communicators are perceived as having expertise and trustworthiness, and as displaying goodwill (Perloff 2020). There is often a healthy skepticism by reporters toward information provided by PR people (Supa 2014). Consequently, in the business beat, perceived credibility of a source can influence journalists' usage of source-provided resources (Ragas and Tran 2019).

## Journalists' Characteristics and Perceptual Variations

Journalism studies find that individual-level factors (traits, roles, demographics) could lead to perceptual variations among journalists, even within the same beat (Willnat et al. 2017). According to the hierarchy of influences model, "in spite of the traditional notion of professional 'objective' detachment, we assume these characteristics affect [journalists'] work" (Reese and Shoemaker 2016, p. 398). This proposition has been tested within the business news beat. The demographics of business journalists and their professional backgrounds have been found to contribute to some perceptual variations within this group (Ragas and Tran 2015).

## Mutually Beneficial Relationships

Much of modern public relations and strategic communication theory is based upon the importance of establishing and maintaining mutually beneficial relationships with key stakeholders, including the news media (Nothhaft et al. 2020). Leading public relations associations also embrace this perspective. The Public Relations Society of America (PRSA 2022) defines public relations as a strategic communication process that builds mutually beneficial relationships between organizations and their publics. The Arthur W. Page Society, a global organization for senior communication leaders, implores its members to tell the truth with honest and good intention as the first principle for the effective practice of public relations.

Unfortunately, PR professionals are viewed by some as "spinmeisters" because they do not always tell the truth (Zoch and Molleda 2006). In an era of social and digital media-driven transparency, those who traffic in "half-truths" and "alternative facts" are doing a disservice to themselves, their clients, and to the reputations of their colleagues and to the field (Kleinnijenhuis 2015; Roush 2022). Such behavior is "bad business" because the misdeeds of these unscrupulous individuals will eventually be found out by enterprising stakeholders, such as activist groups, as well as by investigative journalists. Media relations scholars and experts recommend that communication professionals build mutually beneficial relationships with journalists through responsiveness, accessibility, and professionalism grounded in ethical behaviors (Callison and Seltzer 2010; Supa 2014; Zoch and Supa 2014).

In summary, the extant literature stimulates intriguing questions regarding usage and perception of public relations in business journalism.

- How do business journalists leverage public relations vs. other resources for story ideas?
- How do business journalists perceive the credibility of public relations vs. other sources?
- Which individual characteristics influence business journalists' usage and perception of public relations?
- What is the relationship between credibility perception and usage of public relations, controlling for individual differences?
- What should PR professionals do to improve media relationships?

## Research Method

To address these questions, we employed a programmatic research design in surveying journalists who covered business news in the United States. Spanning five years (2011 through 2015), this project comprised three online surveys, each of which was built on the preceding one to ensure continuity and allow for incremental exploration. We utilized the Gorkana Media Database, a Cision product, as the sampling frame to recruit participants who were listed as business journalists. Each data collection period involved a four-week window with an initial invitation and at least three waves of reminder e-mails. This process resulted in a study sample of 1,265 reporters/writers, columnists, editors, and producers/news directors responsible for covering financial news.

### *Variables*

#### *Use of Resources*

Surveyed journalists were asked how often they used nine different resources for story ideas: personal interest or that of someone on staff; readers/viewers/listeners' e-mails or phone calls; newspapers or other publications; a PR person who pitches a story; corporate news releases; corporate social media; news releases from nonprofit organizations; university news releases; government news releases (Len-Ríos et al. 2009). Responses were recorded on a seven-point scale with 1 being "not at all" and 7 being "very often."

#### *Source Credibility*

Journalists were asked how credible information about a company would be if they heard it from five different types of sources: a news professional, a PR professional, a representative of a nongovernmental organization (NGO), an academic expert, and a government official (Edelman 2021). The response scale ranged between 1 (not at all credible) and 5 (extremely credible).

## Media Relationships

Expanding on 2013 open-ended responses, the 2015 survey sought to quantify journalists' feedback on strategies for better media relationships. Respondents were prompted to indicate the extent to which these six statements accurately described what PR professionals should do: always tell the truth; be more responsive; provide greater access; pitch ideas that are newsworthy and leverage news trends; develop a better understanding of the beats of the journalists, their publications, and audiences; and gain a better understanding of the subject, company, industry they represent. Response options varied from 1 (not at all) to 7 (very much).

## Individual Differences

Journalists differ some in their professional backgrounds and demographics. Professional backgrounds were defined by experience (years of work); editorial rank (junior, senior); newsroom size (six-point scale with 1 being "fewer than 10 reporters/editors" and 6 representing "more than 50 reporters/editors"); news platform (traditional, online); and work location (Northeast, other). Demographics comprised race (white, non-white); gender (female, male); and age (in years).

## Results

### Use of Resources for Stories

We sought evidence of formative agenda building by asking how frequently business journalists used a range of resources for story ideas. A one-way analysis of variance (repeated measures ANOVA) found significant differences in how journalists leveraged those resources (see Table 23.1). Specifically, they relied most heavily on other news media and personal interest or that of someone on staff in this initial stage of reporting. To a lesser degree, they utilized corporate news releases, government news releases, and tips from the news audience. PR

*Table 23.1* Frequent use of resources for story ideas

| Resources | Average usage (seven-point scale) |
| --- | --- |
| Newspapers or other publications | 5.05 |
| Personal interest or that of someone on staff | 4.48 |
| Corporate news releases | 4.06 |
| Government news releases | 3.98 |
| Readers/viewers/listeners' e-mails or phone calls | 3.76 |
| A public relations person who pitches a story | 3.20 |
| News releases from nonprofit organizations | 3.16 |
| University news releases | 2.67 |
| Corporate social media | 2.65 |

professionals who pitch stories and news releases from nonprofit organizations were cultivated less frequently. Respondents rarely acted on university news releases, and they were least
likely to tap into corporate social media. Overall, business journalists found various PR efforts
(except for corporate and government news releases) less useful in generating story ideas.

### Perceived Credibility of Sources

We examined how business journalists rated the credibility of different sources of information. According to a one-way repeated measures ANOVA, credibility perception varied
significantly as a function of source type. On a five-point scale, business journalists ranked
academic experts highest on credibility (3.51), followed by fellow news professionals (3.19),
government officials (3.09), and NGO representatives (2.83). It is noteworthy that PR practitioners were considered the least credible sources (2.60).

Probing further, we found source credibility varied as a function of respondent characteristics as well. Multiple regression analysis showed the significant impact of certain demographic and work-related variables (i.e., age, race, gender, experience, editorial rank,
newsroom size). Essentially, white and senior journalists were more skeptical than their minority colleagues were toward PR professionals. Younger and junior journalists ranked government officials higher on credibility. Participants with less experience were more positive
about the credibility of other news professionals. Male journalists and those who worked
in smaller newsrooms were more likely than their female counterparts to perceive academic
experts as credible sources.

### Individual Differences in the Usage of Public Relations

Looking more closely, we noted variations in the way individual journalists cultivated PR
resources for story ideas. An exploratory factor analysis identified two distinct types of
public relations used by journalists when searching for news topics: corporate PR efforts
(i.e., corporate news releases, public relations professionals who pitch stories, corporate
social media); and non-corporate PR efforts (i.e., news releases from government, nonprofit organizations, and universities). Subsequently, we employed regression analysis
to explore whether individual differences, such as demographics and professional backgrounds, helped explain journalists' reliance on corporate and non-corporate PR efforts for
story ideas. According to the results, age, experience, newsroom size, and work location
were significant predictors. Specifically, younger journalists were more willing to rely on
corporate PR materials, whereas experienced colleagues were much more reluctant to do
so. Older, seasoned journalists and those who operated in smaller newsrooms and away
from the Northeastern financial hub were more attentive to non-corporate PR resources
in finding stories.

### Source Credibility and Usage of Public Relations

These findings imply a three-way relationship among source credibility, respondent profile,
and use of public relations in story idea generation. Therefore, we zoomed in on the unique
contribution of source credibility to formative agenda building by running two regression
models with a selection of corporate and non-corporate PR efforts being dependent variables.

Individual differences (race, gender, age, experience, editorial rank, newsroom size) served as control variables. Credibility perceptions were independent variables.

In the first model, credibility perception of PR professionals explained journalists' reliance on corporate public relations for story ideas. Those who were more likely to rate PR officers as credible sources were also more receptive to using corporate public relations in searching for news topics. Age was a significant contributor with younger journalists using corporate public relations more frequently.

In the second model, perceived credibility for academic experts, government officials, and NGO representatives were significant predictors. The greater credibility of these sources induced greater use of non-corporate public relations. In terms of individual differences, staff size was a contributing factor with heavier reliance on non-corporate PR materials in smaller newsrooms.

### *Improving Media Relationships*

To gain insight into the usage and perception of public relations, we solicited quantitative and qualitative feedback from business journalists regarding ways PR practitioners can enhance media relationships. Based on an analysis of open-ended responses provided by 167 journalists participating in the 2013 survey, we identified the following distinct themes: truth telling; responsiveness; better access; improved knowledge of journalists' beats and audiences; greater knowledge of company/industry; and pitching newsworthy stories and leveraging news trends.

Subsequently, we attempted to quantify journalists' input for better media relationships in order of importance. In the 2015 survey, respondents were asked to use a seven-point scale to rate each of the six strategies PR people should apply to enhance relationships with business journalists. Of 422 participants, 254 provided quantitative responses for analysis. Most respondents highly valued truth telling (90 percent) and better understanding of the beats of the journalists, their publications, and audiences (88 percent). They also emphasized the need for PR professionals to develop greater knowledge of the companies and industries they represent (84 percent) and to provide better access for journalists (83 percent). About 76 percent of respondents agreed on the importance of pitching newsworthy ideas and trending news topics; and 71 percent expected responsiveness. As shown in Table 23.2, the average scores assigned to all six strategies for effective media relationships were on the higher end of the scale.

*Table 23.2* Strategies for improving media relationships

| *Strategies* | *Average score (seven-point scale)* |
| --- | --- |
| Always tell the truth | 6.36 |
| Develop a better understanding of the beats of the journalists, their publications, and audiences | 6.25 |
| Develop greater knowledge of the subjects, companies, industries they (PR professionals) represent | 5.98 |
| Provide better access | 5.96 |
| Pitch ideas that are newsworthy and leverage news trends | 5.64 |
| Be more responsive | 5.44 |

## Discussion

The results reported here come from one of the first empirical studies that employed theory-guided, programmatic research design to examine the dynamic between business journalism and public relations. Not only do our findings help confirm anecdotal observations in the financial news beat, but they also provide new important insights, which are very much reflective of current trends in the broader journalism context. Here are some key takeaways:

First, business journalists must leverage numerous resources for story ideas. Although corporate and government press releases proved useful, PR professionals and corporate social media managers have much to compete with in getting the attention of reporters. This finding is comparable with more recent data in the larger journalism field, demonstrating journalists' greater liking for briefing documents/news announcements over PR people with irrelevant, poorly timed pitches (Cision 2022; Muck Rack 2022). Notably, corporate social media seemed much less effective to business journalism in our study as compared to the more current Muck Rack State of Journalism survey (2022), which stated that 60 percent of surveyed journalists consult a company's social media in their reporting. This divergence might be because our data were collected from a different sampling frame (financial news beat vs. entire news ecology) and/or before the COVID-19 pandemic, which has dramatically altered reporting practices ever since. In addition, companies in recent years have relied more on social media to push news announcements/statements, prompting journalists to consult social media feeds more regularly to keep up with late breaking developments.

Second, despite the symbiosis between business journalism and public relations, it is evident that PR practitioners have a long way to go in fostering a mutually beneficial partnership grounded in trust. According to our findings, business journalists ranked PR people lowest on source credibility, while rating academic experts the most credible sources. This trust perception (or the lack thereof) is further confirmed by survey data in the broader journalism context (Muck Rack 2022).

Another important insight gleaned from our study indicates that individual journalists held different views toward public relations and cultivated different types of PR in certain ways. Junior and non-white journalists were somewhat less skeptical of PR pros. Younger reporters were more open to corporate PR materials, while their older, more experienced colleagues, and those reporting for smaller newsrooms and away from the Northeastern region, were more receptive to non-corporate PR resources. These results should prompt PR practitioners to think through their outreach approach, starting with getting to better know the journalists they are pitching (Cision 2022).

Additionally, we found nuances in how business journalism responds to public relations. Media relationships are built upon trust. Greater credibility of PR sources as perceived by financial journalists, particularly younger ones, increased reliance on corporate public relations for story ideas. Similarly, several reporters – especially those in smaller newsrooms – used non-corporate PR resources more frequently, as they trusted academic experts, government officials, and NGO representatives more. Because media credibility has long been under intense public scrutiny, PR practitioners can be better partners in supporting trustworthy reporting, thereby easing the burden for journalists (Cision 2022).

The aforementioned points to the need for public relations to improve media relationships in the financial beat. Journalists must leverage several resources, having little time to chase down stories. In our study, business journalists' feedback for PR pros predominantly featured references such as "don't lie," "cut the spin," and "keep it honest." Another salient theme emerged from the following comments: "Pitch relevant stories," "research the news outlet BEFORE you pitch" and "learn about the subject areas journalists cover." Business journalists also emphasized to PR people the importance of being "knowledgeable," having "more professional credentials," and "developing expertise in a company or subject area." Moreover, reporters urged PR practitioners to be "more responsive" and to provide "open and unimpeded access" to sources. Finally, financial journalists looked for pitches with "a good angle or timely hook," such as those that are "based on trends or bigger picture events rather than mere corporate self-serving angles." Overall, our qualitative and quantitative data mirror results drawn from a larger sample of journalists across news beats (Cision 2022).

## *Practical Implications*

The findings from this study send a clear message to public relations and corporate communication professionals. Journalists want to work with communicators who traffic in the truth. There must be stronger consequences from both employers and professional associations for those who act deceptively and unethically. Having a code of ethics is good, but not strongly enforcing such a code gives a mixed signal.

Business journalists also cite the importance of PR people developing a better understanding of the beats of journalists, their publications, and their audiences. Public relations and strategic communication programs should consider requiring a media relations course as part of the curriculum. Further, PR agencies and in-house communication departments should bring in current and former journalists as part of internal training/professional development regarding media relations. Many junior and even mid-level PR practitioners do not have journalism backgrounds and would benefit from understanding newsroom norms, cultures and "how the sausage gets made."

The surveyed journalists emphasized the need for PR people to develop greater knowledge of the companies and industries they represent. Recent years have seen the PR and communication profession place a greater focus on improving the business literacy of the field, but there is still much work to be done. Many PR practitioners do not hold business degrees and must learn about the world of business on the job (Ragas and Culp 2021). Teaching young PR professionals to pitch effectively is crucial but teaching them more about the inner workings of the organizations and industries they represent is equally important.

By the same token, business journalists have room for improvement in working with communication professionals. Many PR pros are avid news consumers and some come from journalism backgrounds (Kerrigan 2020). While journalists often operate in the public interest, communicators typically advocate for the organizations and clients they represent. This does not necessarily mean that PR people come with nefarious intent, but that they approach the news from a different vantagepoint. Every PR practitioner has a story of feeling burned by a journalist on a story. The grumbling is mutual.

## *Limitations and Future Research*

As with any study, there are limitations to our findings and the implications that can be drawn from them. These drawbacks provide pathways for future exploration. While the analyzed survey data set is the largest and most detailed of its kind, it was collected before the pandemic. Journalism and public relations practices may have shifted some since then, including greater usage of corporate social and digital media resources. Further, to provide a more complete picture of the corporate source-journalist relationship, a corresponding survey of PR practitioners about working with business journalists would be valuable. While the United States is the world's largest economy, surveys of business journalists and corporate communicators in other top economies would provide for cross-border comparisons. Finally, qualitative research, including focus groups, in-depth interviews, and ethnographies of journalists and corporate communicators, may yield rich insights that online surveys may not capture.

## Conclusion

The pairing of a journalist and a PR professional may never win "Dancing with the Stars." But this "delicate dance" can certainly be improved by each side learning more about the needs, expectations and moves of their partner (and the layout of the dance floor). It is hoped that this chapter contributes to improved media relations, including greater mutual respect in the journalist-PR relationship. Then, maybe somewhere, hacks and flacks will step less on the toes of each other when they hit the dance floor.

## References

Arthur W. Page Society (2022) *The Page Principles, Page.org.* < https://page.org/site/the-page-principles> (accessed: July 27, 2022).

Berkowitz, D. and Adams, D. B. (1990) "Information Subsidy and Agenda-Building in Local Television News," *Journalism Quarterly*, 67(4), pp. 723–731.

Business Roundtable. (2019) *Statement on the Purpose of a Corporation*. Washington, DC: Business Roundtable.

Callison, C. and Seltzer, T. (2010) "Influence of Responsiveness, Accessibility, and Professionalism on Journalists' Perceptions of Southwest Airlines Public Relations," *Public Relations Review*, 36(2), pp. 141–146.

Cision. (2022) *2021 Global State of the Media Report, Cision.* <https://www.cision.com/resources/research-reports/2021-state-of-the-media> (accessed: July 27, 2022).

Edelman. (2021) *2021 Edelman Trust Barometer, Edelman.* <https://www.edelman.com/trust/2021-trust-barometer> (accessed: July 27, 2022).

Fink, L. (2022) *Larry Fink's Annual 2022 Letter to CEOs: The Power of Capitalism, BlackRock.* <https://www.blackrock.com/corporate/investor-relations/larry-fink-ceo-letter> (accessed: July 27, 2022).

Gandy, O. (1982) *Beyond Agenda-Setting: Information Subsidies and Public Policy*. Norwood, NJ: Ablex.

Gans, H. J. (1979) *Deciding What's News*. New York: Patheon.

Kerrigan, K. (2020) *Our Future in Public Relations: A Cautionary Tale in Three Parts*. Bingley: Emerald Publishing.

Kleinnijenhuis, J. (2015) "Public Relations: Media Influence," in Donsbach, W. (ed.) *The Concise Encyclopedia of Communication*. Malden, MA: Wiley Blackwell, p. 507.

Kleinnijenhuis, J. *et al.* (2015) "The Mediating Role of the News in the BP Oil Spill Crisis 2010: How U.S. News Is Influenced by Public Relations and in Turn Influences Public Awareness, Foreign News, and the Share Price," *Communication Research*, 42(3), pp. 408–428.

Len-Ríos, M. E. *et al.* (2009) "Health News Agenda Building: Journalists' Perceptions of the Role of Public Relations," *Journalism & Mass Communication Quarterly*, 86(2), pp. 315–331.

McCombs, M. E. (1992) "Explorers and Surveyors: Expanding Strategies for Agenda-Setting Research," *Journalism Quarterly*, 69(4), pp. 813–824.

McCombs, M. E. and Shaw, D. L. (1972) "The Agenda-Setting Function of Mass Media," *Public Opinion Quarterly*, 36(2), p. 176. Doi: 10.1086/267990.

McCombs, M. and Valenzuela, S. (2021) *Setting the Agenda*. 3rd ed. Cambridge, England: Polity Press.

Muck Rack (2022) *The State of Journalism 2022, Muckrack*. <https://f.hubspotusercontent40.net/hubfs/4272994/State%20of%20Journalism%202022/State%20of%20Journalism%202022_.pdf> (accessed: July 27, 2022).

Neill, J. *et al.* (2018) "The Dash for Gas: Examining Third-Level Agenda-Building and Fracking in the United Kingdom," *Journalism Studies*, 19(2), pp. 182–208.

Nothhaft, H. *et al.* (eds.) (2020) *Future Directions of Strategic Communication*. New York: Routledge.

Perloff, R. M. (2020) *The Dynamics of Persuasion: Communication and Attitudes in the Twenty-First Century*. 7th ed. New York: Routledge.

Perloff, R. M. (2022) "The Fifty-Year Legacy of Agenda-Setting: Storied Past, Complex Conundrums, Future Possibilities," *Mass Communication & Society*, 25(4), pp. 469–499.

Public Relations Society of America (2022) *Learn about Public Relations, PRSA*. <https://www.prsa.org/prssa/about-prssa/learn-about-pr> (accessed: July 27, 2022).

Ragas, M. W. (2014) "Agenda-Setting in the Corporate Sphere: Synthesizing Findings and Identifying New Opportunities in this Growing Domain," in Johnson, T. (ed.) *Agenda Setting in a 2.0 World: A Tribute to Maxwell McCombs*. New York: Routledge, pp. 256–280.

Ragas, M. W. and Culp, R. (2021) *Business Acumen for Strategic Communicators: A Primer*. Bingley: Emerald Publishing.

Ragas, M. W. and Tran, H. L. (2015) "The Financial News Ecosystem: Journalists' Perceptions of Group Hierarchy," *Journalism: : Theory, Practice, and Criticism*, 16(6), pp. 711–729.

Ragas, M. W. and Tran, H. L. (2019) "Peeling Back the Onion: Formative Agenda Building in Business Journalism," *International Journal of Communication*, 13, pp. 4465–4486.

Reese, S. D. and Shoemaker, P. J. (2016) "A Media Sociology for the Networked Public Sphere: The Hierarchy of Influences Model," *Mass Communication & Society*, 19(4), pp. 389–410.

Roush, C. (2016) *Show Me the Money: Writing Business and Economics Stories for Mass Communication*. 3rd ed. New York: Routledge.

Roush, C. (2022) *The Future of Business Journalism: Why It Matters for Wall Street and Main Street*. Washington, DC: Georgetown University Press.

Supa, D. W. (2014) "The Academic Inquiry of Media Relations as Both a Tactical and Strategic Function of Public Relations," *Research Journal of the Institute for Public Relations*, 1(1), pp. 1–15.

Tanzi, A. and Hagan, S. (2019) "Public Relations Jobs Boom as Buffett Sees Newspapers Dying," *Bloomberg*, 27 April. <https://www.bloomberg.com/news/articles/2019-04-27/public-relations-jobs-boom-as-buffett-sees-newspapers-dying#xj4y7vzkg> (accessed: July 27, 2022).

Tran, H. L. and Ragas, M. W. (2018) "Peer Perceptions of Media Elites and Hierarchical Differentiation among Financial Journalists," *Journalism & Mass Communication Quarterly*, 95(1), pp. 258–277.

Walker, M. (2021) *U.S. Newsroom Employment Has Fallen 26% since 2008*, Pew Research Center. < https://pewrsr.ch/3ujBDCi> (accessed: July 27, 2022).

Willnat, L., Weaver, D. H. and Wilhoit, G. C. (2017) *The American Journalist in the Digital Age: A Half-Century Perspective*. New York: Peter Lang.

Zoch, L. M. and Molleda, J. C. (2006) "Building a Theoretical Model of Media Relations Using Framing, Information Subsidies, and Agenda Building," in Botan, C. H. and Hazelton, V. (eds.) *Public Relations Theory II*. Mahwah, NJ: Lawrence Erlbaum, pp. 279–309.

Zoch, L. M. and Supa, D. W. (2014) "Dictating the News: Understanding Newsworthiness from the Journalistic Perspective," *Public Relations Journal*, 8(1), pp. 1–28.

# 24

# BOOSTERISM

## A Test of Commitment

*Dan Trigoboff*

### Introduction

From sports comes the adage "no cheering in the press box." It means, said Mark Gonzales of the Chicago Tribune, "you're strictly objective, with no emotion attached to the outcome" (Linden 2015).

Another Chicago sportswriter, Jerome Holtzman, used the axiom "No Cheering in the Press Box" as the title for his 1974 compilation of sports writers' recollections. Journalists know that great relationships make great stories and great reporters. But writers interviewed for the book acknowledged protecting the images and privileges of star athletes (Holtzman 1974). Some truths about Babe Ruth's myriad excesses, for instance, are likely better known today than in Ruth's own time. The mistake, sportswriter John Kieran said, "is to become a fan of your own team. That warps your judgment" (Holtzman 1974, p. 42).

The definitions of "booster" – other than "boosting" as stealing or shoplifting – describe increasing, amplifying, thrusting, and supporting, and offer applications in radio-television signals, rocket launches, and medicinal potency.

Business journalism raises questions concerning boosterism, acknowledged and alleged. Are businesses favored because they're local, or part of the specialty community that defines the news organization? Are businesses favored because they advertise? Are sources favored because they're prominent, or because they make themselves available? Is boosterism necessary? Is it ethical?

### Journalism Codes

Historians have noted that prior to the 1830s, newspapers were expected to be partisan, and objectivity has emerged over time as a journalistic value – sometimes controversially (Schudson 1978). In The New York Times' first editorial under the management of Adolph Ochs, in 1896, the new publisher pledged to "give the news impartially, without fear or favor, regardless of party sect, or interest involved."

"But almost from the moment that Adolph's famous phrase had first appeared in the paper, the Times had been misquoting it," journalists Tifft and Jones write in their history

DOI: 10.4324/9781003298977-29

of The New York Times and the Ochs family, "The Trust." Ochs' intention, the authors said, "was to reassure Republicans of the paper's political objectivity." The repeated addition of "any" before "interests" – as well as changing "interest" from singular to plural, they wrote – had the effect of "unwittingly stripping the phrase of its political point and changing the meaning to a more general disavowal of prejudice" (Tift & Jones 1999, pp. XIX–XX).

A "more general disavowal of prejudice" appears in key journalism ethics codes. "Act Independently" is one of four sections in the Society of Professional Journalists' Code of Ethics, which cautions about "real or perceived" conflicts, trading information for favors, favoring "advertisers, donors or any other special interests, and resist[ing] internal and external pressure to influence coverage" (SPJ 2014).

The code for the Society for Advancing Business Editing and Writing (SABEW, which also calls itself the Association for Business Journalists) advises that journalists be independent, avoid financial conflicts, and not "alter information, delay or withhold publication or make concessions relating to news content to any source or subject of the story" (SABEW 2015).

The first sentence of the SPJ section reads: "The highest and primary obligation of ethical journalism is to serve the public" (SPJ 2014). Similarly, the "Statement of Purpose" for SABEW states that "we are guardians of the public trust and must do nothing to abuse this obligation" (SABEW 2015).

Journalism's obligation, says the Radio Television Digital News Association's ethics code, "is to the public. Journalism places the public's interests ahead of commercial, political, and personal interests." Editorial independence, the code says, may seem more ambitious than ever. "Media companies, even if not-for-profit, have commercial, competitive and other interests – from which the journalists they employ cannot be entirely shielded." The code stresses "independence from influences that conflict with public interest" and "transparency," so the public can "assess credibility" and "determine who deserves trust." Commercial endorsements compromise credibility, the code says, as does public political activism. The code cautions that transparency is not enough to justify lowering standards of fairness or truth regarding "sponsor-provided content, commercial concerns or political relationships," nor does disclosure justify excluding important perspectives and information (RTDNA 2015).

The American Society of Business Publication Editors appears to acknowledge – and accommodate – a difference between a general public and the more specific public of a targeted business publication. In the introduction to "B2B Journalist Ethics: An ASBPE Guide To Best Practices," ASBPE says, "Business-to-business (B2B) publications, online and in print, exist to serve their audiences in the specialized fields they cover, while being financially viable businesses themselves" (ASBPE 2013).

While the ASBPE code reserves editorial judgments for editors – including determinations on advertiser-recommended story ideas or leads – it advocates "a productive working relationship with the publisher, and with sales personnel. Under ASBPE's best practices guide, editors "may refer potential advertisers to ad sales staff and consult with ad sales staff on story ideas." Editors may accompany business staff on meetings with advertisers, the guide says, and identify such a visit as an "editorial call." But the agenda should be limited to "industry trends, explaining editorial policy and direction, or describing the readership." Editors should not discuss any advertising matters, the guidelines say, and business staff should avoid ambiguous job titles that might suggest editorial functions (ASBPE 2013).

## Wall Came Tumbling Down?

Writing for the Center for Journalism Ethics at the University of Wisconsin-Madison School of Journalism and Mass Communication, Ira Basen (2012) suggested that the proverbial wall between "church and state," while considered a fundamental principle, was "always far more porous than many journalists cared to admit. From the start, there has been a strong whiff of mythology about the separation between the business office and the newsroom."

The revelation that the Los Angeles Times reached an undisclosed agreement in 1999 to split profits with Los Angeles' Staples Center for a Sunday magazine devoted to the new arena brought national headlines. The deal angered a newsroom already distressed by shrinking editorial resources and by a publisher who "ignited controversy with his bottom-line fixation and desire to 'blow... up' the wall between the paper's business and editorial departments" (Jurkowitz 1999).

But it was not profit, but boosterism that drove the deal for the West Coast's largest newspaper, a leading business magazine concluded. "The Times didn't get into trouble because its executives tried to maximize profits (Splitting ad profits means less money, not more.)," wrote Virginia Postrel in Forbes. "The deal wasn't a profitable business exchange. It was cheerleading for a public showcase." In this case, she said, the showcase was a revitalized downtown L.A. Postrel wrote that urban newspapers typically disfavor "suburban sprawl," and favor downtown rail transit, tax-funded convention centers, and downtown attractions – including sports arenas. Beyond policy, "[b]ecause they own downtown real estate," Postrel wrote, "newspapers often have a financial interest in boosterism" (Postrel 2000).

The controversy led reporter David Shaw to undertake a lengthy investigative report about his own paper. Shaw described the newsroom's reaction to the Staples Center revelations as "turmoil," and "an open revolt." Apologies from top management were forthcoming (Shaw 1999).

## Mad Money, Madder Comedian

Perhaps the most dramatic challenge to financial journalism boosterism came – of all places – on cable network Comedy Central. On March 12, 2009, financial analyst and longtime CNBC personality Jim Cramer faced off with "Daily Show" anchor Jon Stewart, who accused Cramer and other financial journalists of using their expertise to serve traders, bankers, and investors, often at the expense of working people and their pensions.

Cramer had defended himself and his network on his own show, "Mad Money," and on MSNBC's "Morning Joe," and took up Stewart's challenge, leading to the highly anticipated confrontation or, "days of mocking" CNBC (Folkenflik 2009). Stewart met Cramer with video in which Cramer shouted "Bear Stearns is fine...Bear Stearns is not in trouble" less than a week before Bear Stearns went under – followed by similar positive reports from Cramer and others regarding Lehman Brothers, Merrill Lynch, Bank of America, and AIG, all of which encountered severe financial problems, and recommendations to buy just before markets declined rapidly. "If I had only followed CNBC's advice," Stewart said, "I'd have a million dollars today...provided I'd started with a hundred million dollars."

Stewart also belittled CNBC's frequent sit-downs with key executives for perceived softball interviews, citing one with Allen Stanford, subsequently sentenced to 110 years in prison for a 20-year, $7 billion investment fraud scheme (a clip from that interview drew a profane response from Stewart). Stewart accused Cramer and CNBC of abdicating credibility as a news outlet because its hosts, analysts and guests were unchallenged cheerleaders for the financial markets (NPR 2009).

Stewart spoke of a "gap between what CNBC advertises itself as, and what it is." Stewart aired advertisements promoting Cramer as an advocate for his viewers – onscreen. Amid tumultuous times, an advertisement for Cramer's show said, "In Cramer We Trust," and a voiceover promised that "Cramer's Got Your Back." When Stewart aired the video of Cramer, as a hedge fund manager, seemingly using deceptive practices, Cramer responded that he had been "inarticulate," Stewart offered another video that appeared to confirm a questionable practice – even endorsing it. "I want the Jim Cramer on CNBC to protect me from that Jim Cramer," Stewart said, pointing toward the monitor.

Cramer appeared conciliatory, defensive, and evasive, as Stewart accused him and financial reporting colleagues for leaving to regulators to expose financial shenanigans, instead of protecting the public as journalists. Rather than using their expertise to expose deception and hyperbole, Stewart said, financial journalists were "in bed" with the finance community, which wrecked the economy while making short-term profits "financed by our 401Ks." It was, he said, "disingenuous at best and criminal at worst" (Quinn 2009).

Cramer admitted mistakes, and said, "I wish that we had done more," he said, and that he and his colleagues had seen dangerous economic signs earlier. NPR called the show "a blistering critique" and "an attack on CNBC's journalism (NPR 2009). Years later, amid negative financial news, Gawker "credited" Cramer with "modulating" from past practice and its attendant criticism, and "choosing mindless panic over mindless boosterism" (Cook 2011).

Writing in The New Yorker, Hamza Shaban noted Cramer's "hysterical boosterism of the stocks he likes," but added that enthusiasm for well-performing companies "isn't unique in business journalism." Shaban listed numerous objectivity-challenged descriptions of favored companies, including "banking powerhouse," "Super-Hot Machine," and "daring and innovative" (Shaban 2014).

Reviewing Dean Starkman's history of business news, "The Watchdog That Didn't Bark," Shaban discussed boosterism in the context of "access reporting." Starkman's history of financial journalism, Shaban noted, discussed how reporters, "dependent on insider sources to inform an élite audience of investors, practice a kind of journalism that is defined by access." Information based on access from the powerful Shaban said, naturally favors, or boosts, the powerful. "News becomes a guide to investing, more concerned with explaining business strategies to consumers than with examining broader political or social issues to the public. Access reporting is friendly to executives because it relies on their candor" (Shaban 2014).

In his book, Starkman said that access reporting "is the longstanding rival of "accountability reporting" – alternatively known, he said, as investigative reporting, public-service reporting, or public-interest reporting. "Confrontational and accusatory," Starkman wrote, "it provokes the enmity of the rich and powerful as a matter of course. When Theodore Roosevelt dubbed it 'muckraking,' he didn't mean it as a compliment." Accountability journalism is also, Starkman wrote, "risky, stressful, expensive, and difficult." Where access reporting –"journalism's dominant strain" – emphasizes inside information, accountability reporting "seeks to gather information not from but about powerful actors," Starkman said, One way to characterize the difference, Starkman wrote, "is that access reporting tells readers what powerful actors say, while accountability reporters tell readers what they do." In business journalism, access focuses on investor interests; accountability journalism focuses on the public interest (Starkman 2014, pp. 8–12).

## Community Defined by Audience

Al Tompkins, who recently retired from The Poynter Institute for Media Studies where he wrote, lectured, and consulted on media ethics, said in response to an email inquiry:

> I really do not see much pressure for positive coverage so much as pressure not to take on big advertisers when the coverage could be negative. But really it is less about advertisers today than political concepts. And mostly, I think, it is self-imposed censorship rather than overt pressure.

Choi and Park (2011) examined two national and two local newspapers and found that while editors evaluated press releases for news value, they also considered advertiser status. The researchers found that in their sample, local newspapers gave more consideration to advertisers than national newspapers.

Whether defined by geography or by professional or financial interests, journalism that addresses an identifiable community may naturally trend toward boosterism, according to Harry Jessell – who covered the television and radio industries for decades and with whom the author of this chapter has worked. "I think when you step out and say I'm going to cover this community, you become a cheerleader for the community," Jessell said in an interview for this chapter. In local journalism, "even on the editorial page, they're rooting for the city," he said (Jessell 2022).

And in business-to-business journalism? "A trade [publication] is just like a general circulation publication, only more so," Jessell said:

> It's probably more of a booster, probably more susceptible to advertiser influence. Some of the worst aspects of journalism may be more pronounced in trade journalism. You're a decades-long member of this community; you're part of the scene. Being in a trade is like being in a small town; you know everybody. You can't screw somebody and not worry about seeing them in a diner.

Jessell was the longtime reporter, editor, and eventually top editor at Broadcasting & Cable magazine (B&C), and later founded the similarly focused website TVNewscheck.com. Unlike news organizations that target general audiences, Jessell said that business-to-business publications exist to serve, and to a large degree, promote the industries they cover. "Our whole mission was to boost the broadcasting industry," Jessell said. "We make no bones about it. Every industry needs a good trade magazine" (Jessell 2022). B&C covered developments in ownership, management, network and syndicated programming, journalism, and related areas.

Many trade publications do not critically cover key players or launch investigative reports, Jessell noted. Company and executive profiles are typically soft. "They're all great men and women," he said facetiously. Such features, he acknowledged, "are beat sweeteners. But it's still a valuable profile." In addition to news sections, he said, trade publication profiles and features can provide important archival information. "We weren't out for blood," he said, "or to be critical of companies. We weren't painting a negative portrait of the industry and people in it." But, he said, on serious issues involving law or regulation, "we were competitive with anyone." And in those areas of coverage, among others, the competition was not only other business-to-business news organizations, but also major news media with general audiences (Jessell 2022).

Jessell said trade publications may:

> tread lightly when the story is about your major advertiser. I'm not denying that. Are newspapers really covering the hell out of the automobile industries, grocery stores… I don't think you're going to hear too many negative stories. They tread pretty lightly on the big retail industries that buy ads. All advertising comes from the community. The bigger the advertiser the louder the voice. With trade publications you're dealing with a narrow pool of advertisers. It makes life difficult.

When a trade publication aggressively reports stories perceived as negative, he said, it would likely be the salespeople or the publisher that gets the blowback. Editors would beg off, citing policy against talking about sales. "Sometimes it's stupid stuff – a story about a lost [station or syndication] sale, or they want to hold up an announcement. And let's say we got a big scoop," Jessell said. "We're not talking about the Pentagon Papers here; we might be talking about the Magic Johnson show ['The Magic Hour']."

### Mile-High Pressure?

Dana Coffield is a veteran reporter with experience in mainstream as well as business-to-business press, including writing and editing for two major Denver newspapers: the now-defunct Rocky Mountain News and The Denver Post.

As an editor for a trade publication, Natural Foods Merchandiser, covering the natural food retail industry, and high-tech magazine Interactive Week, Coffield said in an interview for this chapter that she found less tension with advertisers than in the general press. Companies knew that they would be included in articles inevitably. "We had so many to choose from," she said. "They might not be [included] this time, but they would be another time." She said she "felt less aware" of pressure from advertisers, "which was surprising to me" (Coffield 2022).

"It just didn't feel like I was being told to interview certain people." The publication had its "back-scratching" features, "like the Top 10 widget makers," and friendly profiles. "But it didn't feel like we were being pressured to shape stories to make one company look better than another."

"I can't say that we were doing hard investigations at either [trade] publication" Coffield said. "That was not what it was about. It was more like: here are the trends, here's how you participate in the trends…" (Coffield 2022).

And at the Natural Foods Merchandiser, "it was, 'okay, we know this about your customers, and here's how to get your customers to buy more goji berries ….' That was more or less its function."

"I do think there were times at the Rocky Mountain News where influencers or advertisers had an outsized size influence on what we wrote," she said. As the internet became a retail tool, she recalled:

> There were car dealerships that were trying online car sales. And we did a story about it. And this dealer, who was a major advertiser of ours, lost his nut. We got in trouble for acting like this (online advertising and retail) was going to be a thing.

One of her bosses relayed to her that "Advertiser X says that's not true." Among the issues was the perception that online sales produced less haggling, and one of her bosses told her, "People love to haggle" (Coffield 2022):

> "The concept was just so foreign that they couldn't believe we were writing about it. And we interviewed somebody who had bought a car online and talked about how it worked. So, it was more like a weekly tech section; here's how you use the internet and the things that are going on, on the internet. We did publish the story, but we got in trouble for it internally. But fast-forward three years, and I'm over at The Denver Post in the business news department and that same dealer, won Online Retailer of the Year from some national organization.

The Denver Post, she said, was big enough to resist most pressure. "We prided ourselves on the ability to do investigations and speak truth to power, even if was in the business news. But at the same time there are certain individuals who get a pass." She recalled that the Rocky Mountain News' tech reporter "was summoned" to the office of a local billionaire for an interview. "And then at the end of the interview, he was like, 'this is off the record.' This happened twice."

Advertiser-sponsored content, she said, generated "tons of grief." The "advertorial" pages were labeled, she said, to distinguish them from editorial content. "But consumers don't necessarily understand," especially when the content is designed to resemble news content. When local oil and gas interests sponsored content, "it was seen as 'pro-gas' stories. It's too easily confused with journalism; it's intended to look like journalism. It dilutes our own reporting" (Coffield 2022).

Today, Coffield is the co-founder and senior editor at The Colorado Sun, an independent, journalist-owned online news, mostly supported by subscribers. Its editors/owners need to pay attention to page views, but it's less an issue of whether to run a story as it is about presenting it, she said. "Online delivery-only looks a lot different from home delivery," she said, citing not only web pages, but also social media distribution (Coffield 2022).

## Local Business, Local News

A publication devoted to local business naturally boosts that business community, noted Alexis Muellner, longtime editor of the Tampa Bay Business Journal. The newspaper is one of 44 in the American City Business Journals group of weekly business publications. Beyond providing news, Muellner said in an interview for this chapter, his publication seeks to serve the community – local business – with information that helps its audience prosper.

That doesn't mean, however, that it walks in lockstep with business leaders, he said.

"You need your antenna out," he said. "We are, by and large, writing about people who doing development. We're not covering anti-development groups, unless we need comment. We're talking about business development, economic development…which are pro-business." The Business Journal's readers, he said, "look at every piece of content for what they can build on, to grow and to be successful themselves" (Muellner 2022).

"Everybody in the business community wants to see positive stories," he said. Stories that question local business actions or directions are obviously less popular. But he said, positive news hardly tells the entire story.

"Success alone does not drive business reporting," he said. "If we're fair and accurate, we give people a chance to respond. We write and report about success and about failure. There are a lot of lessons in both."

It is important, he said, to develop relationships "so we get the news first...scoops, exclusives..." Reporters often educate their sources on the purpose of the publication, Muellner said. "They may see the relationship as a partnership, he said. And content is often directed toward readers growing and becoming successful, he said. But "we're not a PR [public relations] firm," he said. "These are people we need to work with," he said. "We don't want to alienate people. But we are not a paid promotional arm," he said (Muellner 2022).

The "usual suspects" are easy to quote, Muellner noted, but "we encourage our reporters to be constantly mining new sources. ...We have to find new sources, new points of view."

Historically, local business publications faced significant competition from metro dailies with larger staffs that covered local government, development, and business. That may have reversed in an era of disappearing newspapers, and cost-cutting institutional investor-ownership.

In 2016, following years of struggling and layoffs, The Tampa Tribune merged into The Tampa Bay Times (Edmonds 2016). Job losses have continued. When The Tampa Tribune shut down," Muellner said, "it took me a while to realize we were filling a bit of a hole. It placed even more responsibilities on us."

Not only in Tampa Bay. "Papers owned by American City Business Journals and Crain Communications have taken over covering many business and economics stories in their towns and cities," noted journalist and academic Chris Roush (2022, p. 6). "But it's impossible to cover all of the news that is occurring with these companies. And when news about companies goes uncovered, it hurts economies" (Muellner 2022).

## Chambers, Cars, and Concealment

Former WRAL Raleigh general manager Steve Hammel said in an interview for this chapter that he typically associates boosterism with sports. He recalled one such promotion, when his station negotiated an agreement with the National Hockey League's local franchise, the Carolina Hurricanes, to provide a weather report for fans as they left the game – featuring the station's chief meteorologist wearing a Hurricanes uniform. Hammel, a longtime journalist, said he wasn't bothered by the obvious local boost of the home team. But it would have been a problem had it been one of the station's news anchors (Hammel 2022).

Some news naturally appears positive, Hammel said, but it's up to the station to delve deeper.

If Apple or Amazon is coming to the Triangle [a reference to the area formed by Raleigh, Durham and Chapel Hill, and to the area's high tech Research Triangle Park], it needs to be reported. Great news for people looking for work.

Not so great, he said, will be the effect on roads and traffic. It will raise housing prices, he said, which will be good for sellers, not so good for buyers. "And so, you report both," he said.

Hammel said he never felt pressure from his own station's upper management toward positive stories, or from the local business community. Hammel represented his company at the local Chamber of Commerce (Hammel 2022). "Like any organization," Hammel said:

> The chamber would put out press releases with their positive spin on it. And we would look at that, and take whatever spin they had, and question it. And never once when I was on the board, or not on the board, did the president of the chamber or anyone with the chamber say, 'Hey, you know, you're connected with the chamber, can you do something about your people and their reporting?' That never happened.

Prominent in most stations' advertising logs, and in most stations' consumer reporting, is the automotive industry. Numerous complaints involving automobiles and automobile dealers came to WRAL's consumer unit 5 On Your Side, Hammel recalled. "And we would report on them. And there were times we lost advertising for some period of time" (Hammel 2022).

One Raleigh-area dealer withdrew advertising over reporting that wasn't about automobiles. Using public records, WRAL had put a tracker on its website, so people could see if there were neighbors with concealed weapons on their street. "We got a lot of flak about that," Hammel recalled. Hammel said he and his general sales manager met with the dealer "who was an ardent fan of concealed weapons, and thought what we did was wrong, He expressed his distaste, and took tens of thousands of dollars away" (Hammel 2022).

In 2017, WRAL battled over boosterism with a local rival. For more than 40 years, WRAL had been the television sponsor for the city's Christmas parade. In 2017, the station lost the contract to rival station WTVD. But WRAL decided to broadcast the parade anyway.

That decision was met with cries of foul play not only from WTVD, but also from the board of the Greater Raleigh Merchants Association, which worried that the two broadcasts would confuse viewers, and that WRAL's siphoning viewers away from the parade's official carrier would reduce the value of the sponsorship, which the merchants' association uses to support the parade (Hammel 2022).

Hammel said other stations could have broadcast the parade when WRAL sponsored it, but none did. "There is no way the hometown station would not broadcast this," Hammel told the Raleigh News & Observer. WRAL is owned by Raleigh-based Capitol Broadcasting; WTVD is an ABC owned-and-operated station.

The controversy may have cost Santa Claus at least part of his annual gig. WRAL filmed and began airing a commercial for its own parade broadcast with the Santa who'd been hired by the merchants' association. That Santa was replaced (Hammel 2022).

## Conclusion: The Inevitably of Boosterism in Local News?

Studying the relationship between local newspapers and corporate malfeasance, Heese, Pérez-Cavazos, and Peter (2022) acknowledged perceived issues with newspapers' monitoring local companies' behavior, including the newspaper's reliance on income from advertisers – which also may employ readers – and the decreasing reach of local journalism. Nonetheless, the study concluded that local newspapers were an important monitor of firms' misconduct, and that the loss of local newspapers had a negative effect on legal compliance. It incorporated previous research, which suggests that the loss of a newspaper can lead to increased crime and corruption, and less-informed and, therefore, less-engaged voters.

Former reporter and media executive Penelope Muse Abernathy has spent years studying the state of local journalism (and potential remedies) as the Knight Chair in Journalism and Digital Media Economics at the Hussman School of Journalism and Media at the University of North Carolina at Chapel Hill, and currently at Northwestern University's Medill School of Journalism.

The reports she's overseen detail the "successive technological and economic assaults [which] have destroyed the for-profit business model that sustained local journalism for two centuries." Hundreds of news organizations – newspapers and, more recently, digital sites, have vanished. Many survivors were "hanging on by the slimmest of profit margins," even before the coronavirus outbreak exacerbated the problem (Abernathy 2020).

In the last decades of the 20th century, the report said, "scholars, policymakers and journalists voiced new concerns about the civic responsibilities of chains" after Gannett, Knight Ridder, McClatchy, and Pulitzer issued stock and attempted to balance those civic responsibilities with the expectations of Wall Street (Abernathy 2020). Over time and trading, the publicly traded chains reduced local connections, continued to cut news staffs – historically, newspapers have employed the largest number of reporters in any community – and centralize many functions in remote locations. And the hedge funds and institutional investor owners? "Their whole goal is shareholder return," Abernathy said in an interview for this chapter. They do not share the dual sense of mission, she said, the sense of commitment to the community of many large and small family corporations that owned media during most of the 20th century (Abernathy interview 2022).

The loss of staff, Abernathy said, means a loss of probing, challenging journalism. "I don't think there's anyone who says, 'Hey, I'm not going to write anything negative.'" More likely, she said, skeleton staffs lack the resources to do real reporting, to follow up on information that begins in a press release. "And they do not have an editor who would say, 'I think this could be a much better story if you held it for three days and asked these questions…'" (Abernathy interview 2022).

Complex stories or editorials challenging prominent local businesses and employers may not bring the best return on investment in a business attempting to shrink to profitability, as newspapers now share local digital revenue with Google and Facebook in even the smallest markets. "I hear this quite often," she said:

> If you're an inexperienced reporter who's being judged on the number of clicks you get and the number of stories you produce, and you don't have an editor telling you to question the press release … [an unchallenging, positive story] is just going to happen. Do I think it's intentional? No.

But local business fallout from negative attention was a reason "editorial writers were the first to go," she said. "Editorials can cause you a big headache" (Abernathy interview 2022).

"Most of the well-known investigative reporters who could take a look at some kind of shenanigans going on with business have retired," she noted. "So, you're losing them. And at the same time, you're losing the editors. So, what you've got, mostly, is younger and somewhat inexperienced reporters being asked to do three and four stories a day."

"Once the hometown paper closes, residents in those markets are left without a reliable source of local information. This has led to the simultaneous rise of news deserts, communities without a local news outlet," the 2020 report said, "and 'ghost newspapers,' with depleted newsrooms that are only a shadow of their former selves" (Abernathy 2020).

The latest report supervised by Abernathy expresses hope in the efforts of "journalists, policymakers, philanthropists, industry executives, scholars and concerned citizens" to save local journalism. But the decline continues. "In communities without a credible source of local news," the report said, "voter participation declines, corruption in both government and business increases, and local residents end up paying more in taxes and at checkout.

"This is a crisis for our democracy and our society" (Abernathy 2022).

# References

Abernathy, P. (2020). "Vanishing readers and journalists". University of North Carolina Hussman School of Journalism and Media. https://www.usnewsdeserts.com/reports/news-deserts-and-ghost-newspa pers-will-local-news-survive/the-news-landscape-in-2020-transformed-and-dimin ished/vanishing-readers-and-journalists/.

Abernathy, P. (Interview, May 24, 2022). Former executive at New York Times, Wall Street Journal, now professor at Northwestern University Medill School of Journalism, Media, Integrated Marketing Communications.

Abernathy, P. (2022). "The state of local news." Northwestern/Medill Local News Initiative. https://local-newsinitiative.northwestern.edu/research/state-of-local-news/report/Basen, I. (2012). "Breaking down the wall." *Center for Journalism Ethics*, December 19, 2012. https://ethics.journalism.wisc.edu/2012/12/19/breaking-down-the-wall/

Choi, J., & Park, S. (2011). "Influence of advertising on acceptance of press releases." *Public Relations Review, 37*(1), 106. https://doi.org/10.1016/j.pubrev.2010.09.010

Coffield. D. (July 18, 2022). Former business writer and editor at *Denver Post, Rocky Mountain News*. Now senior editor, *The Colorado Sun*.

Comedy Central, The Daily Show. (March 12, 2009). https://www.cc.com/video/uc9y5b/the-daily-show-with-jon-stewart-cnbc-financial-advice

Cook, J. (2011). "Jim Cramer chooses mindless panic over mindless boosterism." *Gawker*. https://www.gawker.com/5832212/jim-cramer-chooses-mindless-panic-over-mindless-boosterism

Edmonds, R. (2016). "Tampa bay times buys and folds the tampa tribune." *Poynter*.

Folkenflik, D. (2009). On daily show, stewart, cramer get serious. https://www.npr.org/templates/story/story.php?storyId=101888064Hammel, S. (Interview, July 26, 2022). Retired general manager at WRAL, Raleigh, N.C.

Heese, Jonas & Pérez-Cavazos, Gerardo & Peter, Caspar David, 2022. "When the local newspaper leaves town: The effects of local newspaper closures on corporate misconduct," *Journal of Financial Economics*, Elsevier, 145(2), 445–463.

Holtzman, J. (1974). "No cheering in the press box." Holt, Rinehart, and Winston New York. 1974.

Jessell, H. (Interview, July 12, 2022). Former *Broadcasting & Cable* executive editor. Now editor, co-publisher, TVNewscheck.com.

Jurkowitz, M. (1999). "A cautionary tale about credibility." *Chicago Tribune*. https://login.proxy.lib.duke.edu/login

Justice News. (2012). "Allen Stanford sentenced to 110 years in prison for orchestrating $7 billion investment fraud scheme." https://www.justice.gov/opa/pr/allen-stanford-sentenced-110-years-prison-orchestrating-7-billion-investment-fraud-scheme

Linden, J. (2015). No cheering in the press box [review] *The Hardball Times*. https://tht.fangraphs.com/no-cheering-in-the-press-box/Merriam-Webster, https://www.merriam-webster.com/dictionary/booster

Muellner, A. (Interview, June 13, 2022). Editor, *Tampa Bay Business Journal*.

Postrel, V. (2000). "The ethics of boosterism". *Forbes*.

Quinn, S. (2009). "Stewart destroys CNBC, Cramer, disses "Doucheborough." *Fivethirtyeight*. https://fivethirtyeight.com/features/stewart-destroys-cnbc-cramer-calls/

Roush, C. (2022). *The Future of Business Journalism*. Washington, DC: Georgetown University Press.

RTDNA. (2015). Code of ethics. https://www.rtdna.org/content/rtdna_code_of_ethics

SABEW. (2015). Code of ethics. https://sabew.org/codes-of-ethics/#:~:text=Never%20let%20personal%20investments%20influence,or%20directly%20to%20the%20public.&text=Disclose%20to%20your%20superiors%20and,might%20pose%20conflicts%20of%20interest.

Schudson, Michael. (1978). "Discovering the news: A social history of American newspapers." p. 4.

Shaban, H. (2014). "What has become of business journalism?" *New Yorker*, February 5, 2014.

Shaw, D. (1999). "A business deal done --A controversy born: A Los Angeles Times profit-sharing arrangement with staples center fuels a firestorm of protest in the newsroom--and a debate about journalistic ethics." *Los Angeles Times*, December 20, 1999.

SPJ. (2014). Code of ethics. https://www.spj.org/ethicscode.asp

Starkman, D. (2014). *The Watchdog That Didn't Bark: The Financial Crisis and the Disappearance of Investigative Journalism.* New York: Columbia University Press.

Tifft, S., & Jones, A. (1999). *The Trust: The Private and Powerful Family Behind The New York Times.* New York: Little, Brown and Company.

Tompkins, Al. (Email May 16. 2022). Senior faculty, The Poynter Institute.

# 25

# THE JOURNALIST AND THE TRADER

*Stephen Kurczy*

## Introduction

The idea of ethics in news is foundational to the notion of publishing information. According to scholar Stephen Ward, the invention of the printing press in the 17th century gave way to "printer-editors" who "assured readers they printed the impartial truth based on 'matters of fact' and eyewitness accounts by 'reliable correspondents'" (2010, p. 139).

But what it means to be a "reliable correspondent" who provides "impartial truth" has evolved over the centuries. For the business press, specific ethical guidelines and codes of conduct have only emerged and solidified over the past half-century, with one major impetus being an industry-rocking insider trading scandal at The Wall Street Journal in 1984.

While outlets such as The Wall Street Journal are today known for having strict rules against financial conflicts of interest, speculative investing, and divulging unpublished information, other publications are less rigid. Many outlets have no code at all. Moreover, the often-gray area around financial conflicts and personal investing are largely unmentioned in journalism curricula, raising questions around the profession's pursuit of, and expectations for, that age-old ideal of "impartial truth."

## Ethics Codes Leading Up to the Winans Scandal (1923–1984)

The United States recently marked the 100th anniversary of its first national code of journalism ethics, which debuted in 1923 when the American Society of Newspaper Editors (ASNE) created its Canons of Journalism (Ward 2010, p. 141). It commanded newspapers to be independent of "all obligations except that of fidelity to the public interest" and called on journalists to not take advantage of their positions for personal gain (Brown 2020, p. 233). Those canons were further legitimized when they were adopted in 1926 by the Society of Professional Journalists (Christians 1997, p. 17).

Founded in 1909, SPJ is today the largest professional association for journalists in the United States, and its code has provided a template for newsroom ethics across the country (Boeyink and Borden 2010, p. 17). According to Ward, "By the 1950s these standards [of the SPJ] were operationalized in newsrooms by rules on newsgathering and story

DOI: 10.4324/9781003298977-30

construction… Objective reporters were to be completely detached, to eliminate all of their opinion, and to report just the facts" (2010, p. 142).

When the SPJ updated its code in 1973, a new section titled "Ethics" specifically warned journalists away from financial conflicts of interest: "Gifts, favors, free travel, special treatment or privileges can compromise the integrity of journalists and their employers. Nothing of value should be accepted," the code said (Brown 2020, p. 235). These new rules fit with a trend in the 1970s of press codes taking aim at gifts and freebies. "Up to that time, journalists who took the gifts rationalized that they could still act independently," according to longtime newspaper editor and journalism scholar Gene Foreman (2010, p. 139).

Underscoring the growth of the business press at this time, the Society for Advancing Business Editing and Writing (SABEW, originally called the Society of American Business Editors and Writers), created its first code of ethics in 1974 (Beal 2013). SABEW's code called on business writers to "avoid active trading and other short-term profit-seeking opportunities" and to "not take advantage in his personal investing of any inside information" (Goodwin 1987, pp. 78–79). But a looming scandal at The Wall Street Journal would soon spur news organizations to more specifically address financial conflicts associated with market investing.

## The Winans Case

While not the first journalist to get caught up in an insider trading scheme, R. Foster Winans has become the most well-known. He was hired by Dow Jones News Service in March 1981 to write for its business and financial news wire (Winans 1986, pp. 19–24). He had several years' prior experience reporting for The Trentonian and freelancing for The New York Times, but "business journalism was a specialty I knew absolutely nothing about," as he recounted in his memoir, "Trading Secrets" (ibid., p. 17).

In July 1982, Winans was promoted to Dow Jones's flagship publication, The Wall Street Journal, to write for "Heard on the Street," a popular market gossip column (ibid., p. 31). A fast learner, Winans earned praise for his "Heard" columns (ibid., p. 85). But his inexperience also showed. He was admonished for revealing too much about the contents of a forthcoming column to a source. "You don't **ever** tell people what you're doing," a supervising editor told him (ibid., p. 62). "Be discreet, for chrissakes." This would later become the rub of Winans's legal troubles.

As Winans told the story, in the fall of 1983, he was lured into a trading scheme with a source named Peter Brant, a top broker at Kidder, Peabody. Noting how "Heard on the Street" moved stocks, Brant told Winans, "You know, we could make a lot of money if I knew the day before what was going to be in the column" (ibid., p. 10). The financial lure was especially appealing to a reporter who felt underpaid. Winans's promotion to the Journal had come with a $50 raise, to a weekly salary of $530, "more than I'd ever earned in my life" (ibid., p. 49). But he also learned he earned less than his colleagues, and his disappointment had "festered" (ibid., p. 52). Winans agreed to start tipping Brant about the contents of his forthcoming articles (ibid., p. 120). He asked for an advance of $15,000. Brant agreed and, in a thin attempt to conceal their arrangement, made out a check to Winans's boyfriend, David Carpenter (ibid., p. 121).

This was not Winans's first step into ethically fraught territory. He had already engaged in dubious practices such as buying stocks based on unpublished information gleaned from his reporting (ibid, p. 65). Winans invested in a company called American Surgery Centers, then wrote two "Heard" columns that praised the company; his holdings subsequently gained nearly $3,000 ("United States v. Winans" 1985). He invested in Institutional Investors Trust, wrote about the company, and then sold his stock at a profit of nearly $500 (ibid.). When he learned that his "Heard" colleague was writing a negative column about another company, Winans shorted the stock and pocketed $775 from the trade (Winans 1986, p. 142). Winans also gave investment advice to friends and family who made thousands of dollars from the stock tips (ibid., pp. 48, 70).

Winans believed many people at the Journal were actively trading, with some of this activity possibly based on newsroom information. "At the time, I believe there were other people doing it," Winans later said (2022 interview). "I was not the first person to come up with this idea and act on it." He recalled standing behind a gaggle of Journal editors who, after the market's closing bell, were all checking their stock portfolios on a terminal.

Winans also knew that his bosses "would choke if they learned I was investing in the market" (ibid., p. 65). So, he had Carpenter, who worked at the Journal as a news clerk, make all the stock trades for Winans (ibid., p. 66).

The scheme with Brant took things to a new level. Winans began sneaking out of the Journal's office to call Brant from a payphone and inform him about his forthcoming columns (ibid., pp. 120). In October 1983, Brant traded roughly every other day using inside information about Winans's columns (ibid., p. 131). According to court filings, Brant profited nearly $700,000 from the tips; Winans got $30,000 in kickbacks ("United States v. Winans" 1985).

But an alarm had sounded at the American Stock Exchange, which noticed unusual market movements from Kidder, Peabody just before publication of "Heard" columns (Winans 1986, p. 129). The compliance department at Kidder, Peabody also spotted trades suspiciously timed to Journal articles. To cover his tracks, Brant began funneling trades through a Swiss account (ibid, p. 138; and "United States v. Winans" 1985).

On March 1, 1984, Winans was called into a meeting with Journal managing editor Norman Pearlstine, general counsel Robert Sack, and SEC lawyer Joe Cella of the Enforcement Division (Winans 1986, p. 161–163). Cella asked Winans, "Have you ever told Peter Brant about articles that you were writing?" Winans declined to answer. Cella then asked, "Have you ever received money from Mr. Brant?" "No," Winans lied (ibid., p. 168). Two weeks later, the SEC made its inquiry a formal investigation (ibid., p. 184).

Winans hired a lawyer, confessed to his scheme, and notified the Journal that he had agreed to cooperate with the SEC. The Journal fired Winans and, on March 29, broke the story that he had leaked sensitive information about his articles; days later, a dozen reporters and editors collaborated on a 5,000-word, front-page story excoriating Winans (Goldstein 1985, p. 249).

Paul Steiger was at that time the Journal's assistant managing editor in charge of economics and markets coverage, including "Heard on the Street"; he later served as managing editor from 1991 until 2007. "I just was disgusted by what Foster had done," Steiger would recall years later (2022 interview). "It embarrassed the Journal and his colleagues at the Journal. ... We had to write stories airing our dirty linen."

The SEC filed a lawsuit against Winans in May 1984. That August, he was indicted in the U.S. District Court for the Southern District of New York on 61 counts of mail, wire, and securities fraud for defrauding both the Journal and readers of the Journal (Blumstein 1984). According to District Judge Charles E. Stewart, Jr.:

> The information allegedly stolen from the Journal was the timing, content and tenor of market-sensitive stories scheduled to appear in the paper. This conduct was allegedly

in breach of a fiduciary duty owed to Winans' employer, Dow Jones & Co., the parent company of The Wall Street Journal.

*("United States v. Winans" 1985)*

The trial began in January 1985. The Journal claimed that, as of February 2, 1981, it was company practice to distribute to all new employees "The Inside Story," a 44-page pamphlet that delved into "many ethical grey areas" and had seven pages devoted to conflicts of interest ("United States v. Winans" 1985). In addition, a Conflicts of Interest Policy specifically forbade "the purchase or sale of securities on the basis of articles an employee knows will appear in the newspaper; it also states that employees should not disclose the paper's future contents to anyone outside the company" (ibid.).

Winans argued that he had never received The Inside Story or any formal ethical instruction. "I knew what I had done was wrong and I accepted that I deserved to be fired and probably banished from newspaper work," Winans later wrote (Winans 1986, p. 235):

But I had not seen a conflict policy while I worked at the Journal and neither had [my colleague] Gary Putka, who laughed when he saw a mention of it in the Journal's March 1 package of stories on insider trading.

Steiger also testified at the trial. Interviewed nearly four decades after the fact, he could not recall whether he had received the Journal's ethics policy when he was hired. "But that's beside the point," Steiger said (2022 interview). "Any fool in journalism knew that it was a mortal sin to steal your top secret stuff and trade on it." The judge would agree with Steiger.

In a verdict delivered in June 1985, Judge Stewart found that

Winans knew he was not supposed to leak the timing or contents of his articles or trade on that knowledge. He knew that these columns were likely to affect the price of the stocks to his benefit. This is true even if he had not known of a written policy; he had knowledge of a Wall Street Journal practice, that is, a rule of conduct, which makes this a clear breach of a fiduciary duty... [H]e did not have to be aware of the existence of a Conflicts of Interest Policy, much less a written one, to know that his activities violated a practice, were unethical and would lead to dismissal.

*("United States v. Winans" 1985)*

Winans was sentenced to 18 months in prison and fined $5,000 (Bleakley 1985). He appealed all the way to the U.S. Supreme Court, which in November 1987 unanimously ruled that Winans had committed mail and wire fraud but split as to whether his actions constituted insider trading under securities law ("Carpenter et al. v. United States" 1987). Brant was later sentenced to eight months in prison and fined $10,000 (Yen 1988).

In the end, it hadn't mattered whether Winans had or hadn't formally seen the Journal's code of practice or conflicts of interest policy. The judge determined that Winans was nonetheless aware that the content and timing of his unpublished columns were Journal property, and so he should also have known it was theft to use that property for personal profit:

If you are the writer of what was then the single-most read column in The Wall Street Journal, and you know that when it appears it literally moves markets, and you know that people buy The Wall Street Journal in part because of this wonderful column, then a reasonable judge could conclude you know it's confidential and not supposed to be used in advance for your personal gain,

said Jed S. Rakoff, who was defense counsel to David Carpenter during that case and its appeals (2022 interview). Rakoff was later named a U.S. district judge for the Southern District of New York, where he is now a senior judge and authority on insider trading law.

The Winans case helped contribute to a movement by employers to bind staff to confidentiality agreements and specify all proprietary intellectual property. "To the extent that [the Winans case] had an impact on employers," Rakoff said, "it was to make them reduce to writing what informational property was confidential."

## Impact on the Journal and Codes of Ethics (1984–present)

Almost overnight, the scandal spurred the Journal to update its ethics procedures. Days after the story broke, the Journal's conflict-of-interest policy was handed out to all employees (Winans 1986, p. 221). The newspaper wanted to be sure that no employee could ever again say they'd not been aware of the policy.

"To button that up, we changed the practice so that everybody had to sign an annual acknowledgment that they knew [the ethics policy]," said Richard Tofel, who at that time was a legal assistant to the Journal's general counsel, Robert Sack of the law firm Patterson, Belknap and Webb (2022 interview):

> But let me say that no one I ever met in the newsroom of the Journal thought that doing that changed the rules. No one. Everyone was like, 'This is some bureaucratic bullshit that we have to go through because Foster is trying to confuse people.'

It has been reported that the scandal compelled the Journal "to publicly reexamine and rewrite its code of conduct" (Kovach and Rosenstiel 2001, p. 54). However, Tofel—who in 1989 joined Dow Jones as in-house counsel and later became assistant publisher of the Journal—did not recall the code being rewritten in response to Winans. "I'm pretty sure it wasn't [changed at that time], in part because, very honestly, we wanted Foster to go to jail," Tofel said (2022 interview):

> And we wanted him to go to jail because we thought it was very important to send a message of how wrong this was. If we had changed the policy, there might have been an argument, 'Well they changed the policy because it wasn't clear enough.' So we didn't change the policy.

The scandal reverberated beyond the Journal. "One effect of the Winans episode was that many newspapers began to adopt very tough standards, especially for business writers" (Goodwin and Smith 1994, p. 97). In 1990, for example, The St. Petersburg Times fired a business writer who was short-selling banking stocks; days later, the newspaper also fired its business editor when it was discovered that through an individual retirement account, he owned $42 in stocks in a bank that had been mentioned in the newspaper. Howard Kurtz of The Washington Post interpreted the firings as part of a Winans whiplash, saying, "Many newspapers have adopted strict conflict-of-interest policies since the 1985 insider-trading conviction of former Wall Street Journal reporter R. Foster Winans" (Kurtz 1990).

At a high level, the tightening rules around financial conflicts of interest can be observed in the SPJ's ethics code, which was updated in 1996 to more clearly address the kind of improprieties committed by Winans. In a new section titled Act Independently, the code broadly called on journalists to "avoid conflicts of interest, real or perceived"; "remain free of associations and activities that may compromise integrity or damage credibility"; and "be wary of sources offering information for favors or money" (Brown 2020, pp. 239–241).

It wasn't just the Winans scandal that pushed the business press to update its codes around this time. The rise of online financial news outlets, combined with internet-enabled trading capabilities, fueled concern around insider trading (Pavlik 2001, p. 95). TheStreet.com, founded in 1996, barred editorial staff from holding individual stocks "to avoid any potential problem with its reporters attempting to influence stock prices for their personal gain," according to John Pavlik (ibid., p. 96). "The reasons for prohibiting a reporter from owning stock (except in their own news company) primarily include concerns about insider trading and profiting from promoting the stocks in their own portfolios via their news reports." (One can't help but wonder why a reporter would be permitted to hold his own company's stock, and if that meant it was permissible to profit from stories promoting the company or based on inside information.)

In tandem, press outlets adopted new rules around financial disclosure (Smith 2003, p. 392). In 1995, after Jim Cramer failed to fully reveal his personal holdings in stocks that he wrote about for Smart Money magazine, the publication barred all contributors from writing about companies in which they held more than 1 percent equity (Zuckerman 1995). Around 2000, CNN started requiring a disclaimer if the reporter owned any of the discussed company's stock (Smith 2003, p. 392). By no later than 2001, it was considered "a good guideline for business reporters to avoid owning any stock in companies you might have to cover... at the very least, reporters who own stock should inform their editors (Colón 2001, p. 257). Media ethicist Ron Smith observed in 2003 that,

> Today, nearly all newspapers and TV news organizations require business writers to check with their editors before they buy stocks or sell stocks. Editors can then determine whether the transaction might involve conflicts of interest. Some news outlets, such as CNBC, prohibit business journalists from owning any stocks.
>
> *(Smith 2003, p. 392)*

The Winans scandal still echoes today. When Steiger left the Journal in 2007 to found ProPublica, he recruited Tofel to be the investigative news site's general manager and general counsel. In crafting ProPublica's ethics policy, they adopted the same rules that were put in place at the Journal after the Winans bombshell, part of the long-tail impact of that case. Every year, ProPublica's editorial staff must sign a form indicating they've read and will comply with the code of ethics.

"When we started ProPublica, we adopted the same practices [as Dow Jones] for the same reason," Steiger said (2002 interview). "Once somebody [like Winans] has enormously, disingenuously made these claims, it's enough to say, 'Let's not get ourselves in that discussion again.'"

Tofel now operates a journalism consultancy, Gallatin Advisory, a role that includes advising news outlets on ethical concerns. He said he'd be willing to consult on financial conflicts of interest and insider trading, "but nobody's asked me to. And nobody's asked me because I think everybody knows what the deal is. I am not aware of a single important business news organization that doesn't have a good policy on this" (2002 interview).

## What Today's Codes Say

The Associated Press has some of the most stringent rules around financial holdings, market investing, and real and perceived financial conflicts. The wire service prohibits writers and editors who cover the markets from owning any individual stocks or engaging in any speculative investments, such as short-selling. The AP also warns all employees against acting upon or informing other people of

> Information gained in the course of AP employment, unless and until that information becomes known to the general public. Employees must comply with federal and local laws concerning securities and financial transactions, including those prohibiting actions based upon inside information.

Dow Jones, Bloomberg, and The New York Times prohibit their reporters from holding any investment that overlaps with a company or industry in the reporter's coverage area. As the Times clarifies: "A book editor, for example, may not invest in a publishing house, a health writer in a pharmaceutical company or a Pentagon reporter in a mutual fund specializing in defense stocks." All three outlets also prohibit news staff from buying or selling futures or options or engaging in any short-term trading, though each publication has its own definition of "short-term." At Dow Jones, it translates to a prohibition on selling a security within six months of purchase. At the Times, the rule is three months. At Bloomberg, it's 30 days.

Addressing Winans-like situations, Dow Jones prohibits employees from acting in any way that might invite "suspicion" that they, their families,

> Or anyone else connected to an employee made financial gains by acting on the basis of information obtained through Dow Jones employment before that information was available to the general public; such information includes hold-for-release material or publishing plans with respect to news, advertising, or other information, as well as any other items that might affect movements in the prices of any securities.

ProPublica mirrors Dow Jones's code.

Bloomberg also prohibits all employees from

> Profiting from news, data or information learned in the course of employment that has yet to be made public. ... Journalists may not trade on information they learn in connection with their positions at Bloomberg unless the information has been public and absorbed by the market for at least two full days—and even then, only if they don't cover that company or industry.

The Times tells staffers to "not buy or sell securities or make other investments in anticipation of forthcoming articles that originate with the Times."

National Public Radio's ethics handbook does not prohibit editorial staff from any specific financial activities, but broadly asks reporters to "scrupulously avoid any appearance that we've skewed our journalism to enrich ourselves or our associates" and "disclose to your immediate supervisors any business, commercial, financial or personal interests where such interests might reasonably be construed as being in actual, apparent or potential conflict with our duties." Similarly, the business news radio show Marketplace prohibits staff from short-term trading if they "are in a position to influence stock prices by engaging in primary reporting on a specific company or stock issue."

NPR's code is the only one to specifically mention Winans, noting that he "was investigated by the SEC for using or leaking non-public information he gathered as a reporter for the purpose of making financial investments" and "criminally charged with insider trading."

The codes for USA Today Network and The Washington Post each broadly say the publications seek to avoid real and perceived conflicts of interest, although there are no specific investment restrictions. CNBC, MSNBC, Fox Business, and other business news channels do not have publicly available codes of ethics (Brown 2022 interview).

## Sometimes Permissible?

At first glance, the Winans scandal might appear to have clarified rules around financial conflicts. The reporter was found to have defrauded the Journal by misappropriating proprietary information in breach of a policy on conduct, and the case contributed to a broadening theory around insider trading that the U.S. District Court for the Southern District of New York was developing based on a misappropriation argument (Scheppele 1993, p. 123).

But there appears to be a discomfiting loophole. According to business ethicist Jennifer Moore, the misappropriation argument "is not enough to show that insider trading is always unethical or that it should be illegal" (1990, p. 175). In an article in the Journal of Business Ethics that touched on the Winans case, Moore noted that "if insider information is really the property of the firm that produces it, then using that property is wrong **only when the firm prohibits it** (italics in original). If the firm does not prohibit insider trading, it seems perfectly acceptable." In the Winans case, the government even conceded "that without any [Journal] policy, there could be no prosecution under the misappropriation theory" ("United States v. Winans" 1985).

Further muddying the moral waters, a number of scholars have argued that insider trading is not just not wrong, but good (see Manne 1966; Leland 1992; Macey 2007). In fact, the Journal's own editorial page has routinely espoused the pros of insider trading and argued for its decriminalization. (See "The Case for Insider Trading" (2003) by George Mason University School of Law Dean Henry Manne; "Learning to Love Insider Trading" (2009) by George Mason University Professor Donald Boudreaux; and "Information Is Not a Crime" (2015) by the Journal's longtime editorial writer L. Gordon Crovitz.)

In the 2008 research article "Applying Ethics to Insider Trading," Fayetteville State University accounting professor Robert McGee argued that "insider trading helps the market act more efficiently" and asserted that the Winans case "was seen as having a potential chilling effect on the first amendment freedom of the press—a regulation of a reporter's behavior" (McGee, p. 213).

# Future Directions

## *Stronger Codes?*

As noted above, press codes are not always explicit regarding financial investments, conflicts of interest, and the use of non-public information. Many news outlets lack any ethics policy. A 2010 study found that half of all investigative reporting centers in the United States have no formal ethics or editorial policies (Hochberg 2014, p. 132). This author discovered a similar result when he conducted an informal survey of reporters and editors working across city, state, and national publications in the United States, with ethics policies running the gamut.

From a sampling of current and former employees at 17 U.S.-based news outlets (all of whom spoke on condition of anonymity), nearly half said they never received a copy of their company's ethics policy; this included staff from one of the largest dailies in the country and several prominent business publications. A reporter at a banking news service said: "I requested a copy of the code of conduct prior to onboarding but was never sent one. Ethics aren't discussed much, if at all." An editor at a prominent legal news service referenced an "unwritten rule" against short-term stock-investing or political donating, though the person added that "these policies have never been formalized and I personally do not adhere to them."

The survey also found confusion within some outlets about their ethics policies. At a premium business news service, one editor outlined a rigorous compliance training program and annual review policy that contained, among other things, rules against paying for information, sharing unpublished information, and short-term trading. Another editor at the same publication received no formal ethics training and said he subscribed to a "don't want to know policy" when it came to reporters' personal investments.

To end the discrepancies between codes and publications, would it behoove the industry to ban all editorial staff from holding any individual stocks or making speculative investments? There is arguably a potential conflict when any journalists do any market trading, just as there's a potential conflict when any journalists wear political pins or participate in political campaigns—regardless of whether that journalist covers politics. For this reason, it may be reasonable to prohibit all editorial staff from investing in anything but blind funds, according to Fred Brown, editor of the SPJ's "Media Ethics" textbook and former president of the organization (2022 interview). Such would help regulate the appearance of a conflict of interest, which is something that many news organizations already do (Elliott 1997, p. 91).

However, Pavlik argues that a blanket ban could backfire:

> Reporters have historically been underpaid… Prohibiting reporters from owning stock might be just enough to make some talented reporters leave for greener pastures. Besides, maintaining a disclosure policy in which each reporter's stock portfolio is fully revealed may be sufficient to permit audience members to understand where conflicts of interest may lie.
>
> *(2001, pp. 96–97)*

Christians et al. (2017) argue that banning journalists from engaging in secondary financial interests is treating the symptom rather than the cause, which is that journalists' salaries are low: "For journalists to be truthful at all costs, their salaries should be competitive. Journalists who have good salaries won't solicit gratuities. When journalism is poorly remunerated, insisting on purity is only moralism from an upper class" (p. 57).

A similar critique was leveled against the Journal by Tom Goldstein, former dean of the Berkeley Graduate School of Journalism and the Columbia Graduate School of Journalism. In "The News At Any Cost" (1985), Goldstein wrote that the Journal never explained

Why Winans was entrusted with the column when he was relatively inexperienced in business reporting. Nor did they wish to explain why he was paid so modestly given the importance of his assignment and compared to salaries received by reporters working on other New York City papers.

*(p. 251)*

## Better Education?

Winans was a college dropout who quit McGill University his freshman year (Winans 1986, p. 15). Could a better education have helped keep him out of jail?

Evidence is mixed to suggest that educators play a major role in influencing newsroom ethics. According to a U.S. survey of several thousand journalists conducted in 1982 and 1992, journalism teachers were influential in matters of media ethics for about half of reporters; instead, newsroom learning and family upbringing were the most influential shapers of ethics (Weaver and Wilhoit 1996, p. 154). A 2005 study found no correlation between education and willingness to engage in journalistic deception (Lee 2005, p. 112).

In any case, journalism textbooks appear to devote scant attention to insider trading or financial conflicts. This author reviewed more than two dozen media ethics textbooks and found that most addressed conflicts of interest in terms of political affiliations, schmoozing with sources, and overlap between a publication's editorial and business operations. Few textbooks touched on conflicts involving personal investments. Only three texts mentioned the Winans case: Goodwin's "Groping for Ethics" (1987, and its succeeding editions), Foreman's "The Ethical Journalist" (2010), and Christians et al.'s "Media Ethics" (2017). There was no mention of financial conflicts of interest in several prominent media law textbooks. While conflicts of interest are typically considered an ethical matter, not a legal concern, the Winans case highlights how financial conflicts, specifically around the use of newsroom information, can rise to a legal concern.

In the decades since getting out of prison, Winans has spoken a number of times at Columbia Law School at the invitation of Judge Rakoff, who teaches there. Despite Winans's transgressions, Rakoff calls him "a man of considerable ethical standards," in part because Winans always said that he knew what he did was wrong and expressed remorse (Rakoff 2022 interview). To the students, Winans tells his story as a way of helping the future attorneys understand those who will come under prosecution.

"It's a helpful learning session for the students," said Rakoff, a former federal prosecutor who headed the Southern District's unit combating business crimes and securities fraud:

I think what they learn is, first, that even very good people can, because of financial pressures or otherwise, succumb to temptations to break the law. That doesn't mean they shouldn't be prosecuted, but it does mean that we should be much more forgiving of them than our society usually is.

If a well-respected judge at a prestigious law school sees benefit from hearing from Winans and discussing his case, one has to wonder why journalism textbooks and educators don't discuss it more, too. No journalism school or journalism teacher has asked Winans to share his cautionary tale (Winans 2022 interview).

## A Personal Anecdote

This author has a final, personal anecdote to encourage educators and editors to get specific on financial conflicts of interest, perhaps especially with younger staff who have not absorbed the lessons of past scandals. Early in his career, this author was a reporter for an upstart financial news service. To get scoops from sources, many of whom were traders and investors, this reporter routinely engaged in a playful exchange along the lines of, "I hear this, what do you hear?" In all likelihood, the author may well have said, "I'm working on an article about this, does it sound right to you?" This reporter does not recall being warned about being discreet, nor that he was wading into murky terrain.

At the time, this author was also actively trading, sometimes toggling between his work screen and his online trading account. While none of his investments overlapped with his coverage, by nature of his work the reporter was privy to nonpublic information that informed his overall investment strategy. At one point in conversation with a friend, this reporter noted how easy it would be to pass along investment tips based on market-moving information yet to be published. The conversation ended there, with this reporter failing to appreciate how he was peering across a red line. Nor does this author recall ever receiving, reading, or signing any policy that suggested such actions would have been unethical, or worse.

## The Journalist and the Insider

Despite new rules put in place after the Winans incident, financial scandals involving journalists hardly ended. Here are some notable cases that followed his:

- In 1989, BusinessWeek editor S. G. (Rudy) Ruderman was sentenced to six months in prison for trading on inside information obtained from proofs of his magazine (Hirsch 1989). This came during a larger investigation into about two dozen Wall Street firms for trading on advance knowledge of articles in BusinessWeek, specifically its "Inside Wall Street" column.
- In 1995, Jim Cramer—then president of money management firm Cramer & Company and an editor-at-large for Smart Money magazine, owned by Dow Jones & Company and the Hearst Corporation—faced scrutiny for touting stocks in his columns without fully disclosing his positions. After publication of Cramer's column about three companies, his holdings jumped in value by more than $2 million. "His actions raise both ethical and legal issues about the proper handling of unpublished investment advice that have plagued financial journalism for years," according to The New York Times (Zuckerman 1995).
- In 2005, CBS MarketWatch columnist Thom Calandra agreed to pay more than $540,000 to settle SEC charges that he used his investment newsletter The Calandra Report to pump up the prices of certain stocks and then illegally profit by secretly selling them (SEC 2005).
- In 2018, British journalist Geoff Foster of the Daily Mail was fined by the French market regulator for telling his sources about soon-to-be-published articles regarding takeover rumors of French companies. In 2022, the European Court of Justice overturned the

decision, ruling that Foster was allowed to discuss the content of his upcoming columns with sources to substantiate rumors (Quell 2022).

- In 2021, Bloomberg reporter Ed Hammond found his reporting dragged into a federal indictment for securities fraud (U.S. Attorney's Office Eastern District of New York 2021). A source had "cultivated" Hammond and repeatedly fed him insider tips, including about a potential takeover of a major chemicals company. Hammond's subsequent articles "were often followed by increases in the prices of the companies' stock" to the source's "significant benefit." Hammond was not charged with wrongdoing, but the case "shed light on the uneasy interplay between Wall Street reporters and their sources, who may have a financial interest in the consequences of certain stories," according to The Washington Post's media critic (Wemple 2021).

## Conclusion

In surveying how media ethics codes and educational textbooks address financial conflicts of interest, this chapter argues that the issue should be clearly addressed in all press codes and included more often in educational resources.

"It's one of those areas where people tend to assume that an ethical person just wouldn't do this, so there's no need to get specific," said Fred Brown, the former SPJ president. He noted how plagiarism would also seem obviously wrong; yet, The New York Times' Jayson Blair scandal now appears in nearly all media law and ethics textbooks. "As we have seen," Brown said, "sometimes you need to get specific about what's permitted and what's not."

While insider trading among corporate executives has been widely scrutinized, there is a virtual absence of research into potential insider trading in journalism. This issue is worth further study given that insider trading is considered a much bigger problem than is publicly known (see Patel and Putnins 2020; Vaughan 2021; Arif et al. 2022). The seemingly endless cycle of insider trading scandals in the U.S. Congress and the Federal Reserve (see Slodysko 2021; Saphir and Dunsmuir 2022) begs the question of why – or whether – such scandals don't happen more with business journalists.

## References

Arif, S. et al. (2022) "Audit Process, Private Information, and Insider Trading," *Review of Accounting Studies*, 27(3), pp. 1125–1156.

Beal, D. (2013) "SABEW: From 1963 to Today and Beyond." Available at: https://ahbj.sabew.org/story/04042013-sabew-from-1963-to-today-and-beyond/ (Accessed July 2022).

Bleakley, F. (1985) "18-Month Term For Winans," *The New York Times*, 7 August. Available at: https://www.nytimes.com/1985/08/07/business/18-month-term-for-winans.html (Accessed July 2022).

Blumstein, M. (1984) "Ex-Wall St. Journal Reporter Indicted in Stock Fraud Case," *The New York Times*, 29 August. Available at: https://www.nytimes.com/1984/08/29/business/ex-wall-st-journal-reporter-indicted-in-stock-fraud-case.html (Accessed October 2022).

Boeyink, D. and Borden, S. (2010) *Making Hard Choices in Journalism Ethics*, New York: Routledge.

Boudreaux, D. (2009) "Learning to Love Insider Trading," *The Wall Street Journal*, 24 October. Available at: https://www.wsj.com/articles/SB10001424052748704224004574489324091790350 (Accessed July 2022).

Brown, F. (2022), phone interview with Stephen Kurczy, 22 June.

Brown, F. et al. (2020) *Media Ethics: A Guide for Professional Conduct* (5th edition), Indianapolis, IN: Society of Professional Journalists.

Christians, C. (1997) "Chronology," in Cohen, E. and Elliot, D. (eds) *Journalism Ethics: A Reference Handbook*, Santa Barbara, CA: ABC-CLIO, pp. 15–27.

Christians, C. et al. (2017) *Media Ethics: Cases and Moral Reasoning* (10th edition), New York: Routledge.

Colón, A. (2001) "Ethics in Business Journalism," in Thompson, T. (ed) *Writing About Business*, New York: Columbia University Press, pp. 255–262.

Crovitz, L.G. (2015) "Information Is Not a Crime," *The Wall Street Journal*, 12 April. Available at: https://www.wsj.com/articles/information-is-not-a-crime-1428876543 (Accessed July 2022).

Elliott, D. (1997) "Conflicts of Interest," in Cohen, E. and Elliot, D. (eds) *Journalism Ethics: A Reference Handbook*, Santa Barbara, CA: ABC-CLIO, pp. 91–96.

Foreman, G. (2010) *The Ethical Journalist*, West Sussex: Wiley-Blackwell.

Goldstein, T. (1985) *The News At Any Cost: How Journalists Compromise Their Ethics to Shape the News*, New York: Simon and Schuster.

Goodwin, H. E. (1987) *Groping for Ethics in Journalism* (2nd edition), Des Moines, IA: Iowa State University Press.

Goodwin, G. and Smith, R. (1994) *Groping for Ethics in Journalism* (3rd edition), Des Moines, IA: Iowa State University Press.

Hirsch, J. (1989) "Broadcaster Gets 6-Month Prison Term," *The New York Times*, 6 April. Available at: https://www.nytimes.com/1989/04/06/business/broadcaster-gets-6month-prison-term.html (Accessed July 2022).

Hochberg, A. (2014) "Centers of Investigative Reporting: New Model, Old Conflicts," in McBride, K. and Rosenstiel, T. (eds) *The New Ethics of Journalism*, Thousand Oaks, CA: Sage, pp. 123–135.

Kovach, B. and Rosenstiel, T. (2001) *The Elements of Journalism*, New York: Three Rivers Press.

Kurtz, H. (1990) "Media Notes," *The Washington Post*, October 13. Available at: https://www.washingtonpost.com/archive/lifestyle/1990/10/13/media-notes/c08d01ca-353d-4e32-97ab-2b440e0a114e/ (Accessed July 2022).

Lee, S. T. (2005) "The Ethics of Journalistic Deception," in Wilkins, L. and Coleman, R. (eds) *The Moral Media*, Mahwah, NJ: Lawrence Erlbaum Associates, pp. 92–113.

Leland, H. E. (1992) "Insider Trading: Should It Be Prohibited?" *Journal of Political Economy*, 100(4), pp. 859–887.

Macey, J. (2007) "Getting the Word Out about Fraud: A Theoretical Analysis of Whistleblowing and Insider Trading," *Michigan Law Review*, 105, pp. 1899–1940.

Manne, H. (1966) *Insider Trading and the Stock Market*, New York: The Free Press.

Manne, H. (2003) "The Case for Insider Trading," *The Wall Street Journal*, 17 March. Available at: https://www.wsj.com/articles/SB104786934891514900 (Accessed July 2022).

McGee, R. (2008) "Applying Ethics to Insider Trading," *Journal of Business Ethics*, 77(2), pp. 205–217.

Moore, J. (1990) "What Is Really Unethical about Insider Trading?" *Journal of Business Ethics*, 9(3), pp. 171–182.

Patel, V. and Putnins, T. (2020) "How Much Insider Trading Happens in Stock Markets?" American Finance Association Annual Meeting.

Pavlik, J. (2001) *Journalism and New Media*, New York: Columbia University Press.

Quell, M. (2022) "Top EU Court Rules Financial Reporters Can Disclose Insider Information," *Courthouse News Service*, 15 March. Available at: https://www.courthousenews.com/top-eu-court-rules-financial-reporters-can-disclose-insider-information/ (Accessed July 2022).

Saphir, A. and Dunsmuir, L. (2022) "Federal Reserve Adopts Strict Trading Rules After Ethics Scandal," *Reuters*, 18 February. Available at: https://www.reuters.com/business/fed-adopts-strict-trading-rules-after-ethics-scandal-2022-02-18/ (Accessed July 2022).

Scheppele, K. (1993) "'It's Just Not Right': The Ethics of Insider Trading," *Law and Contemporary Problems*, 56(3), pp. 123–174.

SEC. (2005) "SEC Brings Fraud Charges Against Former CBS MarketWatch Columnist Thom Calandra for Illegal Trading Scheme," 10 January. Available at: https://www.sec.gov/litigation/litreleases/lr19028.htm (Accessed July 2022).

Slodysko, B. (2021) "Sen. Burr under Investigation Again for Pandemic Stock Sales," *The Associated Press*, 28 October. Available at: https://apnews.com/article/coronavirus-pandemic-donald-trump-business-health-richard-burr-8294ed00c4098b295f7c5b21eac4614b (Accessed July 2022).

Smith, R. (2003), *Groping for Ethics in Journalism* (5th edition), Ames, IA: Iowa State Press.

Steiger, P. (2022), phone interview with Stephen Kurczy, 14 June.

Tofel, R. (2022), phone interview with Stephen Kurczy, 16 June.

U.S. Attorney's Office Eastern District of New York. (2021) "Brooklyn Man Charged in Long-Running International Insider Trading Scheme," 23 March. Available at: https://www.justice.gov/usao-ednv/pr/brooklyn-man-charged-long-running-international-insider-trading-scheme (Accessed July 2022).

U.S. District Court for the Southern District of New York (1985) "United States v. Winans," 24 July. Available at: https://law.justia.com/cases/federal/district-courts/FSupp/612/827/1575678/ (Accessed July 2022).

Vaughan, L. (2021) "Most Americans Today Believe the Stock Market Is Rigged, and They're Right" in Bloomberg Businessweek, 29 September. Available at: https://www.bloomberg.com/news/features/2021-09-29/is-stock-market-rigged-insider-trading-by-executives-is-pervasive-critics-say (Accessed July 2022).

Ward, S. (2010) "Inventing Objectivity: New Philosophical Foundations," in Meyers, C. (ed) *Journalism Ethics: A Philosophical Approach*, New York: Oxford University Press, pp. 137–152.

Weaver, D. and Wilhoit, G. (1996) *The American Journalist in the 1990s*, Mahwah, NJ: Lawrence Erlbaum Associates.

Wemple, E. (2021) "Insider Trading Indictment Highlights Contacts with Bloomberg Reporter," *The Washington Post*, 1 April. Available at: https://www.washingtonpost.com/opinions/2021/04/01/insider-trading-indictment-highlights-contacts-with-bloomberg-reporter/ (Accessed July 2022).

Winans, R. F. (1986) *Trading Secrets: Seduction and Scandal at the Wall Street Journal*, New York: St. Martin's Press.

Winans, R. F. (2022) phone interview with Stephen Kurczy, 25 July.

Yen, Marianne (1988) "Insider Trading Figure Peter Brant Sentenced to 8 Months, Fined $10,000," *The Washington Post*, 27 February. Available at: https://www.washingtonpost.com/archive/business/1988/02/27/insider-trading-figure-peter-brant-sentenced-to-8-months-fined-10000/dfa581ab-7c33-49e0-a253-c2c96408c577/ (Accessed July 2022).

Zuckerman, L. (1995) "Smart Money Rethinks Conflict Rule," *The New York Times*, 20 February. Available at: https://www.nytimes.com/1995/02/20/business/smart-money-rethinks-conflict-rule.html (Accessed July 2022).

## References for ethics codes

Associated Press, *Statement of News Values and Principles*. Available at: https://www.ap.org/about/news-values-and-principles/downloads/ap-news-values-and-principles.pdf (Accessed: July 2022).

Dow Jones Company, *Dow Jones Code of Conduct*. Available at: https://www.dowjones.com/code-conduct/ (Accessed: July 2022).

Marketplace, *Our Code of Ethics*. Available at: https://www.marketplace.org/ethics-code/ (Accessed July 2022).

Micklethwait, J. *et al.* (2017). *The Bloomberg Way*. 14th ed. Hoboken, New Jersey: John Wiley & Sons.

National Public Radio, *NPR Ethics Handbook*. Available at: https://www.npr.org/about-npr/688405012/independence#conflictsofinterest (Accessed July 2022).

New York Times, *Ethical Journalism: A Handbook of Values and Practices for the News and Opinion Departments*. Available at: https://www.nytimes.com/editorial-standards/ethical-journalism.html#introductionAndPurpose (Accessed July 2022).

ProPublica, *Code of Ethics*. Available at: https://www.propublica.org/code-of-ethics (Accessed July 2022).

USA Today Network, *Principles of Ethical Conduct For Newsrooms*. Available at: https://cm.usatoday.com/ethical-conduct/ (Accessed July 2022).

Washington Post, *Policies and Standards*. Available at: https://www.washingtonpost.com/policies-and-standards/ (Accessed July 2022).

# 26

# SHAREHOLDER ACTIVISM AND THE BUSINESS MEDIA

*Desiree J. Hanford*

## Introduction

Activist shareholders want to get things done. Whether it's convincing a company's board of directors to shake up management or sell parts or all of a company or attempting to elect their own slates of directors, activist shareholders want action, and they don't always have a lot of patience for that action to occur. They typically believe a company's share price is less than it should be and are convinced they have the remedy that will bring about greater shareholder value. Perhaps not surprisingly, the executives of many companies don't agree with shareholder activists and that's when companies and activists find themselves in the news often in the form of a proxy battle.

When the term activist shareholder is used, some names likely immediately come to mind, including Carl Icahn, Nelson Peltz or T. Boone Pickens. Icahn has tangled with a long list of companies over the decades, including RJR Nabisco, Trans World Airlines Inc., Time Warner Inc. and many others. He lost a proxy fight with McDonald's Corp. in the spring of 2022 over the fast-food giant's treatment of pigs (Hirsch 2022). Peltz co-founded his hedge fund investment firm, Trian Fund Management L.P., and is known for, among other activist activities, waging the most expensive proxy battle to date with Procter & Gamble Co. in 2017 (Creswell 2017). Pickens, who died in 2019, made a name for himself and his hedge fund, BP Capital, by targeting oil and gas companies and was the chief executive of Mesa Petroleum Co. (Gelles 2018).

Icahn and Peltz are still active and questioning and cajoling companies, but they aren't the only shareholder activists grabbing headlines. Investment firm Blackwells Capital LLC has pressured the board of directors at Peloton Interactive Inc., maker of exercise equipment, to sell the company even after a new chief executive office took the reins in February 2022 (Terlep 2022). Christopher James, founder and executive chairman of Engine No. 1 LP, may not have been as well-known as Icahn or Peltz, but that changed in 2021 when the investment firm went toe-to-toe with oil giant Exxon Mobil Corp. in a proxy battle and came out on top on its demand that the oil giant address climate change concerns (Matthews 2021a).

## Definitions

It's not unusual to see the term hedge fund associated with the term activist shareholder. Hedge funds take money from investors and invest with the goal of making money. There are rules in place that many financial products must follow so that investors aren't taken advantage of or risk an amount of money they cannot afford to lose (Securities and Exchange Commission 2013). This is particularly important because "many hedge funds seek to profit in all kinds of markets using leverage (in other words, borrowing to increase investment exposure as well as risk), short-selling and other speculative investment practices" (Securities and Exchange Commission 2013).

Public companies are required to have a meeting once a year that all shareholders are allowed to attend, vote on matters and ask questions of a company's management. When a company has an annual meeting or even a special meeting, the company must first send its shareholders a proxy statement as required by the Securities and Exchange Commission, the advocate for investors which oversees and implements securities laws (Securities and Exchange Commission 2011). The Securities and Exchange Commission requires that a proxy statement contain accurate information that will be voted upon by shareholders (Securities and Exchange Commission 2011). A proxy statement is called a Form DEF 14A. "The term 'proxy' comes from the legal right a shareholder has to designate an agent – or a proxy – to vote their shares and act on their behalf" (Holton 2006, cited in Ragas 2010, p. 40).

## Proxy Contests

An activist shareholder can initiate a proxy battle with a company by nominating individuals the shareholder wants on a company's board of directors, individuals who would replace some or all of a company's current directors (A. Miller 1986, Holton 2006, cited in Ragas 2010, pp. 40–41). A company's shareholders receive proxy statements and cards from both the company – which wants shareholders to vote for directors it backs – and the activist shareholder, each side trying to convince shareholders of the merits of their nominees (Holton 2006, cited in Ragas 2010, p. 41). A proxy contest or battle is "the most aggressive and expensive form of shareholder activism" (Manne 1965; Ikenberry & Lakonishok 1993; Dasgupta & Nanda 1997; Bagley & Savage 2006; cited in Ragas 2010, p. 34).

Proxy battles between activist shareholders and public companies are not uncommon in the U.S. For example, two numbers stand out between 2005 and 2009. During that time frame, the number of these contests "more than doubled, totaling a record 133 contested elections in 2009" (Laide 2010, cited in Ragas 2012, p. 92). In that same year, the number of shareholder activism cases "identified" totaled 371 (Laide 2010, cited in Ragas 2012, p. 92).

An increase in shareholder activism stems from several factors, including financial products that didn't exist several decades ago and which are much more complicated than are stocks and bonds (Anabtawi & Stout 2008). "Today, the capital structures public firms have become far more complex. Investors can purchase not only stock and bonds but also various alternative forms of equity, debt, and hybrid instruments" (Hu 1991, cited in Anabtawi & Stout 2008, p. 1280).

## Historical Perspective

The history of shareholder activism goes back more than 100 years (Talner 1983, cited in Ragas 2010, p. 33). Shareholders of Broadway and Seventh Avenue Railroad Co. banded together in 1855, pressing the company to be more transparent about its finances (Pound 1992, cited in Ragas 2010, p. 33). Benjamin Graham, who eventually became the patriarch of value investing, waged a proxy battle in 1927 with Northern Pipeline Co. to get himself elected to the board because he thought the company was sitting on excess cash that should be given to shareholders (Gramm 2016).

The proxy contests are not cheap endeavors. Pershing Square Capital Management L.P. and Target Corp. spent what was then a record $20 million in 2009 trying to convince shareholders to support their respective stances (Crosby 2009, cited in Ragas 2012, p. 93). Hedge funds that are activist shareholders know that proxy battles aren't cheap so they typically get involved only "when the ex-ante estimated benefits of such interventions are higher than its expected costs" (Ganguly 2020, p. viii).

History was made on December 15, 2017, when the board of Procter & Gamble announced Peltz would be added to the board ending "the most expensive proxy battle ever" waged, with Peltz's Trian Fund Management firm and the consumer products maker spending "at least $60 million" arguing back and forth (Terlep & Benoit 2017). Peltz wanted Procter & Gamble, among other things, "to streamline" its business "and bring in outside talent" (Terlep & Benoit 2017). Trian Fund Management had taken a roughly $3.5 billon stake in Procter & Gamble (Terlep & Benoit 2017).

While Trian Fund Management's fight with Procter & Gamble may have been the most expensive, Peltz's proxy war with DuPont de Nemours Inc., better known as DuPont, in May 2015 may have been one of the most well-known because the company was able to defeat Peltz's push to gain four seats on the company's board of directors (Mordock 2015). All dozen DuPont incumbent directors were re-elected, despite Peltz's push to get four of the seats (Mordock 2015). DuPont and Trian Fund Management spent a total of $23 million, with DuPont spending $15 million and Peltz spending $8 million (Mordock 2015). Peltz sought to break up the company to "unlock more value for shareholders" (Hals 2015).

Icahn and his firm Icahn Enterprises L.P. have tangled with a long list of well-known companies, including eBay Inc. and Apple Inc., pushing them to do anything from change their strategies, repurchase their stock or sell themselves in whole or parts (Farrell 2014). Icahn was involved with tobacco and food company RJR Nabisco between 1995 and 2000, buying and selling stock and initiating proxy battles as he tried to convince executives to separate the company into two pieces (Farrell 2014). In the process, he made more than $850 million in profit (Farrell 2014). Icahn pushed for Time Warner to break into pieces in the 2000s, after then-investment bank Lazard said the media giant should split into four pieces (Farrell 2014).

Icahn was on the winning end of a battle in June 2023 with Illumina Inc., a company that does DNA sequencing, after Chief Executive Officer Francis deSouza stepped down following pressure for his ouster by Icahn (Alfaro 2023). The company's decisions to sell and later repurchase at a higher price Grail Inc., a cancer detection company, and to do so even though European regulators opposed the move, led Icahn to get involved in the company (Alfaro 2023). A study showed that between 1995 and 2007, Icahn had invested in 22 different sectors, including pharmaceuticals, technology and oil and gas and airlines (Venkiteshwaran, Iyer, & Rao 2010). In general, he started as a passive investor, although he did communicate his ideas for "increasing value" to management (Venkiteshwaran, Iyer, & Rao 2010, p. 53).

In other cases, he has started out seeking changes in corporate strategy or governance – at times using the threat of a hostile proxy contest, or even a sale of the company or replacing management ... And Icahn's extensive use of amended 13D filings (roughly four for every initial filing) show clearly that he will change his objectives and approaches if the circumstances warrant it.

*(Venkiteshwaran, Iyer, & Rao 2010, p. 53)*

## Critical Issues and Topics

Hedge funds aren't the only activist shareholders, but they are some of the most well-known for better and for worse. Hedge funds attempt to make money "by aggressively taking a role in directing the business strategies and activities in which they invest" (Hong, p. 194). They use their roles to influence a public company's board of directors to make determinations "that may change the nature of the company substantially and, perhaps, harmfully" (Hong, p. 194).

Changes that hedge funds sometimes seek include the sale of businesses that aren't related to a company's main business, a company buying back its own stock, "extraordinary dividends," or a sale of the entire company (Slawotsky 2015–2016, p. 275). "Such campaigns often involve an implicit or explicit threat of a proxy contest to remove some or all of the target board members and senior management if the activists' demands are not met" (Slawotsky 2015–2016, p. 275).

Supporters of activist shareholders and smaller shareholders claim that activist shareholders have an important watchdog-type role and that "corporate mismanagement and managerial misconduct" would go unchecked without activist funds (Rushton 2014, cited in Slawotsky 2015–2016, p. 275). Large activist shareholders give a voice to smaller shareholders, who alone wouldn't have the ability to tackle a matter (Klein & Zur 2009, cited in Slawotsky 2015–2016, p. 280). Hedge funds are not without their critics, including those who are on the receiving end of their efforts. Critics claim that boards of directors must spend a lot of time and money addressing the complaints lodged by hedge funds (Mordock 2015; Slawotsky 2015–2016, p. 278).

## Role of the Media

Media coverage can affect the actions a company's executives and management take (King & Soule 2007; King 2008; Sobieraj 2010, cited in Bednar, Boivie & Prince 2013). All parties involved want to sway other parties to agree with their view, and the media sometimes serve as vehicles for their attempts at persuasion (Andrews & Biggs 2006; Fiss & Zajac 2004; Kennedy 2008; King 2008; Sobieraj 2010, cited in Bednar, Boivie & Prince 2013). "Even though external groups may be affecting the amount and tone of media coverage, this line of work suggests that the media coverage itself is an important determinant of firm action" (Bednar, Boivie & Prince 2013, p. 912). Research about the role that the media have on shareholder activism has compared it to political elections, with different parties vying for media attention in an effort to get across their message to the people and organizations they want to reach (Ragas 2010).

The number of items such as press releases or story ideas that are circulated during a proxy contest seems to have little effect as to how much attention the media gives the proxy battle. (Ragas 2010). However, media attention was connected to financial metrics. The bigger the company is and the more the company is worth, the more the media pays attention to a proxy battle (Ragas 2010).

The coverage that hedge funds in particular garner in the press can be problematic, because if it's bad press, a company's reputation and worth could be hurt (Soo Young Hong 2019). And when prominent activists such as Icahn and Bill Ackman are involved, shareholders may find that the heightened media coverage sways "their judgment on what is truly in the best interests of the corporation" (Soo Young Hong 2019).

## What's Happening Now

Activist shareholders haven't shown any sign of ending their involvement in either U.S.-based or global companies (Herbst-Bayliss, Murugaboopathy & Jessop 2022). For the first six months of 2022, through June 22, research firm Insightia, which was acquired by Diligent Corp., found there were 669 activist movements started at companies with headquarters in the U.S., up from 503 started during the same period in 2021 (Herbst-Bayliss, Murugaboopathy & Jessop 2022). Worldwide, Insightia found that 999 activist movements were started in the first months of 2022, which was down from 825 campaigns in 2021 (Herbst-Bayliss, Murugaboopathy & Jessop 2022). Still, activist investors slowed their campaigns in late spring 2022, becoming more measured in their actions (Herbst-Bayliss, Murugaboopathy & Jessop 2022). Insightia found that there were

> 22 activist campaigns at U.S.-headquartered companies between May 20 and June 20, down from 25 during the same time in 2021 and 42 campaigns launched in 2018, the year with the most campaigns during that period in the last seven years.
> *(Herbst-Bayliss, Murugaboopathy & Jessop 2022)*

Even with the slowing number of campaigns in late spring, activist shareholders garnered headlines in 2022. Activist investor hedge fund Macellum Advisors GP, LLC tried to replace as many as ten board of directors at Kohl's Corp., but all 13 of the company-backed directors were re-elected in May (Kapner 2022). Macellum Advisors had wanted the retailer to consider number of changes, including selling the entire company (Kapner 2022).

Two well-known names in the activist shareholder universe tangled in a proxy battle that ended in May 2022 when Icahn lost his bid to have two nominees whom he supported voted onto McDonald's board of directors (Hirsch 2022). Instead, the dozen nominees backed by the company won their re-elections. Icahn had argued that the fast-food giant had failed to keep its commitment to slowly end using small crates for pregnant sows (Hirsch 2022).

Peltz and Trian Fund Management were also active in 2022. Unilever PLC announced in May that Peltz would be added to its board in July, saying that his firm had a 1.5 percent stake in the company (Chaudhuri 2022a). Unilever had tried to purchase the consumer-healthcare business of GlaxoSmithKline PLC for $68 billion but announced in January that it wouldn't raise its offer (Chaudhuri 2022b). The company weathered criticism from shareholders about both how well the purchase would fit within Unilever and how much it was willing to pay for the business (Chaudhuri 2022b).

Other activist shareholders and companies who tangled in 2022 include Elliott Investment Management L.P. and PayPal Holdings Inc. (Deveau & Surane 2022); SOC Investment Group and Tesla Inc. (Kolodny 2022); D.E. Shaw group and FedEx Corp. (Fung and Lombardo 2022); Zendesk Inc. and Jana Partners LLC (Cimilluca 2022); and Hasbro Inc. and Alta Fox Capital Management LLC (Deveau & Wanna 2022).

## ESGs

Third Point LLC was also active in 2022, pressuring oil company Shell PLC to break into several pieces, including one for its traditional fossil-fuel refining business and one on renewable energy and liquified natural gas (Strasburg 2022). Third Point, a hedge fund owned by Daniel Loeb, took a stake in Shell in 2021 when it initially stated the company should be divided (Strasburg 2022). Third Point claimed that breaking up Shell would benefit investors "amid a shift to lower-carbon energy sources" (Strasburg 2022).

Third Point's showdown with Shell comes amid a period when activist shareholders – both those that are well-known and several that are not – are putting a greater focus on environmental, social and governance issues. Indeed, Icahn claimed that BlackRock Inc. and other activist investors focused on environmental, social and governance issues should support his effort to convince McDonald's not to use small crates for pregnant pigs (Lombardo 2022).

Engine No. 1 garnered headlines and made a name for itself in 2021 in its battle with Exxon Mobil Corp., grabbing three seats on the oil giant's board of directors in an effort to convince Exxon Mobil to be a more environmentally friendly company (Phillips 2021).

Engine's victory stands out in both shareholder activism and ESGs because the hedge fund owned a small amount of Exxon Mobil's stock yet still came out on top (Matthews 2021a, 2021b; Lombardo 2022). Engine No. 1 was able to convince larger firms such as State Street Corp., Vanguard Group and BlackRock to support its position (Phillips 2021; Lombardo 2022). "The firm is among a new breed of shareholder activists, ones driven by the idea that social good also benefits the bottom line, just as policy and public sentiment on the environment are evolving" (Phillips 2021). Although Engine No. 1 hasn't launched a proxy battle, it has thrown its support behind General Motors Co. (GM) and its ambitions to lead the auto industry in electric vehicles (Colias 2021).

Still, there are signs of a bumpy road ahead for ESG proposals. In addition, on average, backing by shareholders at annual meetings for ESG proposals reached about 22 percent in 2023, 11 percentage points lower than the peak in 2021 and the lowest point since 2017, according to vote tallies compiled by the Sustainable Investment Institute through June 8, 2023 (Green & Kishan 2023). The decline is attributed to the opposition of EGS proposals by the Republican Party (Green & Kishan 2023).

Work conducted by the Center for Active Stewardship shows that in 2023 shareholder "support for climate-related proposals has essentially halved to about 23 percent from two years ago" (Green & Kishan 2023). "Before, investors were merely asking for reporting disclosing emissions goals and energy-transaction plans. Recent proposals are much more specific about executing those plans," said Nolan Lindquist, executive director of the center (Green & Kishan 2023).

## Future Directions

While tactics and names may change, activist shareholders look to remain a bee in the bonnet of some company executives. Icahn, in his quest to influence McDonald's and Kroger Co., won media attention for his more subtle approach in pressuring the pair compared with his strategies over the past decades with other companies. In Pershing Square Holdings Ltd.'s 2021 annual report, Bill Ackman wrote in a letter to investors that the hedge fund has "permanently retired" from activist short selling, a tactic he called the "noisiest form of activism" that the fund has rarely engaged in (Pershing Square Holdings Ltd. 2022, p. 15; Sorkin et al. 2022). The strategy brought media attention to Pershing Square, Ackman said

(Pershing Square Holdings Ltd. 2022, p. 15). Investors in the fund inquired about whether the fund's approach had changed, viewing the fund as having become a "quieter investor" (Pershing Square Holdings Ltd. 2022, p. 15). This approach doesn't garner media attention, particularly compared with proxy contests, Ackman noted (Pershing Square Holdings Ltd. 2022, p. 15).

Peltz has found himself on the receiving end of shareholder activism. Invesco Ltd., Janus Henderson Investors UK Ltd., Pelham Capital Ltd. and Global Value Fund – all investors in Trian Fund Management's Trian Investors 1 Ltd – claim the company has taken a detour from its original purpose and wants current directors replaced (Steinberg 2022). Trian owns shares of both Invesco and Janus Henderson (Steinberg 2022).

Icahn is also in the crosshairs of activist shareholders (Maloney & Gordon 2023). Hindenburg Research LLC, a short-selling firm with Nathan Anderson at the helm, said in a May 2023 report that shares of Icahn Enterprises are overvalued and the company can't continue paying dividends at its current rate (Maloney & Gordon 2023 and Hindenburg Research). The report noted that the company's current dividend yield, at the time the report was published, was about 15.8 percent, "making it the highest dividend yield of any U.S. large cap company by far, with the next closest at ~9.9%" (Hindenburg Research).

While activist shareholders try to force companies to make a public commitment on a topic the shareholders support, advocacy groups are raising red flags on "companies' adoption of policies that some view as being overly political" (Vanderford 2023).

> Such proposals questioning companies' stances on social and environmental issues have come in record numbers, surging to 74 for annual meetings held before May 31, up from 43 last year, according to data from ISS Corporate Solutions, a unit of proxy-advisory firm ISS.
>
> *(Vanderford 2023)*

Given the state of political affairs in the U.S. in 2023, proposals from the far left to the far right in politics are entangling companies in culture wars, a trend that is likely to continue (Vanderford 2023).

## Conclusion

There is little doubt that activist shareholders believe strongly in what they are doing. They spend the money to purchase shares of a company's stock, take the time to nominate individuals to boards of directors and attempt to influence shareholder voting for both board membership and proposals.

In addition, a rule change that went into effect September 1, 2022, requires the usage of universal proxy cards by companies in contested board of director elections (Securities and Exchange Commission 2021). The rule means that a nominee for a company's board of directors – whether the individual was nominated by the company or a shareholder – must be listed on the universal proxy card. The change by the SEC allows shareholders to vote for their choice of directors either by proxy or in person (Securities and Exchange Commission 2021).

Given their extensive involvement in public companies for many decades, activist shareholders, including those focused on ESG, aren't likely to disappear anytime soon. But that doesn't necessarily mean there will be a spike in the number of proxy battles launched by activist shareholders in the coming months and years, according to David J. Collis, adjunct professor at Harvard Business School.

> [Proxy battles] are driven by the state of the economy and by vehicles likes the capital markets. When stock prices fall, that creates an opportunity to say 'Current management isn't doing a very good job. Look at how much the stock price has gone down. We can suggest an alternative way forward and try to create more shareholder value.'
>
> *(Collis 2022)*

Kevin Kaiser, senior director of the Harris Family Alternative Investments Program and adjunct full professor of finance at the Wharton School of the University of Pennsylvania, separates governance from environmental and societal in ESG (Kaiser 2022). Governance exists to make sure company executives don't allow owners to influence management and instead assure that management is driven by what serves the customer and the well-being of the business, not simply the pet projects of the owners (Kaiser 2022).

> [While] 'E' and 'S' are things that sensible people may or may not agree with, it doesn't change the fact that it doesn't honor the principles of putting the customer first. Just because you're the owner doesn't mean you get to decide. That was the old world. The new world is the customer decides, and we don't tell the customers if they're right or wrong. We listen to the customers and try to allocate resources accordingly.
>
> *(Kaiser 2022).*

ESG is going to become more important going forward, and it will be a challenge for boards of directors to incorporate it into their decision making (Kaiser 2022). If maximizing the value of a company is consistent with carrying through on ESGs because it's what customers, employees and communities want, there is no challenge or battle to fight (Kaiser 2022). "Just keep doing what you're supposed to do, which is maximize value, and you will naturally take these things into account" (Kaiser 2022). But if ESGs don't represent the interest of those three groups and a company does the EGSs anyway, challenging or compromising shareholder value, that's where the "G" bumps up against the "E" and the "S" for a board of directors (Kaiser 2022).

> Because now your board, your fiduciary duty, is about to be compromised by your interest in doing this other thing that isn't maximizing the value, the well-being, of the company but instead is implementing a policy you personally believe in or somebody you talked to or your shareholder believes in. And that's where you're going to have difficulty. But [ESG] is not going away. It's going to be an increasing pressure and challenge for board for a long time.
>
> *(Kaiser 2022)*

## References

Alfaro, T. R. (2023). Illumina CEO DeSouza Resigns Following Pressure From Icahn. *Bloomberg* [online]. Available at https://www.bloomberg.com/news/articles/2023-06-11/illumina-ceo-desouza-resigns-after-facing-pressure-from-icahn?sref=XfJMvH3v (Accessed 11 June 2023).

Anabtawi, I. and Stout, L. (2008). Fiduciary Duties for Activist Shareholders. *Stanford Law Review*, Volume 60, Issue 5, p. 1280 (Accessed 16 May 2022). Available at: http://www.stanfordlawreview.org/wp-content/uploads/sites/3/2010/04/AnabtawiStout.pdf

Bednar, M., Boivie, S. and Prince, N. (2013). Burr Under the Saddle: How Media Coverage Influences Strategic Change. *Organization Science*, Volume 24, No. 3, May-June. Available at: https://pubsonline-informs-org.turing.library.northwestern.edu/doi/epdf/10.1287/orsc.1120.0770 (Accessed 1 May 2022).

Chaudhuri, S. (2022a). Unilever to Add Activist Investor Nelson Peltz to Board. *The Wall Street Journal* [online]. Available at: https://www.wsj.com/articles/unilever-to-add-activist-investor-nelson-peltz-to-board-11653980567 (Accessed 15 June 2022).

Chaudhuri, S. (2022b). Unilever Walks Away From Glaxo Consumer-Healthcare Deal. *The Wall Street Journal* [online]. Available at: https://www.wsj.com/articles/unilever-walks-away-from-glaxo-consumer-healthcare-deal-11642615204?mod=article_inline (Accessed 15 June 2022).

Cimilluca, D. and Lombardo, C. (2022). Zendesk Is in Settlement Talks With Activist Investor Jana. *The Wall Street Journal* [online]. Available at: https://www.wsj.com/articles/zendesk-is-in-settlement-talks-with-activist-investor-jana-11655239833 (Accessed 20 June 2022).

Colias, M. (2021). Activist Investor Engine No. 1 Commends GM's Electric-Vehicle Push. *The Wall Street Journal* [online]. Available at: https://www.wsj.com/articles/activist-investor-engine-no-1-says-it-backs-gm-s-electric-vehicle-push-11633355636 (Accessed 20 June 2022).

Collis, D. (2022). Interview by Desiree Hanford [phone], 16 August.

Creswell, J. (2017). Nelson Peltz Declares Victory in Procter & Gamble Proxy Fight. *The New York Times* [online]. Available at: https://www.nytimes.com/2017/11/15/business/procter-gamble-nelson-peltz.html (Accessed 20 June 2022).

Deveau, S. and Surane, J. (2022). Activist Elliott Investment Holding Truce Talks with PayPal. *Bloomberg* [online]. Available at: https://www.bloomberg.com/news/articles/2022-07-27/activist-elliott-investment-said-to-hold-truce-talks-with-paypal?sref=XfJMvH3v (Accessed 28 July 2022).

Deveau, S. and Wanna, C. (2022). Hasbro Fends Off Activist Alta Fox's Push for Board Shake-Up. *Bloomberg* [online]. Available at: https://www.bloomberg.com/news/articles/2022-06-07/hasbro-is-said-to-fend-off-activist-s-push-for-board-shake-up?sref=XfJMvH3v (Accessed 18 June 2022).

Farrell, M. (2014). Carl Icahn Gets His Way … Eventually: A Brief History. *The Wall Street Journal* [online]. Available at: https://www.wsj.com/articles/BL-MBB-27642 (Accessed 8 May 2022).

Fung, E. and Lombardo, C. (2022). FedEx Boosts Dividend, Adds Directors in Deal With Activist D.E. Shaw. *The Wall Street Journal* [online]. Available at: https://www.wsj.com/articles/fedex-adds-board-members-in-deal-with-activist-d-e-shaw-11655212122 (Accessed 20 June 2022).

Ganguly, A. (2020). *Essays in External Corporate Governance*. Ph.D. Thesis. Indiana University. Available at: https://www.proquest.com/docview/2426559907?parentSessionId=tFRBc5YV5%2FQFCbWkBg%2B9L2vLAP9lRHnZp2p%2BvVhBfNE%3D&accountid=12861 (Accessed 15 July 2022).

Gelles, D. (2018). T. Boone Pickens, a Texas-Size Businessman, Calls It Quits. *The New York Times* [online]. Available at: https://www.nytimes.com/2018/01/20/business/t-boone-pickens.html (Accessed 16 May 2022).

Gramm, J. (2016). The Activist Playbook Is Nearly 90 Years Old – and the First Chapter Was Written by Warren Buffett's Mentor. *Insider* [online]. Available at: https://www.businessinsider.com/benjamin-graham-was-the-first-shareholder-activist-2016-6 (Accessed 1 May 2022).

Green, J. and Kishan, S. (2023). Support for ESG Shareholder Proposals Plummets Amid GOP Backlash. *Bloomberg* [online]. Available at: https://www.bloomberg.com/news/articles/2023-06-09/support-for-esg-shareholder-proposals-plummets-amid-gop-backlash?sref=XfJMvH3v (Accessed 11 June 2023).

Hals, T. (2015). DuPont Wins Board Proxy Fight Against Activist Investor Peltz. *Reuters* [online]. Available at: https://www.reuters.com/article/us-dupont-trian/dupont-wins-board-proxy-fight-against-activist-investor-peltz-idUSKBN0NY1JI20150513 (Accessed 15 June 2022).

Herbst-Bayliss, S., Murugaboopathy, P. and Jessop, S. (2022). Where Have All the Shareholder Activists Gone? Campaigns Slow Amid Market Turmoil. *Reuters* [online]. Available at https://www.reuters.com/business/where-have-all-shareholder-activists-gone-campaigns-slow-amid-market-turmoil-2022-06-29/ (Accessed 1 July 2022).

Hindenburg Research LLC. (2 May 2023). Icahn Enterprises: The Corporate Raider Throwing Stones From His Own Glass House. *Report* [online]. Available at https://hindenburgresearch.com/icahn/ (Accessed 11 June 2023).

Hirsch, L. (2022). Carl Icahn Gets Only 1 Percent of McDonald's Investors to Support His Campaign on Pigs. *The New York Times* [online]. Available at: https://www.nytimes.com/2022/05/26/business/carl-icahn-mcdonalds-pigs.html (Accessed 1 June 2022).

Kaiser, K. (2022). Interview by Desiree Hanford [Zoom], 11 August.

Kapner, S. (2022). Kohl's Investors Reject Activist's Push to Overhaul Board. *The Wall Street Journal* [online]. Available at: https://www.wsj.com/articles/kohls-investors-vote-on-activists-push-to-overhaul-board-11652266800 (Accessed 15 May 2022).

Kolodny, L. (2022). Activist Investor Group Asks SEC to Investigate Tesla Over Plan to Shrink Board. *CNBC* [online]. Available at: https://www.cnbc.com/2022/07/01/activist-investors-ask-sec-to-probe-tesla-over-plans-to-shrink-board.html (Accessed 6 July 2022).

Lombardo, C. (2022). BlackRock, Other ESG-Minded Investors Should Back His McDonald's Campaign, Icahn Says. *The Wall Street Journal* [online]. Available at: https://www.wsj.com/articles/blackrock-other-esg-minded-investors-should-back-his-mcdonald-s-campaign-icahn-says-11650503034 (Accessed 15 May 2022).

Maloney, T. and Gordon, A. L. (2023). Carl Icahn Is $15 Billion Poorer After Hunter Becomes the Hunted. *Bloomberg* [online]. Available at: https://www.bloomberg.com/news/articles/2023-05-22/carl-icahn-s-net-worth-takes-15-billion-hit-but-he-s-ready-to-fight-back?sref=XfJMvH3v (Accessed 23 May 2023)

Matthews, C.M. (2021a). Activist Wins Exxon Board Seats After Questioning Oil Giant's Climate Strategy. *The Wall Street Journal* [online]. Available at: https://www.wsj.com/articles/activist-wins-exxon-board-seats-after-questioning-oil-giants-climate-strategy-11622050087 (Accessed 15 May 2022).

Matthews, C.M. (2021b). Activist Likely to Gain Third Seat on Exxon Board. *The Wall Street Journal* [online]. Available at: https://www.wsj.com/articles/activist-likely-to-gain-third-seat-on-exxon-board-11622664757?mod=article_inline (Accessed 15 May 2022).

Mordock, J. (2015). DuPont Spent $15M to Keep Activist Investor Off Board. *USA Today* [online]. Available at: https://www.usatoday.com/story/money/business/2015/05/19/dupont-spent-15m-proxy-fight/27575179/ (Accessed 1 June 2022).

Pershing Square Holdings Ltd. (2022). 2021 Annual Report, p 15. Available at: https://assets.pershingsquareholdings.com/2022/03/29140526/Pershing-Square-Holdings-Ltd.-2021-Annual-Report.pdf (Accessed 1 July 2022)

Phillips, M. (2021). Exxon's Board Defeat Signals the Rise of Social-Good Activists. *The New York Times* [online]. Available at: https://www.nytimes.com/2021/06/09/business/exxon-mobil-engine-no1-activist.html (Accessed 18 May 2022).

Ragas, M. W. (2010). *Agenda-Building and Agenda-Setting in Corporate Proxy Contests: Exploring Influence Among Public Relations Efforts, Financial Media Coverage And Investor Opinion.* Ph.D. Thesis. University of Florida. Available at https://www.proquest.com/docview/743817385?parentSessionId=wdVpVv2UGXQ76NTwhOUGU1gIhiUk5BdLIe8Y8xFtfeU%3D&accountid=12861 (Accessed 16 May 2022).

Ragas, M. W. (2012). Issue and Stakeholder Intercandidate Agenda Setting among Corporate Information Subsidies. *Journalism and Mass Communication Quarterly,* Volume 89, No. 1, pp. 92–93. Available at https://www.proquest.com/docview/1026654795/fulltextPDF/4E07D48DA65448ECPQ/1?accountid=12861 (Accessed 18 May 2022).

Securities and Exchange Commission. (2011) Proxy Statement. Available at: https://www.sec.gov/answers/proxy.htm (Accessed 1 May 2022).

Securities and Exchange Commission. (2013) *Investor Bulletin: Hedge Funds* (SEC Publication No. 139). Available at: https://www.sec.gov/files/ib_hedgefunds.pdf (Accessed 1 May 2022).

Securities and Exchange Commission. (2021) Fact Sheet. Available at: https://www.sec.gov/files/34-93596-fact-sheet.pdf (Accessed 3 November 2022).

Slawotsky, J. (2015–2016). Hedge Fund Activism in an Age of Global Collaboration and Financial Innovation: The Need for a Regulatory Update of United States Disclosure Rules. *Review of Banking & Financial Law,* Volume 35, p. 275, 278, 280. Available at https://www.bu.edu/rbfl/files/2016/05/Slawotsky-Final-Formatted-2.pdf (Accessed 18 May 2022).

313

Soo Young Hong (2019). Curb Your Enthusiasm: The Rise of Hedge Fund Activist Shareholders and the Duty of Loyalty. *Fordham Journal of Corporate and Financial Law*, Volume 24, No. 1, Article 6. Available at: https://ir.lawnet.fordham.edu/jcfl/vol24/iss1/6/ (Accessed 18 May 2022).

Sorkin, A.R., Karaian, J., Gandel, S., de la Merced, M.J. Hirsch, L. and Livni, E. (2022). An Activist Investor Goes Quiet. *The New York Times* [online]. Available at: https://www.nytimes.com/2022/03/30/business/dealbook/ackman-shareholder-activism.html (Accessed 8 June 2022).

Steinberg J. (2022). Activists Target Nelson Peltz's Trian Over U.K. Fund. *The Wall Street Journal* [online]. Available at: https://www.wsj.com/articles/activists-target-nelson-peltzs-trian-over-u-k-fund-11655740646 (Accessed 1 July 2022).

Strasburg, J. (2022). Activist Investor Third Point Continues Push for Shell to Restructure. *The Wall Street Journal* [online]. Available at: https://www.wsj.com/articles/activist-investor-third-point-continues-push-for-shell-to-restructure-11652118646 (Accessed 1 June 2022).

Terlep, S. (2022). Peloton Needs to Explore a Sale, Investor Says. *The Wall Street Journal* [online]. Available at: https://www.wsj.com/articles/peloton-needs-to-explore-a-sale-investor-says-11649855894 (Accessed 15 June 2022).

Terlep, S. and Benoit, D. (2017). P&G Concedes Proxy Fight, Adds Nelson Peltz to Its Board. *The Wall Street Journal* [online]. Available at https://www.wsj.com/articles/p-g-concedes-proxy-fight-adds-nelson-peltz-to-its-board-1513377485 (Accessed 18 June 2022).

Vanderford, R. (2023). Shareholder Activists Drag Companies Into U.S. Culture Wars. *The Wall Street Journal* [online]. Available at https://www.wsj.com/articles/shareholder-activists-drag-companies-into-u-s-culture-wars-775804cd (Accessed 11 June 2023).

Venkiteshwaran, V., Iyer, S., and Rao, R. (2010). Is Carl Icahn Good for Long-Term Shareholders? A Case Study in Shareholder Activism. *Journal of Applied Corporate Finance*, Volume 22, No. 4; a Morgan Stanley Publication. Available at https://onlinelibrary-wiley-com.turing.library.northwestern.edu/doi/epdf/10.1111/j.1745-6622.2010.00301.x (Accessed 16 May 2022).

# 27

# FOLLOWING THE MONEY, NOT THE BALL

## Toward a Redefinition of Sports Business Coverage

*José Luis Rojas Torrijos*

### Introduction

For many decades, sports media coverage focused on delivering final scores, standings and reports about athletic performances in competitions to both general and specialized audiences (English 2018). Despite this "stick to sports" vision that many reporters long assumed to be their main or only mandate (Moritz 2019), sports journalists have become more aware that they are in a position to report about political, social and financial aspects around clubs and tournaments (Broussard 2020), especially when these issues have grown in importance and fans want to see the whole picture, eager to better understand what happens off the field.

As reporters have worked to put their coverage into the larger context, they've found that money is relevant everywhere on the beat. Sports has become a multi-billion-dollar industry and a unique business that has evolved, as Conrad (2017, p. 1) asserts, "into a dynamic economic juggernaut of high revenues, lucrative compensation and high visibility," in which "professional and amateur sports are not only watched, but financed, broadcast and streamed domestically and around the world."

"Financial concerns permeate every decision made in the sport industry," it's been said (Fried, DeSchriver & Mondello 2013, p. 19), and this reflects the increasing importance of business issues as a central component in the sports media coverage. As a matter of fact, "sports journalism covers a topic that is now regarded as having great economic value" (Lambert 2019, p. 7), to such an extent that "sport sits predominantly on the economic capital side of the axis in the journalistic field" (English 2016, p. 1004).

Nevertheless, the transformation of sport into what Serazio (2019, p. 15) coins as "a highly lucrative, multi-branched transnational economy of enormous scope and influence" is recent. Westerbeek and Karg (2022, p. 1) consider that there were "two value explosions in a global industry that is only decades old." According to these authors, the first one took place since the 1980s when television channels decided to broadcast more many major sports events to attract and enlarge their audiences, and this resulted in an exponential growth of media revenues for sport organizations. The second value explosion, which is currently in process, happened after sports clubs, federations and professional leagues began to fully

  DOI: 10.4324/9781003298977-32

embrace the possibilities of the internet and digital technology to better reach fans and increase their influence.

Today, clubs are global brands with supporters in every corner of the planet (Chadwick & Arthur 2008), while the revenues for major sports leagues continue to rise, "spurred by consistently rising media rights fees and the creation and dissemination of content in new platforms" (Conrad 2017, p. xiii). According to SportBusiness Consulting (2021), the global value of sports media rights soared up to $52.1 billion in 2021. Soccer continues to be the world's most-valuable discipline, earning just under $20.8 billion in media rights revenue (almost 40 percent of the total).

In the meantime, the World's Most Valuable Teams list that Forbes publishes annually indicates that American sports franchises such as Dallas Cowboys (NFL, $6.5 billion), New York Yankees (MLB, $6 billion) or New York Knicks (NBA, $5.8 billion) are clearly ahead of the rest, whereas European soccer teams such as Real Madrid ($5.1 billion) and FC Barcelona ($5 billion) are in the Top Ten (Forbes 2022).

## Identifying Domains within Sports Business Journalism

The increasing global impact of sports competitions and the multi-billion turnover this big industry consistently generates have led business journalists to cover such aspects more in depth, and sports media now see the business of sport as a core part of their journalistic coverage. Therefore, we may consider it appropriate to refer to Sports Business Journalism as a significant journalistic subfield (English 2018; Schoch & Ohl 2021) or niche (Perreault & Bell 2020; Smith 2020) that has gained relevance in news organizations positioned at the intersection of sports and business journalism.

The full meaning of "sports business journalism" may still be developing for both practitioners and scholars, but it would include financial stories behind competitions, as well as sports features and news written from business angles and approaches. In both cases, stories published either in financial or sports media outlets employ a similar lens through which specialist reporters select sources, gather information and describe facts to make them meaningful to readers or viewers. This is an example of audience-oriented journalism (Paulussen & Van Aelst 2021) that is provided whether in specialized media, in a section of a general news outlet or in general broadcast news.

Although reporting on money in sport often focuses on such specific areas as transfers data, broadcasting rights deals, sponsorships, merchandise sales and other contracts regarding events, clubs and sportspeople, reporters often look more broadly at the topic. As Berlin (2021, p. 238) notes, "at a broader level, money also shapes the way sport is organized, where and when it is played, the competitive balance and the accessibility to fans."

This implies that business sports journalism also includes the coverage of political, ethical and legal issues (Rosner & Shropshire 2011), such as scandals and corruption in the recent history of sport or in the ownership and governance of sports franchises. Thus, "sports universe has resulted in the expansion and growing sophistication of the business side" (Conrad 2017, p. 3).

## Historical Perspectives and Research

The coverage of the business of sport is, however, an underexplored topic in the academic literature. For this reason, it is necessary to evaluate the boundaries of this subfield.

Over the years, a great deal of research about the dividing line between "hard" and "soft news" has accumulated in media studies. This theory traditionally demarcated a clear distance in news production between finance, regarded as hard news – along with war reporting, political affairs or investigative journalism – and sports, considered as soft news. Sports coverage was regarded in much the same way as entertainment or human-interest stories were, as interesting but not necessarily central to the media mission. This dichotomy reflects "the hierarchy that separates the higher and lower forms of journalistic genres, professional practices, ethical issues, and journalism's potential socio-democratic impact" (Sjøvaag 2015, p. 101).

However, there is no consensus about what this hard and soft news exactly is, or how it should be redefined or measured in the current media landscape. This is the reason why some authors suggest using terms such as "softening of news," "tabloidization" and "growing infotainment" as synonyms (Reinemann et al. 2012) and also raise doubts about the validity of this theory.

In fact, sports journalism has been traditionally viewed as a field where reporters are perceived "as having low professionalism and status and are often accused of being controlled by sources" (English 2018, p. 1). Similarly, financial journalism is far from being exempt from critics and the most frequent accusations leveled against it are related to superficiality (Tambini 2010), sloppy practices (Shaban 2014) or even underreporting (Manning 2013).

With all this in mind, sports business journalism, as "mixed content" delivered within a bundled product, seems to challenge any theory based on former assumptions or categorizations employed in previous research.

On top of that, sports media scholarship has played a key role over the last decades in understanding and analyzing the increasingly complex world of sports, which is no longer "the toy department" of news outlets (Rowe 2007), but rather is big business with serious consequences and a high impact in society (Billings 2012). From this perspective, changes in the sports communication domains have been studied as "a major reason for the rapid growth of the sport industry" (Ruiz 2021, p. 7).

However, previous research highlights the interdisciplinary nature of sport and "opens up the range of ways in which the study of sports journalism connects with wider issues" and non-sports contexts (Boyle et al. 2010, p. 248). In this regard, sports business media appear to enlarge the volume and diversify the range of sports journalism that one now finds across the media (Boyle 2006).

## Critical Issues and Topics

As with other areas of journalism, sports news is being reshaped in the current media landscape due to a number of factors. These include the advent of new creators coming from adjacent fields such as bloggers, streamers or youtubers, who adopt norms and practices historically attributed to sports journalism (Perreault & Bell 2020; McEnnis 2022), the proliferation of digital platforms that are acquiring rights and developing their own content (Westerbeek & Karg 2022) and the heavy use of mobile devices and social media and their impact on sports viewing patterns (Lopez-Gonzalez et al. 2019).

All these elements act as drivers of change in the globalized industry of sport as well as in sports media production. The internet and the 24/7 sports news cycle have forced sports media to adjust their coverage to changes resulting from the technology of the field, from requirements and expectations among media consumers and from "wider structural economic and cultural shifts in what can be called the sports economy" (Boyle 2006, p. 27). As Thorpe (2017, p. 554) explains, new media technologies are playing a key role in building a sense of community among fans and audiences and "contributing to new relationships between corporations, action sporting bodies, and communities."

Besides, new relationships between media and audiences in the digital ecosystem strongly determine news selection decisions and, consequently, criteria when considering a story's newsworthiness. Regarding sports and business media coverage, editorial choices are ever more based on real-time viewer figures and engagement with followers through social media (Bradshaw & Minogue 2020). This means a more varied range of concerns and issues, such as celebrity affairs, human-interest stories and entertainment, may find representation in the agenda.

Although what is judged newsworthy in business news usually differs between mainstream and specialist media outlets, in some cases, "it is difficult to be sure whether what is being offered is financial news in the guise of entertainment or vice versa" (Doyle 2006, p. 448). In this regard, Manning (2013) points out that while specialist news outlets operate with distinct news values on the assumption that their target audience is more inclined to absorb technical analysis, many journalists tend to approach financial stories with mainstream selection criteria. According to this author (2013, p. 179), this prevents their news organizations from covering "stories which involve high levels of complexity and appear to lack a 'personality' around which to hang information."

Therefore, sports journalists need to be able to explain complex financial stories, which has become an important goal, while making them attractive and accessible to public at large. Sports business journalists and media, moreover, face a great challenge once they decided to broaden their area of operations and adapt their content to digital audiences.

## The Blossoming of Sports Business Journalism

Indeed, the irruption of the internet and digital technologies pushed most legacy media to rethink their business models, which became more and more audience-oriented to build news subscriptions. As a result of this, at the beginning of the 21st-century financial news outlets pivoted from niche to general interest editorial formulas and expanded their coverage in political and sports news (Vara 2010, p. 42).

That was precisely the case of The Wall Street Journal, which created a sports desk as a strategy to reach new readers (Berlin 2021). Similarly, the weekly magazine The Economist also broadened its scope to include new content such as technology, science or sports, always from the business angle (Soriano-Llobera 2012).

Bloomberg launched in 2010 Bloomberg Sports as a vertical division focused on technology and data analysis opportunities in sports that also deliver services for teams, broadcasters and athletes. Bloomberg Sports includes subscription products that are complemented by Stats Insights, the sports analysis blog created two years later by this company (Bloomberg 2012). Likewise, Money, Australia's longest-running finance magazine, was launched in 1999 and later built its own sports business section.

Sports also has gained stature at the Financial Times, where this content traditionally had been part of leisure industry coverage. In 2018, Murad Ahmed became the first Sports Editor at the newspaper, where he has led the coverage of sport while steering a team of reporters who write across all sections of the paper. To differentiate FT's sports coverage from others, they focus on the business around competitions instead of reporting about the action.

To make this clear, they repeat a phrase internally, which is "We follow the money, not the ball" (Rojas-Torrijos 2020a).

The recognition and acceptance of sports referred to as business in financial media owe much to pioneers in the field such as SportBusiness International, a magazine founded in 1996 and whose reports "have had a revolutionary impact upon the dissemination of information in this industry" (Westerbeek & Smith 2003, p. x). So, too, has the Forbes Sports Money section had a big impact with its annual value estimates for sportspeople and franchises in major leagues for a quarter of a century and has become "the most popularly cited source for team values" (Swayne & Dodds 2011, p. 1200).

With all these outlets paving the way, sports business journalism expanded as a journalistic niche in the midst of the COVID-19 pandemic (Rojas-Torrijos 2022). When there was any sport during the shutdown, the most important stories to cover for sports reporters became the ones coming from the business side of this industry as a part of a global financial crisis. As a consequence, many sports journalists moved their focus to financial issues and dove into them in a much more considered and profound way than they had previously.

In addition, some new sports business projects emerged. The website Sportico began operations in June 2020 to provide specifically sports industry breaking news, data and insights, with a digital platform, newsletters and events. As that happened, other news organizations positioned at the intersection of sports and business such as Business Insider were reinforced and increased the volume of stories around the sports industry. Even Front Office Sports, a digital-only media outlet launched in 2019, became a specialist agency shortly after and started to deliver sports business content to other outlets like Digiday, Fast Company or Fox Business.

Also in 2020, Financial Times launched "Scoreboard," a weekly premium newsletter designed to house the publication's best sports business content. Following this model, the Spanish news agency EFE opened in April 2021 its own sports business bulletin. Both FT "Scoreboard" and "EFE Sport Business" are very revealing because they function as verticals or mini-brands rather than sports business desks within their newsrooms, and also indicate the increasing importance of email newsletters as journalistic products to explore niches of interest and help media conquer new audiences (Rojas-Torrijos 2020a).

## Conclusion

The coverage of the sports business world is an increasingly competitive arena where there are not only new specialist publications and financial news organizations covering sports more in depth than before, but also a larger number of digital sports media outlets, such as Bleacher Report, The Athletic, Axios Sports and The Player's Tribune, entering the subfield (Adgate 2020).

Money is currently understood as an essential part of a sports reporter's beat. Indeed, a group of highly respected journalists across the sports media trade have been working on these issues for a very long time. Among others, those reporters are David Conn at The Guardian, Martyn Ziegler at The Times, Rob Harris at the Associated Press, Matt Slater at The Athletic UK and Tariq Panja at The New York Times. Berlin (2021, p. 248) refers to them as the "Sports News Lobby" and remarks the fact that "none of these have the word 'financial' in their job titles."

Moreover, the coverage of the business of sport is being redefined and expanded in the current media environment through the use of data-driven techniques and visual journalism solutions (Segel & Heer 2010) being constantly refined and developed by media labs (López-Hidalgo & Ufarte 2016, Mills & Wagemans 2021) and graphics departments in newsrooms. These innovative units are leading the transformation in media organizations (García-Avilés 2021; Hogh-Janovsky & Meier 2021) and they have always considered sports as a perfect field to test "experiments with new formats, as well as storytelling techniques and disruptive ways of engaging audiences" (Rojas-Torrijos 2020b, p. 29).

It seems clear that news organizations are finding ways to differentiate themselves in a new ecosystem crowded by emergent actors coming from the periphery of journalism and where the professional boundaries have become blurred (Lewis 2012; Carlsson 2017). This radical changing process is being especially significant in the sports field where bloggers and other creators raise questions concerning the expertise and distinctiveness of sports journalism (McEnnis 2022).

In this context, as most news operations are reshaping media business models, a more dedicated sports business journalism may offer audiences added value with content that they previously did not have. So this enhanced coverage, based on crunched numbers, fact-checked data and appealing graphics, gives media outlets an opportunity to attract new readers, build loyalty and reach out to audiences who had not been subscribers or members in the past.

## Further Reading

Berlin, P. 2021, Money. In Steen, R., Novick, J. & Richards, H. (eds.), *Routledge Handbook of Sports Journalism*, Routledge, London, 237–250.
Conrad, M. 2017, *The Business of Sports. Off the Field, In the Office* (5th ed.), On the News, Routledge, New York.
Westerbeek, H., & Karg, A. 2022, *International Sports Business. Current Issues, Future Directions*, Routledge, London.

## References

Adgate, B. 2020 (July 8), How New Publication Sportico Plans To Fit In The Sports Business World, *Forbes*, https://www.forbes.com/sites/bradadgate/2020/07/08/sportico-a-new-launch-joins-the-sports-business-world/?sh=42e7755c44bd
Berlin, P. 2021, Money. In Steen, R., Novick, J. & Richards, H. (eds.), *Routledge Handbook of Sports Journalism*, Routledge, London, 237–250.
Billings, A. 2012, Reaction Time: Assessing the Record and Advancing a Future of Sports Media Scholarship. In Billings, A. (ed.), *Sports Media: Transformation, Integration, Consumption* (1st ed.), Routledge, London, 181–190.
Bloomberg. 2012 (December 10), Bloomberg Sports Launches "Stats Insights," Sports Analysis Blog, *Bloomberg.com*. https://www.bloomberg.com/company/press/bloomberg-sports-launches-stats-insights-sports-analysis-blog/
Boyle, R. 2006, *Sports Journalism. Context and Issues*, Sage, London.
Boyle, R., Rowe, D., & Whannel, G. 2010, 'Delight in Trivial Controversy'? Questions for Sports Journalism. In Allan, S. (ed.), *The Routledge Companion to News and Journalism*, Routledge, London, 245–255.
Bradshaw, T., & Minogue, D. 2020, *Sports Journalism. The State of Play*, Routledge, London.
Broussard, R. 2020, "Stick to Sports" Is Gone: A Field Theory Analysis of Sports Journalists' Coverage of Socio-political Issues, *Journalism Studies*, 21(12), 1627–1643. https://doi.org/10.1080/1461670X.2020.1785323
Carlson, M. 2017, *Journalistic Authority: Legitimating News in the Digital Era*, Columbia University Press, New York.
Chadwick, S., & Arthur, D. (eds.) 2008, *International Cases in the Business of Sport*, Elsevier, Oxford.

Conrad, M. 2017, *The Business of Sports. Off the Field, In the Office* (5th ed.), On the News, Routledge, New York.

Doyle, G. 2006, Financial News Journalism: A Post-Enron Analysis of Approaches Towards Economic and Financial News Production in the UK, *Journalism*, 7(4), 433–452. https://doi. org/10.1177/1464884906068361448

English, P. 2016, Mapping the Sports Journalism Field: Bourdieu and Broadsheet Newsrooms, *Journalism*, 17(8), 1001–1017. https://doi.org/10.1177/1464884915576728

English, P. 2018, Sports Journalism. In Nussbaum (ed.), *Oxford Research Encyclopedia of Communication*, Oxford University Press, Oxford, 1–18.

Forbes. 2022 (May 26), The World's Most Valuable Soccer Teams 2022: Real Madrid, Worth $5.1 Billion, Is Back On Top, *Forbes.com*. https://www.forbes.com/sites/mikeozanian/2022/05/26/the-worlds-most-valuable-soccer-teams-2022-real-madrid-worth-51-billion-back-on-top

Fried, G., DeSchriver, T., & Mondello, M. 2013, *Sport Finance* (3rd ed.), Human Kinetics, Champaign, IL.

García-Avilés, J. A. 2021, Review Article: Journalism Innovation Research, a Diverse and Flourishing Field (2000–2020), *El Profesional de la Información*, 30(1), e300110. https://doi.org/10.3145/epi.2021.ene.10

Hogh-Janovsky, I., & Meier, K. 2021, Journalism Innovation Labs 2.0 in Media Organisations: A Motor for Transformation and Constant Learning, *Journalism and Media*, 2(3), 361–378. https://doi.org/ 10.3390/journalmedia2030022

Lambert, C. M. 2019, *Digital Sports Journalism*, Routledge, London.

Lewis, S. 2012, The Tension Between Professional Control and Open Participation: Journalism and its Boundaries, *Information, Communication & Society*, 15(6), 836–866. https://doi.org/10.1080/1369118X.2012.674150

Lopez-Gonzalez, H., Stavros, C., & Smith, A. C. 2019, The Transition of Second Screen Devices to First Screen Status in Sport Viewing, *Sport in Society*, 22(12), 2077–2088. https://doi.org/10.1080/17430437.2018.1554649

López-Hidalgo, A., & Ufarte, M. J. 2016, Laboratorios de Periodismo en España. Nuevas Narrativas y Retos de Futuro, *Ámbitos: Revista Internacional de Comunicación*, 34, 1–11. https://revistascientificas.us.es/index.php/Ambitos/article/view/9360

Manning, P. 2013, Financial Journalism, News Sources and the Banking Crisis, *Journalism*, 14(2), 173–189. https://doi.org/10.1177/1464884912448915

McEnnis, S. 2022, *Disrupting Sports Journalism*, Routledge, London.

Mills, J., & Wagemans, A. 2021, Media Labs: Constructing Journalism Laboratories, Innovating the Future: How Journalism Is Catalysing its Future Processes, Products and People, *Convergence*, 27(5), 1462–1487. https://doi.org/10.1177/1354856521994453

Moritz, B. 2019 (December 18), The End of "Stick to Sports", *Nieman Lab*, https://www.niemanlab.org/2019/12/the-end-of-stick-to-sports/

Paulussen, S., & Van Aelst, P. 2021, News Values in Audience-Oriented Journalism: Criteria, Angles, and Cues of Newsworthiness in the (Digital) Media Context. In Temmerman, M. & Mast, J. (eds.), *News Values from an Audience Perspective*, Palgrave Macmillan, London, 37–55.

Perreault, P., & Bell, T. R. 2020, Towards a "Digital" Sports Journalism: Field Theory, Changing Boundaries and Evolving Technologies, *Communication and Sport*, 10(3), 398–416. https://doi.org/10.1177/2167479520979958

Reinemann, C., Stanyer, J., Scherr, S., & Legnante, G. 2012, Hard and Soft News: A Review of Concepts, Operationalizations and Key Findings, *Journalism*, 13(2), 221–239. https://doi.org/10.1177/1464884911427803

Rojas-Torrijos, J. L. 2020a (June 26), Murad Ahmed (FT Sports Editor): "We Follow the Money, Not the Ball", *Periodismodeportivodecalidad*. https://periodismodeportivodecalidad.blogspot.com/2020/06/murad-ahmed-ft-sports-editor-we-follow.html

Rojas-Torrijos, J. L. 2020b, Gamification of Sports Media Coverage: An Infotainment Approach to Olympics and Football World Cups, *Communication & Society*, 33(1), 29–44. https://doi.org/10.15581/003.33.1.29-44

Rojas-Torrijos, J. L. 2022 (December 1), El Auge del Periodismo Deportivo de Negocios: dos Newsletters Convertidas en Algo Más Que Secciones, *mip.umh.es*. https://mip.umh.es/blog/2022/01/12/auge-periodismo-deportivo-negocios-newsletters-secciones/

Rosner, S., & Shropshire, K. 2011, *The Business of Sports*, Jones & Bartlett Learning, Burlington, MA.

Rowe, D. 2007, Sports Journalism: Still the 'Toy Department' of the News Media? *Journalism*, 8(4), 385–405. https://doi.org/10.1177/1464884907078657

Ruiz, N. 2021, Rising to the Top in Sport Communication in the Digital Age. In Pedersen, P., Laucella, P., Geurin, A. & Kian, E. (eds.), *Strategic Sport Communication*, Human Kinetics, Champaign, IL, 3rd ed., 4–22.

Schoch, L., & Ohl, F. 2021, How Can They Like Doing That?" The Ambivalent Definition of Legitimate Work in Sports Journalism, *Journalism Studies*, 22(3), 263–281. https://doi.org/10.1080/1461670X.2020.1861474

Segel, E., & Heer, J. 2010, Narrative Visualization: Telling Stories with Data, *IEEE Transactions on Visualization and Computer Graphics*, 16(6), 1, 139–148. https://doi.org/10.1109/TVCG.2010.179

Serazio, M. 2019, *The Power of Sports. Media and Spectacle in American Culture*, New York University Press, New York.

Shaban, H. 2014, February 5, What Has Become of Business Journalism? *The New Yorker*, https://www.newyorker.com/business/currency/what-has-become-of-business-journalism

Sjøvaag, B. 2015, Hard News/Soft News. The Hierarchy of Genres and the Boundaries of the Profession. In Carlsson, M. & Lewis, S. C. (eds.), *Boundaries of Journalism*, Routledge, London, 101–117.

Smith, A. L. 2020, *Niche Journalism: Successful Steps in a Saturated, Modern Market*, Honors College Theses, Wayne State University. https://digitalcommons.wayne.edu/honorstheses/63

Soriano-Llobera, J. M. 2012, *Prensa Económica, ¿Ángel o Demonio? De la Democracia a la Actualidad*, Fundación Juan Manuel Flores Jimeno, Huelva.

SportBusiness Consulting. 2021, *Global Media Report 2021.* https://www.sportbusiness.com/global-media-report-2021/

Swayne, L. E., & Dodds, M. 2011, *Encyclopedia of Sports Management and Marketing*, Sage, Los Angeles, CA.

Tambini, T. 2010, What Are the Financial Journalists for? *Journalism Studies*, 11(2), 158–174. https://doi.org/10.1080/14616700903378661

Thorpe, H. 2017, Action Sports, Social Media, and New Technologies: Towards a Research Agenda, *Communication & Sport*, 5(5), 554–578. https://doi.org/10.1177/2167479516638125

Vara, A. 2010, Periodismo Económico: Del Modelo de Nicho al Generalista. El Caso del WSJ.com. In Esteve, F. & y Blanco, E. (eds.), *Tendencias del Periodismo Especializado*, Servicio de Publicaciones de la Universidad de Málaga, Málaga, 31–48.

Westerbeek, H., & Karg, A. 2022, *International Sports Business. Current Issues, Future Directions*, Routledge, London.

Westerbeek, H., & Smith, A. 2003, *Sport Business in the Global Marketplace*, Palgrave McMillan, New York.

# PART V

# Globally Speaking

# 28

# VIVE LA DIFFÉRENCE? BUSINESS JOURNALISM IN ITS GLOBAL UNIFORMITY AND VARIETY

*Ángel Arrese*

## Introduction

Business journalism has developed around the world with the clear reference of the British and American media. For almost two centuries, with English as the lingua franca of economics and business, and with Great Britain and the United States as the great superpowers, media outlets such as The Economist, Reuters, the Financial Times, The Wall Street Journal, Forbes, Business Week, Fortune, Bloomberg and CNBC, among others, have had a great global projection. Not only have they been, due to their reach, truly international media – more than has been the case in any other journalistic field – but they have also acted as reference models for national publications and media. The "Economists" of the 19th century, the "pink" financial newspapers (emulating the Financial Times), or the national "Business Weeks" are identifiable in almost any country we analyze.

However, beyond these global references, the evolution of this sector in each country and in different areas of the planet, also shows a good number of peculiarities, as could not be otherwise. The national journalistic cultures and the different media systems, the particular evolution of political and economic contexts, the different degrees of development of business and finance, of the journalistic profession itself, etc., allow us to speak of different traditions of business journalism, and also of relevant particularities in its practice. Although it is beyond the scope of this work to develop specific national or regional features in detail, this chapter shows some relevant differences in the practice of business journalism in its different facets.

To begin in the most general way – and leaving aside aspects of the sector's historical development – the first thing that stands out when reviewing the academic literature on this news field in different countries is the different ways of designating it, with greater or lesser emphasis on the economic, financial or business dimensions of coverage.

## Economic, Business or Financial Journalism?

Since the last major economic crisis, interest in business journalism has not stopped growing, and more and more research is analyzing different aspects of this journalistic specialty

DOI: 10.4324/9781003298977-34

(Damstra and Vliegenthart 2018; Damstra et al. 2018; Lee 2014; Schiffrin 2015). Generally speaking, authors working in this field accept that there is an umbrella concept that allows them to address specificities across the news field. In fact, depending on their historical evolution and tradition when referring to this beat, different terms are used for the same reality. Thus, the British-influenced academic literature generally uses the concept of "financial journalism" (Brand 2010; Doyle 2006; Knowles 2020; Parsons 1989; Porter 1998; Tambini, 2008; Taylor 2012), the American one prefers to speak of "business journalism" (Elfenbein 1969, Gussow 1984; Roush 2006, 2022; Shaw 2016) and in continental Europe and in other latitudes such as Latin America it is most common to speak of "economic journalism" (Arrese and Vara 2011; Basile 2002; Duval 2004; Mast 1999; Poggiali 2001). In other cases, combinations of these terms are used to refer to the whole ("economic and financial journalism," "economic and business journalism"), or also the three terms together ("economic, business and financial journalism") (Kareithi and Kariithi 2005; Kirsch 1978; Kluge, 1991; Merrill 2019). All of them, except on very rare occasions, are used in a generic way to refer to "news about financial markets, macroeconomic data and trends, government economic policy, corporate news (especially earnings announcements), personal finance, and commentary about all of the above" (Timmermans 2019).

However, especially when referring more explicitly to certain types of content, the terms "economic news" (Adoni and Cohen 1978; van Dalen et al. 2017), "business news" (Davis 2000; Grünberg and Pallas 2012) and "financial news" (Kleinnijenhuis et al. 2013; Schuster 2006; Strauß and Smith 2019) often cease to be used generically (or so generically), and come to characterize categories of news that have special peculiarities, and which also present diverse problems and challenges from a journalistic point of view. Thus, for example, "economic news" is described by Van Dalen et al. (2019) as "information reported by the news media about the state of the micro- meso- and macro-economy at home or abroad" (p. 13), including "business and corporations," but leaving out financial information and markets. Recently, Pollach and Hansen (2021) have distinguished between "financial news" for news on corporate financial results, and "economic news" for news on the economy. In the corporate communication world, studies on "business news" address the special circumstances that concur when covering companies, and the effects they have on issues such as reputation, brand or business management processes (Carroll and McCombs 2003).

This terminological variety will help us to comment on some of the particularities that can be observed in different traditions of business journalism, without losing sight of the great uniformity that can be found in different markets, not only due to the influence of the great international brands in English, but also to the specific features of this news beat: the complexity of economic issues; the heavy reliance on sources and experts that are part and parcel of the news; the close interdependence between the media and the economic, business and financial players; the intensity of conflicts of interest surrounding news stories; the peculiar effects of the news in economic and financial behaviors; the tension between the elitist and mainstream approaches to news (Arrese and Vara 2011).

For the rest of the chapter, with the idea of differentiating the three subfields from the "umbrella" concept of business journalism, and to avoid the repetition of the "economic, business and financial journalism," when we refer to the latter, we will use the expression "EBF journalism," following the suggestion of Merrill (2019).

## Economic News/Journalism

In continental Europe and in other latitudes (Latin America and Africa, for example) the emphasis on "economic" to refer to this field is surely a reflection of the importance of an integrated vision of economic activity, with a strong weight of public economics in relation to the functioning of private business and finance. Historically, economic newspapers of reference in Europe such as Il Sole or the Frankfurter Zeitung reflected well the idea of an economic publication, as opposed to the format of more financial newspapers such as Financial Times or The Wall Street Journal. After World War II, the economic reconstruction led by the nation states required that this dominant "economic focus" be central in the development of this journalistic specialization (see as examples the cases of France and its economic modernization (Riutort 2000; Salmon 1963), that of the Germanic world and the development of the "social marking economy" (Kutzner 2019; Nanrendorf and Waldemar 1996), or the Nordic one and the evolution of its social-democratic economic model (Ainamo 2006; Kjaer 2007).

The framework of analysis of the production and dissemination of economic news is that of political economy and economic policies, as well as their impact on society as a whole. It is the subfield of EBF journalism focused on the interaction between economic decisions and political decisions, and for this reason, it follows the logic of journalistic coverage very similar to that of political journalism. Its central sphere of action is the decision-makers in public life, and the effect of economic news in the society. From the professional point of view, the relationship of economic journalists with decision-makers and economic experts is significantly different, as will be seen below, from that established with other sources and actors of current affairs in the world of business and finance. Of course, economic news often focuses on complex and technical issues of great public relevance, which leads, for example, to giving precedence to the opinions of the elites while disregarding less powerful sources, etc. But it would be inappropriate to state that this dependence always ends up in a phenomenon of "capture," as the relationship between media and sources in other news subfields as business and finance is often described (Schiffrin 2021). This means that the ethical dilemmas and pressures faced by journalists doing "economics" tend to be more conventional – similar, for example, to those of political news – compared to those faced by journalists covering those subfields.

But this is only true in markets where there are full democratic systems and well-developed economies (much of Europe, North America, Oceania, Japan, India and specific democratic countries in Latin America, Asia and Africa). In many others, state "control" of economic news has been (and it is) the order of the day, by a combination of censorship, ownership, and corruption.

Although economic news has historically enjoyed more "freedom" than political news in authoritarian regimes (Arrese 2017), its intimate relationship with political news continues to put it in the spotlight of the authorities. Economic news is subject to various forms of "control," increasingly sophisticated, in places such as China and Russia, or in many Arab countries, to cite a few examples (Gibbs 2021; Rozenas and Stukal 2019; Shuli 2011). That is also so in the growing number of "illiberal regimes" (e.g. Turkey, Venezuela, Singapore, Philippines) defined by Guriev and Treisman (2019) as "informational autocracies," whose key element is the gap in political and economic knowledge between the "informed elite" and the "general public." Public control over how this general public is informed about government economic policies and their consequences becomes in these countries a key mechanism for promoting populist messages.

Finally, economic news has historically played (and continues to play) a central role in the processes of economic development in the most depressed areas of the planet, which often also have weak political systems (Djankov et al. 2002). A paradigmatic case is that of Africa in the last decades (Schiffrin 2009), although there have also been others in the past, such as the countries of Southeast Asia since the 1960s (Mowlana 1967). In Africa, where economic journalism is incipient, in the last decades economic news on development processes has tried to make its way in many countries in recent decades, despite lacking material and human resources. However, with some exceptions – such as South Africa – it has done so with the difficulties inherent to dual markets, with very relevant state-controlled media and great problems of access to public and private information. As a result of that, in Africa, "most independent media are still emerging or in their infancy" (Kareithi and Kariithi 2005, p. 260).

## Business News/Journalism

Business news took shape mainly in the 19th century with the specialization of certain publications in new industries, and it acquired specific features from the end of that century and the first decades of the 20th, with phenomena such as the muckrakers and the birth of publications such as Forbes, Business Week and Fortune, to cite the most paradigmatic business magazines. The performance of companies, management issues, businesses investment and growth decisions, their successful or failed strategies, corporate governance issues, the personality of entrepreneurs, the battles between competitors, the analysis of their products and services, etc., are among the central contents of publications, sections, audiovisual programs or online outlets in this business journalism subfield. The centrality of business news within EBF journalism derives to a large extent from the tradition of American publications and journalism in this field, and from the importance of big business in that country during the 20th century. As President Coolidge noted in 1925 before the American Society of Newspaper Editors in Washington, "after all, the chief business of the American people is business. They are profoundly concerned with producing, buying, selling, investing and prospering in the world" (Coolidge 1925).

The impact of business news on different areas of company management, and the complex and difficult relations between media and companies from a journalistic perspective, with public relations activities at the center of the system, have been of constant interest among researchers, at least from the 1970s to the present day. Also, since the muckrakers, the extent to which the media cover various corporate problems (such as fraud, business malpractices, negative impacts of companies' activities on the community, on the environment, and on labor rights) in a more or less in-depth way has been a central topic of analysis (Aronoff 1979; Carroll 2010; Finn 1981; Rubin 1977; Simons and Califano 1979).

Pressure from businesses to try to control the news is stronger around business issues than around economic and financial issues. Since its beginnings, in the 19th century, there has been a vicious circle in this news beat, which is further aggravated by the more generic relationship between the media and their advertisers. The main targets of the news (companies and businessmen, to use these generic terms) are also the protagonists of business current affairs; they are the ones who – especially in large companies – make advertising investment decisions as advertisers, and sometimes they can even become shareholders or creditors of the media companies that report on them. Of course, this happens more clearly in the case of large corporations, which are the ones that attract most media interest and attention. In this sense, it is not surprising that business news generates ethical problems of special intensity in this type of coverage – in contrast to economic and financial journalism – from "red envelopes" to advertising pressures (withdrawal of advertising from the media), including the "purchase" of professionals or lists of "untouchable companies."

While business journalism cheerleading of big business during periods of economic prosperity is a universal phenomenon, the tradition of more or less incisive and critical business news varies greatly among countries, although a lenient attitude towards companies is common even in markets with well-developed business journalism. Kjaer and Morsing (2010), for example, point out how in Denmark – a good representative of the Nordic countries – businesses historically have not been exposed to the same criticism, skepticism, and anti-corporate activism as companies in the United States. In South Korea, to refer to another latitude, the increasing focus on business news versus economic news has also been accompanied by the fact that the media indirectly support the interests of individual corporations rather than the public interest (Lee & Baek 2018). In Japan, the peculiar system of access and distribution of information to the media through business press clubs ("kisha clubs"), and the rigorous system of legal guarantees that makes, for example, defamation a criminal offense, favor making the tone of business news to be very uniform and not very inquisitive (Freeman 2000; Ishii & Takeshita 2010).

In the continuum from watchdog to lapdog of business, and with the Anglo-Saxon reference as perhaps the historically more skeptical of business (Carson 2014; Haggerty and Rasmussen 1994; Levi 2006; Miller 2006; Tumber 1993), in most countries a certain connivance between business journalism and "national champions," strategic sectors or companies with high visibility and public influence (depending on the countries, banking, big industrialists, big energy companies, etc.) is usual (Almiron 2007; Lee et al. 2019; Pansa 1986; Tienari et al. 2007; Valentini and Romenti 2011). As Verhoeven (2016) points out in his extensive review of studies on the relationship between media and corporations, and its effect on business news, a multi-leveled process of co-production of business news with the key idea of interdependence is the dominant model in a large number of countries. It is not surprising that in this context it is quite common that the most scandalous business wrong-doings of a country's large companies are not scoops in the domestic media, but in the large global media (such as Bloomberg, Reuters, the Financial Times and The Wall Street Journal). It is enough to recall the recent case of Wirecard, one of the biggest corporate scandals ever experienced in Germany (Haseborg & Bergermann 2020), uncovered by the Financial Times. The Economist commented on the role of the domestic media in this story: "The German press, including Handelsblatt, the business newspaper of record, mostly swallowed the firm's line that the attacks on it were illegal moneymaking schemes, or part of an Anglo-Saxon plot to destroy a continental European champion" (The Economist 2022).

The usual interdependence between media and business, which turns business news into a process of continuous "negotiation" (Grafström & Pallas 2007; Kjær & Langer 2005), is significantly aggravated when – in addition to interests such as advertising – other deeper links are added between them. A paradigmatic case is that of ownership. The exercise of a freer and more independent business journalism is or can be seriously threatened when large non-media corporations, state-owned companies or businessmen closely linked to power own or actively participate in the ownership of media that are committed to quality journalism in this news beat (Arrese 2005). It is striking, for example, that in countries such as Italy a large part of the media is controlled by industrial conglomerates, and that the main shareholder of the leading economic daily, Il Sole 24 Ore, is the Cofindustria (the Italian employers' federation and national chamber of commerce) (Colby 1989), or that in France the main specialized daily, Les Echos, is also in the hands of the country's richest man, Bernard Arnault, main shareholder, among others, of the luxury giant LVMH (Davidson & Chazaud 2010). This pattern is also found in other countries, from some with a mature business journalism, such as South Korea (Lee & Baek 2018) or India (Narisetti 2021), to others that have recently developed it, such as Eastern European countries (Zielonka 2015). Finally, in more authoritarian regimes in areas of Africa, Latin America and in Southeast Asia, and in countries such as China or Russia, along with the state media, it is common for business media to fall into the hands of businessmen or oligarchs closely related to the political power. The leading economic newspapers in Russia, for example, have become the property of two oligarchs close to the Kremlin, Alisher Usmanov (Kommersant) and Ivan Eremin (Vedomisti) (Buckley 2011; Seddon 2020).

A final aspect of diversity in the practice of business journalism is the variety of culturally determined professional practices that pose important ethical challenges. As an example – among the many practices that could be analyzed in this field – one can consider the case of the various forms of "cash for news coverage." While this practice is generally unacceptable in business journalism in most Western countries and in Japan, its extension is very significant in other latitudes. "Brown envelopes" in much of Africa (Ndangam 2006; Skjerdal 2010) and in Arab countries (Onyebadi & Alajmi 2021), "red envelopes" in China and other Asian countries (Hanitzsch 2005; Kurambayev & Freedman 2020; Li 2013; Romano 2000; Tsetsura 2015; Zhang 2009), "zakazukha" in Russia and other Eastern European countries (Klyueva & Tsetsura 2015), "chayotes" or "mordidas" in Mexico and Latin American countries (Márquez Ramírez 2012) are some of the denominations for many of the bribery modalities that are commonplace in business desks across the planet (see as a global reference the International Index of Bribery for News Coverage (Kruckeberg & Tsetsura 2003) and Ristow (2010)). Given such diversity, as pointed out by Yang (2012), we must be careful when making comparisons or categorical moral and professional judgments, since there are many factors (cultural, economic, educational, etc.) that somehow determine the "possible" journalistic practice in each country.

## Financial News/Journalism

News on markets, and in particular on stock exchanges, is at the very origin of EBF journalism. From Tulip Mania (XVII) to the dotcom bubble (XX), through the South Sea Bubble (XVIII) or the crash of 1929, financial news has been a central element in the emergence and subsequent explanation of financial booms and crashes, especially in stock markets, but also around markets of other financial assets. It is not surprising that the first way of referring to this journalistic specialty, back in the 19th century, was "financial press/journalism" (Schifferes 2020), and that it was in Great Britain and its colonies where this focus on financial news, up to the present day (with the City as the main reference point), ended up symbolizing better than any other the peculiar nature of EBF journalism. More than a century ago, Charles Diguid (1901) synthesized in the work of the City journalist and in the genre of the "Money article" the evolution of the "old" to the "new" financial journalism, which ranged from The Economist and the two London financial dailies (the Financial Times and the Financial News) to the money columns and notes of the Daily Mail, the Daily Express or the Evening Standard.

The relationship between financial news and market developments generates very special types of interactions and information effects (Davis 2006). The impact that financial news can have on the evolution of individual stocks or on the stock market as a whole is very specific; it can translate into gains and losses for investors, and therefore there is enormous interest in managing it in a certain direction (Barber & Odean 2008; Tetlock 2007). It is, moreover, a field of information very determined by momentum, by news in real time, and in which phenomena such as speculation, the spreading of rumors, spectacularization or the leaking of interested information are the order of the day (Lee 2012; Strauß 2019). All this means that financial news is particularly sensitive (much more so than economic and business news), and peculiar professional problems arise, accordingly.

Journalists who work in this realm deal with a universe of sources, which produces considerable informative asymmetry (Stiglitz 2015), addressed through a process of "recursive mediation" (Grünberg & Pallas 2012). Company insiders, brokers, institutional investors, financial analysts, etc., constitute an informational ecosystem that feed back on each other. Davis (2005) and Thompson (2009, 2012) synthesize these peculiarities of the markets for financial news in the concept of "reflexivity," according to which specialized media and journalists are an essential part of the process of seeking the consensus necessary for the efficient functioning of markets. Both journalists and financial players "are structurally predisposed to reinforce market consensus by focusing market attention on particular stories or frames and providing the context for interpreting financial news" (Thompson 2012, p. 222). As a consequence, it is in this news beat where more doubts are raised about role of EBF journalism, which moves between its contribution to the achievement of markets efficiency and its traditional watchdog and informed-citizenry functions (Doyle 2006; Tambini 2008).

The City, Wall Street, and major stock exchanges worldwide (Japan, Hong Kong, Shanghai, Frankfurt, Toronto, etc.) are the epicenters of financial news, both in general and in specialized media. There are also some exceptional cases, such as that of Switzerland, with a very influential publication in this field, the Neue Zürcher Zeitung (NZZ), where it is traditional for most of the journalists in the Wirtschaft and Finanzen desks to have doctoral degrees in economics and/or finance. It is understandable that in these markets – with special emphasis in the cases of the British and U.S. markets – the complex interaction processes described in the theory are more clearly in place, in a context of quite differentiated financial outlets, hyper-specialized professionals and a special centrality of financial news. Elsewhere, financial journalism has historically been less developed and more routine, at least until the decades prior to the 2008 financial crisis. In fact, especially from the 1980s to 1990s onwards, in all corners of the planet there was a process of markets deregulation and financialization of economies that also translated into a growing financialization of EBF journalism (Coloma-Pinglo & Atarama-Rojas 2014; Cox 2022; Fiera 2018; Greenfield & Williams 2007; Iddins 2021; Kareithi and Kariithi 2005; Knowles 2020; Lee and Baek 2018; Mast 2012; Shaw 2016). The logic of finance, both high finance and personal finance, and its almost magical ability to create value and generate wealth, came to the center of the economic life and economic news. As Foroohar (2021) points out, referring to the American case, "Wall Street used corporate mythology, opacity, complexity, and sheer size to distort the marketplace and make us think that what was good for Goldman Sachs was good for America" (p. 23). But the phenomenon, as commented, was global. Kjaer (2007), in his analysis of the evolution of economic content in the Danish press between 1960 and 2000, points out that until the last decades of the 20th century

Finance was a peripheral issue dealt with in routine stock market reports or treated as a minor aspect of stories concerned with other issues. In 2000, most business stories about business and industry regarded financial performance as a key concern, even when writing about other issues.

*(p. 169)*

In a completely different market from those cited so far, Sesebo (2005) notes that in Nigeria in the early 1990s financial journalism suddenly began to grow at a fast rate as a consequence of a substantial move to liberalize the economy.

The professional problems of financial journalism have also become paradigms of the ethical challenges of the EBF journalist, especially in countries with highly developed stock exchanges and very important financial services industries. Although many of these problems are common to those described for business journalism, there are certain professional mal-practices in financial news that are particularly relevant. Two very special examples are insider trading and market manipulation/abuse.

As for insider trading, it is a practice of corruption in financial news with a very long his-tory, although its regulation as a criminal act is relatively recent, especially in some countries (Bhattacharya and Daouk 2002). The most striking cases that have ended up in court – many others, which undoubtedly occur, go unnoticed – have taken place in countries with a more developed financial journalism, such as the always cited case of R. Foster Winans in The Wall Street Journal in the 1980s, or other more recent ones such as those of an employee of the advertising department of the Nihon Keizai Shimbun (Endo 2006), or the still ongoing case of a New York investor who made use of news not yet published written by a Bloomberg journalist (Grueskin 2021).

As for market abuse practices, the temptation to manipulate markets with news is also almost as old as the emergence of stock exchanges, and it is well known that authors such as Daniel Defoe or Jonathan Swift, already in the 18th century, favored or criticized in their newspaper columns the shares of certain companies, in which they themselves had interests (Chacellor 2000; Odlyzko 2018). As in the case of insider trading, nowadays market ma-nipulation/abuse is a crime today in most countries (Bromberg et al. 2017). Still, there have been notorious cases of financial journalists who have fallen into this temptation, such as the authors of the column "City Slickers" in the British Daily Mirror (Porter 2003), or, to cite an example in other latitudes, the owner and editor of the newspaper Estrategia in Chile, con-victed of enriching himself by publishing biased information about the company Schwager (Leiva and Tamblay 2008).

The seriousness of these crimes, which are very difficult to prove in court, means that according to the Codes of Ethics and Best Practices of the media, especially those with ex-tensive coverage of finance, financial journalists are subject to special limitations regarding their ability to trade in financial products, the obligation to register their investments and economic interests, etc. But there is also broad geographical diversity regarding the ethi-cal requirements of financial journalists, and not only between markets with very different development of the financial news beat, but even among the most advanced ones. Tambini (2013) explains how in Hong Kong financial journalism works in theory with standards and legal obligations similar to the British and American ones, but in practice the reality does not conform to them. This author comments that almost half of the journalists he interviewed for his study "openly said that they or close relatives actively traded in shares or markets that they wrote about, and several others reported a relaxed attitude to such practices" (p. 25).

If we look at places with less advanced financial journalism, such as Kenya or South Africa, to cite two major developing nations, Mare (2018) notes that "insider trading remains a gray area in both nations' newsrooms, with no firm ethical rules in place to address it," while market manipulation "is not specifically addressed in the codes of ethics in Kenya and South Africa" (p. 222). In fact, it can be stated that in very few markets – leaving apart the domestic laws affecting journalists in these matters – is there the professional and ethical sensitivity developed in the codes of ethics and conduct by the most respected international companies and media in this field, such as Dow Jones (Wall Street Journal), Nikkei (Nikkei and Financial Times), Bloomberg or Reuters, to cite the most significant ones. In short, there are universal principles and standards widely accepted by the profession, embodied in best practices such as those of the cited benchmark media, but the application of them is distributed in a very wide gray scale, even among the news outlets of the same country.

## Conclusion

The global development of EBF journalism shows many uniform traits among countries derived from the very nature of this journalistic field and from the existence, throughout history, of some publications and media, especially Anglo-Saxon ones, which have acted as reference models for the sector. However, the practice of EBF journalism in different latitudes also has its own characteristics, depending on multiple factors (different journalistic cultures, degree of economic and political development, the importance of stock markets and certain industries, etc.). This chapter has focused on these differences and has done so by analyzing separately the three main fields of EBF journalism: economic journalism, business journalism and financial journalism. Although in reality many news events should be covered according to their economic, business and financial dimensions, in an integrated way, the truth is that these three news subfields are often practically worked in a differentiated way, in specialized desks. In fact, their configuration as media contents has also occurred with a certain degree of autonomy, and the main professional challenges they pose are also diverse.

**Economic journalism**. The challenges and differential problems of economic journalism among countries are related in most cases to the level of political freedom, which means that this type of content is subject to different processes of control by the authorities. Censorship, difficulties in accessing public economic information, propaganda disseminated through state-owned media, and other sophisticated forms of influence on the messages that reach the population are still very common in a large part of the planet. The consolidation of authoritarian political systems and the rise of illiberal regimes in recent decades have favored the development of a type of "economic populism" that is not necessarily negative from an economic point of view (Rodrick 2018), but is often really negative from the perspective of the exercise of free and critical economic journalism.

**Business journalism**. The capture of business journalism by corporate interests can be described as a global phenomenon, and in this case the differences among countries, although important, are a matter of degree. From the cheerleading of big companies in times of prosperity and the defense of "national champions," to the direct control of media ownership by a few large corporations, business news is produced in an environment of growing conflicts of interest. As explained in this chapter, the Western way to deal with these issues can be a theoretical reference for good practices, but it is not the dominant view worldwide. In the majority of African countries, a good part of Asia and Latin America, and in many countries in Eastern Europe, corporations find the way to pay for good coverage, directly to journalists (envelope journalism) or through other mechanisms (withdrawal of advertising, financing new media projects or acquiring current media outlets). Even in countries with a long tradition of good business journalism, the sophistication of the procedures to influence corporate news has grown in the last years, as can be observed when analyzing the interest in "journalism" by the great tech players (Google, Facebook, Apple, etc.) (Bell 2021).

**Financial journalism**. Financial journalism could be described as the "pretty girl" of EBF journalism, as the area where the special characteristics of EBF journalism are most strongly and clearly concentrated. Extraordinarily developed around the big stock exchanges, and very technical and routine elsewhere, financial news lives in real time, glued to the market momentum, to the complexity and certain "witchcraft" of financial products and services, and to the human passion for easy enrichment. In this sense, professional rules of conduct and specific laws have been developed around the practice of financial journalism, such as those affecting insider trading and market manipulation. However, the different degree of development of this news beat in different countries means that many of them, although generally accepted, are not operative in practice, which turns this professional field into a gray area. The logic of financial journalism was extended in the years prior to the 2008 crisis to the rest of EBF journalism contents, a phenomenon that has been criticized as one of the causes of the poor coverage of that crisis by the media, especially the specialized media.

In the three fields analyzed, in addition to national peculiarities, problems such as the lack of training of journalists in economic matters, the scarcity of material and human resources dedicated to this news beat, and the differences in the level of interest that current EBF affairs arouse in citizens, have conditioned the greater or lesser weight given to these contents in the media agendas.

In summary, from a global perspective, EBF journalism has a long way to go to become a journalistic field that improves its capacity to act as an economic watchdog, to contribute to a more efficient and transparent functioning of markets, and to help citizens to be better informed and make better decisions around economic, business and financial issues.

# References

Adoni, H. and Cohen, A. A. (1978) "Television Economic News and the Social Construction of Economic Reality," *Journal of Communication*, 28(4), pp. 61–70.

Ainamo, A., Tienari, J. and Vaara, E. (2006) "Between West and East: A Social History of Business Journalism in Cold War Finland," *Human Relations*, 59(5), pp. 611–636.

Almiron, N. (2007) "La Convergencia de Intereses entre Banca y Grupos de Comunicación: El caso de SCH y PRISA," *ZER: Revista De Estudios De Comunicación*, 22, pp. 41–67.

Aronoff, C. W. (ed.) (1979) *Business and the Media*. Santa Monica, CA: Goodyear Publishing.

Arrese, Á. (2005) "Corporate Governance and News Governance in Economic and Financial Media," in Picard, R. (ed.) *Corporate Governance of Media Companies*. Jónkoping: JIBS Research Reports, pp. 77–125.

Arrese, Á. (2017) "The Role of Economic Journalism in Political Transitions," *Journalism*, 18(3), pp. 368–383

Arrese, Á. and Vara, A. (2011) *Fundamentos de Periodismo Económico*. Pamplona: Eunsa.

Barber, B. M. and Odean, T. (2008) "All That Glitters: The Effect of Attention and News on the Buying Behavior of Individual and Institutional Investors," *The Review of Financial Studies*, 21(2), pp. 785–818.

Basile, S. (2002) *Elementos de Jornalismo Económico*. Rio de Janeiro: Campus.

Bell, E. (2021) "Do Technology Companies Care About Journalism?" in Schiffrin, A. (ed.) *Media Capture: How Money, Digital Platforms, and Governments Control the News*. New York: Columbia University Press, pp. 291–296.

Bhattacharya, U. and Daouk, H. (2002) "The World Price of Insider Trading," *The Journal of Finance*, 77(1), pp. 75–108.

Brand, R. (2010) "The Business of Business News: South Africa's Financial Press and the Political Process," *Ecquid Novi: African Journalism Studies*, 31(1), pp. 24–41.

Bromberg, L., Gilligan, G. and Ramsay, I. (2017) "Financial Market Manipulation and Insider Trading: An International Study of Enforcement Approaches," *Journal of Business Law*, 8, pp. 652–679.

Buckley, N. (2011) "Russia: Oligarch Media Dilemmas," *Financial Times*, December 13.

Carroll, C. E. (ed.) (2010) *Corporate Reputation and the News Media*. New York: Routledge

Carroll, C. E. and McCombs, M. (2003) "Agenda-Setting Effects of Business News on the Public's Images and Opinions About Major Corporations," *Corporate Reputation Review*, 6(1), pp. 36–46.

Carson, A. (2014) "The Political Economy of the Print Media and the Decline of coRporate Investigative Journalism in Australia," *Australian Journal of Political Science*, 49(4), pp. 726–742.

Chancellor, E. (2000) *Devil Take the Hindmost: A History of Financial Speculation*. New York: Plume.

Colby, L. (1989) "Italy: When Big Business Shapes the News," *Columbia Journalism Review*, 27(5), p. 14.

Coloma-Pinglo, E. and Atarama-Rojas, T. R. (2014) "Panorama del Periodismo Económico Peruano en los Medios Impresos. Análisis de sus Relaciones con los Actores más Relevantes," *Palabra Clave*, 17(3), pp. 920–945.

Coolidge, C. (1925). *Presidential Address to the American Society of Newspaper Editors*, Washington, DC. https://www.presidency.ucsb.edu/documents/address-the-american-society-newspaper-editors-washington-dc

Cox, A. (2022). *News Media and the Financial Crisis: How Elite Journalism Undermined the Case for a Paradigm Shift*. London: Routledge.

Damstra, A., Boukes, M. and Vliegenthart, R. (2018) "The Economy. How Do the Media Cover it and What Are the Effects? A Literature Review," *Sociology Compass*, 12(5), p. e12579.

Damstra, A. and Vliegenthart, R. (2018). "(Un)covering the Economic Crisis?" *Journalism Studies*, 19(7), pp. 983–1003.

Davidson, R. and Chazaud, N. (2010) "Corporate Reputation and the News Media in France," in Carroll, C. E. (ed.) *Corporate Reputation and the News Media*. New York: Routledge, pp. 62–75.

Davis, A. (2000) "Public Relations, Business News and the Reproduction of Corporate Elite Power," *Journalism*, 1(3), pp. 282–304.

Davis, A. (2005) "Media Effects and the Active Elite Audience. A Study of Communication in the London Stock Exchange," *European Journal of Communication*, 20(3), pp. 303–326.

Davis, A. (2006) "Media Effects and the Question of the Rational Audience: Lessons from the Financial Markets," *Media, Culture & Society*, 28(4), pp. 603–625.

Diguid, C. (1901) *How to Read the Money Article*. Wilson: London.

Djankov, S., Islam, R. and McLeish, C. (eds.) (2002) *The Right to Tell: The Role of Mass Media in Economic Development*. Washington, DC: WBI development studies - World Bank Group.

Doyle, G. (2006) "Financial News Journalism A Post-Enron Analysis of Approaches Towards Economic and Financial News Production in the UK," *Journalism*, 7(4), pp. 433–452.

Duval, J. (2004) *Critique de la Raison Journalistique. Les Transformations de la Presse Économique en France*. Paris: Le Seuil.

Elfenbein, J. (1969) *Business Journalism*, 2ª Ed. Revised. New York: Greenwood Press.

Endo, S. (2006) *The Business/Financial Journalism: The Role and the Ways to be Independent from the News Sources*. Master Disseration. University of Leeds, 2006.

Fiera, L. (2018) *Jornalismo Econômico e os Lobos das Finanças – Grupo Folha e o Governo Lula*. Florianópolis: Insular.

Finn, D. (1981) *The Business-Media Relationship: Countering Misconceptions and Distrust*. New York: American Management Association.

Foroohar, R. (2021). "How Silicon Valley Copied Wall Street's Media Capture Playbook," in Schiffrin, A. (ed.) *Media Capture: How Money, Digital Platforms, and Governments Control the News*. New York: Columbia University Press, pp. 23–29.

Freeman, L. A. (2000) *Closing the Shop: Information Cartels and Japan's Mass Media*. Princeton, NJ: Princeton University Press.

Gibbs, J. (2021) "Business News in a Loyalist Press Environment," *Journalism*, 22(10), pp. 2654–2669.

Grafström, M. and Pallas, J. (2007) "The Negotiation of Business News," in Kjaer, P. and Slaatta, T. (eds.) *Mediating Business: The Expansion of Business Journalism*. Copenhagen: Copenhagen Business School Press, pp. 217–233.

Greenfield, C. and Williams, P. (2007) "Financialization, Finance Rationality and the Role of Media in Australia," *Media, Culture & Society*, 29(3), pp. 415–433.

Grueskin, B. (2021) "An Insider-Trading Indictment Shows Ties to Bloomberg News Scoops," *Columbia Journalism Review*, April 1. https://www.cjr.org/business_of_news/an-insider-trading-indictment-shows-ties-to-bloomberg-news-scoops.php

Grünberg, J. and Pallas, J. (2012) "Beyond the News Desk- the Embeddness of Business News," *Media, Culture & Society*, 35(2), pp. 216–233.

Guriev, S. and Treisman, D. (2019) "Informational Autocrats," *Journal of Economic Perspectives*, 33(4), pp. 100–127.

Gussow, D. (1984) *The New Business Journalism: An Insider's Look at the Workings of America's Business Press*. New York: Harcourt Brace Jovanovich.

Haggerty, M. and Rasmussen, W. (1994) *The Headline vs. the Bottom Line: Mutual Distrust Between Business and the News Media*. Nashville, TN: Freedom Forum.

Hanitzsch, T. (2005) "Journalists in Indonesia: Educated But Timid Watchdogs," *Journalism Studies*, 6(4), pp. 493–508

Haseborg, V. and Bergermann, M. (2020) *Die Wirecard-Story: Die Geschichte einer Milliarden-Lüge*. München: FinanzBuch Verlag.

Iddins, A. (2021) "Economic Life: Global Capital, Financial Journalism, and Independent Media," *Media, Culture & Society*, 43(4), pp. 716–732.

Ishii, K. and Takeshita, T. (2010) "Corporate Reputation and the News Media in Japan," in Carroll, C. E. (ed.) *Corporate Reputation and the News Media*. New York: Routledge, pp. 129–141.

Kareithi, P. M. and Kariithi, N. (eds.) (2005) *Untold Stories: Economics and Business Journalism in African Media*. Johannesburg: Wits University Press.

Kirsch, D. (1978) *Financial and Economic Journalism. Analysis, Interpretation and Reporting*. New York: New York University Press.

Kjaer, P. (2007) "Changing Construction of Business and Society in the News," in Kjaer, P. and Slaatta, T. (eds.) *Mediating Business: The Expansion of Business Journalism*. Copenhagen: Copenhagen Business School Press, pp. 159–185.

Kjaer, P. and Langer, R. (2005) "Infused with News Value: Management, Managerial Knowledge and the Institutionalization of Business News," *Scandinavian Journal of Management*, 21(2), pp. 209–233.

Kjaer, P. and Morsing, M. (2010) "Corporate Reputation and the News Media in Denmark," in Carroll, C. E. (ed.) *Corporate Reputation and the News Media*. New York: Routledge, pp. 17–35.

Kleinnijenhuis, J., Schultz, F., Oegema, D. and van Atteveldt, W. (2013) "Financial News and Market Panics in the Age of High-Frequency Sentiment Trading Algorithms," *Journalism*, 14(2), pp. 271–291.

Kluge, P. H. (ed.) (1991) *The Columbia Knight-Bagehot Guide to Economics and Business Journalism*. New York: Columbia University Press.

Klyueva, A. and Tsetsura, K. (2015) "Economic Foundations of Morality: Questions of Transparency and Ethics in Russian Journalism," *Central European Journal of Communication*, 8(1), pp. 21–26.

Knowles, S. (2020) *The Mediation of Financial Crises. Watchdos, Lapdogs or Canaries in the Coal Mine?* New York: Peter Lang.

Kruckeberg, D. and Tsetsura, K. (2003) *International Index of Bribery for News Coverage*, Institute for Public Relations. https://instituteforpr.org/bribery-news-coverage-2003/

Kurambayev, B. and Freedman, E. (2020) "Ethics and Journalism in Central Asia: A Comparative Study of Kazakhstan, Kyrgyzstan, Tajikistan and Uzbekistan," *Journal of Media Ethics*, 35(1), pp. 31–44

Kutzner, M. (2019) *Marktwirtschaft Schreiben: Das Wirtschaftsressort der Frankfurter Allgemeine Zeitung 1949 bis 1992*. Tübingen: Mörh Siebek.

Lee, M. (2012) "Time and the Political Economy of Financial Television," *Journal of Communication Inquiry*, 36(4), pp. 322–339.

Lee, M. (2014) "A Review of Communication Scholarship on the Financial Markets and the Financial Media," *International Journal of Communication*, 8, pp. 715–736.

Lee, N. Y. and Baek, K. (2018) "Squeezing Out Economic News for Business News? Changes in Economic Journalism Over the Past 20 Years in South Korea," *Journalism*, 19(9–10), pp.1220–1238.

Lee. W.-S., Lee, M.-K., Kang, S. and Yoo, J.-W. (2019) "The Samsung–Apple Patent War: Socio-Cultural Comparative Study of News Frames in a Business Conflict Issue," *International Communication Gazette*, 81(1), pp. 46–65.

Leiva, R. and Tamblay, M. E. (2008) "Dilemas éticos y Profesionales del Periodismo Económico Actual," *Cuadernos de Información*, 23, pp. 96–111.

Levi, M. (2006) 'The Media Construction of Financial White-Collar Crimes', *The British Journal of Criminology*, 46(6), pp. 1037–1057.

Li, R. (2013). "Media Corruption: A Chinese Characteristic," *Journal of Business Ethics*, 116, pp. 297–310.

Mare, A. (2018). "'Caught Between a Rock and a Hard Place'? A Comparative Study of How Business Journalists Negotiate Ethical Policies in Kenya and South Africa," in Mabweazara, H. M. (ed.) *Newsmaking Cultures in Africa Normative Trends in the Dynamics of Socio-Political & Economic Struggles*. London: Palgrave Macmillan, pp. 207–228.

Márquez Ramírez, M. (2012). "Bribery, Freebies, Moonlighting and 'Media Attentions' in Postauthoritarian Mexico: Perceptions of Journalists about Ethical Behaviour,' Paper presented for the Conference "Journalism Ethics: Individual, institutional or cultural?", Reuters Institute for the Study of Journalism, University of Oxford, September 27–28.

Mast, C. (1999). *Wirtschaftsjournalismus: Grundlagen und Neue Konzepte für die Presse*. Wiesbaden: VS Verlag für Sozialwissenschaften.

Mast, C. (Hrsg.) (2012). *Neuorientierung im Wirtschaftsjournalismus Redaktionelle Strategien und Publikumserwartungen*. Wiesbaden: Springer VS.

Merrill, G. J. (2019). *The Political Content of British Economic, Business and Financial Journalism*. London: Palgrave.

Miller, G. S. (2006). "The Press as a Watchdog for Accounting Fraud," *Journal of Accounting Research*, 44(5), pp. 1001–1033.

Mowlana, H. (1967) "Cross-National Comparison of Economic Journalism: A Study of Mass Media and Economic Development," *Gazette*, 13(4), pp. 363–378.

Nanrendorf, R. and Waldemar, S. (Hrsg.) (1996) *Wegmarkierungen. 50 Jahre Wirtschaftsgeschichte mi Handelsblatt*. Stuttgart: Schäffer-Poeschel Verlag.

Narisetti, R. (2021) "A Loud Silence," in Schiffrin, A. (ed.) *Media Capture: How Money, Digital Platforms, and Governments Control the News*. New York: Columbia University Press, pp. 160–187.

Ndangam, L. N. (2006) "'Gombo': Bribery and the Corruption of Journalism Ethics in Cameroon," *Ecquid Novi: African Journalism Studies*, 27(2), pp. 179–199,

Odlyzko, A. (2018) "Isaac Newton, Daniel Defoe and the Dynamics of Financial Bubbles," *Financial History*, Winter, pp. 18–21.

Onyebadi, U. and Alajmi, F. (2021) "Unethical but Not Illegal: Revisiting Brown Envelope Journalism Practice in Kuwait," *Journalism*, 24(3), pp. 616–632. https://doi.org/10.1177/14648849211019566

Pansa, G. (1986) *Carte False*. Milano: Rizzoli.

Parsons, W. (1989) *The Power of the Financial Press. Journalism and Economic Opinion in Britain and America*. Aldershot: Edward Elgar.

Poggiali, V. (2001) *Giornalismo Economico. Dottrina e Tecnica Dell'informazione sui 'Fatti' Dell'economia*. Roma: Centro Documentazione Giornalistica.

Pollach, I. and Hansen, L. V. (2021) "Tone variation in financial news: A comparison of companies, journalists and financial analysts," *European Journal of Communication*, 36(5), pp. 511–526.

Porter, D. (1998) "City Editors and the Modern Investing Public: Establishing the Integrity of the New Financial Journalism in Late Nineteenth-Century London," *Media History*, 4(1), pp. 49–6.

Porter, D. (2003) "'City Slickers' in Perspective: The Daily Mirror, its Readers and Their Money, 1960–2000," *Media History*, 9(2), pp. 137–152.

Ristow, B. (2010) *Cash for Coverage: Bribery of Journalists Around the World*. Washington, DC: Center for International Media Assistance.

Riutort, P. (2000) "Le Journalisme au Service de L'économie. Les Conditions D'emergence de L'information Économique en France à Partir des Années 50," *Actes de la Recherche en Sciences Sociales*, 131–132, pp. 41–55.

Romano, A. (2000) "Bribes, Gifts and Graft in Indonesian Journalism," *Media International Australia*, 94(1), pp.157–171.

Roush, C. (2006) *Profits and Losses. Business Journalism and Its Role in Society*. Oak Park, IL: Marion Street Press.

Roush, C. (2022) *The Future of Business Journalism*. Washington, DC: Georgetown University Press.

Rozenas, A. and Stukal, D. (2019) "How Autocrats Manipulate Economic News: Evidence from Russia's State-Controlled Television," *The Journal of Politics*, 81(3), pp. 982–995.

Rubin, B. (1977) *Big Business and the Mass Media*. Lexington, MA: Lexington Books.

Salmon, R. (1963) *L'information Économique. Clé de la Prospérité*. Paris: Collection Entreprise, Hachette.

Schifferes, S. (2020) "The Financial Press," in Conboy, M. and Bingham, A. (eds.) *The Edinburgh History of the British and Irish Press*. Edinburgh: Edinburgh University Press, Vol. 3, pp. 189–210.

Schiffrin, A. (2009) "Power and Pressure: African Media and the Extractive Sector," *Journal of International Affairs*, 62(2), pp. 127–141.

Schiffrin, A. (2015) "The Press and the Financial Crisis: A Review of the Literature," *Sociology Compass*, 9(8), pp. 639–653.

Schiffrin, A. (ed.) (2021) *Media Capture: How Money, Digital Platforms, and Governments Control the News*. New York: Columbia University Press.

Schuster, T. (2006) *The Markets and the Media*. Lanham: Lexington Books.

Seddon, M. (2020) "Pro-Kremlin Entrepreneur Buys Leading Russian Business Newspaper," *Financial Times*, May 31.

Sesebo, J. (2005) "Nigeria," in Kareithi, P. M. and Kariithi, N. (eds.) (2005) *Untold Stories: Economics and Business Journalism in African Media*. Johannesburg: Wits University Press, pp. 25–28.

Shaw, I. S. (2016) *Business Journalism. A Critical Political Economy Approach*. London: Routledge.

Shuli, H. (2011) "The Rise of Business Media in China," in Shirk, S. (ed.) *Changing Media, Chaging China*. Oxford: Oxford University Press, pp. 77–90.

Simons, H. and Califano, J. A. Jr. (eds.) (1979) *The Media and Business*. New York: Vintage Books.

Skjerdal, T. S. (2010) "Research on Brown Envelope Journalism in the African Media," *African Communication Research*, 3(3), pp. 367–406.

Stiglitz, J. E. (2015) "The Media and the Crisis: An Information Theoretic Approach," in Schifferes, S. and Roberts, R. (eds.) *The Media and Financial Crisis*. London: Routledge, pp. 140–152.

Strauß, N. (2019) "Financial Journalism in Today's High-Frequency News and Information Era," *Journalism*, 20(2), pp. 274–291.

Strauß, N. and Smith, C.H. (2019) "Buying on Rumors: How Financial News Flows Affect the Share Price of Tesla," *Corporate Communications: An International Journal*, 24(4), pp.593–607

Tambini, D. (2008) *What Is Financial Journalism For? Ethics and Responsibility in a Time of Crisis and Change*. London: Polis-London School of Economics.

Tambini, D. (2013) "Financial Journalism, Conflicts of Interest and Ethics: A Case Study of Hong Kong," *Journal of Mass Media Ethics*, 28(1), pp. 15–29.

Taylor, J. (2012) "Watchdogs or Apologists? Financial Journalism and Company Fraud in Early Victorian Britain," *Historical Research*, 85(230), pp. 632–650.

Tetlock, P. C. (2007) "Giving Content to Investor Sentiment: The Role of Media in the Stock Market," *The Journal of Finance*, 62(3), pp. 1139–1168.

The Economist. (2022) "How One Journalist Exposed the Wirecard Scandal," *The Economist*, June 16.

Thompson, P. (2009) "Market Manipulation? Applying the Propaganda Model to Financial Media Reporting," *Westminster Papers in Communication and Culture*, 6(2), pp. 73–96.

Thompson, P. (2012) "Invested Interests? Reflexivity, Representation and Reporting in Financial Markets," *Journalism*, 14(2), pp. 208–227.

Tienari, J., Vaara, E. and Erkama, N. (2007) "The Gospel According to the Global Market. How Journalists Frame Ownership in the Case of *Nokia* in Finland," in Kjaer, P. and Slaatta, T. (eds.) *Mediating Business: The Expansion of Business Journalism*. Copenhagen: Copenhagen Business School Press, pp. 187–213.

Timmermans, J. (2019) "Financial Journalism." *Oxford Research Encyclopedia of Communication*. https://doi.org/10.1093/acrefore/9780190228613.013.812

Tsetsura, K. (2015) "Guanxi, Gift-Giving, or Bribery? Ethical Considerations of Paid News in China," *Public Relations Journal*, 9(2), pp. 1–26.

Tumber, H. (1993) "'Selling Scandal': Business and the Media," *Media, Culture & Society*, 15(3), pp. 345–361.

Valentini, C. and Romenti, S. (2011) "The Press and Alitalia's 2008 Crisis: Issues, Tones, and Frames," *Public Relations Review*, 37(4), pp. 360–365

van Dalen, A., de Vreese, C. and Albæk, E. (2017) "Economic News Through the Magnifying Glass," *Journalism Studies*, 18(7), pp. 890–909

van Dalen, A., Svensson, H., Kalogeropoulos, A., Albæk, E. and de Vreese, C. H. (2019) *Economic News. Informing the Inattentive Audience*. New York: Routledge

Verhoeven, P. (2016) "The Co-production of Business News and its Effects: The Corporate Framing Mediated-Moderation Model," *Public Relations Review*, 42(4), pp. 509–521.

Yang, A. (2012) "Assessing Global Inequality of Bribery for News Coverage: A Cross-National Study," *Mass Communication and Society*, 15(2), pp. 201–224

Zhang, S. I. (2009) "What's Wrong with Chinese Journalists? Addressing Journalistic Ethics in China Through a Case Study of the BeijingYouthDaily," *Journal of Mass Media Ethics*, 24(2–3), pp. 173–188.

Zielonka, J. (2015) *Media and Politics in New Democracies*. Oxford: Oxford University Press.

# 29

# THE EMERGENCE OF ECONOMIC JOURNALISM IN THE U.K. IN THE 1970S AND THE TRIUMPH OF NEO-LIBERALISM

*Steve Schifferes*

## Introduction

The coverage of economics in the U.K. was transformed in the 1970s as the country faced its biggest economic crisis since the Second World War. A new breed of economic correspondents emerged who aimed to challenge the fundamentals of how the U.K. economy had been managed. In the course of this debate, the role and prestige of economic reporting itself was transformed. In the process, many became prominent figures, often rivaling political correspondents in their influence, and putting economic coverage at the center of both the business and opinion pages in the major national newspapers. Working closely with newly established right-wing think tanks, they played a major role in the rejection of Keynesianism by both political parties, paving the way for rise of free market economics and monetarism in the 1980s under the Conservative government of Margaret Thatcher.

As the number of economic reporters employed by major newspapers and broadcasters increased, they coalesced into an elite group dubbed "the commentariat," often sharing the same interpretation of economic events. Although there were some outliers, they were broadly supportive of neo-liberalism and the benefits of globalization. This consensus was particularly important during times of economic crisis, when the commentariat's role was most prominent. Their views helped shape public opinion, raise questions about the government policy, and reflect market pressures. Both in the 1992 European Exchange Rate Mechanism (ERM) crisis and in the 2008 Global Financial crisis, these interpretations had serious political consequences, calling in question the economic competence of both Conservative and Labour governments and contributing to their defeat in subsequent elections.

## Historical Background: Business Coverage in the U.K. Press

Business reporting has been a part of the British newspaper tradition since its inception at the end of the 17th century. The oldest continuously published newspaper in the U.K., Lloyds List, covering shipping news vital to merchants and insurers, dates back to 1743. For a long

DOI: 10.4324/9781003298977-35

time, most business reporting was centered on market reporting of movements in shares, commodity prices, government debt and currency rates – all relevant for Britain's growing trade (Schifferes 2020). By the 1820s business newspaper coverage had been regularized by the creation of a daily "City" news page, reflecting the concentration of financial activity in a small district of London known as "the City," Britain's equivalent of Wall Street (Taylor 2015). By 1914, there were 30 national dailies and Sunday papers published in London, with a combined circulation of 10 million, topped by the Daily Mail at 1 million. Nearly all of them covered money and finance, from a "money article" in the popular press to a full City page in all fifteen of the serious papers (Roberts 2015b). Coverage had become more objective as the principles of the New Journalism filtered through, reducing the amount of speculative boosting of company shares (Nye 2015; Porter 1998; Weiner 1988). Two specialist financial newspapers, the Financial Times and the Financial News, emerged in the late 19th century, but their circulation was very small and limited to City traders and other professionals (Kynaston 1988; Porter 1986).

Throughout the first half of the 20th century, the City pages provided investors and businessmen with reports on price movements across an extraordinary range of markets both in the U.K. and around the world, from the price of onions at London's Covent Garden market to interest rates on Argentinian bonds and the price of mining shares in the United States – reflecting Britain's global investments and the increased access to financial information as global telegraph networks were completed (Schifferes 2020; Winseck and Pike 2007). However, the City pages were seen as designed for a particular specialist audience of middle class investors. They operated separately from the editorial output of the main pages of their newspaper, and some even had their offices in a different location from the main newsroom. As late as the early 1960s, the editor of The Times met with his City editor only once a week for tea (McDonald 1984, pp. 377–80).

For a long time, economics itself was not a separate category of reporting, as little macroeconomic data was available. Another key barrier to reporting on economic policy was the reluctance of economic policymakers to speak publicly. Neither the Treasury nor the Bank of England welcomed any intrusion from the press that might question their economic judgments (Kynaston, 2017). For many years, the function of the Bank of England's press office was defined as "to keep the Bank out of the press, and the press out of the Bank" (Lambert 2005). Finally, up until the 1960s, the press was reluctant to criticize the government during a time of economic crisis, preferring to defer to their better judgment in the interest of national unity.

## Economic Ideology of the Press before 1945

Insofar as there was discussion of economic policy, it fell not to the business journalists but to the editorial pages to formulate a view. By the mid-19th century, they offered support for classic economic liberalism. This rested on three pillars: free trade, sound money, and a limited role for the state. Indeed, the influential Economist magazine was founded in 1843 to back free trade, which was the subject of a fierce political debate (Edwards 1993; Zevin 2019). By the late 19th century, free trade was seen as the cornerstone of Britain's economic success (Trentmann 2008). Drawing on the views of the U.K.'s founding fathers of economics, Adam Smith, David Ricardo and Thomas Malthus, the press popularized the belief that laissez-faire – leaving the economy to its own devices – was the best policy to ensure prosperity and economic growth. Both the theory of competitive advantage and the division of labor seemed to be vindicated by Britain's industrial dominance in the world economy. And sound money, and in particular maintaining the gold standard which irrevocably linked the pound sterling to a fixed quantity of gold, was seen as essential in maintaining stability in global financial markets, which London also dominated (Kynaston 2011).

While Britain's economy weakened after the First World War and during the Great Depression, as it was hit by a series of economic crises, this ideology remained dominant through the 1930s. Newspaper editors and proprietors were still reluctant to challenge government economic policy during times of crisis, and felt it was their patriotic duty to support the government of the day during an economic crisis while reassuring the public. This is apparent during the two most severe economic crises that struck Britain in the first half of the 20th century.

When, on the outbreak of war in 1914, the U.K. stock market stopped trading and The Bank of England stopped paying out gold to panicked depositors holding pound notes, the press rallied to support the Chancellor of the Exchequer, David Lloyd George (Grigg 1997; Roberts 2013). To stem the panic, he called all the editors and financial editors of the major newspapers into his Downing Street office, asking them

> To insert special articles in their papers appealing to the public to assist us at the present moment, and pointing out that the duties of patriotism are not confined to those who have to fight either by sea or on the battlefield.
>
> *(Roberts 2015a, p. 236)*

The editors responded enthusiastically with articles appearing with headlines such as "The Duty of Every Britisher" (The Globe) and "The Folly of Hoarding" (The Times). At the same time, the financial specialist press refrained from openly reporting on the perilous state of the banking system and instead went directly to the Chancellor to warn privately of the need for intervention. So little news of the crisis appeared in the press that when a Financial News reporter spotted a newsboy shouting "Run on the Bank" near the Bank of England, he asked a passing policeman to arrest him (Roberts 2015a).

In 1931, in the midst of the Great Depression, Britain was again hit with a major crisis that challenged its adherence to the gold standard. As currency reserves flowed out of the country, the government was forced to seek a loan from American bankers, who demanded cuts in public spending, including a reduction in unemployment benefit, in return. The press enthusiastically endorsed this approach, which split the Labour government (Godden 2008; Marquand 1977; Roberts 2015b). In a rare briefing for journalists, the Permanent Secretary of the Treasury gave short shrift to a suggestion from a junior reporter from the Labour-supporting newspaper, the Daily Herald, that the cost of maintaining the gold standard might be too high:

"To suggest we leave the gold standard," Sir Warren Fisher declared, majestically rising to his feet and pacing backward and forward, "is an affront not only to the national honour but to the personal honour of every man and woman in this country."

"There was nothing for us to do but to slink away," reporter Francis Williams noted (Williams 1965, quoted in Roberts 2015b p. 250).

But, in fact, the loan and public spending cuts failed to save the pound, which was devalued shortly afterward. The newspapers then did a complete U-turn to back the wisdom of the government's new policy (Roberts 2015b).

## Second World War and the Rise of Keynesianism

Among the leading critics of the Gold Standard was the economist John Maynard Keynes, one of the few economists who wrote widely in newspapers and political magazines. His view that government intervention was needed to cure high unemployment and end the depression through increased public spending was not accepted by either policymakers or journalists in the 1930s (Clarke 2009; Godden 2013; Harrod 1951; Skidelsky 2013; Tribe 2009). But after the Second World War, during which the government played a central role in managing the wartime economy, views shifted. Keynes himself had demonstrated the effectiveness of his approach while a senior advisor to the Treasury during the war. Meanwhile, his disciples developed the tools that allowed economists to measure the macroeconomic variables that were needed for active government economic management. In 1945 the Labour government accepted that reducing unemployment by Keynesian methods was the main goal of economic policy. The Atlee government also vastly increased the role of the state by introducing a comprehensive welfare state to support all citizens "from the cradle to the grave" (Bew 2017; Symonds 2022; Timmins 2017). Many industries were nationalized, and the role of trade unions was strengthened. The increased role of the state in managing the economy was endorsed in broad terms by subsequent Conservative governments in the 1950s (Horne 2012; Richards 2021). It was seen as the key to higher growth and spread of prosperity during the post-war boom years (1945–1970). The Keynesian consensus was soon embedded in the views of the academic community and accepted by key policy makers and officials as well as the politicians.

Members of the press, however, were reluctant converts rather than evangelists for Keynesianism. The first major paper to endorse the Keynesian approach was The Times in 1944 (McDonald 1984). Within the financial press, the influential editor of the Financial Times, Gordon Newton (1950–1972), moved to accept the Keynesian approach in the post-war years, although its leading columnist Harold Wincott was more skeptical (Kynaston 1988). The Economist was even slower to acknowledge the usefulness of the Keynesian approach, rejecting any approach by Keynes himself in the 1930s under its long-standing editor Walter Layton. But by the 1950s, under Geoffrey Crowther's reforming editorship (1938–1956), it began to accept the necessity of government economic management and increased its economic coverage, while keeping the magazine's long-standing commitment to free trade and classic liberalism intact (Edwards 1993; Zevin 2019).

Unlike in the United States, where prominent Keynesian academics such as Paul Samuelson and John Kenneth Galbraith had regular newspaper columns to explain the new approach to the general public, British economists generally keep their debates within the academy (Parsons 1990).

The Keynesian paradigm had always had its critics. The "Austrian school" led by Frederick Hayek had long worried that the growing size of the state would restrict individual freedom and the entrepreneurial spirit, as he pointed out in his influential book "The Road to Serfdom," published in 1945 (Hayek 1945; Jones 2012; Tribe 2009; Plehwe 2015). But by the 1960s, a more powerful academic critique of Keynesianism, monetarism, emerged in the United States, led by Milton Friedman and the Chicago school (Edenstein 2015; Jones 2012). It argued that Keynesian spending measures would be inherently inflationary, and that the government's role should be limited to controlling the money supply to expand or contract the economy.

But the adoption of this new and radical paradigm shift did not happen overnight. It took both an economic crisis and an organized campaign by prominent economic journalists, working with a new group of right-wing think tanks closely linked to Conservative politicians, to challenge the Keynesian paradigm. And in Britain it was this new breed of economic commentators who led the charge, challenging the views of most U.K. academic economists and policymakers who maintained their Keynesian stance. The result was the election of a radical, reforming Thatcher government, whose legacy has cast a long shadow over subsequent British economic policy.

### The Economic Crisis of the 1970s

By the 1970s, the U.K. economy was facing unprecedented challenges on multiple fronts, calling into question the post-war consensus (Caves 1968). The 1973–1974 oil embargo led to a recession in Britain just as in other Western countries, with rising unemployment. At the same time, the economy was facing high and rising inflation throughout the decade, which peaked at 27 percent annually in 1975. There were a growing number of strikes with workers demanding higher wages to compensate for higher prices. The miners (the most militant trade union) paralyzed the country with strikes in both 1972 and 1974, preventing coal reaching power stations and leading to power cuts, blackouts and a three-day work week. At the same time, the external position of sterling – Britain's balance of payments deficit – was weakening further. Britain had already had to devalue the pound in 1967, and it came under pressure again in the 1970s. The Labour government, which came to power in 1974, was forced to make spending cuts to balance the budget.

The crisis came to a head in 1976 when Britain was forced to go to the IMF for an unprecedented $4.8 billion bailout to rescue the pound, with the IMF demanding more spending cuts. In contrast to 1931, when the papers had rallied 'round the government, they now uniformly denounced the Labour Chancellor, Dennis Healey, with long features on "the day the pound died" and headlines such as "Britain's shame" and "The Chicken Chancellor" (Healey 1989; Needham 2015; Roberts 2016).

To make matters worse, with soaring inflation, Labour's attempt to reach agreement with the trade unions to moderate wage settlements failed, despite an offer of a "social contract" of increased state benefits in return for restraint in collective bargaining. The winter of 1979, "the winter of discontent," brought widespread strikes by public sector workers that closed hospitals, prevented rubbish being collected, and disrupted public transport, and further discredited the government (Beckett 2009; Cairncross and Burk 1992; Healey 1989; Roberts 2016). Many observers believed that Britain was becoming ungovernable and democracy itself was under threat.

### The Rise of the Economic Correspondent

The groundwork for this harsh critique was the work carried out by a new breed of economic correspondents, who were willing to challenge the prevailing orthodoxy and propose new ways of managing the economy. Its leaders were Peter Jay, Economics Editor of The Times, and Samuel Brittan, the chief economics commentator for the Financial Times.

One precondition for the rise of the economic correspondent was the dramatic improvement in the fortunes of the national newspapers. Increased circulation and higher advertising revenues led to a major expansion of the size, design and content of newspapers. There was a big increase in staffing and the development of more specialist reporting, as more sections and bigger weekend editions with color supplements required more reporters.

In particular, business coverage was rapidly expanding, with the newspapers creating new sections on personal finance, investment, and property, driven by growing affluence which increased interest in these subjects. As business coverage expanded, more specialist business reporters were hired, including industrial and labor correspondents, personal finance reporters and corporate reporters as well as economics correspondents, whose work began to appear in the editorial section rather than being confined to the City pages. Overall, the number of financial journalists grew by 30 percent between 1978 and 1986. The specialist business press also grew rapidly, with the number of periodicals devoted to "finance and investment" growing from 41 in 1970 to 235 in 1995 (Schifferes 2020). And the readership of both The Economist and the Financial Times expanded even more, with the FT exceeding a circulation of 250,000 by 1986 and reaching over 400,000 by 2008, including a quarter overseas (Kynaston 1988, pp. 506–507). The circulation of The Economist grew even faster, from 68,000 in 1963 to 530,000 in 1993, with over half in the United States (Edwards 1993, p. 951).

In this new environment, Peter Jay sought to define what should distinguish the role of the new-style economic journalist:

> [He would] bring some specialist [economic] knowledge with him to the reporting, interpreting and comment on an unbroken chain of connected events … and it excludes both academic and business economists who occasionally write for the newspapers, and the much larger tribe of City, financial, industrial and labour correspondents.
>
> *(Jay 1972)*

Jay was also clear about his audience: policymakers and opinion formers, not the general public. He famously told his Times subeditor that he was writing for an audience of three – the Chancellor of the Exchequer, the governor of the Bank of England, and the editor of The Times (Grigg 1993, pp. 69–73).

A strong spur to the more assertive tone of the new breed of economic journalists in the 1970s was a concern that they had failed to speak out about the botched devaluation of the pound in the 1960s on the grounds that it would harm the government. As two other prominent economic correspondents put it:

> There are two ways economic journalists can influence economic policy … by what they discuss and what they do not discuss … the biggest blot on the reputation of the financial press in economic matters, and still haunts all who lived through it, was the conspiracy of silence over the devaluation issue in 1964–7. The establishment managed to persuade the serious press that mere discussion of the issue would be harmful to the national interest.
>
> *(Keegan and Rea 1979, p. 139)*

In fact, it was Peter Jay himself, writing in The Times just **after** the 1967 devaluation, who fired the opening shot for the new economic journalism by explicitly criticizing the policies of both the Labour government under Harold Wilson and the previous Conservative government for ignoring the growing problems with the pound sterling for political reasons. The Treasury was so incensed by the criticism that it sent a formal letter of complaint to the editor of The Times (Grigg 1993, pp. 386–387).

One reason why the new breed of economic correspondents had the confidence to question government economic policy was that many of them had worked in key government departments themselves: Peter Jay had just left the Treasury; Samuel Brittan had worked in the Department of Economic Affairs; William Keegan (another Financial Times economic reporter, later the economics editor of The Observer), at the Bank of England; and the influential economics correspondent, and then editor, of The Economist, Rupert Pennant-Rea, had started his career at the Bank of England and later returned as deputy governor.

Many of these economic correspondents also had close links both with monetarist economists and with leading politicians. Samuel Brittan studied with Milton Friedman at Cambridge. His younger brother, Leon Brittan, was the Home Secretary in the Thatcher government, and his cousin, Malcolm Rifkind, was also a Cabinet minister. Peter Jay, who gained a first-class honors degree from Oxford and was president of the Oxford Union, was the son-in-law of Labour Prime Minister Jim Callaghan; his father, Douglas Jay, had served as a Treasury minister in the Attlee government. Jay, who was also a television presenter for the influential political interview program Weekend World, developed a close relationship with Milton Friedman, appearing in two episodes of his television series "Free to Choose." Jay was appointed U.K. ambassador to Washington in 1977, but later returned to economic journalism as the BBC's Economics Editor from 1990 until 2001. Brittan carried on his column in the Financial Times for nearly 50 years until his retirement in 2014 (Budd and Hill 2020).

## The Rise of the Think Tanks

The political influence of the new economic correspondents was amplified by their close relationship with a group of new and influential right-wing think tanks that had the ear of the Thatcher government-in-waiting (Cockett 1995). Both Jay and Brittan wrote regularly for these think tanks and participated in their seminars. Their support helped legitimize their radical critique of economic orthodoxy, and, in turn, gave them the ability to influence the Conservative Party as it moved to embrace Thatcherism.

The most well-established think tank was the Institute of Economic Affairs (IEA), founded in 1955, which had been inspired by Hayek's free market approach. It particularly promoted the academic critique of Keynesianism. In the late 1960s, under its research director, Arthur Seldon, a former left-winger, it came to play a key role in the emerging academic debate around monetarism. Alan Walters, the monetarist economist who became Thatcher's economic advisor, was closely associated with the IEA. Jay and Brittan both contributed several essays to IEA publications, including in a volume of essays on inflation which also featured articles by Milton Friedman and Frederick Hayek (Brittan 1974; Jay 1974). Brittan detailed his support of monetarism in another IEA pamphlet (Brittan 1981).

The Adam Smith Institute, founded in 1976 by Madsen Pirie and Eamonn Butler, had close links to its right-wing American counterparts such as the Heritage Foundation. It concentrated on practical policy proposals for implementing the neo-liberal agenda, rather than its theoretical underpinnings, and came up with a number of policy recommendations later adopted by the Thatcher government.

Even more important was the Centre for Policy Studies (CPS), a right-wing think tank set up by Sir Keith Joseph in 1974 with the backing of Margaret Thatcher to provide the intellectual backbone for the development of a new, free market approach to Conservative economic policy. Many of key policymakers and politicians in the Thatcher government

346

got their start, including David Young, the architecture of the privatization program, John Hoskyns, head of Thatcher's policy unit, and Norman Strauss, who wrote the key blueprint for taking power and weakening union power. David Willets, a close aide of Thatcher and Nigel Lawson, later headed the CPS. Its research director, Alf Sherman, was often quoted in newspapers and opinion columns, in major newspapers such as the Times, The Financial Times and the Daily Telegraph. The first pamphlet it published was by Samuel Brittan. In it he explained his conversation to monetarism:

> It was Professor Milton Friedman who removed the scales from my eyes – not by his more technical views on money, but by his analysis of the effects of demand management on unemployment ... I no longer believe that conventional full employment policies pursued through monetary expansion and deficit finance help either growth or employment ... On the contrary, they are likely to bring about an even more rapid inflation, which has many severe consequences of its own, not least of which is the much greater likelihood of heavy unemployment when the rate of inflation eventually has to be checked.
>
> *(Brittan 1975, pp. 11–12)*

In the introduction to the pamphlet, Alf Sherman explained the aim of the CPS:

> Experience and logic combine to convince us that by working with and through the market our society can maximise welfare, liberties and control over our destiny. Conversely, arbitrary intervention motivated by short-term political expediency ... wreaks economic havoc and intensifies the very social and political tensions it is designed to reduce. Policy makers and opinion-formers who expressed these expedients for years, sometimes decades, can hardly be expected to admit with good grace that they had misled us. But we cannot afford to allow their political pre-occupations to perpetuate ruinous fallacies.
>
> *(Sherman 1975, p. viii)*

The Keynesian establishment attempted to fight back. Sir Alec Cairncross, the chief economic advisor to the government for many years, wrote that the critics of Keynesianism were "teenage scribblers" whose debate "took place at times in an atmosphere of hysteria ... there was a tendency to propose extreme measures, predict catastrophe, and accept the preposterous." However, he had to concede that "the central problem of economic policy ... was the torrent of comment and analysis at all levels from the purest of pure theory to articles in the daily press" (Cairncross 1981, p. 174).

And, indeed, the critique of the new breed of economic journalists went beyond the mere criticism of technical aspects of government economic policy. They believed that what they were seeing was an existential crisis of democracy itself. Peter Jay argued in an essay for the IEA that political democracy might be incompatible with sound economic decision making (Jay 1975). By the 1980s, Jay's views had become even more apocalyptic. In a thinly disguised novel, "Apocalypse 2000," he prophesised the complete collapse of Western civilization and economic chaos unless there were fundamental economic reforms. "We are not saying that this will happen...what we are saying is that something like this is likely to happen unless Western democracies learn to cope with their fundamental economic problems more successfully than they have done so far" (Jay and Stewart 1987, p. ix).

Similarly, Samuel Brittan argued that:

> There has been an underlying doubt about the ability of government system to cope... both class and political tensions are greater in the early 1970s than any time in living memory...the pragmatic policies of the 1950s and 1960s have been replaced by a renewed verbal battle between collectivism and capitalism ... the resulting anxiety about the future is not confined to politicians, officials, academics and journalists.
>
> *(Brittan 1977, p. 128)*

But the impact of the new economic correspondents was not just felt in influencing the Conservative Party. Perhaps their greatest success was in persuading the Labour Party itself to question Keynesianism. In 1976, Labour Prime Minister Jim Callaghan, in a passage written by Peter Jay, told the Labour Party conference:

"We used to think that you could spend your way out of a recession and increase employment by boosting government spending ... I tell you in all candour this option is no longer available" (Callaghan 1987; Meridith 2013).

When the Thatcher government took power in 1979, it introduced many of the measures advocated by the new breed of economic correspondents. However, their influence was somewhat diminished by the failure of their key policy proposal, monetarism, as it proved more difficult to control the money supply than expected. However, many other free market policies, such as privatization of state industries, the deregulation of the financial sector, the sale of public housing to existing tenants, and the weakening of union power were successfully introduced (Lawson 1992; Moore 2016). And the electoral popularity of many of these Thatcher reforms made it difficult for the subsequent "New Labour" government under Tony Blair to reverse them. Meanwhile, Samuel Brittan, while supporting free market economic reforms, became increasingly disillusioned with the Conservative's authoritarian tendencies and reasserted his belief in classic liberalism (Brittan 1988, 1995).

### The Economic Commentariat and the New Orthodoxy

When they started, Jay and Brittan were radical outliers both among economists and among economic journalists. But over time, as more newspapers and broadcasters appointed economic reporters, the group began to coalesce into what was sometimes dubbed "the commentariat" (Hobsbawm and Lloyd 2008), whose consensus views were influential both politically and with financial markets, particularly during economic crises. In 1992, the press's vociferous criticism of the Conversative government's forced exit from the ERM and devaluation of the pound damaged their economic credibility and contributed to their electoral defeat in 1997 (Keegan et al. 2017). The then-Chancellor, Norman Lamont, was so discouraged by the relentlessly negative coverage of the crisis that he stopped reading the newspapers (Lamont 2000). After the 2008 Global Financial Crisis, the commentariat's view that public spending cuts were needed in order to tackle the huge U.K. budget deficit helped to undermine the credibility of the Labour government under Gordon Brown, despite his prompt and decisive intervention at the beginning of the crisis to rescue the banking system, and contributed to the Conservative-Liberal Democrat coalition victory two years later (Schifferes and Knowles 2015).

Despite some questioning of the wisdom of deregulating the financial sector, the crisis did not precipitate the major realignment of the existing economic paradigm by journalists, as had happened during the 1970s crisis. Criticism instead focused on individuals, such as the greed of bankers or the incompetence of the regulators. Indeed, there was widespread press support for the austerity program introduced by the Coalition government in 2010 (Basu 2018a, 2018b; Knowles 2020; Schifferes 2018).

A new orthodoxy emerged, that although broadly favorable to the operation of free markets, had some differences from the radical proposals of the 1970s (Mirowski and Ple-hwe 2015; Tribe 2009). Indeed, neo-liberalism has never had a fixed definition. In the new consensus, there was an acceptance that the government did have some role in the economy, as opposed to the radical individualism of the Thatcher years. Very few still supported monetarism. There was a greater emphasis on integrating the global economy and persuading other countries to accept neo-liberal consensus (sometimes called "The Washington Consensus"). This included reforming the international economic system, abandoned fixed exchange rates, allowing the free movement of capital, and promoting free trade, for example by supporting China's membership in the World Trade Organization (Martin 2022; Slobodian 2018). Domestically, the U.K. economic commentators generally supported privatization and further deregulation of the financial sector. They endorsed the apparent return of sound money through the creation of an independent Bank of England whose monetary targets gained more credibility by their support. But the dominant ideology was now centered around controlling government spending, and the dangers of too-high government deficits causing inflation and threatening the value of the pound. This critique of the danger of government borrowing also further weakened the case for Keynesian deficit spending and emphasized the power of financial markets (also the key lesson drawn from the 1992 ERM crisis).

In shaping this view, the economic commentariat developed close links with another think tank which became – and continues to be – highly influential and much quoted (Anstead and Chadwick 2017; Harjuniemi 2023). The Institute for Fiscal Studies (IFS), which was founded in 1969, came to prominence from the 1990s with its forceful and press-savvy director Andrew Dilnot (later head of the U.K. Statistics Authority). Its influence grew under Robert Chote (later head of the Office for Budget Responsibility) and Paul Johnson (director since 2011). The IFS developed its Green Budget as an independent critique of the government's tax and spending plans, particularly its targets for controlling the budget deficit. It was highly successful in producing an academically sound, but rapid-fire response to changes in government economic policy that gained widespread credibility as well as massive publicity. It was particularly influential in its critique of the short-lived Liz Truss government (September–October 2022) which only lasted 44 days after introducing a "mini-budget" that called for huge unfunded tax cuts, which (the IFS argued) would have led to an unsustainable budget deficit (Jessop 2022; Partington 2022; Schifferes 2022).

Many of the key economic journalists of the last few decades got their start at the IFS, including Chris Giles, the Financial Times economics editor; Stephanie Flanders, head of Bloomberg Economics; Evan Davis, a long-term economics editor at the BBC; Soumaya Keynes, the U.K. economics editor at The Economist, and Robert Chote himself, economics editor of The Independent before being appointed to head the IFS. IFS alumni also include Rupert Harrison, chief of staff to Chancellor George Osborne, who shaped the austerity program of the Coalition government from 2010 to 2015 and Steve Webb, who became a Liberal Democrat MP and played a key role in the Coalition government as Secretary of State for Work and Pensions.

## Conclusions and Further Research

The rise of the economic correspondent in the 1970s was a key part of a fundamental paradigm shift in economic policy that occurred not just in Britain but around the world, and especially in the United States. It was a product of its times: deriving from both a profound and accelerating political and economic crisis, and the rise of a powerful new critique of the economic orthodoxy that appeared to offer a solution and was implemented in the 1980s with great political success. It led to a shift of power from a closed circle of government mandarins and academic advisors, bringing the policy debate into the public domain. But while in the United States public intellectuals, notably economists such as Milton Freedman, fronted the public debate, in the U.K. journalists such as Samuel Brittan and Peter Jay played an indispensable role in shifting policy and perceptions. Skillfully drawing on their expertise and contacts, they expanded their role from pure journalism to political and social commentary, with a huge outpouring of books and articles, using their involvement in the world of think tanks to expand their political and intellectual influence.

There has been remarkably little research on economic journalism, and even less on its history, compared to scholarly work on political journalism and the coverage of foreign affairs. There has also been little research that uses a comparative approach, which can challenge assumptions – particularly that the U.S. business journalism sets the pattern which is duplicated in other advanced economics. The particular circumstances in the U.K., for example, with a highly concentrated press, a powerful central government, and a very large financial sector, all centered in London, may have both increased the power of the London-based financial press to influence elite political opinion, and may have led it to focus more on economic policy and its effect on financial markets, with relatively less coverage of individual companies or regional economic developments.

It is also clear that the way economic journalists define their roles will vary over time and in different countries, from investigative journalists critiquing the system, to opinion formers writing analysis piece, to those just reporting on published data or supporting the existing system. The Anglo-American model of fact-based investigative journalism is far from universal (Aresse and Vara-Miguel 2022; Hamilton and Tworek 2017; Tambini 2015).

A key lesson that emerges from this chapter is the importance – and rarity – of paradigm shifts in economic policy, and the key role of economic journalists can play in shaping public, political and market perceptions and expectations. There needs to be more research on when and why such shifts occur, and the interaction between journalists, politicians, markets, and public opinion. In the U.K. case, a smaller elite group within the body of economic reporting, whom we have labeled the "economic commentariat," have had an inordinate influence on policy. The U.K. experience also stands out in showing how important a role think tanks can play as "primary definers," serving as one of the key sources for economic journalists.

This study is an attempt to bring a deeper historical perspective to the study of economic journalism and its impact on society. The debates of the past still play a significant part in shaping the present-day practice and ideology of economic journalism.

## References

Anstead, N. and A. Chadwick. (2016) "A Primary Definer Online: The Construction and Propagation of a Think Tank's Authority On Social Media," *Media, Culture and Society*, 40(2), pp. 246–266.

Arrese, A. and A. Vara-Miguel. (2022) "The Role of Economic Journalists After the 2008 Financial Crisis, paper presented to the ECREA Conference, Panel discussion Learning from crises or stuck on repeat? Ideology, working practices and the mediation of economics," Aarhus, Denmark, 21 October.

Basu, L. (2018a) "Media Amnesia and the Crisis," in Basu, L., S. Schifferes and S. Knowles, editors, *The Media and Austerity: Comparative Perspectives*, Routledge, London.

Basu, L. (2018b) *Media Amnesia: Rewriting the Economic Crisis*, Pluto Press, London.

Beckett, A. (2009) *When the Lights Went Out: What Really Happened to Britain in the Seventies*, Faber and Faber, London.

Bew, J. (2017) *Citizen Clem: A Biography of Attlee*, Riverrun, London.

Brittan, S. (1974) "Inflation and Government," in *Inflation; Causes, Consequences, Cures*, IEA Readings 14, Institute for Economic Affairs, London.

Brittan, S. (1975) *Second Thoughts on Income Policy*, Centre for Policy Studies, London.

Brittan, S. (1977) "The Failure of Social Democracy," in Tyrrell, R. E., editor, *The Future That Doesn't Work: Social Democracy in Britain*, Doubleday, Garden City, LI.

Brittan, S. (1981) *How to End the Monetarist Controversy*, Hobart Paper 90, Institute for Economic Affairs, London.

Brittan, S. (1988) *A Restatement of Economic Liberalism*, Macmillan, London.

Brittan, S. (1995) *Capitalism with a Human Face*, Edgar Elgar, London.

Budd, A. and A. Hill. (2020) "Obituary: Samuel Brittan, Economics Editor, 1933–2000," *Financial Times*, October 12, 2000.

Cairncross, A. (1981) "Academics and Policy Makers," in Francis Cairncross, editor, *Changing Perceptions of Economic Policy: Essays in Honour of the 70the Birthday of Sir Alec Cairncross*, Methuen, London.

Cairncross, A. and K. Burk. (1992) *Goodbye Great Britain: The 1976 IMF Crisis*, Yale University Press, New Haven, CT.

Callaghan, James. (1987) *Time and Chance*, Harper Collins, London.

Caves, R., editor. (1968) *Britain's Economic Prospects*, George Allen and Unwin, London.

Clarke, P. (2009) *Keynes: The Twentieth Century's Most Influential Economist*, Bloomsbury, London.

Cockett, R. (1995) *Thinking the Unthinkable: Think Tanks and the Economic Counter-Revolution 1931–1983*, Harper Collins, London.

Edenstein, L. (2015) *Chicagonomics: The Evolution of Chicago Free Market Economics*, St Martins Press, New York.

Edwards, R. (1993) *The Pursuit of Reason: The Economist 1843–1983*, Hamish Hamilton, London.

Godden, C. (2008) "The Exchange Rates and the Financial Press," September 1931–April 1932. https://ideas.repec.org/p/ehs/wpaper/8039.html

Godden, C. (2013) "Observers, Commentators and Persuaders: British Inter-war Economists as Public Intellectuals," *History of Political Economy*, 45, Supplement 1, pp. 38–67.

Grigg, J. (1993) *A History of The Times, Volume VI: The Thomson Years*, Times Books: London.

Grigg, J. (1997) *Lloyd George: From Peace to War 1912–1916*, Harper Collins, London.

Hamilton, J. and H. Tworek. (2017) "The Natural History of News: An Epigenetic Study," *Journalism*, 18(4), pp. 391–407.

Harjuniemi, T. (2023). The power of primary definers: How journalists assess the pluralism of economic journalism. *Journalism*, 24(4), 877–893

Harrod, R. F. (1951) *A Life of John Maynard Keynes*, Macmillan, London.

Hayek, F. (1945) [republished 2001] *The Road to Serfdom*, Routledge, London.

Healey, D. (1989) *The Time of My Life*, Methuen, London.

Hobsbawm, J. and J. Lloyd. (2008) *The Power of the Commentariat*, Editorial Intelligence, London.

Horne, A. (2012) *Macmillan: The Official Biography*, Picador, London.

Institute for Economic Affairs (IEA). (1975) *Crisis '75..?*, IEA Occasional Paper Special 43, IEA, London.

Jay, P. (1972) On Being an Economist Journalist," *The Listener*, 24 August.

Jay, Peter. (1974) "Do Trade Unions Matter?" in *Inflation; Causes, Consequences, Cures*, IEA Readings 14, Institute for Economic Affairs, London.

Jay, P. (1975) "A General Hypothesis of Employment, Inflation and Politics," in Jay, P, *The Crisis for Western Political Economy*, Andre Deutsch, London.

Jay, P. and M. Stewart. (1987) *Apocalypse 2000: Economic Breakdown and the Suicide of Democracy*, Sphere Books, London.

Jessop, J. (2022) "IFS Must not Become a Politically Motivated Attack Dog," *The Daily Telegraph*, 23 September.

Jones, D. S. (2012) *Masters of the Universe: Hayek, Friedman and the Birth of Neo-Liberal Politics*, Princeton University Press, Princeton, NJ.

Keegan W., D. Marsh and R. Roberts. (2017) *Six Days in September: Black Wednesday, Brexit, and the making of Europe*, OMFIF, London.

Keegan, W. and R. Pennant-Rea. (1979) *Who Runs the Economy: Control and Influence in British Economic Policy*, Maurice Temple Smith, London.

Knowles, Sophie. (2020) *The Media of Financial Crises: Watchdogs, Lapdogs or Canaries in the Coal Mine?* Peter Lang, London.

Kynaston, D. (1988) *The Financial Times: A Centenary History*, Viking, London.

Kynaston, D. (2011) *City of London: The History*, Chatto and Windus, London.

Kynaston, D. (2017) *Till Time's Last Stand: A History of the Bank of England 1694–2013*, Bloomsbury, London.

Lambert, R. (2005) "Inside the MPC," *Bank of England Quarterly Bulletin*, May.

Lamont, N. (2000) *In Office*, Time Warner Books, London.

Lawson, N. (1992) *The View from No 11: Memoirs of a Tory Radical*, Biteback, London.

Marquand, D. (1977) *Ramsey MacDonald*, Jonathan Cape, London.

Martin, J. (2022) *The Meddlers: Sovereignty, Empire and the Birth of Global Economic Governance*, Harvard University Press, Cambridge, MA.

McDonald, I. (1984) *A History of the Times, Vol. V: Struggles in War and Peace*, Times Books, London.

Meridith, S (2013) "The Oratory of James Callaghan: We Used to Think You Could Spend Your Way out of Recession," in A. Crines and R. Haydon, editors, *Labour Orators from Aneurin Bevan to Gordon Brown*, Manchester University Press, Manchester.

Mirowski, P. (2015) "Postface: Defining Neo-Liberalism," in Mirowski, P. and D. Plehwe, editors, *The Road from Mount Pelerin: The Making of the Neoliberal Thought Collective*, Harvard University Press, Cambridge, MA.

Mirowski, P. and D. Plehwe, editors. (2015) *The Road from Mount Pelerin: The Making of the NeoLiberal Thought Collective*, Harvard University Press, Cambridge, MA.

Moore, Charles. (2016) *Margaret Thatcher, Volume Two: Everything She Wants*, Penguin, London.

Needham, D. (2015) "Goodbye Great Britain? The Press, The Treasury and the 1976 IMF Crisis," in Schifferes, S. and R. Roberts, editors, *The Media and Financial Crises: Comparative and Historical Perspectives*, Routledge, London.

Nye, J. (2015) "Boom, Crisis, Bust: Speculators, Promoters and City Journalists, 1880–1914," in in S. Schifferes and R. Roberts, editors, *The Media and Financial Crises: Comparative and Historical Perspectives*, Routledge, London.

Parsons, W. (1990) *The Power of the Financial Press: Journalism and Economic Opinion in Britain and America*, Rutgers University Press, New Brunswick, NJ.

Partington, R. (2022) "The Mini-Budget That Broke Britain – and Liz Truss," *The Guardian*, 20 October. https://www.theguardian.com/business/2022/oct/20/the-mini-budget-that-broke-britain-and-liz-truss

Plehwe, D. (2015) Introduction, in Mirowski, P. and D. Plehwe, editors, *The Road from Mount Pelerin: The Making of the NeoLiberal Thought Collective*, Harvard University Press, Cambridge, MA.

Porter, D. (1986) "A Trusted Guide to the Investing Public: Harry Marks and the Financial News 1884–1916," *Business History*, 18, pp. 1–17.

Porter, D. (1998) "City Editors and the Modern Investing Public: Establishing the Integrity of the New Financial Journalism in Late Nineteenth Century London," *Media History*, 4.1, pp. 49–60.

Richards, S. (2021) *The Prime Ministers We Never Had: Success and Failure from Butler to Corbyn*, Atlantic Books, London.

Roberts, R. (2013) *Saving the City: The Great Financial Crisis of 1914*, Oxford University Press, Oxford.

Roberts, R. (2015a) "Run on the Bank: Covering the 1914 Financial Crisis," in S. Schifferes and R. Roberts, editors, *The Media and Financial Crises: Comparative and Historical Perspectives*, Routledge, London.

Roberts, R. (2015b) "The Pound and the Press 1919–1972" in S. Schifferes and R. Roberts, editors, *The Media and Financial Crises: Comparative and Historical Perspectives*, Routledge, London.

Roberts, R. (2016) *When Britain Went Bust: The 1976 IMF Crisis*, OMFIF, London.

Schifferes, S. (2018) "The U.K. News Media and Austerity: Trends Since the Global Financial Crisis," in Basu, L., S. Schifferes and S. Knowles, editors, *The Media and Austerity: Comparative Perspectives*, Routledge, London.

Schifferes, S. (2020) "The Financial Press," in Conboy M. and A. Bingham, editors, *The Edinburgh History of the British and Irish Press in the 20th Century*, Edinburgh University Press, Edinburgh.

Schifferes, S. (2022) "Mini-Budget: Lessons from the U.K.'s Long History of Financial Crises," *The Conversation*, 3 October. https://theconversation.com/mini-budget-lessons-from-the-U.K.s-long-history-of-economic-crises-191696

Schifferes, S. and S. Knowles. (2015) "The British Media and the First Crisis of Globalisation," in S. Schifferes and R. Roberts, editors, *The Media and Financial Crises: Comparative and Historical Perspectives*, Routledge, London.

Sherman, A (1975) "Introduction," in Brittan, S., editor, *Second Thoughts on Income Policy*, Centre for Policy Studies, London.

Skidelsky, R. (2013) *John Maynard Keynes 1883–1946: Economist, Philosopher, Statesman*, Penguin, London.

Slobodian, D. (2018) *Globalists: The End of Empire and the Birth of Neo-Liberalism*, Harvard University Press, Cambridge, MA.

Symonds, N. (2022) *Attlee: A Life in Politics*, I.B Tauris, London.

Taylor, James. (2015) "The Birth of the Financial Press, 1825–1880," in S. Schifferes and R. Roberts, editors, *The Media and Financial Crises: Comparative and Historical Perspectives*, Routledge, London.

Tambini, D. (2015), "What Are Financial Journalists For?" in S. Schifferes and R. Roberts, editors, *The Media and Financial Crises: Comparative and Historical Perspectives*, Routledge, London.

Timmins, N. (2017) *The Five Giants: A Biography of the Welfare State*, William Collins, London.

Trentmann, F. (2008) *Free Trade Nation*, Oxford University Press, Oxford.

Tribe, K. (2009) "Liberalism and Neoliberalism in Britain 1930–1980," in Mirowski, P. and D. Plehwe, editors, *The Road from Mount Pelerin: The Making of the Neo-Liberal Thought Collective*, Harvard University Press, Cambridge, MA.

Weiner, Joel, editor, (1988) *Papers for the Millions: The New Journalism in Britain 1880–1914*, Greenwood Press, Westport, CT.

Winseck, D. and R. Pike. (2007) *Communications and Empire: Media, Markets and Globalisation 1860–1930*, Duke University Press, Durham, NC.

Zevin, A. (2019) *Liberalism at Large: The World According to the Economist*, Verso, London.

# 30

# BUSINESS JOURNALISM IN CHINA

*Jeffrey Timmermans*

## Introduction

A graph of China's gross domestic product from 1960 to the present shows a stratospheric rise after the country joined the World Trade Organization (WTO) in 2001 – the scale of the Y-axis required to show this surge renders the years before 2000 as almost a flat line:

Considering that China had already been enjoying rapid economic growth for several decades before 2000, thanks to Deng Xiaoping's policy of "reform and opening up" adopted in 1978, the gains after 2001 are all the more impressive (Figure 30.1). The stunning rise of China's economy as it integrated into the global trade network was a compelling story and a triumph for China's ruling Communist Party – a story the leadership was happy to see transmitted across the globe. This opened up a huge opportunity for financial news organizations in China, both foreign and domestic, who rushed in to take advantage of the relatively liberal regulatory environment for business news. Chinese officials also felt more comfortable with financial news because, as Arrese argues, economic and financial publications traditionally have served an elite, not a general, audience. As in other autocratic states, this gave business publications

> A number of privileges over other types of newspapers, especially under circumstances in which some of them, that is, the political ones, caught the attention and interest of the public authorities, who redoubled their efforts to keep them under control.
>
> *(Arrese 2017)*

But perhaps the most important reason for the Chinese leadership's more relaxed approach to business journalism was their realization that sustained economic growth would be impossible without access to reliable financial information. As Keatley writes:

> Although Beijing has never said so explicitly, many domestic and foreign correspondents in China believe the government does more than tolerate, may in fact even encourage, this relatively aggressive and independent business journalism—something seldom permitted regarding social and political issues. If so, the presumed reason is to

DOI: 10.4324/9781003298977-36

**China's Gross Domestic Product**

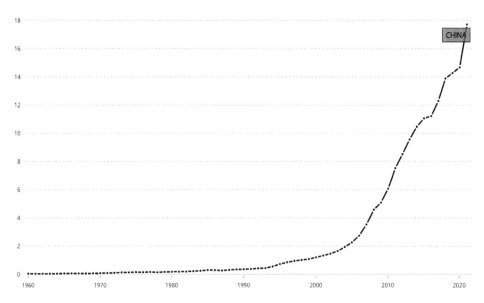

*Figure 30.1*  Gross Domestic Product (current US$) – China

let the press play an important role in giving the financial system added transparency and accountability. Without these, many experts believe, the Chinese economy cannot gain the credibility needed to attract new investors at home and from overseas.

*(Keatley 2003, p. 5)*

## The Golden Age

Thus, business journalism in China was burdened with fewer restrictions than coverage of other fields, particularly politics, just at the time demand for financial information about investing in China began to explode: net inflows of foreign direct investment into China also boomed from 2001 onward as businesses and investors rushed to take advantage of the new opportunities afforded by the country's entry into the WTO:

If there was a Golden Age for journalism in China, it lasted from the late 1990s until the accession of Xi Jinping as General Secretary in 2012 and was led by the generation of journalists who came of age during Deng's "reform and openness" period (Figure 30.2). While the Chinese Communist Party has always imposed strict controls on all media, maintaining state ownership of periodicals and a licensing system for media workers as well as extralegal measures, this generation kept "pushing the envelope" and "mastered the high art of navigating the Chinese media control system" in the words of veteran journalist and journalism educator Yuen-ying Chan (Chan 2010, p. 3). This was especially true in business journalism: it was in that Age that the most famous Chinese business publication, Caijing, was born and upstart outlets such as Chengdu Business News found freedom to pursue investigative journalism. Despite remaining under state control, and lacking any independent legal status, these publications were distinct from "Party organs" (i.e., newspapers directly

**Foreign Direct Investment, Net Inflows (Current US$)**

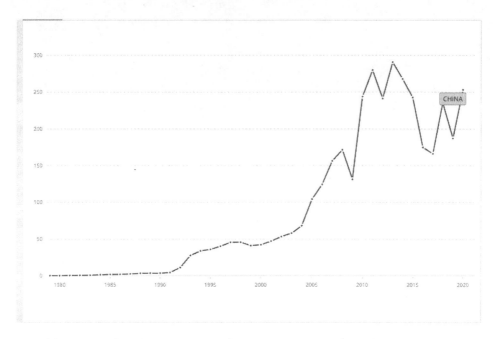

*Figure 30.2*  Foreign direct investment, net inflows (BoP, current US$) – China

controlled by the Communist Party's propaganda department) and enjoyed considerable leeway in editorial and personnel decisions with funding coming from both advertising and circulation revenue – not the state (Huang 2000). Huang refers to these publications as "semi-independent media." They were also extremely popular with readers and advertisers. These publications would have been unthinkable in the Mao era, when all media were nationalized and journalists were effectively propaganda bureaucrats. It was Deng, Mao's successor, who ended government subsidies for media and allowed newspapers to hire journalists on private contracts as part of his broader push toward a more free-market economy (deBurgh 2000).

Chengdu Business News was founded in 1994 and within four years its newsstand sales alone reached 200,000 copies per day, with ad revenue hitting RMB120 million in 1997. By 1998, total circulation had climbed to 500,000 and annual ad revenue to RMB160 million, far surpassing by both measures the local Party organs Sichuan Daily and Chengdu Evening News.

The newspaper's management instituted innovative personnel and anti-corruption procedures to attract and retain talented journalists and keep them honest. News organizations from throughout China paid visits to Chendgu to study its success.

That success made local authorities happy, albeit somewhat wary. "The paper's considerable financial success, without any government investment, has been interpreted widely as an important political achievement of local authorities. In its early stages, local media officials even refused to invite the paper to attend industry meetings because it was too small to be noticed. Now the editor-in-chief of the paper is often invited by officials to "speak some words" ("shuo ji ju") at industry meetings (Huang 2000, p. 649).

## Caijing and Caixin

Caijing founder Hu Shuli is perhaps the most prominent business journalist in China's history, not least thanks to her reputation for "pushing the envelope." The biweekly magazine was founded in 1998 and focused on business and financial topics, although it didn't shy away from controversial topics – especially if there was a finance angle involved. The magazine published a damning account of the corruption and ineptitude of local officials that exacerbated the death toll in Sichuan's devastating 2008 earthquake, including thousands of children who died when their shoddily constructed schools collapsed. Hu was quoted in a glowing 2009 New Yorker profile as saying: "If it's not absolutely forbidden, we do it" (Osnos 2009).

However, that comment underplays Hu's considerable savvy in determining what stories were "absolutely forbidden" in a system that relies on vague regulations and the sometimes-capricious application of those rules by bureaucrats. Caijing's biggest non-business-related scoop was a 2003 investigation into the government cover-up of the SARS outbreak. Authorities responded by removing that issue of the magazine from some newsstands, but Caijing avoided the fate of other publications that published on the same topic: Nanfang Daily Newspaper Group in Guangdong, another media organization known for its hard-hitting coverage, had one of its publications closed by authorities and several top executives sentenced to lengthy terms in jail, ostensibly for embezzlement (French 2004). And if there was any doubt of the government's real intention, the editor of Nan Fang's popular Southern Weekend magazine was replaced with the local propaganda official chiefly responsible for the SARS cover-up (McGregor 2003).

While Hu was widely admired for pushing the envelope, she also was careful to avoid topics such as the banned spiritual group Falun Gong or the anniversary of the 1989 Tiananmen Square massacre and stuck primarily to business stories (Osnos 2009). That and her reported close ties to Communist Party heavyweight Wang Qishan are the reasons most commonly cited for Hu's longevity as an editor (Shih 2018).

In fact, Hu achieved even more success with her second media start-up, Caixin. The name is a combination of the Chinese character for "wealth" or "finance," also used in Caijing, with the character for "new." Hu formed the new venture in 2009 after a dispute with Caijing's parent company S.E.E.C. Media. She took most of the staff with her and continued pushing the envelope (Tsang 2015).

In 2017, Caixin put all its content behind a paywall – the first Chinese online publication to do so. Despite this, readership continued to grow strongly and by 2021 Caixin had amassed more than 700,000 digital subscribers, placing it among the top ten international sites ranked by the International Federation of Periodical Publishers (FIPP).

Just a year later, Caixin surpassed 850,000 subscribers, making it the biggest non-English-language site in the world, according to the FIPP (Turvill 2022).

But not even Hu Shuli proved able to navigate the far more restrictive media environment ushered in by Xi Jinping (see "The Crackdown" below). Hu stepped aside from her editorial role in 2018 and by many accounts has since been much less outspoken (Shih 2018). That hasn't saved Caixin from the crackdown. In 2021, it was removed from a list of media organizations approved for domestic republishing, limiting its distribution in China (White 2021).

## Foreign business news organizations in China

Foreign business news organizations in China proved much less willing and/or able to stay within the red lines, and their efforts to attract a domestic readership have been routinely thwarted. A major hurdle in this regard is the long-standing ban on hiring Chinese nationals as reporters. Ever since foreign media re-entered China in the post-war period, they have relied on local employees to serve as news assistants or "researchers." While these employees performed much of the key behind-the-scenes work required in reporting stories, such as monitoring Chinese media and serving as an interpreter during interviews, they are not allowed to report independently and can't be named on a byline. The bigger problem, though, is government censorship.

The Wall Street Journal launched a Chinese-language website in 2003, but the site was blocked periodically by authorities and remains unavailable in mainland China without the use of a virtual private network to jump the country's "Great Firewall" (see https://cn.wsj.com). The New York Times' efforts were even less auspicious: its Chinese-language site launched in June 2012 but was blocked permanently in October of the same year after the paper published an investigation (see https://www.nytimes.com/2012/10/26/business/global/family-of-wen-jiabao-holds-a-hidden-fortune-in-china.html) into the hidden wealth of the family of then-premier Wen Jiabao (Saba 2013).

Reporting on such "sensitive" topics invariably led to swift punishment, even if the news only appeared overseas and in English, and that forced some foreign news organizations to make difficult editorial choices. Bloomberg News, also in 2012, published an investigation into the wealth of the family of soon-to-be Party leader Xi Jinping. Like The New York Times, Bloomberg's website was blocked in China and its reporters denied visas for a period of time. News reports quoting Bloomberg staffers suggested that the company subsequently became more wary of crossing red lines, declining to publish several other investigations into the hidden wealth of prominent Chinese citizens (Wong 2013). Bloomberg executives rejected that characterization.

## Dodgy Data, Scared Sources

One perennial struggle all business journalists in China face is with the reliability and accuracy of economic statistics – and sometimes even getting access to these data, or the necessary context from expert sources. The gross domestic product figures published by China's National Bureau of Statistics have been criticized for decades – even by the country's own leadership. Li Keqiang, who became premier in 2013, was quoted in a leaked U.S. diplomatic cable in 2007 (when he was party secretary of Liaoning Province) saying China's GDP data were "man-made" and unreliable (U.S. Embassy Beijing 2007). The Liaoning Provincial Government subsequently admitted in 2014, well after Li moved on to a national role, that it had been faking economic data for years, inflating its fiscal revenues by around 20 percent (The Economist 2017). As provincial figures are fed into the calculation of national GDP, such distortions have an impact well beyond individual provinces.

In a report for the U.S.-China Economic and Security Review Commission, Koch-Weser (Koch-Weser 2013) highlighted a long list of issues with how China's GDP data are calculated, starting with incomplete survey data and an outdated system of direct reporting, to outright falsification for political reasons. A 2014 analysis of Chinese provincial economic data showed GDP growth diverged significantly from electricity consumption in years of provincial leadership turnover. As the two indicators should normally correlate, the study concluded that gaps during transition years were "consistent with the hypothesis that political cycles lead to upward-biased reporting at key moments" (Wallace 2016, p. 14).

It's not just GDP figures that are suspicious in China, due largely to the same political factors. Since promotion up the ranks of Party cadres in China tends to be based on compliance with central policy goals, there is a strong incentive to manipulate data. A study of the careers of 967 mayors in 258 prefectures and 28 provinces between 1985 and 2000, done for the U.S. National Bureau of Economic Research, demonstrated that self-reported performance in enforcing the One Child Policy predicted mayoral promotion (Suárez Serrato et al. 2016).

In 2015, Quartz published an extensive list of Chinese economic data sets that were "doctored" (Guilford 2015). While reforms to China's GDP methodology have cleared up some of the problems with that key indicator, the political incentives to fudge all kinds of data remain: in 2022, experts accused China of understating the number of fatalities from COVID-19 in the country (Olcott et al. 2022).

The private sector has attempted to address the lack of reliable statistics by creating alternative economic indicators based on proprietary data. IHS Markit, a unit of S&P Global, publishes a purchasing managers' index for 40 countries, including China. The widely followed China series was sponsored for five years by HSBC, a global financial institution that makes most of its profit in Greater China, and frequently disagreed with the official PMI figure published by the government. HSBC and Markit ended their relationship with the PMI data in 2015; neither organization cited a reason for the termination, but Reuters cited sources suggesting that the discrepancies with the official data upset government officials (Sweeney and Price 2015).

Use of and access to a wide variety of financial data in China is restricted under national security grounds, from pre-release economic indicators to the work product of corporate auditors, i.e., notes and files used in the auditing process. The regulations surrounding data security were revamped and consolidated under two major pieces of national legislation: the Cybersecurity Law of 2017 and the Data Security Law of 2020. The latter singled out "core" data for the highest level of protection, defining "core" quite broadly as "any data that concerns Chinese national and economic security, Chinese citizens' welfare and significant public interests" (Skadden, Arps, Slate, Meagher & Flom LLP 2021).

And sometimes, data simply disappear. Following a record sell-off in Chinese sovereign bonds in March 2022 by foreign investors, accompanied by a decline in the value of the Chinese currency (Bloomberg News 2022c), the data provider relied on by foreign investors "quietly stopped providing data on their transactions." The reasons were unclear, but the timing of the unusual halt in a key financial information system raised concern that the government was trying to stem the losses by making it impossible for investors to trade (Bloomberg News 2022a).

Human sources of information can also become targets of official wrath if their prognostications stray from the party line. The public social-media accounts of a prominent China strategist, Hong Hao of Bocom International Holdings, were abruptly suspended in April 2022 and their contents blocked. A notice on Hong's WeChat account cited unspecified violations of the Chinese social-media giant's public account service rules. As Bloomberg News reported:

> While it's unclear which of Hong's posts may have crossed the line, China has in recent weeks censored social media posts related to economically disruptive lockdowns. The benchmark CSI 300 Index fell to a two-year low last week – one of the world's worst-performing equity gauges this year with a 19 percent loss. That hasn't stopped state-run media from publishing a series of articles projecting confidence in markets.
>
> *(Bloomberg News 2022b)*

Official wrath can result in severe punishment when journalists are considered to have "leaked state secrets" or committed other national-security crimes. The vagueness of the charges and the difficulty lawyers, diplomats and journalists face in contacting detainees make it extremely difficult to ascertain the true nature of the offense. To cite just one example, in August 2020 authorities detained Cheng Lei, an Australian national and prominent on-air presenter for state-run broadcaster China Global Television Network (Committee to Protect Journalists 2020). After being held for almost two years, Cheng was tried behind closed doors on charges of leaking state secrets. The court didn't immediately announce a verdict, leaving Cheng in limbo (Uribe 2022). A similar fate befell Bloomberg News staffer Haze Fan: she was detained in December 2020 by plainclothes security officials and officially arrested after more than six months in detention "on suspicion of committing crimes endangering national security." Fan was released on bail in June 2022, but her employer was unable to immediately contact her (Lim 2022).

## Corrupt Corporations

Reporting on Chinese corporations offers other challenges. China's corporate world is dominated by state-owned enterprises and large private firms, some of which thrive on corruption and plunder of state resources. Rithmire and Chen call these types of private firms "mafia-like" organizations that rely on mutual endangerment with corrupt officials to protect their ill-gotten assets. Such companies tend to be highly secretive, even those with publicly traded shares, and feature opaque, multi-layered ownership structures – making it difficult to obtain accurate information (Rithmire and Chen 2021).

When things go wrong with such business groups, the government steps in behind a veil of secrecy. One example is the government takeover of Tomorrow Group, formerly headed by Xiao Jianhua, a tycoon who was conspicuous even in his flamboyant peer group for his all-female team of bodyguards. Xiao's Tomorrow Group had interests in 44 financial institutions, including a stake in Ping An, one of China's largest insurance companies, and thousands of affiliated companies (ibid). A 2014 investigation by The New York Times revealed he paid $2.4 million for a stake in an investment firm controlled by the sister and brother-in-law of Xi Jinping. That was one of three transactions the newspaper documented that "appear to have benefited the relatives of China's highest-ranking leaders" (Barboza and Forsythe 2014).

Unfortunately for Xiao, neither his political connections nor his female bodyguards could protect him from the wide-ranging crackdown on corruption that Xi implemented after becoming China's president. In 2017, Xiao was taken away from his apartment in Hong Kong's Four Seasons Hotel by Chinese police and smuggled across the border to mainland China – a flagrant violation of Hong Kong and international law (Xiao is a Canadian citizen and also holds a diplomatic passport from Antigua) (Forsythe 2017). After three years in detention, Chinese regulators began dismantling Xiao's corporate empire, seizing companies worth hundreds of billions of dollars (Stanley 2020).

Chinese state-owned enterprises (SOEs) present similar challenges for journalists, but for different reasons. Because they answer to the Party instead of shareholders, they have little incentive to share information with outsiders and much of their internal operations and accounting can be considered state secrets. The size of the biggest make them systemically important in China, and their influence extends throughout the world. There are more than 150,000 SOEs in China, and of the companies on the 2017 Fortune Global 500 list (FG500) 102 were Chinese SOEs. In that year, the revenues of FG500 Chinese SOEs reached a total of $6.1 trillion, amounting to 22 percent of the total revenues of all FG500 corporations ($27.7 trillion) (Lin et al. 2020).

Businesses in China can also have a corrupting influence on reporters through the widespread practice of "red-envelope journalism." This is especially true for financial journalists, whose coverage can often influence share prices. Xu defines the practice, and its appearance in journalistic routines, as follows:

> The giving of red envelopes is a Chinese cultural tradition in which a monetary gift, usually contained in a red envelope symbolizing good luck, is given to friends or relatives during festivals, such as the Lunar New Year, or on special occasions, such as weddings. In the context of journalism, red-envelope cash refers to cash wrapped in an envelope given to journalists by news sources and other agents such as public relations companies or brokers.
>
> *(Xu 2016, p. 231)*

Xu cites a 1997 survey of Chinese journalists showing that

> 34.8 percent of respondents agreed or strongly agreed that accepting cash from sources was prevalent in Chinese journalism. In addition, 56 percent agreed or strongly agreed that taking free gifts was prevalent; 78.8 percent viewed accepting free meals as prevalent, 31.3 percent agreed that accepting free travel was common, and more than 65 percent regarded it as common for journalists to solicit advertising or sponsorships.
>
> *(ibid., 232)*

## Belt and Road

One of the biggest business stories from China in the early 21st century is the country's "Belt and Road Initiative" (BRI, also called "One Belt, One Road") to promote infrastructure development across a wide swath of the globe, and the difference in coverage between domestic Chinese media and overseas publications on this trillion-dollar program is illuminating.

The "belt" in the title refers to traditional overland trade routes linking China and Europe through central Asia, while the "road" is in effect a "maritime silk road" connecting China with Southeast Asia, Africa, and Europe (Yu and Wallace 2021). Xi Jinping announced vague outlines of the plan in 2013, but it wasn't until several years later that the first concrete investment plans began to take shape. Huang (Huang 2016) notes that China's motivation for the BRI centers on the plan's potential to spur domestic growth and bolster the country's international influence.

Even still, the Chinese government has never issued a full list of projects or details on the terms of loans extended to client governments to pay for them. As a Chatham House "explainer" notes:

> It is important not to think of the Belt and Road as a unified, coherent strategy, but rather as a fragmented collection of bilateral arrangements made on different terms. This is illustrated by the fact that governments receiving Chinese loans are not always sure which authority in China they are dealing with. Fifteen different Chinese government ministries claim some responsibility for Belt and Road projects; Chinese provinces

have their own competing agendas, businesses and projects; Chinese diplomats sign up client governments to major projects in order to demonstrate loyalty to the party as opposed to promote a viable project; and even the Chinese central government is still unable to produce a list of what projects are part of the BRI and which are not.

*(Yu and Wallace 2021)*

Unsurprisingly, the BRI coverage in Chinese state-controlled media has been uniformly positive. A critical discourse analysis of BRI stories in state-run China Daily and the U.K.'s Financial Times showed that "China Daily, like other Chinese mainstream media, has attempted to emphasize the initiative's positive attributes and construct positive images of China as a peace-loving nation, an international cooperator, and an emerging global economic and responsible power" (Zhang and Wu 2017). In contrast, the Financial Times' coverage was more mixed. Zhang and Wu note: "We can observe that a prominent image of China represented in FT involves uncertainty, as seen in the expression 'China casts cloud and silver lining...' and in the frequent use of question marks related to events and stories about China in headlines. Furthermore, the image of China as an authoritarian and hegemonic state is well represented, as evidenced in the expression "a new empire" (Zhang and Wu 2017, p. 36). Another critical discourse analysis on BRI news coverage, this one focusing on a BBC News podcast series, paints a similar picture of ambiguity: "While the news value of Positivity is prevalent in the episodes, it has been observed that the construction of Negativity is mostly in the foreground" (Apirakvanalee and Zhai 2022).

## Business Journalism Education in China

While the first journalism school in China was established along American lines – the Missouri School of Journalism established a department at St. John's University in Shanghai in 1921 – the founding of the People's Republic of China presaged a shift to the Marxist, or Soviet, view of journalism's role as a key supporter of the Communist Party, requiring media workers' "absolute acceptance of the party's guiding ideology and leadership and adherence to the party's press policies and censorship" (Xu 2018, p. 177).

The American model's emphasis on professionalism and truth-telling in journalism wasn't completely eliminated, however, leading to a hybrid journalism education that in some ways was contradictory: "Journalism education in China has to struggle between the US and Soviet models to pursue a balance between journalistic professionalism in the Western sense and political orientation" (Xu 2018, p. 177).

Deng's reforms beginning in 1978 were followed by further liberalization of the media by his successor, Jiang Zemin, who understood the importance of journalism to economic growth. "The main concern of the Jiang era," according to deBurgh, "has been to promote the free market as the best means by which the economy may develop; the media are seen as liberating minds and inciting entrepreneurialism" (deBurgh 2000, p. 549). Journalism education also expanded rapidly in the post-Mao era, with the number of journalism graduates soaring from just 453 in 1982 to 9,200 in 1996 (ibid.). The prestige of journalism also grew:

There is eager competition to study to be a journalist, particularly a tele- vision journalist, in China today. They enjoy high pay, status and opportunities to advance in many directions. A typical undergraduate student studies for 4 years, across seven semesters. The eighth semester is a placement in a media organization which takes place in the third year. This is the "Culminating Placement". Students will usually have carried out one or more "Taster Placements" of a few weeks much earlier in their Course. The placements are chosen in consultation with the student and it is expected by all parties that a successful placement will lead to a job upon graduation.

*(deBurgh 2000, p. 549)*

Thus, journalists educated in the post-Deng era were exposed to Western ideas of journalism in a Western style of tertiary journalism education, which they put to good use when "pushing the envelope" of investigative and business journalism in the profession's "Golden Age."

The high point for business journalism education in China probably was in 2007, when the International Center for Journalists (ICFJ), based in Washington, D.C., established a "Global Business Journalism" master's degree program at Tsinghua University in Beijing, one of China's top universities. The English-language program was designed to meet "the highest international standards" and was modeled on the U.S. business-journalism curriculum, featuring courses in ethics and accounting as well as the standard business-reporting courses. The program was also well funded, with financial sponsors, including Merrill Lynch, Bloomberg, and the John S. and James L. Knight Foundation (Maloney 2009). More than 250 Chinese and 200 international students completed the program during its first 15 years.

### The Crackdown

The Golden Age of journalism, and particularly business journalism, in China ended soon after Xi Jinping rose to power in 2012. Xi has in many ways halted, or even reversed, China's path toward Western-style capitalism (Wei 2021). He has taken a hard line against rivals, critics, private enterprise, and restive regions such as Xinjiang and Tibet. He also has re-emphasized the traditional Marxist/Maoist view of journalism as the servant of the state, contrasting with the greater latitude his predecessors allowed for "semi-independent" commercially oriented publications. In 2016, Xi paid a widely publicized visit to the top State-run media outlets and delivered a crystal-clear message: "The Chinese news media exists to serve as a propaganda tool for the Communist Party, and it must pledge its fealty to Mr. Xi" (Wong 2016). And in 2020, the Party introduced a new credentialing system for journalists at State-run publications, requiring all news workers to pass an exam on "Xi Jinping Thought" (Tang 2020).

Even before those two initiatives, Xi's tougher oversight was having a devastating impact on Chinese journalism in general:

The result of these controls is that commercial media as a progressive force have been effectively neutralized over the past few years in China. We have seen, as a result, an exodus of experienced journalists and editors. And because traditional media remain the core of professional journalism practice in China — not least because most online media are still prohibited from having reporting teams — this exodus has meant a very real erosion of professional capacity.

*(Bandurski 2015)*

The crackdown extended to Hong Kong, which reverted to China's control in 1997 under a framework promising the former British colony "a high degree of autonomy, except in foreign and defence affairs" and that the British legal system in place there would "remain basically unchanged" for at least 50 years (United Nations 1985). Those promises were (mostly) kept for almost half that time, allowing for the development of a vibrant free press in Hong Kong that routinely challenged the government and vested corporate interests.

One of the most aggressive watchdogs was Jimmy Lai's Apple Daily, a daily tabloid featuring local politics and scandal, business news, and (for a time) a pornography page. Launched in 1995, it grew to become one of the territory's most popular newspapers with a circulation of more than 350,000 by 2001 (Pottinger 2001). Lai had fled mainland China for Hong Kong as a young boy, arriving penniless but eventually amassing a fortune from manufacturing clothing – a prototypical Hong Kong success story. He and his newspaper were especially critical of the Chinese Communist Party, which made Lai one of the first high-profile targets of a sweeping National Security Law (NSL) imposed on Hong Kong by Beijing on June 30, 2020. In early August, more than 200 police officers raided Apple Daily's headquarters, arrested Lai along with several top executives and charged them with national security offenses. The police then froze the paper's bank accounts, forcing it to shut down in June 2021. Authorities also targeted another vocal critic, the outspokenly pro-democratic Stand News, which was forced to shut down several months later (Wang 2021). The closure of Apple Daily and Stand News had a chilling effect throughout Hong Kong media, spurring local news outlet Citizen News to preemptively shut down in early January 2022 (Pang and Ng 2022).

Even international business publications felt the chill. Because of Hong Kong's global importance as a financial center and gateway to mainland China, not to mention its sturdy legal system and transport links, many international news organizations, including The Wall Street Journal, Financial Times, and The New York Times, used the city as their Asian headquarters. Hong Kong also provided a base for Western reporters expelled from China due to critical coverage. That began to change as China started exerting more direct control over Hong Kong, culminating in the passage of the NSL. Within weeks, The New York Times announced it would move its Hong Kong-based digital news operations to Seoul (Grynbaum 2020). The newspaper cited the uncertainty about the NSL's impact on its journalistic work, but the move also came after several of its Hong Kong-based reporters experienced delays or outright rejection of visa renewals, a long-standing issue in mainland China but unprecedented in Hong Kong before 2018 (Ramzy 2018).

## Conclusion

China's stunning economic growth since "opening up" in the late 1970s and 1980s was accompanied by an equally impressive growth in business journalism. Despite keeping a tight rein on general news reporting, Chinese officials granted business and financial news organizations more room to pursue investigative and watchdog journalism (implicitly rather than explicitly); these officials understood that sustained economic growth, and vitally important foreign direct investment in the country's nascent industries, required a (relatively) free flow of accurate news and information. Domestic and international news organizations rushed to take advantage of the favorable environment, launching extensive coverage of China's financial world and, occasionally, how that world intersected with politics. While financial publications were punished for straying across "red lines" and publishing politically sensitive stories, the late 1990s and early 2000s saw some remarkable investigative journalism published by both domestic and international publications. China's preeminent financial publication, Caixin, has in less than 12 years of operations become one of the world's most viewed websites and publishes news in both Chinese and English. However, Xi Jinping's tight controls over the media has stifled its ability to report independently and discouraged young graduates from pursuing careers in journalism. The "eager competition to study to be a journalist" that deBurgh noted in 2000 has since been replaced by despair.

## Further Reading

Anderson, P.J. & Ward, G. (2007) *The Future of Journalism in the Advanced Democracies.* Ashgate Publishing Company, Hampshire.

Chang, L.T. (2008) *Factory Girls: From Village to City in a Changing China.* Spiegel and Grau, New York.

Huang, Y. (2017) *Cracking the China Conundrum: Why Conventional Economic Wisdom Is Often Wrong.* Oxford University Press, New York.

Li, Z.-S. (1994) *The Private Life of Chairman Mao.* Random House, New York.

McGregor, R. (2010) *The Party: The Secret World of China's Communist Rulers.* Harper Collins, New York.

Osnos, E. (2014) *Age of Ambition: Chasing Fortune, Truth, and Faith in the New China.* Farrar, Straus and Giroux, New York.

Schuman, M. (2020) *Superpower Interrupted: The Chinese History of the World.* PublicAffairs, New York.

Shum, D. (2021) *Red Roulette: An Insider's Story of Wealth, Power, Corruption, and Vengeance in Today's China.* Scribner, New York.

## References

Arrese, Á. (2017) The Role of Economic Journalism in Political Transitions. *Journalism*, 18, 368–383.

Bandurski, D. (2015) How China's Government Controls the News: A Primer. *Foreign Policy*, July 21, 2015, https://foreignpolicy.com/2015/07/21/china-media-xi-jinping-crackdown-newspaper/

Barboza, D. & Forsythe, M. (2014) With Choice at Tiananmen, Student Took Road to Riches. *New York Times*, June 3, 2014. https://www.nytimes.com/2014/06/04/world/asia/tiananmen-era-students-different-path-to-power-in-china.html

Bloomberg News. (2022a) China Stops Reporting Bond Trades by Foreigners After Selloff. *Bloomberg News*, May 17, 2022. https://www.bloomberg.com/news/articles/2022-05-17/china-stops-reporting-bond-trades-by-foreigners-after-selloff?leadSource=uverify%20wall

Bloomberg News. (2022b) China Analyst Hong Hao Has Social Media Accounts Frozen. *Bloomberg News*, May 1, 2022. https://www.bloomberg.com/news/articles/2022-05-01/china-strategist-hong-hao-has-social-media-accounts-frozen?leadSource=uverify%20wall

Bloomberg News. (2022c) Global Funds Cut China Bond Holdings by Record as Premiums Erode. *Bloomberg News*, April 7, 2022. https://www.bloomberg.com/news/articles/2022-04-08/foreigner-exodus-from-china-bonds-deepens-as-yield-premium-fades?leadSource=uverify%20wall

Chan, Y. (2010) Introduction: The Journalism Tradition. In *Investigative Journalism in China: Eight Cases in Chinese Watchdog Journalism*, Eds. Bandurski, D. & Hala, M., Hong Kong University Press, Hong Kong, pp. 1–18.

Committee to Protect Journalists. (2020) Cheng Lei. *Journalists Imprisoned*, August 14, 2020. https://cpj.org/data/people/cheng-lei/

deBurgh, H. (2000) Chinese Journalism and the Academy: The Politics and Pedagogy of the Media. *Journalism Studies*, 1, 549–558.

Economist. (2017) Potemkin Province: A Big Chinese Province Admits Faking its Economic Data. *Economist*, January 26, 2017. https://www.economist.com/finance-and-economics/2017/01/26/a-big-chinese-province-admits-faking-its-economic-data

Forsythe, M. (2017) Billionaire Is Reported Seized From Hong Kong Hotel and Taken Into China. *New York Times*, January 31, 2017. https://www.nytimes.com/2017/01/31/world/asia/xiao-jianhua-china-hong-kong-billionaire.html

French, H.W. (2004) China Tries Again to Curb Independent Press in South. *New York Times*, April 15, 2004. https://www.nytimes.com/2004/04/15/world/china-tries-again-to-curb-independent-press-in-south.html

Grynbaum, M. (2020) New York Times Will Move Part of Hong Kong Office to Seoul. *New York Times*, July 14, 2020. https://www.nytimes.com/2020/07/14/business/media/new-york-times-hong-kong.html

Guilford, G. (2015) The Most Egregious Examples from the Chinese Government's Long, Sordid History of Data-Doctoring. *Quartz*, October 29, 2015. https://qz.com/530096/china-data-tricks

Huang, C. (2000) The Development of a Semi-Independent Press in Post-Mao China: An overview and a case study of Chengdu Business News. *Journalism Studies*, 1, 649–664.

Huang, Y. (2016) Understanding China's Belt & Road Initiative: Motivation, framework and assessment. *China Economic Review*, 40, 314–321.

Keatley, R.L. (2003) *The Role of the Media in a Market Economy.* National Committee on United States-China Relations, Washington, DC. https://www.ncuscr.org/wp-content/uploads/2008/02/page_attachments_Role-of-the-Media-in-the-Market-Economy.pdf

Koch-Weser, I.N. (2013) The Reliability of China's Economic Data: An Analysis of National Output. *U.S.-China Economic and Security Review Commission*, January 30, 2013. https://www.uscc.gov/research/reliability-chinas-economic-data-analysis-national-output

Lim, M. (2022) China Has Released Bloomberg News Staffer Haze Fan on Bail. *Bloomberg News*, June 14, 2022. https://www.bloomberg.com/news/articles/2022-06-14/china-has-released-bloomberg-news-staffer-haze-fan-on-bail

Lin, K.J. et al. (2020) State-Owned Enterprises in China: A Review of 40 Years of Research and Practice. *China Journal of Accounting Research*, 13, 31–55.

Maloney, W.A. (2009) Business Journalism Education in a Changing China. *Academe*, 95, 24–27.

McGregor, R. (2003) China Moves to Control Liberal Paper. *Financial Times.*

Olcott, E. et al. (2022) China 'Playing Games' with Covid Statistics. *Financial Times*, 4.

Osnos, E. (2009) The Forbidden Zone: How Far Can a Provocative Editor Go? *New Yorker*, July 13, 2009. https://www.newyorker.com/magazine/2009/07/20/the-forbidden-zone

Pang, J. & Ng, E. (2022) Hong Kong's Citizen News Says Closure Triggered by Stand News Collapse. *Reuters News.*

Pottinger, M. (2001) Hong Kong Tabloid Brings Back Sex To Please Readers. *The Asian Wall Street Journal*, 5.

Ramzy, A. (2018) Journalist's Expulsion From Hong Kong 'Sends a Chilling Message'. *New York Times*, A9.

Rithmire, M. & Chen, H. (2021) The Emergence of Mafia-like Business Systems in China. *The China Quarterly*, 248, 1037–1058.

Saba, J. (2013) New York Times CEO says Chinese Language Site under Review. *Reuters*, November 26, 2013. https://finance.yahoo.com/news/york-times-ceo-says-chinese-003411147.html

Shih, G. (2018) *AP Interview: Chinese Editor Hu Shuli Steps Aside, Not Down.* Associated Press.

Skadden, Arps, Slate, Meagher & Flom LLP. (2021) China's New Data Security and Personal Information Protection Laws: What They Mean for Multinational Companies, November, 3, 2021, https://www.skadden.com/insights/publications/2021/11/chinas-new-data-security-and-personal-information-protection-laws

Stanley, A. (2020) China Is Dismantling the Empire of a Vanished Tycoon. *New York Times*, July 18, 2020. https://www.nytimes.com/2020/07/18/business/china-xiao-jianhua.html

Suárez Serrato, J.C., Wang, X.Y. & Zhang, S. (2016) *The Limits of Meritocracy: Screening Bureaucrats Under Imperfect Verifiability*, February 2016. https://www.nber.org/system/files/working_papers/w21963/revisions/w21963.rev3.pdf

Sweeney, P. & Price, M. (2015) UPDATE 2-HSBC Ends Marketing Tie-up with Markit for PMI indices. *Reuters*, June 26, 2015. https://www.reuters.com/article/china-pmi-hsbc-markit/update-2-hsbc-ends-marketing-tie-up-with-markit-for-pmi-indices-idINL3N0ZC1WK20150626

Tang, J. (2020) China's Shiny New Press Card Means Total State Control of Media: Journalists. *Radio Free Asia*, November 11, 2020. https://www.rfa.org/english/news/china/press-11112020092314.html

Tsang, A. (2015) Caijing Journalist's Shaming Signals China's Growing Control Over News Media. *New York Times*, September 6, 2015. https://www.nytimes.com/2015/09/07/business/media/caijing-journalists-shaming-signals-chinas-growing-control-over-news-media.html

Turvill, W. (2022) Ranked: The World's Top Ten Non-English Digital News Subscriptions. *Press Gazette*, June 10, 2022. https://pressgazette.co.uk/news/caixin-china-subscriptions-ranking/

United Nations. (1985) Joint Declaration on the question of Hong Kong. 1399, 61.

Uribe, A. (2022) Journalist's China Trial Ends With No Verdict. *The Wall Street Journal*, p. A12.

U.S. Embassy Beijing. (2007) FIFTH GENERATION STAR LI KEQIANG DISCUSSES DOMESTIC CHALLENGES, TRADE RELATIONS WITH AMBASSADOR. *Wikileaks Cable: 07BEIJING1760_a*, March 15, 2007. https://wikileaks.org/plusd/cables/07BEIJING1760_a.html

Wallace, J.L. (2016) Juking the Stats? Authoritarian Information Problems in China. *British Journal of Political Science*, 46, 11–29.

Wang, V. (2021) Hong Kong Police Raid Office of Pro-Democracy News Site and Arrest 7. *New York Times*, A8, December 28, 2021. https://www.nytimes.com/2021/12/29/world/asia/hong-kong-stand-news-arrest.html

Wei, L. (2021) Xi Jinping Aims to Rein In Chinese Capitalism, Hew to Mao's Socialist Vision. *The Wall Street Journal*, September 20, 2021. https://www.wsj.com/articles/xi-jinping-aims-to-rein-in-chinese-capitalism-hew-to-maos-socialist-vision-11632150725

White, E. (2021) Beijing Targets News Outlet Caixin in Media Crackdown. *Financial Times*, 3, October 20, 2021. https://www.ft.com/content/3f6575a5-048c-411d-8103-162d4b27fcbb

Wong, E. (2013) Bloomberg News Is Said to Curb Articles That Might Anger China. *New York Times*, November 8, 2013. https://www.nytimes.com/2013/11/09/world/asia/bloomberg-news-is-said-to-curb-articles-that-might-anger-china.html

Wong, E. (2016) Xi Jinping's News Alert: Chinese Media Must Serve the Party. *New York Times*, February 22, 2016. https://www.nytimes.com/2016/02/23/world/asia/china-media-policy-xi-jinping.html

Xu, D. (2016) Red-Envelope Cash: Journalists on the Take in Contemporary China. *Journal of Media Ethics*, 31, 231–244.

Xu, J. (2018) The Return of Ideology to China's Journalism Education: The 'Joint Model' Campaign Between Propaganda Departments and Journalism Schools. *Asia Pacific Media Educator*, 28, 176–185.

Yu, J. & Wallace, J. (2021) What Is China's Belt and Road Initiative (BRI)? September 13, 2021. https://www.chathamhouse.org/2021/09/what-chinas-belt-and-road-initiative-bri

Zhang, L. & Wu, D. (2017) Media Representations of China: A Comparison of China Daily and *Financial Times* in Reporting on the Belt and Road Initiative. *Critical Arts*, 31, 29–43.

# 31

# ENTREPRENEURIAL BUSINESS JOURNALISM IN SPANISH-SPEAKING COUNTRIES

*Alfonso Vara-Miguel and James Breiner*

Spanish-language digital natives differentiate themselves from legacy media by conducting business journalism in niches defined by topic, geography or both. They define their mission along a broad spectrum with public service at one end and commercial success at the other, sometimes with the latter subsidizing the former. Many successful examples have emerged in Spanish-language media, which attract limited attention from an industry dominated by global corporations in the Anglo-Saxon world.

Still, many of these Spanish media have created viable models with innovative elements worth emulating. This chapter presents a series of examples of innovative media and discusses how these innovations create value for users as well as models that can be replicated around the world.

## Introduction: Business Journalism and Entrepreneurship

John J. Kiernan was a notable figure in business journalism in the 19th century, being an innovator in the delivery of financial news over electric wires in the industrial era (Wells 2020). His agency, the Kiernan News Agency, which operated from 1869 to 1893, was also known for training Charles Dow, Edward Jones and Charles Bergstresser, before they founded the Dow Jones News Service (in 1882) and later The Wall Street Journal (in 1889), which became the most influential media in financial (and business) journalism. These men are examples of 19th-century entrepreneurs who started news businesses, taking full advantage of the new technologies of that age, in particular the advance of the telegraph (Chalaby 1998; Rafter 2016). As Rafter stated, "the history of journalism is marked by entrepreneurial spirit" (Rafter 2016, p. 140). This is particularly the case in business journalism. Throughout the 20th century, business journalism became, in a certain way, a reference for how to resolve the problems and challenges currently facing journalism. The Financial Times, The Wall Street Journal, The Economist, Bloomberg and Reuters, to mention the most significant journalistic brands in this field, are often cited as cases of news organizations that have found their way, by betting on journalism, at the crossroads of the technological and economic developments of the last decades (Arrese 2016).

DOI: 10.4324/9781003298977-37

In recent years, the media industries have undergone tremendous changes due to technological advancements, deregulation and privatization in the information and communication sectors (Hang 2020). The overabundance of information due to the development and popularization of the Internet and social networks, the collapse of old media business models, based almost exclusively on advertising revenues, and the new ways for audiences to receive news, which are more personal, digital and mobile, have led to a crisis in current journalism (Medina-Laverón et al. 2021; Usher 2017). The Internet has changed the rules of the game because audiences have found new outlets for free information and because marketers have identified more effective online channels. However, most news organizations have not changed their revenue model, at least not in the first years of the crisis (Picard 2010).

However, as happened in the 20th century, the field of financial and business information has managed this crisis better. At this point, it is appropriate to differentiate between digital media in general and digital native media and even digital-only media. Following Salaverría et al. (2019), digital media encompass all publications that, regardless of their origin, are published on the Internet. The term digital native media refers to media born directly on the Internet, without being a digital version of any offline publication. Finally, by digital-only media, we mean digital media that come from an extinct offline publication, for example those newspapers and magazines that, due to the crisis, have discontinued their print editions but kept their digital ones. This distinction is important because, as we will see, within the digital media industry, digital native outlets are shaking the market with their new financial and business contents.

On the one hand, the legacy brands have adapted technologically, launching Internet versions of printed publications or broadcast media but preserving their main value proposition: to select, edit and distribute valuable, relevant and quality news. To achieve this, they have strengthened the ability of their journalists to navigate the huge flow of information and events and search for what it is necessary for the audiences to know, to work with their own agendas, to separate the relevant from the superficial and to provide context to the most important events (Arrese 2016; Benson 2019).

On the other hand, digital native outlets have adopted forms and models that have become increasingly specific and are not inspired by publications elsewhere (Brown et al. 2018). As Hang stated, "the increasing use of social media, mobile, Internet and development in streaming technology has brought tremendous opportunities to foster new media business" (Hang 2020, p. 191). New financial media that are smaller and have fewer resources and capabilities than legacy brands have emerged in the business news arena to bring something new and different to their audiences (Arrese & Kaufmann 2016; Vara-Miguel 2020). Some examples are Talking Points Memo and ProPublica (USA), Mediapart (France), El Confidencial (Spain), De Correspondent (Netherlands) and JOTA (Brazil).

## New Digital Journalism in Spanish-Speaking Countries

All the far-reaching changes that the media industry has experienced and that were unimaginable a couple of decades ago have been global, affecting both developed countries and, albeit at a slower pace, the world's least developed countries, especially those with emerging economies. In all of them, there has been a burst of new forms of digital communication. According to Salaverría et al. (2019), one of the regions where this evolution has been most profound is Latin America (Mioli and Nafría 2017; Salaverría 2016;

Salaverría et al. 2019). This region, composed of 20 countries where Spanish is the main language plus Portuguese-speaking Brazil, has experienced a significant change in its media landscape in the last 20 years. By 2000 (see Table 31.1), the median usage of the Internet among the 20 countries was 4.3 percent. Two decades later, this figure has grown to 81 percent. Nevertheless, there is still a difference of 40 points between the leading and the lagging ones. As Salaverría et al. (2019) stated, "not surprisingly, the Latin American countries with higher Internet penetration rates are those where the digital media industry has developed faster."

In May 2017, the "Observatorio de Nuevos Medios" (New Media Observatory, nuevosmedios.es), a comprehensive directory of Spanish-language digital native media, recorded 1,678 publications, of which 875 were distributed among the 19 Spanish-speaking Latin American countries (Salaverría et al. 2019). Besides the Latin American countries, Spain is a market of 47 million people, and its Internet penetration rate is 92.5 percent (Internet World Stats 2022). According to the Digital Media Map prepared by researchers from the Diginativemedia 2019–2021 project, in April 2021, there were 3,949 digital media in Spain, of which 72.8 percent were active (regularly updating content). Of these, 1,361 (47.3 percent) were digital native media and 1,513 (52.6 percent) were non-native media; that is, they had a traditional origin in addition to offering an Internet service (Negredo Bruna & Martínez Costa 2022).

The professional practices of digital native newspapers, both in Latin America and in Spain, were initially not very different from those used by non-natives, except that most

*Table 31.1* Percentage of individuals using the Internet in Latin America (2000–2022)

|  | Population (Est. 2022) | Internet usage (July 31, 2022) | 2000 | 2005 | 2010 | 2015 | 2022 |
|---|---|---|---|---|---|---|---|
| Argentina | 45,873,172 | 42,000,000 | 7.0 | 17.7 | 45.0 | 69.4 | 91.6 |
| Bolivia | 11,935,560 | 8,902,400 | 1.4 | 5.2 | 22.4 | 45.1 | 74.6 |
| Brazil | 215,016,658 | 178,100,000 | 2.9 | 21.0 | 40.7 | 59.1 | 82.8 |
| Chile | 19,383,887 | 18,835,100 | 16.6 | 31.2 | 45.0 | 64.3 | 97.2 |
| Colombia | 49,464,683 | 43,416,500 | 2.2 | 11.0 | 36.5 | 55.9 | 83.9 |
| Costa Rica | 5,170,019 | 4,425,600 | 5.8 | 22.1 | 36.5 | 59.8 | 85.6 |
| Cuba | 11,315,552 | 8,373,508 | 0.5 | 9.7 | 15.9 | 37.3 | 74.0 |
| Dominican Republic | 11,025,942 | 8,489,975 | 3.7 | 11.5 | 31.4 | 54.2 | 77.0 |
| Ecuador | 18,086,232 | 15,769,600 | 1.5 | 6.0 | 29.0 | 48.9 | 87.2 |
| El Salvador | 6,539,150 | 4,895,400 | 1.2 | 4.2 | 15.9 | 26.9 | 74.9 |
| Guatemala | 18,467,149 | 10,750,400 | 0.7 | 5.7 | 10.5 | 27.1 | 58.2 |
| Honduras | 10,165,384 | 5,546,700 | 1.2 | 6.5 | 11.1 | 20.4 | 54.6 |
| Mexico | 131,249,817 | 110,400,000 | 5.1 | 17.2 | 31.1 | 57.4 | 84.2 |
| Nicaragua | 6,753,914 | 4,272,300 | 1.0 | 2.6 | 10.0 | 19.7 | 63.3 |
| Panama | 4,427,158 | 3,411,900 | 6.6 | 11.5 | 40.1 | 51.2 | 77.1 |
| Paraguay | 7,276,583 | 6,177,748 | 0.7 | 7.9 | 19.8 | 48.4 | 84.9 |
| Peru | 33,729,630 | 29,601,700 | 3.1 | 17.1 | 34.8 | 40.9 | 87.8 |
| Puerto Rico | 2,747,603 | 3,047,311 | 10.5 | 23.4 | 45.3 | 79.5 | 110.9 |
| Uruguay | 3,493,160 | 3,261,800 | 10.5 | 20.1 | 46.4 | 64.6 | 93.4 |
| Venezuela | 28,887,118 | 22,735,000 | 3.4 | 12.6 | 37.4 | 61.9 | 78.7 |
| *Median (%)* |  |  | 4.3 | 13.2 | 30.2 | 49.6 | 81.1 |

*Source:* Internet World Stats.

of them lacked financial and human resources. However, thanks to their ability to adapt to new times and technology and their organic development models, many of them managed to consolidate. Paradoxically, the Great Recession from 2008 to 2013 meant that, at a time when the legacy brands were cutting projects and laying off professionals, some entrepreneurs recognized an opportunity to launch new digital projects.

As Salaverría et al. concluded, "the cutbacks by traditional media have created opportunities for new digital news organizations to fill the gaps in coverage or to broaden and deepen topics long-neglected by the established media" (Salaverría et al. 2019). Many of the new sites were founded by laid-off journalists or those frustrated with censorship, low pay and poor working conditions. They were senior journalists, with considerable professional experience and excellent source agendas. However, some digital native media outlets were founded by people with no journalistic experience but a keen interest in informing the public and serving their community. The result was a varied and dynamic information market.

## Some Cases of New Business Journalism

The field of economic information has not been left out of the digital transformation of the information market that has occurred in Spanish-speaking countries. The aim of this chapter is to present some cases of digital native media with contents that, totally or partially, cover events mainly related to the economy, finance or business. The objective is to determine whether there are common elements in the selected business and financial media and provide examples from different cultural, political and economic contexts.

We selected 16 business media from eight countries for our study, (Argentina, Bolivia, Colombia, the Dominican Republic, Ecuador, Mexico, Spain and Venezuela). We based the selection on the media database prepared by SembraMedia, a digital media research and training platform (Warner et al. 2017), which contains data from more than 1,100 digital media in Spanish. SembraMedia employs 15 researchers on the ground covering 17 countries, including the United States and Spain. Their job is to identify digital-native Spanish media. The selected cases fulfill the following main criteria: (i) they should be digital native media, without any relationship with traditional brands; (ii) they should be based in a Spanish-speaking country; (iii) financial, business or economic news should be totally or partially the core of their coverage, even if they publish articles on issues that are not related to their coverage of accounting, taxes, legal, economy, business, international trade, corruption, labor markets and so on; (iv) and, finally, they should have a monthly audience higher than 5,000 monthly visits, according to SimilarWeb.com.

Table 31.2 shows the main data of the 16 cases, ordered by the year when they were founded. Ten of the 16 selected are at least ten years old, suggesting their durability. The table also shows the news focus, type of revenues and monthly visits (according to SimilarWeb.com, as of June 2022). Four of the 16 had at least 1 million monthly visits while six had between 100,000 and 600,000; the two that had only 6,000 have prospered for at least 14 years and are highly regarded for their content, according to our research. It was not possible to obtain the financial results of each medium or the income from each financing channel.

The 16 publications compete in media markets with different specific characteristics. In Latin America, although traditional news media throughout the region have tended to be concentrated in powerful families and political groups (Márquez-Ramírez & Guerrero 2017),

Table 31.2 Business and financial news digital sites

| Publication | Year | Website, distribution | Content | Revenues | Country | Monthly visits (1,000) |
|---|---|---|---|---|---|---|
| Actualícese | 2001 | https://actualicese.com | Accounting, taxes, legal | Subscriptions, ecommerce, training | Colombia | 1,5 |
| El Confidencial | 2001 | http://www.elconfidencial.com | Economy, finance, business | Subscriptions, branded content, advertising, ecommerce, conferences | Spain | 67,4 |
| InfoNegocios | 2003 | https://infonegocios.info | Business | Advertising, branded content, others | Argentina | 205 |
| El Blog Salmon | 2005 | http://www.elblogsalmon.com | Economy, finance, business | Advertising | Spain | 385 |
| Descifrado | 2006 | http://www.descifrado.com | Finance, economics, corruption | Advertising | Venezuela | 228 |
| MarketingActivo | 2007 | https://marketingactivo.com | Marketing, business, training | Advertising, Conferences, others | Ecuador | 6 |
| Pymes y Autónomos | 2007 | http://www.pymesyautonomos.com | Taxes, legal, accounting | Advertising | Spain | 121 |
| Marketingaholic | 2008 | http://marketingaholic.com | Marketing | Advertising | Argentina | 6 |
| Economía Digital | 2008 | http://www.economiadigital.es | Economy, finance, business | Advertising, branded content, ecommerce | Spain | 1,2 |
| El Productor | 2011 | https://elproductor.com | Agriculture, technology, science | Advertising | Ecuador | 27 |
| Bichos de campo | 2014 | https://bichosdecampo.com | Agriculture, exports | Advertising | Argentina | 583 |
| Economía Femini(s)ta | 2015 | https://ecofeminita.com | Gender equality in salary, opportunity | Membership, training | Argentina | 40 |
| El Dinero | 2015 | https://eldinero.com.do | Finance, energy, agriculture | Advertising, branded content | Dom. Rep. | 147 |
| El Contribuyente | 2015 | https://www.elcontribuyente.mx | Business, advice | Advertising | Mexico | 1,3 |
| Economy | 2018 | https://www.cconomy.com.bo | Finance, business, agriculture | Advertising, branded content, print outlet, others | Bolivia | 32 |
| El Mercantil | 2019 | https://elmercantil.com | Logistics, transport, import, export | Advertising, branded content | Spain | 71 |

the past decade has witnessed the flourishing of new independent digital media (Warner et al. 2017). Those in Spain follow the model of liberal economies and democratic values, with a strong public broadcast corporation and polarized press. In this context, the main characteristics of all selected media are the following:

- Commitment to independent journalism: All the analyzed media emphasize their commitment to independent journalism and the absence of ties with the main political, economic and media groups in their countries. In their mission, they benefit from the dissatisfaction of a part of the public with the legacy brands due to the lack of coverage of certain specific or sensitive topics.
- Editorial priorities: The coverage analysis showed three main types of content. In the first place are those topics that the newsroom considers to be of greater news value. This group includes the niche coverage of specialized topics such as agriculture (El Productor and Bichos del campo), logistics (El Mercantil), marketing (Marketing Activo and Marketingaholic), law and accountancy (Actualícese and Pymes y Autónomos) and taxation (El Contribuyente). Together with these media, the more general economic information model survives, structured around the three classic sections of business, markets and economy (El Confidencial, Digital Economy, El Blog Salmón, El Dinero, Economy and Info Negocios). In the second place are those media that offer news that can generate social change to benefit society: giving a voice to silenced social groups. The most obvious case is Economía Femini(s)ta. In the last place, we find media that act as a watchdog of politicians and business people, which frequently cover corruption and misuse of public funds (El Confidencial and Descifrado).
- Nationally focused: Practically all the media analyzed focus on national issues, and the coverage of local or international issues is relatively less than the coverage of issues that affect the respective nations as a whole. The only exception is InfoNegocios, which concentrates on the economy of the Córdoba region and the interior regions of Argentina.
- Multiple revenue streams: All the selected cases have diversified their revenue streams. The most common source of income is advertising, both in its conventional format, used by all the media except two (Acualícese and Economía Femini(s)ta), and in the new branded content formats, used by six media. Only two of the cases have some form of subscription model: El Confidencial offers a freemium model in which the most valuable content is available only to premium subscribers; Economia Femini(s)ta has a unique membership model that offers all the content free to everyone, but members and donors can obtain discounts on the training courses offered by the firm and on products and services offered by partner companies. This is a collaborative model that tries to generate a community involved in the promotion of women and the combating of the gender gap. Finally, six of the selected media obtain income through other formulas, such as training courses, events, the sale of printed products (yearbooks) and electronic commerce.
- Small communication groups: All the media analyzed are independent of the leading legacy companies of each country. Their growth models are usually organic, and their investments are highly conditional on their results. Of all of them, the trajectory of El Confidencial, in Spain, stands out: 20 years after its very modest birth, it has established itself as a reference media brand in the Spanish market, and its financial situation is better than the other Spanish legacy media (Breiner 2022; Vara-Miguel 2016).

## Three Business Journalism Models

The 16 media analyzed base their editorial model on three axes (niche, social commitment, and watchdog), and quality prevails over quantity. Conversely, their revenue model, although diversified, relies especially on advertising, and the weight of payments by users is very low. Although each company has its own specific model, we could identify three models that can be summarized as follows.

### *Model 1. First Niche, Then Broader Interest*

In this model, we found media companies that began by offering quality economic and business information, different from what could be found in traditional economic media. As they grew in audience and income, they expanded their product portfolio to more general topics (politics, science, sports and celebrities) but without neglecting their core business – economic and financial information and independent investigation of political and business corruption. The best example is El Confidencial. Born in 2001 with just ten people, 20 years later, it has a newsroom of more than 100 journalists and has established itself among the leading media in the country (Vara-Miguel 2016). These companies have a strong commitment to a community and good journalism: they publish relevant news that is unavailable anywhere else. On a more modest scale, this model is that of Economía Digital, Economy, Descifrado, El Blog Salmón and InfoNegocios.

### *Model 2. Companies With Great Focus and Low Costs*

For the ten companies that follow this model, technological advances have allowed them to offer a differentiated product at a lower cost than that of traditional news companies. They do not aim to cover all the relevant financial and business information for a given audience but rather focus on very specific issues (marketing, agriculture, logistics, taxation or accounting) that are barely covered by the competition or the more general media. In this second model, we find Actualícese, Marketing Activo, Pymes y Autónomos, Marketingaholic, El Productor, Bichos del campo, El Dinero, El Contribuyente and El Mercantil. All of them try to offer coverage at the service of niche audiences and build communities around those specific issues.

### *Model 3. Non-Profit Journalism*

This model is characterized by journalism at the service of certain social causes that are not usually covered by traditional media. The practitioners aim not to make money but to give visibility to certain problems, influence policy and modify the perception of public opinion. They are usually financed with donations from both institutions and individuals. The case of Economía Femini(s)ta is the most relevant of those studied.

## Conclusions and Limitations

The journalism model as it was known for centuries has been disrupted, and business journalism has not been immune to that change. Technological development and innovation have made possible the creation of new economic and financial media that have tried to plug a gap in the digital market, fulfilling the role of providing good journalism as a public service to their communities.

Additionally, these media are trying to survive by betting on organic growth models, diversifying their sources of income despite the threat posed by legacy brands, with dominant positions in their respective markets. Their viability depends on offering content that adds value to their users, providing them with relevant information for their daily lives and highly differentiated content that helps them to make decisions and that is independent and critical of economic and political powers. However, each medium is unique. Its future is based on the size and resources of its target market, the legal, political and economic context and, above all, the experience of its newsroom and the technological limitations of the production and distribution of its content.

The study has some limitations. The first is the selection of the cases: the differences in their size, their editorial objective and the markets in which they operate make comparisons difficult. Second, the analysis is based mainly on the information available on the companies' respective websites, but their internal information is lacking, especially that referring to their financial results and viability. A deeper qualitative study of each of them would be necessary, through in-depth interviews with their managers, to know their historical evolution and their expectations for the future.

## References

Arrese, A. (2016), "Retroperiodismo, o el retorno a los principios de la profesión periodística", In: Rodríguez, J.M. (Ed) *Sociedad Española de Periodística*, Zaragoza: Ediciones de la Universidad de San Jorge, pp. 15–28.

Arrese, Á. and Kaufmann, J. (2016), "Legacy and native news brands online: Do they show different news consumption patterns?" *International Journal of Media Management*, Vol. 18, No. 2, pp. 75–97. https://doi.org/10.1080/14241277.2016.1200581.

Benson, R. (2019), "Paywalls and public knowledge: How can journalism provide quality news for everyone?" *Journalism*, Vol. 20, No. 1, pp. 146–149. https://doi.org/10.1177/1464884918806733.

Breiner, J.G. (2022), "Redescubrimiento del periodismo como servicio público", In: Salaverría, R. and Martínez-Costa, M.P. (Eds) *Medios Nativos Digitales en España. Caracterización y Tendencias*, Salamanca: Comunicación Social, pp. 95–106. https://doi.org/10.52495/c6.emcs.7.p92

Brown, D.K., Harlow, S., García-Perdomo, V. and Salaverría, R. (2018), "A new sensation? An international exploration of sensationalism and social media recommendations in online news publications", *Journalism*, Vol. 19, No. 11, pp. 1497–1516. https://doi.org/10.1177/1464884916683549.

Chalaby, J. (1998), *The Invention of Journalism*, London: Palgrave.

Hang, M. (2020), "Media and entrepreneurship, a revisit with a decade of progress: A bibliometric analysis of media entrepreneurship research between 2005 and 2017", *Nordic Journal of Media Management*, Vol. 1, No. 2, pp. 187–207. https://doi.org/10.5278/njmm.2597-0445.4295.

Internet World Stats, Available from https://www.internetworldstats.com/stats2.htm [Accessed 25 August 2022].

Márquez-Ramírez, M. and Guerrero, M.A. (2017), "Clientelism and media capture in Latin America", In: Schiffrin, A. (Ed) *In the Service of Power: Media Capture and the Threat to Democracy*, Washington, DC: National Endowment for Democracy, pp. 43–58.

Medina-Laverón, M., Sánchez-Tabernero, A. and Breiner, J. (2021), "Some viable models for digital public-interest journalism", *Profesional de la Información*, Vol. 30, No. 1. https://doi.org/10.3145/epi.2021.ene.18.

Mioli, T. and Nafría, I. (2017), *Innovative Journalism in Latin America*, Austin, TX: Knight Center for Journalism in the Americas.

Negredo Bruna, S. and Martínez-Costa, M.P. (2022), "Tipos de medios nativos digitales: plataformas, alcance geográfico, lenguas y grupos empresariales", In: Salaverría, R. and Martínez-Costa, M.P. (Eds) *Medios Nativos Digitales en España. Caracterización y Tendencias*, Salamanca: Comunicación Social, pp. 35–54. https://doi.org/10.52495/c2.emcs.7.p92

Picard, R.G. (2010), *Value Creation and the Future of News Organizations. Why and How Journalism Must Change To Remain Relevant in the Twenty-First Century*, Lisbon: Media XXI.

Rafter, K. (2016), "Introduction: Understanding where entrepreneurial journalism fits in", *Journalism Practice*, Vol. 10, No. 2, pp. 140–142. https://doi.org/10.1080/17512786.2015.1126014.

Salaverría, R. (Ed) (2016), *Ciberperiodismo en Iberoamérica*, Madrid: Fundación Telefónica & Editorial Ariel.

Salaverría, R., Sádaba, C., Breiner, J. G., and Warner, J. C. (2019), "A brave new digital journalism in Latin America", In: Túñez-López, M., Martínez-Fernández, V. A., López-García, X., Rúas-Araujo, J. and Campos-Freire, F. (Eds) *Communication: Innovation & Quality*, Cham: Springer International Publishing, pp. 229–247. https://doi.org/10.1007/978-3-319-91860-0_14.

Usher, N. (2017), "Venture-backed news startups and the field of journalism: Challenges, changes, and consistencies", *Digital Journalism*, Vol. 5, No. 9, pp. 1116–1133. https://doi.org/10.1080/216 70811.2016.1272064.

Vara-Miguel, A. (2016), "El Confidencial: Innovar en contenido como clave del éxito", In: Sádaba Chalezquer, C. et al. (Eds) *Innovación y Desarrollo de los Cibermedios en España*, Pamplona: Eunsa, pp. 166–177.

Vara-Miguel, A. (2020), "Cross-national similarities and differences between legacy and digital-born news media audiences", *Media and Communication*, Vol. 8, No. 2, pp. 16–27. https://doi.org/10.17645/mac.v8i2.2733.

Warner, J., Iastrebner, M., LaFontaine, D., Breiner, J. and Peña Johannson, A. (2017), *Inflection Point: Impact, Threats, and Sustainability: A Study of Latin American Digital Media Entrepreneurs*, Los Angeles: SembraMedia. Available from https://www.data.sembramedia.org.

Wells, R. (2020), "John J. Kiernan: Business journalism pioneer, 1845–1893", *Journalism History*, Vol. 46, No. 4, pp. 321–338. https://doi.org/10.1080/00947679.2020.1787780.

# 32

# BUSINESS JOURNALISM IN GHANA

## How the B&FT Has Evolved over Three Decades

*Theodora Dame Adjin-Tettey*

### Introduction

Established in 1989, the Business and Financial Times (B&FT) newspaper is the biggest daily business and economic newspaper in Ghana. In the past decade, the B&FT has established itself as a competitive brand with affiliations to and collaborations with international publications. The B&FT was recognized as a super brand in 2012. Having established a strong online presence, B&FT has transitioned from a weekly publication to a daily newspaper, covering varied beats across local and international financial, business, and economic news and information.

This chapter looks at this business journalism niche to understand how it has evolved and remained viable over the years when other similar journalism projects within the Ghanaian media landscape have collapsed. The chapter discusses the business model of B&FT and how different it is from other similar models in Ghana, and possibly Africa. It also discusses how the B&FT has been able to grow its audiences over the years, how impactful it has been, the present challenges it may be encountering and how it is positioning itself to be a viable business entity. To establish the above goals, some key employees of the B&FT, who had been working in the organization for not less than ten years and who occupy top positions within the news organization, were interviewed. They included the managing editor who was in his 17th year at the B&FT. The next section briefly attempts to situate Ghana's business journalism enterprises within the broader media landscape of Ghana, after which the issues emerging from interviews conducted are discussed.

### Business Journalism Niches in Ghana

Ghana's media have contributed immensely to the country's democratization and beyond. The media has consistently set the agenda on crucial issues, sustained dialogue, and impacted change through its strong advocacy during the country's struggles for independence and democratic governance to its current watchdog role for society (Asare 2009, p. 51).

There are many unregistered newspapers in Ghana. Out of the 45 officially registered newspapers, only 35 had renewed their annual registration as of September 2021 (National

 DOI: 10.4324/9781003298977-38

Media Commission 2022). The state-subsidized Graphic Corporation is a major player within the print media space. It produces eight print publications, including two daily newspapers and two weekly entertainment papers – Daily Graphic, Ghanaian Times, The Mirror, Weekly Spectator, respectively. The Daily Graphic is the most widely circulated current affairs and political news publication, covering all 16 regions of Ghana and controlling over 60 percent of the newspaper market (Graphic Communications Group Limited n.d.). While the government subsidizes the Ghanaian Times, the Daily Graphic is operated as a commercial entity that pays dividends to government the closing of each financial year (Kuwornu 2014, p. 4).

With the increasing interest of private actors in the economy and the opening of the economy to global markets, and public-private partnerships in the early 2000s, some media establishments started curating both print and electronic content that cater to business, economic, and financial interests of audiences. Some newspapers which specialize in this area are The Business Chronicle, Business and Financial Concord, B&FT, Business Eye, and Financial Guardian.

The Graphic Communications Group also publishes a business newspaper called Graphic Business. Many of the aforementioned newspapers have lost ground in recent times or are no more on newsstands nor online. Initially, Daily Graphic and the Ghanaian Times had just a page in each paper dedicated to business news (Kuwornu 2014, p. 6), which was sometimes dropped.

Notably, print publications are ranked after online and personal contacts, while radio is the most popular source of news in Ghana, followed by television (MFWA 2018, p. 17). The B&FT started operations when business journalism was not an attractive revenue-generation enterprise. It has, however, stayed its course of pursuing business and economic-related stories. It arguably opened up the market for business news, to the extent that Daily Graphic was also obliged to start a dedicated business issue, Graphic Business.

Ghana has developed a reputation as one of the world's most media-friendly countries, climbing progressively from 67th place to 23rd place in 2018, and from 19th place among African countries to first place in 2018 (Reporters Without Borders 2002, 2018). However, in 2022, Ghana's position on the World Press Freedom Index significantly dropped 30 places to the 60th position (out of 180 countries) and from 3rd to 10th in Africa (Reporters Without Borders 2022). Ghana dropped further in ranking in 2023, to 62nd in the world (Reporters Without Borders 2023). This downward spiral has been attributed to several factors, including the poor economic environment in which the media operate in the country and the impact of digitalization/digital technologies on journalism practice and the business of media (Yeboah-Banin and Adjin-Tettey 2023).

Against this background, it is useful to ascertain how the B&FT has been able to maintain its relevance over the years amid the various challenges the media have to grapple with and especially so when business and economic journalism are not niches deemed common in Ghana.

## A Historical Overview of the B&FT

The B&FT was set up by Chartered Accountant Johnny Hanson in 1989. It was then a once-weekly newspaper (Monday issue) *Business and Financial Times* and remained so for about a decade. In 1999, the paper was later sold to a Nigerian businessman, Everest Ekong. This acquisition led to a rebranding, including change of the masthead, paper size and type, as well as staff restructuring, all designed to make the paper more appealing (Kuwornu 2014, p. 6) and to attract more readership. The B&FT became a 12-to-16-page business newspaper covering the stock market and other relevant business news on the economy.

It was relaunched in 2001, when ownership and management changed hands again. The relaunch was also meant to make a clear statement that the new management was set to forge a new future for the newspaper, mainly with the intent to transform the paper to suit modern trends.

As part of its new strategic direction, the newspaper's masthead, which used to be green, was changed to its present color (blue). The scope of the newspaper expanded after the relaunch which made it a 24-page newspaper. During this time, the economy of Ghana was booming, with a lot of interest from foreign investors and significant interest in the political economy of Ghana. The telecommunications and banking sector had also started expanding. To cater to the buoyant economy, including other emerging sectors, the newspaper introduced news from the telecommunications, insurance, and other emerging sectors, publishing three times weekly.

In 2001, the B&FT started running special supplements focused on specific industries and providing a critical analysis of how they were faring, what challenges they faced and what could be done to improve them. This included special supplements that carried survey reports on the banking, fintech or insurance sectors. Special supplements also provide the opportunity to rope in advertisements from sectors that are captured in the issues. This was run once a year and has continued.

The paper moved from three to four issues each week in 2013 and finally, in 2016, to five issues a week, leveraging on the printing machines they had procured to print in-house. In the previous years, they had used a service provider.

In 2008, there was another relaunch with the strategic intent of drawing the public's attention to B&FT's continuous existence and relevance in the market and the fact that the paper was further advancing its business news reportage. The full name, Business and Financial Times, which appeared on the masthead was changed to its abbreviated form, B&FT, and has remained so since then. In that same year, the media outlet started Business Times (a bimonthly issue) and Energy Today (a quarterly issue). Production of Energy Today was halted during the COVID-19 pandemic. Management intends to revive it when the economy picks up again.

## Targets of the B&FT

The B&FT targets upper-middle class readers interested in the finances and economy of the country, such as investors, entrepreneurs, business leaders and the managers of the economy (state enterprises). It also targets sectors/people who seek to be informed on finance, business and economic news and information, such as university students who are studying for degrees in business and economics as well as business schools.

The managers of the newspaper adopted this strategy because they believe that people outside the above-stated scope are unlikely to need and use the kind of information the newspaper provides. Thus, targeting them will not be a good business decision. During an interview with the Managing Editor of B&FT, William Selassy Adjadogo, he said:

> We do middle-upper class because the lower class is too much, we won't have time for them, and they will also not have time for us. The middle class we do because we know

in the next four or 10 years, they will be signing checks as business leaders, and they will need the kind of information we provide.

*(Adjadogo 2022)*

It is for this reason they have built relationships with major airlines that fly into Ghana and key financial institutions such as banks and insurance companies to draw visibility to the newspaper, through their subscriptions.

## Competition, Challenges, and Strategies to Mitigate Challenges

When the B&FT began, it was unique because it was practically the first wholly business newspaper to be started in Ghana. The Daily Graphic and Ghanaian Times had business sections but not fully fledged business newspapers. Later in 1995, The High Street Journal was launched and competed with the B&FT. The High Street Journal collapsed in time. Just about when the High Street Journal fizzled out, B&FT changed management and began to pick up quite well. Then came the Business Week and Business Finder, which currently are not vibrant in the market. A few other newspapers attempted to venture into similar enterprises but have not been successful, a possible indication that business journalism in Ghana is not an easy sell.

Later, the Graphic Business newspaper came onto the scene. As a subsidiary of the biggest state newspaper outlet, Graphic Business seems to currently be the main competitor of B&FT due to the wide coverage and grounding of the holding company. Both newspapers cover similar beats, tap from the same market, and feature similar advertisements.

When the B&FT began publications in the 1980s and 1990s, one of its main challenges was getting information from credible sources to provide context for its stories. Public officials were generally hesitant about sharing information because of certain institutional policies and the fear of victimization. It was even difficult getting information related to the stock market because there was no official stock market in the country.

The strategy management adopted was to build relationships with key stakeholders. They consciously used that as a basis to gain the confidence of key individuals who had access to information which gradually eased the difficulty in accessing information. Confidentiality was kept for those who were anxious about sharing information.

The other challenge was getting people to be interested in the kind of journalism the B&FT did. Politics and entertainment in Ghana generally sell better than other genres of journalism. A purely business and economic newspaper competing in such a socio-political economy required major whipping up of interest to be able to thrive. According to the lead designer at the B&FT, Alistair Arthur-Don, it has been a hectic journey trying to make impact in an economy where many are not interested in business, economics, and accounting. He argues that the number of people studying business-related courses in schools and universities at the time the paper began was evidence that the newspaper needed to go beyond the ordinary to thrive.

The newspaper saw an opportunity in the early 2000s when private sector investment increased in the Ghanaian economy, and it tended to draw more interest in business and economic information and news. Recognizing the electronic media as a key player within the news and information space, the new management of B&FT took a decision to collaborate with electronic media, especially radio, to engender public interest in their news coverage. They formed partnerships with various radio and television stations to feature B&FT on the newspaper review segments of morning shows which are widely patronized across the country. The newspaper also began giving complimentary copies to schools and embassies. The result of this strategy was a gradual growing interest in the newspaper while subscriptions also increased.

The other challenge is that although there are lots of investments that go into electronic media, little is realized with regards to print publications. With advances in digital technologies which afford print publications to move online, the story is no different as online news portals have tended to be extensions of radio and television (news) outlets. Most digital news (print) start-ups are entertainment focused. Compared to radio and television, many newspapers generally merely break even because investments do not come in that direction. "People do not have interest in investing in the media and since people prefer to listen and view things, the little investment there goes to radio and TV" (Adjadogo 2022).

Adjadogo contends that it is tough running a newspaper in Ghana, especially when it is a business or economic newspaper. The general perception is that social and political issues generate audience interest. This, Arthur-Don thinks, is possibly linked to the culture or the social makeup of the people and the kind of agenda the media sets. Business and economic issues are not ordinarily included in the daily discourses of Ghanaians because the media mainly sets a political agenda. Many cannot relate to the business language and statistics business publications provide. Adjadogo argued that this accounts for why the B&FT enjoys more patronage in the business journalism market. The paper makes a conscious effort to break down business language and statistics, making them more relatable. "Not many understand. So, instead of merely focusing on what the numbers are saying, we look at the impact of the numbers" (Ashiadey 2022).

The other challenge is manpower. Many who are interested in business journalism opt to work for radio or television, where they will gain personal brand visibility. It has also been difficult for the B&FT to maintain interns that they get due to the lack of zeal they exhibit.

The drastic shift to online content consumption is also another challenge B&FT has had to grapple with. It has become more difficult to sell newspapers because online stories are often shared in real time and updates are easily done as and when they are available. By the time a newspaper publishes, audiences would have most likely seen the stories elsewhere – online.

To overcome this challenge, the B&FT has revised its business model. It now has a strong online presence. On its social media platforms, news is shared as and when necessary and on demand. It also shares news in other formats that digital platforms allow for, such as videos, to generate more interest. The B&FT also has a digital newspaper which has a significant subscriber base. On the newspaper's website, there are dedicated sections for Economy (Green Economy) and Business (including insurance, banking and finance, agribusiness, education, energy, and health), catering to different interests. There are dedicated menus for chats and explainers in video formats. There are also dedicated tabs for special features and reports on special projects that readers can subscribe to for a fee.

By adopting this strategy, the B&FT has been able to reach audiences that would ordinarily not buy the physical newspaper.

## Sources of Revenue

Advertising is the primary stream of revenue for the B&FT. The B&FT also generates revenue from subscribers (digital and offline). Since the emergence of COVID-19, digital subscriptions have become the key component of subscriber revenue. Sales from vendors is a rather negligible revenue source. But advertising and subscriptions are not enough to help the B&FT stay viable. Adjadogo put it this way: "Nobody breaks even with newspaper sales in this country." Consequently, about a decade ago, the B&FT decided to venture into other enterprises that will allow it to serve related needs but remain focused on its core mandate, while raking in additional revenue. Managers started organizing events that serve the needs of industry and business/industry leaders. This has been the second driver of revenue for the B&FT.

Their flagship event, the Ghana Economic Forum (GEF), is a platform for government, policy makers, business leaders, business owners and Civil Society Organizations (CSOs) to come together to talk about the Ghanaian economy. A quarterly event is also organized for Ghana's most respected CEOs. These events are centered around specific areas where issues in the field are teased out and solutions identified.

Two years ago, the B&FT added the Money Summit (TMS) to its portfolio of events. This centers on financial management. Thematic areas have been investment, insurance, the stock exchange, equities, pensions, payments among others. Another prominent event is Brand-CON Africa, an annual conference about branding. The events, Ashiadey said, are influencing decisions and policies across the African continent.

> This year [2022] for example, we talked about payments, and we discussed at length what the Pan African Payment and Settlement System can do if it is put to its intended use, and you would not believe the feedback we got. As we speak, the African Union, the African Development Bank, the Afreximbank and the Pan African Payment and Settlement System Secretariat are ensuring some of the solutions that were proffered at the Summit are implemented.
>
> *(Ashiadey 2022)*

These events attract sponsorship and attendance fees in some instances. During the early days of the COVID-19 pandemic, the events had to be switched to hybrid formats.

Additionally, the B&FT engages in projects that are solely associated with the B&FT brand. One such project is the publication of annual industry surveys that rope in a sizable fraction of revenue. The projects attract sponsorships and special features that are paid for. Sponsorships are based on the trajectory of the projects. If it is insurance survey, for example, insurance companies are targeted for sponsorship. It is the case for other business sectors. Many businesses have vested interest in the surveys conducted as they serve as the basis for measuring their performance in the market, making projections, and making strategic decisions.

## Impact of COVID-19 on the B&FT

Back in 2015, some subscribers to the B&FT complained of running out of physical space to hold the newspapers. They suggested finding a way to digitize the paper, so they can access the publication whenever or wherever they wanted to, without a compromise on the quality of the content. The decision was made that each day, even before readers would wake up, they would receive the electronic issues of the newspaper in their email.

When COVID-19 surfaced, the newspaper already had a database of about 100,000 email addresses. Although the pandemic compelled the B&FT to reduce production, the editors had the opportunity to share digital content with their digital subscribers because they already had a database. This meant that the B&FT did not suffer the kind of impact the pandemic had on other media organizations who were compelled to shut down completely or suspend production because they did not have any back-up.

During hard lockdown, the B&FT was producing and circulating only digital copies of the newspaper in addition to an online version (website). The digital copies were distributed to subscribers via email. When lockdown measures were eased, the paper eventually resumed printing, but the volume was slashed.

The few print copies catered mainly for those who were subscribers but were not on the digital newspaper subscription list. This category was served on Mondays, Wednesdays, and Fridays, while Tuesdays and Thursdays were dedicated exclusively to digital subscribers. Although the B&FT survived, revenue shrank during the period. But management made a deliberate decision to ensure that no employee lost their job. There was an attempt at halving pay but that ceased only after a month.

Beyond these issues, COVID-19 came as a benefit in disguise, as it opened an opportunity for management to accept a new work logic – with staffers working remotely and still meeting timelines and expectations. The new work arrangement that the B&FT adopted allowed management to keep all employees on the payroll, even though most worked remotely. Staff were given specific tasks/quotas they had to fulfill each week while they were at home. New work schedules, coupled with the opportunity to serve digital audiences, permitted employees of B&FT to keep their jobs, even as their colleagues in other news organizations lost their jobs. Presently, many staff continue to work remotely and attend the office as and when needed.

## What Sets B&FT Apart from Other Business and Economic Journalism Niches

One of the strengths of the B&FT has been the space it has created over the years for in-depth analysis of various sectors of the economy. The opportunity given to experts to engage in critical analysis and to provide information that helps businesses to make good business decisions has positioned the newspaper as a reliable and credible source of business news and information.

> In this organization, we always tell our journalists that you can be on a beat for so long but that does not make you an expert. There are experts who have been practising and researching into the field for so many years. But we expect you to be knowledgeable about the beat you cover, so you can serve the audiences well and not take any information that sources give you as the ultimate.
>
> *(Adjadogo 2022)*

The B&FT also serves as a useful resource to researchers who sometimes find it difficult accessing information. By focusing on various sectors of the economy, the paper positions itself as a credible medium for investors to obtain information on the most viable sectors to invest in.

"We're unique because our focus is to help grow businesses, rather than break them down. It will be difficult to see us doing stories that are sensational or meant to needlessly bring down businesses" (Arthur-Don 2022).

An employee recounted an incident when someone drew their attention to a product that had been contaminated. The B&FT independently investigated the mishap and found that the mistake did not affect the whole batch of products. The journalists contacted the company in question to draw attention to the mishap. The company admitted the error and corrected it immediately. "Assuming we did a sensational story on that, the company would have collapsed, jobs would have been lost. Maybe that is why people have a certain level of trust for the paper" (Arthur-Don 2022).

B&FT journalists are groomed to become authorities in specific areas they report on. This way, the reporters produce quality content. By concentrating on particular beats over a substantial period, reporters also look for innovative ways to report on their stories to sustain the interest of their readers.

Reporters have also had the opportunity to go on exchange programmes with the Commonwealth Press Union. One reporter, for instance, got the opportunity to practice with the Financial Times in London. These are avenues that have exposed staff to different practices and deepened their expertise in sourcing and writing business and economic stories.

Further, employees are encouraged to take advantage of other opportunities to learn and to stay up to date with current trends. A staff is currently on a B&FT-funded stock exchange course. Many employees take the Bloomberg Market Concepts (BMC) self-paced e-learning courses to help them better appreciate the beats they report on. The B&FT also collaborates with Project Syndicate, the International Monetary Fund (IMF) and the World Bank, which provide data for the B&FT.

A recent editorial decision to include content covering other interests of business leaders beyond hardcore business news and information is another factor that positions the B&FT as a unique brand.

> Businesspeople are also regular people. So, what we have done is to provide turnkey content for that businessperson or that business organization. On Tuesdays, we have a four-page insert purely dedicated to sports. In turn, it has spurred businesses to look to sports as an avenue to build their brands. That gives opportunity to business organizations to also look to the B&FT to cover sports event they may have. Then, on Fridays, we have dedicated content for entertainment, including travel, food, and lifestyle.
>
> *(Ashiadey 2022)*

The quality of content of the B&FT also sets it apart. All interviewees agreed that the B&FT thrives on quality content which is rooted in its ability to make business information easy-to-understand. In one of its publications on June 27, 2022, the newspaper used an everyday commodity, bread, to illustrate the impact of the Russian-Ukraine war on the economy of Ghana in an article titled:

> Bread prices take a hit from Russia-Ukraine war." In another instance, while many business newspapers reported Ghana's inflation figures, the B&FT used another common commodity in the country, fuel, to illustrate the rising costs in an article titled "Fuel price hikes keep inflation high at 29.8%.
>
> *Published on July 14, 2022*

Given that many people find it difficult to comprehend technical economic information and news, this strategy converts the abstractions in economic news and information into accessible terms.

## Impact of the B&FT

The result of B&FT's strategic targeting, business model, editorial policies, and collaborations is that the B&FT has become a notable source of business data for businesses, researchers, and individuals with interest in business and the economy. Stories covered often go beyond mere reportage to empirically based statistics/figures on key areas of the economy. Experts in specific business areas are given the opportunity to share their views and data on critical areas of the economy that become the basis for making business decisions.

Another key feature of the B&FT is that it provides daily updates on the stock market, making a significant number of readers to buy the B&FT solely because of that data. Management of the newspaper believe that this data is not provided by other business journalism endeavours in Ghana. They believe that the newspaper has made significant impact because such data has been able to influence certain government policies and business decisions in Ghana. The editorials and analysis provided by expert columnists have also informed the state on how to manage certain sectors of the economy.

> Our flagship program, the Ghana Economic Forum, is a solutions-delivering event. As much as possible, our communiques and final reports deliver tangible recommendations. So, we were not surprised when somewhere in 2013, some of our speakers suggested something in the shape of the Ghana Infrastructure Investment Fund (GIF) and when government heard it, it saw the value in it and established the GIF. The YouStart initiative by government that gives grant to young entrepreneurs came about because of a recommendation from our Youth Economic Forum we organized last year. Even though Government had been thinking about a similar innovation, it was at our Youth Economic Forum that they secured enough clarity about it.
>
> *(Ashiadey 2022)*

The daily market reports of key investment funds, such as mutual funds and exchange-traded funds (ETFs), are useful for readers who want to keep updated on their investments. "Some people buy our paper just for that data to keep tabs on their investments" (Arthur-Don 2022).

## The Role of Management

One of the driving forces behind the success of the B&FT, according to those interviewed, is the strict adherence to organizational policy of no editorial interference of any form, including pressure from the Board Chair, Edith Danquah, and the Chief Executive Officer, Godwin Acquaye. The strong ethical disposition of unit/line management also ensures that they do not compromise this principle. Speaking on how the board chair distances herself from the day-to-day running of the organization, Adjadogo said: "She doesn't even know how the paper comes out. There is no interference with regards to what content we feature in the paper. The only time she comes in is when there is a problem" (Adjadogo 2022).

Also, the expertise of top management has been instrumental in promoting the B&FT brand. Management, under the leadership of the then CEO who is now the Board Chair, has been visionary and has contributed enormously to the financial sustainability of the newspaper. Her marketing background has immensely contributed to the initiation of innovative revenue generation projects to keep the business financially viable.

A key reason the B&FT has remained relevant is its management's proactive responses to the growing needs of readers as the economy expands. Target readers are able to find content that speaks to their needs, which makes them stick with the brand. Content has value because it is relevant to target readers.

The other factor is how responsive the paper has been as consumption news patterns change. The decision of management to compile the emails of subscribers, when some requested for digital copies, provided a window to still be in business during the pandemic when there were restrictions of movement and physical association. Even though not all subscribers were sent digital copies prior the pandemic, when the pandemic came, the B&FT responded swiftly by falling on the bigger data base it had to disseminate its content.

## A Look into the Future

The B&FT is working toward becoming Africa's leading provider of business and financial news. To achieve this, its managers plan to invest in content that engenders more interest in business, financial and economic news and information. Building on the success of their already established events, they intend to organize events that target those outside their current target group to get them interested in such information and ultimately, all the content the B&FT provides. Beside this, they want to build on the ongoing initiative of providing explainer content ("street economics") both in print and in video formats that are widely disseminated on social media platforms.

Additionally, as digital spaces reduce advertising revenues of print outlets, the B&FT is currently working on a mobile application to serve as another source of revenue from readers who prefer accessing content via mobile phone.

## Lessons/Recommendations for Practice

Like every business entity, newspaper organizations must target well and provide targets with needed information and news. To effectively meet the demands of targets, it is essential that they research into the changing news and information needs of targets on a regular basis and respond to them. It is equally important to find innovative ways, such as targeted events, to build interest in content which may not necessarily be appealing to targets but useful to them.

Considering the economic challenges currently being faced by media organizations (which could jeopardize the quality of their work), media organizations can no longer rely solely on advertising. This demands that media organizations look to homegrown innovations that meet the demands of readers, while keeping them focused on their mandate and brand and raking in revenue in return. For business and economic journalism enterprises, the B&FT model of event organization could be a useful cue.

## Further Reading

Abdul-Basit, M. (2017). An Investigation into the economic activities of radio stations in Wa. Doctoral thesis. University of Ghana.

Asare, A.A. (2016). Exploring the funding of public service broadcasting in Ghana's democracy. Doctoral dissertation. University of Ghana.

Obijiofor, L. (2003). 'New technologies and journalism practice in Nigeria and Ghana,' Asia Pacific Media Educator, 14, pp. 36–56.

Schiffrin, A., Clifford, H. & Adjin-Tettey, T.D. (2022). *Saving journalism 2: Global strategies and a look at investigative journalism*. Washington, DC: Konrad-Adenauer-Stiftung USA. Available at: https://www.kas.de/documents/283221/283270/Saving+Journalism+2+-+Global+Strategies+and+a+Look+at+Investigative+Journalism.pdf/a8ec2655-5636-8d69-00e5-c698c76c3845?version=1.0&t=1642517860288

# References

Asare, G. (2009). The media liberalization and democracy: Experiences from Accra, Ghana. Master of Philosophy Thesis. Centre for Peace Studies, Faculty of Social Sciences University of Tromso, Norway.

Graphic Communications Group Limited. (n.d.). Daily graphic. Available at: https://corporate.graphic.com.gh/daily-graphic-newspaper.html (Accessed 7 April 2022).

Kuwornu, Y.E. (2014). The Advertising factor in the growth and development of independent newspapers in Ghana–A case study of business and financial times. Master's Thesis. School of Communication Studies, University of Ghana.

MFWA. (2018). Media consumption in Ghana. Online. Available at: https://ghana.mom-gmr.org/en/media/ (Accessed 22 May 2022).

National Media Commission. (2022). Medium-term expenditure framework (MTEF) for 2022–2025. Online. Available at: https://mofep.gov.gh/sites/default/files/pbb-estimates/2022/2022-PBB-NMC.pdf. (Accessed 24 August 2022).

Reporters Without Borders. (2002). 2002 World press freedom index. Available at: https://rsf.org/en/index?year=2002 (Accessed 15 May 2022).

——— (2018). 2018 world press freedom index. Available at: https://rsf.org/en/rsf-index-2018-regional-analysis (Accessed 15 May 2022).

——— (2022). 2022 World press freedom index. Available at: https://rsf.org/en/country/ghana (Accessed 15 May 2022).

——— (2023). Ghana. Available at: https://rsf.org/en/country/ghana (accessed 10 June 2023).

Yeboah-Banin, A. A. & Adjin-Tettey, T. D. (2023). Financial viability of Ghanaian media. In *State of the Ghanaian Media Report* (31–46). Accra, University of Ghana.

## *Interviews*

Alistair Arthur-Don (2022). Interviewed by Theodora Dame Adjin-Tettey (in person), June 20.

Bernard Yaw Ashiadey (2022). Interviewed by Theodora Dame Adjin-Tettey (in person), June 27.

William Selassy Adjadogo (2022). Interviewed by Theodora Dame Adjin-Tettey (in person), July 7.

# 33

# MISSING THE BIG PICTURE

## Journalists in Sierra Leone Provided Incomplete Coverage of the Economic Effects of the COVID-19 Pandemic and the Russia-Ukraine War

*Ibrahim Seaga Shaw*

### Introduction

External shocks such as the disruption of international trade links, increases in the price of fuel, declines in tourism, declines in Diaspora remittances, declines in foreign direct investment, declines in development aid, etc., and internal shocks such as increases in morbidity and mortality, decreases in domestic tax revenue, increases in public expenditure on health and poverty reduction, etc., that resulted from the COVID-19 pandemic and the Russia-Ukraine War have all had a devastating impact on the economies of African countries.

According to the 2022 African Economic Outlook released by the African Development Bank in May 2022, the pandemic and the war could impact economies of African countries for a long time to come. The report states that about 30 million people in Africa were pushed into extreme poverty and 22 million jobs were lost in 2021 due to the pandemic. The report adds that the economic disruptions caused by the Russia-Ukraine War could push a further 1.8 million people in Africa into extreme poverty (AFDB 2022). The situation was further complicated by the high dependence on wheat imports from Russia or Ukraine by several African countries, including Sierra Leone, with the Food and Agriculture Organization of the United Nations estimating that 30 percent of wheat consumed in Africa comes from these two countries at war

United Nations Assistant Secretary-General Ahunna Eziakonwa is reported to have said:

Russia's war in Ukraine has disrupted Africa's promising recovery from the COVID-19 pandemic by raising food and fuel prices, disrupting trade of goods and services, tightening the fiscal space, constraining green transitions and reducing the flow of development finance in the continent.

*(Sen 2022, p. 1)*

A report released by the Energy for Growth Hub titled "New Headwinds to Clean Energy" provides a first of its kind analysis of the interlocking disruptions caused by COVID-19 and the Russia-Ukraine War in the global supply chains, rising costs, fixed power purchase agreements, tightening monetary policies, and pandemic drained budgets (Chang 2022). Moreover, according to Angela Lusigi (2022), by far the most visible impact of the Russia-Ukraine War "is the rising fuel and food prices, inflation and financial instability. The poorest are the hardest hit as a large proportion of their consumption expenditure is on food and transport."

Heads of programs at Action Aid in Africa sent a joint letter in April 2022 to their heads of state and regional bodies raising "concerns about the impact of soaring food prices following Russia's invasion of Ukraine on hundreds of millions in Africa," and called for "urgent action to tackle rising hunger." The U.K.-based 9 News TV 6 p.m. nightly program reported in January 2022 that the immediate post-COVID-19 period had seen a dramatic nearly 500 percent increase in the cost of ocean freight with the cost of moving a container from Asia to Australia rising from US$1,200 about a year ago to US$7,000.

According to a World Bank Sierra Leone Economic Update released on June 21, 2022, the partial economic recovery of that country following COVID-19, especially in tourism and manufacturing, was severely disrupted by "downside risks and uncertainties due to the war in Ukraine, global inflationary pressures, and the continued treatment of COVID-19 outbreaks" (World Bank 2022).

Drawing on the foregoing, I argue that the recent spike in the prices of essential goods in Sierra Leone is a result of a global crisis that requires a critical global business journalism approach to educate the public and help it understand the global context of the local crisis in the increase of prices of goods in the country.

However, preliminary investigations have revealed that very little, if any, of that global context was reflected in reporting by the African press of the recent economic hardship that has hit the continent; on the contrary, the media have focused on the local context. Drawing on a content analysis of the coverage of the economic crisis in Sierra Leone by three local newspapers spanning the period since the start of the Russia-Ukraine War in February 2022 to December of the same year, this chapter explores the extent to which journalists in that country failed to use global business journalism from a critical political economy approach in their reporting of the economic hardship and suffering that came to Sierra Leone in the wake of the COVID-19 pandemic and the Russian-Ukraine War. This has produced an incomplete picture of the reality on the ground.

The chapter provides a brief overview of the concept of global business journalism from a critical political economy approach. It also provides an exploratory content analysis of the coverage of the economic crisis in Sierra Leone spanning February–December 2022 by three local newspapers to determine the extent to which they employed, or failed to employ, global business journalism from a critical political economy approach in their reporting of the economic crisis in Sierra Leone during the period under review.

## Critical Political Economy of Global Business Journalism

In the 20th century, business journalists alerted the public to safety problems in vehicles and in chemicals. Business journalists warned the public about investment schemes and poorly run businesses that take the money of gullible investors. The United States Food and Drug Administration, which ensures that Americans eat healthy foods, was set up following business journalism's exposure of spoiled meat being sold to unsuspecting consumers. Business journalism has ensured that killer drugs are not stocked for consumers to buy. Media have had a profound effect on business and the economy. The development of the newspaper contributed to the widening of markets, effectiveness of competition, lowering of the costs of production, the spread of the price system, etc.

However, despite its important role to people and society, business journalism is often not taken seriously by some journalists and consumers. This is because business stories are often less dramatic and therefore boring. They are often full of numbers and statistics that make them difficult. They may lack depth, understanding, and context. Normal business stories do not necessarily attract mass readership and mass advertising. Most business stories are therefore limited to a small space in a mainstream daily newspaper and very limited airtime on radio and TV.

By far the most scathing criticism mainstream business journalism has faced over the years, despite all its great achievements in the building of modern industrial society, is its failure to serve as a proper watchdog of business and the political class, and by extension to strike a balance between meeting the business bottom line and the public interest.

Former Wall Street Journal Deputy Managing Editor Byron "Barney" Calame, a former president of the Society of American Business Editors and Writers (now called the Society for Advancing Business Editing and Writing), said: "Especially in times of financial pressure, there is a temptation to create coverage whose primary objective is to attract advertisers rather than serve readers...Good journalism can and should do both" (cited in Roush 2011, p. 9).

Mosco (2009, p. 2) provides two main definitions of political economy. The first, a narrow view, sees political economy as "the study of the social relations, particularly the power relations that mutually constitute the production, distribution, and consumption of resources, including communication resources." Mosco argues that the extent to which his definition calls attention to how the business of communication operates underscores its practical value. It provides us an idea of how a product of communication moves through a chain of production and distribution processes and structures before finally getting to the consumer. It also illuminates how the choices consumers make about the communication products such as a news item, a movie, a comedy, etc., are fed back into policies and decisions politicians and businessmen make and take, respectively, in producing new or similar products. This definition invites us to consider how not just the communication product, but the very attention of the consumers is put in the marketplace. It helps us see the approach as facilitating our understanding of how power relations operate, how people use and abuse power to make some people get what they want, albeit sometimes at the expense of some people denied what they want. It gives us an idea of how power relations interact, and sometimes clash, in the chain of production, distribution and consumption of goods and services.

A much broader definition of political economy, according to Mosco (2009), sees it as the "study of control and survival in public life." The key words in this definition are **control** and **survival**; control relates to how a community runs and manages its affairs while survival refers to what people do on a daily basis (for example, producing, distributing and consuming goods) to keep their society on the move. While control relates to a political process as it involves community power relations, survival relates to an economic process as it involves economic power relations that shape or influence the production and reproduction, as well as the distribution and consumption of goods and services.

Broadly speaking, when we talk about the political economy of communication we are talking about how political and economic power relations are influenced, or vice versa, within the context of agenda-setting by our "systems of mass media, information, and entertainment" (Mosco 2009, p. 6). Since journalists work within these mass communications systems, the political economy of journalism can be defined as the way in which journalists are influenced by political and economic forces, within an agenda-setting context, and how that affects their roles as watchdogs, rather than mere lapdogs or cheerleaders. This definition suggests a resonance between the concept of the political economy of journalism and that of public business journalism, especially in the context in which a public business journalist can take a political economic perspective to explore the political and economic power relations in the production, distribution and consumption of goods and services in the public interest.

Yet, empirically, business journalism is informed by the business model of journalism, which is based on pushing the bottom line over that of the public interest. This failure makes the business journalist little, or no, different from those in specialized business newspapers that solely cater to their readers and sources. In order to address this problem, this chapter critically explores the failure of business journalists to strike a balance between the bottom line of the business model and the public interest, especially during periods of global financial crisis. Drawing inspiration from a political economy perspective, I blame this failure of some Sierra Leonean business journalism on its increasing dwindling social responsibility role in holding power – political and corporate – to account. I also propose public business journalism as an alternative to the problematic mainstream business journalism. "Public business journalism is informed by the alternative models of journalism that strike a balance between financial performance and the welfare of the real producers of wealth and consumers of the end products" (Shaw 2016).

I argue that public business journalism has the potential not only to narrow the gap between reporting for the bottom line (the interest of the investor with the capital) and the public interest (society at large, including workers, consumers etc.), but to tip the balance in favor of society. As I emphasize above, the public business journalist needs to adopt a critical political economy perspective to be in a better position to achieve a proper balance between the corporate, or political, bottom line and the public interest, and to tip the balance in favor of the public interest.

A business journalist with a critical political economy perspective would be interested in interrogating the interaction between the political and economic relations that threaten the interests, or very survival of members of the public, including producers and consumers of goods and services, as well as the investors. The savvy business journalist needs to adopt the critical political economy approach in researching and writing a business story or news program.

When something dramatic happens – for instance, a sudden increase in taxation to pay for public services – the business journalist with a critical political economy perspective would not only be interested in reporting it but in looking at the "bigger picture of such a policy." He would want to know the "implications of such a policy for the public, the politicians and the businessmen, and not just for the last two" (Shaw 2016). Similarly, when prices of essential goods dramatically increase (as we have seen in Sierra Leone and many other countries in recent times), the business journalist should not only look inward (the local context) when looking for answers to explain this but should also look outward (the global context), what Berglez (2008) called "the global outlook," to be able to give a complete picture of what is really going on. This is what I call critical global business journalism. However, as the following content analysis of the coverage of the economic crisis in Sierra Leone between February and December 2022 by three local newspapers shows, very little, if any, of this type of journalism was practiced in the country.

## The Reporting of the Economic Crisis in Sierra Leone in 2022

This section attempts an exploratory content analysis of the reporting of the economic crisis in Sierra Leone between February and December 2022 by three leading local newspapers: Politico, Awoko, and Global Times. The first two are among the few politically neutral newspapers in the country while the latter, a pro-government newspaper, was selected to see whether its political orientation and that of the other two provided a global context in the reporting of the economic crisis in Sierra Leone. The content analysis takes two forms; the first is a quantitative content analysis to determine how often each paper foregrounded the global context in reporting on the economic crisis in the study; the second is a qualitative analysis of selected discussions foregrounding the local or global contexts of the economic crisis. Only articles published by these newspapers that focused on the economic crisis with specific references to increases in the prices of essential commodities such as food and fuel, and the hardships of inflation, were shortlisted for this study. In all, 43 articles that met the criteria indicated above were downloaded from the web sites of these three newspapers in the following order: Politico (26), Awoko (13), and Global Times (four).

## Quantitative Analysis of the Global and Local Contexts

Using De Boneville's quantitative analysis approach (2000), 43 articles selected from the three newspapers were analyzed to determine how many of them foregrounded the global context, or local context, in explaining the economic hardship caused by increasing inflation and price of essential commodities such as food and fuel, or how many of them were neutral.

Figure 33.1 presents data of the quantitative analysis of the 26 articles selected from Politico, 13 articles selected from Awoko, and four articles selected from Global Times.

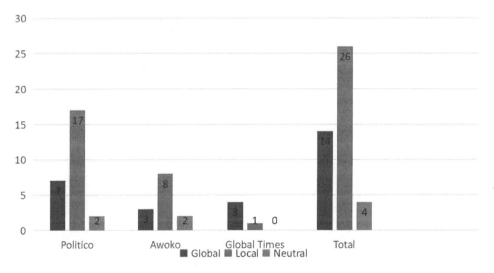

*Figure 33.1* Three newspapers.

## Discussion

As presented in Figure 33.1, Politico had not only the most number of articles (26) focusing on the issues associated with the economic hardship or crisis in Sierra Leone, such as increasing inflation, increasing price of essential commodities, especially food and fuel, but also published the largest number of articles (17) that foregrounded the local context to explain the economic crisis, as opposed to the global context, which stood at seven with two considered to be neutral because they reflected both the global and local contexts. Awoko newspaper published the second largest number of articles focusing on economic hardship (13), and also with the second largest number of articles (eight) that foregrounded the local context to explain the economic crisis as opposed to the global context which stood at three with two considered to be neutral for reflecting both the global and local contexts. Global Times had the third largest number of articles (four) focusing on the economic hardship in the country, and unlike Politico and Awoko, it had more articles (three) at least in relative terms that foregrounded the global context and just one that foregrounded the local context.

Overall, the analysis shows that all the three newspapers put together foregrounded the local context with 26 articles, far more than the global context with 14 articles, with only four articles taking a neutral position. This finding confirms the hypothesis that there was more focus on the local context, such as pointing fingers at the local dynamics such as bad government policies, unhealthy business environment, too much domestic taxation, etc., as opposed to the global context, such as blaming it on the economic disruptions caused by the COVID-19 pandemic and later the Russia-Ukraine War. Although Global Times had by far the lowest number of articles that focused on the economic crisis (four), three of those foregrounded the global context over the local context, which was foregrounded by only one article. This finding did not come as a surprise since Global Times openly leans toward the ruling government. It rigorously foregrounded the global context which was more or less the official line, pointing fingers at COVID-19 and the Russia-Ukraine War to explain the economic hardship with increasing inflationary trends and prices of essential commodities.

Considering that both Politico and Awoko are among the most established independent newspapers in the country, one would expect them to score high in foregrounding the neutral or balance representation of both the global and local contexts of explaining the economic hardship in the country. This was unfortunately not the case, as the balance tipped heavily in favor of the local context as opposed to the global context. If anything, it is reasonable to argue that these two newspapers, as far as this analysis is concerned, did lean more toward the populist government opposition position in terms of putting the blame of the increasing economic hardship at the doorstep of the government of President Bio for what they call poor management of the economy.

In a very large way therefore, these newspapers were leveraged by the political power relations of the opposition and government, respectively, and in this way failed to practice global business journalism with a critical political economy perspective. They failed to survive the control and manipulation of the political and corporate classes of the opposition and ruling government in their reporting of the economic crisis in Sierra Leone during the period under review.

Global Times employed more global context in its reporting, but the limited nature of this reflection and the fact that it had only one article that foregrounded the local context made it fundamentally lacking in global business journalism with a critical political economic perspective. This shows that Global Times was a victim of the political manipulation of the government. Similarly, Politico and Awoko did well by employing more local context in their reporting, but the very wide margin between this local context they foregrounded and the global context which they backgrounded, and the fact that they had such a very small number of articles (just two) that provided a balanced perspective made them fundamentally lacking in global business journalism with a critical political economic perspective. A global business journalist with a critical political economic perspective is expected to be critical and sensitive to the control and manipulations of the political and corporate classes of society and is therefore in a better position to produce a more critical global business journalism with a more balanced and complete picture of the reality that serves the public interest.

## Qualitative Analysis of Some Global and Local Contexts

This section includes a critical analysis of randomly selected articles from all the 43 articles of the three newspapers in this study to tease out some of the global context and local context frames drawing on Robert Entman's (1993) frame analysis approach.

## Global Context Frames

An issue that dominated the global context frames in most of the articles analyzed here is the fluctuating pump price of fuel in Sierra Leone, largely attributed to the fluctuating global oil price. Sierra Leone's Information and Communications Minister Mohamed Rahman Swaray was quoted in an article published by Politico on July 1, 2022, and authored by M.M Kamara (2022) titled: "Hike in Fuel Price is a global crisis – Sierra Leone Info Minister" as saying that the sharp increase in the price of fuel was not unique to Sierra Leone and that it was a global problem caused by the COVID-19 pandemic and the Russia-Ukraine War. The article further reported that Sierra Leone experienced a 76 percent increase in the price of fuel between May 2021 and May 2022 from Le 8,500 to Le 15,000. This increased further by 112 percent from Le 8,500 to Le 18,000 between June 2021 and June 2022. The information minister said that in order to cushion the impact of the global price increase of fuel on the people, the government had made efforts to improve oil storage facilities and supported oil importers with foreign exchange. However, reference was made to the practice of hoarding fuel by some unscrupulous petroleum dealers who always take advantage of fuel shortages to create artificial scarcity, thereby causing unnecessary queues at fuel stations.

The fuel crisis frame, with its attendant hoarding of petroleum products, was even more visible in another Politico article published on August 15, 2022, titled: "As fuel pump price drops to NLe 18, gas stations close" largely based on a joint press release by the Petroleum Regulatory Agency (PRA), Ministry of Finance (MOF), Ministry of Trade and Industry (MTI), and oil companies officially announcing a drop in the price of fuel from NLe 19 to NLe 18 with immediate effect. The press release added that the drop in fuel price was a result of the drop in the global oil price, which seems to underscore the importance of the global context in explaining the economic crisis not only in Sierra Leone but in most African and other countries that rely on oil imports. As explained in the joint press release, the drop in fuel price also led to a corresponding decrease in local transport fares which, in turn, would have a knock-on effect on the prices of essential commodities.

There was at least one article published by Awoko on October 20, 2022, and authored by M. Bah (2022) titled: "Fuel pump price increases to NLe 20" that reflected the fuel crisis frame. The article, largely based on a joint press release signed by the PRA, MOF, MTI and oil companies, announced the increase from NLe 18 to NLe20, which they said came "as a result of the increase in price of the product in the global market in the last couple of months and the depreciation of the Leone against the dollar." So here, unlike the press release published earlier by Politico referring to the decrease of fuel price from NLe19 to NLe 18, reference was made not only to the drop in the global oil price but also to the depreciation of the local Leone currency against the U.S. dollar as reasons for the increase of the fuel price. The inclusion of the depreciation of the local currency against the U.S. dollar to justify the increase of fuel price further underscores the importance of the global context in explaining the economic crisis in Sierra Leone.

Global Times, for its part, published a much stronger agenda-setting fuel crisis frame earlier in an editorial published on February 23, 2022, titled: "Due to soaring Global Oil Prices, Petrol Price may go up," which further explained that fuel pump prices are "determined by the combined effects of the international reference price (Platts) and the value between the U.S. dollar and the Leone." The article spun the official line by reporting that government has spent Le 240 billion to stabilize the fuel crisis in the country.

The notorious August 10 protests in the eastern parts of Freetown, Makeni and Kamakwei also dominated the global context frame in all the three papers. In a Politico article published on the August 23, 2022, and authored by C.A. Kamara(2022) titled: "Alpha Kanu Preaches Peace, National Cohesion in Sierra Leone," newly appointed presidential spokesman Alpha Kanu called on Sierra Leoneans to be peaceful about two weeks following the notorious August 10 protests, especially when, as he put it, the world is going through "turbulent waters," adding that during the August 10 protests, no responsible people were out in the streets protesting because they understood that the problems of the economic hardships that "face the country are not unique, but of a global nature." Global Times came out with an even more emphatic article, an opinion piece by its publisher and editor-in-chief, Sorie Fofana, dated March 31, 2022, titled: "Cost-of-living Crisis: Don't blame President Bio," in which he compared the spiraling cost of living in the U.K., where he was then visiting and where people were struggling with increasing energy bills and higher costs for essential goods and services, to the economic hardship hitting Sierra Leone. This further underscored the importance of the global context in explaining what was happening in Sierra Leone.

## Local Context Frames

The August 10 protests that left about 31 people dead, among them six police officers, dominated the local context frames in all the three newspapers, especially Politico and Awoko. An article in Politico on August 12, 2022, with the headline "Black Wednesday in Sierra Leone as 27 die in violent protests," reported that the protesters expressed dissatisfaction over the current economic situation, corruption, and police brutality as they chanted: "Maada Bio must go, we want peace."

As discussed in the quantitative analysis earlier, most of the articles published in Politico and Awoko foregrounded the local context, such as bad economic policies, high domestic tax, inflation, corruption, etc., to explain the economic crisis and all these frames were particularly dominant in the reporting of the August 10, 2022, protests in these two newspapers.

## Conclusion

Drawing on quantitative and qualitative content analyses of the reporting of the economic crisis in Sierra Leone between February 2022, when the Russia-Ukraine War broke out, coming on the heels of the last days of the COVID-19 pandemic and December 2022, this chapter found that two newspapers in the study, Politico and Awoko, foregrounded the local context. They stressed bad government policies, corruption, high taxation, inflation, rather than the global context to explain the economic crisis in Sierra Leone, and thus produced an incomplete picture. The study also found that two independent newspapers, Politico and Awoko, failed to practice objective and balanced journalism in their reporting of the crisis as they foregrounded the local context far above the global context. They published only two articles each that reflected a balanced representation of the local and global contexts. Finally, the study found that Politico and Awoko, and Global Times, which had fewer articles that foregrounded the global context over the local context, failed to practice global business journalism with a critical political economic perspective. It is reasonable to contend that this was because they were largely controlled and manipulated by the power relations of the opposition and government, respectively.

## References

AFDB.ORG (2022) African Economic Outlook 2022.

Bah, M (20 Oct. 2022) "Fuel Pump Price Increases to NLe 20". In Awoko *Newspaper*, Sierra Leone.

Berglez, P. (2008) "What Is Global Journalism? Theoretical and Empirical Conceptualisations." *Journalism Studies*, Vol. 9, pp. 6, 845–858.

Chang, A. (August 23, 2022) "New Analysis Demonstrates How Covid Crisis and Russia's Invasion of Ukraine Are Derailing Energy Development in Emerging and Frontier Economies." *Rockefeller Foundation* web site.

De Bonville, J. (2000) *L'analyse de Contenu des Medias: De la Problematique au Treatment Statistique*. Quebec: De Boek Universte.

Global Times Editorial (Feb. 23, 2022) "Due to Soaring Global Oil Prices, Petrol Price May Go Up," In Global Times, Sierra Leone

Entman, R. (1993) Framing Towards Clarification of a Fractured Paradigm. *Journal of Communication*, Vol. 43, No. 4, pp. 51–58.

Fofana, S. (March 31, 2022) "Cost-of-Living Crisis: Don't Blame President Bio." *Global Times*, Sierra Leone.

Kamara, M.M. (July 1, 2022a) "Hike in Fuel Price Is a Global Crisis-Sierra Leone Info Minister." *Politico Newspaper*, Sierra Leone.

Kamara, M.M. (August 12, 2022b) "Black Wednesday in Sierra Leone as 27 Die in Violent Protests." *Politico*, Sierra Leone.

Lusigi, A. (August 30, 2022) "Africa and the Russia-Ukraine Conflict: Seizing the Opportunity in the Crisis." *Africa Renewal e-magazine*.

Mosco, V. (2009) *The Political Economy of Communication*. London: SAGE.

Politico Staff Writer. (August 15, 2022) "As Fuel Pump Price Drops to NLe 18, Gas Stations Close." *Politico*, Sierra Leone.

Roush, C. (2011) *Profits and Losses: Business Journalism and Its Role in Society*. Second Edition. University of North Carolina, Chapel Hill.

Sen, A.K. (June 15, 2022) "Russia's War in Ukraine Is Taking a Toll on Africa: UN Assistant Secretary-General Ahunna Eziakonwa says inflation and trade disruption have put countries in a "very precarious situation."" *Analysis and Commentary*.

Shaw, I.S. (2016) *Business Journalism: A Critical Political Economy Approach*. UK: Routledge.

World Bank. (June 21, 2022) *Sierra Leone's Economy is Recovering from the COVID Shock Although Uncertainties Persist*.

# PART VI

# Economics

# 34

# BREXIT AND MURDOCH – A MARRIAGE MADE IN HELL

*Ivor Gaber*

## Introduction

It would be foolish to suggest that the decision by the U.K. electorate in June 2016 to vote in favor of leaving the European Union was the work of one man – Rupert Murdoch. It would be equally misguided to suggest that the Australian-born media magnate had nothing to do with the decision; indeed, if one person could be said to have played the decisive role, then that person's name would be Rupert Murdoch.

Looking back to the pattern of news consumption at the time of the Brexit referendum, we see, according to the media U.K.'s regulator Ofcom (2021), that of those whose principal source of news was newspapers (or news websites) the Daily Mail/Mail Online was the most read with 26 percent of the total readership, Murdoch's Sun on 22 percent, was the next most read title and some way behind was the Daily Mirror on 11 percent. Of the so-called quality newspapers, Murdoch's The Times was on 9 percent, as was The Guardian with The Daily Telegraph on 7 percent. However, television news was overwhelmingly the main source of news, with 69 percent citing it as such, and 70 percent saying it was their most trusted source of news. On the face of it, newspapers with just 29 percent citing them as their main source of news, and a trust figure of just 51 percent, were far less significant players.

However, this is to ignore the substantial agenda-setting effect that leading newspapers exercise, not just over their actual readers but, through amplification and repetition on television news and social media. (Cushion & Lewis 2017; Phillips 2019) This is the key to understanding the influence of Murdoch and his publications on the Brexit decision. Looking at the 2017 U.K. General Election, Cushion et al. (2018) found that broadcasters tended to follow the policy agendas of right-wing newspapers in particular: "a range of structural constraints and professional routines encouraged broadcasters to feed off stories that were more likely to be supplied by right-leaning newspapers" they found; and researchers, Cushion and Lewis (2017), in their analysis of how broadcasters covered the Brexit campaign, noted: "Our findings should also be considered against the wider backdrop of how U.K. news media have reported the EU over several decades. The EU has long been the bête noir of a significant section of the U.K. press. While far less vituperative, research has shown that broadcast news has not been impartial. Wahl-Jorgensen and colleagues (Wahl-Jorgensen 2013), in an

 DOI: 10.4324/9781003298977-41

impartiality review for the BBC Trust, found that coverage of debates about the EU tended to focus on Europe as a problem for the UK, particularly in terms of national sovereignty [with] very little room for sources presenting a broader range of views, and for substantive information about what the EU actually does" (Ibid pp. 51–52).

## Discussion

The Brexit referendum campaign took place between May and June in 2016, culminating in the 52 percent to 48 percent vote to leave. However, in truth the campaign to get the U.K. to leave the European Union had been taking place, in one form or another, ever since the British voted to remain in what was then the European Economic Community in 1975, just two years after joining.

There had long been an ambivalence in Britain toward the notion of the U.K. being part of a European "community" or "union"; hence, it was hardly surprising that Britain opted out of signing the 1957 Treaty of Rome which involved France Germany, Italy, Netherlands, Belgium and Luxembourg, nations that formed the European Economic Community (EEC). Britain did try to join in 1961 but, due to the hostility of President de Gaulle of France, its efforts were rebuffed and it wasn't until 1973 that it was finally allowed to join the club.

Britain was never a contented member. It was blighted by how it saw itself and its place in the world, in the memorable words of former U.S. Secretary of State Dean Acheson, "Great Britain has lost an Empire and has not yet found a role." This was the driving narrative behind the U.K.'s relations with Europe – never seen as fully "communitaire" by its EEC partners.

And so, we come to Murdoch and his role in a nation's psychodrama.

Murdoch first came to the U.K. in 1968 to buy Britain's biggest selling Sunday paper, The News of the World, which he followed up a year later by buying the then-ailing daily, The Sun, rapidly turning it into Britain's biggest selling daily newspaper. There is no evidence that the issue of the U.K.'s relations with Europe was then of concern to Murdoch; indeed in 1975, when Britain faced its first referendum on continued membership, his papers joined the rest of Fleet Street in campaigning for a Yes vote.

All that began to change following Murdoch's purchase of the prestigious broadsheets The Times and The Sunday Times in 1981. Buying the papers was not straightforward. Because he already owned two national newspapers, Murdoch's purchase needed approval from the competition regulator, the Monopolies and Mergers Commission. Under the existing regulations approval was expected to be withheld – he already controlled a significant section of the newspaper market – but Murdoch was given an exemption, it is widely assumed, as a result of a direct intervention by then-Prime Minister Margaret Thatcher.

Both parties have always denied that any deal was done but within days of their meeting approval for the merger was given. Harold Evans, former Times and Sunday Times editor under Murdoch, displayed his skepticism about the denials when he told the Leveson Inquiry[1]: "A newspaper merger unprecedented in history went through in three days," and went on to say: "I was told by someone I know that Mrs. Thatcher had determined it must go to Mr. Murdoch because she valued his support" (Leveson 2012, p. 1243). Apparent confirmation of the "secret deal" came when Murdoch told Mrs. Thatcher's official biographer that he thought she had given her approval because "she liked the political stance of The Sun, she knew where I stood" (Greenslade 2013). In approving the takeover, the Monopolies and Merger Commission made one proviso – that the papers' editorial direction should be overseen by a board of "independent directors." Such a board was appointed but, in the words of another of Murdoch's editors, Andrew Neil of The Sunday Times: "They were not that independent, after all, Rupert had hired them" (Neil 1997, p. 38). Murdoch has always vehemently denied that any such deal with Mrs. Thatcher was made. A few months after the Brexit referendum, in a letter to The Guardian, a paper that did not attempt to hide its antipathy to Murdoch and his apparent Euroskepticism, he wrote:

> On a number of occasions now your paper has quoted me as saying: 'When I go into Downing Street, they do what I say; when I go to Brussels, they take no notice.' There is much fake news published about me but let me make clear that I have never uttered those words. I have made it a principle all my life never to ask for anything from any prime minister.
>
> *(Murdoch 2016)*

One of Murdoch's great gifts, if that is the right word, is his ability to sense the public mood and to play to it. In the 1980s Britain's public mood was souring. Despite the harsh dose of monetarist medicine doled out by Mrs. Thatcher, most of the economic indicators were pointing in the wrong direction; in particular unemployment rates were at record levels for much of the decade. Once the trade unions – which Mrs. Thatcher frequently blamed for much of the country's economic woes – were vanquished, a new scapegoat needed identifying and slaying, and that was Europe.

Murdoch, using his newspapers, led the anti-European charge. Oliver Daddow talks about "a Murdoch effect" in terms of Britain's relations with Europe (Daddow 2012), which he characterizes as "a move from permissive consensus to destructive dissent." He identifies what he describes as a "symbioses between the Euroskepticism which was part and parcel of Mrs. Thatcher's political DNA with Murdoch's identification of an underlying xenophobia (some might say racism) which was the inheritance of Britain's confused post-colonial role." Daddow describes how "the media, led by tabloid alarmism" (which he attributes to the "Murdoch effect")

> Played a crucial enabling role in encouraging the Europskeptic cause by legitimating political criticism of the EU.... Not least, the media have worked synergistically with politicians to articulate a workable language of Euroskepticism that has taken hold of the popular imagination.
>
> *(Daddow 2012)*

Whether his antagonism toward Europe stemmed from his dealings with Mrs. Thatcher, or whether from some sense that Britain being closer to Europe meant being more distant from Australia, and his adopted home of the United States, one can only guess at, but his antipathy was plain to see. Stephen Castle suggested an additional reason – the obstacle that the EU appeared to present to his plans to expand his media empire in Europe (Castle 1988). This was sharpened by threats of measures against media concentration in 1992 and in the 1997 the directive, "TV Without Frontiers," which proposed to restrict exclusive rights to sporting events in Europe, a move that would have stymied Murdoch's plans to make live football a crucial part of his Sky TV offer.

Whatever the cause, as Andrew Neil observes: "He [Murdoch] dislikes Europe … and barely even visits as a tourist. He despises the idea of the European Union: hence the Sun's strident anti-European line" (Neill, p. 174). His anti-Europeanism came to be almost an article of faith for him, which found its focus in his opposition to the U.K. having anything to do with European monetary union – the Euro.

In 1990, making her last appearance in Parliament as Prime Minister, Mrs. Thatcher, in answer to a question about Britain joining a European currency replied: "No, no. no." But following her ejection from office, her successor, John Major, was less strident about the issue and this clearly alarmed Murdoch. According to the testimony that Major gave to the Leveson Inquiry, Murdoch tried to bully him to fall into line:

> In the run-up to the 1997 election, in my third and last meeting with him on 2 February 1997, he made it clear that he disliked my European policies which he wished me to change. If not, his papers could not and would not support the Conservative Government.... Both Mr. Murdoch and I kept our word. I made no change in policy, and Mr. Murdoch's titles did indeed oppose the Conservative Party.
>
> *(Leveson, p. 1131)*

It is no coincidence that in the year before, Murdoch had begun wooing Labour leader, Tony Blair. He was invited to Murdoch's annual "away day" with his editors and executives on a luxury island off the coast of Australia. Blair addressed the gathering and Murdoch was apparently impressed (he was no doubt equally impressed with Labour's commanding lead in the opinion polls – backing winners was not a philosophy unknown to Murdoch).

In the run-up to the election the following year Blair held further meetings with Murdoch; after one such session, he told Alastair Campbell, his media adviser, that while "... he felt we got a fair crack on some issues, but not on Europe...he [Murdoch] hated the idea of the single currency (the European Currency Union) (Campbell 2011, p. 795). According to David McKnight in his book "Murdoch's Politics: How one man's thirst for wealth and power shapes our world," Murdoch told Blair: "Let me make my position on Europe absolutely clear. I will have no truck with a European super state, full stop. If there were moves to create that dragon I would slay it" (McKnight, p. 168).

Murdoch has always displayed a rather ambiguous, some might say disingenuous, position as to the extent to which he influences the editorial line of his papers. In the Witness Statement he submitted to the Leveson Inquiry (Murdoch 2012) he asserted: "On editorial matters, I observed the limitations imposed by the undertakings given by NI [News International] with respect to both The Times and The Sunday Times" (Murdoch 2012, p.76), a statement that should be taken with a large spoonful of salt according to his former editors, Harold Evans and Andrew Neill. In his evidence, Murdoch wrote: "With respect to The News of the World and The Sun, when it comes to political endorsements, I do not believe that I have dictated an editorial stance or interfered with the work of our editors" (Op Cit, p.75). But under questioning he changed his tune, telling the Inquiry: "If you want to judge my thinking, look at The Sun" (Discover Leveson 2012). He went on to assert: "I certainly do take part in the policy decisions of the Sun. I think that is my job" (Ibid.). And asked about the decision of The Sun to endorse New Labour in 1997, Murdoch said, "Well, it certainly would have been with my approval" (Ibid.).

He was more reticent about the extent to which he sought to influence The Times and The Sunday Times, describing his supposed "non-intervention" in The Times he said: "If an editor is sending a newspaper broke, it is the responsibility of the proprietor to step in for the sake of the journalists, for the sake of everybody. And particularly his responsibility to his many thousands of shareholders" (Ibid.). With respect to The Sunday Times, Murdoch, somewhat coyly, told the Inquiry: "Sometimes when I was available on a Saturday, I would call and say, 'What's the news today?' It was idle curiosity, perhaps" (Ibid.).

Indeed, Andrew Neil, who was the then editor of The Sunday Times, recalled that while Murdoch was still enthusiastic about Blair, "he started getting cold feet about the prospect of a Labour government, particularly as its pro-Europe stance became more apparent" (Neill, p. 172.) But he did eventually switch his papers' support to Labour after Blair wrote an article in The Sun declaring his opposition to a European "super state." Labour won the election in a landslide, but subsequent polls suggested this would have happened, irrespective of support from The Sun.

Throughout Blair's term in office, which ran from 1997 to 2007, Murdoch, either directly, or through his papers, sought to block closer European integration, specifically by trying to ensure that Britain did not join the European Currency Union (the precursor to the Euro). Murdoch sought constant assurances from Blair that he would not join the Euro without first calling a referendum. Just one year after enthusiastically backing Blair for Downing Street, The Sun ran a front-page headline denouncing his apparent support for the single European currency: "As Euro looms The Sun asks this question: Is this the most dangerous man in Europe?" (The Sun, June 24, 1998). The newspaper, though more probably Murdoch himself, felt particularly outraged about suggestions that Blair was beginning to favor Britain joining the Euro because, according to Lance Price, then head of Communications for the Labour Party, Blair "promised News International we won't make any changes to our Europe policy without informing them" (Price 2011, p. 347).

Early in 1999, Prime Minister Blair had dinner with Murdoch and his senior colleagues, in an attempt to persuade him that his papers should take a less hostile line on Europe. After the dinner Blair told Alastair Campbell that it had been a futile operation. He told Campbell: "Murdoch's position was so fixed and OTT [over the top]. Murdoch said at one point he thought Britain could be like Switzerland [a neutral country outside the European Union]." Campbell goes on to observe: "It was faintly obscene that we even had to worry what they thought, but we had to do what we could to get a better debate going on Europe" (Campbell 2011B, p. 944).

According to McKnight, Murdoch did manage to get undertakings from Blair that he would not commit the U.K. to joining the Euro without first calling a referendum – the Labour leader agreed to this even though he was riding high in the polls and was not dependent on Murdoch for continuing support (McKnight, p. 168). In 2002, Blair let it be known that he was not opposed to Britain joining the Euro; this led to Murdoch threatening to break with him unless he restated his pledge to hold a referendum on the issue. Murdoch never got this specific pledge but in 2004 Blair publicly committed himself to a referendum, not on the Euro (which by now was not an option, as a result of the sustained opposition not just of Murdoch but of Blair's most senior colleague, Gordon Brown) but on the enactment of a new constitution for the European Union. McKnight claims he made this decision as the price for Murdoch's continuing electoral support and indeed, in the 2005 election The Sun did endorse Blair (he was still way ahead in the polls), but simultaneously praised the Conservative leader, William Hague, because of his campaign to oppose the Euro and "Save the Pound" (McKnight 2013, p.164).

This obsession with the Euro could be seen most vividly in the output of The Sun's then-Political Editor, Trevor Kavanagh, whom colleagues described as "obsessed" with Europe (Firmstone 2008). In evidence submitted to a 2003 Treasury Select Committee, which was investigating British attitudes to joining the Euro, he said The Sun would campaign against Britain's entry to the Euro: "We have declared that we would fight it very strongly" (Stationery Office 2003).

In the 2010 election, Labour, then under Gordon Brown, who was more of a traditional social democrat than Blair, did not get Murdoch's backing and lost power. The election was won by Conservative David Cameron under a manifesto that promised a referendum if there were any further attempts to extend the powers of the European Union, or if the government wanted to join the Euro. However, Cameron did not have a majority and, because his coalition partners, the Liberal Democrats, were enthusiastic supporters of Europe, the issue faded from the headlines. However, in 2015, Cameron won an absolute majority and this time his manifesto contained a commitment to hold a referendum on Britain's membership of the EU. This reflected both the growing strength of Euroskepticism among members of the Conservative Party, and particularly among its MPs, a direct result of the growing electoral success of the UKIP, the United Kingdom Independence Party.

In the 2014 elections for the European Parliament UKIP finished first, pushing the Conservatives into third place behind Labour. The success of UKIP was far from overnight. Under its charismatic leader Nigel Farage, UKIP had been campaigning against British membership of the EU since 1993. Between 1992 and 2016, the authoritative British Social Attitudes survey found substantial changes in the attitudes of the British public toward EU membership. In 1992, only 10 percent favored withdrawal, but by 2016 this had risen to 41 percent (in the subsequent referendum, Leave won by 52 percent to 48 percent) (British Social Attitudes 2016).

The constant drumbeat that accompanied these developments was the Euroskepticism that emanated from much of the British popular press. The Sun, one of the leading Euroskeptic voices, was, as he told the Leveson Inquiry, the voice of Murdoch. The Sun has many faults but hiding its editorial opinions under a bushel is not one of them, as evidenced by the lack of ambiguity of its front-page headlines. Perhaps the most infamous, in terms of Europe, came in 1990 in response to the efforts of the then head of the European Commission Frenchman Jacques Delors to persuade Britain to join the common currency. In a front-page headline The Sun, with a distinct lack of subtlety, wrote: "Up Yours Delors: at midday tomorrow Sun readers are urged to tell the French fool where to stick his ECU [the European Currency Union]".

But The Sun was at its propagandist best when it used tongue-in-cheek humor to attack the EU. Over the years it "discovered" ever-more outrageous initiatives by the hated "Brussels bureaucrats." These included claims – all comprehensively refuted by the EU – that bananas must not be excessively curved, cows would have to wear nappies, Euro coins will make you sick, Euro notes will make you impotent and women will have to hand back old sex toys. More seriously, and with a little more rationality, The Sun complained about the EU's Common Agricultural Policy which appeared to be responsible for the creation of vast wine lakes and huge butter mountains which, the paper claimed, benefited French farmers at the expense of their British counterparts.

A more subtle drumbeat emanated from The Sunday Times – Britain's biggest selling quality paper, and one seen as having great political influence – described as "the paper that leads the weekly agenda in Westminster more often than any rival" (Urso & Wickham 2020). It was no coincidence that shortly after taking it over Murdoch appointed Andrew Neil as editor. Neil, who had previously been the U.K. editor of The Economist, came with a robust neo-liberal agenda and an antipathy to what he saw as the collectivist, corporatist mindset that, he claimed, had largely been responsible for Britain's decline prior to Mrs. Thatcher assuming office in 1979. In his memoir of his time working for Murdoch, Neil reflected: "He picks his editors, people like me, who are generally on the same wavelength as him. We started from a set of common assumptions about politics and society" (Neill, p. 171). However, Neil went on to note: "Stray too far often from his general outlook and you will be looking for a new job. It can be strangely oppressive even when you agree with him the man is never far from your mind" (Ibid., p. 174).

Under Neil, The Sunday Times did not initially dance to Murdoch's Euroskeptic tune, indeed Neil describes himself at the time of becoming editor as pro-European. However, during his editorship, which ran from 1983 to 1994, his, and the paper's, disillusionment with Europe began to grow, until 1991, when in an editorial entitled "Eurolunacies" he declared: "It was not meant to be like this … It was never envisaged that we would be increasingly ruled by Brussels … The great European experiment has gone sour" (Sunday Times 1991).

Looking specifically at the coverage of the Brexit referendum, it is impossible to make any specific assumptions about the direct impact of the Murdoch press on the campaign. Media research investigating the relationship between news coverage during an election campaign and people's voting habits has found that it is usually the long-term impact – the constant drip, drip of stories – that plays a larger role in the formation of public opinion than any specific campaign stories. The former Deputy Editor of The Sun, Roy Greenslade, discussing the Brexit referendum result, noted that: "…[the] forty years of anti-European stories The Sun has run that will have had the bigger impact" (Greenslade 2016).

Researchers at the University of Loughborough investigated how newspapers had covered the Brexit campaign. Of the 1,127 newspaper cuttings they looked at over the two-month campaign they found that while there was a broad balance in terms of the numbers of Pro-Remain and Pro-Leave stories, once newspaper circulations were taken into account and the strength of the newspaper's backing for or against Brexit, there was an 82 percent to 18 percent advantage in favor of Brexit (Loughborough 2016). The other significant factor was that Leave voters tended to make greater use of newspapers as their principal source of news than did Remain voters: 71 percent compared with 55 percent (Fletcher & Selva 2019).

The Reuters Institute also monitored newspaper coverage over six months before and during the campaign. It found that its sample of 3,403 articles contained 41 percent pro-Leave articles against 27 percent pro-Remain. After factoring in the reach (i.e., the circulation plus readership figures) of the different newspapers, but not seeking to adjust for newspapers' pro or anti-Brexit position, they found a pro-Leave majority of 48 percent to 22 percent (with the remainder of the articles favoring neither one side nor the other) (Levy et al. 2016).

There is little doubt that the brazenly vulgar Sun, with all its crudity, created and sustained a Euroskeptic, some would say xenophobic, mood against Europe that must have influenced the long-term opinions of its regular readers – indeed, prior to the campaign the overwhelming majority of The Sun's readership had told pollsters that they were intending to vote Leave. The readership of The News of the World, Murdoch's populist Sunday paper gave little coverage to politics other than urging its readers to vote to Leave. And The Sunday Times, as has been noted, had been openly Euroskeptic, since 1990 and also campaigned for a Leave vote. However, it is The Times that makes for an arguably more interesting case study.

Ostensibly, The Times, unlike its Sunday stablemate, was in favor of the U.K. remaining in the EU. However, when one looks at its actual coverage of the campaign, a somewhat different picture emerges. The Loughborough researchers ranked Britain's ten national newspapers in order of their Brexit partisanship – the volume of pro-Remain and pro-Leave coverage. They found that the Financial Times was the most pro-Remain of all the papers while The Times, in fifth place, was the weakest Remain-supporting paper. Reuters Institute researchers found that The Times actually carried more pro-Leave than pro-Remain articles in the six months [prior to the vote – 36 percent compared to 22 percent (Levy et al. p. 16). Yet in a front-page editorial, headlined "Why Remain is Best for Britain," published just five days before the vote, The Times declared, "The best outcome of next week's referendum would be a new alliance of sovereign EU nations dedicated to free trade and reform, led by Britain." And then, it seemingly gives its readers "permission" to vote for Brexit when it said, "This referendum has rightly been a thunderous rebuke to Europe and a solid Brexit vote should shake Brussels out of its complacency." It concluded by admitting that staying in "may not sound as exhilarating or romantic as a defiant march to Brexit, but it is the better choice for Britain and Europe" (The Times 2016).

Even The Times' half-hearted endorsement of the EU was sometimes challenged by its own columnists. On the eve of the poll it carried an opinion piece by one of its most prominent columnists, Melanie Phillips, who opined:

> The EU has metastasized into a full-blown superstate project. In the intervening years, the damage it has done to core British industries such as fishing, its crippling effect on Britain's economic bedrock of small businesses and its increasing subjugation of domestic to European law have steadily ratcheted up public fury.
>
> *(Phillips 2016)*

It is thus hardly surprising then that the National Centre for Social Research found that of all the quality newspapers The Times, at 30 percent, had the highest percentage of readers of quality newspapers who said they had voted Leave. Less surprising is their finding that 70 percent of Sun readers – the highest for any national newspaper – said they had also voted Leave (NatCen 2016). During the campaign, Murdoch attempted to avoid stating his own position, but this probably fooled few and it came as no surprise that after the vote he finally broke his silence and told an invited audience of business leaders that Britain had made a "momentous decision." Brexit "was a bit like prison break … we're out" (Saul 2016).

## Conclusion

So, overall, what can we conclude about the role of Rupert Murdoch in Britain's decision to leave the European Union? Proving a direct causal relationship between media consumption habits and political choices is a notorious minefield and one in which it is advisable to avoid coming to any hard and fast conclusions. However, as this analysis has demonstrated, a number of trends are clear. First, that from 1979 onward, when Thatcher and Murdoch were playing leading roles in the nation's politics and media, hostility to Europe became a dominant theme of British public life. Second, that Murdoch effectively spiked the guns of Tony Blair's New Labour government should it have sought to bring Britain closer to Europe, either politically or economically. Third, Murdoch was not only able to ensure that three of his four newspapers argued the Euroskeptic case, not just during the referendum campaign but in the years leading up to the vote, but also ensured that the fourth, The Times, was anything but wholehearted in its support for remaining in the EU.

However, despite the importance of the Murdoch press, we also have to look at the media as a whole before coming to any conclusions about the influence of one person – admittedly a person with a high degree of political and media power – on the Brexit decision. It can be argued that, given the pre-eminent position of broadcasting in terms of the public's consumption of news, it is possible, even likely, that Murdoch's influence may be exaggerated. However, this ignores the important role newspapers still play, and most certainly did play, in 2016, in setting the news agenda for the broadcast and social media. Once this is taken into account, it is reasonable to conclude that, at the very least, the influence of Rupert Murdoch on the decision by the British public to leave the European Union was of enormous significance.

## Note

1 The Leveson inquiry was a judicial public inquiry into the culture, practices and ethics of the British press established by the British Government following the News International phone hacking scandal. It was chaired by Lord Justice Leveson, who was appointed in July 2011.

## References

Campbell, A. (2011A) *Diaries Volume One: Prelude to Power: 1994-97.* London, Random House.

Campbell, A. (2011B) *The Alastair Campbell Diaries, Volume Two: Power and the People 1997-99.* London, Random.

Castle, S. (1988) "Get Into Bed With Rupert, And Think Of Europe'," the *Independent* 4 April 1998

Cushion, S. & Lewis, J. (2017) "Impartiality, Statistical Tit-For-Tats and the Construction of Balance: U.K. Television News Reporting of the 2016 E.U. Referendum Campaign," *European Journal of Communication*, Vol. 32(3): 208–223

Cushion, S., et al. (2018) "Newspapers, Impartiality and Television News," *Journalism Studies*, Vol. 19(2): 162

Daddow, O. (2012) "The UK Media and 'Europe': From Permissive Consensus to Destructive Dissent," *International Affairs Oxford, Royal Institute of International Affairs*, Vol. 88(6): 1219–1236.

Discover Leveson. "Morning Hearing, 25 April 2012" University of Kingston. https://discoverleveson.com/hearing/2012-04-25/987/?bc=4 Accessed 1 November 2022.

Firmstone, J. (2008) "The Editorial Production Process and Editorial Values as Influences on the Opinions of the British Press," *Journalism Practice*, Vol. 2(2): 212–229.

Fletcher, R. & Selva, M. (2019) *How Brexit Referendum Voters Use News.* Oxford, Reuters Institute for the Study of Journalism. https://reutersinstitute.politics.ox.ac.uk/risj-review/how-brexit-referendum-voters-use-news

Greenslade, R. (2013) "Murdoch, The Times Takeover and the Minister Who Read the Tea Leaves," *The Guardian*, 9 May 2013.

Greenslade, R. (2016) "Why Does Rupert Murdoch Want a Brexit?" *NewsTalk Breakfast Show Ireland*, 15 June 2016, Newstalk.Com.

Leveson, B. (2012) *An Inquiry into the Culture, Practices and Ethics of the Press* Volume III. London, The Stationery Office.

Levy, D., Aslan, B. & Bironzo, D. (2016) *UK Press Coverage of the EU Referendum.* Oxford, Reuters Institute for the Study of Journalism.

McKnight, D. (2013) *Murdoch's Politics: How One Man's Thirst for Wealth and Power Shapes Our World.* London, Pluto Press.

Murdoch, R. (2012) *In the Matter of the Leveson Inquiry into the Culture, Practice and Ethics of the Press: Witness statement from Keith Rupert Murdoch,* Leveson Inquiry. https://discoverleveson.co.uk/evidence/Witness_Statement_of_Keith_Rupert_Murdoch/6089/media

Murdoch, R. (2016) – Letter: "I Have Never Asked for Anything from any Prime Minister," *Guardian*, 19 December 2016.

NatCen. (2016) "The Vote to Leave the EU: Litmus Test or Lightning Rod?" *British Social Attitudes 2016*. London, The National Centre for Social Research https://bsa.natcen.ac.uk/media/39149/bsa34_brexit_final.pdf https://www.newstalk.com/business/why-does-rupert-murdoch-want-a-brexit-592236

Neil, A. (1997) *Full Disclosure*. London, Pan Books.

Phillips, A. (2019) "The Agenda-Setting Role of Newspapers in the UK 2017 Elections," in Wring, D. Mortimore, R. & Atkinson, S. (eds.), *Political Communication in Britain: Campaigning, Media and Polling in the 2017 General Election*. Basingstoke, Palgrave Macmillan.

Phillips, M. (2016) The Times, June 21, 2016, Opinion, 28.

Price, L. (2011) *Where Power Lies: Prime Ministers v The Media*. London, Pocket Books.

Ofcom. (2021) *News Consumption in the UK*. London, Office of Communications. https://www.ofcom.org.uk/research-and-data/tv-radio-and-on-demand/news-media/news-consumption

Saul, H. (2016) "Rupert Murdoch Gives His Verdict on 'Wonderful' Brexit Billionaire Media Mogul Says Decision to Leave the E.U. Is Like a 'prison break,'" *The Independent*, 29 June 2016.

Stationery Office. (2003) "Treasury Sixth Report: the UK and the Euro," 24 April. http://www.parliament.thestationeryoffice.co.uk/pa/cm200203/cmselect/cmtreasy/187/3031101.htm

The Sun. (1998) "Is This The Most Dangerous Man in Europe," (headline) 24 June 1998.

The Sunday Times. (1991) "Eurolunacies," (Leader Column) 3 November 1991.

The Times. (2016) "Remaking Europe the Best Outcome of Next Week's Referendum Would Be a New Alliance of Sovereign EU Nations Dedicated to Free Trade and Reform, Led by Britain," 18 June 2016.

Urso, J. & Wickham, A. (2020) "Rupert Murdoch's Sunday Times Backed Brexit And Boris. Now Number 10 Sees It As The Most Hostile Paper In The Country," *Buzzfeed*, 25 April 2020. https://www.buzzfeed.com/joeydurso/rupert-murdoch-sunday-times-boris-johnson-coronavirus

Wahl-Jorgensen, et al. (2013) *BBC Breadth of Opinion Review Content Analysis* BBC Trust, https://downloads.bbc.co.uk/bbctrust/assets/files/pdf/our_work/breadth_opinion/content_analysis.pdf

# 35

# CALAMITIES UNFORESEEN

*Joe Mathewson*

## Introduction

Three painful débacles: the very costly savings and loan crisis of the 1980s. The wildly speculative dot-com bubble of the 1990s. The Great Recession of the late 2000s. Did the financial press see them coming?

These calamities were all aided, encouraged or even caused by very public official acts – by Congress, regulatory agencies, or government-sponsored mortgage buyers. Their critical decisions and policies unmoored the economy from its historic norms and standards. And, of course, in time the results of these faulty decisions were duly reflected in woeful economic indicators compiled and published by that same federal government.

There was another common denominator in the three contractions: unsupportable debt, or what economists call leverage. Although it would be unfair to assert today that a journalist covering the economy in the months and years before the collapse should have recognized when a business, especially a regulated business, was taking too much risk, the form as well as the substance of growing risk was readily seen to be, well, out of the ordinary. And stimulated by those same unwise official actions.

Accordingly, bearing in mind the time and space constraints of daily journalism, especially the challenge of understanding and reporting clearly on often-complex subjects under deadline pressure, it's instructive to look at the very public economic and regulatory harbingers of these three painful calamities. We do this in the hope of encouraging future journalists covering such critical matters to be more sensitive to unusual forms and levels of debt, and less satisfied with aberrational pronouncements by authoritative government officials and reputable business sources.

## The Savings and Loan Crisis of the 1980s

Official actions, first by the Federal Reserve, the nation's central bank, then by federal and state regulators of this traditionally sleepy but stable and important industry, caused a colossal meltdown and destruction of thousands of thrift institutions, including savings banks and credit unions, as well as savings and loan associations. These specialized institutions

 DOI: 10.4324/9781003298977-42

had been created by government authority to confront the Great Depression of the 1930s, to safely corral individual savings (insured by the government) and put them to work financing home mortgage loans. They did both. The typical thrift was a mutual association owned by its depositors rather than shareholders, so there was no stock price, no quarterly dividends to distract from their hallowed mission: facilitating home ownership, the American dream. Thrifts were government regulated, subject to surprise examinations to make sure they weren't taking excessive risks with their depositors' money, and savings and loans were actually granted an advantage in their competition with banks for those personal savings. The Federal Reserve, regulating both industries, allowed S&Ls to pay one-quarter of a percentage point more on savings accounts than banks. For instance, for many years banks were limited to paying 5½ percent while thrifts could pay 5¾ percent. Thrifts prospered, in their very quiet way. By 1980 they were making nearly half of the nation's home mortgage loans. Importantly, they were well supported by two federal agencies, the Federal National Mortgage Association, or Fannie Mae, and the Federal Home Loan Mortgage Corporation, or Freddie Mac. These organizations, created by Congress, bought or insured the home loans generated by the thrifts, providing a steady source of liquidity, or new money, that the thrifts could use to make more loans. The system worked.

The S&L disaster didn't start with the thrifts themselves. It started with severe inflation in the 1970s. In August 1979, President Jimmy Carter, vexed by relentless cost of living increases nearing double digits, purposefully appointed a prominent economist, Paul Volcker, then president of the Federal Reserve Bank of New York, to become chairman of the Federal Reserve. Carter's mandate to Volcker: rein in the inflation. He did. Through its open-market operations, buying and selling government securities, Volcker's Fed contracted the money supply and brusquely escalated the "fed funds" rate – the rate banks pay each other for overnight loans – from an already-high 11.2 percent to a stupefying 21.5 percent in mid-1981. Rates jumped accordingly everywhere. Even the government had to pay more – 15 percent on short-term Treasury bills. Predictably, savings began moving from thrifts to investment firms offering "money market" funds paying high rates.

So, what about those thrifts? And what about home mortgage financing?

What, indeed? Thanks to the Fed, the thrifts confronted a fundamental, potentially fatal problem: their funds were tied up in traditional, long-term, fixed-rate home mortgages, paying previously prevailing low rates, while the thrifts were still dependent, to finance current and future operations, on attracting short-term savings deposits from the public. But those regulated savings account interest rates were no longer competitive. As one history of the S&L calamity states, "The savings and loan industry exploded when an unexpectedly sharp rise in interest rates in the late 1970s and early 1980s drove virtually all savings and loans into massive economic insolvency" (Barth 2004, p. xii).

An unexpected result of this bizarre threat was that federal and state regulators of thrifts, ostensibly their disciplinarians, became instead their friends, advocates and protectors. Helpfully, the regulators set out to remake the thrift industry as a viable, competitive force. They did this by bending their own rules, prudent rules that had served both the industry and the public very well over several decades. Among other supportive actions, the regulators, with occasional help from a compliant Congress, authorized thrifts to offer market-rate savings certificates of at least $10,000; authorized checking-like NOW accounts; relaxed downpayment requirements and other mortgage terms; permitted thrifts to invest some funds in consumer loans, corporate bonds and commercial paper; eased branching restrictions; allowed thrifts to convert their charters to a new category of "federal savings banks" with more bank-like operational flexibility; and authorized renegotiable-rate mortgage loans. President Carter proposed and signed a new law suspending all state usury laws. In other words, the regulators authorized the thrifts to become more like commercial banks, taking on more risk with their depositors' savings.

Traditionally, more risk – in any business, but especially in banking – would call for more capital, to cushion these risks. Capital is the most important measure of any business's financial strength, its ability to withstand a reversal. But the regulators zigged when they should have zagged. Most importantly, they relaxed their historic minimum capital requirement of 6 percent of a thrift's assets (also the commercial bank standard) – those assets being the total of its mortgage loans plus investments – to just 3 percent. This meant that a thrift with, say, $6 million in capital, while previously limited to making loans and investments of $100 million, could now double that risk to $200 million. Leverage!

Congress thoughtlessly added fuel to the fire by abruptly increasing the limit of Federal Deposit Insurance from $10,000 to $100,000 per account. "Congress needs to recognize," wrote Edward J. Kane of Ohio State University, "that its decision to increase account coverage to $100,000 in 1980 was a serious mistake that it should strive to rectify as soon as possible. Fully insuring large denomination deposits effectively permits banks to issue high-denomination, federally guaranteed debt that in divisibility and liquidity is actually superior to ordinary Treasury securities." (Kane 1985, p. 157) Kane observed later, "for a long while federal regulators and federal politicians let accounting gimmicks render the damage invisible to the ordinary citizens. Hiding the strains and deferring the cleanup for so long greatly compounded the aggregate mess" (Kane 1989, p.1).

The regulators relaxed accounting rules, too, to permit weak thrifts to appear healthy and continue to operate. One such accommodation facilitated the acquisition of weak thrifts by stronger thrifts, transactions enthusiastically encouraged and assisted by the regulators. When a thrift acquired a lesser thrift whose liabilities, mostly loans gone bad, exceeded its good assets, the buyer could book the difference as "goodwill," an "asset" deemed part of capital. One historian wrote later, "Unfortunately, phony accounting and the administration's decision to avoid closing insolvent thrifts prevented market forces from working. Thrifts remained in business whether good, bad, or ugly" (Day 1993, p. 100).

Such regulatory practices, with rather arbitrary rules, could be perverse. The regulators pushed First Federal Savings and Loan Association of Chicago, the biggest S&L in Illinois, to acquire smaller, troubled thrifts, winking at the resulting dilution of First Federal's capital, only to turn later on First Federal, declaring its capital inadequate, and forcing it to merge into the still-larger Citicorp.

Although the press chronicled these numerous events and government actions, it gave little attention to the progressive weakening of S&Ls' capital. For instance, timely articles in The New York Times in April and July 1980 on changes in the thrift industry, including the merger trend, made no mention of capital levels (Hollie 1980, p. 27; Miller 1980, p. B3). A story in Newsweek fretted about the capital of New York City savings banks, pointing out that much of it was in bonds whose market value, at a time of increasing interest rates, was well below book value, but the story ignored the much larger problem of shrinking S&L capital (Anderson 1980, p. 56).

Things got worse. Much worse. The regulators encouraged thrifts to convert from the traditional mutual form to stock corporations, hoping to help them raise much-needed capital. But what it facilitated, sadly, was acquisition of thrifts by newly formed holding companies with authority to invest S&L assets in all sorts of baubles and wild schemes, notably speculative real estate developments, that in turn led to colossal scandals and losses, then prosecutions of a number of malefactors of great wealth. Most prominent among those convicted was one Charles Keating, a wealthy and rapacious insurance executive with no respect for the important mission of the S&L industry, and who had openly compromised several well-placed U.S. senators with gargantuan campaign contributions. They became known as "the Keating five." He went to jail.

The malignant catastrophe enveloped other banking institutions as well. According to a later recounting by James R. Barth, former chief economist of S&L overseer Federal Home Loan Bank Board and its successor Office of Thrift Supervision, and Glenn Yago of the Milken Institute:

> Our nation's banking institutions were in a constant state of turmoil throughout the 1980s. During that period and into the early 1990s, 1,273 saving and loans with assets of $640 billion failed, 1,569 commercial and savings banks with $264 billion in assets failed, and 2,330 credit unions with $4 billion in assets failed. The cost of resolving the crisis eventually surpassed $190 billion, the majority of which was paid for by the taxpayers.
>
> *(Barth 2004, p. xi)*

The press could hardly have been expected to anticipate this horrendous cascade of disaster upon disaster, which dragged on for eight years. But, again, was it remiss in failing to sense the inevitable dangers to thrift institutions inherent in the Fed's credit crackdown (which in fact precipitated a recession), and the higgledy-piggledy deregulation, notably capital debasement and aggravated risk, that followed? One expert observer wrote later:

> It was all too complicated and boring to interest many mainstream journalists. Regulatory changes – such as the accounting tricks and reduced capital requirements that helped paper over the first phase of the savings and loan crisis in the early 1980's – weren't big news.

This writer, Ellen Hume, executive director of Harvard's Shorenstein Barone Center on the Press, Politics and Public Policy, quoted Gregory Hill of The Wall Street Journal as saying that "not one paper covered it thoroughly from beginning to end." In mitigation, Hume expressed some sympathy for the press in coping with the complexities of the long-drawn-out horror story:

> Government regulators had special reasons for keeping quiet about the problem. With the exception of the former chairman of the Federal Home Loan Bank Board, Edwin J. Gray, high-level regulators were reluctant to disclose the facts, often for political reasons. They said they were afraid of triggering runs on lending institutions.
>
> *(Hume 1990, p. 25)*

A trio of independent investigative journalists, on the way to writing a highly-detailed book called Inside Job: The Looting of America's Savings and Loans, tried without much luck to interest other reporters in this monumental story: "With the exception of a handful of other reporters around the country, we couldn't find anyone who understood what was happening or seemed to care. Major newspapers we tried to interest in the story routinely snubbed us" (Pizzo et al. 1989, p. 464).

Perhaps the article closest to the truth in the early days of the S&L disaster was this Wall Street Journal editorial in June 1981: "Indeed, the whole idea that we need specialized institutions to deal in home mortgages probably deserves re-examination" (Day 1993, p. 80). But that didn't happen, and it was too late anyway.

## The Dot-Com Bubble of the 1990s

With the stench of the savings and loan crisis still fresh in their nostrils, investors and speculators nevertheless plunged ahead. From the late 1980s, when the Standard & Poor's 500-stock index stood at 250 on a very comfortable price/earnings ratio less than 12, the stock market doubled, then doubled again. The price-to-earnings ratio, always a good measure of stock price rationale, ballooned past its traditional normal of about 18 into the high 20s.

The white-hot advance was led by technology-based stocks, notably those denominated dot-coms, as the internet blossomed. Many small start-up companies with no profits went public, selling shares to the public for the first time, at unheard-of multiples of **revenues** (radically debased from the traditional measure of multiples of **earnings,** or profits), which market analysts unaccountably "justified" as a fair measure of the value of an unprofitable company. In 1995 alone a stock appropriately called General Magic went public at $14 and soared to $32 before the end of its first-day trading. Premisys Communications came out at $16, leapt to $36 and shortly to $52. Tivoli Systems launched at $13 and went promptly to $31, then $37. All soon died.

Even after the usually circumspect chairman of the Federal Reserve Board, Alan Greenspan, in 1996 declared the market obsessed with "irrational exuberance," it continued upward. In 1998 science and technology mutual funds jumped 51 percent, and the tech-heavy Nasdaq 100 Index sold for 100 times earnings. In the following year, America Online stock traded at 347 times earnings. In 1999, as the Nasdaq index advanced further to what would prove to be its peak, Qualcomm, a purveyor of wireless communications, gained 1,700 percent. A fledgling company called Pets.com went public with no earnings at all – and collapsed before the end of the year.

If corporate earnings didn't justify the seemingly endless advance, what was going on? And where was the press?

Some observers pointed to the Fed. Robert Shiller, a Nobel-prize-winning economist, wrote later:

> During the boom years of the late 1990s, Alan Greenspan and his Federal Open Market Committee (FOMC) did nothing to stop the growth of the stock market until the very end, watching the dramatic bull market charge by for over four years without any effort to rein it in.... It was on February 2, 1995, that the FOMC increased the interest rate for the last time until August 24, 1999... [T]he generally supportive stance of Alan Greenspan and other central bankers was a contributing factor to the millennium stock market boom and to the real estate price boom that came on its heels.
>
> *(Shiller 2005, pp. 40, 41)*

Part of that support was the Fed's rigid continuation of its long-standing policy of permitting investors to purchase stocks with only half the price in cash; this 50-percent "margin" could have been tightened to cool the market but wasn't. Greenspan "suggested in passing to his colleagues that increasing 'margin requirements' – that is making it harder to borrow money to buy stocks–might take the air out of the market" (Mallaby 2016, p. 498). But he left that very public rate at 50 percent, and the press unaccountably ignored the issue.

Shiller, the Nobelist, didn't stop at criticizing the Fed. He found the press irresponsibly complicit, not just in the 1990s advance but in affecting stock prices generally. The news media, he declared, "play an important role in setting the stage for market moves and in instigating the moves themselves." In catering to a broad audience, he went on, "the media seem often to disseminate and reinforce ideas that are not supported by real evidence." He castigated the media for trying to explain market moves by "quotes from a few well-chosen 'celebrity' sources" such as the then very influential analyst Abby Joseph Cohen of Goldman, Sachs & Co. When Cohen

> coins a quotable phrase – as with her warnings against the 'FUDD' (fear, uncertainty, doubt and despair), or her phrase 'Silly Putty Economy' – it is disseminated widely. Beyond that, the media quote her opinions but pay no critical attention to her analysis.... [I]t is the nature of the sound-bite-driven media that superficial opinions are preferred to in-depth analyses.... A sequence of news stories about Joseph Granville, a flamboyant market forecaster, appear to have caused a couple of major market moves. The only substantive content of these media stories was that Granville was telling his clients to buy or sell, and that Granville himself was influential.
>
> *(Shiller 2005, pp. 85, 87, 88, 93)*

Still not finished, Shiller castigated the press for quoting people who had taken to proclaiming a "new era" in the market and the economy generally:

> The popularity of the term *new era* to describe the economy took hold after the 1990s stock market had advanced far enough that it was beginning to amaze people, and all the new era stories featured the stock market. It was not as if some economists proclaimed a new era after looking at national income data or other data relevant to the real economic outlook. The new era theory emerged principally as an after-the-fact interpretation of a stock market boom.... In fact, it appears that the stock market often *creates* new era theories, as reporters scramble to justify stock market price moves.
>
> *(Shiller 2005, pp. 108, 109)*

To be fair, not all the news media blindly devoured the gossamer new theories of stock valuation. In late 1998, as the S&P Index roared past 1,200, The Wall Street Journal was skeptical. "Either it is a new era of technology-driven growth, or it is a bubble," wrote Greg Ip. He quoted Donaldson Lufkin & Jenrette analyst Stephen Koffler as predicting a further increase in the stock of Cisco Systems, already priced at 100 times earnings. "'On the face of it, we certainly agree the stock is in uncharted valuation territory,' Mr. Koffler wrote. But, he argued, 'As an Internet stock, Cisco is cheap!'" Prudently, Ip's story went on:

> This sort of talk alarms William Meehan, chief market analyst at Cantor Fitzgerald. 'It tells me there's an asset bubble on Wall Street. We've run out of rationalizations for current levels so the next step is to project earnings far, far ahead with commensurate

price targets and justify it with newfound ties to the Internet and how it's all going to be wonderful'.

*(Ip 1998)*

Market analyst James Grant wrote presciently in July 1999:

> According to the Federal Reserve's own stock valuation model (as maintained and interpreted by economist Ed Yardeni), the S&P 500 was 50% overvalued in early July. In recent congressional testimony, Alan Greenspan brushed aside the risk that a crash would cripple the U.S. economy. In effect, said the chairman, America could work through it. Japan, of course, has not worked through it.

*(Grant 1999)*

But these cautionary tales went unheeded. The beat went on. In early 2000 the S&P 500 topped 1400, five times its starting point in 1988, buoyed by an unheard-of price/earnings ratio of 32, almost double the norm. The tech-heavy Nasdaq index was up by a multiple of 15 over the decade.

At that point, finally, the tide turned. With no prompting by the press, in March 2000 investors panicked, apparently recognizing that the economy simply didn't support the lofty stock prices. They fell. As the decline continued, in April The New York Times quoted Byron R. Wien, U.S. investment strategist at Morgan Stanley Dean Witter, "The market was levitating on hope and irrational concepts of stock market value, and now it's coming down to earth, but it's probably not down yet" (Fuerbringer 2000). It wasn't.

In 2000–2001 the S&P 500 Index sank 37 percent, the Nasdaq 72 percent. In 2000 alone $2.4 trillion in market value was wiped out, meaning huge losses for millions of stockholders. The impact on individuals and families was calamitous. Newspapers told of a young father who lost $50,000 and was selling his tech stocks at huge losses to buy a car, and of a man who had retired early on his stock market profits, an incredible $1 million in 1999 alone, but lost it all in 2000. Now the press was on the dénouement, if not the precipitants.

## The Great Recession 2007–2009

There was no secret about what was happening, and why. Home prices were soaring in the early 2000s. A major stimulant was a proliferation of easy credit – risky "subprime" mortgage loans to less-qualified borrowers – loans with small down payments, or even none, at low but temporary "teaser" rates that escalated sharply after just two or three years.

The press duly reported the remarkable rise in both home prices and mortgages. Along with government officials, newspapers applauded the increase in home ownership rates from 65 percent of the population to 69 percent. In 2005 the Richmond Times Dispatch published a recommendation to buy real estate "regardless of price," and USA Today reported that economists saw no national downturn and that housing builders were irritated by "sky is falling" predictions.

However, in the last half of 2006, the press did report an occasional dire comment. Economist Mark Zandi of Moody's was quoted as saying that the "housing peak was a year ago," and fabled bond manager Bill Gross of PIMCO remarked that housing was "not looking good." In early 2007 Lewis Ranieri, who had gained fame two decades earlier as an imaginative creator of bonds secured by huge packages of home mortgage loans, was described by

The Wall Street Journal as "worried about the proliferation of risky mortgages and convoluted ways of financing them. Too many investors don't understand the dangers" (Hagerty 2007).

There was even some talk of a recession, but it was all just background noise. A U.S. Bank economist predicted a recession. An often-dour New York University economist named Nouriel Roubini warned, in a speech to an international gathering of economists, that the U.S. was soon likely to face, as The New York Times put it later:

> A once-in-a-lifetime housing bust, an oil shock, sharply declining consumer confidence and, ultimately, a deep recession. He laid out a bleak sequence of events: homeowners defaulting on mortgages, trillions of dollars of mortgage-backed securities unraveling worldwide and the global financial system shuddering to a halt.
>
> *(Mihm 2008)*

In the pages of The Wall Street Journal, where there appeared lots of red flags flying in real estate – mortgage foreclosures at a new high, sharp downgrades of bonds secured by mortgages, bank writedowns of mortgage loan portfolios –

Martin Feldstein, chairman of the White House Council of Economic Advisers under President Reagan, wrote ominously, "In my judgment, the probability of a recession in 2008 has now reached 50%. If it occurs, it could be deeper and longer than the recessions of the recent past" (Feldstein 2007).

Nevertheless, Alan Greenspan, now the former Fed chairman, wrote reassuringly in The Journal that although real estate was in crisis, the market would readily adjust: "Very large losses will, no doubt, be taken as a consequence of the crisis. But after a period of protracted adjustment, the U.S. economy, and the world economy more generally, will be able to get back to business" (Greenspan 2007).

The government, which had facilitated the spree, failed to sense the enormity of the danger. New York Fed President Timothy Geithner wrote reassuringly, "there are few signs that the disruptions in this one sector of the credit markets will have a lasting impact on credit markets as a whole" (Geithner 2014, p. 112).

The real estate jitters – mortgage defaults and foreclosures, mortgage bonds collapsing, mortgage buyers Fannie Mae and Freddie Mac in distress, even mortgage insurers unable to pay – did in fact unhinge the entire economy. In October 2007 the S&P 500 Index went down, and down and down – ultimately 57 percent over the next 17 months. Unemployment jumped to 10 percent. Gross domestic product and household wealth declined. The U.S. was in serious trouble.

In a dramatic move without precedent or clear authority under existing law, Fed chairman Ben Bernanke, Geithner, and Treasury Secretary Hank Paulson conceived and persuaded both President George W. Bush and Congress to approve a $700 billion government purchase of underwater mortgage-backed securities and other "troubled assets" from hurting financial institutions. Even with such a forceful government intervention, one major investment bank, Lehman Brothers, which had plunged enthusiastically into subprime mortgage debt, collapsed. Another, Bear Stearns, and the country's largest securities broker, Merrill Lynch, were rescued by abrupt acquisitions at rock-bottom prices. The principal insurer of mortgage-backed bonds, American International Group, faced insolvency but was saved by a huge, direct government investment.

Bernanke, Geithner and Paulson wrote later:

> It was, again, a classic financial panic, a run of the financial system triggered by a crisis of confidence in mortgages. It was fueled, as crises usually are, by a credit boom, in which many families as well as financial institutions became dangerously overleveraged, financing themselves almost entirely with debt.
>
> *(Bernanke, Geithner, Paulson 2019, p. 3)*

Outside observers were less charitable. "A notable culprit was Federal Reserve chair [2006–2014] Alan Greenspan," declared Nolan McCarty, Keith T. Poole and Howard Rosenthal in their 2013 book, "Political Bubbles: Financial Crises and the Failure of American Democracy."

> Greenspan pumped up the housing bubble with easy credit and failed to exercise his responsibility to investigate and regulate deceptive 'teaser loans' and outright fraud in the origination of subprime mortgages. His successor, Ben Bernanke... was curiously passive until the September 2008 collapse of the financial sector.

"Here again, the use of effective leverage was prevalent," later wrote Vikram Mansharamani, a Yale lecturer.

> It was the 'pay only 10 percent to get economic exposure to 100 percent of an asset' mind-set. By simply putting down a deposit that was 90 percent less than the actual price, speculators in Florida were able to achieve 10X leverage on the price movement of the properties they had supposedly committed to purchasing ... The house of cards, which was built on a precarious foundation of extreme leverage, eventually imploded.
>
> *(Mansharamani 2011, p. 199)*

The authors also took aim at the three principal credit-rating agencies' generous assessments of complicated mortgage-backed securities.

> Despite the low quality of the underlying loans, credit rating agencies uniformly issued ratings at AAA, as safe as U.S. government debt.... With the blessings of Standard & Poor's, Moody's, or Fitch, these securities were then marketed by financial institutions and peddled to investors around the world.
>
> *(McCarty, Poole, Rosenthal 2013, pp. 5, 9)*

Historian Niall Ferguson later observed:

> The main problem lay with CDOs [collateralized debt obligations], over half a trillion dollars of which had been sold in 2006, of which around half contained subprime exposure. It turned out that many of these CDOs had been seriously overpriced, as a result of erroneous estimates of likely subprime default rates.
>
> *(Ferguson 2008, p. 271)*

Another tart analysis observed, "recessions are a product of a financial system that fosters too much household debt" (Mian and Sufi 2015, p. 13). And another, by Dean Starkman of

Columbia Journalism Review, who conducted a detailed review of business articles preceding the crash, which began in 2007:

> The lending industry from 2004 through 2006... had become unhinged—institutionally corrupt, rotten, like a fish, from the head.... [B]reathtaking corruption overran the mortgage business—document tampering, forgery, verbal and written misrepresentations, changing of terms at closing, nondisclosure of fees, rates, and penalties, and a boiler-room culture reminiscent of the notorious small-stock swindles of the nineties.
>
> *(Starkman, in Schiffrin ed. 2011, p. 47)*

Starkman's review of the 2004–2006 press found numerous but occasional stories that disclosed weaknesses in the economy and in business corner-cutting, but "Missing are investigative stories that confront directly powerful institutions about basic business practices while those institutions were still powerful. This is not a detail. This is the watchdog that didn't bark" (Starkman, in Schiffrin ed. 2011, p. 42).

Michael Lewis wrote later in the best-seller "The Big Short" that two investment bankers became alarmed very early about the prospects for a tumultuous collapse, telling him, "either the game was totally rigged, or we had gone totally fucking crazy. The fraud was so obvious that it seemed to us it had implications for democracy. We actually got scared." Lewis went on, "They both knew reporters who worked at the New York Times and the Wall Street Journal--but the reporters they knew had no interest in their story."

The human results of the crash were devastating. Economic historian Adam Tooze wrote later:

> From their peak in 2006, by 2009 US house prices had fallen by a third. At the worst point of the crisis, 10 percent of home loans across the United States would be seriously in arrears and 4.5 percent of all mortgages crashed into foreclosure. More than 9 million families would lose their homes. Millions more suffered years of anxiety as they struggled to make payment on homes that were no longer worth the mortgages secured on them. At the worst point in the crisis more than a quarter of US homes had negative equity.
>
> *(Tooze 2018, p. 156)*

Looking back, former Treasury Secretary Henry M. Paulson, Jr. observed that the basic cause was well-meaning, pro-home ownership government policies that deviated from historical norms: "These initiatives fed an unsustainable housing boom, even as market and regulatory discipline fell away.... Regulators failed to police this mess until the housing bubble burst, triggering the financial crisis." (Paulson 2010, p. 441).

Once again, the problem was debt – shaky, excessive debt, or leverage – fostered directly by unscrupulous lending businesses and indirectly by government itself over several years. Leaders of the Federal Reserve and financial regulators declined to exercise their authority to thwart deviations from the norms of the past. Mortgage buyers Fannie Mae and Freddie Mac abandoned their historic mission to support sound home financing, participating aggressively in stoking the subprime mortgage fires, to their peril and shame. The deviations from reliable past norms of business and government conduct were all out in the open, totally public.

## Recommendations for Practice

In light of the contractions and pain that devolved in the decades of the 1980s, 1990s and early 2000s, is it reasonable, or fair, to suggest that journalists should have sensed and spotlighted the economic and regulatory peculiarities that presaged trouble? After all, journalists are not economists, and shouldn't be.

But think about debt, or leverage. It's a fact of economic life, which means there are historic patterns and practices that at least suggest what levels are reasonably prudent (though debt is never without risk). Debt data is ubiquitous. Banks report debt. The Department of Commerce reports debt. The Bureau of Labor Statistics reports debt. The Treasury reports debt. Securities markets report debt. The Fed has power to regulate investor debt. Credit card issuers report debt. At the working end of the economy, most consumers have debt, or have had. Watching debt, especially imaginative new forms of debt like the opaque derivatives of the real estate crisis, is surely warranted.

Then there are economists, market analysts and other professionals who watch over the economy and the markets. Whatever the state of the economy, their thinking is never unanimous. There are always contrarians, which is good. Still, there's a tendency among journalists everywhere to follow the crowd, to accept the consensus, on anything, including politics and the arts. But, fortunately, there are also resourceful journalists who are always looking elsewhere for good stories that don't fit within the prevailing fad, or don't readily accept all pronouncements from high government officials, like the S&L regulators who said 3 percent capital was adequate. In covering the economy, that independence should include resisting the ordinary human inclination to be awestruck by amazing profits in business or the markets. Ask instead, what are the conditions that enable such extraordinary good fortune? Clearly, we need more such journalistic iconoclasts, especially their ability to sense when the unconventional is not only interesting but important. Nouriel Roubini, now celebrated for predicting the Great Recession, drew little attention at the time for his lonely forecast, even though it was well reasoned and delivered in an auspicious forum, a meeting of the International Monetary Fund.

It's worth noting that the harbingers of these three disasters weren't the first to be downplayed by the press. A study by Christopher W. Shaw of the University of California, Berkeley, found that:

> [A]lthough bank failures were pervasive during the early 1930s, the media accorded these dramatic events surprisingly limited attention.... The large-circulation daily newspapers... articulated a dominant media narrative that blamed small depositors seeking to salvage their savings for the banking crisis.... Investigations of banking crises on the local level have found that poor management and white-collar crime occupy a conspicuous place in these events.... If the press had addressed the financial situation more forthrightly, banking reforms might have been implemented earlier.

When the new Roosevelt administration responded to public pressure by creating the Federal Deposit Insurance Corporation, the results were striking, Shaw declared. "Bank failures fell from 4,004 in 1933 to only sixty-two the following year" (Shaw 2019, pp. 26, 27, 37).

A traditional and continuing aspect of good journalism is skepticism. In today's increasingly complex financial world, more skepticism is clearly warranted. Apply it especially to debt and government regulation.

## Further Reading

Abramson, J. 2019. *Merchants of Truth: The Business of News and the Fight for Facts*. Simon & Schuster, New York.

Carlson, M., S. Robinson and S. C. Lewis. 2021. *News After Trump: Journalism's Crisis of Relevance in a Changed Media Culture*. Oxford University Press, Oxford, London and New York.

Goodwin, D. K. 2013. *The Bully Pulpit: Theodore Roosevelt, William Howard Taft and the Golden Age of Journalism*. Simon & Schuster, New York.

Rauch, J. 2021. *The Constitution of Knowledge: A Defense of Truth*. Brookings, Washington.

Roush, C., L. Stovall and C. Stovall. 2022. *The Future of Business Journalism: Why It Matters for Wall Street and Main Street*. Georgetown, Washington.

Starkman, D. 2014. *The Watchdog That Didn't Bark: The Financial Crisis and the Disappearance of Investigative Journalism*. Columbia University Press, New York.

Srote, R. 2010. *Wildfire: The Legislation That Ignited The Great Recession*. Tate Publishing, Mustang, Okla.

Sullivan, M. 2020. *Ghosting the News: Local Journalism and the Crisis of American Democracy*. Columbia Global Reports, New York.

Wells, R. 2019. *The Enforcers: How Little-Known Trade Reporters Exposed the Keating Five and Advanced Business Journalism*. University of Illinois Press, Urbana, Chicago, and Springfield.

## References

Anderson, H., with P. L. Abraham and R. Thomas. 1980. "The S&Ls in Deep Trouble," *Newsweek*, December 29, 56.

Barth, J. R., S. Trimbath and G. Yago, eds. 2004. *The Savings and Loan Crisis: Lessons From a Regulatory Failure*. Milken Institute, Santa Monica.

Bernanke, B. S., T. F. Geithner and H. M. Paulson Jr. 2019. *Firefighting: The Financial Crisis and Its Lessons*. Penguin, New York.

Day, K. 1993. *S & L Hell: The People and the Politics Behind the $1 Trillion Savings and Loan Scandal*. W. W. Norton, New York.

Feldstein, M. 2007. "How to Avert Recession," *The Wall Street Journal*, December 5. https://www.wsj.com/articles/SB119682440917514075?mod=Searchresults_pos5&page=5

Ferguson, N. 2008. *The Ascent of Money: A Financial History of the World*. Penguin, New York.

Fuerbringer, J. and A. Berenson. 2000. "The Markets: Stocks; Stock Market in Steep Drop as Worried Investors Flee; Nasdaq has its worst week," *The New York Times*, April 15. https://www.nytimes.com/2000/04/15/business/markets-stocks-stock-market-steep-drop-worried-investors-flee-nasdaq-has-its.html?searchResultPosition=19

Geithner, T. F. 2014. *Stress Test: Reflections on Financial Crises*. Crown, New York.

Grant, J. 1999. *Grant's Interest Rate Observer*, July 30, 1999, vol. 17, no. 15.

Greenspan, A. 2007. "The Roots of the Mortgage Crisis," *The Wall Street Journal*, December 13. https://www.wsj.com/articles/SB119748692103824231?mod=Searchresults_pos2&page=4

Hagerty, J. R. 2007. "Mortgage-Bond Pioneer Dislikes What He Sees," *The Wall Street Journal*, February 24. https://www.wsj.com/articles/SB117227957162518036?mod=Searchresults_pos3&page=32

Hollie, P. G. 1980. "Merger Trend in Thrift Industry," *The New York Times*, July 5, 27.

Hume, E. 1990. "Why the Press Blew The S & L Scandal," *The New York Times*, May 24, 25.

Ip, G. 1998. "Internet Stocks Are No Longer A Sideshow to the Real Market," *The Wall Street Journal*, December 28. https://www.wsj.com/articles/SB914805685755050?mod=Searchresults_pos4&page=1

Isaac, W. M. with P. C. Meyer. 2010. *Senseless Panic: How Washington Failed America*. John Wiley & Sons, Hoboken.

Kane, E. J. 1985. *The Gathering Crisis in Federal Deposit Insurance*. MIT, Cambridge and London.

Kane, E. J. 1989. *The S&L Insurance Mess: How Did It Happen?* The Urban Institute, Washington.

Lewis, M. 2011. *The Big Short: Inside the Doomsday Machine*. W. W. Norton, New York and London.

Mallaby, S. 2016. *The Man Who Knew: The Life and Times of Alan Greenspan*. Penguin, New York.

Mansharamani, V. 2011. *Boom Bustology: Spotting Financial Bubbles Before They Burst*. John Wiley & Sons, Hoboken.

McCarty, N., K. T. Poole and H. Rosenthal. 2013. *Political Bubbles: Financial Crises and the Failure of American Democracy*. Princeton, Princeton and Oxford.

Mian, A. and A. Sufi. 2015. *House of Debt: How They (and You) Caused the Great Recession, and How We Can Prevent It from Happening Again*. Chicago, Chicago and London.

Mihm, S. 2008. "Dr. Doom," *New York Times Magazine*, August 15, https://www.nytimes.com/2008/08/17/magazine/17pessimist-t.html

Miller, J. 1980. "Jay Janis and the 'Unshackling' of the Thrift Industry," *The New York Times*, April 13, B3.

Paulson, H. M. Jr. 2010. *On the Brink: Inside the Race to Stop the Collapse of the Global Financial System*. Business Plus, New York.

Pizzo, S., M. Fricker and P. Muolo. 1989. *Inside Job: The Looting of America's Savings and Loans*. Harper Perennial division of HarperCollins, New York.

Schiffrin, A., ed. 2011. *Bad News: How America's Business Press Missed the Story of the Century*. New Press, New York and London.

Shaw, C. W. 2019. "'The Story Was Not Printed': The Press Covers the 1930s Banking Crisis," *Journalism History*, vol. 45: 1, March, 26–44.

Shiller, R. J. 2005. *Irrational Exuberance*, second edition. Doubleday, New York.

Starkman, D. 2014. *The Watchdog That Didn't Bark: The Financial Crisis and the Disappearance of Investigative Journalism*. Columbia, New York.

Tooze, A. 2018. *Crashed: How a Decade of Financial Crises Changed the World*. Viking, New York.

# 36

# THE MEDIA AND ECONOMICS

## Still an Unmet Challenge

*David R. Davies*

## Introduction

In the early 1970s, Washington Post assistant managing editor Richard Harwood was asked whether his newspaper gave more space to sports than to weightier topics of business and economics. The answer was a very emphatic yes. "I guess it is because we think sports is more interesting to readers than business and economics," Harwood said. "I know it is to me." Harwood's views were widely shared; a Columbia Journalism Review quoting him and other editors about the poor state of the coverage of pocketbook issues was entitled "The Bleak Wasteland of Financial Journalism" (Welles 1973).

While financial and business journalism has emerged from the "wasteland" to achieve greater prominence in the intervening decades, reporting on economics remains problematic. Despite the subject's importance to readers' and viewers' everyday lives, today's new coverage of economics nonetheless remains dwarfed by sports and entertainment and many other categories of news that editors still perceive as being of far wider interest to readers. Coverage also remains hampered by the same systemic and professional factors that relegated economics to the "wasteland" of a half-century ago. This chapter explores the reasons that economics is often so poorly covered, describes some of the highlights and pitfalls of coverage as it has evolved in recent decades, and looks ahead to prospects for further shifts in coverage of economics as media industries have accommodated themselves to the internet in the 21st century.

## Discussion

The importance of economics to the public is obvious. "This is people's pocketbooks, their paychecks, their homes, and their lives," New York Times reporter Shaila Dewan observed about coverage of the economy (Tenore 2012, #2). Economic news has the potential to have a profound effect on the daily lives of everyone, scholars Damstra et al. (2018) concluded in a wide-ranging review of economic news research in recent decades. The effects extend well beyond the obvious effects the twists and turns of the economy have on everyone's pocketbook. "[P]eople learn about the economy by reading and watching the news. Economic

DOI: 10.4324/9781003298977-43

news stories shape people's economic perceptions," they noted, "which, in turn, have profound impacts on a range of other attitudes and behaviors, and sometimes even again on the economy itself."

Nonetheless, coverage of business and economics was a backwater of journalism for decades. When Benjamin Bradlee joined The Washington Post as an editor in 1965, the newspaper had a one-person business section and just one specialist who covered economic issues. Business reporters of this era served a relatively small audience of the managerial class and "were far down the status ladder," recalled longtime Post economics reporter Robert J. Samuelson (2002). The business news they covered was "tucked behind the sports section" and amounted to no more than a page and a half a day, including advertising. Economics reporters, what few there were, "were something of outcasts, seen as specialists dealing with esoteric and murky matters." These reporters had often been assigned to cover economics without having had any formal education in the subject. That description certainly fit Samuelson, who had been drafted to cover economic issues but had no formal training in economics beyond a few courses in college (Samuelson 2002).

But coverage of economics increased throughout the 1970s due to a confluence of factors. Parker (1997), in a detailed overview of the intersection between journalism and economics, explained that coverage of American business and economic news doubled in the 1970s. This was primarily due to the chaotic economic events of that decade, when "stagflation, repeated energy crises, eroding productivity and wages, the explosion of public debt and deficits" and other issues gave increasing prominence to economic news nationally. Cable television's growth in the ensuing years led to even more coverage in specialized television programs such as Wall Street Week and Moneyline. At the same time, the business press expanded significantly, both through circulation increases in established publications such as The Wall Street Journal and Forbes and the sprouting of specialized business titles. Newspapers increased their coverage of economic news, too. Taken together, these factors resulted, Parker concluded, in an "explosive growth in the volume and variety of economic and business news available to the public" (Parker, p. 4). Samuelson (2002) agreed that the volume of business and economic news increased in these years due to the greater prominence of economic issues on the national agenda. But he also cited an additional factor – the increasing percentage of Americans who owned stocks and who therefore paid attention to the economy. Just 15 percent of Americans owned stock in 1970, while more than half own stocks today (Samuelson 2002).

But Samuelson said problems remained with modern coverage. "Business and economics reporting is still seen as a specialty" somewhat out of the mainstream, and reporters who don't cover these issues tend not to know much about them, nor do their editors (Samuelson 2002).

Indeed, economists rankle at what they see as journalists' lack of understanding of basic economic principles. In a nationally syndicated newspaper column published in 2004, economist and Hoover Institution fellow Thomas Sowell maintained that "journalists don't know about economics" (Sowell 2004). Specifically, Sowell criticized a front-page Wall Street Journal article, which he didn't identify. He said the author showed a lack of basic understanding about the relationship of a commodity's price to the laws of supply and demand. Journalists "first and foremost ought to know what they are talking about," Sowell complained, and said that economic illiteracy was a significant deficiency in journalism. He argued that because journalists habitually report on so many issues with economic implications, they should be required to take at least a year of introductory economics in their undergraduate years.

"The time is long overdue for schools of journalism to start teaching economics," he said. "It would eliminate much of the nonsense and hysteria in the media, and with it perhaps some of the demagoguery in politics" (Sowell 2004).

More recently, a Media Matters study of economic news coverage faulted television news broadcasts for their failure to rely upon economic expertise. In an analysis of three months of weekday and evening broadcast news programs in early 2014, Media Matters found that economists were seldom invited on these programs (Kleine and Harrington 2014). Economists – defined as economics professors, experts with advanced degrees in economics, or those who worked in the economics profession – accounted for only 2 percent of network news program guests in segments dealing with economics, while 58 percent of the guests interviewed were journalists and 29 percent were political guests, i.e., current or former government officials or political strategists (Kleine and Harrington 2014). Commenting immediately after the study's release, communication professor Jeffrey McCall of DePauw University observed that the statistics were a troubling example of "the vacuous manner in which television covers the important topic of the economy" (McCall 2014).

Economists are consistently critical of journalistic coverage of economic news. An early and prominent critic was Herbert Stein, a former chair of the Council of Economic Advisers under presidents Richard Nixon and Gerald Ford. His pointed criticism of journalists, published in a 1975 issue of the Columbia Journalism Review, is frequently quoted in scholarly articles about economic news. "The model of the economic story, especially as told on television, is the soap opera," Stein wrote (1975, p. 40). Stein said while the media adequately reported routine day-to-day economic news – commodity prices, layoffs, dividend payments and the like – news outlets tended to overdramatize macro-economic trends and therefore to confuse the public about the true state of the economy. Specifically, he said, "the media concentrate on the short-term aspects of the economy, and they also dramatize them in ways that further exaggerate their importance" (Stein, p. 39). Journalists, Stein said, tend to communicate and to exploit anxiety about economic events "when there is no basis in fact, or no adequate basis, for being worried" (pp. 39–40).

While Stein's criticism may have reflected his frustration with critical press coverage of the American economy during the Nixon and Ford years, other economists have leveled similar criticism at journalists. As economics professor William C. Wood summarized economists' complaints in 1985, "Economists consider much reporting done on economic matters to be uninformed, and in some cases, misleading." Wood attributed much of the deficiency to what he called "the journalist's thought pattern" (p. 29), the inclination to consider each news story as having winners and losers and therefore quoting both sides in an account. This conflict-resolution model, he said, was beneficial in covering two-sided conflicts but less useful in covering something as complicated as economics. He also said that coverage of complex economic events takes more time and money than most journalistic organizations can afford. According to Wood, economists accuse journalists of multiple errors of omission and commission: Journalists "do not get their facts straight"; they cover personalities to the exclusion of issues; they cover events rather than larger underlying issues or trends; they "oversimplify and sensationalize"; they are "obsessed with distribution and indifferent toward inefficiency"; and they emphasize bad economic news to the exclusion of good news (P. 28). Wood argued that the best way to overcome these shortcomings was for economics educators such as himself to do a better job of educating audiences so that news consumers would ultimately demand a better journalistic product.

Economists also fault what they describe as "negativity bias" in journalists' coverage of economics. This is the tendency to focus on bad economic news, which obviously reflects the journalistic norms of finding and emphasizing conflict in the day's news. Damstra et al. (2018), in an article summarizing how the media cover the economy, observed that a wide range of economic studies had observed negativity bias in journalists in their coverage of both macroeconomic news and unemployment rates. The finding was consistent across broadcast and print news and found a particular sensitivity among journalists to any change in unemployment rates.

This tendency to emphasize negative economic trends, these scholars concluded, "might lead to a distorted information environment for citizens, at least in modern Western democracies" (Damstra et al. 2018, p. 3). Indeed, Jonkman et al. (2019) conducted a 15-year study of news coverage of economic issues in the European Union and determined that negative economic news coverage was negatively associated with consumer confidence. Similarly, Canadian economist Glen Hodgson observed in 2009 that Canadian media portrayals of the economy strongly affected how Canadian consumers viewed the economy (Bouw 2009). The Conference Board of Canada, an economic research group for which Hodgson was chief economist, concluded that coverage of economic troubles in Canada had created a "psychology of recession" (Bouw, p. C1). "If (the media) keep saying the sky is falling, well, people think the sky is falling," Hodgson said (Bouw, p. C1).

Scholars also have argued that the negativity bias varies according to which political party is in power. In a 2019 study, scholar Eric Merkley studied 400,000 articles on inflation and unemployment from large-circulation American print publications as well as the Associated Press wire service and found "a bias in favor of Democratic presidents" after controlling for economic performance (2019). Merkley also noted that the "media's bias toward novelty and negativity" means that economic news coverage focuses on short-term rather than long-term economic changes and on negative rather than positive economic developments (2019, p. 2).

Still other studies have accused the news media of other kinds of biases in economic news coverage. Jacobs et al. argue that media coverage of the economy is "attuned almost entirely to the fortunes of the most affluent" (2021). The study analyzed 30 years of news articles about economics from 32 U.S. newspapers and found that:

> Across the board, economic news is more positive in tone during periods when the top 1 percent is seeing their incomes rise. Conversely, the economic news is worse when those at the top are facing income losses. In both situations, evaluations of the economy by the news media are almost entirely unrelated to the economic experiences of the bottom 99 percent when their fortunes diverge from those at the top.
>
> *(Jacobs et al. 2021)*

Jacobs et al attribute this dynamic to the fact that journalists use aggregate measures of economic growth – such as Gross Domestic Product – to gauge the health of the economy, as well as the unemployment rate and the value of the stock market. But in the past 50 years in the United States, increases in stock valuations and GDP have far outpaced real income growth for average Americans, rendering these measures less than ideal for understanding the economic conditions of all income groups. "A news media fixated on GDP growth and other top-line figures will thus miss the real story of how the economy is working for most families," Jacob et al. argued (2021). The scholars urged journalists to use other economic data – such as median earnings as reported by the U.S. Department of Labor – in order to adequately report on the financial health of typical American families.

The global economic downturn of 2007 to 2009 was a milestone in the coverage of economic issues. The Great Recession, the most severe downturn in the American economy since the Great Depression of the 1930s, elevated economic issues to the forefront of both the nation's and journalists' agendas. Economic news dominated newspapers, television, and internet news for much of the three-year period, showing that journalists could in fact cover economics in depth after all.

But the coverage proved problematic in some ways as well.

Despite the extensive coverage of the recession, journalists' attention to economic news, nonetheless, lagged behind public interest in the story. The Pew Research Center's Project for Excellence in Journalism examined more than 5,000 economic news stories from 48 media outlets across five media sectors during the earliest months of the recession (Pew Research Center 2008). In the months leading up to the recession, fully one-quarter of Americans said they were following the economic story very closely, but only 3 percent of the media coverage examined by Pew concerned the economy. Even as coverage of the economy as well as public interest in the subject spiked during 2008 as the recession took hold, the media nonetheless spent five times as much time covering the presidential campaign as they did the economy (Pew Research Center 2008). Moreover, Pew found that the recession could be somewhat difficult to cover. The government data that journalists used to explain the recession was often out of date, meaning that journalists were often reporting on past economic conditions rather than current ones.

Interestingly, Pew found that different types of media emphasized different elements of the recession. In particular, older established media such as newspapers and television tended to devote the most attention to the recession and its effects. Newspapers devoted much attention to the housing crisis, and television devoted considerable airtime to the recession's effects on the energy sector (Pew Research Center 2008). Gas prices were covered consistently because they were easier to track than other large-scale economic changes. A follow-up study by Pew said that coverage of the recession diminished substantially in early 2009 after economic conditions improved (Pew Research Center 2009). Coverage of the crisis dropped by more than half by mid-2009.

While economics coverage in the aggregate ebbs and flows in small and mid-size media outlets, economics gets prominent and consistent treatment by national publications. The Wall Street Journal, for example, is known for the depth of its economic coverage and carries a daily feature, "Real Time Economics," that serves as a roundup of each day's important economic stories along with links to in-depth articles by the newspaper's staff of journalists. Similarly, the New York Times offers regular coverage of economics from its correspondents and distributes an economics newsletter authored by one of its veteran journalists, Peter Coy. In the United Kingdom, The Economist and the Financial Times each offer in-depth coverage of subjects reflected in their titles. Economics coverage, then, is at its healthiest at the largest and most prestigious publications that have had the most success in the internet era.

## Conclusion

In the decade since the Great Recession, news industries have contracted and shed jobs as the internet has undermined the established media's advertising base, further diminishing

426

the news industry's ability to devote coverage to a topic as specialized as economics. The News Media Alliance reports that nearly half of all counties in the United States have just one newspaper. Moreover, the country has lost half of its newspapers since 2005. The coronavirus pandemic that began in March 2020 further weakened news outlets as advertising plummeted. The economic future of newspapers is so threatened that the U.S. Congress is considering legislation, the Journalism Competition and Preservation Act, that would provide a temporary antitrust exemption allowing newspapers to negotiate as an industry with Google and Facebook on compensation (A devasting trend 2022).

The trends of the 21st century do not bode well for adequate coverage of economics. As one observer of financial journalism put it:

> There is this … vicious downward circle: You have fewer journalists paid less with less time and they don't have the luxury of spending the time you need to come up with information that is required.
>
> *(Tambini 2010, p. 166)*

Yet the demand for good, reliable information about the economy remains strong; the Great Recession proved that readers want economic news. "Our audience demands the velocity of real-time economy coverage," the executive editor of CNNMoney once observed, "and the insight we can provide" (Tenore 2012). As the modern media marketplace continues to rapidly evolve, it's unclear exactly how today's media will meet that need.

## References

"A devastating trend: Local newspapers are shrinking or disappearing," Congress must act (2022). *USA Today*, 19 July. Available at: https://www.usatoday.com/story/opinion/todaysdebate/2022/07/19/local-news-organizations-financial-crisis/10085190002/ (Accessed: 23 July 2022).

Bouw, B. (2009) "Experts: Media coverage adding to economic woes", *New Brunswick Daily Gleaner*, 8 January, p. C1. Available at: https://advance.lexis.com/api/permalink/c9bb10da-c889-4d8a-9a23-b36d19ac7dc4/?context=1516831 (Accessed: 23 July 2022).

Damstra, A. *et al.* (2018) "The economy. How do the media cover it and what are the effects? A literature review," *Sociology Compass*, 12(5), pp. 1–14. https://doi.org/10.1111/soc4.12579

Jacobs, A.M. *et al.* (2021) *Opinion: Media coverage of the economy ignores the plight of most Americans.* Available at: https://www.marketwatch.com/story/media-coverage-of-the-economy-ignores-the-plight-of-most-americans-11623501181?mod=newsviewer_click_seemore (Accessed: 27 August 2022).

Jonkman, J. et al. (2019) "When do media matter most? A study on the relationship between negative economic news and consumer confidence across the twenty-eight EU states," *International Journal of Press/Politics*, 25(1), pp. 76–95. https://doi.org/10.1177/1940161219858704

Kleine, A. and Harrington, C. (2014) *Report: Weekday broadcast and cable evening news economic coverage lacks context, economists.* Available at: https://www.mediamatters.org/msnbc/report-weekday-broadcast-and-cable-evening-news-economic-coverage-lacks-context-economists (Accessed: 27 August 2022).

McCall, J. (2014) "Serious economic analysis scarce on network TV," *Indianapolis Star*, 25 April. Available at: https://www.indystar.com/story/opinion/2014/04/25/serious-economic-analysis-scarce-network-tv/8169713/ (Accessed: 27 August 2022).

Merkley, E. (2019) "Partisan bias in economic news content: New evidence," *American Politics Research*, Partisan Bias in Economic News Content: New Evidence. Available at: https://advance.lexis.com/api/document?collection=news&id=urn:contentItem:6123-8R81-JBMY-H3J0-00000-00&context=1516831 (Accessed: 23 July 2022).

Parker, Richard. (1997) *Journalism and economics: The tangled web of profession, narrative, and responsibility in a modern democracy.* The Joan Shorenstein Center Discussion Paper D-25. Available at: https://shorensteincenter.org/wp-content/uploads/2012/03/d25_parker.pdf (Accessed: 25 June 2022).

Pew Research Center. (2008) *Tracking the economic slowdown.* https://www.pewresearch.org/journalism/2008/08/18/tracking-the-economic-slowdown/ (Accessed: 27 August 2022).

Pew Research Center. (2009) *Covering the great recession.* https://www.pewresearch.org/wp-content/uploads/sites/8/legacy/Covering-the-Great-Recession.pdf (Accessed: 27 August 2022).

Sowell, T. "Journalists Don't Know About Economics," Federal Reserve Bank of Minneapolis, from a column nationally syndicated by Creators Syndicate Inc. Available at https://www.minneapolisfed.org/article/2004/journalists-dont-know-about-economics

Samuelson, R. (2002) "Moving toward the mainstream: Economics and business reporting has increased in quantity and improved in quality," *Nieman Reports,* Summer, pp. 22–24.

Tambini, D. (2010) "What are Financial Journalists For?", Journalism Studies, 11(2), pp. 158–174.

Tenore, J. (2012) *How journalists are giving people the economic news they want.* Available at: https://www.poynter.org/reporting-editing/2012/how-journalists-are-giving-the-public-the-economic-news-they-want/ (Accessed: 27 August 2022).

Welles, C. (1973) "The bleak wasteland of financial journalism," *Columbia Journalism Review,* 12(2), pp. 40–49.

Wood, W. (1985) "The educational potential of news coverage of economics," *Journal of Economics Education,* 16(1), pp. 27–35. Available at: https://www.jstor.org/stable/1182182 (Accessed: 23 July 2022).

# 37

# BLACK, BROWN, AND THRIVING

## Redefining Economic Podcasting

*Ashia Aubrey and Kelli S. Boling*

### Introduction

Amidst a global pandemic that drove consumers indoors and online, podcast audiences grew 40 percent in 2020 and 2021 ('U.S. podcast listenership continues to grow, and audiences are resuming many pre-pandemic spending behaviors' 2022). According to Nielsen, as of March 2022:

- 56 percent of podcast listeners reported that they listened to podcasts more often in the last two years.
- 52 percent reported increasing the number of podcasts they listened to.

Not only is the medium seeing continued growth, but the podcast audience is also rapidly diversifying ('Podcasts are resonating with diverse audiences' 2021). Since 2018, Nielsen reports that,

- Black podcast audiences have increased by 70 percent.
- Black podcast audiences average a 73 percent brand recall for podcast ads.

Not only are Black listeners tuning in more and recalling ads, but they are most often listening to music, health and fitness, or business podcasts – making them one of only two audiences with business podcasts in their top five most popular genres, with Asian Americans being the second largest audience ("Podcasts are resonating with diverse audiences" 2021).

In addition to racial diversity, Nielsen also reported on gender-based growth amid the pandemic ("Women are driving significant gains in podcast engagement" 2022), finding:

- A 40 percent increase in podcast listeners in the United States can also be attributed to gender-based growth.
- Since 2018, women in podcast audiences have increased by 76 percent, with a 41 percent increase since January 2020.

 DOI: 10.4324/9781003298977-44

The growth is not just represented by the number of women listening. Those women are also listening more often. Women who are heavy podcast users (listening to more than ten per month) have increased by 90 percent since November 2019 ("Women are driving significant gains in podcast engagement" 2022). Like the Black audience, women can recall 73 percent of podcast advertisements, making both audience segments desirable target markets for advertisers ("Women are driving significant gains in podcast engagement" 2022).

This demonstrable growth in audience size and diversity mirrors the increase in the podcast industry. According to Nielsen, there are over 2.1 million total podcasts as of 2022, accounting for over 91 million episodes ("New Listeners Are Giving A Lift To Podcasting's Mainstream Genres, Says Nielsen." 2022). In June 2018, Apple reported only 550,000 podcasts with less than 20 million episodes (Winn 2021a). Business podcasts have grown 39 percent since 2019, placing them in the top 10 podcast genres in 2022 ("New Listeners Are Giving A Lift To Podcasting's Mainstream Genres, Says Nielsen." 2022). This combined growth in genre, medium, and audience offers an interesting opportunity to explore business journalism in podcasts.

## Business Journalism in Economic Podcasts

In his recent book, "The Future of Business Journalism," Chris Roush argues that business journalism needs to focus less on Wall Street and more on what is happening locally, providing coverage that matters to the average citizen and small business owner (2022). Roush says that small businesses are "more than 40 percent of the economy...but they are not anywhere close to being 40 percent of the mainstream business news coverage" (2022, p. 78). Not only is the coverage focused on national markets and global business, but it is also "dominated by white males in virtually every newsroom" (2022, p. 81).

According to the U.S. Census Bureau, as of 2020, 18.7 percent of U.S. businesses were minority-owned, and 20.9 percent were women-owned (Alonzo 2021). Given the increase in podcast audience growth and diversity from a racial and gendered perspective, the popularity of business and economic podcasts, and the ease of access and low barriers to entry for podcasters (Winn 2021b), the podcast medium offers an ideal opportunity for business journalists to connect with these new, diverse audiences ('Podcasts are resonating with diverse audiences' 2021). Roush argues: "Consumers need economics news. They need to understand what is happening in their local economy and how it affects them and their ability to spend money" (2022, p. 177). Without this local, personal coverage reflecting racial and gender diversity, business journalism will continue to "serve[s] the 1 percent, not the 99 percent," and drift further from the audience seeking life-applicable news and data (2022, p. 4). The economic podcasts "Brown Ambition" and "Freakonomics" demonstrate the difference in how topics are framed when podcasters focus on the 1 percent (wealthy and elite) versus the 99 percent (average public). We also explore how podcasters can intentionally include voices of color and diverse perspectives on financial topics.

## Case Study Overview

This case study focuses on "Brown Ambition" and "Freakonomics" as two examples of economic podcasts covering similar topics in distinct ways. "Brown Ambition," launched in 2016, averages 200,000 monthly downloads and was nominated for the 2022 iHeartRadio podcast awards as Best Business and Finance Podcast (Aliche & Woodruff n.d.). "Freakonomics," launched in 2010, averages 15 million monthly downloads as of 2018 (Dubner n.d.). While their audience size and years of experience in the industry differ, the topics they cover only differ in how the conversation is framed and the experts involved in the episodes.

"Brown Ambition" is hosted by two Black women who explore the challenges of finances in the Black community and offer advice on how to best tackle the wealth gap amongst Black and brown people in America (Aliche & Woodruff n.d.). "Freakonomics," hosted by a white male journalist, discusses economics using a more global lens, focusing on government policies and big businesses. Both podcasts concentrate on business and economics, but the focus is shifted based on the podcast host's lived experiences, gender, and race.

The topics covered are technically the same, but the framing of the subjects is distinct. Framing is defined as how the media presents an issue (Goffman 1974) or, more recently, as getting to the root of a situation, determining the cause of the problem, and then figuring out ways to fix the problem (Entman 1993). We're exploring how two podcasts discuss the same topics but frame them differently based on their interpretation of the subject matter. Since the hosts of "Brown Ambition" and "Freakonomics" occasionally use storytelling and their own lived experiences to frame topics, the lens they use to frame the information is critical to how subjects are presented.

With a clear racial difference between the podcast hosts, examining how topics are presented through distinct racial lenses is essential. Interest convergence involves the construct of race, how it impacts our society, and how systemic inequalities continue to exist, especially in laws and government structures (Bell 1980; Crenshaw 1991). The concept centers on the idea that racial equality progresses only if the outcome serves the interest of those in charge, typically white male lawmakers (Bell 1980; Crenshaw 1991; Milner 2008). Specific to this study, "Freakonomics" produced two episodes on reparations ("Brown Ambition" had none). Examining the interest of a white male host when discussing reparations is a key piece of understanding how the wealth gap is framed.

"Brown Ambition" hosts present financial and economic information from their own lived experiences, specifically focusing on how Black and brown people can overcome economic inequality and "Build wealth unapologetically" (Aliche & Woodruff n.d.). "Brown Ambition" aims to educate Black and brown listeners on the economic systems in place in our society and how they can navigate financial freedom successfully.

"Freakonomics" approaches economic conversations from a societal lens, examining how economics broadly impacts the world in which we live (Dubner n.d.). The guests on the episodes of "Freakonomics" that we analyzed are overwhelmingly white scholars or economists discussing the history of financial topics like taxes or debt as opposed to personal impact.

This study conducted a qualitative textual analysis of 25 podcast episodes -13 from "Brown Ambition" and 12 from "Freakonomics". Episodes were selected for analysis based on the topic to compare how each podcast addressed the same information. Topics examined were: debt, student debt, wealth, retirement, gender pay gap, and taxes. Audio files were downloaded from the podcast websites, and episodes were transcribed and imported into MAXQDA for analysis. Transcripts were analyzed using Johnny Saldaña's qualitative coding methods (Saldaña 2016). This coding methodology intentionally explores the text to identify specific codes. A significant part of the coding was comparing how the discussions were framed and if the information could be relatable to a lay audience. We examined patterns and themes in each podcast – looking at how each podcast host talked about topics and who they brought on as guests to join in the conversations. Both authors listened to every episode and coded the transcripts. After coding was complete, the authors met to discuss the key themes and findings.

## Findings

Three significant themes were noted throughout both podcasts: defining an economic problem, solving an economic issue, and financial prosperity. For this analysis, we discuss general differences between the two podcasts, then move to the thematic analysis and framing differences by topics.

In 13 episodes of "Brown Ambition," there were six total guests, four women (66 percent) and two men (33 percent), all Black. In 12 episodes of "Freakonomics," there were 40 total guests, 13 women (32.5 percent) and 27 men (67.5 percent). Of those 40 guests, six were Black (15 percent), 30 were white (75 percent), and four identified as neither white nor Black (10 percent). Notably, all Black guests on "Freakonomics" appeared during the two episodes on reparations. There were no Black or brown guests on any of the other "Freakonomics" episodes analyzed. The "Brown Ambition" guests were financial literacy experts, entrepreneurs, non-profit owners, and podcasters. The "Freakonomics" guests were mostly professors (28, 70 percent) or industry experts (10, 25 percent). Those numbers clearly indicate the prominent voices on each podcast and how the topics would likely be framed.

## Debt and Student Loan Debt

The difference in how guests impacted the conversation was apparent in the student loan debt discussions. "Brown Ambition" invited Angela Howze onto an episode to answer questions submitted by audience members. Howze is the founder and CEO of the Financial Literacy Institute, a nonprofit in Mississippi. She aims to help people attend college debt-free or manage their loans properly after graduation.

A mom of three sons approaching college age asked for advice on managing college expenses. She said:

> My college-age child graduated from one of the top high schools in our state, so we thought he'd be assisted with scholarships. However, the schools who offered him money still wanted two to three times of the amount of the scholarship offered to pay for attendance...He's been applying for scholarships without success. While we're concerned about our child, we also have one who may be in a similar situation in just three more years.

Howze replied with several different pieces of advice: (1) students can attend Harvard for free if their parents make below a certain income level, (2) students can join AmeriCorps and earn up to $20,000 for college, and (3) multiple federal aid grants worth $4,000 to $5,000. By the end of the episode, she had given that mom ideas for free education at Harvard and around $44,000 in aid from other programs.

On "Freakonomics," the two guests were Mitchell E. Daniels Jr., the former president of Purdue University, and Kristine Bredemeier, who was the head of admissions and enrollment at Holberton School when the podcast aired, a for-profit college. Daniels restructured the business model of Purdue University, and he was proud to say that "the cost of attending our school in 2021 will be less than it was in 2012." While Dubner includes statistics describing the state of the college debt crisis, the focus of the episode is on one college president attempting to lower the cost of college, which is notably different than eliminating student loan debt.

Both Purdue and Holberton tried income share agreements with students. Essentially, the students did not pay to attend school, but upon graduation, after they secure a job, they agreed to pay the school 17 percent of their income for three years (for example). Brede-meier said this income share agreement attracted a diverse student body:

> We have over 60 percent people of color, 30 percent plus women. We have a lot of college dropouts. We have teachers and artists, a lot of musicians, over 40 percent of our students are first-generation, post-secondary students. And 30 percent of our students, English is not the main language spoken at home.

While these two guests attempted to change the costs associated with attending college, the conversation was notably different between academics and a journalist versus a nonprofit financial literacy CEO and a mom of three sons approaching college age. Technically, both discussions centered on student loan debt, but while the facts may have been the same, the framing of these conversations was drastically different. "Freakonomics" focused broadly on solving the economic problem, addressing the 1 percent, while "Brown Ambition" focused explicitly on economic prosperity amid the global student loan debt crisis, helping the 99 percent.

In addition to addressing student loan debt, "Brown Ambition" produced three episodes focused on eliminating debt. In these episodes, the hosts and guests shared their debt-elimination journeys. When discussing debt on "Freakonomics," episodes were aimed at the national debt, payday lenders, credit card companies, and the debt ceiling, so they were not included in this analysis.

## Wealth and Retirement

"Brown Ambition" produced six different episodes on wealth and retirement, and "Freako-nomics" made four, with one focusing on venture capital wealth and one focusing on death as an industry. Again, the guests on the episodes played a crucial role in framing the information. "Brown Ambition" hosted Patrice Washington, America's Money Maven, and "Freakonomics" hosted venture capitalists and economics professors. Washington spoke of her wealth-building journey and the struggle to get to where she is today. The "Brown Ambition" hosts also spoke of their personal experiences regarding wealth and retirement planning. All three women have overcome setbacks in their lives. Washington was transparent about her journey, sharing that she lost her business and all of her money during the recession of 2008. She now defines wealth as "the freedom to do what I want, when I want, with people I want to do it with. It's literally just freedom." She was also open about the crucial role that therapy has played in her financial success:

> [I] use[d] community resources for therapy when I lived in Atlanta because I needed to talk to somebody. My family wasn't getting it. I'm not going to lie, and I'm a big believer and a spiritual person and stuff, but folks telling me to pray about it wasn't helping either...I would pray about it, feel like, okay, I left it on the altar or whatever, and then like a couple hours later, I'd be like, "What happened to my life? How did I get here?" Especially when I was coming home to notices on the door and all kind of stuff. So going to therapy really helped me separate who I was from what had happened, and not make those all one thing.

In addition to the episode with Washington, "Brown Ambition" also took questions regarding wealth and retirement from listeners and answered those in the other five episodes. The four "Freakonomics" episodes on wealth and retirement focused on the canard that all gay men are rich, the death/dying industry, the statistics showing that early retirement can lead to premature death, and venture capitalists.

Again, while all the episodes technically discussed wealth and retirement, "Brown Ambition" episodes focused heavily on financial prosperity leading to wealth-building and retirement, and "Freakonomics" episodes focused on solving economic problems to contribute to a fruitful retirement. While both approaches are helpful and interesting, "Brown Ambition" approached the subject in a much more practical manner, specifically including Black and Brown success stories in their narrative, while "Freakonomics" discussed the topics with a universal perspective, including mostly white voices.

## Gender Pay Gap and Reparations

In the "Brown Ambition" episode on the gender pay gap, the hosts acknowledged that everyone is not afforded the same opportunities, and that not everyone starts from a level playing field. Different advantages like privilege and generational wealth, which everyone is not privy to, can play a part in how success is shaped. This episode revealed how showing up in spaces as a brown woman is a different experience that comes with unique challenges. Woodruff said, "just by having dark skin and a vagina, you are already at a disadvantage in a lot of ways."

The hosts addressed three myths behind the gender pay gap. Highlighting statistics from the Economic Policy Institute, Woodruff and Aliche demonstrated that Black women work more hours than white men, increasing work hours by 18.4 percent since 1979. However, the wage gap has risen continually. The second myth is that "Black women can educate themselves out of the pay gap." Woodruff reminded listeners that 29.4 percent of Black women in the workforce have at least a bachelor's degree. However, "Black women are paid less than white men at every level of education, even if they have a college degree." The third myth is that Black women select careers that pay less than white men. The hosts then compared the earnings of Black female elementary and middle school teachers to white male elementary and middle school teachers, where they found that "Black women earn $25.65 an hour versus white men who earn $30 an hour." The hosts of "Brown Ambition" directly addressed the myths, citing statistics and demonstrating that the racial wealth gap is still prevalent today.

"Freakonomics" produced three episodes on the gender pay gap, focusing on proof that the gender pay gap exists. In the first episode, "What Can Uber Teach Us About the Gender Pay Gap," Dubner and his guests analyzed pay data amongst drivers for Uber. Arguing that the Uber algorithm is gender-neutral, they reviewed pay for men and women Uber drivers examining miles, earnings gap pertaining to gender, hours worked, etc. While Uber's customers did not discriminate against selecting men or women drivers, they did discover that men Uber drivers make 7 percent more per hour than women drivers. The analysis showed that men tend to target neighborhoods where Uber rides were requested frequently and areas where they would make a profit. Also, men were more likely to drive an overnight shift than women and have a longer tenure with the transportation service, resulting in a better understanding of maximizing income.

Policy experts argued that the gender pay gap is not about discrimination but more about "gender preferences." For example, Rebecca Diamond stated, "women prefer to work fewer

434

hours per week than men, on Uber and in the broader economy." While the data showed that men are making more per hour driving for Uber, most of the episode was spent demonstrating that there is not an actual gender pay gap, yet a difference in how women work, resulting in a pay disparity.

The other two episodes on gender pay from "Freakonomics" took similar approaches. One episode compared salaries using census data, again breaking down the statistics behind the data to show that the statistics usually cited are not "quite right." Dubner summarized what his guest (a woman) presents, saying, "women aren't getting paid 20 some percent less than men for doing the same work. They are, however, often doing different work or work that affords more flexibility, which tends to pay less." He continued:

> Now, it may be that if you put a dollar value on flexibility, it could offset a lot of the actual salary dollars. In any case, there would seem to be some sort of good news here, which is that discrimination doesn't seem to be the main culprit in the gender pay gap.

While "Brown Ambition" discussed the gender pay gap from the perspective that it is a "real" problem and even more pronounced for Black and brown women, "Freakonomics" approached the discussion attempting to prove that there is no gender pay gap when you control for differences in the data. "Brown Ambition" cited data from the Economic Policy Institute and their personal experiences, and "Freakonomics" hosted 13 guests, most of whom were women (8, 62 percent) who had collected their own data, to refute the idea that the gender pay gap is a result of discrimination. While discussing the same topic, these two podcasts again took drastically different approaches, with "Brown Ambition" focusing on solving an economic problem and being financially prosperous and "Freakonomics" defining the situation to the point that it no longer exists.

In addition to examining the gender pay gap, "Freakonomics" also produced two episodes focused on the racial pay gap with a discussion centering on reparations. These were the only episodes analyzed from "Freakonomics" that included Black voices, and they were all male. These episodes were structured similarly to the gender pay episodes where the guests debated the definition of the problem, many defining the problem out of existence. Dubner did include opinions and data both supporting and opposing reparations. Many unique ideas for reparations were discussed, including affirmative action programs for housing and heavy investments in early education. However, the episodes leave the audience understanding that not all Black people are pro-reparations, and those reparations may not be the answer to racial financial equality.

## Taxes

There was no topic that more drastically differed in framing than the episodes on taxes. "Brown Ambition" produced two tax episodes, primarily focusing on how to file taxes, save on taxes, and the benefits of using professional tax advisers. "Freakonomics" made one tax episode focusing on how governments can convince people to pay more taxes.

The "Brown Ambition" episodes were almost entirely devoted to preparing for taxes to grow or maintain financial prosperity. Using their experiences and insight from their tax advisers, Woodruff and Aliche discussed problems they have overcome, how they save for tax payments, and how taxes differ for entrepreneurs. They also answered audience tax-related questions. In the second episode, they hosted Terrie Chantel, a Black woman, tax educator, and financial specialist for entrepreneurs, who answered audience questions. One question was from a listener working in the "gig economy" to try and pay off some debt, and they had a question about how much taxes they are required to pay on a "side hustle." Terrie answered with an explanation that is understandable for people who are not professional economists or tax advisers:

> Well, the first thing is we are in a pay-as-you-go system. So whether you're making money with a job or as a side hustle, you're required to pay taxes. So what a 1099 does is require you to report that income to the IRS. So mindset shift number one, I have to pay taxes. The goal is to pay the least amount of taxes…let's say it's Brad's dog walking business, and it's his side hustle. Well, he made $200, but he gets to write off any expense that went into that business. So the flyers that he put out, the website that he built, the leashes that he bought. So he made $200, but he could probably write off half of that and not pay taxes on half of the money that he made. So really, in many situations when it comes to a side hustle, the pro is that it's a business expense.

The "Freakonomics" episode hosted three guests, all professors or industry experts who have conducted experiments either in the United States or other countries on how to get people to be more excited about paying taxes and, in turn, get them to pay more taxes. Dubner described the tax gap as "one of the biggest economic problems in the United States" and defined it as:

> The difference between the tax that is owed the federal government and what's actually paid. The U.S. tax gap is considered quite large for a rich country. IRS says it's around 15 to 20 percent of the total amount due. This adds up to $477 billion. Nearly half a trillion dollars each year in unpaid taxes.

Again, two drastically different approaches on the same topic, with "Brown Ambition" focusing on financial prosperity and "Freakonomics" focusing on solving the economic problem of people not paying taxes.

## Recommendations for Practice

These two podcasts may cover similar topics; however, as we have shown, the hosts' approach to the subjects differs based on their lived experiences and target audience (the 1 percent versus the 99 percent). "Brown Ambition" is a microeconomic podcast that seeks to help Brown and Black women achieve wealth and success. The hosts are intentional about the guest experts they bring on the podcast and how they approach different conversations. "Freakonomics" is a macroeconomics podcast where the discussions have a more global concept of how the economy impacts people.

"Brown Ambition" is unique because the episodes usually dissect topics related to race, class, and finances associated with systemically underserved communities. The hosts and guest speakers provide real-life, practical advice to listeners, like exploring ways Black and brown communities can make investments. Black economists are known to be absent from spaces where their voices are needed, specifically in the media (Anna Gifty 2020). Their voices and expertise are necessary given the economic changes that the world is facing, where people of color are often hit the hardest.

Business and economic stories are topics that are not widely covered by female journalists compared to education and lifestyle stories (Roush 2022). Podcasts such as "Brown Ambition" and hosts such as Woodruff and Aliche can make a difference in communities of color, provide information, and tell stories that can shape how Black and brown women can thrive economically. Roush argued that to attract readers, diversity in who is telling business journalism stories should be put at the forefront (Roush 2022). "Brown Ambition" provides a needed perspective on how people of color can be financially prosperous and how to close racial and gender gaps in the economy.

Talking about these issues and exploring ways people can flourish in these areas is not typical for business journalism (Roush 2022). "Brown Ambition" addresses economic inequalities through open conversation and real-life experiences with guests who can relate to their audience. Business journalism needs more Black and brown voices, specifically women, and to produce content that speaks to the general public, not the wealthy elite. Research has shown that the podcast audience is becoming more diverse, but the journalism and podcast industry does not currently reflect those changes (Roush 2022; 'Podcasts are resonating with diverse audiences' 2021).

### What Should Economic Podcasters Do?

Economic inequality is still prevalent, and the racial wealth gap between white and Black people is increasing (Rosalsky 2022). Podcasts are a growing medium with a viable audience (Brooke 2022). Gallup and the Barbara Bush Foundation for Family Literacy partnered on a study that showed literacy proficiency could contribute to a $2.2 trillion improvement in annual income for the United States (Rothwell 2020). Financial literacy can become a broader pathway to closing economic and financial gaps (Robinson & Rogers 2022).

Understanding the connections between how debt works, saving money, the effects of a pandemic, and inflation ultimately makes consumers more prepared to be economically prosperous. A study from Edison Research shows that 74 percent of people listen to podcasts to learn new things, and 60 percent of people turn to podcasts to stay up to date with the latest topics ('The Infinite Dial' 2019). Economic podcasters are well-positioned to deliver this type of content to interested audiences.

### Conclusion

"Brown Ambition" is forging ways to break the racial wealth gap today by discussing financial stability and encouraging listeners to take better control of their income. Aliche and Woodruff are intentional about the topics they choose to discuss and the experts they bring on. Most importantly, "Brown Ambition" is educating its listeners, providing real-life examples of how to build wealth, and taking questions from listeners to serve them better. While "Brown Ambition" and "Freakonomics" have distinct differences in their approach (micro versus macroeconomics), we have demonstrated that the host's race, gender, and lived experiences can significantly impact how economic topics are framed. "Brown Ambition" is a leader in the economic podcast space, demonstrating how Black and Brown women can achieve financial success.

*Ashia Aubrey and Kelli S. Boling*

## Further Reading

Black Girl Budget Podcast (2021–2022): Nicole Donnell, https://blackgirlbudget.com/, "The Black Girl Budget Podcast Incorporates Social Capital, Life Experiences, and Self Reflection into the Budgeting Lifestyle As a Means of Creating a Well Rounded Community of Financially Stable Women."

Black Girl Finance Podcast (2020–2022): Selina Flavius, https://blackgirlfinance.co.uk/, "The Black Girl Finance Podcast Is Dedicated for Women to Discuss Money, Finances, and Financial Goals."

Debt Free Latina Podcast (2020–2022): Mayra Alejandra Garcia, https://debtfreelatina.com/, "The purpose of this podcast is to inspire and motivate listeners to pursue their financial goals and be wise with their money."

Diversifying Podcast (2022): Delyanne Barros, https://cnn.com/audio/podcasts/diversifying, "Diversifying Explores the Traditional Rules of Money Management and Demystifies and Humanizes Money by Examining the Culture We Make it in and How to Make it Work for You."

Her Dinero Matters Podcast (2015–2022): Jen Hemphill, https://jenhemphill.com/, "Her Dinero Matters Is a Bilingual Podcast for Women That Consist of Interviews and Panel Discussions from la Comunidad Latina as well as Solo Episodes Sharing Simple Actionable Tips and Strategies on How to be Confident with your Finances."

Journey To Launch Podcast (2017–2022): Jamila Souffrant, https://journeytolaunch.com/, "The Journey To Launch Podcast Explores All Aspects of Reaching Financial Freedom; from Increasing Income, Becoming Tax Efficient, Paying Off Debt, Investing, Saving & Learning How to Retire Early and Wealthy."

Side Hustle Pro (2016–2022): Nicaila Matthews Okome, https://sidehustlepro.co/, "Side Hustle Pro Spotlights Bold Black Women Entrepreneurs Who Have Scaled from Side Hustle to Profitable Business."

The Clever Girls Knows Podcast (2016–2022): Bola Sokunbi, https://clevergirlfinance.com/, "The Podcast Shares Open and Honest Conversations With Real Women at Different Stages of Their Financial and Life Journeys to Inspire and Motivate Other Women on Their Own Journeys Too!"

The Dreamers Podcast (2020–2022): Anne-Lyse Wealth, https://dreamoflegacy.com/, "The Dreamers Podcast Shares the Story of Change-Makers Who Bet on Themselves to Design a Wealthy Life, Free of Society's Expectations."

Worth Listening Podcast (2018–2022): Lauryn Williams, https://worth-winning.com/, "Certified Financial Planner and 4x OlympiaLauryn Williams and Guests Share Their Money Memoirs to Offer Insights Into How Money Works for Them."

Yo Quiero Dinero Podcast (2019–2022): Jannese Torres, https://yoquierodineropodcast.com/, "Yo Quiero Dinero Is a Personal Finance Podcast that Empowers Listeners on Topics Like Entrepreneurship, Investing, Financial Independence & Money Mindset."

## References

Aliche, T. & Woodruff, M. '"Brown Ambition" Podcast,' retrieved September 24, 2022, from https://brownambitionpodcast.com.

Alonzo, F. 2021, "Census Bureau Releases New Data on Minority-Owned, Veteran-Owned and Women-Owned Businesses," *Census.gov*, retrieved September 24, 2022, from https://census.gov/newsroom/press-releases/2021/characteristics-of-employer-businesses.html.

Anna Gifty, O.-A. 2020, "Do Black Economists Matter?: The Media Erasure of Black Economic Voices Hurts the Communities Hardest Hit by the Pandemic and Society at Large," *Economic Policy Institute*, retrieved September 15, 2022, from https://epi.org/blog/do-black-economists-matter-the-media-erasure-of-black-economic-voices-hurts-the-hardest-hit-communities-by-the-pandemic-and-society-at-large.

Bell, D. A. 1980, "Brown v. Board of Education and the Interest-Convergence Dilemma," *Harvard Law Review*, vol. 93, no. 3, pp. 518–533.

Brooke, A. 2022, "Podcast Statistics and Data [August 2022]," retrieved September 24, 2022, from https://buzzsprout.com/blog/podcast-statistics.

Crenshaw, K. 1991, "Mapping the Margins: Intersectionality, Identity Politics, and Violence Against Women of Color," *STANFORD LAW REVIEW*, vol. 43, p. 61.

Dubner, S "Freakonomics," retrieved September 24, 2022, from https://Freakonomics.com.

Entman, R. M. 1993, "Framing: Toward Clarification of a Fractured Paradigm," *Journal of Communication*, vol. 43, no. 4, pp. 51–58.

Goffman, E. 1974, *Frame Analysis: An Essay on the Organization of Experience*, Harper & Row, New York.

Milner, H. R. 2008, "Critical Race Theory and Interest Convergence as Analytic Tools in Teacher Education Policies and Practices," *Journal of Teacher Education*, vol. 59, no. 4, pp. 332–346.

"New Listeners Are Giving A Lift To Podcasting's Mainstream Genres, Says Nielsen," 2022, *Insideradio.com*, retrieved September 24, 2022, from https://insideradio.com/podcastnewsdaily/new-listeners-are-giving-a-lift-to-podcasting-s-mainstream-genres-says-nielsen/article_66876324-e101-11ec-84c9-cb0a90a56313.html.

"Podcasts Are Resonating with Diverse Audiences," 2021, *Nielsen*, retrieved September 24, 2022, from https://nielsen.com/insights/2021/podcasts-are-resonating-with-diverse-audiences.

Robinson, B. A. & Rogers, M. 2022, "Literacy Is An Economic Growth Engine – Will We Seize it?" *The Hill*, retrieved September 24, 2022, from https://thehill.com/opinion/education/3598408-literacy-is-an-economic-growth-engine-will-we-seize-it.

Rosalsky, G. 2022, "Why The Racial Wealth Gap Is So Hard To Close," *NPR*, retrieved September 24, 2022, from https://npr.org/sections/money/2022/06/14/1104660659/why-the-racial-wealth-gap-is-so-hard-to-close.

Rothwell, J. 2020, "Assessing the Economic Gains of Eradicating Illiteracy Nationally and Regionally in the United States," *Barbara Bush Foundation for Family Literacy*.

Roush, C. 2022, *The Future of Business Journalism*, Georgetown University Press, retrieved September 24, 2022, from http://press.georgetown.edu/book/georgetown/future-business-journalism.

Saldaña, J. 2016, *The Coding Manual for Qualitative Researchers* 3rd edition., SAGE Publications Ltd, London.

"The Podcast Consumer 2019," 2019, *The Infinite Dial*, retrieved September 29, 2022, from https://edisonresearch.com/infinite-dial-2019/.

"U.S. podcast Listenership Continues to Grow, and Audiences Are Resuming Many Pre-Pandemic Spending Behaviors," 2022, *Nielsen*, retrieved September 24, 2022, from https://nielsen.com/insights/2022/u-s-podcast-listenership-continues-to-grow-and-audiences-are-resuming-many-pre-pandemic-spending-behaviors.

Winn, R. 2021a, "2021 Podcast Stats & Facts (New Research From Apr 2021)," retrieved September 24, 2022, from https://podcastinsights.com/podcast-statistics.

Winn, R. 2021b, "How To Start A Podcast: A Complete Step-By-Step Tutorial (2022 Guide)," retrieved September 24, 2022, from https://podcastinsights.com/start-a-podcast.

"Women Are Driving Significant Gains in Podcast Engagement" 2022, *Nielsen*, retrieved September 24, 2022, from https://nielsen.com/insights/2022/women-are-driving-significant-gains-in-podcast-engagement.

# PART VII

# On the Move

# 38

# BUSINESS JOURNALISTS ON THE MOVE

## Transitioning Out of the Trenches

*Ron Culp*

### Introduction

Media-to-public relations (a.k.a. communications) career shifts have grown dramatically since the beginning of the 20th century when Ivy Lee, a 26-year-old newspaper reporter in New York, became the best-known journalist to transform into a full-time PR professional (Herbert 1966).

Because of his training as a New York Times reporter, Lee is believed to have written the first corporate press release covering a tragic Pennsylvania Railroad derailment in Atlantic City on October 6, 1906, according to Shelley Spector, founder and director of the Museum of Public Relations. "As a former reporter, he instinctively knew that hiding the incident from the press would only lead to more distrust," Spector explained.

> So, he insisted on inviting down the photographers and writing up a 'Statement from the Road,' to give the public an objective, first-hand account of the incident. The 'statement' -- which eventually was regarded as the world's first press release -- was printed verbatim by the Times, since it was written in the same balanced and succinct style a reporter would use.
>
> *(Spector 2022)*

This basic training and experience for most journalists explains why they became the early, turn-to pool of talent for public relations.

Talent migration from journalism to public relations and corporate communications has intensified in recent years due to media consolidation, cost cutting and downsizing of news organizations. We explore such moves here.

### Discussion

As traditional and business reporting jobs vanish, aspiring journalists must work even harder to remain in the field of their dreams. But an increasing number of them decide to move onto other occupations where their skills are recognized.

DOI: 10.4324/9781003298977-46

An analysis of Bureau of Labor Statistics data by Northwestern's Medill School of Journalism, Integrated Media, Integrated Marketing Communications underscored the significant drop in local journalists since 2005, when newspaper revenues topped $50 billion. By 2021, total newspaper revenues declined 60 percent to $20 billion. During the same period total newspaper employment dropped 70 percent, from 375,000 in 2006 to 104,000, and journalist jobs declined some 60 percent from 75,000 to 31,400 (Abernathy 2022).

Fortunately, graduates of college journalism programs continue to land jobs in electronic, digital media and specialty publications. But those jobs are not growing at a rate to offset massive declines in traditional media. Many of the markets once served by now-shuttered newspapers do not get a print or digital replacement.

While journalists employed by digital-only news operations have risen by 10,000 since 2008, it has not compensated for the loss of 34,000 newspaper journalists" (Walker 2021). Even the largest local and state news sites employ fewer than a dozen journalists, and many are solo practitioners. Once robust newspaper business sections have been relegated to one page, often buried within other sections such as sports, and much of the business news is obtained from other news outlets, including cable financial networks like CNBC, Bloomberg, and Fox Business. And another disrupter in business media is the growing use of computer-driven AI systems that interpret and write both routine and complex data (Schmelzer 2019).

Adding to the woes of business journalism today is a growing "knowledge issue," according to Chris Roush, former dean of the School of Communications at Quinnipiac University and author of "The Future of Business Journalism: Why It Matters for Wall Street and Main Street."

"Despite gains in business journalism in the last three decades, many business reporters and editors at smaller publications lack the skills and knowledge required to provide nuanced and analytical coverage," Roush noted. "There is no formal business journalism training required, and many media organizations have cut their training budgets in the past decade." As a result, the traditional pool of corporate and agency talent is not as reliant on recruiting reporters as in the past. This comes as university public relations programs start to increase the number of business-focused courses (Roush 2022).

In 2013, my DePaul University colleague Matthew Ragas, Ph.D., wrote a provocative article for the Chronicle of Higher Education titled, "Colleges Should Require Business 101 for Every Student," submitting that all students (not just those enrolled in business schools) would benefit from coursework in business fundamentals (Ragas 2013). Based on positive feedback and interest from our students, Ragas invited me to collaborate on our first book, "Business Essentials for Strategic Communicators" (Ragas & Culp 2014). That book was followed by "Mastering Business for Strategic Communicators" (Ragas & Culp 2018) which consists of essays contributed by current and former chief communications offers. Our third book, "Business Acumen for Strategic Communicators" (Ragas & Culp 2021) underscores the critical need for any communicator – journalist, advertising, and public relations professional – to have a sound foundation of business knowledge. Once relegated to finance or investor relations professionals, business comprehension is fast becoming a key attribute when leaders consider hiring communications talent.

As Ragas determined in a 2019 Delphi panel of 40 senior leaders in corporate communications and prior research, business acumen has risen to the top spot of desired expectations of hiring managers. And Ragas' Delphi panel arrived at this definition of business acumen which can help guide journalism and public relations course development and training programs:

Business acumen means becoming knowledgeable about business functions, stakeholders and markets that are critical to the success of one's organization or client; using this understanding to access business matters through a communications lens; and then providing informed strategic recommendations and actions. As such, professionals should demonstrate a commitment to ongoing learning about a range of business subjects, including interpreting financial statements and information; strategy; operations; supply chain; organizational behavior, culture, and structure; marketing and sales; human resources; technology, data and analytics; economics; legal, public policy and regulatory; stakeholder management; and corporate governance and social responsibility.

Fortunately, business-focused reporting in several major markets thrives due to niche publishers including Crain's Business Journal in major markets including New York, Chicago, Detroit and Cleveland and digital editions in other cities. As local newspapers in other cities decrease emphasis on business news, publications such as the Indianapolis Business Journal and the Dallas Business Journal also take up the slack.

Despite specialized and innovative ways of covering business news, the exodus of top talent over the years has been a boon to public relations and other professions that rely on experienced writers. "I love to hire journalism students because they know how to write well, think quickly, and rely on facts to create the story without the use of adjectives and promotional language," said the Museum of PR's Spector, who also is founder of her own agency, Spector & Associates. "They can gather the stats that make a story stronger, will ask the right questions (from a reporter's perspective) and understand instinctively how to make a story newsworthy" (Spector 2022).

In preparation for writing this chapter, the author surveyed nearly 30 former business journalists and sought specific insights from several of them to assess the decision-making process of switching career paths or seeking ways to alter their jobs within the Fourth Estate.

All former journalists surveyed expressed fond memories of their journalism careers that ranged from two years to 31 years. Many said they would have stayed in their media jobs if the industry didn't face low wages, significant consolidation and downsizing.

## Options for Today's J-Students

Despite fewer traditional media jobs, major college journalism programs remain strong thanks to purpose-driven students who know they want to pursue their passion. Some also know the lessons learned can open doors to other fallback opportunities, if necessary (Bauder 2019).

Recent DePaul University journalism graduate Jason Grapenthin is one of the many students who passionately studied journalism before completing a master's degree in 2023 in public relations and advertising.

"While I believe I can excel in journalism, public relations or advertising, I realized journalism is market restricted whereas public relations and advertising are market expansive — meaning most companies and agencies of all sizes need communications talent," Grapenthin told me (Grapenthin 2022).

He and others believe they are enhancing their longer-term job options by becoming familiar with other communication disciplines. And most of those non-journalism opportunities are in public relations and corporate communications. Today, public relations pros in the U.S. outnumber journalists by a ratio of 7.6-to-1, according to the U.S. Bureau of Labor Statistics. That ratio was 1.9-to-1 20 years ago. Employment of public relations specialists is on track to grow at a projected rate of 11 percent from 2020 to 2030, faster than the average for all occupations (U.S. Bureau of Labor Statistics 2022).

Grapenthin and other journalism majors have learned from the experience of former journalists such as Jennifer Delgado, a University of Iowa journalism major who was a reporter for the *Chicago Tribune* before realizing what was happening at that one-time significant employer of journalists. She moved into a public relations role with a major school system in the northwest Chicago suburbs where she realized additional training and insight might prepare her for a corporate PR career.

"I knew the skills I gained as a journalist transferred to public relations, but I wanted more guidance on how to work with the C-suite," Delgado explained. "My graduate program at DePaul really focused on building students' business acumen so we could become trusted advisors. It was especially helpful that our professors arranged for us to regularly meet with PR practitioners across industries so we could network and get a better understanding of career opportunities in the field.

"Going back to school for my graduate degree is one of the best investments I have made in myself," she said. "Doing so led to my current job in financial communications at Discover. It strengthened my skills so I can be a better leader. And I now have a clearer picture of what I want for my career" (Delgado 2022).

### Shifting Careers: Successful Case Studies

No two career shifts are alike, and some former reporters and editors boomerang back to media organizations that create new opportunities, or they simply decide to return to their first love at any cost. Here are some of their career stories and advice:

- **From The Wall Street Journal to PR and Now Nonprofit Leadership: Calmetta Coleman, Chief Operating Officer, Chicago Urban League**

While a student at Dillard University, Calmetta Coleman began her newspaper career via a part-time job at The Times-Picayune newspaper in New Orleans, writing obituaries. She moved on to earn a master's degree at Northwestern University's Medill school. Coleman said:

> My first job after finishing graduate school at Medill was writing for The Wall Street Journal. I was incredibly fortunate to land the dream job that I often joked about in college when explaining my co-majors (mass communications and business management) to family and friends.
>
> *(Coleman 2022)*

Coleman made her career shift into public relations after seven years as a staff reporter in the Chicago bureau of the Journal. Her decision to accept a job as media relations manager for Bank One (now JPMorgan Chase) was based on having become a new mother and wanting to reduce the travel that was required as a national business journalist.

From banking, Coleman was recruited into a senior vice president role at Ketchum, a public relations firm, where she provided communication and editorial support, as well as strategic media relations counsel and media training for clients spanning a wide range of industries. After her five-year agency stint, Coleman joined the University of Chicago where she served as director of communications for civic engagement. During her nearly six years in academia, she developed and executed communications strategies to increase awareness of the university's impact through civic engagement. She also served as a spokesperson on community and civic issues.

Seeking an even greater sense of purpose in her career, Coleman became intrigued by the opportunity to do more for her city, so she pursued a position with the influential Chicago Urban League, a civil rights organization dedicated to achieving equity for Black families and communities through social and economic empowerment. She joined the Urban League as senior vice president of external affairs. During her first four years, Coleman's efforts were recognized with frequent promotions, and she was named chief operating officer in 2022. She credited her journalism career for teaching her to write clearly and concisely while covering key points.

What does she wish she knew before making a career transition? Coleman said:

I don't regret anything about the path that has gotten me to where I am now; however, I wish I had understood earlier the power of simply asking for what you want. Whether it is more money or a specific role or responsibility, we have not because we ask not.

*(Coleman 2022)*

**Her Advice**: "The skills required to be a good journalist – knowing how to write well, speak effectively and ask the right questions – are assets in any field. Be deliberate in strengthening these skills; as you consider any potential new career opportunity, make moves that will allow you to be a strong contributor while continuing to learn and grow."

- **From Financial Journalist to Financial PR: Mark Veverka, Partner, FGS Global**

Upon graduating with a journalism degree from the University of Oklahoma, Mark Veverka started his career as a local television news reporter before completing a master's degree at Medill. Upon graduation, he began a succession of significant financial media roles over 30 years at some of the country's leading publications known for financial news coverage, including The Orange County Register, Crain's Chicago Business, the San Francisco Chronicle, The Wall Street Journal and Barron's.

Like many other journalists at the time, Veverka was laid off in 2013 after 13 years at Barron's when News Corp.'s Dow Jones closed the entire San Francisco bureau in a cost-cutting move. Noting that the outlook for traditional news outlets was "bleak, uncertain and fraught with continuing layoffs," Veverka decided to shift gears to public relations.

With increasing high demand from agencies and corporations for business-savvy public relations talent, Veverka didn't have difficulty landing roles in the San Francisco offices of some of the top financial and strategic communications firms. Today, he is a partner in the San Francisco office of FGS Global, where he practices strategic communications, specializing in financial and transactional matters, shareholder activism, leadership transitions, reputation management, crisis management, and related communication challenges.

While recalling myriad positives about his long media career, Veverka said journalism-to-PR career shifts are not easy for everyone.

"The importance of pivoting to a client-facing role in a professional services industry is something everyone should recognize," Veverka said. "This is a dramatic and difficult adjustment for any journalist, of which many journalists fail to accomplish."

Veverka noted that the media landscape is quite different today than during his early career. "Yet, it is still possible to earn a decent living as an independent entrepreneurial journalist," he said (Veverka 2022).

**His Advice**: "Build a strong personal network, keep your skill set current and remain nimble as media organizations, public relations agencies and corporate communications are ever-evolving and changing at high velocity."

- **From Major Business Media Roles to Freelance: Judith H. Dobrzynski, Independent Writer**

A highly regarded business journalist for more than three decades at Business Week (now Bloomberg BusinessWeek), The New York Times and CNBC, Judith Dobrzynski fits the freelance model of a successful independent entrepreneurial journalist. After serving as a senior executive at CNBC, she decided to create a portfolio career that initially included writing about the arts, serving as an instructor in journalism at Columbia University, and as a program consultant to a major start-up arts foundation where she initiated programs and dispersed grants.

In recent years, Dobrzynski has laser-focused her freelance efforts on the arts, mostly at the Wall Street Journal, where she reviews exhibitions and occasionally writes other visual arts news features. Her other articles have appeared in various arts publications.

Although Dobrzynski stopped full-time journalism jobs after an impressive, high-pressure career, she reminded the author that she never really left the Fourth Estate. As she told me, she advises those considering freelancing to realize that it seldom provides the financial rewards possible at major media outlets, agencies, foundations, or corporations (Dobrzynski 2022).

**Her Advice:** "(1) Always try to leave a job on good terms; you may want to return to journalism. (2) Never take a job just for the money."

- **From Correspondent and News Editor to Top Global PR Gigs: Björn Edlund, Self-Employed Writer**

Born and raised in Europe, Björn Edlund began his journalism career as a freelance reporter during his college days at Stockholm University.

Upon graduation, he became a schoolteacher until moving into journalism, where he excelled in an array of international media assignments with UPI and Reuters that took him to Hamburg, Madrid, Mexico City, Buenos Aires and Bonn. During his media career, roles included general news correspondent, bureau chief, regional news editor and chief correspondent.

After more than a dozen years in journalism, Edlund decided to switch careers to public relations. His reasoning: "I wanted to get inside rooms where decisions were made instead of reporting on them and their consequences, and global corporations seemed more open to change and new ideas than government or international organizations," he said.

And making change happen is a hallmark of Edlund's career. He credits his journalism experience for being a highly recognized global public relations leader. His last corporate assignment was chief communications officer of Royal Dutch Shell, followed by a three-year stint as chairman of Edelman Europe and CIS before returning to independent consulting.

"The top contribution of the CCO is to help the company's leaders think things through," Edlund said. "As a correspondent and news editor, I learned to think in contingencies and see around corners."

What does he wish he knew before making his career transition? Edlund noted, "No one outside journalism really understands the value of language and truly believes that the choice of words matters" (Edlund 2022).

**His Advice**: "Operate with complete integrity and do the right thing. Learn to handle disagreement and pressure and understand that keeping a sound distance to those in power is as important in your role in business as it is in journalism."

- **BusinessWeek Bureau Chief Turned Agency Head: Richard Melcher, Founding Principal of Melcher + Tucker Consultants**

Upon graduation from Duke University with a history degree, Rick Melcher landed his first media job as a general assignment reporter for the Akron Beacon Journal in Ohio. Two years later, he began a remarkable 21-year career at BusinessWeek magazine that included bureau chief roles in London and Chicago.

Melcher then turned to one of the early internet content companies for a quick year before eventually hanging up his own agency shingle in July 2000 with Anne Tucker, who had considerable marketing experience with an internet company.

Melcher described his leaving BusinessWeek as a "two-step transition."

"First, attracted to early movers in web-based content development, I left traditional journalism for an opportunity to grow an upstart national news and policy information internet site," Melcher said. "Funding challenges turned that into a very short-term opportunity when the company went out of business. I quickly decided to start my own shop, in tandem with Anne Tucker."

"Boiling that moment down to a sentence: I needed to find a new job, wanted to do something entrepreneurial and figured that storytelling – the heart of journalism – would serve me well in pursuing another communications field," Melcher said.

He credits his journalism career with influencing his agency career by teaching him to "stay curious, always listen, filter and analyze." Reflecting on the rapid pace of the changing media landscape and how it affects public relations, Melcher said, "What that tells me is how crucial it is to be flexible and adaptable, exploring all channels for communicating your client's message" (Melcher 2022).

**His Advice**: "Appreciate that the skills you develop in journalism – especially the ability to think and write clearly, maybe never more important than now – can serve you well across many job sectors. Be persistent. As you would in reporting a story, never stop asking questions and follow wherever those answers may lead you, including to other careers."

- **From Financial Reporter to Non-profit Leadership: Laura Washington, Chief Communications Officer/VP Strategic Partnerships, New-York Historical Society**

Upon graduating with her history degree from Vassar College, Laura Washington did what most only dreamed about. She traveled through Europe for 13 months, splitting her time between working with the European tour of Duke Ellington's "Sophisticated Ladies" musical review and exploring with friends.

When she returned to New York, she said her mother was anxious for her to find "real" work. That first "real" job was a copy editor at Vogue magazine. While gaining hands-on training at Vogue, Washington started freelancing for local community publications, including City Limits magazine where she covered the revitalization of Downtown Brooklyn. This was her launch pad to getting hired as a reporter for a start-up publication called Smart-Money, which was jointly published by The Wall Street Journal and Hearst Publications. Ensuing jobs led her to Money magazine.

On September 11, 2001, Washington and her family were vacationing on Fire Island as they witnessed the attacks on the World Trade Center in real time on CBS. Seeking more purpose when she returned to Brooklyn, Washington said, "I started volunteering with the Partnership for New York City, a nonprofit organization whose members are some of the most prominent business leaders in New York." She eventually joined the staff at Partnership's spinoff – ReStart Central, a redevelopment nonprofit charged with helping small businesses rebuild. It was her first paid nonprofit job.

When the ReStart's 18-month grant expired, Washington returned to journalism as finance editor at Consumer Reports before moving back into the nonprofit world to become vice president of communications for the New-York Historical Society for ten years. She then joined the $8 billion Andrew W. Mellon Foundation as the first-ever head of communications, charged with building a PR department. She was recruited back to the New-York Historical Society in 2021 as chief communications officer and vice president of strategic partnerships, where she is responsible for all facets of brand, marketing, and communications.

Citing her departure from the Fourth Estate as "pure luck," Washington said. "Many former colleagues tell me my timing was impeccable. I have to agree, but it was not planned. The field of journalism has been disrupted and is still finding its way in this brave new world."

Washington credited every aspect of her journalism career with influencing her current work.

> Not accepting anything at face value is one skill I developed as a journalist covering personal finance. You must always dig deeper to find the full story. As a journalist, your job is to become expert at whatever it is you are covering. I apply that to my job in communications.

Washington applauded the shift in how communications officers today are viewed and valued as "partners for leaders of their respective institutions" (Washington 2022).

**Her Advice:** "Journalists who can do analysis and who can decipher data are in demand. While anecdotal stories and leads remain valuable, it is also important to interpret and incorporate data as a source."

- **Boomerang from Media to Corporate and Back: Greg Burns, Editor, Medill Local News Initiative & Freelance Editorial Writer, The Chicago Tribune**

Upon receiving both bachelor's and master's degrees from Northwestern's Medill School of Journalism, Greg Burns set off for his first job as an education reporter for the Anderson Independent-Mail in South Carolina. Some 30-plus years later after several major media roles (Chicago Sun-Times, BusinessWeek and Chicago Tribune), Burns made his career transition into corporate America as director of financial communications, executive media and sustainability at insurance giant Allstate.

In explaining his decision to leave journalism, Burns said, "I escaped a sinking ship, plus I needed to pay for my three children's college and grad school."

Burns credits his media experience for building a broad knowledge of business that was extraordinarily helpful in his corporate role. "You learn a lot of management lessons from wrangling a 50-person newsroom staff," he said.

One of the major takeaways from his Allstate role was a corporation's commitment to training. "Personal training and development at a corporate job is much greater than in the sink-or-swim, learn-by-doing world of newsrooms."

Upon retirement from Allstate, Burns took on a portfolio of part-time roles, including editor of the Medill Local News Initiative, an innovative a digital publication of news and research on local journalism. In addition, he writes editorial content for his newspaper alma mater, The Chicago Tribune (Burns 2022).

**His Advice:** "People skills matter."

- **Smooth Sailing from TV Newsroom to Agency Leader to Corporate Communications: Bill Zucker, Vice President, Public Relations & Communications, Holland America Line**

At the University of Wisconsin, Bill Zucker's double major in journalism and political science proved to be a great combo for his first job covering politics at the State Capitol in Madison.

Upon graduation, Zucker moved to Milwaukee to become a reporter/anchor for WTMJ Radio where he churned out three to four stories a day ranging from floods to politics. On weekends, he anchored and produced the twice-hourly newscasts. A succession of other media jobs took him to other cities, including New York before landing an executive producer job at WBBM-TV where he created and oversaw the first morning news program on CBS Chicago. He later oversaw daytime newscasts and special projects programming.

Explaining his decision to leave broadcasting after 15 years, Zucker said:

> I loved news, but got to a place where it was starting to feel repetitive and formulaic so I wanted to pursue a career that would build on my journalism skills but offer me new challenges and perhaps fewer geographic moves.

The next move, indeed, allowed him to stay in Chicago when Zucker moved into his first agency role at global public relations firm Burson-Marsteller, now BCW Global. After a decade of positions at Burson, Zucker moved over to head the Chicago office of Ketchum, another global PR firm. Through a series of promotions, his last agency role was partner and managing director of the agency's executive advisory and media services.

Zucker was recruited in 2021 to Holland America Line, a premier cruise brand in the Carnival Corporation portfolio of companies.

Asked to reflect on elements of his journalism career that influenced his current position, Zucker said:

> My role as an executive producer taught me how to make quick decisions based on the facts I had in front of me and that has always served me well in public relations,

whether advising clients in my agency roles or now advising leadership at Holland America Line.

Zucker added that his broadcast roles prepared him well for making decisions dozens of times a day, "even in the midst of a live broadcast, and there is no better training ground for the fast-moving nature of reputation work than that." He also credits journalism with creating his fervent passion for accuracy in his media, agency, and corporate roles.

Zucker said many journalists don't understand how open corporations are to creative ideas, change and new ways of working. "But only if you help show the 'why' and build within a brand's strategy." To be effective, Zucker said, "understanding the business you are consulting or working for and its stakeholders will be your biggest guide to success" (Zucker 2022).

**His Advice**: "Lean on your skills and trade on your knowledge to help learn the career you are transitioning to. When I entered PR, I found colleagues and clients acutely interested in my opinion and background as a journalist and therefore more than willing to help mentor and teach me a new industry."

## Conclusion

While college public relations programs, internships and prior PR jobs form the main pipeline for agency and corporate public relations talent, journalism experience continues to hold a special place in the minds of hiring managers who understand the value this background brings to real-world communication challenges.

Oscar Suris, Chief Communications Officer of Duke Energy, agreed. Suris' 11-year media career reflects the experience of others who left the Fourth Estate for careers in agencies, foundations, and corporations. "The two biggest professional gifts from my years in journalism were my development as a writer and a love of reading that fueled a curiosity and willingness to learn that continues to serve me today" (Suris 2022).

**His Advice:** "Value your strengths. Dream big. And wholly embrace being better at a profession that is not journalism."

## References

Abernathy, P. (2022). *The State of Local News, Executive Summary*, Northwestern University Medill Local News Initiative.

Bauder, D. (November 9, 2019). *Fake News? No Jobs? Prospective Journalists Soldier On*, Associated Press.

Herbert, R. (1966). *Courier to the Crowd: The Story of Ivy Lee and the Department of Public Relations*, Iowa State University Press.

Roush, C. (2022). *The Future of Business Journalism*, Georgetown University Press.

Ragas, M. and Culp, R. (2014) *Business Essentials for Strategic Communicators: Creating Shared Value for the Organization and its Stakeholders*, Palgrave Macmillan.

Ragas, M. and Culp, R. (2018) *Mastering Business for Strategic Communicators*, Emerald Group Publishing.

Ragas, M. and Culp, R. (2021) *Business Acumen for Strategic Communicators: A Primer*, Emerald Publishing Ltd.

Ragas, M. (2013). *Colleges Should Require Business 101 for Every Student*, The Chronicle of Higher Education.

Schmelzer, R. (August 23, 2019) "AI Makes Waves in News and Journalism," *Forbes*.

U.S. Bureau of Labor Statistics. (April 18, 2022). *Occupational Outlook Handbook: Public Relations.*
Walker, M. (2021). "U.S. Newsroom Employment Has Fallen 26% Since 2008," Pew Research Center.

## Interviews

Burns, G. Interviewed by Ron Culp, July 19, 2022
Coleman, C. Interviewed by Ron Culp, June 3, 2022.
Delgado, J. Interviewed by Ron Culp, August 11, 2022.
Dobrzynski, J. Interviewed by Ron Culp, July 17, 2022.
Edlund, B. Interviewed by Ron Culp, July 17, 2022.
Grapenthin, J. Interviewed by Ron Culp, December 8, 2022.
Melcher, R. Interviewed by Ron Culp, July 16, 2022.
Spector, S. Interviewed by Ron Culp, July 2, 2022.
Suris, O. Interviewed by Ron Culp, July 2, 2022.
Veverka, M. Interviewed by Ron Culp, July 22, 2022.
Washington, L. Interviewed by Ron Culp, July 22, 2022.
Zucker, B. Interviewed by Ron Culp, July 16, 2022.

# 39

# GOING ACADEMIC

## Issues and Topics for Business Journalists Who Move into Higher Education

*Melony Shemberger*

### Introduction

Much of the research on journalism has studied the journalism industry, the profession, education, and the curriculum. In addition, debates between journalism educators and professional journalists over the content of media education are studied, often referred to as "the dialogue of the deaf" because journalism educators and working journalists typically fail to work with each other to advance future generations of business journalists (Lovell 1987; Dennis 1988). However, crossing the divide from the newsroom to the classroom is a crucial theme that has not been explored fully in the literature; arguably, it is under researched (Russell & Eccles 2018). One reason might be that scholars still are confronting the changing landscape of journalism in an effort to figure out what updates and new approaches should occur (Peters & Broesma 2017). A focus on this transition is necessary to gain a greater understanding of the role, value and views that a journalism instructor has in the context of an evolving profession and curriculum (Russell & Eccles 2018).

Those who switch from the professional newsroom to the college classroom to teach journalism – hybrid journalist-academics, if you will – face opportunities and challenges in their academic roles. Since the 1880s, journalists and former journalists have been recruited to teach journalism (Winston 2010, p. 121). By the 1920s, the members of the American Association of Teachers of Journalism debated whether journalists or scholars were best suited to teach journalism (Singer 2008, pp. 145–147). Much of the journalism curriculum in higher education is determined and taught by journalists, typically those in the middle of their career who leave the profession for academia (Greenberg 2007, p. 298; Kenny 2009, p. 41).

The literature on career changes discusses altruism because journalists seek ways to serve as mentors to students looking to pursue journalism as a career either early in their entrance to college or near the end, when they begin to start their work at a news outlet (Lachman 2004; Williams 2013). Journalists who enter the academy undergo a change in their professional identities, although a calling to service is strong for both journalists and academics. This tends to occur for those from any profession who join academia (Van Lankveld et al. 2017). Further, these "hardy hybrids … have moved from newsroom to classroom … to

DOI: 10.4324/9781003298977-47

develop new skills in teaching, research and academic publication" (Errigo and Franklin 2004, p. 43). Therefore, a journalist's decision to teach is "essentially about the construction of a new professional identity" (Williams 2013, p. 25).

Transitioning out of the trenches, business journalists are finding new careers through teaching in higher education. Yet, "there remains a distressing gap between the acknowledgement of the need for education and the actual training of reporters" (Ureneck 2010). Therefore, this chapter explores the challenges that business journalists might encounter in their decision to move into teaching in colleges and universities. Once in the classroom, business journalists must crack reluctance among students to explore business journalism and encourage them to take courses in a field few students know about, and that challenge is also examined here. Professional moves to the academy can provide journalists opportunities to do a different sort of journalistic work, such as writing academic articles and books, than they were accustomed to doing. However, taking on the role as a scholar also presents difficulties for the journalist. The themes of journalism education and the switch from business journalist to business journalism professor are shaped as the critical issues and topics explored here.

## Critical Issues and Topics

Three chief topics present difficulties or challenges to faculty who teach business journalism. These are journalism education, specifically addressing courses and the curriculum; textbooks and instructional materials; and the expectations that colleges and universities might place on business journalism faculty to build a record of research and scholarly activity.

## Journalism Education: Courses and Curriculum

Journalism courses often are taught by former news reporters and editors, who likely spent many years in the field. As emerging instructors, the former journalists often use standard textbooks, some of which have not been updated. In addition, internships or campus media work experience are encouraged to reinforce and preserve an idea of what journalism should be (Macdonald 2006; Mensing 2011; Bloom and Davenport 2012; Evans 2014). Unfortunately, opportunities for students to immerse themselves in business news reporting tend to be limited or not available, in part because relatively few journalism schools see the area as appealing and necessary for students, viewing it more as a niche that draws too few students.

This shortcoming in schooling has consequences for news outlets that either specialize in or devote attention to business and economic news. Cowdin (1985, p. 18) wrote that one of the reasons why journalists are dissatisfied with journalism graduates is that "they don't know enough about field that they are going to be writing about." Mabrey (1988) noted the same criticisms that Cowdin did, adding that graduates have little knowledge about history, economics and government. However, the perception of this could depend on the size of the news publication. Large newspaper editors were more likely to rate journalism graduates as having strong knowledge of current events, media law, a second language, and business and economics, among other categories (Dickson 1996).

Business dominates political, civic, and cultural affairs, making business journalism a crucial specialized news beat. Chakravartty and Schiller (2011) discussed how an increasing emphasis has been placed on features and infotainment at the expense of hard news, distracting public attention to from the reality of global economies. Chakravartty and Schiller (2011) also contend that rigorous scrutiny of business by the news media is vital to global economic health. Therefore, the need is great for business journalism to thrive in all kinds of media markets. Research since the early 2000s points to the need for business journalism, but students must be educated enough in business to cover the issues, events and challenges of the U.S. economy (Ludwig 2002; Roush 2006).

However, the poor instruction that students often receive about personal finance (an area of business journalism) before entering college complicates the problem. The Council for Economic Education reported in 2022 that 25 states require high school students to complete an economics course, and students in 23 states must take a class in personal finance to graduate (Council for Economic Education 2022). Further, the National Center for Education Statistics reported in 2020 that 20 percent of 15-year-olds in the United States lack basic money concepts (Taylor 2020).

Classes in business and economics journalism have been added to journalism and mass communication degree programs in recent years (Roush 2006). These courses are designed for an instructor to teach skills and knowledge, such as how to read a financial statement, which students can apply to any facet of their journalism or communication career. However, few schools with journalism or mass communication programs require that their students take a business or economics course. These courses might be part of a menu for general education requirements in which a student can select which courses to take, but this means that students still could avoid business and economics courses.

Complicating the inclusion of business courses in the journalism curriculum is the rise of what Wahl-Jorgensen (2015, p. 25) calls "subjective journalism," in which personal perspectives rather than objective reports are presented. This is a critical challenge for a faculty member who teaches business journalism, which relies on data and numbers to help tell a story. Such a movement "represents a direct challenge to the journalistic paradigm of objectivity so central to professional identity and appears to draw on an epistemological vocabulary which equates truth with authenticity, emotional integrity and immediacy" (Wahl-Jorgensen 2015, p. 6).

## Textbooks and Instructional Materials

The field of business journalism expanded in the 1990s with the rise of the stock market and the development of the internet and technology-related companies, making the year a prime one for journalism schools to add business courses to their curricula (Roush 2006). In 1988, an estimated 4,200 reporters worked in business journalism. That figure increased by the year 2000 when the estimate was 12,000 (Henriques 2000). However, many journalists were unprepared to cover the top business stories from the 1980s through 2000 (Roush 2006).

One reason for the gap between academia and profession has been the lack of textbooks that focus on business journalism. Since 2000, textbooks on business journalism have been published. These include "Bottom Line Writing: Reporting the Sense of Dollars" (2000) by Conrad Fink, "Show Me the Money: Writing Business and Economics Stories for Mass Communication" (2004) by Chris Roush, with the third edition of this title published in 2016, and "Writing About Business: The New Columbia Knight: Bagehot Guide to Economics & Business Journalism" (2001) edited by Terry Thompson.

However, other published textbooks on journalism and mass communication overlook or only briefly mention the critical role of reporting about the economy, business and industry. Roush (2006) reviewed several textbooks used in mass media history courses and found that these lacked a robust focus on business journalism-related events and publications.

## Business Journalists Becoming Scholars

What makes teaching on the higher education level different from working in other professions is the inclusion of theoretical scholarship, which is critical in journalism education to protect the profession as the fourth estate and to maintain ethical standards (McNair 2005; Deuze 2006; Witschge and Nygren 2009; Evans 2014). However, journalism educators are scrutinized, perceived as out of touch with the needs of the profession and lacking in modern knowledge and practice (Dickson and Brandon 2000; Deuze 2006; Greenberg 2007; Picard 2015; Wake and Farrer 2016). Further, journalists-turned-educators might be viewed as "practitioners" by their academic colleagues in an insulting way (Harcup 2011). Such an unhelpful perspective could cause a business journalism professor to feel isolated and create an unproductive teaching and learning environment.

Publication or conference presentations of scholarly activity are key for both career growth, such as tenure and promotion, and the development of a rich curriculum that combines theory and practice (Errigo and Franklin 2004; Macdonald 2006; Bromley 2013; Wake 2015; Frost 2017). Although the hybrid journalist-academics who leave the newsroom to teach journalism on the higher education level likely have been recruited by journalism departments in universities, the extent to which they are expected to produce the scholarly activity that is expected in academia remains murky (Harcup 2011). This tends to create a "dissonance" between journalism as a practice and journalism as an academic field to study, one that leads to "existential uncertainty underlying journalism's co-existence with the academy" (Zelizer 2009, p. 29).

## Future Directions

While the critical issues might cast business journalism education in a negative light, the topics actually provide a stage of opportunities for the business journalist joining the higher education ranks to teach business journalism. Several recommendations and directions are offered in response to the critical issues and topics discussed previously.

Business journalism is not a subjective field, since the work of a business journalist is dependent on data, statistics, and other numbers. Weber (2016) studied how teachers of business and economic journalism are developing creative approaches to attract and educate students in a field many find daunting. To recruit, some business news educators avoid using the terms "business" or "economic" in course titles, preferring "financial basics" and "financial literacy" (Weber 2016). Although students often choose journalism and media as programs of study to avoid majors in mathematics, economics or business, several pedagogical approaches exist for a business journalism instructor to help students overcome their anxiety with numbers. This includes scaffolding business concepts and applications throughout the journalism curriculum, rather than lumping it all into a course or two. This could begin in an introductory course in which fundamental topics – history of business journalism, the difference between public and private companies, a study of economic indicators, the contributions to business news by female journalists as well as those of diverse races, and the inclusion of nonprofits as businesses – are woven into writing assignments as basic news stories throughout the term or semester. In a journalism course taught on an intermediate level of the curriculum, exploring business topics on a more intensive level – such as how to read a financial statement – could be the foundation for enterprise or analytical reporting assignments.

A standalone course on business journalism, either as a required core course or an elective, or an advanced journalism course would provide an immersive capstone experience for the student as an emerging business journalist. To teach students about stock markets, for instance, some business journalism educators organize competitions where students vie to develop the most profitable portfolio (Weber 2016). Trips to news organizations that have a dedicated business news desk or team or invitations for business journalists to serve as guest speakers also open doors more widely for the student to explore business journalism more in depth.

Despite all the criticisms against journalism education raised by working journalists, the business journalist-turned-educator can redesign any course as a way to improve the profession. To begin, journalism education – as a way to direct students toward "knowledge, not just a job" – should base a curriculum on learning outcomes rather than career paths as a more appropriate benchmark for success in journalism education (Shapiro 2015, p. 23). The business journalism educator can begin discussions with reporters and editors in the field to identify the knowledge and skills related to business concepts that a journalism graduate should have. For instance, in an introductory newswriting course, a business journalism instructor can plan learning activities and writing assignments in which the learning outcome expects students to write business news stories that feature economic concepts, such as inflation. A newswriting assignment could require a student to interview a customer at a fuel pump for a business story about rising gasoline prices or talk with a young family that is shopping for groceries on a limited income. These kinds of stories not only will help students to report how business affects nearly every facet of daily living, but these start the connection to business at a basic outcome level.

The newsroom can prepare the business journalist for instructional leadership in the classroom, but business journalists entering higher education will need to learn new skills and knowledge – especially in pedagogy – to help aspiring students become business journalists. Given the critical issues that were discussed earlier, business journalists-turned-instructors might consider developing one or more of the following outcomes, many discussed by Roush (2006), into the curricular structure to assist in student learning:

1 **Form academic alignments with programs in the business school.** Work with faculty in business and economics programs to determine which courses might be best for journalism students to take.
2 **Show students how to read a financial statement.** Examine the nuances among the different financial reports (a balance sheet, income statement, cash statement), in addition to differentiate between terms such as revenue and profit.
3 **Partner with other programs within the journalism and mass communication discipline.** Arrange opportunities with other courses, such as mock news conferences, stock market scenarios, or panel discussions in which current issues and trends in business can be discussed and reported.
4 **Design activities and assignments for students to apply business concepts to their lives.** Help students to calculate varying interest rates on a mortgage so that they can relate to the business ideas more personally.
5 **Discuss historical perspectives to business issues reported in the media.** Guide students to explore how business regulations surfaced and how American business scandals have been reported. One example is Ida Tarbell's reporting of the Standard Oil Co., which examined one of the largest global companies in the early 20th century.

Another aspect to consider in enhancing business journalism is the advancements that have been made in technology, such as database access and apps. In fact, technology is essential for business journalism to report financial news effectively. This would assist how business journalists entering higher education should consider the technological ways of reporting business news. Overall, the inclusion of technology sounds a call for curricular opportunities in the development of fact-checking business models, improved media literacy in education, and the reinforcement of core values in journalism that will energize the profession and attack false and misleading news reports (Beckett 2017; Lilleker 2017; Richardson 2017). Specifically, technology in the business news classroom, perhaps at the intermediate or advanced level, would involve a focus on data reporting that would require students to use the Electronic Data Gathering, Analysis, and Retrieval system, commonly known as EDGAR. This online application, available at sec.gov/edgar/search-and-access, performs automated collection, validation, indexing, acceptance, and forwarding of submissions by companies and others who are required by law to file forms with the U.S. Securities and Exchange Commission (SEC). Essentially, EDGAR is a gold mine for business journalists, who can review various financial statements filed by publicly traded companies. Another online tool is the World Bank, which offers a collection of free data sources at data.worldbank.org/, plus some of the other global sources of economic data. Finally, the Bloomberg Terminal at bloomberg.com/professional/solution/bloomberg-terminal/allows journalists to create an endless stream of stories through real-time and historical data available to them for a fee. Many universities have the terminal available for business journalism students to use.

Business journalism professors must consider the availability of textbooks and instructional materials when writing course or unit learning outcomes. Rather than relying on standard textbooks that might be outdated or expensive to students, business journalism faculty might consider finding open education resources for students to use. Often called OERs, these resources are any type of educational materials that are in the public domain. They are published under open licenses, such as Creative Commons, that specify how materials can be used, reused, adapted, shared, and modified according to specific needs. One specific repository is the OER Commons, a public digital library of open educational resources available at oercommons.org. Open educational resources are important in higher education because they can lower the cost of education. OERs are either free or low cost, which result in a greater number of students being less dependent on student loans and may even result in higher program completion rates.

Another idea, albeit requiring a considerable time investment, is for a business journalism instructor to create an open textbook through an open-sourced content management system. Creating an open educational resource is a different process than creating educational materials that will be published and distributed by a traditional publisher or even just distributed to students. Digital platforms such as Pressbooks, which is free and based on WordPress, can help educators to plan and organize materials by exporting content in many formats for ebooks, web-books or print. Plus, educators can update the OER when necessary.

Further, creating open education resources could be an important scholarly task for business journalism educators in the quest for an improved journalism program with a business journalism focus. While the journalism instructor should be encouraged to pursue academic writing, other projects also could be regarded just as highly. Further, the prior news experience of a business journalism instructor is filled with rich opportunities for research and scholarly activity. Such contributions could include an analytical news story that reports on a significant business news trend or a documentary that critically examines a business issue. These types of creative outputs also provide moments of experiential learning for students, from the research phase to fact-checking of information provided in interviews and other sources.

The experiences of the journalism educator after entering higher education tend to be dismissed when discussions about journalism's evolving landscape and challenges surface. This is unfortunate because the future is dependent on having quality business journalism faculty. The professional identities of business journalist and business journalism educator must be embraced by journalism programs for the recruitment of students to carry the torch further into the 21st century. Changes in the practice of business journalism are a key element in efforts to report a current financial crisis (Chakravartty & Schiller 2011), and recruitment of business journalists to the higher education faculty ranks can help students to navigate such changes. The bottom line: Business journalism can help journalism programs make themselves more relevant.

## Further Reading

Bottom Line Writing: Reporting the Sense of Dollars (2000) by Conrad Fink.
Show Me the Money: Writing Business and Economics Stories for Mass Communication (2016) by Chris Roush.
Writing About Business: The New Columbia Knight: Bagehot Guide to Economics & Business Journalism (2001) edited by Terry Thompson.

## References

Beckett, C. (2017) "'Fake news': The best thing that's happened to journalism." Retrieved from https://blogs.lse.ac.uk/polis/2017/03/11/fake-news-the-best-thing-thats-happened-to-journalism/

Bloom, R. and L. Davenport. (2012) "Searching for the core of journalism education: Program directors disagree on curriculum priorities" *Journalism and Mass Communication Educator* 67(1), pp. 70–86.

Bromley, M. (2013) "The 'new majority' and the academization of journalism." *Journalism* 14(5), pp. 569–586. Doi: 10.1177/1464884912453285.

Chakravartty, P. and D. Schiller. (2011) "Global financial crisis: Neoliberal newspeak and digital capitalism in crisis." *International Journal of Communication* 4, p. 23.

Council for Economic Education. (2022) Survey of the states: Economic and personal finance education in our nation's schools[online]. Retrieved from: https://www.councilforeconed.org/wp-content/uploads/2022/03/2022-SURVEY-OF-THE-STATES.pdf [accessed 15 June 2022].

Cowdin, H. P. (1985) "The liberal art of journalism." *Quill* (July/August) 23, pp. 16–19.

Dennis, E. E. (1988) "Whatever happened to Marse Robert's dream?" *Gannett Center Journal* 2, pp. 1–22.

Deuze, M. (2006) "Global journalism education." *Journalism Studies* 7(1), pp. 19–34.

Dickson, T. (1996) "Is journalism education an oxymoron? What editors say about college preparation for journalists." Paper presented at the convention of the Association for the Education of Journalism and Mass Communication, Anaheim, California.

Dickson, T. and W. Brandon. (2000) "The gap between educators and professional journalists." *Journalism and Mass Communication Educator* 55(3), pp. 50–67.

Errigo, J. and B. Franklin. (2004) "Surviving in the Hackademy." *British Journalism Review* 15(2), pp. 43–48.

Evans, R. (2014) "Can universities make good journalists? *Journalism Education* 3(1), pp. 66–95.

Frost, C. (2017) "The United Kingdom juggles training and education: Squeezed between the newsroom and classroom." In: R. Goodman and E. Steyn (Eds.), *Global Journalism Education in the 21st Century: Challenges and Innovations.* Austin: Knight Center for Journalism, pp. 199–218.

Greenberg, S. (2007) "Theory and practice in journalism education." *Journal of Media Practice* 8(3), pp. 289–303.

Harcup, T. (2011) "Hackademics at the chalkface: To what extent have journalism teachers become journalism researchers?" *Journalism Practice* 5(1), pp. 34–50. Doi: 10.1080/17512786.2010.493333

Henriques, D. (2000) "Business reporting: Behind the curve." *Columbia Journalism Review* 39(4), pp. 18–21.

Kenny, C. (2009) "The republic of Ireland journalism education landscape." In: Georgios Terzis (Ed.), *European Journalism Education*. Bristol: Intellect, pp. 35–45.

Lachman, M.E. (2004) "Development in midlife." *Annual Review of Psychology* 55, pp. 305–331.

Lilleker, D. (2017) "Evidence to the culture, media and sport committee 'fake news' inquiry." presented by the Faculty for Media & Communication, Bournemouth University. Documentation. Bournemouth University.

Lovell, R. (1987) "Triumph of the chi-squares. It's a hollow victory." *Quill* (October) 75(9), pp. 22–23.

Ludwig, M. (2002) "Business journalists need specialized finance training." *Newspaper Research Journal* 23(2), pp. 129–41.

Mabrey, D. (1988) "Journalism, liberal arts and editors." *ACA Bulletin* (April), pp. 41–45.

Macdonald, I. (2006) "Teaching journalists to save the profession." *Journalism Studies* 7(5), pp. 745–764.

McNair, B. (2005) "What is journalism?" In: H. de Burgh (Ed.), *Making Journalists*. Abingdon: Routledge, pp. 25–43.

Mensing, D. (2011) "Realigning journalism education." In: B. Franklin and D. Mensing (Eds.), *Journalism Education, Training and Employment*. London: Routledge, pp. 15–33.

Peters, C. and M. Broersma. (Eds) (2017) *Rethinking Journalism*. Abingdon: Routledge.

Picard, R. G. (2015) "Deficient tutelage: Challenges of contemporary journalism." In: G. Allen, S. Craft, C. Waddell and M. Young (Eds.), *Toward 2020: New Directions in Journalism Education*. Toronto: Ryerson Journalism Research Centre, pp. 4–10.

Richardson, N. (2017) "Fake news and journalism education." *Asia Pacific Media Education* 27(1), pp. 1–9.

Roush, C. (2006) "The need for more business education in mass communication schools." *Journalism & Mass Communication Educator* 61(2), pp. 195–204.

Russell, C. and S. Eccles. (2018) "From newsroom to classroom: Exploring the transition from journalism practitioner to journalism educator." *Journalism Education* 7(1), pp. 6–18.

Shapiro, I. (2015) "To turn or to burn: Shifting the paradigm for journalism education." In: G. Allen, S. Craft, C. Waddell and M. Young (Eds.), *Toward 2020: New Directions in Journalism Education*. Toronto: Ryerson Journalism Research Centre, pp. 11–27.

Singer, J. (2008) "Journalism research in the United States: Paradigm shift in a networked world." in: Martin Loffelholz and David Weaver (Eds.), *Global Journalism Research: Theories, Methods, Findings, Future*. Oxford: Blackwell, pp. 145–157.

Taylor, S. J. (2020) Covering personal finance in the classroom. Donald W. Reynolds National Center for Business Journalism [online]. Available from: https://businessjournalism.org/2020/04/covering-personal-finance-in-the-classroom/

Ureneck, L. (2010) "The teaching of business journalism in the United States today." Available from: https://amacad.org/sites/default/files/academy/pdfs/journalism.pdf

Van Lankveld, T., J. Schoonenboom, M. Volman, G. Croiset and J. Beishuizen. (2017) "Developing a teacher identity in the university context: A systematic review of the literature." *Higher Education Research & Development* 36(2), pp. 325–342.

Wahl-Jorgensen, K. (2015) "Challenges to journalistic professionalism: On technological change and epistemologies of journalism." In: J. Sobczak and J. Skrzypczak (Eds.), *Professionalism in Journalism in the Era of New Media*. Logos Verlag Berlin, pp. 21–26.

Wake, A. (2015) "Delay journalism practice until academic scholarship is mastered." *Asia Pacific Media Educator* 25(1), 55–61.

Wake, A. and G. Farrer. (2016) "What is journalism for? Call for journalism educators to think beyond industry practice." *Asia Pacific Media Educator* 26(2), pp. 163–174.

Weber, J. (2016) "Teaching business and economic journalism: Fresh approaches." *Journalism & Mass Communication Educator* 71(4), pp. 470–486.

Williams, J. (2013) *Constructing New Professional Identities*. Rotterdam: Sense Publishers.

Winston, B. (2010) "Book review: The Manship School." *Journalism Practice* 4(1), pp. 121–122.

Witschge, T. and G. Nygren. (2009) "Journalistic work: A profession under pressure?" *Journal of Media Business Studies* 6(1), pp. 37–59.

Zelizer, B. (2009) "Journalism and the academy." In: Karin Wahl-Jorgensen and Thomas Hanitzsch (Eds.), *The Handbook of Journalism Studies*. New York and London: Routledge, pp. 29–41.

# PART VIII

# The Future

# 40

# THE LOOMING SPREAD OF BUSINESS NEWS DESERTS

## An Outlook for Business Journalism

*Henrik Müller*

### Introduction: The Internationalization of Business Media

Let's start with the good news. The media are a valuable source for keeping track of the drivers of the economy. They are important in shaping expectations concerning future developments. Trust in the reliability of media is still fairly strong in Western democracies, but markedly less so elsewhere. Quality is deemed to have been deteriorating somewhat. These propositions are among the key results of a global survey I conducted with colleagues from ifo Institute in Munich in 2020 (Boumans et al. 2023). The people our questionnaire was directed at were representatives of the very core of business journalism's audience: economic experts from private and government institutions all around the world, people who themselves are communicating intensively, thereby playing a central role in shaping other people's views. Our findings underline the notion that business journalism is indeed important, as it provides the public with valuable information about what's going on in the economy and politics, and more generally in the societies in which they operate. They also show that parts of the news media are still in decent shape. When asked which media they used themselves, the participants, who were located in more than 100 countries, displayed a clear preference for Anglo-Saxon brands. As it turned out, The Economist and the Financial Times were by far the most read publications among respondents, with a reach of 48 and 41 percent respectively. The New York Times (17 percent) came in third, followed by Bloomberg (14 percent) and The Wall Street Journal (13 percent).

The overwhelming preference for Anglo-Saxon (business) media is an impressive display of the level of trust and relevance these outlets enjoy. That international top media brands are increasingly consumed in non-English-language countries clearly is a result of markets and politics becoming more interconnected, stoking readers' interest in international issues and perspectives. Improved command of English as a second language has helped these publications to proliferate.

At the same time, the emergence of an upmarket segment of business news dominated by a few international news brands spells trouble for media outlets elsewhere: national and regional media are not only competing amongst each other anymore, but also against potent rivals located in London or New York. Business news outlets that have held up pretty well in

 DOI: 10.4324/9781003298977-49

recent years are now being compared with outlets employing specialized global staffs, outstripping them in terms of scale and scope. Business magazines such as Nouvelle Économiste in France or Wirtschaftswoche in Germany vie for readers, subscribers, and advertising revenues with The Economist. Dailies like the Dutch NRC Handelsbladet or the Italian Il Sole 24 Ore compete with the FT and the WSJ. This constellation is bound to create an awkward situation particularly in smaller countries, where national business media brands are at risk of being driven out of the market. While one could argue that the supreme quality of international media outlets is being rewarded by a more and more receptive global audience, this comes at a price. In a scenario of emerging business news deserts, the toll on the economy could be substantial, as independent scrutiny of companies, governments, and markets at the national and regional level would largely vanish.

This short chapter strives to lay open the dynamics behind these trends (Section "Media Market Dynamics – When Less Is Worse") and highlight potential consequences for journalistic quality and the structure of public spheres (Section "Quality Under Strain – Journalism and its Discontents"). It concludes with considerations regarding possible remedies.

## Media Market Dynamics – When Less Is Worse

News as a product is characterized by a set of market failures (e.g., Hamilton 2004; Fengler and Ruß-Mohl 2005; Nielsen 2016). **Information asymmetries** are pronounced since readers cannot judge the relevance and correctness of news ex ante. **Economies of scale** are strong, as unit costs of news production and distribution fall with increasing readership, raising the bar for newcomers and protecting incumbents behind barriers to market entry. The prevalence of **externalities in news consumption** implies that the benefits of concerning oneself with the broader issues covered by the media largely accrue to society as a whole rather than individual media users; well-informed citizens (consumers, workers, entrepreneurs, company executives, investors, etc.) can be expected to make better choices, thereby enhancing the workings of institutions and markets at large, while consuming news is associated with considerable personal cost (e.g., paying for a subscription, foregone time not spent on more pleasurable alternatives).

Digitalization has fundamentally transformed information goods (Shapiro and Varian 1999), of which journalistic content is a variation. Most importantly, compared to the bygone days of physical products (e.g., printed newspapers, video cassettes, floppy disks) marginal costs of (re)production and distribution have been brought down to zero. Therefore, once enough copies are sold to cover the initial production costs, arising from researching a story and writing or cutting it, huge surpluses can be expected. These funds can be reinvested in more high-quality content. However, if sales fall below the profitability threshold, things start looking bleak – the economies of scale effect. Digital products have another peculiar feature: non-rivalry in consumption, meaning that the quality of a digital news product does not diminish with the number of people using it. Rather, a story may even become more valuable as more and more people take an interest in it and engage in a conversation about it. In some respects, digital news products can be likened to public goods, who typically suffer from under-provision, as economics textbooks teach.

Given these detriments, it is rather astonishing that competitive hard-news markets exist at all. The combination of information asymmetries and externalities in consumption suggests depressed effective demand. Strong economies of scale, in turn, foster concentration on the supply side.

Yet, news markets have flourished in liberal societies in the 20th and early 21st centuries. Recurrent use of media brands is lowering "quality uncertainty" (Akerlof 1970), turning news into an "experience good" (Nelson 1970). Media corporations have invested in trust-building measures regarding content quality, branding and media accountability (Fengler and Speck 2019). Competition authorities have strived to counter concentration, while press laws are meant to ensure that the media behave responsibly. However, since the turn of the millennium, media spheres have undergone profound changes. Digitalization has both rein-forced economies of scale and lowered barriers to market entry; it has also vastly increased the opportunity costs of news consumption as time-consuming digital amusements (streaming, gaming) have spread. Quality uncertainty has become more severe with the rise of social media and the multitude of views they convey, prompting parts of society to consider the news as insincere, false or fake; trust in media content is correlated with trust in public and private institutions in general (Müller 2020, pp. 95–116).

Business journalism is a slightly different story. Content of this type is more specific – and even less fun to concern oneself with. In a survey among users of business media (Mast 2012) most participants indicated that they were looking for "information about current economic, political and social developments" (82 percent), followed by "gaining personal knowledge" (78 percent); the motivation of being able to "converse with colleagues and friends" gained somewhat lower values (56 percent). Among professional readers, such as the economic experts targeted in our ifo survey, the results were even more pronounced. Hence, business and economic journalism can be considered a hardcore variety of hard news. It is seldomly awe-inspiring, exciting, moving, or amusing, but expected to be factual, serious, and sober. That's a problem, because it limits the potential size of its audience, while requiring high reporting standards and accuracy that call for employing large, specialized staffs.

However, depending on the issues, angles and targeted audiences involved, different sub-types of business and economic journalism come with different characteristics. In Müller (2023), a taxonomy of economic journalism is proposed that involves five varieties: consumer journalism, private investor journalism, financial market journalism, business journalism, and economic policy journalism. Table 40.1 compares their product properties with respect to the product characteristics of news.

Consumer journalism is concerned with enhancing individual households' decisions. Private investor journalism focuses on the question of where they should put their money. Financial market journalism covers developments at bourses, banks, and regulators. Business journalism aims at shedding light on what's going on inside companies, particularly large

*Table 40.1* Types of economic journalism and their characteristics

| Type | Potential size of audience | Economies of scale | Information asymmetries | Externalities |
|---|---|---|---|---|
| Consumer journalism | ++ | O | + | O |
| Private investor journalism | + | + | O | O |
| Financial market journalism | – | + | O | + |
| Business journalism | – | ++ | + | + |
| Economic policy journalism | ++ | ++ | ++ | ++ |

*Source:* The author (after Müller 2023, chapter 2).

++ very large/strongly applies + large/applies o medium/neutral – small/applies to a lesser degree
 – – very small/does not apply at all.

ones. Economic policy journalism is concerned with the interplay between politics, households, firms, and markets.

The sizes of potential audiences vary considerably: since everybody has a role both as a consumer and as a citizen (and voter), the first and the last category are the ones with the largest potential userships. Private investor journalism is only relevant for people with spare funds to invest, maybe the upper third of the income distribution, to give an optimistic guess. In turn, readers of financial market and business journalism (e.g., company executives, analysts, fund managers) are small in number, but highly knowledgeable and motivated.

Different degrees of economies of scale stem from the size of staff required to cater to the respective audience in a credible way. More knowledgeable and better-informed readers call for more expertise, and hence dearer personnel. The more reporters and editors with specific expert knowledge are needed, the bigger the fixed cost pool of a media outlet. This effect is particularly pronounced when it comes to in-depth coverage of business and economic policy.

Positive externalities arise where media consumption benefits society as a whole, but individually attributable utility is only limited, a constellation that typically implies a low willingness to bear the costs of consumption – which is characteristic first and foremost of economic policy journalism. In contrast, the benefits of consumer journalism fall predominantly on the individual.

The particular combination of these features is crucial for the viability of a news outlet. A limited audience of readers with a high willingness to pay may generate revenues large enough to sustain sufficiently large, specialized staffs needed to ensure high-quality reporting. However, even a big audience will not generate revenues adequate to cover production costs, if individual willingness to pay is low, as is typically the case for economic policy journalism products.

That's why, in reality, business media bundle several types of economic journalism. A private investor section or the job-and-career pages, for instance, aim at individual interests of high-income readers, adding to their willingness to pay, while an extended economic policy section may be meant to appeal to a broader readership and to signal editorial competence. Given these properties, many business journalism outlets in national media markets have done rather well in fertile niches. Even though digitalization has taken its toll on business media's advertising revenues as well, these brands have been able to tap into other streams of income, such as specialized in-depth information formats for professional users ("verticals") or classy event businesses, i.e., exploiting economies of scale due to large, specialized editorial staffs and trusted brand names by putting them to use for other, related activities. Importantly, national legacy business media brands would differentiate themselves from international ones by relying on language barriers as well as idiosyncratic content catering to the respective national audience.

With English turning into the international (second) language, and international linkages becoming ever more important in times of rising geopolitical and economic tensions, national business media compete with international ones more directly. Thereby, the competitive advantage of the latter is becoming more evident. For example, the Financial Times employed around 700 journalists working in 40 countries in early 2023; it had 1.2 million subscriptions worldwide.[1] By comparison, Handelsblatt employed about 200 journalists and reported 135,000 subscriptions.[2] It's an increasingly unequal game, even for leading business media brands in larger national economies.

## Quality Under Strain – Journalism and its Discontents

If current trends continue, national business media run the risk of being sidelined. This is troubling, because even the best and biggest international outlets are able to cover only major corporations and politics in the most important countries. As a result, medium-sized businesses and institutions in smaller countries are bound to become largely invisible – and un-scrutinized by independent quality media. "News deserts," a phenomenon well-documented at the local level (Miller 2018), are set to spread to the national level for more specific types of economic journalism, most notably the ones where pronounced economies of scale coincide with strong consumption externalities, as is the case for economic policy journalism and business journalism (Table 40.1). In these fields, fixed costs of news production are high (due to the need to employ large numbers of specialists) and consumers' willingness to pay is weak (because benefits from news consumption accrue to society rather than exclusively to individual users).

Without journalistic scrutiny, institutional performance is in danger of degenerating. Gao et al. (2020) find that municipal budgets deteriorate where local newspapers have vanished. Corruption proliferates in places where officials are not held to account by the press (Stiglitz 2002). As information asymmetries between corporate executives and company stakeholders become more severe, company performance and financial market efficiency are being impaired (Goldman et al. 2022). In sum, the spread of **business news deserts** is set to hamper growth, company performance, and overall well-being.

From a normative perspective, journalism should be well-researched, timely, comprehensive and accessible. Economic journalism in particular needs to be forward-looking, pointing to ensuing problems before things turn really bad, e.g., a country becoming overleveraged or a corporation losing its competitive edge. As it deals with grand concepts such as "the economy," "society," "the corporation," or "the financial market," it needs to make the abstract relatable and the invisible graspable (Müller 2023, Chapter 3). Thus-defined journalistic quality is clearly affected by the more difficult market environment.

In the envisioned scenario, increasing competition from international news brands may force national media brands to lower their fixed cost base, i.e., reductions in staff, or replacing experienced, expensive old hands with young, cheap rookies. Employing less well-equipped editorial teams induces crumbling quality: with experienced reporters and contributors lacking, the amount of original and exclusive content diminishes; reporting becomes faulty and prone to herd-behavior as inexperienced staffers seek the safety of banding together, thereby reducing reporters' individual uncertainty in circumstances where they don't have sufficient command of the issues at stake. Therefore, reacting to increased competition by cutting costs and putting quality at risk leads down a dangerous path – with business news deserts as the final destinations.

Business news deserts, however, may not turn out to be uninhabitable arid lands, but places where species flourish that make do with few nutrients. A habitat opens up for partisan and activist media that carry little news in the traditional sense, but thrive on polarizing opinion, which is cheap to produce, easy to understand, and attention-arousing. It's more exciting to read or watch a story about vicious foreign competitors that are to be blamed for industrial decline and the ensuing hardship, than to concern oneself with the particularities of long-term regional development, involving a range of policies such as education, transport and energy infrastructure or the specifics of tax systems. A correct and balanced deliberation of real-world problems and their potential remedies is both harder to fathom and more expensive to produce than the rogue alternative of just blaming someone: foreign corporates, immigrants, or the elites per se. This is where populist media outlets enter the picture. They are low-cost businesses, since producing opinionated content does not require much research and investigation, to the effect that even smallish audiences are able to generate enough revenues to cover operating costs, and maybe even rake in handsome profits.

More extreme media brands have proliferated over the past decade, as the political fringes in western societies have grown. A field has opened up where hard-right publications such as Breitbart in the United States or Compact in Germany and leftist outlets such as Les Crises or Rebellyon in France could flourish (Institut Montaigne 2019). Also, foreign interference, sponsored by the Russian state in particular, has been on the rise. To mimic traditional mainstream media, some of these alternative brands carry economics or business and finance sections, although basic requirements of journalistic quality such as being comprehensive, factual, accurate, balanced, and non-sensational (McQuail & Deuze 2020, p. 217), hardly apply.

Populist tendencies are not confined to extremist "alt" media but have been seeping into the journalistic mainstream as well. Intensified competition in revenue-deprived media markets results in an unjustified over-coverage of radical positions, repeatedly kicking off emotionally charged news cycles, thereby deviating the public from more relevant issues and achievable solutions. The ensuing "spiral of noise" can largely be explained by altered media economic dynamics (Müller 2017). Outlets that refrain from giving in to populist tendencies but keep holding up values such as facticity, impartiality and soberness, may lose parts of their audience to more arousing competitors, as the U.S. news network CNN has experienced in recent years (Barker et al. 2022).

Editorial independence, an indispensable precondition for journalistic quality, is coming under pressure as well. In many Western countries, oligarchic tendencies have been visible for years, as rich individuals, families, companies and business associations have acquired publishing houses. This trend is set to strengthen, as cash-strapped media companies are looking for deep-pocketed long-term sponsors. Examples include Amazon founder Jeff Bezos buying The Washington Post in 2013 and, more recently, Elon Musk of Tesla and SpaceX taking over Twitter, a platform where politicians, business folks, and journalists mingle. In France, luxury conglomerate LVHM, controlled by billionaire Bernard Arnault, owns the country's most influential business newspaper, Les Echos. In Italy, the national business association Confindustria is the major shareholder of Il Sole 24 Ore. Oligarchic ownership structures are particularly problematic in the business news segment, since here influence on public opinion and personal financial interests are closely intertwined. With national legacy media in dire straits, owners exert their influence on editorial boards and media content more ruthlessly. In March 2023, Les Echos' editor-in-chief Nicolas Barré was ousted by LVHM majority owner Arnault, breaking with precedent and the media group's established rules of editorial independence. Apparently, the reason for Barré's demission was a critical article about another billionaire, Vincent Bolloré, who himself owns a sizable media side-business as well (Klasa 2023).

Taken together, strained journalistic quality, populist incentives and oligarchic tendencies pose grave challenges. The development of a two-tier public sphere for business and economic news is conceivable. While a growing upmarket fraction of users turn to Anglo-Saxon international business media that hold up quality standards, struggling competitors at the national level run the risk of being crowded out. In this scenario, an international-minded elite consuming international media would become estranged from the majority of people, who'd be stuck with media pursing populist instincts and/or oligarchic interests. What's more, international media share a distinctly liberal stance with regard to economic issues, a worldview that could be attributed as typically Anglo-Saxon. In contrast, national business news outlets in search of a stable audience are likely to lean toward one political camp or another, abandoning the traditional notion of targeting the vast middle ground at the center of the political spectrum. As a result, an altered business media sphere would widen the already apparent gulf between globalist "citizens of nowhere" (a phrase used by former British prime minister Theresa May to denounce allegedly footloose capitalist elites) and the less fortunate immobile majorities – tendencies that contribute to political polarization and make it ever harder to facilitate deliberating debates as well as holding corporations, politicians, and institutions to account effectively.

## Conclusion – There Must Be Some Way Out of Here

In the preceding sections I've argued that economic factors are key to the specter of spreading business news deserts. As economies of scale are pronounced, size matters greatly for the viability of quality media business models. In the digital era, economies of scale have become even more forceful, now enabling the internationalization of upmarket segments, with Anglo-Saxon media offering hard-to-beat quality coverage supported by huge global readerships. This, in turn, bodes ill for media at the national level. As they give in to the temptation to deviate from expensive independent research and investigation to more attention-arousing, low-cost reporting styles, journalistic quality is being compromised. Likely economic and political implications include diminished public scrutiny of the powerful and aggravated political polarization.

What could possible remedies look like? Welfare economics may hint at an answer. The scenario presented above results in an under-provision of some varieties of economic journalism, particularly business and economic policy journalism. If there is insufficient supply of a good that is deemed necessary for society to function properly, there might be a case for government intervention. After all, that's what states frequently do: enhance the supply of goods that the market by itself fails to produce in sufficient quantity or quality. However, outright state provision, or massive subsidization, of journalistic media is hardly compatible with the requisite of editorial independence. Where governments get to decide on the financing of media outlets, political intrusion is inevitable. Instead of a free and fearless press societies may be getting mere mouthpieces of officeholders. At worst, these media could turn into instruments of shrill propaganda.

To keep the state and politics at bay, an intermediate solution exists: public-service media (PSM), run by institutions separate from the state, supervised by boards comprising members from civil society. These not-for-profit media corporations are mandated to provide impartial information and a basic platform for public discourse. (Whether they live up to these noble standards is a matter of recurring debate.) They are financed by designated household fees, as opposed to state coffers filled by general taxes.

PSM emerged with the introduction of radio broadcasting in the 1920s. The United Kingdom and Scandinavian countries developed this model, which was embraced elsewhere in Europe later. It is a cornerstone of the "Democratic Corporatist Model" of media systems, whereas the "Polarized Pluralist Model" of Mediterranean countries features strong political intervention in broadcasting media, while the "Liberal Model" of Anglo-Saxon countries relies mostly on the private provision of media, except for Britain's and Ireland's public broadcasters (Hallin and Mancini 2004, p. 67). What started out as a PSM monopoly, without allocating bandwidth to private media companies, has turned into an integral part of more competitive media markets, with substantial private sector involvement since the 1980s. In countries where PSM existed before private broadcasting was introduced, they have held up pretty well in what are now dual media systems – accompanied by public disputes about costs, content and the appropriateness of household fees.

Could PSMs be a model for other countries that wish to counter media market deficiencies and the spread of business news deserts? The answer is two-fold: in countries where PSMs exist, they clearly have a role to play in filling ensuing gaps left by diminishing private coverage. In places where no such tradition prevail PSMs can hardly be part of the solution.

In European countries, PSM are typically mandated to report on domestic politics and international affairs, social and economic issues, culture and science. Indeed, traditionally their proponents do not see them as a means to counter market deficiencies at all, but more broadly as a foundation on which culture and humane progress can be built (Donders 2021). Informing and educating the public is an integral part of their mission. Therefore, if the scenario sketched above leads to an undersupply of economic policy and business journalism at the national level, there is a case for more intense and systematic coverage by PSM. In reality, though, this type of content is underrepresented, particularly on television. More coverage would be better. It would be unlikely to crowd out private business media, but users whose interest in business and economic issues has been stoked by PSM reporting can be expected to be more inclined to also turn to more specialist publications.

Alas, trying to mimick the Nordic model doesn't look too promising. Syvertsen et al. (2014, p. 71) stress four key features of PSMs: public ownership and universal availability, institutionalized freedom from editorial interference, an obligation to provide diversity and quality output, and a "broad political compromise." In other words, they need firm moorings in the social and political system at large. That's why introducing PSMs has proved difficult elsewhere. Attempts to convert state broadcasters into public-service ones frequently failed, particularly in southern and eastern Europe (Donders 2016, p. 41).

Where PSMs are not part of the media repertoire, regulation may play a role in promoting business and economic policy content in commercial news media, as well as on digital platforms such as Google, YouTube, Facebook or Instagram. Competition policy, in turn, may hinder harmful concentration in some segments of the news market and across sectors.

Philanthropic involvement in business news media may open another path to promoting diversity in the supply of economic journalism. Clearly, competition tames the concentration of power. The rise of digitalization has not only furthered economies of scale, but also lowered barriers to market entry. In some cases, independent newcomers have been able to benefit. In France, mediapart has earned a reputation for investigative journalism. In Germany, correctiv, a research-focused outfit modeled after Pro Publica in the United States, is mostly philanthropy-financed. While these newish media brands pose a welcome challenge to oligarchic tendencies, they do not offer a broad and continuous coverage of economic and business issues.

In any case, there is no silver bullet. Feasible answers need to differ depending on specific conditions that prevail in each country.

## Notes

1 https://aboutus.ft.com/; https://aboutus.ft.com/press_release/one-million-digital-subscribers
2 https://www.handelsblatt.com/autoren/handelsblatt/12194446.html

## References

Akerlof, G. A. (1970). The Market for "Lemons": Quality Uncertainty and the Market Mechanism. *The Quarterly Journal of Economics*, *84*(3), 488–500. https://doi.org/10.1016/B978-0-12-214850-7.50022-X

Barker, A., Grimes, C., & Nicolaou, A. (2022). CNN wants to stay neutral in a divided America. Will anyone watch? *Financial Times*, November 21, 2022. https://www.ft.com/content/a289eb16-6aa4-4b4c-831a-aa4663b7c9fd

Boumans, D., Müller, H., & Sauer, S. (2023). How media content influences economic expectations: Evidence from a global expert survey. *Journal of Forecasting*, first published online 08 February 2023. https://doi.org/10.1002/for.2961

Donders, K. (2016). Public Service Media and the European Internal Market: Friends or Allies? *Communications & Strategies*, 1 (101), 41–61.

Donders, K. (2021). *Public Service Media in Europe: Law, Theory and Practice*. Routledge. https://doi.org/10.4324/9781351105569

Fengler, S., & Ruß-Mohl, S. (2005). *Der Journalist als "Homo Oeconomicus"*. UVK.

Fengler, S., & Speck, D. (2019). Journalism and Transparency: A Mass Communications Perspective. In S. Berger & D. Owetschkin (eds.), *Contested Transparencies, Social Movements and the Public Sphere: Multi-Disciplinary Perspectives*. Springer, 119–149. https://doi.org/10.1007/978-3-030-23949-7_6

Gao, P., Lee, C., & Murphy, D. (2020). Financing dies in darkness? The impact of newspaper closures on public finance, *Journal of Financial Economics, 135*(2), 445–467.

Goldman, E., Martel, J., & Schneemeier, J. (2022). A Theory of Financial Media. *Journal of Financial Economics*, *145*(1), 239–258. https://doi.org/10.1016/j.jfineco.2021.06.038

Hallin, D. C., & Mancini, P. (2004). *Comparing Media Systems: Three Models of Media and Politics*. Cambridge: Cambridge University Press.

Hamilton, J. T. (2004). *All the News That's Fit to Sell: How the Market Transforms Information into News*. Princeton University Press.

Institut Montaigne. (2019). *Media Polarization "à la Française"? Comparing the French and American Ecosystems*. Institut Montaigne. https://www.institutmontaigne.org/ressources/pdfs/publications/media-polarization-a-la-francaise-report.pdf

Klasa, A. (2023). Les Echos Journalists protest over removal of editor by billionaire owner Bernard Arnault. *Financial Times*, March 23 2023. https://www.ft.com/content/958cb9d8-b9ff-430a-8074-c3e5a5e33b85

Mast, C. (2012). *Neuorientierung im Wirtschaftsjournalismus: Redaktionelle Strategien und Publikumserwartungen*. Springer.

McQuail, D., & Deuze, M. (2020). *McQuail's Media & Mass Communication Theory*. Seventh Edition. Sage.

Miller, J. (2018). News Deserts: No News is Bad News. *Urban Policy*, 2018, 59–76.

Müller, H. (2017). Populism, De-globalisation, and Media Competition: The Spiral of Noise. *Central European Journal of Communication*, 9, 1(18), 64–78.

Müller, H. (2020). *Kurzschlusspolitik. Wie Ständige Erregung Unsere Demokratie Zerstört*. Piper.

Müller, H. (2023). *Challenging Economic Journalism. Covering Business and Politics in an Age of Uncertainty*. Palgrave Macmillan.

Nelson, P. (1970). Information and Consumer Behavior. *Journal of Political Economy*, *78*(2), 311–329. https://doi.org/10.1086/259630

Nielsen, R. (2016). The Business of News. *The SAGE Handbook of Digital Journalism*, 51–67. https://doi.org/10.4135/9781473957909

Shapiro, C., & Varian, H. R. (1999). *Information Rules. A Strategic Guide to the Network Economy*. Harvard Business School Press.

*Henrik Müller*

Stiglitz, J. (2002). Transparency in Government. In Islam, R., Djankov, S. & McLeish, C. (eds.) The Right to Tell. The Role of Mass Media in Economic Development. *World Bank Institute Development Studies*, 27–44. https://doi.org/10.1596/0-8213-5203-2

Syvertsen, T., Gunn, Enli, Mjøs, Ole, J., & Moe, Hallvard. (2014). *The Media Welfare State*. University of Michigan Press.

# CONCLUDING THOUGHTS

*Richard S. Dunham*

More than four decades after it happened, I remember vividly the moment when an assistant city editor at the Dallas Times Herald rushed over to the business news desk. General Motors, mired in a sales slump during the 1979 Arab oil embargo, had announced massive layoffs at its plant in Arlington, Texas. The editor asked a business desk staffer to drive over to the manufacturing facility and talk to some of the newly unemployed workers. The business reporter demurred. "I'm not a reporter. I'm a business writer," he said brusquely.

As a young city desk reporter, I was shocked and puzzled by my business colleague's attitude. But it taught me a lesson about the mindset of at least some business reporters. They were a part of the newsroom, but they were apart. They didn't wear out their shoe leather like those of us who covered floods, shootings, riots and political rallies. They didn't talk to "real people." They lived in a world of corporate press releases, news conferences and the occasional economic analyst.

That world has changed. Completely. As the impressive scholarship in this volume shows, business and economic journalism is now a dynamic and indispensable part of our 21st-century journalism world. Despite its continuing shortcomings – from the calamitous failure to foreshadow the 2008 global financial meltdown to the well-documented resistance to equal pay for women at many business news outlets – economic journalism has emerged as "a vibrant area of news coverage around the world," my colleague Joseph Weber writes in his introduction.

Business reporting is better than ever. It offers a deeper analysis and makes deeper impacts on the communities it serves. It is readily available on the internet, free of cost or for tens of thousands of U.S. dollars each year for businesspeople who want the latest data and in-depth analysis. Despite its shortcomings and challenges, business news remains a bright spot in the economic darkness of the modern media.

The 44 major contributors to this book have documented those changes while offering a healthy dose of history and context. The topics explored in this volume are varied and consistently compelling. There are the success stories: the growth of entrepreneurial journalism and business newsletters, the increasing attention paid to the business of sports and art, the rise of trade publications and the courage shown by women and minorities as they have faced the old-boys network in business journalism.

DOI: 10.4324/9781003298977-50

Business departments no longer are segregated units within newsrooms. They are essential players in multidisciplinary reporting projects. And collaboration extends beyond individual newsrooms. Business journalists are engaging in ambitious partnerships, as described in chapters on the Panama and Pandora Papers efforts. These cross-border partnerships, from Argentina to Zimbabwe, are an "indispensable tool for journalism in general and for business journalism in particular," Dean Starkman writes. The collaborative investigations have real-world impact, hastening the resignations of government officials and, in the case of the hidden wealth of Russian oligarchs, providing a road map for economic sanctions after Vladimir Putin's invasion of Ukraine in 2022.

While business journalism has been expanding in this era of industry contraction, its growth has not been uniform – or universal. Global business journalism is not monolithic, and it varies from country to country based on factors such as national journalistic culture, media system, economic and political systems, the influence of business interests in the society and the level of economic development of the nation. Business journalists face particular challenges in authoritarian regimes, which often create barriers to transparent coverage. "Censorship, difficulties in accessing public economic information, propaganda disseminated through state-owned media, and other sophisticated forms of influence on the messages that reach the population are still very common in a large part of the planet," Ángel Arrese writes in the chapter titled "Vive la difference!"

While the Anglo-American model of business news coverage is still dominant in global journalism, it is not hegemonic and is not applicable to large swaths of the world, for cultural and political reasons. It is important to study best practices of thriving business journalism enterprises in the developing world to seek lessons for "non-Western" nations. Theodora Dame Adjin-Tettey's examination of the Business and Financial Times in Ghana provides best practices clues in the publication's journalistic and financial models: deep, accurate, authoritative coverage of key industry sectors and an adaptable financial model that metamorphosizes as technologies and audience tastes change.

In a way, that's the history of business journalism. Through 5,000 years of human civilization in China, Africa, Egypt, Persia, Mesopotamia, Greece, Rome and beyond, storytellers described commerce and the people who engaged in it. The "modern" history of economic journalism began with Johannes Gutenberg's epoch-altering invention in 1440 and widened in influence with increasing literacy rates in the 19th century and the ubiquity of daily newspapers, radio and television in the 20th century. Today's fragmented media marketplace most closely resembles the turn of the 20th century, when "muckrakers" investigated the abuses of unfettered capitalism, as captured brilliantly by Chris Roush, and advocacy news organizations mingled with corporate media and self-styled "objective" publications.

While today's aggressive business journalism echoes some of the best of a century ago, it has radically different ways of delivering its reports to news consumers. The digital news world has marginalized respected "legacy" print publications such as BusinessWeek, Fortune and the Kiplinger Report. Advocacy publications like Mother Jones continue to fill a niche, though always, it seems, on the edge of insolvency. And while daily and weekly print products seem headed for oblivion, and so-called "linear" television is on a glide path to irrelevance, old-fashioned print is thriving in one form. Business-oriented books have boomed over the past four decades, as publishers continue to offer up a steady diet of best-selling chief executive memoirs, business guru books, business narratives and social science research volumes, writes Alan Deutschman.

Despite the economic and technological disruption of recent decades, video news remains a global mainstay, as Ceci Rodgers recounts in a fascinating review of a half-century of economic coverage on television, from "Wall Street Week" and "Nightly Business Report" to 24/7 business news via CNBC and Bloomberg. Rabbit-ear antennas and cable boxes have come and gone, as have numerous digital business news startups. (Remember the Financial News Network or CNNfn?) Although much of the audience for video news is migrating from cable television to streaming video, Rodgers is sanguine about its future. Business journalists, she writes, have "always found new audiences and better ways to deliver news to them, proof of its staying power in an evolving industry."

Serious challenges remain for business journalism. The primary one is an antiquated economic model that is over-reliant on advertising and subscription revenue. To remain solvent, news organizations must develop diverse revenue streams to pay for value-added content that resonates with their audiences.

Within the industry, staffing must better reflect the communities we serve. More attention should be paid to the hiring, promotion and retention of women in business journalism, particularly women of color. Kathleen Graham, the former executive director of the Society for Advancing Business Editing and Writing (SABEW), deserves credit for prioritizing programs "that help women develop their business journalism skills, navigate newsroom culture, and develop as leaders," as Kristin Gilger and Sophie Knowles write. But more is needed to help female journalists deal with the often misogynistic "bro culture" of Wall Street and Silicon Valley.

There should be greater coverage, in quantity and quality, of the Latino community in the United States and the developing nations of Latin America and South America. The Hispanic population of the United States has grown by 325 percent in four decades, and yet the business coverage of Latino consumers or Hispanic-led businesses has lagged behind, particularly in mainstream English-language media. "If it were a company, the Latino community would be a sleeping unicorn," Claudia Cruz writes.

Beyond America's borders, the failure of global media to pay attention to the growing economic importance of the Spanish- and Portuguese-speaking nations of the Western hemisphere stands in embarrassing contrast to the far more extensive and sophisticated English-language coverage of developing nations in Asia.

There is an urgent need for journalism training in the "non-Western" world. Journalists in developing nations need additional tools and resources to provide fact-based information to broader audiences and to create entrepreneurial journalism ventures. Journalists working in autocratic countries need training to help them understand the global economy and their own business environments. And they should be encouraged to provide coverage that is as robust and analytical as possible under the constraints imposed by their governments.

Today's business journalists are better qualified than any generation in history. They have more substantive knowledge of economic issues, world affairs and corporate strategies. They are more adept at data diving and data analysis than previous newsroom hires. And they are more willing to embrace multimedia storytelling than their veteran colleagues.

Still, there is a need for all business reporters to engage in lifelong learning to stay up to date with the rapid changes in journalism technology that are certain to transform modes of news consumption in the decades ahead. The need for intensive technology training begins with university business journalism programs around the world. The demanding combination of a rapidly evolving business world and perpetual new communication technologies calls for business journalism professors who are more highly qualified than ever before. J-school faculty members must understand economic concepts, the global economy, multimedia storytelling techniques and the latest journalism technologies. Faculty members who spent their careers in business and financial journalism are more important than ever. But journalists who switched to academia years ago may find themselves anachronisms if they have not kept up with hot economic topics (Blockchain! E-commerce! Crypto! Generative AI!). Professors with experience in a single medium (print, radio, television) may find themselves struggling to teach the digital natives in their classrooms how to produce multimedia content.

This thick volume is a good way for all of us to catch up in a hurry. If we are willing to embrace change and learn new storytelling tools, we won't find ourselves as useless as that journalist in 1979 who stubbornly believed he was a business writer and not a reporter.

# INDEX

Note: **Bold** page numbers refer to tables; *italic* page numbers refer to figures and page numbers followed by "n" denote endnotes.

Printed in the United States
by Baker & Taylor Publisher Services